Project Management Communication Tools

By William Dow, PMP & Bruce Taylor

Copyright

Table of Contents

COPYRIGHT... II

TABLE OF CONTENTS... III

DEDICATION XXI

ABOUT THE AUTHORS... XXII

CREDITS... XXIII

FOREWORD XXIV

PREFACE XXVI

WHAT'S NEW IN THIS VERSION XXVIII

    IMPORTANT NOTE ABOUT THE TOOL TEMPLATES: XXVIII

HOW TO GET THE MOST OUT OF THIS BOOK XXIX

    HOW THIS BOOK IS ORGANIZED... XXX

PART I: AN INTRODUCTION TO PROJECT COMMUNICATIONS XXXI

    PART II: PROJECT COMMUNICATION TOOLS BY KNOWLEDGE AREAS XXXI

    PART III: PROJECT COMMUNICATION TOOLS BY PROCESS GROUPS XXXII

    PART IV: PROJECT MANAGEMENT BI & PMP® EXAM QUESTIONS... XXXII

INTRODUCTION XXXIII

CHAPTER 1.. 1

    INTRODUCING PROJECT COMMUNICATION.. 1

REVIEWING A PROJECT SCENARIO.. 3

PLAN TO COMMUNICATE, COMMUNICATE THE PLAN 5

    PLAN TO COMMUNICATE 5

UNDERSTANDING PMI'S PROJECT MANAGEMENT KNOWLEDGE AREAS.............. 8

    PROJECT INTEGRATION MANAGEMENT 9

    PROJECT SCOPE MANAGEMENT.. 9

    TIME MANAGEMENT 9

    COST MANAGEMENT... 10

    QUALITY MANAGEMENT... 10

    HUMAN RESOURCE MANAGEMENT 11

    COMMUNICATION MANAGEMENT... 11

    RISK MANAGEMENT.. 12

    PROCUREMENT MANAGEMENT 13

    STAKEHOLDER MANAGEMENT 14

UNDERSTANDING PMI'S PROJECT MANAGEMENT PROCESS GROUPS **15**

INITIATING PROCESS GROUP 16
PLANNING PROCESS GROUP.. 17
EXECUTING PROCESS GROUP... 18
MONITORING & CONTROLLING PROCESS GROUP 18
CLOSING PROCESS GROUP 18

INTRODUCING AGILE METHODOLOGY...**20**

INTRODUCING PROJECT MANAGEMENT BUSINESS INTELLIGENCE **21**

SUMMARY..**22**

CHAPTER 2...**23**

PLANNING PROJECT COMMUNICATION 23

PREVENTING COMMON COMMUNICATION PROBLEMS **30**

DEFINING A PROJECT COMMUNICATION PLAN **31**

CREATING A PROJECT COMMUNICATION PLAN 31

UNDERSTANDING THE CIRCLE-OF-COMMUNICATIONS CHART..........................**36**

DEFINING THE PROJECT COMMUNICATION REQUIREMENTS MATRIX................**38**

UNDERSTANDING HOW TO READ THE MATRIX CHART 38
CREATING A COMMUNICATION REQUIREMENTS MATRIX 40

UNDERSTANDING THE ROLE REPORT MATRIX **41**

CREATING A ROLE REPORT MATRIX 43

DEVELOPING LESSONS LEARNED INFORMATION **45**

COMMUNICATING LESSONS LEARNED INFORMATION.. 45
BENEFITTING FROM LESSONS LEARNED... 46

SUMMARY..**48**

CHAPTER 3...**49**

WORKING WITH PROJECT COMMUNICATIONS 49

INTERACTING FACE-TO-FACE...**50**

MAKING FACE-TO-FACE COMMUNICATION WORK 50
UNDERSTANDING THE VALUE OF FACE-TO-FACE COMMUNICATIONS..................... 51

UNDERSTANDING COMMUNICATION LINKS..**53**

SENDING AND RECEIVING MODELS 55
Sending model.. 56
Receiving model 57

UNDERSTANDING THE STAKEHOLDER RISK TOLERANCE LEVEL...**58**

High risk tolerance level 58
Medium risk tolerance level 58
Low risk tolerance level 59
Determining customer tolerance levels.. 59

PREPARING AND DELIVERING PRESENTATIONS **61**

Preparing for a presentation... 61
Presenting your project materials 62
Avoiding common mistakes... 62

DISTRIBUTING PROJECT INFORMATION **64**

Communicating verbally 64
Communicating in writing.. 65
Communicating visually 66

SUMMARY...**68**

CHAPTER 4...**69**

Exploring Foreign and Virtual Communications 69

PREPARING AND PLANNING FOR PROJECT COMMUNICATIONS IN FOREIGN COUNTRIES **70**

BUSINESS TRAVEL **71**

Preparation 71
Dual-language business cards 71
Culture 71
  Greetings 72
  Gifts 72
  Significance of gestures.. 72
  Negotiating styles... 72
  Differences in business styles 72
Discovering etiquette 72
  United States of America (U.S.) 73
  Belgium.. 73
  China... 73
  France.. 73
  Germany 74
  Italy... 74
  Indonesia 74

EXPLORING VIRTUAL COMMUNICATIONS **75**

Communicating with the virtual project team 76
  Virtual communicating methods.. 76
Managing virtual project teams... 76
Motivating virtual project teams.. 78

COMMUNICATING CONSISTENTLY 78

ESTABLISHING COMMUNICATION GUIDELINES 79

EXPLORING VIRTUAL TEAM MEMBER QUALIFICATIONS 80

SUMMARY **82**

CHAPTER 5 ....**83**

SOCIAL MEDIA AND PROJECT MANAGEMENT COMMUNICATION TOOLS 83

WHAT IS SOCIAL MEDIA? **84**

SOCIAL MEDIA TOOLS 84

MAPPING SOCIAL MEDIA TOOLS TO PROJECT MANAGEMENT PROCESS GROUPS...........................**86**

SHARING PROJECT INFORMATION **91**

CUSTOMERS, STAKEHOLDERS, AND LEADERSHIP ON SOCIAL MEDIA..........**94**

SOCIAL MEDIA EXPERTS...**95**

SUMMARY..**96**

PART II – PROJECT COMMUNICATION TOOLS BY KNOWLEDGE AREA **97**

CHAPTER 6..**99**

COMMUNICATION TOOLS THAT MANAGE PROJECT INTEGRATION 99

INTRODUCTION TO AGILE PROJECT MEETINGS **100**

PLANNING AGILE PROJECT SPRINT MEETINGS.. 101

REPORTING INFORMATION FROM AGILE PROJECT SPRINT MEETINGS............... 102

INTRODUCTION TO THE AGILE PRODUCT VISION STATEMENT **104**

PLANNING THE PRODUCT VISION STATEMENT STRATEGY MEETING 105

PLANNING TO USE A PRODUCT VISION STATEMENT 106

REPORTING USING THE PRODUCT VISION STATEMENT..................................... 106

INTRODUCTION TO THE PROJECT CHARTER..**107**

DEFINING THE ROLES 108

PLANNING THE PROJECT CHARTER 109

REPORTING INFORMATION FROM THE PROJECT CHARTER 109

INTRODUCTION TO THE PROJECT KICK-OFF MEETING **110**

PLANNING A PROJECT KICK-OFF MEETING 112

REPORTING INFORMATION FROM THE PROJECT KICK-OFF MEETING 112

INTRODUCTION TO THE PROJECT MANAGEMENT PLAN **113**

PLANNING A PROJECT MANAGEMENT PLAN 116

REPORTING INFORMATION FROM A PROJECT MANAGEMENT PLAN 116

INTRODUCTION TO THE PROJECT MEETING MINUTES **118**

PLANNING THE PROJECT MEETING MINUTES 120
REPORTING INFORMATION FROM THE PROJECT'S MEETING MINUTES 120

INTRODUCTION TO THE PROJECT STATUS MEETING **122**

PLANNING A PROJECT STATUS MEETING 124
REPORTING INFORMATION FROM A PROJECT STATUS MEETING 125

INTRODUCTION TO THE PROJECT STATUS REPORT **126**

PLANNING A PROJECT STATUS REPORT 128
REPORTING USING A PROJECT STATUS REPORT 128

SUMMARY **130**

CHAPTER 7 131
COMMUNICATION TOOLS THAT MANAGE PROJECT SCOPE 131

INTRODUCTION TO AGILE ESTIMATING TOOLS **132**

INTRODUCING AGILE RELATIVE SIZING 133
INTRODUCING AGILE STORY POINTS 133
INTRODUCING AGILE PLANNING POKER 134
INTRODUCING AGILE TEAM VELOCITY 134

INTRODUCTION TO THE AGILE USER STORY **135**

PLANNING THE PRODUCT VISION STATEMENT 136
PLANNING A USER STORY 137

INTRODUCTION TO THE AGILE USER STORY BACKLOG **138**

INTRODUCING AGILE PRODUCT BACKLOG 139
INTRODUCTION TO THE AGILE RELEASE BACKLOG 139
INTRODUCTION TO THE AGILE SPRINT BACKLOG 140

INTRODUCTION TO THE BUSINESS CASE **143**

PLANNING TO USE A BUSINESS CASE 144
REPORTING FROM A BUSINESS CASE 144

INTRODUCTION TO THE CUSTOMER REQUIREMENTS **146**

PLANNING TO USE CUSTOMER REQUIREMENTS 148
REPORTING CUSTOMER REQUIREMENTS 149

INTRODUCTION TO THE DESIGN SPECIFICATION DOCUMENT **150**

PLANNING TO USE A DESIGN SPECIFICATION DOCUMENT 152
REPORTING FROM THE DESIGN SPECIFICATION DOCUMENT 152

INTRODUCTION TO THE EXECUTIVE SUMMARY **154**

PLANNING TO USE AN EXECUTIVE SUMMARY 155

REPORTING FROM THE EXECUTIVE SUMMARY 155

INTRODUCTION TO THE FEASIBILITY STUDY **157**

PLANNING TO USE A FEASIBILITY STUDY 159
REPORTING FROM THE FEASIBILITY STUDY 159

INTRODUCTION TO THE SYSTEM REQUIREMENTS DOCUMENT **160**

PLANNING TO USE A SYSTEM REQUIREMENTS DOCUMENT 163
REPORTING FROM A SYSTEM REQUIREMENTS DOCUMENT 164

INTRODUCTION TO THE WORK BREAKDOWN STRUCTURE **165**

THE WORK PACKAGE 167
WBS DICTIONARY 167
WBS FUNCTIONAL LEVELS 167
WBS IN A PROJECT MANAGEMENT OFFICE ENVIRONMENT 168
PLANNING TO USE A WBS 170
REPORTING FROM A WBS 170

SUMMARY **173**

CHAPTER 8 .... **175**

COMMUNICATION TOOLS THAT MANAGE PROJECT TIME 175

INTRODUCTION TO THE BASELINE SCHEDULE **176**

PLANNING TO USE A BASELINE SCHEDULE 178
REPORTING FROM A BASELINE SCHEDULE 178

INTRODUCTION TO THE GANTT CHART **179**

PLANNING TO USE A GANTT CHART 181
REPORTING FROM A GANTT CHART 181

INTRODUCTION TO THE LOGIC NETWORK DIAGRAM **185**

PURE LOGIC DIAGRAM 186
TIME SCALE DIAGRAM 186
PLANNING TO USE A LOGIC NETWORK DIAGRAM 188
REPORTING FROM A LOGIC NETWORK DIAGRAM 188

INTRODUCTION TO THE PROJECT SCHEDULE **192**

PLANNING TO USE A PROJECT SCHEDULE 195
REPORTING FROM A PROJECT SCHEDULE 196

SUMMARY **197**

CHAPTER 9 .... **199**

COMMUNICATION TOOLS THAT MANAGE PROJECT COSTS 199

INTRODUCTION TO THE BUDGET SPREADSHEET **200**

PLANNING TO USE A BUDGET SPREADSHEET 202
REPORTING FROM A BUDGET SPREADSHEET 203

INTRODUCTION TO EARNED VALUE ANALYSIS **205**

MEASURING A PROJECT'S EARNED VALUE 207
CALCULATING EARNED VALUE ANALYSIS PERFORMANCE 207
PERFORMING AND INTERPRETING EARNED VALUE ANALYSIS 207
PLANNING TO USE EARNED VALUE ANALYSIS 208
REPORTING FROM EARNED VALUE ANALYSIS 208

INTRODUCTION TO THE EARNED VALUE ESTIMATING TOOL **211**

CALCULATING FORMULAS FOR ESTIMATING 212
PLANNING TO USE AN ESTIMATING TOOL 213
REPORTING FROM THE ESTIMATING TOOL 213

SUMMARY **214**

CHAPTER 10 ....**215**

COMMUNICATION TOOLS THAT MANAGE PROJECT QUALITY 215

INTRODUCTION TO THE COMPREHENSIVE TEST PLAN **216**

PLANNING TO USE A COMPREHENSIVE TEST PLAN 218
REPORTING FROM A COMPREHENSIVE TEST PLAN 218

INTRODUCTION TO THE CONTROL CHART **219**

PLANNING TO USE A CONTROL CHART 221
REPORTING FROM A CONTROL CHART 221

INTRODUCTION TO THE DESIGN SPECIFICATION DOCUMENT **223**

PLANNING TO USE A DESIGN SPECIFICATION DOCUMENT 224
REPORTING FROM THE DESIGN SPECIFICATION DOCUMENT 225

INTRODUCTION TO THE QUALITY MANAGEMENT PLAN **227**

PLANNING TO USE A QUALITY MANAGEMENT PLAN 229
REPORTING FROM A QUALITY MANAGEMENT PLAN 230
Understanding the Shewhart cycle *230*

INTRODUCTION TO THE QUALITY METRICS TOOL **232**

PLANNING TO USE A QUALITY METRICS TOOL 233
REPORTING FROM QUALITY METRICS 233

INTRODUCTION TO THE SCATTER CHART **235**

PLANNING TO USE A SCATTER CHART 239
REPORTING FROM A SCATTER CHART 239

SUMMARY **241**

CHAPTER 11..**243**

CoMMUNICATION TOOLS FOR HUMAN RESOURCE MANAGEMENT..243

INTRODUCTION TO THE CIRCLE-OF-COMMUNICATIONS CHART...**244**

PLANNING TO USE A CIRCLE-OF-COMMUNICATIONS CHART 246
REPORTING FROM THE CIRCLE-OF-COMMUNICATIONS CHART 246

INTRODUCTION TO THE HISTOGRAM REPORT **247**

PLANNING TO USE A HISTOGRAM REPORT 249
REPORTING FROM A HISTOGRAM REPORT 249

INTRODUCTION TO THE PROJECT ORGANIZATION CHART **252**

PLANNING TO USE THE PROJECT ORGANIZATION CHART 254
REPORTING FROM A PROJECT ORGANIZATION CHART 254

INTRODUCTION TO THE RESPONSIBILITY MATRIX **256**

PLANNING TO USE THE RESPONSIBILITY MATRIX 260
REPORTING FROM THE RESPONSIBILITY MATRIX 260

SUMMARY..**261**

CHAPTER 12..**263**

DEFINING COMMUNICATION TOOLS THAT MANAGE PROJECT COMMUNICATIONS 263

INTRODUCTION TO AGILE INFORMATION RADIATORS **264**

INTRODUCING LOW-TECH, HIGH-TOUCH AGILE INFORMATION RADIATORS..264
INTRODUCING HIGH-TECH, LOW-TOUCH AGILE INFORMATION RADIATORS..265
PLANNING TO AGILE INFORMATION RADIATORS 266
REPORTING FROM AGILE INFORMATION RADIATORS 267

INTRODUCTION TO THE COMMUNICATION PLAN...**268**

PLANNING TO USE A COMMUNICATION PLAN 270
REPORTING FROM THE COMMUNICATION PLAN 270
COMMUNICATION PLAN MATRIX TEMPLATE 270

INTRODUCTION TO THE CHANGE READINESS ASSESSMENT DOCUMENT................................**272**

PLANNING TO USE A CHANGE READINESS ASSESSMENT 274
REPORTING FROM A CHANGE READINESS ASSESSMENT 275

INTRODUCTION TO THE DAILY PROGRESS REPORT **277**

PLANNING TO USE A DAILY PROGRESS REPORT 278
REPORTING FROM A DAILY PROGRESS REPORT 279

INTRODUCTION TO THE PARETO CHART...**280**

PLANNING TO USE A PARETO CHART...282

REPORTING FROM THE PARETO CHART 282

INTRODUCTION TO THE PROJECT CALENDAR **283**

PLANNING TO USE A PROJECT CALENDAR TOOL 285
REPORTING FROM THE PROJECT CALENDAR TOOL 285

INTRODUCTION TO THE PROJECT PRESENTATION **288**

PLANNING TO GIVE A BETTER PROJECT PRESENTATION 290
REPORTING FROM PROJECT PRESENTATIONS 290

INTRODUCTION TO THE SPIDER CHART **292**

PLANNING TO USE A SPIDER CHART 293
REPORTING FROM A SPIDER CHART 294

INTRODUCTION TO THE STOPLIGHT REPORT **296**

PLANNING TO USE A STOPLIGHT REPORT 298
REPORTING FROM A STOPLIGHT REPORT 298

INTRODUCTION TO THE WORK PACKAGE **300**

PLANNING TO USE A WORK PACKAGE 301
REPORTING FROM A WORK PACKAGE 301

SUMMARY **305**

CHAPTER 13 ....**307**

DEFINING COMMUNICATION TOOLS TO MANAGE PROJECT RISK 307

INTRODUCTION TO THE EXPECTED MONETARY VALUE **308**

PLANNING TO USE THE EXPECTED MONETARY VALUE 310
REPORTING FROM EXPECTED MONETARY VALUE 310

INTRODUCTION TO THE ISSUES LIST **312**

PLANNING TO USE AN ISSUES LIST 315
REPORTING FROM AN ISSUES LIST 315

INTRODUCTION TO THE RISK ASSESSMENT FORM **317**

PLANNING TO USE THE RISK ASSESSMENT FORM 320
REPORTING FROM A RISK ASSESSMENT FORM 320

INTRODUCTION TO THE RISK MATRIX **322**

PLANNING TO USE A RISK MATRIX TOOL 325
REPORTING FROM THE RISK MATRIX TOOL 326

INTRODUCTION TO THE RISK MODEL **327**

PLANNING TO USE A RISK MODEL 329
REPORTING FROM A RISK MODEL 330

INTRODUCTION TO THE RISK REGISTER **331**

PLANNING TO USE THE RISK REGISTER 334

REPORTING FROM THE RISK REGISTER 334

SUMMARY **335**

CHAPTER 14 ....**337**

DEFINING COMMUNICATION TOOLS TO MANAGE PROJECT PROCUREMENT 337

INTRODUCTION TO THE DOCUMENT CONTROL SYSTEM **338**

PLANNING TO USE THE DOCUMENT CONTROL SYSTEM 341

REPORTING FROM A DOCUMENT CONTROL SYSTEM 341

INTRODUCTION TO THE FORMAL ACCEPTANCE DOCUMENT **342**

PLANNING TO USE A FORMAL ACCEPTANCE DOCUMENT 345

REPORTING FROM THE FORMAL ACCEPTANCE DOCUMENT 345

INTRODUCTION TO THE LESSONS-LEARNED DOCUMENT **347**

PLANNING TO USE A LESSONS-LEARNED DOCUMENT 351

REPORTING FROM THE LESSONS-LEARNED DOCUMENT 351

INTRODUCTION TO THE PROJECT PROPOSAL **353**

PLANNING TO USE A PROJECT PROPOSAL 355

REPORTING FROM A PROJECT PROPOSAL 355

INTRODUCTION TO THE USER ACCEPTANCE DOCUMENT **356**

PLANNING TO USE A USER ACCEPTANCE DOCUMENT 358

REPORTING FROM THE USER ACCEPTANCE DOCUMENT 358

SUMMARY **359**

CHAPTER 15 ....**361**

DEFINING COMMUNICATION TOOLS FOR WORKING WITH STAKEHOLDERS 361

INTRODUCING TO THE CHANGE CONTROL PLAN **362**

UNDERSTANDING CHANGE CONTROL PLAN...364

PLANNING TO USE A CHANGE CONTROL PLAN 365

REPORTING FROM THE CHANGE CONTROL FORM 365

INTRODUCING TO THE CHANGE REQUEST FORM **367**

CHANGE REQUEST FORM 368

CHANGE REQUEST LOG 369

PLANNING TO USE A CHANGE REQUEST FORM..370

REPORTING FROM A CHANGE REQUEST FORM..370

INTRODUCING THE DASHBOARD TOOL **372**

PLANNING TO USE A DASHBOARD REPORT 374
REPORTING FROM A DASHBOARD REPORT 374

INTRODUCING TO THE PROJECT NEWSLETTER...375

PLANNING TO USE A PROJECT NEWSLETTER... 377
REPORTING FROM A PROJECT NEWSLETTER 377

INTRODUCING TO THE STAKEHOLDER REGISTER 378

PLANNING TO USE A STAKEHOLDER REGISTER 379
REPORTING FROM A STAKEHOLDER REGISTER 380

INTRODUCING TO THE STAKEHOLDER MANAGEMENT PLAN 381

PLANNING TO USE A STAKEHOLDER MANAGEMENT PLAN 382
REPORTING FROM A STAKEHOLDER MANAGEMENT PLAN 382

SUMMARY...384

PART III – PROJECT COMMUNICATION TOOLS BY PROCESS GROUPS.................385

CHAPTER 16..387

USING COMMUNICATION TOOLS DURING THE INITIATING PROCESS 387

MASTERING THE AGILE PRODUCT VISION STATEMENT 389

CREATING AN AGILE PRODUCT VISION STATEMENT... 389
PRODUCT VISION STATEMENT 393
PRODUCT VISION STATEMENT EXAMPLE 393
USING AGILE PRODUCT VISION STATEMENT 393

MASTERING AGILE ESTIMATING TOOLS...395

CREATING AGILE RELATIVE SIZING 395
USING AGILE RELATIVE SIZING 398
CREATING AGILE STORY POINTS 398
USING AGILE STORY POINTS 399
CREATING AGILE PLANNING POKER 399
USING AGILE PLANNING POKER 401
CREATING AGILE TEAM VELOCITY 401
USING AGILE TEAM VELOCITY 402

MASTERING AGILE USER STORIES..403

CREATING AGILE EPIC USER STORIES... 403
USING AGILE EPIC USER STORIES 406
CREATING DETAILED AGILE USER STORIES 407
USING DETAILED AGILE USER STORIES... 409

MASTERING AGILE USER STORY BACKLOGS..410

CREATING THE AGILE USER STORY PRODUCT BACKLOG 410

USING THE AGILE USER STORY PRODUCT BACKLOG 412
CREATING THE AGILE USER STORY RELEASE BACKLOG 413
USING THE AGILE USER STORY RELEASE BACKLOG 415
CREATING THE AGILE USER STORY SPRINT BACKLOG 415
USING THE AGILE USER STORY SPRINT BACKLOG 419

MASTERING THE BUSINESS CASE **420**

CREATING THE BUSINESS CASE 421
USING THE BUSINESS CASE 421

MASTERING THE CIRCLE-OF-COMMUNICATIONS CHART **422**

CREATING THE CIRCLE-OF-COMMUNICATIONS CHART 422
USING THE CIRCLE-OF-COMMUNICATIONS CHART 423

MASTERING THE COMMUNICATION PLAN **424**

CREATING THE COMMUNICATION PLAN 424
USING THE COMMUNICATION PLAN 425

MASTERING THE CUSTOMER REQUIREMENTS DOCUMENT **427**

CREATING A CUSTOMER REQUIREMENTS DOCUMENT 427
USING A CUSTOMER REQUIREMENTS DOCUMENT 429

MASTERING THE DOCUMENT CONTROL SYSTEM **431**

CREATING THE DOCUMENT CONTROL SYSTEM 431
USING THE DOCUMENT CONTROL SYSTEM 435

MASTERING THE EXECUTIVE SUMMARY **436**

CREATING THE EXECUTIVE SUMMARY 436
USING THE EXECUTIVE SUMMARY 437

MASTERING THE FEASIBILITY STUDY **438**

CREATING A FEASIBILITY STUDY 438
USING A FEASIBILITY STUDY 439

MASTERING THE PROJECT CHARTER **441**

CREATING THE PROJECT CHARTER 441
USING A PROJECT CHARTER 443

MASTERING THE PROJECT KICK-OFF MEETING **444**

CREATING THE PROJECT KICK-OFF MEETING 445
USING A PROJECT KICK-OFF MEETING 448

MASTERING THE PROJECT MANAGEMENT PLAN **449**

CREATING A PROJECT MANAGEMENT PLAN 450
USING THE PROJECT MANAGEMENT PLAN 453

MASTERING THE PROJECT ORGANIZATION CHART **454**

CREATING A PROJECT ORGANIZATION CHART.. 454

USING A PROJECT ORGANIZATION CHART 455

MASTERING THE PROJECT PROPOSAL **456**

CREATING A PROJECT PROPOSAL.. 456

USING A PROJECT PROPOSAL 458

MASTERING THE QUALITY MANAGEMENT PLAN **460**

CREATING A QUALITY MANAGEMENT PLAN 460

USING A QUALITY MANAGEMENT PLAN.. 462

MASTERING THE STAKEHOLDER REGISTER **463**

CREATING THE STAKEHOLDER REGISTER 463

USING THE STAKEHOLDER REGISTER 464

MASTERING THE STAKEHOLDER MANAGEMENT PLAN **466**

CREATING THE STAKEHOLDER MANAGEMENT PLAN 466

USING THE STAKEHOLDER MANAGEMENT PLAN... 467

SUMMARY..**469**

CHAPTER 17..**471**

USING COMMUNICATION TOOLS TO ADMINISTER THE PLANNING PROCESS 471

MASTERING THE CHANGE READINESS ASSESSMENT..**472**

CREATING THE CHANGE READINESS ASSESSMENT 472

USING THE CHANGE READINESS ASSESSMENT 474

MASTERING THE DASHBOARD REPORT **475**

CREATING A DASHBOARD REPORT.. 475

USING A DASHBOARD REPORT... 477

MASTERING THE RESPONSIBILITY MATRIX **479**

CREATING A RESPONSIBILITY MATRIX.. 479

USING THE RESPONSIBILITY MATRIX 481

MASTERING THE RISK MODELING PROCESS...**483**

CREATING A RISK MODEL 483

USING A RISK MODEL 485

SUMMARY..**486**

CHAPTER 18..**487**

USING COMMUNICATION TOOLS TO PLAN AND DEVELOP PROJECT DELIVERABLES 487

MASTERING THE BASELINE SCHEDULE..**488**

CREATING A BASELINE SCHEDULE 488

USING A BASELINE SCHEDULE 489

MASTERING THE CHANGE CONTROL PLAN **490**

CREATING A CHANGE CONTROL PLAN 490

USING A CHANGE CONTROL PLAN 492

MASTERING THE COMPREHENSIVE TEST PLAN **494**

CREATING A COMPREHENSIVE TEST PLAN 494

USING A COMPREHENSIVE TEST PLAN 496

MASTERING THE DESIGN SPECIFICATIONS...**497**

CREATING DESIGN SPECIFICATIONS 497

USING DESIGN SPECIFICATIONS 498

MASTERING THE EXPECTED MONETARY VALUE...**500**

CREATING AN EXPECTED MONETARY VALUE... 500

USING AN EXPECTED MONETARY VALUE 501

MASTERING THE PROJECT CALENDAR **502**

CREATING A PROJECT CALENDAR 502

USING A PROJECT CALENDAR.. 503

MASTERING THE PROJECT SCHEDULE **505**

CREATING A PROJECT SCHEDULE 505

USING A PROJECT SCHEDULE 507

MASTERING THE SYSTEM REQUIREMENTS DOCUMENT **508**

CREATING A SYSTEM REQUIREMENTS DOCUMENT... 508

USING A SYSTEM REQUIREMENTS DOCUMENT 511

MASTERING THE WORK BREAKDOWN STRUCTURE (WBS) **513**

CREATING A WORK BREAKDOWN STRUCTURE 513

Basic rules or guidelines to follow when you are creating a WBS............................ *514*

Identifying functional levels of the WBS *515*

USING A WORK BREAKDOWN STRUCTURE 516

SUMMARY..**517**

CHAPTER 19..**519**

USING COMMUNICATION TOOLS FOR PROJECT REPORTING DURING THE PLANNING PROCESS.................... 519

MASTERING THE BUDGET SPREADSHEET...**520**

CREATING A BUDGET SPREADSHEET 520

USING A BUDGET SPREADSHEET 522

MASTERING THE EARNED VALUE ANALYSIS TOOL **523**

CREATING THE EARNED VALUE ANALYSIS PERFORMANCE TOOL... 523
USING THE EARNED VALUE ANALYSIS PERFORMANCE TOOL 527

MASTERING THE EARNED VALUE ESTIMATING TOOL...**529**

CREATING AN EARNED VALUE ESTIMATING TOOL.. 529
CREATING A PROJECT FORECAST 530
USING THE EARNED VALUE ESTIMATING TOOL 530

MASTERING THE LOGIC NETWORK DIAGRAM...**532**

CREATING A LOGIC NETWORK DIAGRAM... 532
USING A LOGIC NETWORK DIAGRAM 533

MASTERING QUALITY METRICS **535**

CREATING QUALITY METRICS 535
USING QUALITY METRICS 537

MASTERING THE RISK REGISTER...**538**

CREATING A RISK REGISTER.. 538
USING A RISK REGISTER 539

MASTERING THE RISK MATRIX **541**

CREATING A RISK MATRIX.. 541
USING A RISK MATRIX 542

MASTERING THE SCATTER CHART **544**

CREATING A SCATTER CHART 545
USING A SCATTER CHART 546

SUMMARY...**548**

CHAPTER 20...**549**

USING COMMUNICATION TOOLS DURING THE EXECUTING AND CONTROLLING PROCESSES TO ADMINISTER THE PROJECT. 549

MASTERING AGILE PROJECT MEETINGS..**550**

AGILE PROJECT MEETINGS OVERVIEW 551
AGILE SPRINT PLANNING MEETING 551
AGILE DAILY STANDUP MEETING 553
AGILE SPRINT REVIEW MEETING 554
AGILE SPRINT RETROSPECTIVE MEETING 556

MASTERING THE CHANGE REQUEST FORM..**559**

CREATING A CHANGE REQUEST 560
USING A CHANGE REQUEST 561

MASTERING THE CONTROL CHART 563

CREATING A CONTROL CHART 563
USING THE CONTROL CHART 566

MASTERING THE PROJECT NEWSLETTER 568

CREATING A PROJECT NEWSLETTER 568
USING THE PROJECT NEWSLETTER 569

MASTERING PROJECT PRESENTATIONS 570

CREATING PROJECT PRESENTATIONS 570
USING PROJECT PRESENTATIONS 571

MASTERING THE PROJECT STATUS MEETING 573

PLANNING THE PROJECT STATUS MEETING 573
FACILITATING THE PROJECT STATUS MEETING 575

SUMMARY 576

CHAPTER 21 577

USING COMMUNICATION TOOLS DURING THE EXECUTING AND CONTROLLING PROCESS 577

MASTERING THE ISSUES LIST 578

CREATING THE ISSUES LIST 578
USING AN ISSUES LIST 579

MASTERING PROJECT MEETING MINUTES 580

CREATING PROJECT MEETING MINUTES 581
USING PROJECT MEETING MINUTES 581

MASTERING THE RISK ASSESSMENT FORM 583

CREATING A RISK ASSESSMENT FORM 583
USING A RISK ASSESSMENT FORM 584

MASTERING THE WORK PACKAGE 586

CREATING A WORK PACKAGE 586
USING A WORK PACKAGE 587

SUMMARY 589

CHAPTER 22 591

USING COMMUNICATION TOOLS DURING THE EXECUTING AND CONTROLLING PROCESS TO REPORT PROJECT INFORMATION 591

MASTERING AGILE INFORMATION RADIATORS 592

CREATING THE AGILE PRODUCT ROADMAP 592
USING THE AGILE PRODUCT ROADMAP 595

CREATING THE AGILE KANBAN BOARD...596
USING THE AGILE KANBAN BOARD..597
CREATING THE AGILE BURNDOWN CHART 597
USING THE AGILE SPRINT BURNDOWN CHART 599
CREATING THE AGILE RELEASE BURNUP CHART 600
USING THE AGILE SPRINT BURNUP CHART..601

MASTERING THE DAILY PROGRESS REPORT...**603**

CREATING A DAILY PROGRESS REPORT 603
USING A DAILY PROGRESS REPORT..604

MASTERING THE GANTT CHART...**605**

CREATING A GANTT CHART 605
USING A GANTT CHART REPORT 606

MASTERING THE HISTOGRAM REPORT...**607**

CREATING A HISTOGRAM REPORT 607
USING A HISTOGRAM REPORT 609

MASTERING THE PARETO CHART...**610**

CREATING A PARETO CHART 610
USING A PARETO CHART...613

MASTERING THE PROJECT STATUS REPORT...**614**

CREATING A PROJECT STATUS REPORT 614
USING A PROJECT STATUS REPORT 615

MASTERING THE SPIDER CHART..**617**

CREATING A SPIDER CHART...617
USING A SPIDER CHART 619

MASTERING THE STOPLIGHT REPORT..**620**

CREATING A STOPLIGHT REPORT 620
USING A STOPLIGHT REPORT..624

SUMMARY...**626**

CHAPTER 23...**627**

USING COMMUNICATION TOOLS DURING THE CLOSEOUT PROCESS 627

MASTERING THE FORMAL ACCEPTANCE DOCUMENT **628**

CREATING THE FORMAL ACCEPTANCE DOCUMENT...628
USING THE FORMAL ACCEPTANCE DOCUMENT..630

MASTERING THE LESSONS-LEARNED DOCUMENT..**632**

CREATING THE LESSONS-LEARNED DOCUMENT 633

USING THE LESSONS-LEARNED DOCUMENT 633

MASTERING THE USER ACCEPTANCE DOCUMENT...**635**

CREATING THE USER ACCEPTANCE DOCUMENT 636
USING A USER ACCEPTANCE DOCUMENT 637

SUMMARY...**638**

PART IV – PROJECT MANAGEMENT BI & PMP® EXAM QUESTIONS.......................**639**

CHAPTER 24...**641**

PROJECT MANAGEMENT BUSINESS INTELLIGENCE 641

INTRODUCING BUSINESS INTELLIGENCE AS A TOOL FOR PROJECT COMMUNICATIONS **642**

PLANNING TO USE BUSINESS INTELLIGENCE AS A TOOL FOR PROJECT MANAGEMENT COMMUNICATIONS **644**

THE PROJECT MANAGEMENT BI PROCESS **646**

USING BUSINESS INTELLIGENT REPORTS **648**

REPORT INFORMATION DECISIONS AND ASSESSMENT—PROJECT RISK DASHBOARD 649

SUMMARY...**652**

CHAPTER 25...**653**

SAMPLE PMP® EXAM QUESTIONS FOR PROJECT COMMUNICATIONS 653

SAMPLE PMP® EXAM QUESTIONS: COMMUNICATIONS.......................................**654**

SUMMARY...**657**

CHAPTER 26...**659**

BIBLIOGRAPHY 659

CHAPTER 27...**661**

APPENDIX 661

SAMPLE PMP® EXAM ANSWERS AND EXPLANATIONS **662**

ANSWERS EXPLAINED: 662

PROJECT MANAGEMENT COMMUNICATION TOOLS MASTER LIST **664**

CHAPTER 28...**669**

INDEX.. 669

Dedication

To Our Wives & Families

We want to thank Kath and Nancy for their constant dedication and never-ending support while we wrote this book. The development of this book became a major project for all of us and we spent many hours apart. We both thank you for being so understanding and giving us that time. It was truly a team effort.

About the Authors

Bill Dow has worked in Information Technology (IT) for the last 23 years, with 21 years focusing on project management. He built two Project Management Organization (PMOs) from the ground up by using Project Management Institute's (PMI) best practices and core principals and he's led countless projects. He has worked in Canada, the United States, and across a variety of industries.

Bill is the co-author of the book, *Project Management Communications Bible*, published in 2008 by Wiley Publishing Inc. This book, Project Management Communications book is a major update to the Communication Bible, where we have incorporated new material, updated PMI references, and added exciting new chapters.

Bill's second book, *The Tactical Guide for Building a PMO,* encapsulates 10 years' experience building and implementing PMOs into an easy read and text book for any PMO manager, portfolio, program, or project manager.

Bill is currently the Project Management Discipline Owner for Microsoft Corporation in the IT department, as well as an Adjunct Professor at Bellevue College in Bellevue, Washington. Bill also owns his own book publishing company, Dow Publishing LLC.

Contact Bill Dow at: billdow@dowpublishingllc.com

Bruce Taylor is an expert in the field of project management. He regularly provides professional assistance to top management and has accumulated impressive experience in developing project scheduling and cost control systems continuously since the mid-1960s. He has worked worldwide on some of the largest projects, including some major offshore platforms in the North Sea and the Northwest shelf of Australia.

Bruce is a pioneer in project management software tools. He and a partner founded a small project management consulting and software development company, which quickly grew internationally. Using his experience, the company developed and marketed an automated project scheduling and cost control system. Included in this development was the first automated network logic diagram chart using the critical path method of scheduling. He built a client base of over 150 major companies worldwide, including branch offices in France and Australia.

Over the past 40+ years, he has conducted many project management classes and seminars throughout the United States, Canada, Europe, Japan, Australia, South America, and the Near and Far East.

Contact Bruce Taylor at: brucehtaylor@hotmail.com

Credits

Book Front, Back, and Side Cover(s) Design— **Elysia Chu**

Book Foreword— **Tammo T. Wilkens, P.E., PMP**

Book Editor—**Sarah Rogers**

Project Management Leadership, Mentor, Friend—**Al Callan, PMP**

Agile Project Management Communication Tools—**Kevin W. Reilly, PMP, PMI-ACP, CSM, CSPO**

Project Management Body of Knowledge® (*PMBOK® Guide*) Exam Questions—**Dan Yeomans, PMP**

Project Management Business Intelligence—**Michael Hopmere**

Foreword

The Project Management Institute's *PMBOK® Guide* devotes an entire knowledge area to communications. Why? Communications is such a general and pervasive process; we all do it naturally. Why do we need a communications standard? As part of my Project Management Certificate program at Cal State Dominguez Hills, I naturally cover communications. I ask the students, "What are Project Managers supposed to do?" Of course, I get the usual answers about producing plans, producing schedules, reviewing designs, managing risks, and so on. I then tell them that while project managers are certainly involved in those endeavors, they are not supposed to "do" anything. All that project managers *should* do is communicate and facilitate. It's the rest of the project team that "does" everything.

As you most likely realize, the reality is that project managers do indeed get their hands dirty producing the above mentioned items. But, one needs to realize that when project managers do perform these tasks, they temporarily remove their management hat and swap it out for a worker's hat. The whole point is that communications is a central effort to managing projects, so skills in that arena are essential to being a successful project manager.

No human social process is as pervasive, or as important, as communications. It affects all human relationships and endeavors; be it a marriage, a football game, the classroom, or a project. Somehow, we all seem to be able to recognize poor communication or the lack of any communication, but we can't seem to see it coming, and we're not sure just what makes good communications. That makes it difficult to intercept the problem because it is generally too late by the time we identify the problem. One solution might be proper planning. You have likely heard the old adage that, "Those who fail to plan, plan to fail!" Yet even planning requires some forethought, help, and proper tools.

Project teams and stakeholders require information as rapidly as possible. Receiving a monthly progress report long after the status date is like reading last week's newspaper. Team members require accurate and comprehensive details on the scope of their work and they need it "now." Stakeholders want to know the status and the performance of the project execution. Contractors need to have clarification on ambiguous issues in the specifications and drawings. Funding agencies want to know that their funds are being used as planned. Participants want to know what to expect at upcoming meetings so they can prepare. International teams face the added challenge of different time zones and cultural issues, such as perceptions and practices.

Communications technology has evolved and allowed for much greater speed in communicating. Similarly, the newer technology for executing the project activities has allowed for more rapid production and execution of the work. Along with this speed increase, we are faced with problems and issues arising more rapidly and in increasing volume. This, in turn, requires more rapid capabilities with which to respond, and tools for dealing with the vast array of data and information. Nothing has revolutionized human communication capability as much as the Internet, and since Gutenberg invented the printing press. Radio and television come close, but even they are limited in scope by the presentation format, the geographic boundaries of broadcasts, and the regulatory limitations of governments. And with the ever expanding use of the Internet, even these media have resorted to streaming their content over the Internet. This continuing evolution of technology seems to have no end in sight. This new edition will help you deal with these technological changes.

Communication is the key to keeping team members, managers, and stakeholders informed and on track to pursue the project objectives. Communication is also the key to identifying issues, risks, misunderstandings, and other challenges to project completion.

The task of dealing with all of these challenges and demands can be daunting; however, there is abundant help available. The literature is full of books on communication skills and methodologies. The challenge is to find a single, comprehensive publication that covers the subject from head to toe, for project management in particular.

Add to all this, the vast array of options for what, when, and how to communicate project information, and it can quickly become a bit overwhelming on just what to do and how to do it right. A comprehensive guide that is well organized and attuned to PMI's *PMBOK® Guide* is a tool that will only enhance your success as a project manager.

I am delighted to congratulate you on reading a volume that has met that challenge. Bruce Taylor and Bill Dow, PMP have concluded a superb effort to bring the subject into focus while covering all aspects of the issues. This second edition brings the topics up to date as technology has advanced ever further. Using the *PMBOK® Guide* as a framework, they have organized the material in a logical fashion that will aid you in honing your skills in a particular subject. You will also find the material broken down into two major parts: tools and processes.

Whether you are looking to gain insight about specific tools and techniques that can help you, you will find the answer here. The material is also current in light of the ever-changing technologies that we humans use to communicate with others. Just as the technology of communications tools has evolved, so has the type of information and the formats used to present information. Performance reports, earned value techniques, information distribution systems, document control systems, configuration control processes, and risk handling are just a few of the many project communication tools used around the globe. Many of these have evolved over time. This volume covers it all.

So please, keep this book within reach, mark the pages, use paperclips or self-stick notes as bookmarks. It will be your friend for life. Enjoy! And may your future communication problems all disappear before they really are problems.

Tammo T. Wilkens, P.E., PMP

Preface

This book is a guide for all project managers, team members, and customers or clients regardless of the project's size, industry, or complexity. The book acts as a single source of project communication tools for immediate use on your projects.

As a project manager, one of your top priorities is to ensure that you have a handle on all of your project's communications. It's critical that you control every "major" message flowing in and out of your project. There is an old, but wise, saying, "A project that communicates poorly is going to perform poorly." That's such a true statement, and one that should guide you on your projects.

This book maps various communication tools to PMI's *PMBOK® Guide* knowledge areas and life-cycle process.

The mapping between the methodologies and the tools allows you and your team members to easily understand which tools to use when communicating during a particular area of the project.

As you start to look at the mapping between the communication tools and the knowledge areas, there can be a great debate over where a tool will live. Should the tool be in the planning or executing phase? Should a tool be assigned to integration or closing? Regardless of where a tool should or shouldn't live, your job is to find the right tool for what you are trying to communicate. If you are stuck trying to communicate a budget issue, look in the cost section to find the budgeting tools. We understand that there cannot be a perfect match on where a tool will live, but that's really not the point of the mapping. The point is to get you thinking about your projects in a different way and to be able to quickly find a tool based on your project's current knowledge area or life cycle. We mapped both the *PMBOK® Guide's* knowledge areas and life-cycle processes for every communication tool.

When reviewing the tools in this book, you will see the terms "customer" or "stakeholder," and it is important to understand who these individuals are. The project customer, or stakeholder, is the individual who has commissioned you to do the project. Some people use the term "client," but regardless of the term used, this individual is the "customer." The other assumption that we make is that you, the reader, are a project manager. You will see a lot of "you" must do this, or "you" should do that, well, that's because we are speaking to you, the project manager. You could be running a large IT project, a construction project, or a research project. It doesn't matter the project type, what matters is you understand that we are trying to help you be more successful.

This book includes an appendix with a table called, "Project Management Communication Tools List" that provides you with an instant reference of the various communication tools located throughout the book. The spreadsheet contains tool name, chapter # for part II chapter # for part III, knowledge area, life cycle, and its' purpose for use with social media tools. You'll likely find this spreadsheet priceless in managing your project's communications!

If you are not a project manager, and you are playing the role of a customer or a client of a project, having this knowledge and understanding of the mapping between communication tools and knowledge areas or life-cycle processes will be valuable to you as well. This will give you great insight and allow you to have meaningful conversations with your project manager or team members about which tools are available to use on the project. You can request that the project manager use tools that you need for particular areas of the project that you previously didn't know existed. If you ever feel you are not getting good information on a particular area of the project from your team, you now have access to solutions and several tools at your fingertips that you can share with your project manager for use on the project. This information is valuable and will help you get the information you need from the project manager in a format you can use to make project decisions. It is important that you are getting the information you need to make project decisions and guide the project to completion. Using the tools in this book, you can suggest to the project manager, or team members, the tools you would like them to use on your project. The project manager will have examples readily available that they can show you and that you can jointly agree to use on your project. Without you having the knowledge of all the different kinds of communication tools available, you may not know what project information you are missing (budget spreadsheet, risk register...and so on) and, therefore, may not be getting all the data you need to make project decisions. This book will become valuable to you in ensuring your project manager or project team members are continually sending you the information you need in the format that you need.

To communicate more effectively, this book offers a series of communication tools to anyone involved in the project. There are times when project managers, or team members, are unfamiliar with how to communicate certain aspects of their project. That happens to even the most seasoned project managers. However, there is a solution, and that is for the project manager to grab the mapping chart for communication tools to knowledge areas (or life-cycle processes) to help resolve that communication issue. The project manager can reference any one of the tools in this book to help communicate across any of those areas. Because there are many tools in this book, there is a high likelihood that one of the tools will be applicable for a particular projects scenario. The communication tools in this book are applicable for across various projects and most industries. That is the great aspect about project communication management; it is not industry specific—a status report is a status report. You need one in IT, you need one in construction, and you need one in manufacturing. The content is different, but the tools are essentially the same.

What's New in this Version

Anytime a new version of a book is published, the first question people ask is, "What is in the new edition—should I buy this edition when I already own the first version?" These are great questions and we would say, yes, yes, yes...

We updated this edition to include some new and exciting chapters while removing some outdated tools. For example, we removed the critical chain tools, which were much more popular and relevant five or six years ago, but not as relevant today. There are other tools we removed, but let's not spend time looking back, let's look forward. The complete list of tools is in the **Project Management Communication Tools** table located in the Appendix.

Here is the list of new chapters and sections we added in this edition:

- Agile Project Management Communication Tools
- Chapter 5 - Social Media and Project Management Communication Tools
- Chapter 24 - Project Management Business Intelligence
- Chapter 25 - PMBOK Exam Questions (Project Communications)

We are excited to bring you this new edition as we believe it is going to help you drive your projects as effectively as possible, while keeping communications as your top priority.

Important Note about the Tool Templates:

Tool templates will be available online at Dowpublishingllc.com website.

How To Get the Most out of this Book

Here are some areas to consider that will help you get the most out of this book:

- For general knowledge of project communications in a working environment, review and analyze Part I of the book.
- For information about communications tools and how they relate to knowledge areas, review and analyze Part II of the book.
- For information about communications tools and how they relate to life-cycle processes, review and analyze Part III of the book.
- The Agile Project Management Communication tools are contained in Part II and Part III of the book.
- For general knowledge of Project Management Business Intelligence (BI), Social Media and Project Management, and Project Management Professional (PMP®) Exam Prep questions (communication questions only), review and analyze Part IV of the book.
- Refer to the Appendix to review the PMP® Exam Prep Answers and Project Management Communication Tools table as a reference to ensure that you are using the right communications tools for your project.

Tip
Tips offer you extra information that further explains a given topic or technique, often suggesting alternatives or workarounds to a listed procedure.

Note
Notes provide supplementary information to the text, shedding light on background processes or miscellaneous options that aren't crucial to the basic understanding of the material.

Cross-reference
Cross references help you find related information to a given topic in another chapter.

Tool Value
Tool values show you the value of the tool for the project manager, customer, team members, and other stakeholders.

Social Media Tools
Social media information provides the common communication purposes and the most applicable social media tools.

Caution
Caution provides extra information to about tool that the project manager should watch out for when using the tool.

How this Book Is Organized

The book is broken down and organized in four main parts. In the first part, we discuss general project management communication. The second part covers communication tools that support the project knowledge areas. The third part includes the same communications tools; however, it demonstrates the creation and use of the tools across the life-cycle processes. Finally, the fourth part provides a different look at communication tools. This section covers areas such as project management BI, PMP® exam prep questions (communication questions only) and social media and project management. We hope that you find this extra information helpful. Finally, in the Appendix you will find answers to the PMP® exam prep questions and the Project Management Communication Tools table that documents every tool we discuss in the book. Feedback from the first version of the book indicated that many readers found the table useful; it quickly became a critical resource for project managers and team members when researching the appropriate tool to use when communicating project information.

Part I: An Introduction to Project Communications

Project communications planning is the task of identifying the information needs and requirements of the project's customers. Customers need information about the project, such as risk events, budget data, and schedule information. You are the project manager, so you must be proactive and plan for your customer's needs. Most project managers do not plan their communication needs and often struggle when times get tough on their projects. When project managers don't spend the time to properly plan their communications, they are forced to scramble to communicate effectively to their customers when project problems occur. It happens all the time, many project managers do not see the value of planning their communications and end up paying for it with failed projects, loss of customer confidence, and occasionally, removal from the project.

One of the most challenging parts of being a project manager is project communications. Many project managers fail at being good communicators. As projects become complex and more challenging, project managers need to step up and become effective communicators. The challenges that project managers face today are greater than in the past. These challenges include virtual project teams, shorter product times to market, and technology advancement. The project manager also deals with changes in the middle of the project, and the diversity of product availability (new products coming out daily). During communication planning, the project manager must document project information such as: who, what, where, when, and how. Occasionally, but not in the communication plan, documenting the *why* can also be valuable to you and your customer. Communication planning will guide you, your team, and the customer through the project life cycle.

The next area that we cover includes communicating in foreign environments and with virtual teams. Project management is now much more global than it ever has been. You may be responsible for driving virtual teams and travelling to foreign markets. Some of your project manager peers are spending 100% of their time traveling from country to country. In this section, we cover both virtual teams and some common customs of working and living in different countries around the world. This chapter is not a comprehensive list of all the customs or behaviors across every country. Rather, it provides a review for you and your team members who have not worked abroad and may need some basic tips about working in different countries. Even having some awareness of different customs can help individuals who must work in a different country. In the virtual communication section, we cover case studies, managing and motivating virtual teams, and virtual team member qualifications. This section provides a light review of managing virtual teams and working and communicating in a virtual environment. There are many books dedicated to leading and managing virtual teams that go into much deeper detail that we don't cover in this book. If your full-time job is managing virtual project teams, we recommend that you read books that are dedicated to this topic area.

Part I also covers social media and project management and how far we have come in a short period of time with social media tools and the impact they have on project communications. It would not be wise to ignore the various social media tools for communicating project information. For more information about social media and project management, head over to *Chapter 5 - Social Media and Project Management Communication Tools*.

Part II: Project Communication Tools by Knowledge Areas

The second part of this book describes and highlights the communication tools applicable to the nine knowledge areas. Communication tools can have primary knowledge areas and secondary knowledge areas. For example, a communication tool can be a primary tool in the cost knowledge area, and a secondary tool in the quality knowledge area. Using best-practice techniques and historical reference will help you decide where each communication tool fits within what knowledge area. This tool mapping to knowledge area is not perfect (it was never intended to be perfect!), but can be considered a best fit for most projects. As you manage your project, you will use the tools that are most applicable for your needs.

The second part of the book also covers Agile software development communication tools. We also mapped the Agile tools to the knowledge areas and life-cycle processes. We hope you will find this mapping easy to follow.

Part III: Project Communication Tools by Process Groups

This part describes and highlights the communication tools applicable to the five life-cycle processes. In this section of the book, the goal is for you to master the creation and use of these tools. This process is the same one used for mapping communication tools to knowledge areas. Communication tools can map across one, or many, of the project life cycles. Therefore, there are no hard rules that indicate when you should use one communication tool over another. As with the knowledge area process, use just the tools you need for your project. The more places you use communication tools without overloading your customer, the better, which often leads to improved communications on your project. More is not necessarily better, but selecting the right tool for the right situation is what is most important.

Part IV: Project Management BI & PMP® Exam Questions

This part covers two main areas: project management business intelligence (BI) and PMP® exam prep questions (communication-related questions only) for taking the PMI® exam. In this section of the book, we move past communication tools (as covered in the previous chapters), and go into the power of information (project management BI) that using communication tools provides. Think about all of the data and information contained in a simple project status report. In this part of the book, we have also included some PMP® exam questions. We feel that by adding these questions and answers, you will get a feel for what the PMP® exam is like. We only added a few communication-related questions (this is a communications book), but the questions provide a good sampling if you are new to the PMP® exam process. We have listed ten common questions from the communications chapter that you will likely face in the exam. We also felt the individuals who already have their PMP® certification may run into these same scenarios on their projects and could use a refresher. The answers to the exam questions are provided in the Appendix. For more information about the project management BI and exam questions, head over to chapters 24 and 25.

Introduction

Projects mainly fail for one reason only: poor project communications. A lack of clear and concise communications prevents projects from succeeding. It is that simple! Regardless of what you read or what experts on the web say, when you or your team do not communicate effectively, you will have a hard time completing a successful project. This is also true for clients or customers of the project. They too also own the responsibility for communicating effectively on their projects by providing you and your team members the information needed to execute the project. Project communications is a two-way effort and both parties are responsible for ensuring that their messages are clear and concise. Without that, project failure is inevitable!

There are countless surveys on the web that document all the reasons projects fail. These surveys pop up all over the web. Sometimes they say project failure is due to communication issues, sometimes they say it is due to something else. But the results are the same; the projects are failing repeatedly for one reason or another. However, what survey results lack when they state one reason or another is the *why*. That's the downside of these surveys. You will often see reasons such as poor requirements, poor scope control, but you won't see them call out poor communication as one of the reasons. One way or another, poor communication will be a reason in "project failure" surveys. You don't have to look too deeply at the survey to recognize that communicating more effectively could have prevented different situations (poor scope control, for example) from occurring. For example, let's look at how "poor requirements" as a reason for project failure could be a communications issue as well.

Poor Project Requirements – 45%

- If I decide to capture my requirements over email, and only over email, would that be a communication problem?

- If I decided to never meet face-to-face to capture my project requirements with my customer, would that be considered a communication problem?

Given these two examples, clearly the entire 45% would not fall under "poor project requirements" when some of the percentage should also fall under communication issues. In these two examples, it was *how* the business analyst decided to capture the requirements that lead to the problem with poor project requirements. There will be some situations where your project has poor project requirements. That is going to happen, but it will be limited and will most likely fall back on how the communications were initially collected.

It is important for you and your team to consider the importance of communications when looking at "project failure" survey results. It would not be wise to simply take the percentage you are given as the entire reason for the issue because, as we just covered in the poor project requirements example, communication played a role in that outcome as well. When you start looking at the various reasons from a communications perspective, you will have a different view of the issue. You will quickly see how important communication is and how you can potentially reduce the impact of these issues occurring on your project.

There is a common saying in the project management profession, "Project communication is the most important area of managing a project." If you are a poor communicator, this can make it difficult to be successful running projects. If you are a great communicator, and proactive in managing your communications, your life as a project manager will be much easier.

The most important part of project communications is the way you approach it. Most of your project manager peers just let communications happen; they do not plan for it. Don't be like your peers. It is common for project managers to send out project status reports, issues lists, and risk registers as their continuing and regular project communications. On average, we don't think they are considering whether the customer is even viewing this information. Do you think the average project manager stops in the middle of the day to decide whether the reports that he/she is sending are valuable? Does this information provide the customer with what they need? We don't think so, and that is why so many project managers run into trouble. If you are not properly planning or understanding your customer's communication needs (before starting any project work) you could run into some serious issues down the line. These regular communications that you are sending to your customers may not be getting the job done for them or your leadership team. If that is the case, you could get in some serious trouble with your customers.

For you to be successful, it is important for you to look at the tools you are using today on your project and ask yourself if you are communicating effectively. Really ask yourself that question and seek an honest response. Then, ask your customers and see how they respond. If they don't respond to that question positively, you have your answer. You know right then that you need to do a better job planning which communication tools would be most effective for your customers. Then go forward and work directly with your customers or clients to ensure that they are receiving the information they need. This early planning work and getting with your customers or clients to fully understand their needs will help ensure effective communications between both parties. This "planning for communications" idea might be new to you and your peers, but it is slowly taking hold in our industry. More and more project managers are starting to adopt this process, and the ones who do are becoming much more successful with their projects.

Planning communications is a fundamental change for most of you and your project manager peers, and it is important to understand this culture shift immediately. Changing the way you think about project communications will allow you to be more successful. You must understand what information you need to manage your project successfully. Typically, most project managers ask team members for project information, but they don't explain how or why they want it. When you do not take the time and explain how you want project information, you are not properly communicating to your team members and it can be frustrating for everyone. Successful communicators change the way they think about communicating by planning how they are going to communicate project information. When your team members send you the basic project information, they are not necessarily thinking how to communicate that information properly; they are just sending it because you are asking for it. Usually, they do not even consider whether the information they send is even usable, they just send it over. Often, you will find that team members send the information and hope you go away and stop bugging them from getting their real work done. If you worked closely with them and explained why and how you want the information from them, it opens and improves the communication between both parties. It also sets up a trusted relationship between you and your team members, which is critical to a successful project.

Without making that paradigm shift (planning your communications), you can complete your projects, but just not as effectively as possible—especially if you don't do communication planning with your customers and team members. You could have made a huge difference to your customers if you had just given some thought about how you were going to communicate the project information to them throughout the life of the project.

Your customers can benefit from this effective and proactive communication style. When you are proactive and plan communications with your customers, they are confident that they will get the information they need for effective project decision making throughout the life of the project. Proactive project managers are more in control of their project communications. Project managers who don't control their communications are more reactive and in firefighting mode. You are in much greater control of your projects when you are a proactive communicator rather than a reactive communicator. That's been proven over many years by project management professionals across every industry. Being a proactive communicator also establishes a much better rapport with your customers and team members and will go a long way in helping you run a successful project. Let's move now into the main book and help you become a much more effective communicator on your projects.

Chapter 1

Introducing Project Communication

IN THIS CHAPTER

- ♦ Reviewing a Project Scenario
- ♦ Plan to Communicate, Communicate the Plan
- ♦ Understanding PMI's Project Management Knowledge areas
- ♦ Understanding PMI's Project Management Process Groups
- ♦ Agile Methodology
- ♦ Introducing Project Management Business Intelligence

Many project managers take good communication for granted. They start working on a project without even thinking about how to communicate with others. The lack of a communication plan is the biggest mistake you and your team members can make, yet it happens on most projects. It is important to understand that just because you finished a project doesn't mean you did a good job communicating your project information; it just means you finished it. That's all. Don't think that because you didn't focus on communication that it is not important, because those are the project managers who often run into the most trouble. When facing project problems, the project manager who has planned and prepared for them should see the least amount of negative impact or damage to his or her project.

Project communication management is comprised of three components:

- Communicating project information in a timely manner

- Generating the right level of information for the customers, leadership, and team members

- Collecting, distributing, and storing project information

Tip
The combination of these areas results in proper project communication. Take the time to see the bigger picture and fully understand the project communication areas of your project.

Each team member communicates daily with other team members about various subjects, issues, and processes. One common challenge that project teams face is that everyone assumes they communicate properly with each other. When, in fact, that is often not the case and they are miscommunicating rather than communicating. In this chapter, we cover why you, the project manager, should plan your project's communication strategy and review the communication tools to knowledge area and life cycle process mapping.

The core of this chapter and the take-away for you is the mapping communication tools to knowledge areas and process group charts. You are going to love these charts! This is so important for you and your team members when planning your project's communications because these two charts give you the starting point to build out your communication strategy for the project. You no longer have to think about which tools you need to communicate cost information or risk management; that information is located in the charts for you to use immediately. That work has already been completed for you. All you have to do is use the two process charts to see which tools are available to use right away.

Let's get started planning your project communications.

Reviewing a Project Scenario

A typical scenario in the day in a life of a project:

1. A stakeholder requests an unexpected report.

2. A team member who is familiar with the data or has the skills to run a tool produces the report.

3. The stakeholder wants to receive the report every week. Therefore, the team member who created the report is now on the hook to update it and send it weekly indefinitely.

This scenario happens every day on thousands of projects. The stakeholder requests a report, and it gets created, printed, and then sent off as soon as possible. This is simple for a project manager because it requires no thinking or planning, just getting the information to the stakeholder as soon as possible.

However, what just happened here? Or rather, what did not happen? Absolutely no planning occurred. The project manager was randomized with another request from the customer as they have been a hundred times before. The project manager has no idea why they are providing the report; he or she just provides it because the customer requested it.

Well, if you think about this scenario and what happened, you can see how a project manager could have applied some communication planning techniques to this situation. The customer would still get the information needed, but the project manager and team members would have been much smarter about why. They also could have suggested more efficient tools and processes to the customer to get the information they needed.

Here is a better way to handle this scenario. Put yourself in the role of the project manager for this scenario and ask yourself these questions:

1. What information does the report provide?

2. What are you trying to achieve with this information?

3. Who needs this report and how will they use it?

4. How often is the information needed?

5. How quickly do you need the report developed?

6. Do you have the budget to develop this report?

7. Is there an existing report that includes similar information?

Using the questions and answers technique develops the customer requirements for the requested report. This technique saves time and potentially hours of clarifying the needs of the customer. You then ensure that you have the report requirements long before anyone develops anything. That way, if nobody requests it, nobody has wasted time creating something that isn't useful. It is a good idea for you and your team members to look at the requested report to evaluate whether other stakeholders would value from it. Usually, if it is good for one stakeholder, it will be good for others. That is a win-win for everyone!

When you or your team members do not gather all the information needed for the request and simply develop the report on the fly, you are setting a bad example. This behavior is one that encourages continual randomization of you and your team. Completing a short-term request while not considering the long-term use of the information doesn't make sense. That's not something that you or your team would want to do continually, for any customer, on any project. Why? Because it takes away from your real project work, which is never a good idea! Extra work increases timelines, increases costs, and causes other project-related issues.

Note

There are some reports that should be created quickly, especially if executives are asking for them. But you have to be thinking about communication planning when these requests are made. Often, these short-term reports quickly become long-term reports. Then they never go away! Planning how project information is communicated is not only your responsibility, but that of your project team members and the customer.

Plan to Communicate, Communicate the Plan

We recommended that, as you begin new projects, you step back and determine how you will communicate project information effectively. This technique of planning of your project communications is still considered pretty new in the project management industry. Using this approach and mindset forces you and your team—as well as your customers—to think in a completely different way about how to deliver or receive project information. Each communication tool (such as a status report), is going to present different project information. Therefore, you should plan how you will communicate this information to your customers, and customers should plan how they will use the information after they receive it. The days when project customers received and accepted generic status reports from project managers are over! For example, customers who plan the information they need for project-level, decision-making purposes will no longer accept a status report that does not provide the information they need. If customers are not seeing the information they require, then you have failed to communicate properly. Customers will not accept randomly created status reports that may or may not include the information they need—especially if it is just a generic template. Customers will treat this situation in a number of different ways, and you must be aware of what some customers might do if they are not getting the information they need in a format that they can use. Here are some of the ways customers or clients will deal with the information that is in a format they don't want or never agreed to.

- The will simply ignore it.

- They will take the report the way it is and add to it or put it in a format that works for them.

- They will send it on as-is and spend their own time creating a new format, essentially making your information useless.

Don't be surprised how customers and clients react if you continue to send them the same information in a format they can't or won't use. Also, you will quickly lose credibility with your customers or your leadership team if you continue to send them information in such a format. Your job is to ensure that you are communicating effectively. It is going to take some time to plan your communications with you customers, leadership, and your project team members.

Cross-reference
In Chapter 2 – Planning Project Communication, we cover the different ways customers want to receive project information.

Caution
Use your communication tools correctly. These tools enable you to deliver various project statuses to stakeholders and leadership. Therefore, make sure you are using the right set of tools for your customers.

Plan to communicate

Normally, you provide the project status to your customer, but rarely do both parties spend time together to actually plan the information that is going back and forth between them. You or your team members send the information to your customer without knowing if the information is valuable or helpful. That is the fundamental problem with project communications today, and we see it all the time on projects. What you need to do is sit down with your customer and ask them what information they need from the project. When that occurs, there is a much better understanding of the data that should flow between them. Then, you just have to plan accordingly and get the tools ready for use.

Project planning is not new; project managers have been planning projects for years. However, project communications planning is new, but sadly, it is rarely done by project managers or project team members. We recommend that you and your project management peers plan not only your projects from end to end, but plan your communications as well. There is a project management saying, **"When you plan your project, spend the time and plan your communications as well. Project communication tools are just as important as planning your resources, your schedule and your budget."** We suggest you learn the various communication tools in this book, and then select the right tools based on the size of the project, the knowledge area you are communicating, and the particular life cycle process you are in at the time. Communication planning goes a long way in effectively communicating your project information with your customers, leadership, and team members. Using the tools in this book will give you a huge advantage and go a long way in helping you become a great communicator on your projects. Your customers, leadership, and team members will value the time and effort you put into planning your communications, and you will increase your chance of success on your projects.

After the project management communication planning is complete, and you and your customers agree on which communication tools will work for the project, you should send out the communication plan for approval. The communication plans should go to all customers, clients, and leadership and include the agreed upon information and communication tools for the project. It is best practice for you to get signoff on the communication plan by all parties. That way, when there are issues on the project, you can refer to the agreed upon communication plan and respond accordingly. Without signatures, the project is open to random changes, which makes it much harder for you to be successful.

In this book, we also cover some new communication tools in the project management industry. The first tool is the *circle-of-communications chart*. This chart highlights the various roles on the project with the project manager role being in the center. This chart shows the project manager's name in the center circle, which indicates that you are the center of all project communications. All project information and data must flow through you. Nothing officially goes out about the project unless you send it or you approve it. You own all official communications on the project. You do not have to be a bottleneck, or involved in every email, but by putting your name in the center of the circle, you at least have to be involved in controlling official communications. The last thing you want to do is make yourself the roadblock. That would not be effective for anyone; however, it is critical that you are the last stop and the person ultimately accountable for all official project communications.

The second tool we cover is the *project communication requirements matrix*. This tool documents project roles, reports timing and frequency, and includes the names of the staff members receiving project information. The names of project team members and customers come directly from the circle-of-communications chart.

The next tool we cover is called the *role report matrix*. This tool is a table that displays the project roles and the different reports those roles receive for the project. The role report matrix also captures the reports distribution time table (weekly, monthly, quarterly, and so on). This allows anyone to view, at a glance, who is receiving which report and how often. This tool is helpful when your customer calls you about not getting project information. You'll know exactly what they are getting by looking at the names on the role report matrix. Therefore, by taking the time to create the role report matrix for your project, you will always know what kind of information is being sent to your customers and leadership team. For your project, you should control all incoming and outgoing project information. That's the purpose of the role report matrix. The tool stores the communication requirements coming from the customers and leadership team. Often, customers ask for data they are already receiving, they just don't know which report it is in. That's where you would use the role report matrix with your customer to tell them where the data is that they're looking for. This is a good example of what was mentioned earlier about customers getting information in a format they don't like or can't use themselves. What customers often do is ignore the reports and turn around and randomly ask you or your team members for the information directly.

Finally, we highlight and discuss in detail the impact and benefits of using a *project communication plan*. As we all know, project communication plans are one of the most important tools you can use on a project. It is also a tool that establishes the rhythm of project communications for every project. Without having a solid communication plan, the project manager, team members, or customers have no idea who is managing, controlling, or reporting project information.

Cross-reference

See Chapter 2 – Planning Project Communication for more information about the project communication requirements matrix and the people-report matrix.

One method you can use to plan project communications is to gather the project team members and customers, or clients, in a communication planning meeting. This meeting allows the group to jointly plan who will be involved in communicating project information. During the meeting, you drive creating the following tools: circle-of-communications chart, the communication requirements matrix, the role report matrix, and the project calendar. When finalized, they go into the communication management plan. The group selects the various communication tools for the project. This allows everyone from the start to be on the same page about the project's communication tools and who is responsible for creating them. After the planning meeting occurs, you can complete the communication management plan and ensure that everyone agrees and signs off on the document. Make sure you send the communication management plan to all customers, clients, leadership (upper management), and your project team members for signoff. The communication management plan is the official plan for the project. However, if changes need to be made, you would go through the formal change control process.

The Project Management Office (PMO) is important in the role of project communication. PMOs support all of the company's projects and all of their different methodologies. PMOs must support and stay on top of the industry methodologies in order to stay relevant and survive. Normally, a project or program director runs the PMO with project managers and administrative support. The size of the PMO will vary depending on the company size and the number of projects being executed. Large corporations have used PMOs for many years. Often, PMOs set the standard for project communication tools, such as status reports, issues lists, risks, communication plans, project schedules, and so on. As a project manager, your job is to know your PMO's governances and processes. By auditing projects, most PMO directors ensure that they are adhering to the PMO's rules and guidelines.

Understanding PMI's Project Management Knowledge Areas

The project manager and team members are involved in all aspects of the project; therefore, one of the most important things you and your team members can do is understand the project's knowledge areas. Knowledge areas are documented within the Project Management Institute's (PMI) *PMBOK® Guide* and widely used across most projects, regardless of size or industry. To be a successful project manager, you should know and understand each of these knowledge areas well and consider them when running your project on a day-to-day basis. It is a little tricky to understand. But, when you are communicating project information, you are doing so under a particular knowledge area—could be one or two areas, but it is at least one, every time and in every case. Everything within a project falls into a knowledge area. Let's think about that for a second and go over a sample table with that in mind to make it easier to understand.

Table 1.1 Project Deliverables to Knowledge Area mapping covers a sampling of a project deliverable and the associated knowledge area. As you can see, a budget spreadsheet would fall under the cost management knowledge area. The communication plan would fall under the communications management knowledge area. It is pretty logical, but it's surprising how many project managers don't look at their communications in that manner.

Table 1.1 Project Deliverables to Knowledge Area

Project Deliverable	Project Knowledge Area
Budget Spreadsheet	Cost Management
Communication Plan	Communications Management
Resource Plan	Human Resource Management
Project RACI	Human Resource Management
Issue List	Risk Management

Does that make sense? Every project deliverable you create will be for one knowledge area or another, guaranteed! So, with that logic in mind, when you think about planning your communications and the overall project management, you need to think about managing the different knowledge areas. We will cover this again in the next chapter, but for now, start thinking about the connections and the tools you are using today and which particular knowledge area those fall into on your project.

This concept is so important because after mapping all of the communication tools in your project to their respective knowledge areas, you might find that a knowledge area isn't represented, so you can aggressively go after that knowledge area and start to communicate using the tools available for that area. What happens if you build the same version of **Table 1.1** for your project and you find you are missing, one, two, or three knowledge areas? Do you think you would be communicating effectively on your projects if you are missing any of the knowledge areas? Not likely. It is possible, but not likely, and again, you would have a plan to go after those areas and start to communicate using the tools from those areas.

Let's look into those knowledge areas now.

Project Integration Management

The *project integration management* knowledge area is the art of pulling the various knowledge areas and life cycle processes together to drive a successful project. The integration knowledge area includes the work required to integrate all areas of project management: integration, scope, time, cost, quality, human resources, communication, risk, procurement, and stakeholder management. Most projects undergo continuous changes that require constant integration; the activities in this area pull everything together. Your typical day might have you shifting attention from communication issues to cost and budget concerns, and then to addressing quality issues, and so on. You will spend the day spread thin across each knowledge area, so you must have a solid understanding of each knowledge area so that you can address each situation properly. Project managers who are unsure of a particular knowledge area will struggle until they learn that area well enough to work effectively in it. It is important that you understand the knowledge areas well to help you be successful in your job.

Project Scope Management

The *project scope management* knowledge area identifies how to manage all the work that is required to complete the project. Creating a work breakdown structure (WBS) helps tremendously in project scope control. These WBS's consist of project activities, costs associated with activities, project resource names, and so on. The project schedule acts as a central repository for the entire project's scope and holds the WBS numbering information. Therefore, using the WBS for project scope management is a valuable tool. The other important communication tool within the scope management area is the project communication plan. The communication plan documents and describes how you or your team members will communicate project information throughout the life of the project. Project scope control is a critical task that you will undertake while managing your projects. Ensure that your projects have a well-defined scope and that customers and management approve that scope before getting too far along in the project. Without approval, the project's scope can easily get away from you, resulting in negative impact to the project. To prevent scope getting out of hand, ensure that at the beginning of the project you have a *change control process* defined and in place. A change control process is an important method of scope control. A common term within scope management is *scope creep*. Scope creep is adding extra work items to the original scope without going through a change control process.

Note
Scope creep is a common risk to projects today. Scope creep can consist of a small change like adding two or three new reports to a software development project, to complex changes where designers add 1000 square feet to the building.

The project scope approval process is normally project-specific and is important for every project manager to understand and continually drive. There are two major groups that handle scope approval. The first group is the customer, or client requesting the added work, and the second group is the project manager or the team members who perform the work. Traditionally, the customers or clients have the final say on any additional scope items added to the project. These items often come with a price; it is either the price of extending the project schedule or adding more costs or resources to the project.

Time Management

The *time management* knowledge area includes all aspects of managing the project's time. Activity estimating is difficult for most project managers to manage successfully. Often, these estimates are pessimistic best guesses from the team members. Your project team members normally give these to you as the basis to build the project schedule. The team members give a best-guess estimate as to how long they think it will take to complete their assigned deliverable. Unless your project is using machines, such as in manufacturing, where scheduling the time it takes to perform a task is exact, activities estimating and working with your project team members' best guesses can be challenging. As a project manager, you are basing the success of your project on the best-guess estimates given by your team members. If there are miscalculations from anyone who provided an estimate, your project timelines can increase.

Time management consists of many different aspects of your project, ranging from project activity dates to resource allocation (such as equipment used on a construction project). Time management also includes schedule development and resource schedule management.

Cost Management

The *cost management* knowledge area includes all aspects of managing project costs. There are many cost management components in a project, such as reviewing estimates from team members, reporting budget, negotiating vendor rates, and so on. Cost management is another key component of your project and is one of the core areas managed tightly by most project managers. Because cost management can be challenging, you should watch it closely throughout the life of the project.

Successful cost management requires cost estimating and tracking tools. Without tools in place, cost management can be difficult, and sometimes impossible. We have included several cost tracking tools in this book to help you be successful. It is important that companies provide suitable cost estimating tools for their project managers to manage costs. Without the proper tools, project managers would find it very challenging to effectively oversee cost management. For cost-driven projects, you must perform cost management activities in order to be successful; there is no other way. If costs are a driving factor to the success of a project, we also strongly recommend that you learn the accounting practices of your organization. In some companies, money is not an issue, so cost management is not a factor in driving a successful project. Such cases are much easier for project managers in that they are given one less area on which to focus. As project manager, you should know at the beginning of the project if budget isn't an issue. Make sure you have approval from the customer and leadership team to not focus your efforts on the budget where cost is not a factor. Never assume that budget is a non-issue and get formal approval first.

Quality Management

The *quality management* knowledge area includes all of the aspects of managing project quality. The quality level of a project is a subjective measurement without solid metrics. By putting metrics in place, however, you can quantify these measurements to help your project team and customers understand the project's quality level. In software development projects, a common quality measurement is the bug count (number of issues) in a software program, based on the severity level. For example, one milestone might have 10 severity 1 bugs and 23 severity 2 bugs. A software project manager measures quality by measuring the number of bugs at the severity 1 level. If a project has 5 severity 1 bugs, and the target measurement of quality is 3, then the project would have failed its quality measurement. In that case, the project manager must keep working to improve the quality level.

All areas of the project should measure quality, and project documentation is no exception. All projects include many documents as part of the project life cycle, and those documents should be of the highest quality. The project team reviews each document for content as well as acceptable levels of quality before giving their final approval. This is an area that we have seen lacking in software development projects. Typically, team members accept project documents based on the content and project objectives. What they often miss is reviewing how well the document is put together and ensuring there are no missing sections in the document. Team members should check for spelling errors, readability, and the right level of quality. As you and your team members mature your quality management practices, it is a best practice to challenge document quality. You should ensure project team members are producing the highest level of quality, and if they are not, send documents back until the quality is higher.

Most project managers overlook the quality management on their projects, or it is something they review much later in the project; often, when it is too late. Your main responsibility is to ensure the highest acceptable level of quality on the project. Quality should equal, but never exceed, what is in the scope of the project. For example, the project manager would never approve to build a more expensive project than is in scope for the project.

Human Resource Management

The *human resource management* knowledge area includes all aspects of managing the team members on the project. There are several complexities around managing project team members, and each belongs in the human resource management knowledge area. On most projects, managing project team members can be challenging because often, you are not a team member's direct supervisor. In that case, you are working under a weak matrix structure. You must then work closely with the functional manager for the resource's time on a project. This makes it difficult for you to be successful, but unfortunately, it is the norm in most companies.

Note
A weak matrix structure is a structure where the project manager does not have any formal reporting responsibilities or authority, but acts more as a coordinator when leading the project. A weak matrix structure organization is not a project-driven organization, but more of a functional-driven organization.

An important aspect of human resource management is consultant management. Project managers often have consultants or vendors working on their projects as regular members of the team. Consultants or vendors assigned to projects are managed differently than company employees. You must be aware of these differences and look to your own human resources rules and policies to determine your management responsibilities. For example, consultants do not normally receive end-of-the-year formal performance reviews as this is more of an employee-only activity. Another example is that you can't formally train consultants or send them to a training class even though it may be directly project related. Again, refer to your human resources policies at your company.

Project human resource management is not the equivalent of the standard human resource manager. A human resources manager manages the hiring, firing, and training of company resources. They assign resources to projects and work closely with the project manager on these assignments. Human resources managers don't manage their staff on a day-to-day basis; they leave that to the project manager to cover. If, as project manager, you have issues with a resource, you'll have to work directly with the human resources manager for resolution. It is important to course-correct the individual sooner rather than later to prevent any long-term project problems.

Communication Management

The *communication management* knowledge area includes all aspects of managing the project's communications. Communication management is the most important knowledge area for your project. Project managers who fail to communicate effectively can negatively affect their projects, which occasionally can lead to failure. Make sure you are constantly communicating with your customers, clients, and leadership team.

Project communication management is important because it covers every aspect of the project. For example, from the project's first approval to the final closeout, you will consistently communicate various aspects of the project to the project team members, leadership, and customers or clients. If you cannot communicate effectively, you will struggle as a project manager, which could lead to project failure. We have seen it before. However, constant communication with project team members and customers or clients increases the chance of a successful project. Ongoing communication gives your project customers or clients the information they need to make project-level decisions, thus moving the project forward and most likely toward a successful outcome.

Tip
Communication management is providing the right information to the right people at the right time.

Risk Management

The *risk management* knowledge area includes all aspects of managing project risks. You must be watching regularly for risks to ensure that there is no negative impact to the project. Another component of risk management, rarely called out in the risk management area, is issue management. Issue management is just as important as risk management. When risks occur, they become issues. It is just as important for you to track and monitor the issues as it is for you to track and monitor potential risks. Issue management is often overlooked by project managers and project team members, but can quickly lead to project failure if the issues are not controlled. It is an industry best practice for project managers to put the same rigor and attention to issues as they do with risks. It is also a best practice to report and track risks and issues separately. Many project managers track risks and issues together, which is wrong. Risks and issues have completely separate fields and information. For example, you wouldn't track a risk exposure score for issues and you wouldn't track a probability percentage for issues. Take the time to separate your project's risks and issues into separate tracking tools and record the right level of information for each.

Risk management is important. You must be diligent in risk tracking on your projects. Often, project managers use a risk assessment form for tracking project risks. This form allows for easy sharing with anyone interested in the project. Make sure you are tracking risks on a constant basis and, at a minimum for smaller projects, discussing the risks with the team members on a weekly basis. Tracking project risks weekly for a multiyear project may not make sense. The project's length and how often risks are discussed and reviewed with the project team members makes a difference. As project manager, you should spend the time reviewing project risks with your team members regularly (for example, weekly status meetings). In doing so, you will get assurance that team members are staying on top of risk management. Without a regular review, project risks can go undetected and could negatively affect the project.

In the project risk management knowledge area, there are many tools available to help you plan, analyze, and control project risks. We have included several of these tools in the book.

Cross-reference
See Chapter 13 - Defining Communication Tools to Manage Project Risk for more information about these tools.

Risk classification is simple. Risks have three main categories: low, medium, or high. The project team weighs in on the risk classification. For example, in the construction industry, a tilt-up building (warehouse) is a fairly low-risk project because warehouses are rather easy to build from a construction prospective. A hospital or research lab is a high-risk project because of the number of complexities and customizations that go into these types of buildings. In a construction project, a medium-risk effort would be somewhere between building a warehouse and building a hospital. For example, a residential complex could be a medium-risk project. The project manager, project team members, and customer or client decides the risk level at the beginning of the project and decides the meaning of the low, medium, and high categories. To classify a risk correctly, the project team, customers, and leadership should agree on the definitions and rating factors of these three classifications. When the classification is determined and understood, the team can work jointly to assign risk classifications to every risk event and place them in a risk matrix tool, which we cover in chapters 13 and 19 later in this book.

Procurement Management

The *procurement management* knowledge area includes all aspects of managing your project's procurement activities. For example, procurement management activities include everything from when to hire resources (from outside your company), to ordering weekly lunches, or managing contracts. On construction projects, your procurement activities are critical because they include managing and coordinating many contracting companies—much more than working on a software development project. Procurement management requires your endless involvement in the process throughout the project. Tasks such as hiring, firing (vendors or consultants, not employees), scheduling work tasks, and negotiating contracts are just a few of the procurement management activities you'll perform.

Project procurement can be a difficult area to manage, especially when working with consultants or vendors and outside contracting companies. Further, change requests impact the contract or budget and engage the project manager to drive the change through the approval process. Ongoing change requests usually put a strain on relationships between the two parties—especially when money is involved and someone is waiting for or expecting payment. If one company continues to submit change requests and expects payment for every additional work item, then there are usually problems. Often, both parties should have an understanding that not every work item is chargeable to the project. Even in fixed-bid projects, some work is completed free of charge by the contracting company. When both sides understand that not everything results in a change request, there is goodwill between both companies, which improves the chance of future projects between them. Most change requests occur on fixed-price (fixed-cost) contracts when additional project work items are requested and contractors are expecting payment, but the customer requesting the work expects the requests to be already in scope. When such a situation occurs, it is scope creep and handled through the change request process. If the change request extends beyond the original agreement on the project's cope, and additional work is required, the contractor is going to expect additional payment for this work. This is totally acceptable and fair to the contractor.

One important aspect of procurement management is the contract management. Contract management includes negotiating and creating contracts. Contracts can include the following:

- Labor

- Equipment

- Materials

- Agreement between two parties

Note
A contract is a great communication tool and is legally binding.

One aspect of the procurement knowledge area is administrative closeout. Administrative closeout is different from the technical aspects of closeout because administrative closeout pertains to closing down the activities on the project. Closing out a project includes tasks such as budget auditing, inspection and final approval, sign-off on a subcontractor's contract, archiving documents for long-term storage, and project turnover. You must ensure that there is legal closeout of your project before its final turnover.

Contract administration includes the activities to start the engagement process between two parties, and then managing it throughout the project until closure. After the project is complete, contract administration includes the activities to formally accept and close the contract.

Caution

Ignoring one knowledge area, or leaving it for someone else to take care of, may hurt your project's chance of success.

Tip

Knowledge areas are not created equal. As a project manager, you might not spend equal time on all areas. That's ok because as you progress through your project, sometimes your time will be spent in one knowledge more than the other knowledge areas which is perfectly acceptable.

Stakeholder Management

The *stakeholder management* knowledge area includes all aspects of managing the relationship with your stakeholders, such as stakeholder communications, management, and control. Project success depends on a good relationship between you and the stakeholders, every time. When the relationship is good, you will have the support and backing to be successful. When relations are not good, or even bad, you will have a much more difficult time managing the project. We have seen many projects fail when relations are strained, or people don't get along or trust each other. It happens all the time. If needed, you might need to work with management to move to a different project.

You must proactively manage your stakeholders throughout the life of the project. Your goal is to be a trusted advisor to your stakeholders. A proactive project manager is constantly providing communications to their stakeholders. Stakeholders expect this level of communication and will know they can turn to you and get the information they need, when they need it. When they don't get it, there can be problems between the two individuals, which you will usually hear about. A hands-off project manager—one who is not engaged—will find that a strong stakeholder will see right through them. They will lose the stakeholder's confidence immediately and lessen their chances of running a successful project. Losing a stakeholder's confidence is horrible for any project manager and difficult to turn around for anyone.

A large part of stakeholder management is project communications. Which tools and processes you choose to send your stakeholders the information they need is critical. You will provide this information from the beginning to the end of the project. There are several communication tools available in this book to help you communicate effectively with your stakeholders. The goal is to send the stakeholders the information they need to make decisions and to help you drive things forward. It's important to have a planning meeting where you sit down with your stakeholders at the beginning of the project and go over the possible communication tools available. You can both look at the various tools and agree on which ones will be valuable for the project. This exercise helps ensure that you are using communications tools that the stakeholder values and can use. This upfront planning for communication tools is a best practice for all project managers. Your stakeholders will appreciate it and it will go a long way in your becoming a trusted advisor to your stakeholders.

Don't under estimate the importance of stakeholder management for running a successful project!

Understanding PMI's Project Management Process Groups

Project managers can use many different methodologies to manage projects, and each industry has a unique methodology for managing its specific types of project. For example, a software development project has a couple of different industry-specific methodologies (waterfall, Agile). Each methodology has its own unique set of process groups. Regardless of the methodology you choose, there are common processes among them all. For example, most methodologies have initiating, and closing processes. This book outlines just the descriptions and details for PMI's process groups below. There are many books and materials available for a deeper and more in-depth understanding of any methodology.

The project management industry has many different methodologies. Each methodology has defined different core processes for the life of a project. PMI defines five core processes for any project: Initiating, Planning, Executing, Monitoring & Controlling, and Closing.

Figure 1.1 – Typical Project Management Process Groups Chart shows the *project life cycle* process from PMI. As you can see, the five processes in this chart relate to one another. The Initiating process starts a project, and then moves to the Planning process. Then the Executing process starts, which is the actual creation of the project's scope. There, you go back-and-forth between the Executing process and the Planning process throughout the life of the project. Finally, as the project approaches the finish and the scope of the work is done, you move into the Closing process. It is important to note that the Controlling process is an overarching process that oversees the activities occurring throughout the project. The Controlling process provides rigor and structure to the team members while they accomplish their tasks.

Figure 1.1 – Typical Project Management Process Groups Chart

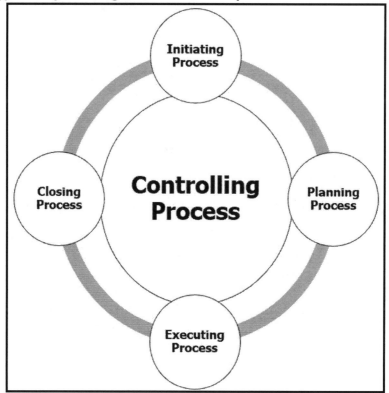

Tip
It is critical that you understand the project process groups, which can certainly increase your chances of success.

Initiating Process group

The project initiation activities are the startup tasks required on every project to get it under way. A wide range of activities are included in project initiation tasks for every project. These activities include initial project setup documents, creating budget forecasts, hiring consultants, and creating project schedules. It typically takes time to start a project correctly, so do not rush through creating the work deliverables; it will only hurt your project. If you forget something important early on in the project, it may be difficult to go back and make corrections. For example, the schedule baseline tool is a good one to consider. If you do not create it before any work begins on the project, it cannot be re-created easily. The project schedule would require having its performance data deleted for all completed work, to date, on the project. Schedule baselines are created and taken from the project schedule before recoding any progress on the project. When the project moves to the executing phase, it is next to impossible to go back and take a baseline snapshot.

Ensure every deliverable you complete is the highest level of quality for the project. To ensure a high level of quality, you need to document the quality standard for the team members to follow for each major deliverable. For example, when the analyst develops a systems requirements document, it is a best practice to complete all sections in full. When there are sections of the document that are not applicable to the project, they should be noted by the author and not deleted. Sections of the document that are not applicable should remain empty. When there are empty sections in the document, they look like they have not been completed by the author, which may not be the case. When driving a high level of quality for the project, document quality management is important.

Depending on the methodology selected for your project, these activities can take weeks or months to complete. On larger construction projects, the start-up activities can sometimes take years before the project actually starts. Small to medium software projects often take a couple of weeks to a month to begin. Documentation for a particular methodology describes, in detail, the activities required to move from phase to phase. Usually, the startup tasks for different methodologies are consistent and generally the same across project types. It is a best practice to find the documentation or training materials for the methodology that you are using on your project.

Planning Process group

Project planning activities include expanding the project charter to gather necessary information to plan and design the main product of the project. You and your team members plan the project execution during this phase. During the planning phase, you might perform a sampling of the following items:

- Plan and define project scope

- Develop work breakdown structure (WBS)

- Create the project schedule and assign resources

- Create a project budget

- Generate a risk plan and analysis

- Develop a quality plan

- Create a communication plan

- Develop a procurement and contract administration plan

Note
Each activity is part of the planning phase. You decide in what order to perform each activity, but each activity needs to be complete before you consider the planning phase complete.

It is crucial that you take the time to plan your projects. Many project managers ignore the planning process for one reason or another, which usually ends badly for the project manager and hurts the project's chance of success... If you get pushback or negative feedback from management or the customer, you need to advise them of the importance of proper project planning and the issues that the project will likely encounter if you don't. Any experienced project manager knows that improper resource planning, scheduling, budgeting, or scoping can cause project problems. You should have to do little justification to management or customers about the importance of project planning.

Earlier, we noted that successful project communication management requires you to plan your communications. The planning process is the best time for you to plan your project communications—not only communications, but all the parts of the project. The planning process is not something you are going to be able to come back to once you start the execution process. You just can't stop the project to create project deliverables (for example, project status reports or project newsletters) after the project execution has begun. The planning process is the best time to create these deliverables; otherwise, it just won't happen. You will be too busy with scope issues, resource issues, and budget issues to stop the project at this point. What generally happens in this case is that you will have to scramble and perform some heroic efforts to keep the project moving forward. It is never a good sign when a project manager has to be heroic due to their own improper planning. Don't put yourself in that position; plan your project properly across the various areas of your project.

Executing Process group

Project execution is the process of executing the activities of the project. This is where the real work of the project is completed. During this process, you assign each work item or project deliverable to project team members—or other individuals, where applicable. Project work includes the activities you documented in the project management plan, and no other. The executing phase of the project is one of your top responsibilities.

One of your tasks at the beginning of this phase is to create and build the project team. Throughout the execution phase, you mentor the project team members. During this phase, your role is to ensure that project team members execute their high-quality work activities in a timely manner. The execution phase is also the most difficult and time-consuming for you because most of the project work activities occur during this phase and you must stay on top of problems and issues as they arise.

Quality assurance is also an important part of the executing phase. All project team members who have work assignments complete quality assurance activities. Your ultimate responsibility is to ensure the highest level of quality on the project.

Monitoring & Controlling Process group

Project monitoring and controlling includes the work of ensuring that the project is on track and executing as expected. You play a big role in this process by performing activity oversight and control throughout the life of the project. Work monitoring and controlling spans all process group activities. You must monitor and control project activities from project initiation to closeout. When you monitor and control project work, your chance of success increases; otherwise, it decreases. This phase of the project is the most time consuming because you need to understand every component of the project and how it's tracking to completion. You need to know whether the individual project activities are under control at all times. If not, you will step in and take control of the process until it has recovered and is back on track.

Tip
The controlling process spans across the entire project life cycle.

Monitoring and controlling the process requires you to be actively engaged at all times. All of your projects will include the monitoring and controlling process to ensure there is oversight by the project management team. Project monitoring and controlling is where project managers are either successful or fall down and perform miserably. If you constantly monitor and control your project's activities, you will increase your chance of having a successful project.

Closing Process group

The project closeout process includes the work of shutting down a project and releasing the resources. These activities include: closing contracts, reassigning staff, archiving documents for long-term storage, obtaining final signatures for documentation, performing project audits, and other shutdown activities.

There are two types of closeouts on a project:

- Technical closeout includes the activities performed to deliver the product. The final product must meet the agreed-upon technical specifications. To confirm that they have, project team members should refer to the technical documentation and the final product to ensure it meets the required specifications. During this phase, you and your team members verify the quality of the product.

- Administrative closeout refers to signing off and archiving all of the project documents and open contracts. One critical task of this closeout is capturing the final approval and acceptance signatures on all contract conditions by the project customer and any team members. It also includes reassigning project staff and any final budget transfer or closeout processes. Often, the administrative closeout process has a formal audit of the project work's activities to ensure that the project team completed the project satisfactorily.

Capturing and reporting lessons learned is an important part of the project closeout process. Normally, captured at the end of the project, the lessons learned are invaluable for the future projects that might be similar. However, waiting until the end of the project to capture this data is not a good idea. You might miss capturing valuable information that occurred throughout the project if you wait until the end. The time to capture lessons learned is at the time it happens, not after the project ends. A best practice you should adopt immediately is to start collecting lessons learned from the kickoff activity throughout the project. This information is great for historic knowledge of the project's events. This information should not be lost or forgotten and is valuable to the organization. Actually, the PMO should be compiling lessons learned data from all projects so the leadership team can see all-up what is happening across the organization. By collecting this data throughout the project, you can course-correct along the way. When you reach the end of the project, you have a wealth of data at your fingertips that you have collected and reporting on it is simple. If team members leave during the project, you won't have to chase them down for their feedback because you've been collecting it all along. It is important to store the lessons learned as part of an overall knowledge base repository for other project teams to review.

Cross-Reference
See Chapter 14 - Defining Communication Tools to Manage Project Procurement for more information about the lessons learned document.

Finally, you should remember how important the warranty period is on a project. The warranty period starts after product delivery to the owner. You should be alert and have the project's maintenance team ready to respond to any issues or problems with the delivered product after the warranty period begins. The warranty period is going to be different for each project based on the industry, priority, and the impact to the customer. A lower-priority project may not have a long warranty period; whereas, a high-priority, high-criticality project would. Another example is the project warranty on a construction project that would have a much longer period than a software project. Warranty periods are not applicable to every project.

Introducing Agile Methodology

Although the majority of the project management communications tools covered in this book are specific to traditional/waterfall projects, there are several communications tools used in Agile project management that we feel are of equal importance. Similar to traditional project management, each Agile project is also preceded by a series of strategy meetings that occur during the initiation phase before any actual development work is performed on the project.

In Agile, these meetings are sometimes referred to as "events" or "ceremonies." The initial strategy meeting is held to kick off the project and is driven by a vision associated with a strategic business need or goal. This vision is typically framed in the context of a strategy and its associated goals and objectives, which often result in specific deliverables being created in the form of documents, referred to as "artifacts." Throughout this book, we point out the specific meetings and documents created for an Agile project, as well as some of the specific tools used with Agile projects to communicate project status to team members, customers, and all project stakeholders.

We have included the following Agile tools in this book for your reference:

- Agile Product Vision Statement

- Agile Estimating Tool

- Agile User Stories

- Agile User Story Backlogs

- Agile Team Dynamics

- Agile Meetings

- Agile Information Radiators

These seven tools are placed in the most applicable areas for the project. As with other tools in the book, you might debate about a tool being placed with the life cycle process or with the specific knowledge area, and that is something you will have to decide for yourself. It was our intention to place them in the most relevant and applicable area, but that may not be true for every project.

From a communications tool perspective, these seven tools were the most relevant from a communication perspective and, therefore, added to the book. We understand that there are additional Agile tools beyond the seven listed, but we intentionally left those out. We wanted to add the most critical tools from a communications perspective rather than offering a complete list of all Agile tools.

Introducing Project Management Business Intelligence

Throughout this book, we talk in great detail about the many communications tools and instruments that might be applied to a given project. For certain types of communications and for certain stakeholder groups, these separate documents, reports, and files may be overwhelming and confusing. This is where project management business intelligence (BI) might be useful. Using BI techniques and tools, you can quickly and economically bring together data from various sources, combine related data sets, create simplified data visualizations, and share these reports for viewing and consumption by your various stakeholders. Because projects are rarely exactly alike, the flexibility of BI to connect vastly different data sources and yet create views that people can understand and act on is invaluable.

You can imagine, over the course of a project, how much information is contained in status reports, spreadsheets, newsletters, and other project artifacts. Project managers face the challenge of putting it all together, from the various sources, to make something meaningful to customers, leadership, and project team members.

In *Chapter 24 - Project Management Business Intelligence*, we explore project management BI and walk you through the step-by-step process to create your very own project summary dashboard. All you need to get started is a copy of Microsoft Excel® and Microsoft Project® and you too will be creating project management BI reports for your projects in no time.

We have included the following BI tools in this book for your reference:

- Project Summary Dashboard

- Project Risk Dashboard

Obviously, there are many more project dashboard reports that can be created for your project, but the two shown in *Chapter 24 - Project Management Business Intelligence* are great starting points for any project manager. Once you start creating and using these dashboards on your project, you and your customers will want to run these types of reports on other project data. BI reports are great communication tools for your projects.

Summary

This chapter covered the importance of project knowledge areas and life cycle process for every project manager. Successful project managers use knowledge areas and process groups to communicate project information. Understanding and using the knowledge areas and process groups are fundamental to your success as a project manager. It is important that project managers and team members understand their roles and are comfortable with communicating project information.

The most important aspect this chapter covers is communication planning. This is a paradigm shift for the project management industry—and to the average project manager. You should spend time at the beginning of the project to plan your projects and, specifically, plan the communication tools you will use. The communication tools you select will affect the overall outcome of the project. The selection process has you and your customer or client spending time to select the tools everyone feels necessary for communicating effectively on the project. A lack of communication planning can have the team scrambling and producing information that may or may not be valuable and could potentially become a time waster.

Chapter 2

Planning Project Communication

IN THIS CHAPTER

- ◆ Struggling with Proper Project Communication Planning
- ◆ Preventing Common Communication Problems
- ◆ Creating a Project Communication plan
- ◆ Understanding the Circle-of-Communications chart
- ◆ Defining the Project Communication Requirements matrix
- ◆ Understanding the Role Report matrix
- ◆ Developing Lessons-Learned information

Project communication planning involves identifying your customer's information requirements. Customers require information about the project, such as risk events, budget data, and schedule information, to name a few. As project manager, you must be proactive and plan for your customer's needs throughout the life of the project. As you progress through the project, be aware that those needs will change and that you will need to adapt and change depending on the needs of your customers, clients, or leadership team.

Most large companies have project management organizations (PMOs) or project management groups that set standard requirements for company projects. These standards include areas such as scheduling when to send status reports, capturing data for budgets, creating templates for risk and issue tracking, and formatting for the monthly newsletters. For example, one common standard that PMOs set is the day that project teams are required to send status reports. Typically, the data collection is due by the end of the workday on Thursday so that the status report can be compiled and sent on Friday. Most companies want project status reports due on Friday.

One important task of communication planning is deciding who produces the project information and how they will do it. Oftentimes, the project manager and his or her team members jointly produce project information for the customer. Occasionally, a project team lead must create project information specifically for a particular customer. For example, in a software project, a development lead will create a report that lists all of the bugs in the development phase. Capturing the specifics of who is responsible for creating project information is important. It is also important to let the team know which tools they are responsible for creating. That way, you reduce confusion and any possible rework for the team members. This is a best practice for any project manager and helps ensure that everyone is on the same page. To do so, you can use a tool called the project communications tools RACI. For more information, see **Figure 2.3 – Project Communications Tools RACI in** this chapter.

Struggling with Proper Project Communication Planning

Project managers often struggle to communicate their project information effectively. They often send too many reports and produce status information that makes little sense or doesn't provide value. Communication planning can be difficult. Understanding your customer's or client's information needs can be challenging. It takes years to become an effective communicator and hours of practicing and working with customers to understand their communication needs.

Most project managers either ignore or struggle to properly perform project communication planning. The following list explores some of the common reasons this occurs:

- Bringing together the various parties involved in the project is challenging. These parties include you as the project manager, team members, customers or clients, and any other stakeholders. Bringing everyone together is difficult. Everyone is busy working on many different activities; some team members work offsite or in a different country and are not easily available. However, to have a fully documented project communication plan, you need as many people involved as possible for the best chance of success.

- Project managers and team members have been communicating all their lives. Most project managers, therefore, wrongly assume that they can communicate project information just as naturally as they communicate any other information. Don't avoid or ignore the communication planning techniques. Recognize that effective project communication is one of your highest priorities so that you will be an effective communicator for your project team members or your customers.

- Project managers often fail to plan project communication requirements by not allotting the proper time to effectively understand and document the communication needs of their customers. Oftentimes, the project manager feels forced to start the project sooner, or has higher priorities, such as deciding a budget or finding team members. The task of identifying the project's communication requirements becomes overlooked or not addressed. Due to this pressure, most project managers usually complete just the planning task, and then dive right into the details of the project. This is a bad practice. In the end, this lack of planning negatively impacts the project.

- Some project managers have no idea how to create a communication plan. This is often because they do not have the proper training or experience on this subject. From the beginning, the project manager struggles to start the process of creating the communication plan. The techniques in this section will help you and your project team members create a communication plan. We will also cover the basics of how to present project information and be an effective communicator.

Project managers who don't plan their project communications may find themselves in a tough situation when trying to communicate project status. Without up-front communication planning, the project manager or their team members lack a full understanding of their customer's requirements. The project manager and customers may have different ideas about how the project team will communicate project information. This leads to a communication breakdown, which could lead to project failure.

To be successful at planning your project's communications tools, there is a common approach that has proven to be effective. One best practice is to look at your projects from the knowledge area perspective. For example, "cost management is important in my project because I have a tight budget." Using this knowledge area approach, the focus is to use the different communication tools under the Cost Management knowledge area specifically for this project. Make sense? By using this approach and focusing on which tools are in each knowledge area, you ensure the best chance of communicating effectively across each of the areas in your project. This is a different approach to tackling your project, but one that will increase your chance of success. Closely consider the different knowledge areas—especially those that are most impactful to your projects (for example, Cost Management).

Let's look at **Figure 2.1 — Communication Tools by Knowledge Areas** chart for the mapping between tools and knowledge areas for every project. Remember, projects usually touch on each knowledge area, so you will use some of the communication tools. You won't use all of them, but you need to at least consider which ones you will use for your project. This chart gives you an early start in helping you understand which tools to use for each knowledge area. Go over the tools for the different knowledge areas with your team members and customers to select the set of tools that you will use on the project. After you've selected the tools, you can add them to the Project Communication Tools RACI, seen in **Figure 2.3 – Project Communications Tools RACI** later in this chapter.

Figure 2.1 — Communication Tools by PMI Knowledge Area

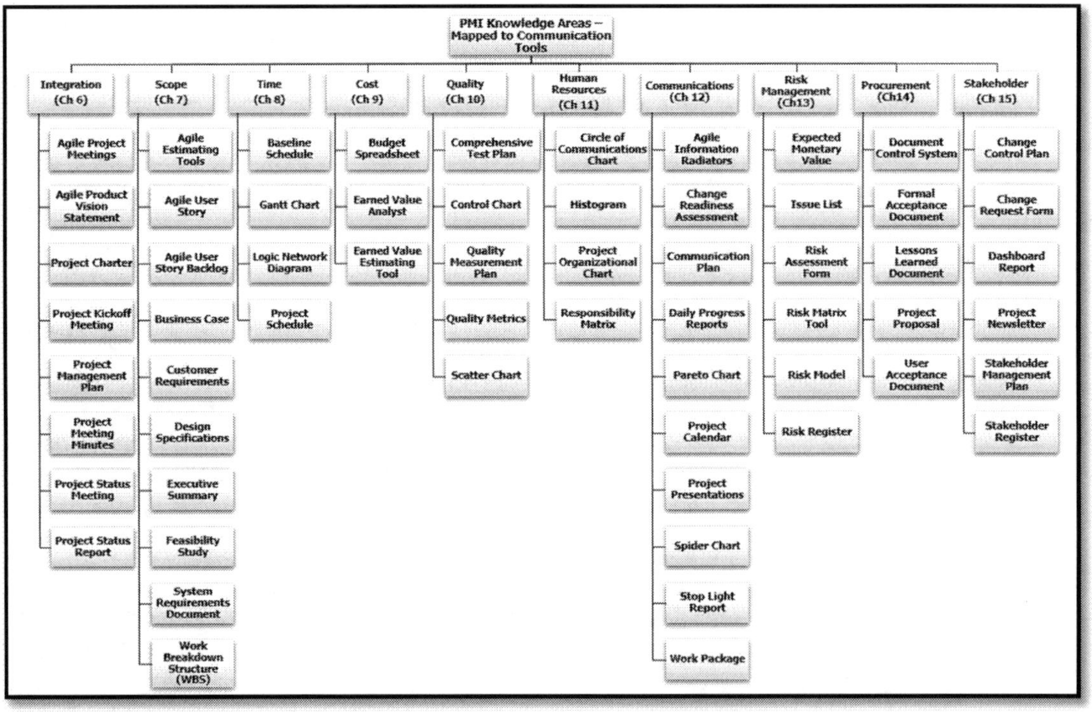

Now, let's look at the same communication tools by pivoting on the process groups instead of the knowledge areas. The idea remains the same, you need to consider which communication tools you and your team will use during each process—just as you do for each knowledge area. For example, which tools should you use during the Initiation process and which tools should you use during the Planning process, and so on? Every project proceeds through each process (rarely are there exceptions!); therefore, you need to determine which communication tools are most applicable for each.

Figure 2.2 — Communication Tools by PMI Process Group chart maps the communication tools to process groups. It looks similar to the knowledge area mapping chart, but this one includes life cycles processes—not the knowledge areas. As you did with the knowledge areas, it is important that you consider which communication tools to use during each life cycle process. This chart will help you with that process.

Figure 2.2 — Communication Tools by PMI Process Groups

PMI Process Groups – Mapped to Communication Tools

PMI - Initiation Process		PMI - Planning Process			PMI - Executing & Controlling Process			PMI - Closing Process
Project Initiation Process (Ch16)		Planning Admin (Ch 17)	Planning Developing (Ch 18)	Planning Reports (Ch 19)	Administration (Ch 20)	Monitoring (Ch 21)	Reporting (Ch 22)	Project Closeout (Ch 23)
Agile Product Vision Statement	Feasibility Study	Change Readiness Assessment	Baseline Schedule	Budget Spreadsheet	Agile Project Meetings	Issue List	Agile Information Radiators	Formal Acceptance Document
Agile Estimating Tools	Project Charter	Dashboard Report	Change Control Plan	Earned Value Analysis	Change Request Form	Project Meeting Minutes	Daily Progress reports	Lessons Learned Document
Agile User Story	Project Kickoff Meeting	Responsibility Matrix	Comprehensive Test Plan	Earned Value Estimating Tool	Control Chart	Risk Assessment Form	Gantt Chart	User Acceptance Document
Agile User Story Backlog	Project Management Plan	Risk Model	Design Specifications	Logic Network Diagram	Project Newsletter	Work Package	Histogram	
Business Case	Project Organization Chart		Expected Monetary Value	Quality Metrics	Project Presentations		Pareto Chart	
Circle of Communications Chart	Project Proposal		Project Calendar	Risk Matrix Tool	Project Status Meetings		Project Status Report	
Communication Plan	Quality Management Plan		Project Schedule	Risk Register			Spider Chart	
Customer Requirements	Stakeholder Management Plan		System Requirements Document	Scatter Chart			Stoplight Report	
Document Control System	Stakeholder Register		Work Breakdown Structure (WBS)					
Executive Summary								

The chart is pretty clear, isn't it? It shows the process groups that every project follows and the different communication tools for each process. It is the same mapping that we used for knowledge areas (shown previously). From a communications planning perspective, these charts show you which tools you should be using to communicate project information. This chart shows the best possible process area for the different communication tools, but that is not to say it is the only place the tool can be mapped. Some tools could be mapped across many different processes. You might have your own opinion about where a particular tool should fall, and that's fine, it shows that you understand the importance of project communication tools and how they are used in each process area. You are on your way toward understanding which tools you can use for each process area. We recommend that you print the chart so that you can continually reference it when you have an issue and need a communication tool for your project.

For the best chance of success on your projects, approach your project communication planning with the process group's tool mapping concepts in mind (knowledge areas and process groups). Your project manager peers may struggle because they haven't thought about looking at their projects in this manner, and therefore they have no idea how to communicate effectively in the various stages of their projects.

After you review the communication tools in the various knowledge areas and process group charts, you are ready to start the next important step on your project, deciding with your project team and customers which tools to you use for your project. More importantly, you also need to decide who will create the tools.

Remember, when adding work for a team member, you will need to add the additional time in the schedule for the team member doing the work.

To document the added workload, use the Project Communications Tools RACI. **Figure 2.3 — Project Communication Tools RACI** shows an example of this tool. This will come in very handy for you and your team members to document who is building what tools for the project. This tool documents the different types of reports for the project, by category (administrative reports, requirement reports, and technical reports) and stores the name of the report in the associated category. The tool also stores the project role associated with creating the communication tool across the top of the table. It is important to store the name of the individual and the role. This tool works exactly like a project RACI, you place the A's, R's, C's, and so on in the associated intersecting cell between the role and the communication tool. This is the same process as using the standard project RACI you use today. So, "accountable" is "accountable," "responsible" is "responsible," and so on. Some skeptics will immediately ask you, why do I need another tool? Can't I just add these to the project RACI I am already using? The answer is yes, you certainly can, but if you want a cleaner and more concise communication tool that focuses just on the project's communications tools, then add those tools to the RACI. In some cases, there may be some duplicate entries between the project RACI and this tool; however, that will be minimal and does not devalue the use of this tool. You can easily copy and paste between the Project Communication Tools RACI and the formal project RACI.

Let's look at the tool now. You will quickly see how easy it is to create for your project. Think about how valuable it will be to have a conversation with your customers or clients using the completed Project Communication Tools RACI—especially when you are trying to communicate which tools you will use on the project. This is a great communication tool for all projects and an extremely valuable tool for you to help drive your communication planning.

Figure 2.3 Project Communication Tool RACI

PROJECT COMMUNICATION TOOL RACI **Responsibility Definitions:** **R- Responsible** **A - Accountable** **C - Consult** **I - Inform**	Project Manager	Team Member #1	Team Member #2	Team Member #3	Team Member #4	Team Member #5
Project Administration Reports						
Status Report	A	R	R	R	R	R
Financial Reports	A	R	R	R	R	R
Risk Report	A	R	R	R	R	R
....ETC	A	R	R	R	R	R
Requirement Reports						
Business Requirements Document	R	A	R	R	C	C
	R	A	R	R	C	C
	R	A	R	R	C	C
...						
...						
Technical Reports						
Funcational Requirements Document	R	R	A	R	C	R
Quality Reports	R	R	A	R	C	R
Bug Defect List	R	R	A	R	C	R
....etc						
....						
...						
...						
...						

You should take advantage of this communication tool on all your projects.

Project communication planning is a relatively new concept in the project management industry, but one that will change the way you manage projects forever. The project's success can depend on how well you embrace project communication planning and how willing you are to take a chance on doing things a bit differently than you have in the past. A tool like the Project Communication Tool RACI will help you move forward and will let you focus on project communications from the very start of the project.

Preventing Common Communication Problems

Communication problems occur throughout a project's life cycle. These problems include anything and can have a large impact on the project.

The following common communication techniques can help you be successful on your projects.

- Hold weekly, in-person status meetings with key project customers to establish a rhythm of project communications. Regular project communication creates confidence by showing your customers that you are in charge of their project and watching it closely. Some project managers never spend any time with their customers, so when issues and concerns arise, they have no relationships to fall back on. Take the time to work closely with your customers to form a good working relationship; these relationships can last forever.

- Establish a cadence for delivering project status reports on the same day, at the same time. In doing so, you build yet another level of confidence and trust with your customer by showing them that you can deliver the information on time and on a regular basis. Customers will come to expect that reporting cadence from you and will appreciate receiving the information on a consistent basis. Your customers will feel like they can rely on you, which makes for a great relationship.

- Disperse status reports and meeting agendas prior to the day of the meeting—a best practice is one day ahead. You should allow enough time for your customers or leadership team to absorb the information before the actual meeting. By doing so, you allow everyone to prepare for the meeting. If anyone is required to bring additional information, or talk about a particular subject, you've taken the surprise out of the meeting by allowing them to prepare ahead of time. This technique helps speed up the meeting because attendees have had the opportunity to review the material ahead of time; less important items can be discussed briefly and the meeting can move to other agenda items.

- Follow up with attendees after a status meeting by asking questions, sending meeting minutes, and being available. If questions arise, be sure to respond in a timely manner. Doing so goes a long way in great project communication, and your customers will appreciate it!

- Create a project communication control room and assign team members for the duration of the project, especially for large projects. Large construction projects or high profile projects, for example, often use communication control rooms for standard operating procedures. Large projects typically have the time, budget, and complexity to establish project communication control rooms because of the critical role project communications plays. The control room is the central communication room for displaying and discussing project information, in addition to being the area where the press or outside agencies can gather project information.

- Use the two-question technique (for small stakeholder groups only). After reading the status report, project customers or stakeholders bring two questions to the meeting. This is a fun way to get the stakeholders engaged in the project and ensures that they read the status report.

Defining a Project Communication Plan

A project communication plan is the document that defines the process and procedures involved with communicating project information. The communication plan outlines the process for managing the project information and distributing the information to the project stakeholders. Contrary to popular belief, the communication plan does not communicate project information; it simply outlines the processes to follow to produce and deliver the information, but does not contain status. The project communication plan includes areas such as the timeframe to receive data, project data recipients, distribution and storing methods, and the information collection process. One piece of the communication plan to watch closely is the timely delivery of project information. If you distribute project information late, the information becomes useless for your customers; they will not be happy or put up with the delay for long. Ensure you send the most recent information possible. For example, timely information is important for budget data and the frequency of reporting that type of data. Financial and cost information can swing radically from week to week; therefore, timely reporting of financial information is critical in keeping the project budget on track.

Note
Part of creating a project communication plan is to understand the proper generation of project information. This ensures the right people receive the right information at the right time.

Creating a project communication plan

One of your earliest tasks when initiating and kicking off a project is to create the project communication plan. Complete the following steps to create a project communication plan.

1. **Plan and document the communication components of your project.** For example, document the information you believe necessary to communicate effectively, such as:

   - Why do the customers need project information?

   - Who is working on the project?

   - What information do the customers need?

   - When do the customers need it?

   - In what format do the customers want it generated?

   - How will communication materials be stored? How will materials be retrieved?

   - Why is the information needed? Sometimes this history is beneficial.

When creating your project's communication plan, think about virtual communications as well. When managing virtual teams, this information is critical and requires a whole new level of project planning. In corporations today, virtual communication has been commonplace for many years, yet many project managers struggle to effectively communicate with virtual teams.

Compile the following questions and answers when documenting and planning your project communications. These questions and answers give you a huge start and advantage in creating a solid and comprehensive communication plan.

2. **Consolidate and plan using the results from the planning activities in Step 1.** Gather the information from Step 1 to create specific activities for creating those requirements. For example, the customers have asked for a monthly newsletter. The project manager must figure out the process for generating a newsletter in their project environment. The project manager works with the customers to ensure the information in the newsletter is what they want. The newsletter, in this case, represents the vehicle for delivering project information. The project manager continues working with the customer until he or she knows all the communication requirements (documented in Step 1).

3. Document the customer communication requirements within the project communication plan. For example, in Step 1, the customer requested a project website, a monthly newsletter, and quarterly press conferences. The project manager would document those requests within the communication plan. After getting customer approval, the project manager's task is complete and the communication plan is done.

4. Record your findings in your communication management plan. **Table 2.1 — Communication Plan Table of Contents** shows a sample table of contents for a communication management plan.

Every company that practices formal project management should have a form or a template of a project communication plan. Review the communication plan and make sure that it works for your projects; otherwise, adjust accordingly—not every section will apply to the project. For unique projects, you may need to add sections that are not in the communication plan template today. The main communication plan template should be sufficient for most project customers or clients for most projects. After completing the information in the document using the processes just described, you will have a very comprehensive communication plan.

Table 2.1 — Communication Plan Table of Contents represents a table of contents for a communication plan that uses five critical communication tools. Most communication plan templates include other sections, which is fine, just make sure additional communication tools are added to the communication plan. Without including specific tools, you do not capture all of the information you need for an effective communication plan. Remember the critical questions covered in Step 1 noted above? Without asking these questions and capturing the answers in the communication tools, you will not fully capture your customer's communication requirements. Later in the book, we cover each of the five communication tools; however, capturing the empty sections and placeholders in the communication plan document now is important.

Table 2.1 — Communication Plan Table of Contents

#	Description
1	Circle-of-Communication Chart
2	Project Communication Requirements Matrix
3	Role Report Matrix
4	Timeframe
5	Lessons Learned

The following tips can increase your chance of success and can be used as a checklist when creating a communication plan.

- Follow any procedures outlined by your PMO or company when capturing your customer's communication requirements. Most PMOs set the cadence for how often project reporting is required for project teams. You need to understand that cadence and use this information when gathering customers' communication requirements. For example, if the PMO establishes a monthly cadence for producing newsletters, and the customer wants a weekly newsletter instead, you will have to work with both parties to resolve.

- Hold brainstorming sessions with project team members and project customers or stakeholders to capture their communication requirements for the project. In these sessions, you or your administrative assistant will document the customer's communication requirements, such as which reports, forms, websites, communication tools, and specifically, the documents or spreadsheets the customer requires for the project. The goal of every communication plan identified in these sessions is to provide the customer with the information they need to make project-level decisions and gain status of the project.

- When the project customer's requirements include communicating with the media, you need to know the steps and processes for working with the media. This can be difficult for most project managers. Often, these messages must be approved by the legal department and can be quite complex to handle. Dealing with the media can be tricky and is common for large construction, research, or IT projects.

- Understand your customer's expectations and find out how often they want to receive project data. For example, the project customer requests a project status report, and your role is to determine how often the customer will receive that status report—weekly, monthly, quarterly? You need to work directly with the customer for this information and jointly agree on an acceptable timeframe for delivery.

- Understand exactly who the audience is for each communication deliverable. Ensure that you do not misjudge the recipients of the project when sending out project information. Take time to ensure the right people have the latest project information, always.

- Use the company's standard template if possible; do not create your own version of the communication plan if there is already one available. However, we suggest that you add the various communication tools we discussed in this chapter to the existing plan. Companies often have a generic communication plan that might be missing the key steps and processes outlined above, but it could be a good starting point.

Case Study - Kingdome roof replacement project and the media

A project that received much media attention was the Kingdome roof replacement project in Seattle, Washington, back in 1994. The Kingdome was Seattle's multipurpose stadium for professional baseball, football, concerts, and many other events. The problem arose when the roof tiles inside the Kingdome started randomly falling on the baseball field and were endangering the players during a regularly schedule practice. Team members were immediately removed from the field, and the safety manager of the Kingdome closed the stadium for safety reasons. This drew instant media attention to the Kingdome. An investigation determined that the tiles in the Kingdome needed to be replaced before any concerts or athletic events could continue. The media agencies actively tracked this high-profile project and demanded up-to-date information throughout the life of the project. The project office decided the best way to handle the constant pressure of replying to the media was to create a PMO. So, they took over a conference room and posted all relevant project information on the walls for review by team members, media, and the public. This information was always current because of the demand from the press to be updated. The media had the latest project information at all times. The room was open 24 hours a day, seven days a week. The project team worked around the clock to meet a tight deadline; the latest information was available to the media at any time without having to bother the project manager or owners.

Understanding the Circle-of-Communications Chart

The circle-of-communications chart identifies the resources you will work with throughout the life of the project; it's a simple chart to create, and effective when used on projects. You create the chart based on the specific project methodology you use. Because each project methodology has its own resource requirements, it is important that you create a project-specific chart. For example, a research project is different from a construction project; therefore, the circle-of-communication charts would be different as well. One area common to all projects is that they all have resources, and they all have a "lead" person who drives a specific group. The leads work closely with you rather than every individual team member. On large projects, working with everyone may not be scalable for you to handle successfully. Regardless of project type—construction project, a software development project, or a research project— the circle-of-communications chart works for any project type.

As you review **Figure 2.4 — Example of Circle of Communication Chart (Software Project)**, you will see the project manager role (you) in the center of chart, which represents you as the "center of communications" for the project. Connected to the project manager role are various leads (different for each methodology) who have team members working for them. The figure shows a software project example where the "Test Lead" has two testers working for him or her.

Figure 2.4 – Example of Circle of Communication Chart (Software Project)

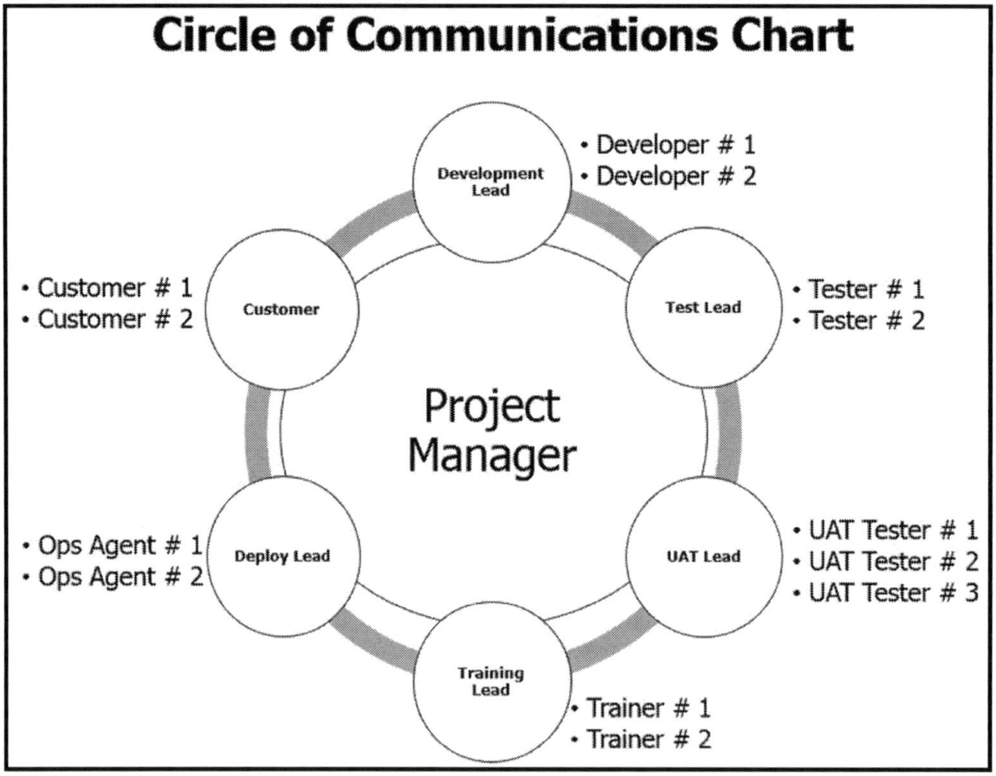

The circle-of-communications chart is not an organization chart. We have all seen hierarchical organization charts with a common structure of a single lead person on top, and the other resources shown under the lead person. For a project manager, however, a typical project structure does not look like an organization chart at all. Most project team members do not formally report to a project manager. How many teams have you worked on where everyone directly and functionally reported to you? There are cases where it happens, but not often. The circle-of-communication chart removes the view of who formally reports to whom, and puts the project manager in the center to represent that he or she owns the project communications only—not the team members. In today's project environment, the circle-of-communications chart becomes highly valuable and is used instead of an organization chart. This tool is beneficial to the project by helping you avoid politics while letting you establish and drive the project's communications. It's tackling communication planning from a different angle—one that takes the emotions of someone reporting to someone else out of the conversation.

Defining the Project Communication Requirements Matrix

A *project communication requirements matrix* is a chart that shows how communications flow on a project. It shows who communicates with whom and which tool they use to communicate. It also shows who develops the information and who receives it. As you read the chart, the direction and flow of information is from left to right, bottom to top. The communication matrix is easy to understand and build. However, before you start to create the matrix, there are several pieces of information you need. It takes a lot of time to build the tool and collect the information, but the process of gathering the information and asking the questions from the different parties is priceless. Gathering information and building the communication requirements matrix helps you and your team members understand the real communication needs of everyone on the project; no other tool can offer that level of information about a project's communication needs. By not creating the tool, you lose a wealth of data about how to communicate effectively with your customers. You never want to be in a place where you don't know what or how to communicate to you customers, clients, or leadership team.

Figure 2.5 Communication Requirements Matrix is a small example of this tool. This matrix represents who receives what information on the project and lists project stakeholders across the top and down the side. Also noted are any company-specific applications that require project status. The actual information or reports that you or the project team produce are documented in the cell of the matrix.

Understanding how to read the matrix chart

The first row in the matrix, the Project Manager, shows the project manager role sending the Stakeholders (Internal/Core Team) weekly status reports and attending monthly stakeholder meetings. The intersecting cell documents the specific communication requirements between the project manager and the particular role, in this case the Stakeholder (Internal/Core Team). As you read the matrix, look closely at the intersecting cells; they tell you the information passed between the two parties. This continues for every role on the project. As you read across the row for the Project Manager, specifically, note that he or she is responsible for entering status in the company's financial and reporting systems. This data includes color status (green, yellow, red), project dates, budget information, risks, issues, action items, and so on. Continue to review each row for every role on the project and review the intersecting cells for each role. You will also note that "No need to communicate" is a valid entry when two roles have nothing to communicate

Tip
You'll find that the communication requirements matrix is a valuable tool. This tool takes time to complete, so plan for this time in the planning process. Don't be intimidated by the complexity of the tool, just dive into it and get started right away on your project.

Figure 2.5 — Communication Requirements Matrix

Role / Role Communication Requirements	Project Manager	Stakeholder (Internal/Core Team)	Stakeholder (External)	Owner	Estimator / Estimating Team	Project Team Members	Company Financial and Reporting System(s), Estimator System(s)
Project Manager		Communicates Status weekly and participates in Monthly Stakeholder meeting		Communicates Status weekly and participates in bi-weekly			Project Status, Project Financials, Project Budget, Risks, Issues
Stakeholder (Internal/Core Team)	Feedback, Issues/Concerns		Feedback, Issues, Concerns		No need to communicate	No need to communicate	No need to communicate
Stakeholder (External)	Feedback, Issues/Concerns			No need to communicate	No need to communicate	No need to communicate	Add Budget information
Owner	Feedback, Issues/Concerns				No need to communicate		No need to communicate
Estimator/ Estimating Team	Project Estimates	Feedback, Issues, Concerns					
Project Team Members	Real time project data						Project Status, Project Financials, Project Budget, Risks, Issues
Company Financial and Reporting System(s), Estimator System(s)	Status Reports, Financial Reports	Status Reports, Financial Reports	Status Reports, Financial Reports	Status Reports, Financial Reports	Status Reports, Financial Reports	Status Reports, Financial Reports	

You benefit from using the communication requirements matrix by being able to see, on a single page, the information needed from the various roles. No other communication tool provides the same information to everyone on the project.

Creating a communication requirements matrix

Complete the following steps to create the communication requirements matrix.

1. **Plan and document the roles needed for the project.** Once you have identified all of the required project roles, add each role across the top and down the side cells of the matrix. This establishes the project roles needed to obtain or distribute project information. Create the circle-of-communication chart before you create the communication requirements matrix so you already have the roles you need. For the first step, think about the circle-of-communications chart, and then the communication requirements matrix as step two.

2. **Document individual communication requirements for every project role.** You will work directly with each role to gather information needs for the project. For example, you will meet with the customer to discuss communication needs. The information you capture during the session is added in the intersecting cells on the communication requirements matrix between the roles. The interview process continues as you meet with each role and document what they require for project information. You also set up and coordinate the meetings between the other roles of the project. For example, the customer and the team members require someone to coordinate the meeting between those roles, and in every case, that person should be you. Different project managers will tackle this process differently, but in the end, you need to address every intersecting cell. At the end of every session, enter the requirements directly in the intersecting cells between the two roles. You are finished with the communication requirements matrix tool when you have interviewed, captured, and entered all the data into the matrix. Often, you will work with various company systems on your projects. These systems have data entry requirements as well as reporting requirements and the system information should also be added to the matrix. It is a best practice to document both the data going in and reports coming out of the system. For example, the financial system produces weekly cost reports; however, the project manager had to enter the data into the system. Documenting both interactions for the various project systems is beneficial.

3. **When the communication requirements matrix is complete**, store it with the project documents and send it to customers for approval and future reference. If the project has a control room, hang the matrix on the wall for everyone to see and update when applicable. Another best practice is to continually review and refine the tool throughout the project. If a project team member leaves the project, you will need to update the communication requirement matrix with the new team member's information.

Understanding the Role Report Matrix

A role report matrix identifies which reports you will create for the various project roles. The role report matrix is different from the communication requirements matrix. The main difference is that the communication requirements matrix contains the information that is sent between the two roles (either people or applications), while the role report matrix only documents the reports between the parties. The communication requirements matrix includes areas where you can enter data into a financial reporting system; whereas, such data would never go in the role report matrix. The role report matrix describes and documents the various reports the stakeholders receive. Many project managers want to combine the two tools into one, which is definitely possible, but not recommended. The more information you put in one tool, the harder it is to read and understand. You'll find it worth the extra effort to keep the tools separate and the information clean in each tool.

Table 2.2— Role Report Matrix shows an example of a role report matrix. This table shows the project reports sent to the different roles and the people involved with the project. The matrix lists the different types of reports across the top of the table and the project roles and people's name down the side of the table. Just like the communication requirements matrix tool, the intersecting cells show the core information that is passed between the two people on the project.

In this example, the first row of data shows the CEO/CFO for the project. In reviewing that row, the CEO/CFO (John Smith) can request a status report or a cost report at any time (on-demand), and there is a requirement that he would like to see a monthly variance report. As you progress through the table, you will see the roles and their associated project reports.

Another key difference between the communication requirements matrix and the role report matrix are the names of the individuals that are listed. Use actual names so that when someone calls or emails you about receiving project information, you can quickly refer to the matrix to see who is receiving what. Without a role report matrix, you would likely have to search through old emails and look at distribution lists to figure out what information you are sending them.

Table 2.2 — Role Report Matrix

People (who receives the report)	Name	On-Demand Report	Daily Report	Weekly Report	Monthly Report	Quarterly Report
CEO/CFO	John Smith	Status/Cost Report			Variance Report	Quarterly Project Report
Owner	Peter Adams	Status/Cost Report	Daily Status Report		Schedule, Cost Report, Issues/Risks Report	Quarterly Project Report
Stakeholder	Mark Taylor	Stakeholder Report	Daily Status Report	Schedule, Cost Report, Issues/Risks Report		Quarterly Project Report
Project Manager	Bruce Jones		Daily Status Report	Weekly Status Report, Cost Report, Issues/Risks Report		
Risk Manager	Sally Smith	Risks Report	Issues/Risks Report	Risks Report		
Media	Tim Robbins	Media Report				Quarterly Project Report
Project Engineer	Peter Parker			Status Report, Cost Report		
Foreman	Tom Jones		Daily Status Report	Look Ahead or Activity Report		

The benefits of using the role report matrix include:

- It documents who receives which reports and how often the reports are distributed.

- It documents available reports. The matrix displays who is receiving which report. If stakeholders see a report they are not receiving, they can simply ask for it. Stakeholders would have no other way of knowing who is receiving which report without this tool.

- You can control the project information distribution to your stakeholders and team members, while seeing who is receiving what kind of project information.

- You can use it throughout the project to decide whether certain reports are still required by each customer. When a new customer joins the project, you can capture the customer's reporting requirements directly into the report with other stakeholder information.

Creating a role report matrix

Complete the following steps to create a role report matrix.

1. Plan and document the roles and report types available for the project. For example, document the different types of roles and add them, vertically, on the left side of the matrix. Across the top of the matrix, add the various time frames for report delivery. Time frames, at a minimum, include daily, weekly, monthly, or quarterly reports.

2. Document the individual project reports required for every project role. Work directly with each role to determine which type of project information reports they want to receive. A great example is the owner role, in which the owner requests an on-demand status and cost report, a monthly status report, and a quarterly status report. You would then work with each project role to decide which reports each role should receive and the timing. You will continually update the role report matrix by adding the information obtained from interviews directly into the intersecting cells. At the end of the interview process, the role report matrix is complete and ready to use on the project.

Tip
A best practice is to create the role report matrix at the same time you are completing the communication requirements matrix so that you only need to interview the stakeholders once.

3. After the role report matrix is complete, store it with the project documents and send it to customers for approval and future reference. Similar to the communication requirements matrix, if the project has a control room, hang the role report matrix on the wall for anyone to see and update when applicable.

The following list shows the various types of communication reports in a role report matrix. These names would be listed across the top of the table.

- Weekly Status Reports: Provide a status of the project mainly from a scheduling and cost perspective.

- Project Schedule: Provides the time lines for the project's work activities.

- Daily Report: Provides a daily snapshot of the project activities, addressing any risks, issues, or concerns about the project.

- Monthly Report: Provides a monthly snapshot of the project activities, addressing any risks, issues, or concerns about the project.

- Quality Report: Provides a quarterly snapshot of the project activities, addressing any risks, issues, or concerns about the project. This is normally a summary-level report.

- Cost Report: Provides a snapshot of the project costs at the time of running the report. This includes planned and actual costs.

- Variance Report: Provides a snapshot of the variance across cost and time from an established baseline.

- Issues Report: Provides a list of all project issues.

- Risk Report: Provides a list of all project risks and risk issues.

- Performance Report: Provides a snapshot of the current project performance metrics and trends.

- Resource Utilization Report: Provides a snapshot of the resource utilization across all project team members.

- Resource Leveling Report: Provides a snapshot of the project's resource leveling project.

- Quality Report: Provides a current snapshot of quality status and issues for the project.

- Media Report: Provides a media release.

- Lesson Learned Report: Provides ongoing lessons learned for the project.

- Look Ahead Report: Provides a look ahead for short-term activities.

- Stop Light Report: Provides a high-level graphic summary report on the cost and schedule status of the project.

Note

As you develop the role report matrix, it is critical that you determine who will receive which report.

Developing Lessons Learned Information

One of the techniques and best practices that senior and experienced project managers use is to develop and create *lessons learned* information throughout the life of the project—not at the end of the project. Usually, project managers collect lessons learned information in the final days or at the end of the project, which is during the closeout process and the project manager must scramble for bits and pieces of project history to compile into a lessons learned document. Often, because the project is in its closing phase, the project manager has only a few team members remaining, which makes compiling and obtaining project information from the remaining few resources difficult. The challenge is that the lessons learned information is incomplete because the project manager doesn't have the whole team, just the people left in the closing phase. This scenario is common for a project manager who waits until the end of the project before collecting and developing the project's lessons learned information.

A best-practice technique that is starting to gain popularity is collecting lessons learned information during the life of the project. From the kick-off meeting, capture and store the lessons learned information in a central repository for everyone to review. As the project progresses, use the project's status meetings to capture and review lessons learned information since the previous meeting. This is the best time to collect lessons learned information because you and your project team members can provide the week's lessons learned information while you are reviewing it—everyone is present to discuss what is happening, or what happened, during the week. When developing your weekly status meeting agenda, add a lessons learned agenda item. As the meeting progresses to the point where you are ready to collect lessons learned information, ask each team member about their positive and negative experiences for the week. Don't mention the words "lessons learned" to them, though, just capture what went right and what went wrong from every team member. The more you do this, the more the team members will start to provide the data. Eventually, team members will provide lessons learned data without realizing they are doing so. The goal of collecting this information on a weekly basis helps you lead the discussion around the lessons learned information rather than waiting until the end of the project. Having information from past projects or past weeks on the current project will help ensure that your team does not repeat the same mistakes. Each week, be on top of this process and continue capturing what went right and what went wrong from each team member. At the end of the project, compile the information into a final presentation—you won't be scrambling around trying to collect lessons learned information from project team members who may be long gone and working on different projects.

Communicating lessons learned information

When communicating project information, you should have as much knowledge about the project as possible. That way, you ensure that the messages you communicate are as accurate as possible. One method for gathering knowledge is by using the lessons learned information from past projects.

When you review the lessons learned information from past projects, you gain a wealth of knowledge about a previous project's events that might not normally be available. We recommend that you review the lessons learned information from past projects or, if possible, talk to the project manager who ran the previous project to learn more about what happened on the project. Occasionally, you might need to decide what information should be shared or not. Sometimes, sharing too much information can cause unnecessary bias that could negatively impact the project. An example would be capturing information about an individual or a particular group. The information was valuable to capture for the past project from a lessons learned perspective, but does not offer any benefit for this particular project and, therefore, should not be broadly shared.

When planning your project communications, it is advantageous to use lessons learned information wherever possible. If you have a customer that wants you to personally deliver a project status report instead of emailing it, you would want to know that information sooner rather than later. You can get this kind of information from the lessons learned information. When you have that kind of knowledge of what went right and what went wrong on projects similar to yours, you can communicate that information to your team members and be on your way to delivering a successful project.

Benefitting from lessons learned

One of the advantages of sharing lessons learned information is the positive impact that information can have on your project. Sharing these experiences and the specific knowledge that team members gained is beneficial for the next project. One example is when design teams create cost-saving techniques on the earlier project, and then use those same techniques on the existing project. These design and cost techniques save time and money on the current project.

Another important benefit of sharing lessons learned information is the advantage that team members, customers, and other stakeholders gain from understanding the mistakes and benefits from previous projects. Understanding a previous project's mistakes and benefits at the start of your project helps reduce the chance of making similar mistakes. When managing a second iteration of a project, make sure you understand the previous major issues or concerns. When using and reviewing information from past projects, look for the following information to share with your team and customers to help benefit your new project:

- Project budget information. Learn how earlier project managers managed their budgets and what tricks and techniques they used to be successful.

- Project schedule information. Determine the duration of the new project to compare with the previous project schedules. This comparison is important because you can find out if your project can or should be using the same time frames as the previous projects. For example, how long was the last development cycle compared to the current development cycle? Are they radically different for essentially the same project? This information is good to know when managing a project that closely matched another project.

- Project resources. Look for the various usage percentages of each team member, the process for finding team members, and whether those team members were allocated properly across the project life cycle. The more information you can discover and extract from previous lessons learned helps you plan more appropriately for your new project.

- Risks and Issues. Understand the previous project's risks and issues and try to remove the chances of those reoccurring on your project. Try to learn from what went right and wrong on the previous projects, specifically around what risks could occur and what issues did occur. Understand the method that previous project managers used to create, track, and reduce risks.

- Communicate with the previous project manager. One of the techniques that senior project managers often use when reviewing lessons learned is talking directly to the project managers of the previous projects. Those conversations often provide additional ideas that are not documented, but still valuable. Some of the stories and best practices the previous project managers can offer you are undocumented. Without these conversations, you would miss some valuable management points.

While collecting the lessons learned information, enter the data into a central location, such as a database or document. When companies take the time and effort to produce lessons learned information on a project, they build a wealth of information that can benefit future projects for years to come.

Caution
Collecting lessons learned information on a project can be difficult. Do not let lessons learned sessions turn into complaining sessions!

Summary

In this chapter, we explored the essence and importance of planning your project's communications. We covered how various project managers struggle with communication planning and discussed how mapping communication tools with PMI methodologies can help you communicate more effectively. We discovered and discussed some communication challenges, showed you how to solve or work with those challenges, and put you in the best spot possible to deliver a successful project.

Then, we covered creating a communication plan and the critical tools that should be in every communication plan going forward. We felt like it was important for you and your project manager peers to have a solid communication plan for every project and by covering this topic this early in the book, it represents our strong passion and dedication to the importance of this in delivering your projects.

Chapter 3

Working with Project Communications

IN THIS CHAPTER

- ♦ Interacting Face-to-Face
- ♦ Understanding Communication Links
- ♦ Understanding Stakeholder Risk Tolerance level
- ♦ Preparing and Presenting Presentations
- ♦ Distributing Project Information

One of the most challenging areas for project managers is communications management. Project managers own and drive all project communications. As projects become complex and more challenging, project managers need to step up and become effective communicators. The challenges that project managers face today are greater than in the past. These include running virtual project teams, shorter time to market, and advancement of technology and diversity of product availability (new products coming out daily). These complexities make managing projects a challenging task in today's market. When communicating project information, project managers need to focus on these challenges throughout the project life cycle. Project managers must document the "who", "what", "where", "how," and "when" (documenting the W's) of their project's information, which drives communication needs throughout the project life cycle.

In this chapter, we explore the various aspects of working with project communications. Some of the areas we cover include information overload, the importance of communicating face-to-face, challenges of virtual teams, and dealing with personality conflicts on large, diverse teams.

Interacting Face-to-Face

Spending time with each team member, even if it's limited, may help resolve concerns when applicable. We call this method face-to-face communication. Face-to-face communication occurs between at least two people. A group session of at least three people communicating and interacting is also face-to-face communication. As project manager, you should try to regularly establish face-to-face communication with each project team member. These individual sessions will help improve the overall group sessions that you lead with the whole team.

Face-to-face communication cannot prevent problems from escalating, but they can help build good rapport and strong relationships among team members, which can reduce escalations and keep team members working together.

Tip
Establish a good rapport as early as possible, regardless of the roles team members play or where they are in their specific organization. You should allot some time each week to meet with your team members, customers, or stakeholders, and anyone else involved in the project.

The following list outlines some of the various benefits of face-to-face communication, both professionally and personally:

- **Build and establish rapport.** Face-to-face meetings establish a rapport and a working relationship among various parties.
- **Build and establish credibility.** You can establish credibility and respect by communicating face to face. Like trust, earning credibility and respect occurs between the parties over time, and as team members continue to meet commitments and expectations, this respect comes more quickly. Credibility is something that can quickly be lost if someone feels that you are not telling the truth, or that you have betrayed them. It takes a lot of work to maintain credibility!
- **Build and establish friendships.** Face-to-face communication, over time, builds personal and professional friendships. Building rapport and credibility often turns two people into friends.

Tip
Encourage face-to-face meetings among different skill sets. Often, face-to-face communication occurs between the project manager and a team member, but a best practice is to encourage team members to meet regularly themselves. This helps them build rapport, which can be helpful later on when working out issues among themselves.

Making face-to-face communication work

In the following sections, we help you implement and strengthen your face-to-face communications with your project team members, customers, and stakeholders.

In-person meetings

When meeting in person with your project team, remember that your body language and facial expressions are harder to hide than when communicating by phone or email. Avoid making any expressions, comments, or remarks that unintentionally express your true feelings or reveal information—doing so is essential when visiting team members in foreign countries. (See *Chapter 4 - Exploring Foreign and Virtual Communications* for further information about foreign communications.) Incorrect actions or communications by you or your team members can easily offend your customers or leadership team, which can be perceived as inappropriate or even offensive.

When preparing to meet your project team or project stakeholders for the first time in person, remember the following actions and techniques:

- Body language: As a project manager, be careful about how you approach people during the first meeting. Be professional and ensure that your body language is not giving a different message than you are saying. Avoid crossing your arms when communicating to team members, which can be perceived that you are concealing information.

- Emotions: Control your emotions when communicating your project information to project team members and customers. If you cannot keep your emotions in check, you will not be seen as a leader and may be perceived as not strong enough for the role. A best practice is to show some emotion, but make sure to control your emotions when required.

- Facial expressions: Facial expressions tell it all. Be careful because so many things can be "said" with facial expressions—either on purpose or by accident. You must project a strong, confident image; ensure that your expressions do not reflect something that you do not want to reflect. Think positively and always smile when delivering positive project information. When delivering negative information, your facial expressions are also important and should reflect the seriousness of the problem.

- Dress: Dress professionally so you project an image of authority when delivering project information. You will gain confidence if you dress professionally.

Informal conversations with team members and customers can strengthen the project. These conversations can take place just about anywhere, and serve to establish a rapport with team members or stakeholders that is unlikely to happen in a formal setting. Informal conversations also build trust between people and increase the bond between the two parties. Often, long-lasting friendships develop when establishing informal conversations with team members or customers. Try to encourage informal discussions whenever possible to help your team members and customers build stronger relationships.

Social events

Often, you can improve team member communication by scheduling social events. Social settings often lower the working anxiety between team members and create a relaxed and friendly atmosphere for everyone. Another positive aspect of hosting or attending a social event is the opportunity to resolve communication issues with team members or customers.

Business lunch

A business lunch is one of the most valuable venues for one-on-one communication. The low cost of having the occasional business lunch pays off in building rapport and establishing good relations between two people. However, too much can be perceived as a bad thing when the same two people go to lunch too often—daily, for example. The value of the rapport building process decreases when communications happen too often and become too informal, and even unprofessional in some cases.

Understanding the value of face-to-face communications

You cannot assign a dollar value to the benefits of practicing face-to-face communication. Building trust is building credibility among project team members. When you work with team members who are credible, you know you can assign them work and it will be completed and with good quality. Building trust with your team members early in the project can reduce wasted time that could negatively affect the project. If people do not trust each other, they will spend extra time following up and checking up on one another.

This hurts the project and the people who continue to do the checking because it makes for unnecessary work. An ongoing meeting between the two parties can reduce the possibilities of miscommunications.

Understanding Communication Links

In this section, we discuss communication links between people. Do you remember the game everyone called "telephone"? It's the game where someone whispers a sentence to someone else, and that friend whispers it to the next person but adds something to it, and so on until the last person says it out loud and the original sentence is much different from the original sentence. You will deal with your own version of the telephone game on your projects. You don't want your original message to customers, clients, or leadership getting morphed into something completely different. We will talk about using the circle-of-communication chart to reduce some of the communication issues.

The more people in the communication chain, the harder it is to communicate accurately. Adding people almost always guarantees that someone will jumble the information between the parties.

The following formula represents the calculations for communication links. This formula is widely used by project managers around the world. You'll see the number of links that are created when you are communicating and working with so many different people. **Figure 3.1 — Communication Links** and **Figure 3.2 — # of Communication Links Chart (1 to 25 people)** show how quickly the communication links grow as you add more people. For example, if you are communicating with ten people, your links are not just ten, but equal to 45. The following formula demonstrates how many people are in your communication path.

Number of Links = n(n-1)/2 where n = number of people communicating

Example for 10 People: 10 (10 − 1)/2 = (10 x 9)/2= 45 Links

Note
PMI uses the term "channels" where we are using the term "Links" in this book. Either terms are valid and should be considered the same.

Therefore, if you send your communication to ten people, expect the message to be repeated at least 45 times. Repeating information can have a negative impact on your project, especially if the message was unclear to begin with. The result could be a miscommunication of project information being sent to your customers or your leadership team! That's never a good sign and should be avoided.

Figure 3.1 — Communication Links demonstrates how quickly the communication links grow as you add more people to the conversation.

Figure 3.1 — Communication Links

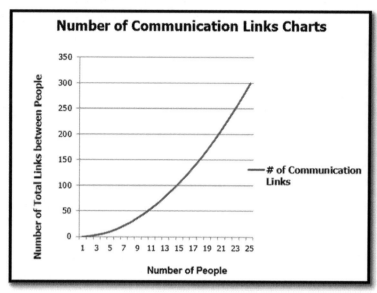

Note

The formula will make sense after you start working with it. Initially, it takes some time to see just how large the impact is on people when sending a message. The formula gives you a number to focus on when creating a message. No longer will you assume your message is going to just ten people, as in our example. Account for your message going to a larger group from the beginning and craft it accordingly.

Figure 3.2 — # of Communication Links Chart (1 to 25 people) shows a line chart of the communication links for 1 to 25 people. You can see how fast the number of people grows.

Figure 3.2 — # of Communication Links Chart (1 to 25 people)

This figure shows that as the number of people involved in your project communication increases, the number of communication channels increases exponentially. The changes in this figure actually hit the 300 mark for 25 people.

Sending and receiving models

There are two components of communication: sending and receiving. This sounds simple, one sends and one receives. It occurs daily in regular conversation. However, understanding and implementing the process of sending and receiving is not quite that simple. The challenge is the "interference" (also known as "noise") that happens when communicating with multiple parties.

Figure 3.3 — Sending & Receiving Model shows several steps that occur during a simple conversation between two people. Both people are transmitting and receiving messages as the conversation occurs. Due to interference, the messages are sometimes altered as they go through filters. Interference could be a personal filter. Interference is just about anything that can alter or interfere with the message sent. Each of us has a *personal filter* that can alter our understanding of the message communicated to us. Personal filters develop over time as our personalities develop and we experience life's daily challenges. These personality traits create and develop a person's communication filter. Therefore, one person can hear a message and experience that message based on their background and experiences, while someone else could interpret the same message a different way. These differences really become evident when two people are communicating from different countries where each person might have a different understanding of the message. These differences are especially true when dealing with two different cultures, such as eastern and western cultures.

Figure 3.3 — Sending & Receiving Model

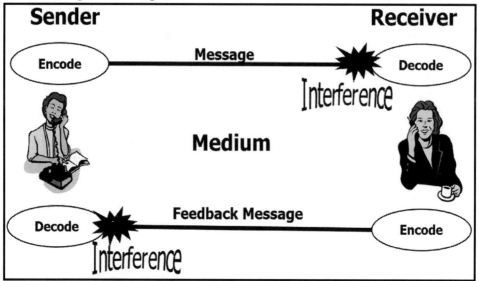

Figure 3.3 — Sending & Receiving Model portrays two women having a conversation. Both women are engaged in encoding and decoding the conversation. Interference is added to the conversation before decoding happens and after the encoding process. Interference could change the sent message. A simple conversation can become complex. Encoding, decoding, and interference throughout a conversation can make communication difficult for everyone.

Knowing the following terms can be helpful:

- **Sender:** Person sending message
- **Receiver:** Person receiving message
- **Encode:** Sending messages that are understood by others
- **Decode:** Translating messages during the thought process
- **Message:** The result of the encoding process
- **Medium:** Any form of conveying the message
- **Feedback message:** The results of the encoding process sent by the receiver

Sending model

Sending information, regardless of the type, can be tricky. When sending a message, put yourself in the place of the receiver to help you avoid miscommunication. Knowing the receiver's background, role on the project, and other information can help you determine how they might interpret your message. Sometimes, it helps to send the same message a couple of times in a slightly different format; people may not clearly understand the message if it is only delivered in one format. The format you choose may or may not be one that your receiver is comfortable with. For the best chance of success, ensure that you cater to more than one style of learning when sending your project messages. For example, use both text and graphics in your messages to enhance not only the message, but the chances of your readers comprehending the information. You should be aware of the cultural differences and personal bias people may possess. Having that knowledge beforehand allows you to tailor the message to that individual, and increases the chance that he or she understands the information.

Receiving model
The line graph in **Figure 3.2 — # of Communication Links Chart (1 to 25 people)** shows that even when you think you are communicating with a small number of people, you are actually dealing with a much larger group. Communicating a specific message to that many people means it must go through everyone's personal filters; to some extent, everyone will filter it differently. It is amazing that any verbal communication accurately transmits at all when going through so many people!

Understanding the Stakeholder Risk Tolerance Level

Risk tolerance level (often called, *risk level*) describes an individual's willingness to take various risks. Usually, the customer's risk tolerance level and your risk tolerance level are different, which can lead to communication problems. Personality conflicts arise when one person is more risk-adverse than the other. It is your responsibility to learn and understand your customer's risk tolerance level as early as possible in the relationship. This will help you make project decisions that align better with your customer's expectations; otherwise, you risk making project decisions that are opposite of what your customer expects.

The three levels of risk tolerance are described in the following list.

- **High risk tolerance:** Willing to take more project risks and make decisions based on that risk level.
- **Medium risk tolerance:** Willing to take some risks, but careful when making those decisions.
- **Low risk tolerance:** Very fearful of project risks and unwilling to make a decision that would increase the project risk.

The following sections describe the three different risk tolerance levels in detail.

High risk tolerance level

A person with a *high* risk tolerance level is someone who has a tendency to take and allow more risks on a project. We call these people "risk seekers." For example, a project customer (in this case, a risk seeker) accepts that the budget forecast has been overrun for the last several months. Because it is only a forecast, the customer is willing to take the chance that the project's forecast will decrease at the end of the project and end on budget. High risk tolerance people generally take more chances on their projects and in their personal lives—these are the bungee jumpers of the world. Therefore, depending on the role the risk seeker is assigned on a project, he or she could jeopardize the project due to the willingness to take risks. Over the years, we have found that high risk tolerance people tend to be optimistic people.

High risk tolerance people (risk seekers) will either not require many status updates from you, or they will make endless project information requests. Risk seekers are not micromanagers and let team members do their jobs and tend not to interfere with the project. Adjust your project communications accordingly for this type of customer. Occasionally, over communicating with a risk seeker actually does more harm than good.

Medium risk tolerance level

A person with a *medium* risk tolerance level is someone who takes and prevents risks on projects. This "risk neutral" person is willing to take some risks, but not high risks. Using the same budget overrun example, someone with a medium risk tolerance level would accept the risk of the project going over budget. But, he or she would try to prevent that from occurring as soon as possible. This person will require constant updates—at least until the issue is resolved.

A risk neutral person requires some level of project reporting, but doesn't request needless or extra reports. Most customers have a medium risk tolerance level. Therefore, most customers don't require excessive reporting or hand-holding. These customers are usually willing to accept the regular cadence of project information that you agreed to when you planned your project's communications. When you work with a risk neutral customer, you will do just fine keeping the customer continually updated with project information.

Low risk tolerance level

A person with a *low* risk tolerance level is someone who does not accept many risks. A "risk avoider" is unwilling to take any kind of risk on a project. This person often worries unnecessarily about all aspects of the project. This type of individual focuses on what could go wrong and puts measures in place to prevent those events from occurring. Using the same budget overrun example, a person with a low risk tolerance would worry about the forecast overage and be insistent about resolving the issues as soon as possible, which potentially causes extra work for team members. A risk avoider is typically a pessimistic person who requires constant attention. The term micromanager is often the label given to these individuals.

A risk avoider requires constant project reporting updates and reassurance that a project is on track. It is common for the project team to produce many on-demand reports and ongoing project information reports. In some cases, it might be best to hire a project assistant to deal with a low risk tolerance customer because of the extra time spent producing reports for them instead of driving the project.

Table 3.1 — Sample Risk Tolerance Versus Reporting Frequency Matrix shows an example of the three risk tolerance levels and the amount of requested reporting for each level. In the matrix, the High (Risk Seeker), requires high-level project information at a lesser frequency (Monthly/Quarterly). Review the other two risk tolerances for an understanding of their requirements. This matrix does not require you to add specific project details. Rather, it as a guide to help you understand and plan how to communicate effectively with each level of risk tolerance.

Table 3.1 — Sample Risk Tolerance versus Reporting Frequency Matrix

Customer's Risk Tolerance Level	Level of Reporting to Provide to Customer	Frequency
High (Risk Seeker)	High level of project information: for example, Project End Date: September 2019, Budget: $1,000,000	Monthly/ Quarterly
Medium(Risk Neutral)	Medium level of project information: Combination of high level and detailed level of project information. For example, Project End Date: September 12-15, 2019, Budget: $1,123,200	At least weekly
Low (Risk Avoider)	Low level of project information: Very detailed project information, covering all aspects of the project. For example, Project End Date: September 15, 2019 @ 5:00pm PST, Budget: $1,123,202.22 +/-5% accuracy	Daily/hourly and on-demand

This matrix is a great communication tool for directing and guiding you when working with different customers and their different risk tolerance levels.

Determining customer tolerance levels

Successful project managers assess a customer's risk tolerance level at the first meeting. You may ask the customer how they deal with project risks, or you may have a general conversation about risk management. If the initial conversations don't work, the next best is email. You should be able to get a feel for how much risk a customer is willing to take from your customer's initial emails. When a customer says, "You must hit x date," or, "You only have limited budget," you will know real fast that this customer has a low risk tolerance, so you should be able to respond and communicate accordingly. These clues in your customer's emails make it easy for you to understand your customers' risk tolerance level. If you are really stuck, have a conversation with the customer that is specifically focused on their risk tolerance levels. Make sure you know your customer's tolerance levels. With this knowledge, you will understand how to communicate more effectively with that customer. By missing this important aspect of your customer's personality and particular tolerance level for handling risks, you may not communicate as effectively with them.

Note

When discussing risk tolerance levels, you may find that some customers have different risk tolerances for different areas of the project. For example, in a cost-driven project, a customer may have a lower risk tolerance around project costs, but a higher risk tolerance for the project schedule or scope. On a completely different project, that same customer might change his or her risk tolerance levels based on the conditions or type of project. On a schedule-driven project, a low-risk person will take fewer risks on the schedule component, but may be freer with the budget and scope components.

Preparing and Delivering Presentations

As project manager, you and your team members are responsible for presenting project data and information during the project life cycle. It is important for project managers to know how to plan and deliver a great presentation. We also cover some tools and techniques to ensure that your presentations achieve their desired goals.

Note
Presentations are a great opportunity for you to shine and show off your presentation skills. Be prepared and give them your best presentation every time!

Tip
If your presentation skills are lacking, we recommend joining Toastmasters International® to improve your skills.

Preparing for a presentation

Preparing for a project presentation is like preparing for anything important. If you are unprepared, you are likely to have some disastrous results. Here are some tips that you can use while planning and preparing for a presentation.

Some of these tips are common sense, but all are helpful reminders that can help you become a better communicator.

- **Know your audience.** Although knowing your audience is important, knowing how knowledgeable your audience is about the subject you are presenting is even better. You can create a more detailed presentation when your audience is familiar with the material. This also determines the amount of time you need to spend on each section. If you feel your audience is going to be fully conversant in one area, you may want to focus more of your presentation in that area and leave the areas that everyone is less familiar with alone. Catering to the needs and wants of your audience will help you deliver a successful presentation.

- **Establish the correct tone.** You need to decide what tone will work best for your presentation. Should it be serious or informal? Will humor work? How much is too much?

- **Dress for success.** Always dress professionally when presenting. Even if every other day you dress informally, the day of the presentation you need to look professional and respectable to your audience.

- **Know the room and facilities.** Familiarize yourself in advance with your presentation room and the equipment that you will use. Upfront planning should help with any technical issues that may arise. Reserve the room at least 30 minutes before the scheduled meeting time to give you enough time to set up and get comfortable.

- **Present your credentials to establish creditability.** Present your credentials at the beginning of your presentation so that your audience knows your background and you build a level of trust and respect with them from the start. If you put your project manager credential slides at the end of your presentation, you may run out of time to cover them. So, we recommend that you present your credentials early and quickly to build creditability with your audience.

- **Schedule informal meetings with stakeholders in advance.** Presenting information to some of the key customers or clients ahead of the actual formal meeting should eliminate any major surprises during the presentation. Schedule "dry run" preview meetings ahead of the final presentation, to give customers and leadership teams the chance to see the raw materials before the formal meeting. "Dry run" meetings should have limited attendance to ensure that only specific people are in the room—not everyone you are inviting for the formal meeting.

- **Practice, practice, practice.** Practicing your presentation is the key to presenting it well. When you think you are done and know the material, practice some more.

Presenting your project materials

After all the preparation is complete, it is time for the presentation. As you continue to hold more and more presentations, you will learn from your mistakes and improve your presentation skills naturally. In the meantime, here are some helpful tips and ideas for presenting your material.

- **Introduce your topic well**. Your introduction will vary in length and detail, depending on the length of your talk, your topic, and the level of audience sophistication. Determine what you are trying to impart. Give the necessary information, but be careful not to include large amounts of extraneous material. Visual aids are particularly important to grab your audience's attention. If you have a snappy photo, an interesting thought, or a catchy phrase, use it here. Your introduction should capture your audience's attention, let them know what you will be presenting, get them ready and excited, and advise them on why your material is so interesting.

- **Limit your use of animation.** Too much animation can be distracting and reduce your presentation's impact. Many presentations have this problem today because animation software has become easier to use. Including just the right amount animation or graphics in your presentations, however, can have a positive impact. Remember, this is your time to shine, and you want your presentations to be fun and exciting, just don't overdo it. Regardless of how serious the message, it may be easier to sell with some levity.

- **Don't overwhelm your audience with information.** Limit the total amount of data you present and limit the amount of information you show on any single slide. Busy slides and complex graphs are not helpful and can end up confusing your audience. A confused audience is not a happy one. Keep slides brief and to the point; never have more than five bullets per slide, but three bullets is recommended.

- **Begin with a title slide and show a brief outline of the topics.** Use text slides to designate the beginning of individual sections or to introduce a major topic. Usually a prominent title in bold letters is adequate. Text slides can be helpful to you and your audience. Text slides demonstrate your organizational skills, help audience members follow the presentation more easily, and let them know where you are heading in your presentation.

Avoiding common mistakes

When making project presentations, it is common to make simple mistakes that detract from the overall presentation. These are frequently made mistakes, but easily avoidable. Here is a list of tips that will help you avoid these common mistakes.

- **Paraphrase your text slides, don't read each major point.** The audience will be reading the slides. Read a point or two, but then go into the details you want your audience to understand.

- Clearly label all axes on figures (if applicable) and give each figure a brief, informative title. Doing so is good practice and makes your slides clear and easy to follow.

- **Choose your graphs carefully.** Graphs should follow a logical progression, and you should be able to fully explain each graph. Use the best graphics available, but be careful not to distract your audience by making the artwork more interesting than the information. Watch for colors, patterns, and the various combinations of each. Make sure you focus on content and clarity.

- **Cite all sources of information, especially if you did not generate the data yourself.** It is important to give credit where credit is due when using material that you did not create.

- **Always give a synthesis or conclusion.** Display a brief summary of your conclusions while you discuss the significance of the material you presented. Your conclusions should match your talk objectives and complete your story.

Make sure to include time for questions and answers following a project presentation. Adding a question and answer period is the key to a successful presentation and allows everyone to walk away with more knowledge about the subject. When you don't provide a question and answer period, the audience can feel rushed and less informed. The question and answer period lets you prove that you really know your subject, so plan and prepare. Try to think about all the questions that could come up and be ready to answer them. Be prepared to answer questions about the materials or the project in general.

Tip
Always remain relaxed and calm throughout the question and answer period, even though you may get stuck on a question or be put on the spot. Do not worry, even the best presenters get stuck, but the more experienced ones can normally get themselves out of it. Usually, this is as easy as saying, "I don't know the answer" or, "I will get back to you." This response gets you off the spot, but gives you an action item to track down the answer after the presentation.

When answering questions during the presentation or during the question and answer period, take time to gain composure, make sure you understand the question clearly, and think about it before you answer. If the question is unclear or does not make sense, ask politely for clarification. Experienced project presenters encourage questions and answers during the presentation. They can control the time remaining for the presentation and move the meeting along.

Distributing Project Information

When distributing project information, you must decide the method, manner, and style for delivery. There are three ways to deliver information: verbally, written, or visually. Each delivery method offers benefits and risks for delivering project information. The challenge is deciding which method to use when sharing specific project information.

We recommend that at the start of a project you ask your customers the communication style they prefer. Customers or stakeholders will often unknowingly tell you. For example, if a customer is drawn to diagrams and pictures when describing something, he or she is often graphics oriented. These individuals will likely say something like, "Draw me a picture; I learn better that way." On the other hand, some customers learn quickly by reading a text document or spreadsheet, so the customer might say something like, "Can you send me the raw data?" In either case, you have discovered their learning preferences without even having to ask them. You are now much better off because you know their preferred method of communication.

Communicating verbally

Verbal communication is simply having a conversation. Verbal communication is something you should excel at with your customers, team members, and leadership team. If you do not communicate well, focus on improving those skills as soon as possible. Strong communication skills are critical to a successful career in project management. There are many courses and training materials available for you to use if you struggle in this area.

One of the challenges of verbal communication is communicating by telephone or working in a global environment. Be aware of your tone when speaking on the phone compared to how you come across in person. Your communication styles may need to be different based on the situation and the communication method (phone versus face-to-face conversation). Something said in person may be inappropriate over the phone (a joke, for example). Some of your customers or stakeholders may prefer to learn and understand the message using verbal communication. They may learn more effectively by having project information explained to them directly in verbal conversations and conference calls rather than receiving the same information nonverbally, in an email, a report, or a document. To help a customer who learns better using a verbal method, try the following:

- Develop status reports, issues, or risks formally on paper or email and send them to the stakeholders before the first face-to-face meeting.
- Go through the report with the customer on the phone or in person. The preferred method, if possible, is in person. That way, you have a formal record on paper, but you also explained the report and addressed any customer questions or concerns.

The following list includes details about verbal communication choices.

- Face-to-face conversation
    - **Formal:** Formal communication includes presentations, status meetings, budget reviews, milestone reviews, providing information to media (interviews), and meeting with customer or stakeholders.
    - **Informal:** Informal communication includes water cooler conversations, hallway conversations, gossip, and conversing during social functions.
- Telephone conversation
    - **One-on-one:** Typical one-on-one conversations are usually informal. Talking on the phone and dealing with project issues, for example, is usually an informal conversation—

unless both parties agree that it is a formal conversation. Permission is needed if someone wants to record a call for future playback, which makes the conversation formal. Recording a phone call can be helpful when you need to go back for future reference. In some cases, the subject is so complex that you might need to listen to the recording to fully understand the information.

- **Conference calls:** Conference calls involve communicating with several people and are usually formal. Costs are often associated with these calls and they are scheduled formally with multiple project team members, customers, or stakeholders. Conference calls usually have multiple participants and might include people from different time zones. For example, a person working on a technical problem might contact his or her peers working in India and Ireland—all three parties are actively on the call at the same time. Conference calls can help you solve problems more quickly than a one-on-one call because there are more people involved to solve the problem.

- **Online meetings:** Online meetings are similar to standard conference calls in which you have a one-on-one conversation or multiple people on the line. Using communication software is becoming a popular way to communicate over the standard telephone call. You can find many products on the Internet to conduct online meetings, and depending on the Internet connection, most of them are free. For global project teams, technology narrows the gap among team members and lets everyone feel connected. Using online meetings, you can communicate verbally, but the presenter can share his or her computer desktop at the same time. Online meetings are wonderful for virtual teams!

Communicating in writing

Written communication is the most popular method of communicating project information. In project emails, or official documents, written communication is by far the most popular choice for project managers. For example, new policies are written and distributed to organizations all the time. Whereas, verbally telling people about a policy change in a large company meeting or through a presentation does not carry the same impact as a document with the same information.

There are three main written communication formats that most project managers use while communicating project information. These formats include:

- **Email:** Email has become the most common form of communication in the 21st century, especially among project teams. Project teams communicate via email more than by telephone or even face-to-face conversations. The downside of email is that you might phrase text in a tone that you may not use in a face-to-face or phone conversation. Email provides distance between the two parties that sometimes can be negative. Framing your email and understanding how your audience might perceive the tone of your email will go a long way in improving your email project communication skills.

- **Paper:** Paper has been around for thousands of years and is the standard for project information reporting. Even in the age of electronic communication, some stakeholders and leadership team members want hardcopy, paper reports. Make sure you understand how your project customers, clients, and leadership teams want to view or receive reports.

  - **Formal:** Project managers use formal reporting for deliverables such as project status reports, presentations, and cost reports. They file and save these documents for long-term storage and future reference.

  - **Informal:** A project memo is an example of informal communication where, for example, no signature is required. Normally, people discard them when no longer needed.

- **Electronic:** You can send your messages instantly using instant messaging tools on your computer and text messaging on your mobile phone. These tools are great communication tools, but should not be used for formal communication. Instant messaging tools are great for quick status, high-level actions, and general communication touch points. Do not communicate formal project information using an instant messaging tool without immediately following it up with an email, document, or telephone call. Another aspect of instant messaging you must consider is the lack of security. Most popular instant messaging tools today do not have strict security standards. Instant messaging and texting were not developed to be formal tools. Be careful how much and what type of information you send with these tools. As the tools improve over time, new security features will likely be added. In the meantime, though, only use these tools for informal communications.

Communicating visually

You have the luxury of presenting data in graphs, charts, and tables—formats that are visually appealing and easy to and understand. Never has there been a truer statement than, "A picture is worth a thousand words." Project customers or stakeholders often find it easier to read and understand project information visually. Use visual communication when possible because customers and team members can see the project information rather than reading pages of text with the same data. It's important to request feedback and comments about your presentations so that you know your material is sending the right message.

Note
Consider feedback obtained about your presentation material as a mini lessons learned session.

A good presentation strategy is to approach your audience as if you are telling them a story. Guide the audience through the story as you present the material. Even though you might be presenting a serious subject, have fun with it. Do not be afraid to add some animation, graphics, and color to your material to help lighten the mood, raise the learning level, and add some fun.

One benefit of visual communications is that customers or stakeholders generally prefer it. They like graphics and charts for showing project information because they can quickly grasp it and make decisions based on what they see. On the flip side, if your customer does not favor graphics or charts, you could produce a text version of the same slides to cater to their preferred learning style. A great example of this is junk mail marketing. Junk mail often contains a large, glossy foldout page of marketing material, but it also contains the same material in a plain text format. Marketing companies have figured out that to market to everyone effectively, they have to cater to everyone's learning styles. As noted earlier in this chapter, this is another opportunity to understand and cater your materials to your of your customers', clients', and leadership team's learning styles.

After you decide to present project information in a visual format, you have several choices to make. With the advancement of technology, and the Internet specifically, you should not be short of choices for deciding which method to use for your presentation. Often, your imagination is the only obstacle you will face. Here are a couple examples of the many visual methods:

- **Presentations:** Some of the most popular tools for developing presentations are Microsoft PowerPoint® and Apple Keynote®. If you are unfamiliar with these two tools, or any other presentation tools, you should gain familiarity with them quickly. If you need it, take some training to learn how to use them to your fullest potential. Presentation software improves your ability to deliver powerful and effective project presentations.
- **Documentary of the project (video or DVD):** One method of delivering a powerful impact for your project is to create a video documentary. Video documentaries can contain valuable project information, but they are usually expensive. However, if you are working on a high visibility

project, using video is a great way to communicate your project information concisely and professionally. Large construction projects often use videos as a standard tool for communication. Large software development companies are producing videos that capture and simulate their software to potential customers. Companies offer short videos of what the software can do and show simulations of their products in action. You can see many examples of these videos on company websites all over the Internet. Microsoft uses many of these videos on their websites for Office products and game suites. Spend some time on the Internet and you will find a variety of products that you can use to create videos for your presentations. One major advantage of using a video format in your presentations is repeating and reusing the same information as a learning aid. If you run the video in a loop, the information is repeating continually for the customers. Videos are often shown in conferences, auto shows, boat shows, home shows, and they even appear in local stores (for example, showing you how to use their product to paint your house). Other advantages include the ability to start, stop, reverse, and fast-forward the information, allowing you to review specific areas of the material several times.

The greatest advantage of using video or DVD media is that it captures time motion photography that captures step-by-step development of the project throughout its various phases. Construction, manufacturing, and security industries all use this photographic technique successfully for various reasons. In construction, for example, time motion photography displays a time-lapsed view of the various stages of development of the building, house, or bridge.

Summary

In this chapter, we explored working with project communications. We covered the importance of face-to-face interactions and the struggles behind communication links. We explored how even a simple phone conversation can have messages being interpreted many different ways based on people's backgrounds and experiences.

Then we covered stakeholder risk tolerances and the importance of project managers learning the risk levels of their customers. We captured how their risk tolerance levels drive how often you and your team members will communicate and how deep the information needs to be for your customers.

Finally, we covered preparing, presenting, and delivering project information and some tips and tricks for you to use. Preparing and delivering project information is a staple for all project managers, and the areas covered in this chapter are going to set up any project manager for success.

Chapter 4

Exploring Foreign and Virtual Communications

IN THIS CHAPTER

- ◆ Preparing and Planning for Project Communications in Foreign Countries
- ◆ Business Travel
- ◆ Learning Virtual Communication

Whether you are negotiating a project budget or listening to a team member's problems, you must always be an effective communicator, regardless of the situation. Effective communication is a mandatory skill set when traveling and working in different countries. In today's work environment, project managers travel for assignments all over the world. When traveling abroad, learn about the culture and customs of the country where you will be working so that you can effectively communicate with foreign team members.

Preparing and Planning for Project Communications in Foreign Countries

If you travel to another country for work, it is important that you spend time learning about that country's religions, cultures, and customs. There are many different customs across many countries, so read about the country you are going to work in prior to traveling. You do not want to get into a situation that is acceptable in your country, but unacceptable elsewhere. For example, in a Muslim country, you do not sit with your legs crossed and the soles of your shoes showing. Be aware of these types of common everyday situations that are problematic in a foreign country. You should be overly aware of your environment and sensitive to your surroundings so you know what is acceptable, or not, in that country.

When projects are short on staff and project managers cannot find local resources, they often look abroad for talented individuals. When you hire team members in a different country, those new team members must also be aware of the different customs of the country in which they are doing work. Team members must also prepare to work aboard. In some cases, new team members might continue to work in their home country, but they are part of a team in a different country. Those team members need to understand the other country's culture. For example, if a group of individuals from China are working on a team that is based in the Canada, the team in China should understand Canadian customs, and the team from Canada should understand the customs relevant to China—especially if people are traveling between the two countries.

As project manager, make sure your team members learn the customs and cultural differences of the new team members. It is time well spent to let team members take time away from their current tasks to learn about the cultural differences of their newest team members. It not only helps the current team members accept the new team members, but it also helps overall morale and teamwork. If each team member learns the different customs, you will have a strong team and the new team members will feel accepted.

Occasionally, you may need to work in a foreign country where the two countries (your home country) and the other country are hostile. If that is the case, you need to be extremely careful and alert to the environment and political unrest of the country. Work closely with your company advisors on security, country protocols, and other procedures to ensure your safety in the new environment.

Business Travel

If you are lucky enough to win a project management assignment on a foreign project, we advise you to learn the customs and cultures of the country you will be visiting prior to traveling there. By doing so, you learn how to act so that you avoid offending anyone.

Preparation

Preparation time varies from person to person. Use the amount of time you are going to be in the country as a guide for preparation. A weeklong trip requires a lot less preparation than someone staying in a foreign country for months or years. Usually, if you are assigned to a long-term project in a foreign country, your company will give you enough time to prepare. Your company should cover expenses related to relocating (for example, visa processing fees). If your project assignment is longer than a year, you might consider taking a class in the country's language to help you communicate with your new team members. The new team members will appreciate your extra effort learning their language.

Dual-language business cards

In most countries, exchanging business cards during the first meeting shows good business manners. It is best to carry business cards printed (front and back) in English and the language of the country you are visiting. If you receive a business card from your foreign counterpart in Japan, for example, make sure to review it; otherwise, it is considered rude and bad manners to immediately put it in your pocket. It is acceptable to ask questions or make comments about the business card after you have reviewed it.

Tip
Even though English is the international business language, getting business cards made in dual languages is a great idea for anyone working in a multinational company. Even if you are at home and staff from your international office visits you, it is a nice gesture to hand out your dual language card.

Many times, international airlines can arrange to have these cards printed and ready for you when you arrive. It is important when visiting Japan or China that you have dual language business cards. This is a standard practice for these cultures.

Culture

Learning the cultural differences between your country and the foreign country is important. Familiarize yourself with basic cultural traits, such as hand gestures, street signs, tipping, and specific rules for women in Middle Eastern countries. Most project managers need flexibility and cultural adaptation before considering work aboard, and you won't be any different. You and your team members traveling abroad for the first time will be surprised by how much business manners, customs, religion, dietary practices, humor, and dress can vary dramatically from country to country. Be alert and observant about the local customs. A quick way for you to become familiar with the country you are visiting is buying a travel guide for that country. Or, borrow one from a friend or coworker who already lives there.

Understanding cultural differences contributes to a successful experience when working in a foreign country. A lack of familiarity with etiquette, social customs, and cultural norms that the country practices can hurt your creditability with local team members—to the point where they don't want to work with you at all. If you arrive and make some major cultural blunder, it could affect the team's overall morale and put you in an awkward position that could take a long time to correct.

It is important to have knowledge of the culture, management attitudes, and customs before traveling abroad. Do your research, read books, get training, and read personal interviews to learn as much as possible about the culture.

Greetings
Traditional greetings may include a handshake, a hug, a nose rub, a kiss on the cheek, placing the hands in praying position, or various other gestures. When cultural lines cross, something as simple as a greeting can be misunderstood between two people and cause issues. You need to be fully aware of the country's accepted form of greeting or it could lead to awkward encounters with your foreign stakeholders.

Gifts
Gift giving is a common custom in China, for example. When you are traveling to China, expect to bring a gift for your host. The gift should be from your home country, or even better, your local area. It does not have to be expensive, just thoughtful. Failure to bring a gift is an insult in some countries; whereas, in other countries, presenting or offering a gift is akin to bribing someone. In sharp contrast, exchanging gifts in Germany is rare and is not usually an appropriate thing to do. Gift giving is not a normal custom in Belgium or the United Kingdom either, although in both countries, flowers and wine are suitable gifts when invited into someone's home. Again, know the customs of the country in which you are going to work.

Significance of gestures
A misunderstanding over gestures is a common event in intercultural communication. Misinterpreting a gesture can lead to a big laugh or it could lead to working through issues and social embarrassment for you. Be careful when using body movements or gestures to convey specific messages because gestures that are common in some cultures may not be common in other cultures and you could end up offending someone. For example:

- Putting your hands on your hips in some cultures indicates a challenge or a combative attitude.
- Crossing your arms in front of someone signals that you disagree or are skeptical of them.

Negotiating styles
Project negotiation is a complex process even between parties from the same nation. It is even more complicated in international transactions due to potential misunderstandings that stem from cultural and language differences. It is essential to understand the importance of rank in the other country, to know who the decision makers are, and to be familiar with working styles. It is also important to understand the nature of agreements in the culture. That way, when you are negotiating agreements, you will have a better understanding of how everything fits together.

Differences in business styles
Pay attention to different styles in accomplishing a project's objective. In some countries, team members are direct, and in others, they are much more laid-back and not aggressive. In Germany, for example, project team members are serious and generally get right down to business when they are working; there is little to no small talk, which could interrupt project performance. Many Germans take the work environment seriously and keep work at a professional level.

Discovering etiquette

Use the following tips as a guide for some of the popular countries for business travel. Your next assignment could be in any one of these countries, so think about how to prepare for that next major move. As you can imagine, though, every situation is different and the following tips may not work in every situation. Be aware and adapt these tips to each situation, as it occurs.

Note
Not all countries are listed here, just some to guide you in preparing for your travels.

United States of America (U.S.)
Acceptable in most cases:

- In general, tipping is not included in the bill or tariff—adding an additional 15 percent tip is considered average.
- When in a crowd, always stand up when the national anthem is played, and if you are wearing a hat, remove it during the anthem.

Unacceptable in most cases:

- Americans tend to be proud of their country, so do not disrespect it or make disparaging comments.
- Slang is unacceptable in business and project communications.

Belgium
Acceptable in most cases:

- Greeting someone with three kisses on the cheek, alternating from one cheek to the other. This is also a custom in France and Greece.

Unacceptable in most cases:

- Yawning, sneezing, or blowing your nose in the presence of others.
- Placing your hands in your pockets while talking to someone—by doing this, you are showing a lack of interest.
- Pointing your index finger at somebody. Pointing in most European countries is impolite and frowned on. If you need to point at something, simply gesture in that direction, usually a nod of the head will work.

China
Acceptable in most cases:

- Address a person using their family name. For example, use "Mr. Li" rather than "Raymond Li". In business, it is traditional to call an Asian person by their surname along with their title, such as, "Director Li" or "Doctor Li".
- Look at the business card from your Asian business associate and note the name and position in the company that this person holds. This is important in China. When putting away the business card, always put it in a front pocket, not a rear pocket. It is an insult to put a business card in your back pocket. If possible, remember to take or receive the business card with both hands.
- Start all business meetings with small talk and avoid getting into the business topic too early.
- Always bring a gift to your host.

Unacceptable in most cases:

- Even though you start meetings with small talk, do not become too friendly too fast. The Asian culture frowns on quick informality.
- Do not be boastful and overbearing. A simple nod, or better yet, a slight bow and an occasional mild handshake are all proper greeting protocols during introductions.

France
Acceptable in most cases:

- For business communications, such as email or letters, use a formal and businesslike format.
- Avoid calling your business associates' personal phone (home or cell) for business-related topics. If you must make the call, make it before 9:00 P.M.

Unacceptable in most cases:

- Arriving late for meetings.
- Using first names during a business meeting. The French are proud of their culture and want a formal business atmosphere. Even if you are a friend, you should still use their last name and title (for example, "Director Brisard").
- In a dinner or meeting environment, delay business discussions until the small talk is finished. Jumping right into business discussions is considered rude.
- A man should never ask a woman what she did over the weekend.

Germany
Acceptable in most cases:

- Always knock before opening a closed door, regardless of the door.
- Always be punctual whether attending a business meeting or a dinner. It is rude to be late to almost any engagement.
- Minimize small talk in business situations.
- Always use the title and family name of your local team members.

Unacceptable in most cases:

- When meeting someone, shaking his or her hand with your other hand in your pocket.
- Being late for a business meeting.

Italy
Acceptable in most cases:

- When greeting each other, you may kiss each other's cheeks and offer a long handshake.
- It is acceptable to shake with both hands.
- Hire an interpreter if you are not fluent in Italian.

Unacceptable in most cases:

- Refusing repeats on your plate if offered.
- Being late for meetings or appointments is considered rude. Especially in northern Italy; they consider time the same as money.

Indonesia
Acceptable in most cases:

- If you are being introduced to several people, always start with the eldest or most senior person first.
- Titles are important in Indonesia as they signify status. If you know someone's title, be sure to use it in conjunction with their name.

Unacceptable in most cases:

- Crossing your legs when you are sitting and showing the soles of your shoes.
- Women should not wear short skirts. Women should dress conservatively, ensuring that they are well covered from ankle to neck.

Exploring Virtual Communications

The project management profession is clearly changing by moving away from boardroom meetings and group gatherings to favoring virtual project teams at various sites around the world. Companies are allowing full- and part-time employees to work from home (home office employees) or a remote office (corporate or remote offices) in another town or state, 100 percent of the time. Many companies moved development and testing teams to offshore countries and left project management at home. Project managers, with little to no virtual team skills or any particular communication tools to help them, can find themselves managing up to 95 percent virtual team members. Project managers must figure out how to manage a virtual team on their own, which can be a tough spot for anyone. Sometimes, training is available, but that is often rare and the project manager must figure out how to manage these teams with little training. If you haven't managed a virtual team, you initially could be in for a big surprise by managing your first virtual project. Virtual team management is difficult; it is something that takes time to master. Communicating with virtual teams is difficult, so make sure to prepare when first starting to manage a virtual project.

Case Study - A real-world project communication lesson

A software development company wanted to find out if it was practical to develop a software system by working around the clock across three different countries, in different time zones. It appeared there were only two choices: work three teams in three shifts (first shift, second shift, and third shift), 24-hours a day in one location; or work three teams located strategically around the world, each working only the first shift.

The objective of the project was to develop a software system in less than half the normal time it would take to develop the software with a single onshore project team. Senior management decided to experiment by using a global project and created three virtual teams to fulfill that objective.

Here is how the virtual teams worked together: the team in the United States developed their portion of the software during their eight-hour shift. Near the end of the shift, they documented what they had accomplished that day. Then, they sent all of the files and documentation for the project to the team in Japan. The two teams would communicate and establish what the Japanese team would accomplish during their shift. At the end of the shift in Japan, those team members repeated the process of documenting the day's work, and then submitted the work to the European team. At the end of the shift in Europe, that team communicated back to the U.S. team on the progress. The U.S. team then took over, working on the remaining tasks. This process continued until the project was finished. It turned out to be a successful project, and the three teams produced the software system in half the time of a single U.S.-based team. The team used the different time zones around the world to their advantage, and to the project's advantage. Using teams in three different countries, the project ended and completed a total of 24-hours a day worth of work, compared to the standard 8 hours worked in the United States and most other countries—passing the project files and information from one team to another continued to keep the project progressing every day.

It became immediately obvious when the teams first started the process that it was critical that communications were concise and accurate for two reasons. The workers needed to communicate the technical information between teams in a way that everyone could understand—in a way that would allow the project work to continue when that team handed over the files to the other team. Additionally, the communications had to be in different languages. The language barrier was especially challenging when translating the work from Japanese to English.

A benefit often missed by using the three time-zone scenario was that overtime payouts were limited because team members handed the work off to the next team at the end of the working day. Thus, overtime payout was reduced in three different countries.

Communicating with the virtual project team

Working with project teams can be challenging, but working with virtual teams is even more challenging. The challenging aspects of virtual teams come in all areas of the project. Challenges include communication challenges (such as time zones), language barriers, resource challenges (do they have the right skills to work in virtual environment) and cost challenges (fluctuating exchange rates). Different religious holidays in different countries also can become an issue. Some of these issues are common to all project managers, so they are not specific to virtual project management. However, these issues magnify tremendously with virtual teams. Communication with virtual teams is an important concern for project managers. The language barrier has a huge impact on the project team. Sometimes language issues takes months to resolve, or in some cases you may need to hire an interpreter to communicate between the two countries. After communications barriers are resolved, the project communications should become easier.

Virtual communicating methods

There are many different methods to communicate effectively with virtual project teams. These methods include:

- Telephone
- Weekly telephone conference calls
- Site visits
- Online conferences or video conferences
- Email and written communications, such as faxes or letters
- Shared company websites, such as Microsoft SharePoint® sites
- Shared applications where project status information is stored and updated (for example, a project server)
- Instant messaging
- Online communication tools, such as Microsoft Skype®
- Online collaboration tools
- File transfer software
- Document control systems

As you gain work experience with virtual project teams, you gain different communication skills and knowledge and will quickly be communicating effectively in this difficult environment. The more time you work with virtual teams the better you become, and you will discover your own methods for working with virtual teams.

Managing virtual project teams

Like working with onsite project teams, managing virtual project teams is often challenging. Actually, managing virtual project teams is usually much more challenging than managing onsite teams. Onsite teams don't have the same issues as virtual teams. The difference is that you can readily help onsite teams resolve issues as they arise; whereas, virtual teams must wait for you to become available. With virtual teams, these issues can last for days or months, often negatively impacting the project.

The following tips and techniques can help you manage virtual project teams:

- **Conduct a kick-off meeting.** At the beginning of a virtual project, you should hold a project kick-off meeting. This meeting may be the first time that some members have a chance to meet each other. In the kickoff meeting, you are responsible for defining the project's scope, goals, and objectives, and to get the team's approval before the meeting finishes. A strong project manager (meeting leader) can accomplish this goal with all team members. This may be the last time some team members meet each other.

Tip

If you do not have strong meeting skills, consider hiring a motivational speaker to help bring project team members together.

- **Build a rapport and establish trust**. Another aspect of people management is building rapport and trust with each team member, which is twice as hard with virtual teams. Establish a strong rapport early in the project's life cycle by ensuring that you establish a relationship with each team member. Put in face time and bond with your team members to form relationships. You might need to periodically conduct onsite visits to accomplish this. Rapport and trust is a two-way street; people must earn the trust by others. Trust that your team members will deliver their respective tasks on time.

- **Create good team dynamics**. In virtual environments, setting up a buddy system is a good idea. When the team spans multiple locations, each team member needs the psychology, morale, and technical support from at least one other person. Establishing a buddy system provides virtual team members a person they can contact when they need help. This partnership between two or more team members creates a buy-in and ownership for the tasks assigned to the project. Having a buddy system provides someone for each member to contact and collaborate. Buddy systems are also valuable to onsite teams, but in a virtual environment, they become a need.

- **Meet in person**. When working in a virtual environment, the team is spread out and does not often meet face-to-face, if ever. Therefore, as a project manager, you must decide how to meet and continue to build the rapport among team members. As the bond with your team increases, the dedication increases. You become even more committed to your team, and therefore, to the project. It is a win-win for everyone. Allocate enough budget and time in the schedule to allow face-to-face meetings. We recommend ensuring that virtual team members show up, in person, to important project meetings so that they gain a connection to the local project team and feel like they are important to the project. It is a great morale booster to virtual team members because you are telling them that they are important enough to the project to attend the meeting.

Tip

Ensure there is budget for virtual team members' travel and expenses. If applicable, have them visit the main office for important meetings.

- **Keep tasks short for early success.** From the beginning of the project, create short project tasks to allow easy tracking and performance reporting. The advantage to virtual team members is that they know exactly what to do, how long it will take, when it is due, and what to deliver. Working and reporting on five short tasks is easier than reporting on one or two long tasks. The short task technique keeps team members motivated to complete tasks.

- **Ensure each team member has enough work.** In a virtual environment, you can feel like you are unclear on what tasks the team members are working on because they are not physically present. This sometimes creates worry and concern for you because you do not know if you are getting the maximum productivity out of your team members. To ensure motivation and ownership from team members, continually ensure that your project team members have enough work to do. If, in the rare case, they don't have enough work to do, point out how valuable it is to offer help to other team members. Your role is to stay on top of your team members' work assignments, regardless of their location, to ensure productivity and motivation toward the project.

- **Give team members more responsibility.** Determining how much work each virtual team member can perform can be tough—especially if you are not working closely with them on a daily basis. It is a best practice to visit the virtual team's location whenever possible to observe their current workload. Nothing is more productive than face-to-face communication with your team to help keep them motivated. During onsite visits, if you find they are lacking work tasks, you can assign more responsibility to the team. This gives them the confidence that they are a valuable part of the team, and it is a great way to keep them engaged and excited about the project.

Motivating virtual project teams

Motivating project teams, either virtual or local, can be challenging, but it can also be fun and rewarding. You must treat both the onsite team and the virtual team members equally.

Use the following events and activities to celebrate and show your appreciation towards your team:

- **Hold morale events.** Create a project environment that includes regular morale-boosting events. Morale events are great pick-me-up events where team members get together to relax and chat about nonbusiness-related topics and get to know each other. Typical morale events include team lunches or after-work drinks. Other events include outings such as miniature golf, attending sporting events, or other fun outings. These events are successful when many team members participate and share their experiences and personalities outside the office. These types of events are critical to larger teams on longer-term projects. When team members work together for long periods and never get to spend quality non-work time together, more personality conflicts arise on the project. Holding the occasional morale event, regardless of the cost, can do wonders toward the success of the project.
- **Recognize and reward people.** If your company has a reward and recognition program, use it whenever possible. If the company does not have a formal program, create or write up rewards for your project team members. Even a simple thank you email can go a long way. It is surprising how far a certificate, toy, or marketing gadget given to a hardworking team member goes toward building morale and a great working relationship. A low-cost reward system pays off in the end for you and your project.
- **Create fun.** It is your responsibility to create fun on the project. Instill a fun environment, but also keep the project team focused to deliver a successful project. There are many ways to have fun on a project, from giving gifts at status meetings, holding morale events, and keeping the environment light and motivating.
- **Monetary rewards and pay raises.** Some team members are motivated by monetary rewards, so you could offer money, gift cards, or a pay raise to a team member, either at the beginning or during the project.

Communicating consistently

Sending regular and timely project communications is a necessity for every project manager. The need is greater for project team members working in a virtual environment. There are some virtual team members who need added communications from you. They may feel that the more connections they have with you, the better they are connected to the project. These individuals need that extra hand-holding and connection with you. Look at the tools and processes you are using to ensure that virtual team members are receiving the information they need. One of the main areas you should look for is inconsistency when sending out project information to your virtual team members, such as the project status report. For example, team leads typically send weekly status reports for their area. However, if the team lead is inconsistent in sending their information, say they send it monthly instead of weekly, it is difficult for you to stay on top of that area. Therefore, make sure you can report updated project information in the weekly project status report so that virtual team members and everyone else is getting the latest project status information.

Case Study - A virtual project team member conflict scenario

A virtual project team member felt that his project manager was nagging him too much about project status information. He decided to stop communicating with the project manager. He stopped answering emails, stopped attending status meetings, and no longer filled out status reports. He believed that if he stopped communicating, he could spend more time on his work and get his tasks done without interruptions. Meanwhile, the project manager told him that this was unacceptable behavior and that he was affecting the progress of the project. The team member and project manager agreed on the following project principals, and it looked like the issue was resolved. First, the project manager could call the team member at any time during working hours and the team member would answer. The project manager would allow the team member to come into the office when he wanted to, but he had to come in three days a week, minimum, until this issue was back to normal. The project manager would also let the team member respond to emails only during a limited window during the day. This helped the team member feel like he could perform his tasks and not have to spend time responding to the project manager, let alone anyone else asking him questions and taking time away from his tasks. This scenario went on for about a week, and the team member went back to his old tricks. The project manager then notified upper management and asked to remove the team member from the project. After continuing communications with the team member and stressing that his behavior was unacceptable, the project manager could no longer work with the team member. Upper management advised the project manager and the team member was removed from the project.

Establishing communication guidelines

We suggest that you develop guidelines for virtual project team members. If guidelines had been in place before the project began, the case study we just covered would not have happened. Look to your project management offices or to specific company policies, if applicable, to decide if there are any virtual project team member guidelines or procedures already in place. If there are, use those policies whenever possible. If there are no policies in place, we recommend the following as a starting point for your project:

- **Establish work hours.** The work hours of a virtual team member are the standard working hours of the company. These hours normally include an eight-hour day with the weekends off. If both parties agree, they can change these hours. Being offsite does not guarantee any extra "away" time from the regular office responsibilities.

- **Create home office infrastructure.** Virtual team members should have company-standard computers that are loaded with the company image of software products. The home office should be a separate location, away from any distractions for the team member to be able to work effectively. A virtual team member cannot have a standard dial-up connection as their only source of connecting to the Internet.

- **Require progress and status reporting.** A team member working virtually will follow the same requirements as onsite team members and must report, at a minimum, project progress and status once a week. This could include completing status reports, one-on-one communications, newsletters, or completing online status information, such as updating the project's schedule.

Note
Establish and document firm guidelines to set the virtual team members' expectations for communication, infrastructure, work hours, and progress reporting. These expectations are set as policies, not guidelines, and ensure that virtual team members follow them when working offsite. The project manager requires the virtual team member to sign and approve these polices

before starting in this virtual work position. If someone does not sign the agreement, he or she should not be eligible to work remotely.

Exploring virtual team member qualifications

It is important to consider the qualifications and skill sets of virtual team members—especially when qualifications for virtual team members and local team members are different. If you are hiring resources for both roles, consider the qualifications for the different positions. There are six basic skills and qualities a person should have before they can work in a virtual environment. If one of these qualities is missing, the project could suffer because that individual may not pull his or her own weight and would slow down the project's progress.

A virtual team member should have the following qualities:

- **Be an excellent communicator.** The number one quality of a person in a virtual role is being a good communicator. If a virtual team member is a poor communicator, he or she is putting the project at risk.
- **Have experience with a similar project or position.** A team member who has worked on a similar project before, or worked virtually in the past, can be a great asset to the project team. If a team member is new or has little experience, starting in a virtual role could be risky.
- **Be a self-starter.** A virtual team member must be a self-starter and proactive. Someone who is a self-starter can immediately jump into their workload and perform without constant supervision. A proactive person is one who will identify problem areas and will jump to address those areas without direction or assistance from you. That person will "just do it" and take on the extra workload.
- **Have self-discipline.** A virtual team member needs a high degree of self-discipline. This person is not easily distracted and can focus on work tasks during fixed working hours.
- **Have a high-level of dedication.** A virtual team member must be highly dedicated to the project. You can test a person's dedication level during the interview process by using psychological tests and in-depth questioning about previous dedication on projects. Contact a candidate's references during the interview cycle to learn about past dedication to projects.
- **Be able to prioritize.** All virtual team members must consider the project as a high priority and focus on delivering their work. If a team member does not feel this project is a high priority or feels like he can only work at a half capacity, this is not the right fit for that person.

Figure 4.1 — Team Member Evaluation Spider Chart shows a spider chart that evaluates the qualifications of potential virtual team members for work on your project. In this case, you can see that Sally B has the highest level for each factor, which makes her the best fit for the project.

Figure 4.1 — Team Member Evaluation Spider Chart

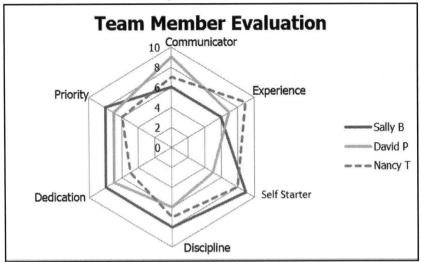

Summary

In this chapter, we explored communicating with team members in foreign countries, preparing for business travel, and virtual communications.

Each area from a project management perspective is important in how successful you will be if you are working in a local environment. Rarely do project managers have the luxury of working with local and onsite team members on projects. More companies are using offshore resources in India, China, and other countries that force project managers to learn how to work with foreign teams. A savvy project manager will begin to understand the importance of communications in these environments and will quickly embrace the customers and the individual team members working in another country. The topics we covered will help you plan and prepare to work in these environments.

We also covered virtual communications and working in a virtual environment. As noted, more companies have offshore companies deliver projects. Local onshore project managers must learn to communicate with virtual teams. The topics covered in this chapter will help you prepare to work in this environment.

Finally, we covered preparing, presenting, and delivering project information and some tips and tricks for you to use. Preparing and delivering project information is a staple for all project managers, and the areas covered in this chapter will help set you up for success.

Chapter 5

Social Media and Project Management Communication Tools

IN THIS CHAPTER

- ◆ What is Social Media?
- ◆ Mapping Social Media tools to Project Management Process groups
- ◆ Sharing Project Information
- ◆ Customers, Stakeholders, and Leadership on social media
- ◆ Social Media Experts

In this chapter, we explore the communication value of social media tools in project management. Social media has been a hot topic for several years, but we are still at the cusp of understanding how powerful social media can be in project management. Before you rush into using social media tools for your project, be aware of their advantages and disadvantages by researching which tools will work for you. Some projects are perfect for using social media and others are not. As project manager, you need to understand how social media can help you. Don't use social media tools for the sake of using them.

In this chapter, we cover the top social media tools, map the tools to the project management process groups, map social media tools to common communication purposes, explore customers' and leadership's opinion about social media, and learn about social media experts.

Let's spend some time exploring social media tools for your project by referencing the communication tools covered in this book.

What is Social Media?

It is important that you understand what social media is before exploring how it may or may not work for your project. There are many definitions of social media. Social media is often described as a website or application that lets users create and share information in an online environment. Definition after definition describes social media as sharing data, exchanging information, and creating content using a set of tools. You may recognize some of the social networking sites out there, such as Twitter®, Facebook®, or Yammer®—the list goes on and on.

What we find when reviewing countless definitions about "social media" is that each one is essentially the same. That's good news because it shows that everyone has the same general understanding about the term, "social media."

It is also important that we call out what social media is *not* in this chapter. We are not talking about online meeting tools such as GoToMeeting® because this chapter focuses on social media and networking tools and how they map to project management. Tools such as WebEx and Web Meeting are online meeting tools and not full-scale project management communication tools.

Social media tools

When you think about social media, there are so many tools to choose from that you might get confused about where to start. Let's start by looking at some popular web-based social media and networking tools. These include:

- Blogs
- Discussion forums
- Facebook®
- Instagram®
- LinkedIn®
- SlideShare®
- Tumblr®
- Twitter®
- VMware® Horizon Socialcast ™
- Yammer®

Many project managers have probably visited some of these sites, but only a handful have regarded them from a pure project management perspective. Few project managers are managing projects using Twitter or Instagram. Why? Customers don't want their private project information on the Internet. There is no way you are telling the public what is happening on our project. The list of reasons is a mile long and for every "no" that someone on the project says about using social media, there is usually a valid reason. However, those "no's" are rapidly changing to "yes's" and we should examine ways of using social media tools so as not to fall behind. Reasons why people who are connected to the project are against using social media remain valid. However, we need to look at ways of using social media while preserving the validity of what those individuals are saying. For example, when a project manager says, "I want to Tweet on Twitter the project's budget," everyone connected to the project will say no. You would likely agree that it's not a good idea to Tweet on Twitter financial information. Now, using the same example, what if the project budget was already on the Internet, like many publicly funded projects are today? Now, it doesn't seem as bad to Tweet on Twitter the information after all because it's already on the Internet and available for anyone who wants to see it. This is a classic example of people's intentions being correct about not wanting to release company information, when in this case, the information is already available. This is just one of the many different examples that you should think about when communicating project information. Occasionally, moving some project information into the social media world may be the right direction for sharing information. For example, when a soda company launches a new brand, chances are high that they will post that information on social media.

Let's continue exploring this complex "project management in a social media world" topic.

Mapping Social Media Tools to Project Management Process Groups

To understand which social media tools to use, one of the first places to start is researching what tools are available. It is also important to understand how social media tools map to project management process groups. Some project managers will want their social media tools to apply to every life cycle process; other project managers are more flexible and will use some tools in some areas and other tools in other areas. In researching social media tools and project management process groups, we found that there are limited tools that work in all areas.

Figure 5.1 — Social Media and Networking Tools Mapped to Project Management Process Groups shows the mapping for some of the social media and social networking tools to the project management process groups. There is no right or wrong mapping, and clearly one tool could be used in an area that it is not already mapped on the chart. Our hope is that this mapping will get you thinking about how to use the social media tools in different areas of your project. The mapping chart is a great way to see which social media tools are most applicable to the five project management process groups. Let's look at this mapping table in more detail.

Figure 5.1 — Social Media and Networking Tools Mapped to Project Management Process Groups

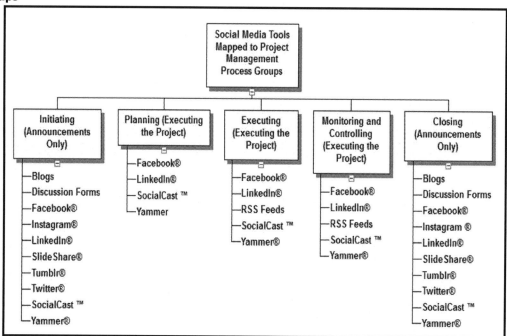

What is valuable about this mapping chart is that you can immediately see that there might be only a few tools applicable in the Planning, Executing, and Controlling stages of a project. Most of the tools in the chart apply to the Initiating and Closing process groups because most social media and networking tools are great for announcing or broadcasting information, but not as good for managing and running a project.

Table 5.1 — Social Media to Process Groups Mapping shows a breakdown for some of the social media and networking tools in each process group. We recommend that you read each row in the table carefully; we added high-level details and related functionality to give you a taste of how you could use a social media tool in a particular process group process. We also added guidance and some of the nuances for each tool. There are many details in the table that you might miss if you don't take the time to read through it.

Table 5.1 — Social Media to Process Group Mapping

Tool	Initiation	Planning	Executing	Monitoring & Controlling	Closing
Blogs (Assuming nothing private)	Make announcements and talk about the project/product	N/A	N/A	N/A	Make announcements and talk about the project/product
Discussion Forums (Assuming nothing private)	Make announcements and talk about the project/product	N/A	N/A	N/A	Make announcements and talk about the project/product
Facebook® (Assuming Private Groups)	Make announcements and talk about the project/product	Store files, have private conversations and share project information.	Store files, chat with team members, post project documents, etc.	Store files, chat with team members, post project documents, etc.	Make announcements and talk about the project/product
Instagram ® (Assuming nothing private)	Post photos about project. Some PR and marketing information could be posted with the photo.	N/A	N/A	N/A	Post photos about project launching. Some PR and marketing information could be posted with the photo.
LinkedIn® (Assuming Private Groups). No ability to store files in groups, but	Make announcements and talk about the project/product	Have discussions, post links and polls about the project, but limited if unable to	Have discussions, post links and polls about the project, but limited if unable to	Have discussions, post links and polls about the project, but limited if unable to	Make announcements and talk about the project/product

Tool	Initiation	Planning	Executing	Monitoring & Controlling	Closing
can on main site.		attach a file in a group.	attach a file in a group.	attach a file in a group.	
SlideShare (Assuming nothing private)	Post presentations about upcoming project. Some PR and marketing information could be posted with the photo.	N/A	N/A	N/A	Post presentations about upcoming project. Some PR and marketing information could be posted with the photo.
Tumblr (Assuming nothing private)	Post text, photo, quote, links, chats, audio and video about the upcoming project or product.	N/A	N/A	N/A	Post text, photo, quote, links, chats, audio and video about the project or product that is launching.
Twitter (Assuming nothing private)	Promote via text or photo of the upcoming project or product. Has email capability, but not possible to run a project with direct messages on Twitter.	N/A	N/A	N/A	Promote via text or photo of the project or product you are launching.
Socialcast ™ (Assuming Private Groups)	This is a full-scale project collaboration system. Features include storing project files, team conversations, chat sessions, and posting project announcements.	All project files and information can be stored throughout the planning process.	All project files and information can be stored throughout the project execution.	All project files and information can be stored throughout the monitoring and controlling phase.	This is a full-scale project collaboration system. Features include storing project files, team conversations, chat sessions, and posting project announcements.

Tool	Initiation	Planning	Executing	Monitoring & Controlling	Closing
Yammer (Assuming Private Groups)	This is a full-scale project collaboration system. Features include storing project files, team conversations, chat sessions, and posting project announcements.	All project files and information can be stored throughout the planning process.	All project files and information can be stored throughout the project execution.	All project files and information can be stored throughout the monitoring and controlling phase.	This is a full-scale project collaboration system. Features include storing project files, team conversations, chat sessions, and posting project announcements.

As you review the table, there are only five social media tools shown that can be used end-to-end on a project. "End-to-end" is considered from the Initiation phase to the Closing phase. Every project will go through those phases during the project life cycle. The areas may be called something different for different methodologies out there today (for example, PMI), but the five phases are the same across projects. It is important that you don't try to force a social media tool to work for a process group process that it isn't designed to support. For example, don't use Twitter during your project's planning process if Twitter does not apply to your planning process. If there is no logical place for Twitter to work during the planning phase, don't use it. Research social media and networking tools so that you don't try to force tools to work in areas that don't make sense.

Note
It is critical that you review the table and understand each tool's functionality. Not every tool will work the way you expect. Understand the tools before implementing them for your project.

Let's examine the information presented in the table:

1. From a marketing, communications, or public relation's perspective, social media and networking tools are ideal during the project initiation phase. For example, you can Tweet on Twitter that you are starting a project or create a YouTube video about your project—social media tools are optimal for evangelizing your project.
2. From a marketing or public relation's perspective, social media and networking tools are beneficial during the project's closing phase too. Similar to using social media to announce the project initiation phase, you could announce the project's completion: "the product is ready to ship"; "the bridge is open"; "the building is ready". Regardless of the message, social media and networking tools are great for announcing the project end and success.

Important
Before sharing project or company information, make sure you get approval from your legal or human resources teams. Do not share any project information without full legal approval.

3. Only some social media and networking tools are appropriate throughout a project's life cycle, for example, Facebook®, LinkedIn®, Yammer®, and Socialcast™. Current functionality for LinkedIn® professional networking services, however, does not let you customize who you want to share files

with; project information is sent to all of your connections. To use LinkedIn® professional networking services, your company could create a LinkedIn® professional networking services profile only for people connected to the project. However, if you're creating workarounds to make a social media tool work for your project, it's probably best not to use it at all. Yammer and Socialcast ™., however, are examples of robust collaboration tools. They let you communicate, share files and information, and they are considered full-scale collaboration tools. Other tools in the table are not appropriate for all project areas. For example, it would be difficult to plan a project using Twitter. On the other hand, it is applicable to Tweet on Twitter, "Just launched new product *xyz*" during the project's closing phase.

4. Before committing to a tool, understand the constraints and nuisances documented in the table and research its current functionality. Social media tools change all the time, and functionality is added and removed regularly. Create your own accounts and try the tools yourself to determine where the tool might fit in your environment. This is not an easy or trivial task, but you need to spend time and effort to understand them so that you are knowledgeable about social media tools and how to use them for your project.

Don't rush into using social media tools for the sake of using social media tools. Consider social media tools as a growing set of communication tools to use on your project, where applicable. There is not a one-size-fits-all scenario for using social media, and your project will have its own constraints for determining where social media might work for your project. If you need to use a social media tool to collaborate (for example, Facebook®), go ahead and use the tool. Otherwise, be cautious about using social media for your projects.

Sharing Project Information

Part of being cautious about which social media tools to use includes determining what information you should share about your projects on social media. Not all project information will be shared, but there might be information you could share and should share. In this age of social media, project managers, customers, and leadership need to start thinking more broadly about sharing project information with the public. Work with your customers, leadership, and legal or human resources teams to understand the types of data that can and cannot be shared about your project.

At this point, you should understand and be excited about the various social media and networking tools that are available for your project. One of the first challenges that you will face about using social media is deciding what information to share. Another challenge you will face is deciding the stakeholder's or customer's role in sharing information.

The first thing you need to do is check with your legal and human resources teams about sharing company information. You may not have the authority to share project information without proper approval. A common theme expressed throughout this chapter is if you're not sure you can share something on social media, then your default answer should be not to share it.

Note
Before sharing any project or company information, make sure you go through your legal or human resources teams. Do not share any project information without full legal approval.

Assuming you have approval to start using social media, you must first understand what information you can share about your project. One way to determine information that is shareable is looking at project information through the lens of communication tools (covered later in Chapters). By doing so, you will understand what kind of project information is stored in which communication tool, and then you can determine which social media tool you can use to share that information.

It is also important when you think about sharing information to understand the communication purposes for sharing that information. There are five main purposes for communicating. These include:

1. **Inform** – to give facts or information, tell someone something.
2. **Persuade** – to cause someone to do something. This could be by reasoning with this person, or by convincing them.
3. **Motivate** – to provide someone with a motive to do something. Stimulate interest in doing something.
4. **Interact** – to act in a way to affect someone or something else. To act upon another.
5. **Inspire** – to fill the urge in someone to do or feel something. To produce or arouse a feeling.

You may not realize it, but you communicate project information from these five perspectives. Likewise, each social media tool has its own way of communicating one of the purposes above. If you use social media for your project, you are responsible for determining which purpose(s) you are trying to fulfill with your communications. Then, once you know the purpose(s), you can figure out which social media tools will help you achieve those communications.

The following table maps the common communication tools and some of the social media tools. The table also includes the five common communication purposes (inform, persuade, motivate, instruct, and inspire). This is just a small sampling of the larger table in the **Appendix – Project Management Communication Tools**.

Table 5.2 — Project Communication Tools - Social Media Tools Mapping Sample maps the project communication tools with the most applicable communication purpose and a social media tool that might satisfy that purpose. For example, in the table, a budget spreadsheet falls under "Inform," and some of the social media tools that store budget spreadsheets include, Yammer®, Socialcast ™., and Facebook®.

Table 5.2 — Project Communication Tools - Social Media Tools Mapping

	Social Media Tools/Communication Purposes				
Tool Name	**Inform**	**Persuade**	**Motivate**	**Instruct**	**Inspire**
Baseline Schedule	Yammer®, Socialcast ™, Facebook®				
Benefits Review Plan	Yammer®, Socialcast ™, Facebook®	Yammer®, Socialcast ™, Facebook®			
Budget Spreadsheet	Yammer®, Socialcast ™, Facebook®	Yammer®, Socialcast ™, Facebook®			
Business Case	Yammer®, Socialcast ™, Facebook®	Yammer®, Socialcast ™, Facebook®			Yammer®, Socialcast ™, Facebook®
Change Control Plan	Yammer®, Socialcast ™, Facebook®			Yammer®, Socialcast ™, Facebook®	
Change Readiness Assessment	Yammer®, Socialcast ™, Facebook®		Yammer®, Socialcast ™, Facebook®		

Cross-Reference
Table 5.2 is a sample of the full table shown in Chapter 27 - Appendix.

As you review the sample table, some trends emerge and you'll note that not all communication tools are applicable across each communication purpose. That's understandable, but it provides insight that you may not have previously considered as to why and how to use social media tools for your project.

Another trend in the table show products such as Yammer®, Socialcast®, Facebook® as full-scale project management tools. These social networking tools include features, functionality, and ability to use private groups and store project information.

The table also shows that you can use multiple tools across multiple communication purposes. For example, you can use the communication plan in the standard set of project management social media tools for both "Inform" and "Instruct" categories. This is a good trend to see because the more you hit different communication purposes, you increase the chance of communicating more effectively with your customers, team members, and leadership.

Finally, as you look through the full table in the **Appendix – Project Management Communication Tools**, you will see other trends and more information to help you understand how and where to use communication tools. As you read the book, the tools will make more sense and you will become more familiar with them, but having the mapping of project management communication tools and social media tools will help you communicate more effectively on your projects.

Customers, Stakeholders, and Leadership on Social Media

Many project managers today are excited about using social media for their projects. Social media is hot, it is the latest trend, and many of your project manager peers are desperate to understand how they can share project information using these tools. In the excitement to use social media for their projects, some project managers may forget about their customers and leadership team. Customers and leadership are going to be a mixed bag about using social media to share project information. Some will be just as excited as you are, and some will not want anything to do with social media or sharing project information. For those who are less adept at using social media, you may need to walk them through the following steps to ease them into the social media world. These steps include:

1. **Be open-minded** – Your customers and leadership must be open to learning about social media tools. It will be easier on you if they are eager and want to learn about the tools.
2. **Explain the purpose of top communication tools** – Explain the social media tools you want to use for your project. This will set a nice foundation for them to learn about the tools and how you think they will benefit the project.
3. **Explain the privacy settings and features of the tool** – Customers and leadership will be concerned about information going out to the public versus what information will be internal. Remember, you probably don't know what your customers or leadership know about social media, so you'll need to explain the privacy settings for each tool.
4. **Explain the tool's functionality and features** – Each tool offers different features and functionality so it will be in your best interest to explain the most common features of each tool.
5. **Work with your customers or leadership to set up accounts** – Have customers and leadership set up their own accounts so they can try out the tools themselves. You may need to help get them started, but by doing so, you are helping them ease into the idea of using these tools for projects.

After walking your customers and leadership through these steps, it is important that you give them time to understand and use the tools before re-introducing the subject of using social media tools for the project. Some individuals will learn the tools right away and be supportive, and others—even after spending time and being open-minded—will not see the need for using social media. As project manager, decide whether you want to fight with your customers about using social media tools for your projects. Sometimes, it just won't be worth it. Other times, you may have valid reasons and it could be something worth readdressing with your customers or leadership.

Over time, customers and leadership will become more favorable about using social media for your projects, but that time may not be today, tomorrow, or in a couple months. But, the time will come, and the tools' functionality and features will continue to grow and become more applicable for a full-scale project environment.

Social Media Experts

When considering social media tools for your project, think about using a social media expert. More companies are hiring social media experts to help create a presence for their companies in the social media world. Social media experts are popping up all over companies that understand the importance of social media and these companies want to connect with communities of people who want to follow the company. Companies are creating Facebook pages, Twitter accounts, and joining LinkedIn® professional networking services to communicate and start connecting online. Let's look at some of the roles and responsibilities of a social media expert:

- Responsible for online marketing on social networking sites.
- Monitors social networking sites and addresses inquiries as necessary.
- Interacts with blog communities via chat, email, and web.
- Manages social media channels to ensure the company is meeting the brand's business goals.
- Ensures information provided on social media reflects current business practices.
- Creates content for feeds and snippets on various social media sites.
- Develops site content and graphics.
- Researches industry trends and best practices. Performs benchmarking and competitive analysis of other sites, social media channels, etc.
- Provides information by collecting, analyzing, and summarizing data and website or blog trends.
- Assists with admissions informational sessions and provides community feedback from blogs.
- Trains and presents social media to other team members.

A social media expert drives the online existence for a company and is dedicated to many areas. Large companies have full social media teams dedicated to this process to ensure that they have a rich user experience. If your company has social media experts, you are in a great position to work with them and learn how you can use social media for your project. Often, social media experts have policies or procedures that you can use for projects. Otherwise, work directly with the social media expert to understand how to communicate project information through various channels.

On large, public-facing projects, it is becoming common for project managers to hire a full-time social media expert who is dedicated to the project and to share project information through various social media and networking tools. For example, a large bridge construction project that is going to impact thousands of commuters a day will have a full-time social media expert on the team to get information out to the public. The social media expert will give the public relevant project updates during the project life cycle and respond to any public questions or opinions about the project. The more information you give to people—in this case, commuters—you help them understand the traffic situation and recognize that there is an end in sight. Public-facing projects usually have social media experts on staff using social media tools to communicate. Another advantage of using a full-time social media expert is that they usually have a direct connection to the legal and human resources teams and will know what information can be shared with the public. Because most social media is public facing, it is critical that the social media expert knows what can and cannot be shared. You can get into trouble if you don't consider what you want to share about your project to the public, and you could get the company in legal trouble. It is a best practice to consider hiring or involving a social media expert on your projects—especially if you are new to using social media tools and you are unsure of what information can be shared.

Summary

In summary, the tools described in this chapter are in the world of social media and project management. This is not an exhaustive chapter on social media and networking tools because social media and full-scale project management is still growing and there is still much to learn. Project managers across the world are desperate to use social media for their projects and our best advice is to do so with caution. Using social media is fun and it's wonderful to share photos or post silly messages, but some of these tools are not ready to run full-scale projects. Don't let that discourage you, though, keep hunting for new tools, watch for functionality changes on current tools.

Be extra cautious about using social media to release project information to the public. If you don't have a social media expert, you need your legal or HR teams involved, but be careful about what information is released and shared to the public or you could open your company to legal problems.

Combining social media and project management is an amazing idea. The industry is moving quickly and you should consider using some of the tools for your projects. But, only a few tools have restrictions (for example, private groups) for running a full-scale project.

PART II – Project Communication Tools by Knowledge Area

Chapter 6

Communication Tools That Manage Project Integration

IN THIS CHAPTER

 ♦ Introduction to Agile Project Meetings
 ♦ Introduction to Agile Product Vision Statement
 ♦ Introduction to the Project Charter
 ♦ Introduction to the Project Kick-off meeting
 ♦ Introduction to the Project Management plan
 ♦ Introduction to the Project Meeting minutes
 ♦ Introduction to the Project Status meeting
 ♦ Introduction to the Project Status report

In this chapter, we explore the project communication tools that support project integration management. Project integration management is one of the knowledge areas recognized by the Project Management Institute® and common across every project.

The project integration management knowledge area pulls together the various knowledge areas and process groups to drive a successful project. The integration knowledge area integrates all areas of project management: integration, scope, time, cost, quality, human resources, communication, risk, procurement and stakeholder management. Most projects undergo continual changes that require constant integration. Complete the activities in this knowledge area to pull everything together. Project managers constantly shift from knowledge area to knowledge area while managing projects. Thus, integration management (the coordination of those activities) is a critical component to any project's success.

Managing project integration is compulsory throughout the project. Any time individual project knowledge areas interact with each other, you need to manage and control the integration.

Introduction to Agile Project Meetings

Schedule *Agile project meetings* so that the Agile project team can assemble periodically to communicate about the Agile project throughout the project life cycle.

There are three types of project meetings on a typical Agile project. First, the *Agile project strategy meeting* occurs at the beginning of each Agile project. This meeting lays the foundation for the project before actual product development begins. The strategy meeting kicks off the project and is driven by a vision associated with a strategic business need or goal. Supporting documents you might use as inputs to the strategy meeting can include: a project concept, a project charter, funding approval, or an implementation strategy. It is not uncommon to use all of the inputs, or a combination of them—this depends on the individual organization and the specific project.

Note
The Project Management Institute's knowledge area for this tool is the integration area. The secondary area that this tool could be associated with is communications.

Tool Value
Using all of the different Agile project meetings ensures that each Agile project for an organization follows the same Agile best practices and principles. Not only does this ensure that the current Agile project is executed successfully, but it also lays the groundwork for the success of future Agile projects as the organization scales Agile project management and product development across its entire enterprise.

Social Media Tools
The communication purposes for Agile daily meetings is to inform, inspire, instruct, and motivate. Communication from Agile project meetings can be posted on social media tools, such as, Yammer, Socialcast, and Facebook (private group).

Note
Agile project meetings are also commonly referred to as "Agile events" or "Agile ceremonies."

Cross-Reference
See the Defining the Agile Product Vision Statement section in this chapter to learn more about the activities performed during the Agile project strategy meeting.

Second, the *Agile release planning meeting* occurs not only at the beginning of an Agile project, but periodically throughout the project when a major feature or set of functionality is released to your customer. During the initial release planning meeting, you plan the specific releases (referred to as the delivery cycle) to determine which features to include (referred to as epic user stories), to decide which order the user stories will be developed within each release (referred to as prioritization), and to create initial high-level estimates for these features (referred to as affinity estimation). This process is repeated for each product release during an Agile project.

Cross-Reference
See Chapter 7 – Agile User Story to learn more about the activities performed during the Agile project release planning meeting.

The third meeting focuses on the Scrum team and occurs during each sprint on an Agile project. The Scrum team usually consists of the project owner, the Scrum master, and the development team. Sprints are short, fixed-length subsets of releases and represent the executing portion of the project. Agile project sprint meetings help guide the Scrum team through the planning estimation at the beginning of each sprint (sprint planning), the daily status of project activities during each sprint (daily standup), the demonstration of the product components that have been developed during the sprint (sprint review), and the lessons-learned activities that are identified at the end of each sprint so that process improvements can be implemented in the next sprint (sprint retrospective). Each Agile project sprint meeting is critical to the success of any Agile project.

Note
Agile project strategy meetings and release meetings are contained in the overall framework of best practices for all of the different Agile methods available, such as Scrum, Extreme Programming, Kanban, and so on. Agile sprint meetings are specific to the Scrum methodology, but many other Agile methodologies also employ these types of meetings because they offer a structure and frequency that is ideal for any type of Agile project.

Planning Agile project sprint meetings

To maximize their effectiveness, Agile project sprint meetings occur at a specific time and in a specific sequence during each sprint on an Agile project. These meetings should also follow a specific format, as dictated by Agile best practices. The following list provides an overview of each sprint meeting on an Agile project.

- **Agile Sprint Planning Meeting.** The first sprint meeting is the sprint planning meeting. This meeting occurs on the first day of each sprint, and the recommended attendees are Scrum team members. This is the core team that performs the work on the user stories during the sprint. They must work together as a cohesive team in order to complete the selected user stories in the sprint. Sprint planning is for team members to plan and agree on the user stories or backlog items that they are confident they can complete during the sprint. The sprint planning meeting also entails identifying the detailed tasks and acceptance criteria (tests) for delivery, according to the "definition of done." The "definition of done" is created by the Scrum team. It is a description of the mandatory steps that must be completed to a user story to indicate that the particular product component's functionality is ready to be delivered to your customer by the end of the sprint.

- **Agile Daily Standup Meeting.** The second sprint meeting is the daily standup meeting. This meeting is held every day during the sprint at the exact same time and location, and the recommended attendees are the Scrum team members. This meeting helps facilitate daily team communication and synchronization, and ensures that everyone is working daily toward the same priorities and end goals. Anyone interested in the project or the specific functionality from the sprint can attend the daily standup meeting. However, only Scrum team members are allowed to speak during this meeting so that each team member's status can be quickly reviewed and that the focus is solely on the team and the status of their current activities.

- **Agile Sprint Review Meeting.** The third sprint meeting is the sprint review meeting. This meeting occurs on the last day of each sprint, and although any project stakeholder can attend this meeting, the recommended attendees include the Scrum team members and your customer, at a minimum. Usually, all members of the Scrum team will participate in this event. The Scrum team ensures all product acceptance criteria have been met and that the product's working functionality is demonstrated to the interested stakeholders in attendance. After functionality is demonstrated, interested stakeholders can ask questions and provide feedback to the Scrum team.

- **Agile Sprint Retrospective Meeting.** The fourth and final sprint meeting is the sprint retrospective meeting. This meeting occurs on the last day of each sprint, immediately after the sprint review meeting ends. Only Scrum team members are allowed to attend this meeting. This is the core team that has actually performed the work on the user stories during the sprint. Scrum team members will delve into the specifics of how to make the team stronger and how to make the next sprint more successful. This is an important meeting because it allows the team to evaluate what was done correctly and what can be improved for the next sprint. It also allows the team to create plans to implement these improvements and to identify potential roadblocks that might surface in the next sprint.

Reporting information from Agile project sprint meetings

Although there are no specific tools for reporting information gathered during Agile project meetings, there are some best practices you can follow to ensure that all information exchanged during these meetings is captured so that it can be communicated to the project team, customers, and other stakeholders. Agile uses a variety of "information radiators" to help radiate information about the project status as a whole, the current release, and the current sprint. The following overview shows the types of information gathered and some of the information radiators used in each meeting.

- **Agile Sprint Planning Meeting.** During this meeting, the product owner chooses specific user stories that the Scrum team will work on during the sprint, starting that day. The product owner is responsible for maintaining the product backlog, which is a repository that contains all of the project's epic and detailed user stories. During this maintenance activity, the product owner works with the customer to prioritize (and reprioritize) all of the user stories according to the highest value to your customer and/or the highest project risk. In the sprint planning meeting, the product owner takes a subset of the overall product backlog (called a sprint backlog), which represents the current highest value and highest risk user stories, and reads each user story to the Scrum team. The team is then allowed to ask questions to clarify the user stories so that they have enough information about the requirements to effectively perform the work. If any changes are needed to the user stories based on this initial discussion, the product owner will update both the product backlog and the sprint backlog. When all of the user stories in the sprint backlog have been read and clarified, the product owner leaves the meeting and the development team and Scrum master spend the rest of the meeting assigning resources, time estimates, and cost estimates to each user story. Usually, the process includes having an electronic copy of the sprint backlog available; the Scrum master updates the sprint backlog as the meeting progresses. When all of the user stories have resources, time estimates, and cost estimates assigned to them, the meeting is adjourned. The product backlog and the sprint backlog are the main documents that are updated during the sprint planning meeting.

- **Agile Daily Standup Meeting.** During this meeting, each Scrum team member talks about his or her own assigned sprint activities by answering the following three questions:

  1. What did I accomplish since our last meeting?

  2. What will I be working on today?

  3. What roadblocks are impeding my progress?

As each Scrum team member answers these questions, a meeting facilitator (usually the Scrum master or product owner) logs a short description of the issues in what is called a "parking lot"—usually a whiteboard or easel pad in the daily standup room. After each team member answers the three questions, anyone who has an issue in the parking lot, or anyone who can help resolve an issue in the parking lot, stays after the meeting to work with the product owner, Scrum master, or any pertinent Scrum team member to determine how to overcome the roadblocks and resolve issues. The Scrum master takes the notes from the parking lot and updates the sprint backlog, detailing the roadblocks and their possible solutions. The sprint backlog is the main document that is updated during the sprint planning meeting, although some Agile project teams also keep a separate issues log for parking lot items.

- **Agile Sprint Review Meeting.** During this meeting, each Scrum member demonstrates the specific user story functionality that he or she completed during the current sprint. The product owner presents the release goal, the sprint goal, and the feature user stories to the attendees. The development team demonstrates each feature or functionality that was completed during this sprint. The development team answers questions from the stakeholders. During this meeting, the product owner takes notes about the discussions that occur from the Scrum team, your customers, and other stakeholders attending the meeting. When all of the questions have been answered, the product owner formally accepts the functionality and closes the sprint. The product owner updates the product backlog and the sprint backlog with the user story acceptance results, as well as the notes from other discussions that occurred during the Agile Sprint Review Meeting.

- **Agile Sprint Retrospective Meeting.** During this meeting, each Scrum member shares ideas about how to improve the processes from the current sprint by answering the following three questions:

    - What went well with the sprint?

    - What did not go well with the sprint?

    - How can we improve what did not go well with the sprint?

As each Scrum team member answers these questions, a meeting facilitator (usually the Scrum master or the product owner) keeps track of the input from all of the team members. After each team member answers the three questions, the facilitator reads each process improvement idea and asks the Scrum team how to improve the processes in future sprints. The facilitator compiles the meeting notes into a business process improvement log to review for both effort and impact, and then decides which process improvements are best to select for implementation in the next sprint. While there is no standard document to log process improvements for an Agile project, this information should be kept separate from the product backlog and the sprint backlog. The product backlog and sprint backlog are product-centric, while the business process improvement log is process-centric, which is why they should be logged separately.

Each of the Agile project meetings discussed here are extremely important to the success of any Agile project because they identify information about the status of the project from an overall project level, release level, sprint level, and activity level. This information is communicated to the project stakeholders using the Agile information radiators selected by the project team to ensure that anyone who is interested in the project can obtain an update about the project's progress in a short amount of time, and in real-time.

Cross-Reference
See Chapter 20 Using Communication Tools During the Executing and Controlling Processes to Administer the Project learn more about the agile project meetings.

Introduction to the Agile Product Vision Statement

The *product vision statement* provides a concise description of the project goals that helps the team remain focused on the crucial aspects of the product. This is normally posted in a conspicuous place so that all team members and stakeholders can refer back to it to ensure that the project is progressing toward the product's specific vision. The product vision statement is the first artifact created on an Agile project and sets the stage for all future scope and development. Although this is not considered a Scrum-specific artifact, it lays the foundation for creating other important Agile and Scrum artifacts. Every project activity must support the product vision statement throughout the project. The product vision statement should be posted in plain sight so that anyone with a stake in the project, who is interested or affected by the project outcome, or who works directly on the project can review it to ensure the product vision is always being supported.

Note
The Project Management Institute's knowledge area for the Agile Product Vision Statement tool is the integration area. The secondary area that the tool is associated with is scope.

Tool Value
The product vision statement is a valuable Agile tool that provides direction and a singular purpose for all that is affected by the product's creation and, completion. The Agile Product Vision statement supports the organization's and the customer's strategic objectives.

Social Media Tools
The communication purposes for the Agile product vision are to inform, persuade, and motivate. Communication from the product vision statement can be posted on social media tools, such as Yammer, Socialcast, and Facebook (private group).

Figure 6.1 — Product Vision Statement Template shows a product vision statement template in a format that was created by Geoffrey Moore in his book, *Crossing the Chasm*. Using this template is generally accepted as a best practice for creating product vision statements on Agile projects.

Figure 6.1 — Product Vision Statement Template

For (target customer)

Who (statement of need/opportunity)

The (product)

Is a (product category)

That (compelling benefit)

Unlike (primary competitive alternative)

Figure 6.2 — Product Vision Statement Example, below, shows an example of a typical product vision statement using the template above.

Figure 6.2 — Product Vision Statement Example

> **For** (Smartphone users)
>
> **Who** (want to journal their daily activities)
>
> **The** (Journal application)
>
> **Is a** (mobile journaling application)
>
> **That** (that allows them to track all of their daily activities)
>
> **Unlike** (the EZ Personal Log mobile journaling application)
>
> **Our Product** (allows users to upload journaling information to ALL current social media, not just the top two most popular forms of social media.

Note
The product vision statement is sometimes called the "elevator pitch statement" because it provides a summary that communicates how your product supports the company's or organization's strategies by articulating the goals for the product.

Planning the product vision statement strategy meeting

To obtain the most value from the time invested, the following roles should attend the strategy meeting where the product vision statement is created:

- **Key upper-management stakeholders.** Because the product vision statement is created during the first strategy meeting on an Agile project, it is important that key upper management stakeholders from your organization who have an interest and/or a stake in the project attend the meeting. This will help them understand the overall project vision to ensure that it matches the organization's strategic objectives. These attendees are usually from key organizational departments, such as finance, marketing, business process improvement, and human resources, to name a few.

- **Project manager.** Some organizations using the Agile methodology may still assign a project manager to an Agile project even though there is not technically a project manager role on an Agile project. Someone in this position is usually working on multiple projects, some of which may be Waterfall, some Agile, and some a combination of both—referred to as a "hybrid" project. A benefit of this person attending the strategy meeting is that he or she can implement the Agile process for strategic project planning in future Agile and hybrid projects.

- **Product owner.** The product owner facilitates the strategy meeting and must attend for it to be successful. The product owner ensures that the meeting output is logged in the proper format.

- **Scrum master.** The Scrum master has an in-depth understanding of the development team's needs and can help with the initial estimate of product scope and requirements during the strategy meeting.

When the product vision statement is final, it should not be changed. This makes it one of the most difficult Agile project management communication tools to use, but also one of the most important, because it guides the product and project from beginning to end.

Planning to use a product vision statement

The product vision statement describes what the product and project will achieve and becomes the beacon that guides all project activities. Because the product vision statement is the first document you create for an Agile project, it is the first communication tool you use to plan the initial scope and requirements of the project at the 50,000-foot level. The product owner and the customer review the product vision statement to acquire a basic understanding of the product and project goals. The product vision statement enables the product owner to help your customer plan the specific project team members needed, the initial high-level requirements, the priority of the requirements in terms of highest customer value and highest risk, the number of releases for each project deliverable component, and the end product itself. These activities set the stage for future strategic meetings, including the project kick-off meeting and release planning meetings, which are crucial for determining which requirements the project team will work on and in what order.

We highly recommended that you conspicuously post the product vision statement for the project team and stakeholders to see during the course of an Agile project. Many teams print the product vision statement on a 24" × 36" poster board and post it in the project war room, the daily Scrum room, and the common area where the team performs most of the project activities. Posting the product vision statement is very useful so that team members or stakeholders involved in a planning activity can easily refer to it to ensure that the artifacts they create are in line with the overall product vision. This is also true of the project team members who are performing Agile activities to develop the product.

As you can see, the product vision statement is not only the first artifact and project management communication tool for an Agile project, but perhaps the most important. It sets the vision and direction for all future aspects of the project and ensures that only those project activities that support the product vision are performed and that project activities that do not support the product vision are eliminated.

Reporting using the product vision statement

There is no real formal reporting of the product vision statement in Agile projects. The vision statement acts as a guide to help the team stay focused on the most important aspects of the project. Some Product Owners or Scrum Masters may post the product vision statement in the team war room, or in the hallways, but there is no ongoing reporting of the vision statement. It an artifact that the team will use to guide them in the project, not necessary something to be reported on

Cross-Reference
See Chapter 16 - Using Communication Tools in the Initiating Process to learn more about the agile product vision statement.

Introduction to the Project Charter

The purpose of the *project charter* is to approve the project, assign a project manager, and officially "kick-off" the project. During the time you are building the project charter and collecting all the information about the proposed project, you may decide to use the company's resources or hire externally when deciding who will complete the work of the project. It is only during the time of creating the project charter and learning more about what the project is going to be about can you decide where the best resources to do the work should come from. The project charter sets up the project's budget and duration. It describes and communicates the project's high-level items, such as scope, goals, and objectives. The project charter is a document that anyone can read to understand the project at a high-level, without needing to understand its details or technical areas. You use the project charter to authorize project material and equipment usage. Think about the project charter as the document that includes the project's major parts that you would usually put in a formal presentation to management. The project charter communicates the project goals to anyone who is involved or interested in learning about it.

Note
The Project Management Institute's knowledge areas for the project charter are the integration area (primary area) and scope area (secondary area).

Tool Value
The project charter document includes the project approval and sets the project in motion. It also states who the project manager is, the budget, the start date, and the project duration.

Social Media Tools
The communication purposes for a project charter are to inform and instruct. Communication from the project charter can be posted on social media tools, such as Yammer, Socialcast, and Facebook (private group).

The project charter, because it sets the project in motion, is the first official document for the project. It describes the project at a high-level and helps you create the scope document. The project charter describes what to do, not how to do it. Without the project charter, the project team has no direction or idea what they should be doing.

A project charter document is generic and adaptable to most projects. The project charter document includes common sections that describe the project's purpose, scope, budget, resource requirements, schedule, and critical success factors. Most project charter templates also include assumptions and constraints. The project sponsor or owner is responsible for developing the charter, but may need help from you and your team members. The project sponsor sends you and your team the project charter document so that you understand what you need to build for the project.

A well thought-out project charter helps you communicate project information to stakeholders, team members and guides the project to successful completion. The project manager uses the project charter to help the team understand what they must do to complete the project successfully. The project charter contains most of the important items of the project, usually at a summary level at this point because so far there has been little, if any, planning. The project charter document helps kick off the project and does not contain many project details. From a communication perspective, each component in the project charter document can stand alone to communicate valuable project information. For example, you communicate in the major deliverables section of the document what the team members are going to build.

Table 6.1 — Example of a Project Charter Table of Contents shows a sample project charter document. This sample covers the major areas of the project. Most project charters have the same information, with changes being company- or industry-specific.

Table 6.1 — Example of a Project Charter Table of Contents

#	Description
1	Introduction
2	Project Overview
3	Project Purpose
4	Project Objective
5	Project Scope
6	Project Budget
7	Project Start and Finish Dates
8	Major Deliverables
9	Resources
10	Business Need or Opportunity
11	Financial Benefits of the Project
12	Critical Success Factors of Project
13	Expected Benefits
14	Assumptions and Constraints
15	Sign-offs

Defining the roles

Many different people can be involved in creating and communicating the project charter. The following roles and descriptions can help you understand who is involved in this process:

- **Project manager.** Supports the project sponsors in developing the project charter. Implements the project charter after leadership approval. Communicates all project charter development activities. In some organizations, the leadership team creates the project charter and assigns a project manager after the document is completed.

- **Team members.** Perform project activities after the project kick off. Team members communicate various sections of the project charter. For example, they could be responsible for describing the project's planning tasks as they relate to the details described in the project charter.

- **Project sponsors.** Develop the initial project idea, communicate the idea by presenting a project proposal, and support developing the project's charter document.

- **Project owner or client.** Holds financial responsibility, is responsible for overall acceptance, and communicates project approval.

Planning the project charter

When planning to use a project charter, work with the sponsor and owner to review the document and get an understanding of the proposed project. Doing so lets you review and accept the project responsibility as described in the project charter document. After you are familiar with the project, you have enough information to build your project team and start the project planning process. As the project kicks off, you and the sponsor or owner will meet with the project team to review the project charter. This gives them time to ask questions and get an understanding of the project.

Reporting information from the project charter

The project owner or customer creates the project charter document. The document guides you and your team members in scheduling, budgeting, and defining the quality areas of the project.

There are two distinct reporting levels for distributing the project charter.

- The project owner(s) who presents the document to their peers and financial leaders for project support and approval.
- You and the project team members use the project charter to drive the work toward completion.

During the project's conceptual and startup phases, you and your team members regularly refer to the project charter to ensure that you are staying on track toward the project's goals. The project charter is developed and shared in a document format for ease of distribution and presentation. Often, you will pull information from the project charter for presentations during the project.

The project charter is usually distributed once; however, it should be available, on demand, in a document repository for long-term storage and accessibility. You typically only use the project charter document during the beginning of the project. You do not report from the project charter because it does not include project status information.

Cross-Reference
See Chapter 16 - Using Communication Tools in the Initiating Process for additional information about how to create and use a project charter.

Introduction to the Project Kick-Off Meeting

The project *kick-off meeting* formalizes the start of the project and the project activities. The project kick-off meeting engages project team members and enables them to become a team. The project kick-off meeting helps set up the atmosphere of the project, and without it, projects can suffer. Some of the benefits of holding a project kick-off meeting include bringing the team together, forming relationships and bonds among the team members, and providing an opportunity to communicate project information for the first time to everyone. The project kick-off meeting is a great time to invite virtual team members to your corporate offices to connect and form relationships with other team members.

The project kick-off meeting gives you and your team the chance to establish a bond. Team members need to feel that they can work together to resolve project issues. By attending the kick-off meeting and getting to know each other, team members establish a bond. Without a project kick-off meeting, team members may never have that bonding experience and you might face challenges with team members working together. This is especially true for virtual team members and onsite team members. If they never have a chance to bond or connect, working together in difficult project situations can be challenging.

Note
The Project Management Institute's knowledge area for the project kick-off meeting is the integration area. There is no secondary area.

Tool Value
Project kick-off meetings set the direction, tone, focus, and goal of the project for all team members and stakeholders.

Social Media Tools
The communication purposes for a project kick-off meeting are to inform, motivate, and instruct. Communication from the project kick-off meeting can be posted on social media tools, such as Yammer, Socialcast, and Facebook (private group).

The project kick-off meeting usually creates positive energy for your team and customers. This is the time when everyone establishes early opinions and first impressions of each other. These opinions can last throughout the project. As mentioned—especially for team members working in a virtual environment—the project kick-off meeting may offer the only opportunity to meet the other team members; they may not get another opportunity to connect with onsite team members again.

Table 6.2 — Example of a Project Kick-off Meeting Agenda shows a typical project kick-off meeting agenda. The agenda items are typical for any project discussion. You can easily add your own sections to the kick-off meeting agenda for your specific project or industry.

Table 6.2 — Example of a Project Kick-off Meeting Agenda

#	Description
1	Project Scope, Goals, Objectives
2	Project Out-of–Scope Goals
3	Project Risks
4	Project Issues
5	Budget Estimate
6	Project Schedule
7	Methodology Deliverables
8	Requirements Deep Dive
9	Design Deep Dive
10	Development Deep Dive
11	Test Deep Dive
12	User Acceptance Criteria Deep Dive

Creating a positive first impression with your team during the project kick-off meeting can help you gain a high-level of respect. Most team members quickly decide if they want to work for you. You must make a good impression with your team and customers when driving the project kick-off meeting.

The project kick-off meeting is the official start of the project. During the meeting, you explain the scope, goals, and objectives to all stakeholders and interested parties. This ensures that everyone has the same information about the project, at the same time, so that everyone can focus on what the team has to deliver. The kick-off meeting is the first chance for the project owner to present his or her expectations about the project and for the team and to explain what they are hoping to achieve. Likewise, the project owner presentation provides an opportunity for the team to ask questions. This connection is important when building relationships between your customer and team members. The project kick-off meeting is often the first and only chance these parties will meet.

Some customers refuse to be involved in running or leading the project kick-off meeting. They might feel that they have turned the project over to you and so they do not want to interfere. Other customers will want to run and lead the meeting. A best practice is for you and the project owner to jointly present at the project kick-off meeting. This will put more of the meeting ownership on you instead of the customer. The customer should feel like a valuable participant in the meeting, rather than owning the whole meeting.

If you decide not to have a project kick-off meeting, team members are much slower to engage in the project. Team members will feel lost and unsure of the project's goals or their role. This uncertainty can have a devastating impact when communicating with team members. Bad morale is not something you want to face during the project—especially at the beginning.

Planning a project kick-off meeting

The project kick-off meeting in many ways, is an example of project planning. The planning work for the project kick-off meeting is required to ensure that you meet both your customer's and your goals and objectives for the meeting. The planning work ensures that you have the information to kick off the project and that you are communicating effectively with everyone.

The following tips can help make your project kick-off meeting a success:

- **Research the project.** Do some preliminary research to help you understand the project objectives. Gather relevant documentation and information.
- **Meet your customers and outline their expectations.** Sit down with your customers to understand and document their expectations. Good communication skills are necessary during customer meetings and discussing their expectations. Make sure to meet with everyone who signed the project charter.
- **Gather lessons learned.** Work with previous project managers to gather lessons learned. Read similar projects' lessons-learned documents to understand the previous project's challenges that might be relevant to your project.
- **List team members' project expectations.** Meet with each team member to explain the project and gather his or her expectations and feelings about the project.
- **Include company-specific tasks.** Include company-specific tasks for the project kick-off meeting, when applicable.

Reporting information from the project kick-off meeting

Usually, at least two groups are involved with creating the presentation materials for the project kick-off meeting: project managers and their customers. Each has specific areas to cover during the meeting. Each party should take ownership for their areas of the presentation materials. For technical projects, it is a best practice to invite a subject matter expert who is responsible for the technical areas of the project. The subject matter expert would also present materials.

The project kick-off meeting is a one-time event; therefore, the document is used only once, at the beginning of the project. All presentations and project materials should be stored in the document control system. The document control system allows for long-term archiving and accessibility to anyone working on the project.

Cross-Reference
See Chapter 16 - Using Communication Tools in the Initiating Process to learn more about how to plan a project kick-off meeting.

Introduction to the Project Management Plan

The purpose of the project management plan is to create and compile a series of management planning documents. These documents guide you through managing and controlling project activities. The various plans include time management, quality management, risk management, and cost management. Each plan covers the specific project knowledge areas and how they will be communicated. It is the collection of those management plans into a single package (volume) that creates the project management plan document. One important section to include in the project management plan is the project strategies. These strategies include the project's scope, goals, and objectives.

Note
The Project Management Institute's knowledge area for this tool is the integration area. The secondary knowledge area for this tool is scope.

Tool Value
The project management plan provides a process for you to follow during the project life cycle.

Social Media Tools
The communication purposes for the project management plan are to inform and instruct. Communication from the project management plan can be posted on social media tools, such as Yammer, Socialcast, and Facebook (private group).

There are two main methods you can use to create a project management plan on a project.

- The first method is to create a single, blank, electronic document titled "Project Management Plan," and then use hyperlinks in the document to link to the major project areas: scope, risk, cost, and schedule. For example, a project management plan using this method has a page dedicated to risk management, but that page only includes a hyperlink to the project's risk management document.

- The second method is to create a fully documented and detailed project management plan by copying and pasting the contents from various management plans (risk, issue, schedule, quality, and so on) into the project management plan document. It is not a good practice to include hyperlinks in this plan. Copy the details from one management plan into the project management plan. For example, the major contents of the risk management plan are copied into the risk management section of the project management plan. The disadvantage of this method is keeping the information current in multiple documents. Another disadvantage is ensuring that your customers or team members are using the most current information from either plan. It can be a problem if you change a process in the project management plan and not make the same changes in the other documents.

Table 6.3 — Example of a Project Management Plan Table of Contents shows an example of a project management plan table of contents. The descriptions in the table are suitable for most projects and industries. If you work for a company that does not have a project management plan, use this project management plan as a starting point. This document should cover all areas of the project in as much detail as possible to avoid any confusion and get everyone on the same page.

Note
*Sections 1 through 19 in **Table 6.3 — Example of a Project Management Plan Table of Contents** should be included in every project management plan.*

Table 6.3 — Example of a Project Management Plan Table of Contents

#	Description
1	Introduction
2	Project Descriptions
3	Application
4	Scope
5	Constraints and Assumptions
6	Risks
7	Issues
8	Relationship to Other Project(s)
9	Mission Statement
10	Project Objectives
11	Project Team Members
12	Project Roles and Responsibilities
13	Project Plan Management
14	Project Approach
15	Conflict Management
16	Project Tasks, Deliverables, and Milestones
17	Planning Approaches/Methodologies
18	Key Deliverables
19	Major Milestone Dates/List
20	Scope Management
21	Issues Management
22	Risk Management/Including Risk Register
23	Problems Management
24	Financial/Cost Management
25	Communications Management

#	Description
26	Quality Management Plan
27	Staffing Management Plan
28	Procurement Management Plan
29	Schedule Management Plan
30	Summary

A project management plan is important for any project, regardless of size, type, or industry. The plan is a communication and support tool that documents and helps team members and customers manage the project. When a situation arises, the project management plan—or one of the various documents within the plan—describes, in detail, what to do to resolve the issue. The project management plan covers, at a high-level, the management plans for each of the project knowledge areas. For example, the risk management plan documents, in detail, the process and procedures for opening and closing project risks. The risk management plan is part of the overall project management plan, so team members can refer to either document for risk management information. Be careful that you don't repeat documentation in two sets of documents. The best approach is for the project management plan to be a consolidated document that brings together all of the plans in one location. Doing this avoids people having to go from plan to plan, or looking for some disparate information.

Note
Some companies refer to the project management plan as a project governance guide. This document represents essentially the same areas of the project management plan. Project governance guides include company-specific information or requirements. Ensure that you capture this extra information for your project.

A common misconception about project management plans is that they are the same as a project schedule. They are not, and it is important to keep the two documents separate. Project schedules include a list of tasks with intended start and finish dates that are normally generated by a project scheduling tool. The contents of the project schedule and the project management plan are different. The schedule contains tasks, dates, and resources—not processes and procedures—which is what the project management plan contains. The project management plan contains the processes and procedures for managing the schedule. You should understand the differences between the two documents and make sure that you are clear when discussing each document with your customers, stakeholders, or team members.

You are responsible for creating and maintaining the project management plan during the project life cycle. You also become one of the main users of the document, and you will heavily rely on it to help other stakeholders manage the project. Project customers or team members also use the project management plan, mainly for guidance on how a particular process should work. For example, a customer would look closely at the change control plan and refer to the change request process within that plan. That way, when your customers have change requests, they have a documented process to follow.

You are responsible for ensuring that your team members approve the project management plan before the project begins. Getting approval from team members can prevent future miscommunication and chaos. The various documents that are contained in the project management plan should include information that team members need to handle most situations that occur on the project.

Planning a project management plan

In preparing to create and use a project management plan, you must decide as early as possible which method to use for the project management plan document itself: a blank shell document that links to each management plan or an all-inclusive document that describes each knowledge area. The next step is to ensure that the knowledge area management plans (risk, scope, quality, and so on) are complete, approved, and stored in the document control system. That way, you can link to the plans directly or go into each and copy and paste the text in the project management plan document. You then need to prepare some of the technical areas of the project management plan, such as where the documents are stored, who receives security access, and long-term archiving. Finally, when planning to use the project management plan, decide who owns each management plan(s) and work with them to complete their documents. After performing these tasks, you have adequately prepared for using the project management plan on your project.

Reporting information from a project management plan

At the beginning of the project, develop the project management plan. As the documents that comprise the project management plan are completed, you will continue to update, monitor, and ensure that everything is accurate. If a company policy or process changes on the project, the project management plan needs to reflect those changes. It is your responsibility to make that happen. If you chose to set up the project management plan as a shell document, you would reflect the changes in the individual management documents as well. Regardless of which method you choose to build the plan, remember to communicate updates and changes to all stakeholders.

The following list shows the management plans included in a standard project management plan. These plans represent the major areas of most projects. Each category represents a document that needs to be created and included in the project management plan.

The following plans are included in a standard project management plan:

- Project scope management plan
- Schedule management plan
- Cost management plan and cost baseline
- Quality management plan and quality baseline
- Staffing management plan
- Communication management plan
- Risk management plan
- Procurement management plan
- Project major milestone list
- Schedule baseline
- Issue list
- Risk register

You will not create reports from the project management plan because it does not include project status information. The project management plan is more of a reference and guidance document that you refer to throughout the project life cycle. This plan, like other documents, is stored in the document control system. This allows for long-term archiving and is accessible by interested stakeholders.

Cross-Reference
See Chapter 16 - Using Communication Tools in the Initiating Process to learn more about how to create and use the project management plan.

Introduction to the Project Meeting Minutes

The purpose of *project meeting minutes* is to capture the activities and action items that occur during a project meeting. Project meeting minutes enable anyone interested in the project to learn what transpired and what was committed to during the meeting. Meeting minutes are helpful for team members who could not attend the meeting. You should take meeting minutes or have someone capture meeting minutes for you. It is best practice to ask or assign someone else to take the minutes because it's difficult to run the meeting and take minutes at the same time. The meeting minute's taker should capture as much relevant information in the meeting minutes as possible and leave out extraneous discussions or "noise." The meeting minute's taker sends the minutes to you for distribution to the project team, customers, and leadership.

Note
The Project Management Institute's knowledge area for this tool is the integration area. This tool also applies to the other knowledge areas.

Tool Value
Project meeting minutes document what occurred and was agreed on during the meeting. This provides everyone a synopsis of what happened during the meeting—especially for those who could not attend.

Social Media Tools
The communication purposes for project meeting minutes are to inform and instruct. Communication from the project meeting minutes can be posted on social media tools, such as Yammer, Socialcast, and Facebook (private group).

Project meeting minutes are the notes that capture the action items and main points that happened during a meeting. You should always review the captured and summarized meeting minutes after each meeting to ensure that they are accurate. Then, share those minutes with your team members and customers so they can review the minutes for their own issues and action items. Creating and sharing project meeting minutes is an important step in project communications management. Sending project meeting minutes and keeping your customers and team members engaged allows for continuous flow of project information. This is important to the health of the project and keeping everyone engaged and current with the latest status.

Tip
You might want to capture a certain part of a meeting, such as a subject matter expert's material, to make sure the communication is accurate. If this is necessary, record only that part of the meeting for future playback. You can use several recording tools, such as the Dictaphone, computer camera, tape recorder, movie, camcorder, and so on.

Figure 6.3 – Meeting Minutes Template shows an example meeting minute's template for a project.

Figure 6.3 – Meeting Minutes Template

Meeting Minutes for PROJECT XXX

Project Name	:	
Meeting Title	:	
Date	:	
Time	:	
Place	:	
Phone Information	:	
Chair Person	:	
Invitee List	:	
In Attendance	:	

AGENDA	
1.	Last week's Minutes Review
2.	Project Schedule Review
3.	Major Area Updates
4.	Project Issues Review
5.	Project Risk List Review
6.	This week's Lessons Learned
7.	Walk-on's

Action Items:

#	Action Item	Owner	Status	Due Date	Comments
1.					
2.					

Carry-Over Items for Next Meeting:

#	Description
1.	
1.	

Next Meeting Details:	:	
Date	:	
Time	:	
Place	:	

An excellent tip when using meeting minutes is to capture the action items from the last meeting and bring them to the current meeting to ensure that nothing is lost from week to week. It is easy to miss this step and assume that your team members performed the action items captured from the last meeting. Most team members need that extra push to ensure they remember the action items assigned to them; bringing them forward once a week reduces the chances of them forgetting.

It is best practice for project managers to communicate meeting minutes at the end of every meeting by distributing meeting minutes and relevant action items to all stakeholders and project team members. You should also post those minutes within the document control system for easy access and review. By doing so, you continue to provide project communications for your interested stakeholders, thus, keeping project information flowing. You should also follow up during the week on each issue or action item to ensure the team is making progress on the items. Communicate to the team when action items are completed.

As the project progresses and you capture weekly meeting minutes, the minutes become valuable. The meeting minutes' repository contains a wealth of project information, which is valuable to the project team, customers, and stakeholders. When you need to look back at past decisions or discussion points, the first place to look is in the historical repository of meeting minutes. The meeting minutes become a source for to-do lists (action items) or formal project tasks. The action items in the weekly minutes carry through each week until they are completed or noted, and then dropped.

Capturing the lessons learned information within the meeting minutes is a best practice technique. In **Figure 6.3— Meeting Minutes Template** there is an agenda item called "This Week's Lessons Learned." During that time in the meeting, you discuss and take note of lessons learned (what went right and what went wrong) for the week.

All project team members should reference the meeting minutes to review and recap what occurred. Each person will have a different reason for how and why they will use the meeting minutes. Most often, team members review the meeting minutes to find action items assigned to them. Make sure the meeting minutes are available to everyone on the project; it is important to have full disclosure for anyone who wants to see what occurred during the meeting.

Note
The accuracy of your meeting minutes is important. Occasionally, these documents are valuable in litigation, so make sure they are current and as accurate as possible.

Planning the project meeting minutes

In preparing to create and use project meeting minutes, you must first develop or use an existing project meeting minute's template from your company or a past project. In doing so, you are showing your project team members what you plan to communicate during the meeting. Next, you need to decide where the meeting minutes will be stored. When storing meeting minutes, there are some technical areas of the process to consider, such as security access, technology solutions (e.g. shared LAN drives on company networks), and non-technology solutions (e.g. paper copies).

The next step is to create a meeting agenda that matches the project meeting minute's template—it can take some time to ensure the agenda and the meeting minute's template are aligned. Make sure you get the information you need from the team members during the meeting, because that won't be possible when the meeting is over. Finally, work with the minutes' taker to go over the template and ensure that they know what to capture. You should never randomly select someone at the start of the meeting to collect the minutes unless they already know how to fill out the template. When you randomly select a team member to take meeting minutes, the person you select may not know how to correctly fill out the template and valuable information could be lost and never captured. Often, there is valuable information that comes out of a status meeting, so make sure whoever you pick knows how to fill out the template correctly.

After performing these planning steps, you are adequately prepared to use meeting minutes on your project.

Reporting information from the project's meeting minutes

If your project is small, team members can take turns each week to capture meeting minutes. This requires that you spend time with team members to ensure they all know how to fill out the template and what to capture. Meeting attendees should receive the minutes no later than 48 hours after the meeting.

It is a best practice for every project manager to use the project meeting minutes to report from those minutes each week or for the duration of the project. This reporting duration could be monthly or quarterly, but whatever cadence you choose, continue reporting on the project using the meeting minute's template to ensure nothing is missed from reporting period to reporting period. The meeting minutes are full of valuable project information, status, current events, and a wealth of project data. The meeting minutes are stored as part of the document control system for long-term storage and archiving, and are accessible by any interested stakeholder on the project.

Cross-Reference
See Chapter 21 - Using Communication Tools During the Executing and Controlling Process to learn more about how to create and use the project meeting minutes.

Introduction to the Project Status Meeting

The purpose of the *project status meeting* is to get and communicate status about the project. There are two types of status meetings for a typical project: project team status meeting or customer status meeting.

In the *project team* status meeting, team members take turns communicating status for their deliverables and discuss any issues, concerns, or risks for those deliverables. These status meetings usually occur weekly and are more like "working" status sessions than pure status meetings. This meeting is one of the only meetings where the project team gets together each week to communicate about the project in person. These meetings are critical to the success of the project, and they must occur throughout the project.

In the *customer* status meeting, you meet directly with your customers to communicate the overall project status. This status meeting communicates high-level information; you should limit the details.

For some projects, you might have one large project status meeting where team members work through project deliverables, issues, and concerns in front of the customer. The project team can ask the customer about specific project areas without having to go through formal communication channels. This meeting is more effective on a monthly basis so that customers are not hearing about the day-to-day project issues. The negative side of having one large project status meeting is that there's no time for the team to work together without the customer present. The team may have issues or concerns, and if they don't have the opportunity to work on those concerns outside of this meeting, your customers will hear all of the problems. It is a best practice to keep these two meetings separate so that team members can work out their issues without being in front of the customer. It also gives you the opportunity to incorporate the issues you hear from the team into the status report. You would be able to talk to your team directly and not in front of the customer. You have few opportunities to work with your team members each week, so remember that working status meetings with your team are valuable.

On high-profile projects that have media attention, you will need to schedule *media-based* status meetings, where you and your team answer questions from the media.

Note
The Project Management Institute's knowledge area for this tool is the integration area. Project status meetings are applicable to all knowledge areas.

Tool Value
The project status meeting ensures constant communication among team members. It keeps the project owner up to date and keeps communication flowing between you and the project owner.

Social Media Tools
The communication purposes for project status meetings are to inform and persuade. Communication from the project status meeting can be posted on social media tools, such as Yammer, Socialcast, and Facebook (private group).

The project status meeting is a decisive communication tool, whether you need to meet with team members once a week, twice a week, daily, hourly, or whenever the project requires. The project status meeting provides you and your team with the most up-to-date information about the project. There is no other opportunity for you and your team to get this much information about the project at one time except in a written status report, which may not include all of the meeting information. Getting everyone in a room or on a call lets project information flow among multiple team members. All projects need status meetings, with few to no exceptions.

Table 6.4 — Example of a Project Status Meeting Agenda shows a typical project status meeting agenda. It contains the most relevant agenda items for most projects. The meeting agenda sets the tone and format for how the meeting will run. Using a formal project meeting agenda makes it simple to create meeting minutes from that agenda.

Table 6.4 — Example of a Project Status Meeting Agenda

Agenda Item	Description	Owner / Responsible
1	Review Last Week's Minutes	Project Manager
2	Review Current Action Items	All Team Members
3	Review Project Schedule	All Team Members
4	Major Area Updates	All Team Leads
5	Review Current Budget Information	Project Manager
6	Project Risks	All Team Members
7	Project Issues	All Team Members
8	Lessons Learned Information	All Team Members
9	Walk-ons	All Team Members

Project status meetings are helpful to you, your team, and your customers. These meetings let the team present status and work together on project-related items. Project status meetings can be fun and can have a playful atmosphere that increases morale and team relationships. You are responsible for the mood and atmosphere of these meetings; therefore, take every opportunity to capture project status, but make the meetings fun and enjoyable. Team members use project status meetings to learn about the health and direction of the project. During the week, leave your team alone so they can work on their deliverables; you can get everyone together in the status meeting to discuss accomplishments or next steps.

Getting team members together regularly to report status and discuss issues, risks, and next steps is critical to the project's success. Without project status meetings, you can easily lose control of the project, and you could have project team members sitting around not knowing how to continue. Typically, for most small to midsize projects, you hold weekly status meetings, but daily checkpoints are common when there are project issues. A daily status meeting is rare and occurs only for a short duration while critical issues need attention. Projects should go back to regular (for example, weekly) status reporting when the critical issues are resolved.

On most projects, weekly project status meetings are required. If you do not meet with your team weekly or biweekly, they can quickly lose sight of what is happening on the project. On the average project, two weeks is a long time to wait between status meetings and too long for you to wait to get updated project information.

There are many different types of status meetings that you can use. The communication requirements for each type can also vary. Look at each meeting from a communications perspective and decide what kind of status you want to communicate in each meeting. The following list shows some of the common status meetings:

- **Daily checkpoint**. A daily checkpoint meeting is for team members to discuss pressing issues or project concerns. This is a helpful meeting from your customer's perspective. Your customer can hear how the project is progressing each day and if they have any issues or concerns, they have the opportunity to voice them at this meeting.
- **Weekly project status**. The regular project status meeting occurs weekly. At this meeting, you typically describe and record the project issues, risks, schedules, and budgets. This meeting is valuable for your customers because it lets them consume project data on a weekly basis. Presenting daily project data to your customers may be overwhelming to them. Frankly, it may cause more of a negative experience than a positive one.
- **Weekly financial and budget review**. This meeting is a weekly financial status and budget review. You and your customers go over project finances, in detail, to decide if the project is running over or under budget. Often, this meeting is biweekly or monthly, depending on the project's financial cycle. If the project is running over budget, you might meet more often. The benefit of this meeting is being able to communicate the project's financial information to your customers on a weekly basis. Usually, the project budget is calculated monthly, but doing a weekly sync allows project customers tighter control or understanding of the project forecasts. Although the budget does not change weekly, keeping a grasp on how the team is forecasting is important.
- **Monthly media status**. This monthly checkpoint meeting with the media where you, the communications manager, and possibly the owner's representative discuss project updates and status. This meeting provides the media with the latest project status and gives them continuing and regular communications. When working with the media, it is important to be as open as possible when providing them the project information they want. Preparation for this meeting is an absolute necessity.
- **Monthly management checkpoints**. This is normally a high-level status meeting where the project team, led by you, discusses project status. This meeting includes schedule, budget, issues, risks, key requests, or challenges. This meeting is valuable because it acts as a monthly status high-level checkpoint session for the executives. The data provided in this meeting is different than they would receive on a weekly basis. The benefit of this meeting, from a communications perspective, is that you provide information about the project to senior-level decision makers that they don't normally receive in a weekly status report. For example, if anything is going on that needs executive support, you have them right there in the meeting. So, if the project needs to change course, you can get the approval to move forward with the change during this meeting— whether you need extra resources or more budget, these monthly meetings are perfect for communicating this to the executives.

Project status meetings are critical to the success of the project because of their communication value. Customers can hear, firsthand, about project issues and can work with the team to resolve them— sometimes immediately.

Planning a project status meeting

In planning a project status meeting, you must first decide the meeting agenda and the items you need to cover in the meeting. After you decide what you want and need to cover, create a meeting agenda based on those areas. The next step is to decide the meeting structure and format. Finally, you need to decide if there will be any co-leaders or co-presenters for the meeting and make sure they are available. Other considerations to think about when planning a status meeting include:

- Booking the meeting room on a regular cadence
- Deciding the duration of the meeting

- Securing audio or video equipment that may not already be in meeting room
- Inviting attendees
- Preparing for food or drinks, if applicable

Reporting information from a project status meeting

On most projects, you will create the agenda and format for the project status meeting. You own the agenda, meeting minutes, preparation, and meeting contents. Project team members are expected to attend, report status, and provide project-related information. On large projects, you can assign support staff as administrative support for the meeting. They can capture and compile the meeting minutes while you drive the meeting.

Project status meetings usually occur weekly. On most projects, this rhythm meets your customer requirements. After the project status meeting is complete, you—or whoever is responsible for creating the meeting minutes—have 48 hours to distribute them. If you wait any longer than 48 hours, team members will have moved on with their work activities and may have forgotten their new assignments or action items. It is important that you distribute the minutes as soon as possible after the meeting so this does not happen.

You report status from the project status meeting by using the meeting minutes on a weekly basis. The project status meeting has a wealth of project information about the progress over the last week. You create the project status meeting agenda by using a document format. The status meeting agenda is stored as part of the document control system. This provides long-term storage and is accessible to interested project stakeholders.

Cross-Reference
See Chapter 20 - Using Communication Tools During the Executing and Controlling Processes to Administer the Project to learn more about project status meetings.

Introduction to the Project Status Report

The *project status report* formally communicates project information to your customers, leadership, and team members. The project status report is one of the most common project communication tools. There are thousands of project status report examples to choose from on the Internet; however, most companies have standard project status reports. The project status report is a live document that is used throughout the project life cycle. However, it is important that the report provides the latest project status at a given time. Set expectations with your customer that you will give them the project status report on the same day each week. Once you set that standard, they will expect this regular project communication. The most common day to send the report is Friday, by the end of the business day (EOD). Selecting a certain day of the week gives the leadership team a "stake in the ground" day when they know you will send the latest project information. Set up a regular cadence for delivering the project status report at the beginning of the project. It is especially important to stick to that reporting cycle throughout the project, and if you do miss it, that would be an exception only.

Note
The Project Management Institute's knowledge area for this tool is the integration area. Project status reports apply to all knowledge areas.

Tool Value
Project status reports provide project stakeholders current project information on a regular basis.

Social Media Tools
The communication purposes for the project status report are to inform and instruct. Communication from this report can be posted on social media tools, such as, Yammer, Socialcast, and Facebook (private group).

The project status report is the project's official plan of record. This report contains relevant project information, in addition to the latest status of each project area. This report is valuable to you because it provides information about what is happening on the project for you to discuss with your team members or customers. Set expectations with your team to discuss project status each week and report that same status to upper management and customers. This practice ensures the verbal and written status reports match and keep consistent information about the project.

Figure 6.4 — Example of a Project Status Report shows a summary-level status report example to use on any project. The report data stays at a high level, with no detail. This is a common format for status reports in the project management profession. There are thousands of different status reports; however, your company should have a template for you or a system in which to enter project status information. Each status report caters to the specific project type and industry of the company managing the effort.

Figure 6.4 – Example of a Project Status Report

<u>Example of Project Status Report (High Level)</u>

Reporting Period: 4/14/2019 – 4/18/2019

Project manager: Bob Smith, PMP

<u>**Accomplishments this Period:**</u>

- Tech specs completed
- Design Started
- 5 Developer Resources hired and started on-boarding process

<u>**Scheduled Items Not Completed:**</u>

- Approvals obtained from customers
- Final Budget approved

<u>**Activities Next Period:**</u>

- Design to Continue
- Developers to continue on-boarding

<u>**Issues:**</u>

- None at this time.

<u>**Schedule Changes:**</u>

- None at this time.

<u>**Budget Changes:**</u>

- Project is running $5,000 under budget at this time.

<u>**Staffing Changes:**</u>

- Two more team members left the project due to unfair working conditions

Notes:

Tip

Every project must regularly produce a status report. Customers expect regular communication about the project.

The project status report provides project status. Depending on the audience for the status report, the information can be detail oriented, or provided high-level information. The details within the report depend on who is requesting the report and their project information requirements.

When implementing a project status report, work with your customer to ensure the report is meeting their reporting and communication needs. Meet with your customer to go over the report together and change it to match your customer's requirements. Your customer may not be happy with a generic status report and could have specific requirements about what they want to see. You cannot assume that a generic report will provide enough information for your customer; that assumption could cause communication problems.

If you create your project status report with too much detail, senior-level management who expects summary-level status will get lost in the details. They won't want to weed through the details to find the particular status they are looking for. On the other hand, if your status report only summarizes status information, you may have problems communicating that information to team members or customers who want details. Your goal is to mix both detailed and high-level information into a single project status report and properly communicate that information.

Usually, the primary audiences for sending status reports are your customers and leadership team. People looking for granular project details won't find them in status reports. Project details should come from talking directly with you or the project team—not relying on a report for detailed information.

Project status report information serves two main purposes: action or informing. When customers or stakeholders receive the report and realize there are decisions or project-related items that they need to address (take action on), they do so by reacting from the data provided on the report. Without a project status report, project issues could sit and, occasionally, negatively affect the project if not attended to. The other purpose of the project status report is to tell customers and upper management the latest project status and information. In this case, the project status report is to inform only and not to decide or take action.

Two main audiences need the project status report: the project team and the customers or stakeholders. Each group has a different need for the report. The project team uses it to document the latest project information and provide status updates about their specific project areas. Project customers or stakeholders use the project status report to make project-level decisions.

Tip
Let your customers decide how often they want to receive the project status report. Usually, most customers choose a weekly cadence for status report delivery.

Planning a project status report

In preparing to create and use a project status report, decide which reporting template to use. Most companies have templates that they use, but you may need to tweak it a little. Make sure to match the project status report with the weekly project status meeting agenda to ensure stakeholders are getting the information they need each week. You should also make sure to review the last meeting's minutes when preparing the next project status report to ensure there are no outstanding items from the last report; in which case, those items are either addressed or closed. Set up a long-term storage repository for the reports, and you may need to add company-level status reports to the repository as well. It's not unusual that you are asked to produce a single project status report that you need to transcribe into a company-wide reporting tool.

Prepare how you will collect project status information because it may not be readily available. You might have to consider what sources you will use for finding the information. For example, the team lead's report is an excellent source of project status information. Those reports include issues, risks, and budget data for their particular area of the project.

Reporting using a project status report

You may not have to develop the project status report—usually, though, you probably will—but you do have accountability for creating and delivering it. On large projects, you can have an administrative assistant, a junior project manager, or a team member help you create and compile the report.

Figure 6.5 — Example of a Detailed Status Report shows a detailed project status report. Stakeholders who want to understand all of the project details will request a status report. The following format is common for status reports in the project management industry.

Note
Many times, there is little or no activity on a project over the weekend, so in most cases status reporting is not required during that period. If deadlines are in jeopardy and work occurs over the weekend, the project manager must report project status updates on those days as well. This occurs rarely and for short periods until the project is back on track.

Figure 6.5 — Example of a Detailed Status Report

Example of Project Status Report (Detailed):

Date:

Project Name: _____   **Prepared by:** _____

Week ending: _____

Planned Tasks for Reporting Period:

Task Name	Start Date	End Date	% Complete	Status	Resources Assigned
Start Foundation	3/12/2019		22	On Track	Bob, Sam, Frank

Conflicts:

- The project is running into a conflict with the Jones project and resources from each project are running into conflicts on which project they should be working on. Joe Smith is spending 100% of his time on the Jones's project but has to develop the detail designs for the walls on the east side of the building next week. We have to determine what we can do about this conflict, or the project could have an impact hit to the schedule.

-

Action Plans:

- Jon Hollenbeck needs to spend time securing the extra budget for the second structure. The change request approved, but the funding taken longer than expected. Jon will spend next week on this funding delta and report back to the stakeholders.

Next Week's Planned Activities:

- Complete foundation work, on the Jones and Smith structures.

- Johnson Stones Company is delivering 20 tons of bedrock for the main structure. That is due next Tuesday between 4 – 5pm. Larry Smith will be on site receiving the rocks and will sign all relevant paperwork.

Other Notes:

Cross-Reference
See Chapter 22 - Communication Tools in Executing and Controlling Process to Report Project Information to learn more about project status report.

Summary

In summary, we explored project communication tools that support the integration knowledge area. The tools in this chapter will help you improve your project communications across the various knowledge areas. Use the tools, such as the project kick-off meeting, project management plan, and the project status report, to ensure you are communicating as effectively as possible. The project status report is the most common tool for project managers across every industry, and it is important to get it right. Talk to your customers about how effective the current project status report is in providing them the information they need to make project decisions. If it doesn't meet their needs, it needs to be updated.

Chapter 7

Communication Tools that Manage Project Scope

IN THIS CHAPTER

- ◆ Introduction to Agile Estimating tools
- ◆ Introduction to the Agile User story
- ◆ Introduction to the Agile User story backlog
- ◆ Introduction to the Business case
- ◆ Introduction to the Customer Requirements
- ◆ Introduction to the Design Specification document
- ◆ Introduction to the Executive Summary
- ◆ Introduction to the Feasibility Study
- ◆ Introduction to the System Requirements document
- ◆ Introduction to the Work Breakdown Structure (WBS)

In this chapter, we explore project communication tools in the scope management knowledge area. Scope management is the processes and procedures you use to manage and track project work tasks. This chapter does not address managing out-of-scope project items because out of scope items are not managed by you or anyone on the team. There are some communication tools that you can use to document and communicate anything that's out of scope, but that's outside the scope of this chapter. Project managers oversee the scope management processes throughout the project life cycle. It is important to understand that without solid project scope, you will struggle with creating a solid project foundation.

Project managers who manage projects that are scope-driven do not focus on project cost and scheduling; they focus on scope. The focus areas for scope-driven projects are scope, quality, and delivering your customer's requirements. Scope-driven projects try and match your customer's requirements one hundred percent, however that can often be very difficult to achieve. An example of a scope driven project is building an airplane engine. In aerospace, an airplane engine must not fail; the project continues regardless of the time or cost it takes to build an airplane engine that meets safety requirements.

In this chapter, we present tools that help you manage and control project scope. These tools will help you communicate effectively. Each tool has its own purpose in the scope knowledge area.

Introduction to Agile Estimating Tools

Agile estimating tools help you estimate the level of effort to complete each project requirement. An estimate is the value assigned to a specific requirement that represents the ease or difficulty to develop that requirement. The first step in Agile estimating (also referred to as "scoring") for requirements is based on the level of effort to develop the estimates. The highest level of Agile project requirements are called *themes*. A theme is a logical group of product features that helps the project team create the initial product roadmap. *Features* are the first level of requirements decomposition. Features describe a new capability that will be included with the final product. Features help further define the product roadmap. *Epic user stories* are high-level requirements that contain multiple actions that are necessary to support a specific feature. Epic user stories are further decomposed into *detailed user stories*, which usually contain a single action and are small enough to develop and implement. *Tasks* are the lowest level of Agile requirement decomposition, which represent each activity that the development team must perform to complete the *detailed user story* and deliver the expected functionality to the customer.

The Agile estimating tool you choose depends on where the project team is in the project's life cycle, as well as the level of detailed requirements that are necessary to perform requirements decomposition. During initial strategy meetings, you create features, themes, and epic user stories, but there is not sufficient information to decompose them into the detailed user story level. The project team can rank them only according to the level of effort relative to other epic user stories that have been created, called *relative sizing,* which is the starting point for Agile project scope and requirements estimation.

When you've determined the relative size of the themes, features, and epic user stories, the product owner, Scrum master, and development team assign each relative size a numeric value, usually based on the *Fibonacci sequence*. The numeric values are called *story points* and become the basic estimation unit for the entire project. When you assign the themes or features a story point value, future requirements estimating is based on those values. User stories are further defined until they have specific tasks assigned to them to complete the user story. Initially, the majority of themes and features are assigned effort scores from 55–144 because they are so large. As the product owner, Scrum master, and development team performs the estimating process and decomposes the requirements, they are broken down into smaller user stories with epic user stories usually scoring between 13–34, and detailed user stories scoring between 1–8 in the amount of effort to develop and complete them. You use the *planning poker* tool to compare and estimate any level of Agile user stories.

Note
The Project Management Institute's knowledge area for this tool is the scope management knowledge area. This tool is also associated with the integration knowledge area.

Tool Value
"Relative sizing" is an important concept in Agile and Scrum; everyone performing Agile estimating should understand and use it. It is also important that the team reaches consensus about the requirements and selects a "medium" value as a benchmark. When scoring other requirements, the team decides which user stories will be easier to develop and which will be more difficult, based on the benchmark comparison. Story points are another important concept because they determine the velocity of a team's performance throughout an Agile project. Velocity is simply the number of story points that an Agile development team completes in each sprint and is the basis for all estimation and forecasting for the Agile development team's future work performance.

The communication purposes for Agile estimating tools is to inform and instruct. Communication from Agile estimating tools can be posted on social media tools, such as Yammer, Socialcast, and Facebook (private group).

Introducing Agile relative sizing

The ideal sizing unit for estimating size requirements on your Agile project is determined by *relative sizing*. You use relative sizing to estimate the level of effort a user story will take to complete, relative to the other user stories you are completing. Relative sizing is an Agile estimating tool based on the relative effort needed to perform the work for a project requirement. It indicates how much effort a requirement will take to complete compared to the effort it will take to complete the other requirements. It's important to understand that relative sizing does not equal a specific unit of time. It's not measured in minutes, hours, days, or years. Relative sizing simply compares the effort required to complete each user story "relative" to the other user stories and determining which of those will take more or less time and effort. Performing this exercise helps provide a high-level estimate of the project difficulty throughout the project life cycle and, therefore, how much time and effort the project will take to complete. Relative sizing is a form of *affinity estimating*, which is a consensus-based technique that is useful to quickly and easily estimate the effort required for a large number of user stories. This technique can be very helpful when you are starting a new project and you need to estimate a large product backlog. A common method of relative sizing and affinity estimating is called "T-shirt" sizing. The product owner, Scrum master, and development team determine which themes, features, or epic user stories represent a "medium" size (relative to the size of the other requirements being reviewed), and then assign a corresponding "T-shirt" size to the remaining requirements, such as extra small (XS), small (S), medium (M), large (L), or extra-large (XL), and even double-extra-large (2XL). This allows the team to sort requirements by their level of effort, relative to each other.

Introducing Agile story points

Story points are the most common unit of measure when estimating the relative size of your Agile project's components, but the measurement should not represent a specific unit of time. Story points are also an Agile best practice and an effective unit of measure for the level of effort to complete user stories. So, how do story points work? First, your team selects a theme, feature, or user story from the product roadmap where they are fairly confident of the level of effort required to complete the particular user story. This may be a user story that team members have previous experience developing and have a fairly good idea how much time and effort it takes to complete. That user story becomes the team's benchmark.

The *Fibonacci sequence* tool is very effective at helping estimate user stories on your Agile project. The Fibonacci sequence is a number sequence you can use in Agile estimating that helps establish the value of story points. The mathematical equation for the Fibonacci sequence is $Fn = Fn-1 + Fn-2$, where "F" is the next number in the sequence and "n" represents the previous numbers in the sequence. In plain language, each number in the sequence is assigned by adding the previous two numbers. Therefore, the Fibonacci sequence starts with one, then one plus one equals two, then two plus one equals three, then three plus two equals five, and so on. For example, let's say your project team reaches a consensus that a medium-sized requirement is assigned the Fibonacci sequence number "55." You will then evaluate all of the other user stories on your project compared to your benchmark of 55 story points. If a specific user story takes about the same time and effort as your benchmark, then it too will be assigned 55 story points. Anything considered smaller than medium is scored as a 1, 2, 3, 5, 8, 13, 21, or 34. Anything larger than medium is scored as an 89, 144, and so on, based on the Fibonacci sequence.

Introducing Agile Planning Poker

Agile *planning poker* is a variation of the Wideband Delphi technique that makes the most accurate estimates as possible and helps you avoid the risk of having one influential or overly persuasive team member controlling the estimates. Team members make their estimates individually and without any undue influence from other team members. When using the planning poker technique, it is an Agile best practice and strongly recommended that you use story points as the unit of work effort.

Planning poker is a consensus-based technique, meaning everyone works together to come up with the most accurate estimate. An estimate calculated by the Agile project team is much more accurate than an individual team member's estimate. Each team member has a deck of planning poker cards with each Fibonacci sequence number printed on them. The product owner (who does not participate in the actual estimating) presents the user story backlog to the project team and answers questions. Each team member estimates the effort required to complete each user story. Team members show their planning poker cards at the same time for each user story. The team discusses the initial estimates, and then each team member votes to revise any estimates. This process continues until they reach a consensus on the story point value for each user story.

Introducing Agile team velocity

Velocity is simply the number of story points that can be completed within a specific Agile project timeframe, such as a sprint. It is the rate at which the development team can deliver value to your customer. In other words, velocity tells you how much work can be done in a given timeframe. This is the Agile team's measure of the throughput, per sprint, and the rate at which they deliver value. Velocity is one of the most common Agile metrics. The principal concept behind velocity is to help teams estimate how much work is required to complete a requirement in terms of user stories in a given time period, such as a sprint. It measures how quickly and how much work was performed during the specific sprint, compared to how quickly and how much work was performed in previous sprints. For the Agile development team, velocity is essential to iterative planning because it helps the team make up-front commitments with confidence, and most importantly, velocity is based on empirical data gathered from velocity performance in previous sprints. There is no formula to calculate velocity; however, after the first sprint is completed, you can use the computed result as a benchmark for subsequent sprints. After each sprint, the project team's velocity changes, requiring them to recalculate their average velocity at the end of each sprint to produce a more accurate estimate. Because velocity is calculated after each sprint, it becomes more accurate over time, typically stabilizing after three to six sprints, and eventually plateauing and becoming constant and predictable.

As you can probably tell by now, Agile project management uses quite a few estimating tools that are distinctly different than those used on traditional or Waterfall projects. Using relative sizing, story points, planning poker, and velocity helps ensure that Agile estimating is an integral part of the overall adaptive planning process for your Agile projects. Agile development teams continuously engage in re-estimation activities after each successive sprint to help them eventually determine the average velocity per sprint, which can be used to forecast future project work performance based on the empirical data from previous sprints.

Cross-Reference
See Chapter 16- Using Communication Tools in the Initiating Process to learn more about the agile estimating tools.

Introduction to the Agile User Story

The Agile *user story* captures, documents, and communicates your customer's wishes and needs for the project and product. Do not start work on the project until you have collected and documented some of your customer's requirements. In Agile project management, the user story is the main vehicle for capturing customer requirements. To create effective user stories, your customer works directly with the product owner. The product owner is an expert at writing user stories and will spend a considerable amount of time with your customer to train them how to create user stories. In Agile, your customer, not the product owner, is responsible for writing user stories, which represent their requirements. In traditional project management, however, a business analyst (or similar role) typically gathers customer requirements and creates the customer requirements document, and later, the work breakdown structure.

Note
The Project Management Institute's knowledge area for this tool is the scope management knowledge area. This tool is also associated with the integration knowledge area.

Tool Value
The Agile user story is a valuable tool that helps the customer and the product owner communicate and document the customer's wants and needs to the project team. Customer requirements are captured in plain language that is easily understood by the development team, enabling them to provide the specific functionality that the customer wants—nothing more and nothing less. The user story is a simple description of product requirements that identifies what must be accomplished.

Social Media Tools
The communication purposes for the Agile user story is to inform, inspire, and instruct. Communication from the Agile user story can be posted on social media tools, such as Yammer, Socialcast, and Facebook (private group).

Agile project management uses two types of user stories. At the beginning of the project, usually during the release planning meetings during the planning phase, very high-level requirements are captured in *epic user stories*. Epic user stories are the 50,000-foot view of the project and product requirements. As the project progresses through each sprint, release-level epic user stories are decomposed into smaller user stories that include project tasks you can assign to specific resources, time estimates, and cost estimates. The decomposed user stories represent the 10-foot view of the project requirements.

The product owner works with your customer to capture the customer requirements, written in the form of user stories. The user stories are given to the project team to help them understand the project and the product. User stories provide detailed descriptions of the project's business needs. The sum of the user stories includes the project scope, goals, and objectives. When the product owner has trained your customer how to write Agile user stories, they can work together to develop user stories that meet your customer's requirements. The product owner asks your customer specific questions to ensure that he or she fully understands your customer's requirements for a user story. This is usually an iterative process and continues until both parties agree that they have fully captured the user story requirements.

Figure 7.1 — User Story Template shows a user story template in a format used by most Agile project management teams. This template is generally an accepted tool for creating user stories for Agile projects.

Figure 7.1 — User Story Template

User Story (front)	
ID #:	
Title:	
As a <user>	
I want to <action>	
so that <benefit>	
Value =	**Priority =**
Estimate =	**Owner =**

Acceptance Criteria (back)	
When I do this:	**This happens:**

Planning the product vision statement

To get the most value from the time invested, the following roles should attend the release planning meeting to help create the epic user stories:

- **Customer or customer representative and end users.** For Agile projects, your customer writes epic user stories during the release planning meeting, so it is critical that your customer attends this meeting. If your customer is unable to meet with the project team, a customer representative can be appointed to create the user stories. If possible, we recommend that end users who will be using the final product attend because they often provide valuable insight and input into creating epic user stories.

- **Project manager.** Some organizations using the Agile methodology still assign a project manager to an Agile or Scrum project. Someone in this position is usually working on multiple projects, some of which may be Waterfall, some Agile, and some a combination of both—referred to as a "hybrid" project. The benefit of this person attending the release planning meeting is that he or she can implement the Agile process for strategic project planning in future Agile and hybrid projects.

- **Product owner.** The product owner facilitates the release planning meeting and must attend for it to be successful. The product owner ensures that the meeting output is logged in the proper format. Again, the product owner is an expert at creating user stories and may need to spend quite a bit of time with your customers to help them create user stories. This is especially true if your customer is new to Agile and has never written a user story.

- **Scrum Master.** The Scrum master has an in-depth understanding of the development team's needs and can help with the initial estimate of product scope and requirements during the release planning meeting.

Tip
Personas help facilitate writing user stories and identifying users who may eventually use the final product. A persona is a fictional character who is based on the expected user. Personas

include a name (first name and sometimes last name), a stock photo or drawing of the character, and a title, role, or job description of the character representing the typical user, such as "cashier" or "administrator." Personas provide the customer and product owner someone to visualize as they are creating user stories so that additional requirements are discovered, which otherwise may have been missed.

Planning a user story

During the release planning process when you prepare to create epic user stories, make sure that the product owner and the customer (and possibly the end user) are trained on how to write user stories. On an Agile project, we recommend that your customer get formal training for writing user stories by attending an accelerated seminar, such as Certified Scrum Master (CSM) and/or Certified Scrum Product Owner (CSPO), which go into specific details about writing effective user stories. These seminars give your customer and the product owner a head start when preparing to write epic user stories. The product owner works with your customer to write epic user stories until both parties agree that they are sufficient. Then, they create more detailed tasks to perform during the sprints for the upcoming release. The number of release planning meetings and the number of epic user stories that are created during these meetings depend on the project's size and complexity. When the epic user stories are ready for the upcoming release, the product owner and customer prioritize which epic user stories to decompose first, based on the highest value to your customer and/or the highest risk to the project. The epic user stories are added to the product backlog and the release backlog, which are repositories for the user stories, and represent the overall product and project requirements.

User stories capture the customer's product and project requirements for an Agile project. Therefore, it is crucial that the product owner and your customer are proficient at creating user stories for both the release level and the sprint level. Understanding the customer's specific requirements and creating appropriate user stories help ensure that your customer's end deliverable is what they need and gives them value to help minimize risk to their organization.

Cross-Reference
See Chapter 16 - Using Communication Tools in the Initiating Process to learn more about Agile user stories.

Introduction to the Agile User Story Backlog

Agile *user story backlogs* are documents, also called artifacts that are repositories for each level of requirements decomposition throughout an Agile project. The levels of requirements decomposition occurs in different stages and are closely linked to various types of Agile project planning that occurs throughout the project. What is Agile project planning? Agile project planning determines the required activities to complete a project within a particular timeframe, and then defines the stages and designates resources to accomplish those activities. Agile project planning embraces change from stakeholders throughout the course of the project. In fact, most Agile methodologies (including Scrum) assert the concept of taking a "just in time" approach to planning, which equates to not doing most of the planning at the front end of the project. Instead, most of the planning is deferred until later in the project where it can be done more collaboratively with the development team. Agile project planning is heavily based on customer involvement with the expectation that your customer will also play an active role in defining and managing the requirements as the project moves along through its life cycle. Ultimately, your customer should feel just as responsible for producing a successful result as the project team. Agile project success is directly related to how well a project is planned.

Note
The Project Management Institute's knowledge area for this tool is the scope management knowledge area. This tool is also associated with the integration knowledge area.

Tool Value
The value of Agile user story backlogs is based on the intrinsic value of the project's Agile user story as the basic tool that helps the customer and the product owner communicate and document the customer's wants and needs to the project team. The Agile user story is the one tool you use to document all of an Agile project's customer requirements. You implement the Agile user story backlog to organize, update, prioritize, and reprioritize Agile user stories throughout the project life cycle. The data you collect in the Agile user story backlogs measures the project team's performance in terms of completed work, as well as budget and schedule performance at the project-level, release-level, and sprint-level. This data also helps determine the development team's average velocity, which increases the accuracy of forecasting future project performance because the forecasts are based on empirical and historical data captured in the Agile user story backlogs.

Social Media Tools
The communication purposes for Agile user story backlogs are to inform, inspire, and instruct. Communication from Agile user story backlogs can be posted on social media tools, such as, Yammer, Socialcast, and Facebook (private group).

The first stage of Agile project planning is to create the *product vision statement*. The product owner creates the product vision statement during Agile strategy meetings. The product vision statement defines what your product is, how it will support your organization's strategic goals, who will use the product, and why they will use the product. This sets the foundation for all future Agile project requirements gathering. Next, and also during Agile strategy meetings, the product owner creates the *product roadmap* document. The product roadmap includes high-level product requirements and a flexible time frame for when those requirements need to be developed. Identifying product requirements and then prioritizing and providing rough estimates for developing those requirements allows the product owner to develop requirement themes and identify gaps in the requirements. In the next stage of Agile project planning, a release planning meeting is held where the product owner creates a *release plan* that identifies a high-level timetable for multiple releases of the product features. Each release serves as a goal around which the

Scrum team organizes their specific sprint activities to support each release. An Agile project may have many releases, each representing a major set of product features, based on the highest customer value and/or highest project risk.

Up to this point, the product owner's activities have progressively decomposed the requirements from a very high level to successively lower levels, resulting in the *product vision statement*, the *product roadmap,* and the *release plan*. Now, the product owner (with the Scrum master and development team's help) can start breaking down the requirements into user stories. There are also several planning phases to create initial user stories and decompose them to a level where they can be assigned specific resources, cost estimates, and time estimates to complete. Each successive phase results in the initial document creation, called *user story backlogs*, which are updated throughout the project life cycle. The other tools that are updated during this process consist of the *product backlog*, the *release backlog*, and the *sprint backlog*.

Introducing Agile product backlog

The Agile product backlog is the first Agile user story backlog that is created on an Agile project. After the product owner creates the product roadmap and the release plan, some high-level features will have been identified. These are the first entries in the product backlog. Even though these entries are still at the feature level, and may not have been decomposed yet at the epic user story level, it is recommended that you still enter the user stories in the product backlog at this time. The following list includes some important product backlog characteristics and suggestions for effectively using them on an Agile project.

- The product backlog is a prioritized features list that contains abbreviated descriptions of the product functionality. It also serves as a release plan and contains high-level customer requirements in the form of features. The features in the product backlog are written in user story format.

- The product owner logs the product roadmap user stories in the product backlog. The product owner prioritizes the user stories based upon certain criteria, such as which pose the highest risk, which offer the highest business value, which do the organization have the most control over, and which will be the easiest to implement and demonstrate.

- The product backlog identifies "what" will be developed and the order in which it should be developed. It is accessible and editable by anyone, but the product owner is ultimately responsible for updating (also called grooming) the product backlog.

- The product backlog contains rough estimates of business value and development effort. These estimates are usually represented in story points using the Fibonacci sequence. The product owner is responsible for the product backlog and each business value item. However, the development team determines the estimated effort to complete each product backlog user story and accompanying tasks.

- The product backlog should be visible to everyone, which aligns with Agile manifesto principles where collaboration and transparency are in the highest regard.

- The product backlog is the single source of requests and represents the entire requirements scope for an Agile project.

- Only keep a single version of the product backlog to prevent updating conflicts from multiple people.

Introduction to the Agile release backlog

The Agile release backlog is the second Agile user story backlog that you create for an Agile project and is a subset of the overall product backlog. As part of the release planning meeting, the product owner presents the initial product backlog that was created during the strategy meeting. The product backlog usually contains features and epic user stories, but may also contain detailed user stories. The user stories are presented with a solicitation for questions from the meeting attendees. It is important for you to pay particular attention during this time to the development team who is more versed on what is involved in user story development and could help you to create the release backlog if needed. At this point, a high-level estimate is assigned to each user story by using a method called relative sizing. After the initial user stories are identified and estimated at a high level using relative sizing estimation, you can determine the length of each sprint. Sprints can last anywhere between one week to four weeks, with four weeks being the absolute maximum—longer sprints pose greater risk to the product and project. You will need to create a release goal that describes the overall release goals and which features you expect to deliver at the end of the release, in support of an overall business objective for the product features. The release goal is based on business priorities, as well as on the speed and experience of the development team. At this point, the product owner takes the user stories that have been identified for the first release from the initial product backlog and adds them to the *release backlog*. The release backlog is a subset of the overall product backlog. These are the user stories you plan to develop and deliver as part of this release. The product owner polls each stakeholder attending the meeting to obtain a consensus on the specific user stories to develop and deliver as part of the release. This is sometimes difficult to achieve, depending on the number of stakeholders attending the meeting. If an impasse is reached, either a majority vote is reached or the product owner makes the final decision, since he or she represents your customer's voice. The product owner states his or her commitment to proceed with the release. This process is then repeated before each release during the overall Agile project. The following list includes some important release backlog characteristics and suggestions for effectively using them on an Agile project.

- A release backlog is a limited set of items that are derived from the product backlog and selected for a specific release.

- The items in the release backlog are focused on specific goals or objectives and adhere to a specific timeframe. This differs from its "parent," the product backlog, which contains the product "wish list" without concern for time.

- The items in the release backlog should be estimated in story points, which, along with the release burndown chart, give the Agile project team visibility into whether the release goal will be achieved as the release progresses.

- The development team's velocity during the release will provide a clearer picture for tracking progress and provides feedback about the sprint estimates during the release and helps to make decisions that pertain to the scope of the requirements.

- The release backlog is dynamic, but once a sprint has begun, the product owner cannot change the work that was selected for that sprint.

Introduction to the Agile sprint backlog

The Agile sprint backlog, a subset of the current release backlog, is the third Agile user story backlog that you create for an Agile project. At the beginning of each sprint, the Scrum team holds a sprint planning meeting to decompose each user story in the release backlog into specific tasks. During the sprint planning meeting, the development team commits to completing a set of user stories in the release backlog that are the highest priority. This commitment defines the specific user stories in the sprint backlog, which is a subset of the release backlog. The product owner works with the development team to create a sprint goal that represents a specific sprint objective that is usually a product component that can be demonstrated to your customer at the end of the sprint. This helps guide the user story selection in the sprint. This goal and the specific user stories are added to the sprint backlog. The product owner presents the stories that are being considered for this sprint to the development team. As the product owner presents each user story, the development team asks questions about the user story to get as much information as possible and to clarify the individual user story requirements. This helps him or her better estimate the level of effort and create the specific tasks that are necessary to complete each user story. After the user story question and answer session, story points are assigned to each user story, usually by using planning poker. The user stories and their corresponding estimates are updated in the sprint backlog, which is the official list for sprint planning and execution.

Now that all user stories have been clarified, estimated using story points, and logged into the sprint backlog, you need to determine the specific tasks that need to be performed to develop each user story. Development team members offer input into each task they believe should be performed for that specific user story. They will also offer estimates, in hours, for each task. Tasks included in the "definition of done" must also be included in the user story estimation hours. After the tasks are finalized and estimated for each user story, you can assign the tasks to development team members. Because the development team is self-organizing by nature, individual team members can select the tasks they would like to perform. The Scrum master will assign any remaining tasks after everyone has made their selections. At this point, the development team conducts a final workload review to determine the feasibility of the work being performed successfully in the sprint. Any user stories that cannot be 100% completed during the sprint are removed from the sprint backlog. At the end of the sprint planning meeting, the development team gives a verbal commitment to the product owner that all of their assigned tasks for each user story will be s completed successfully by the end of the sprint.

The following list includes some important characteristics of the sprint backlog and suggestions for effectively using them on an Agile project.

- The sprint backlog lists the work that the development team must complete during the current sprint. The development team creates the list by selecting user stories from the top of the release backlog until they have sufficient work to fill the sprint.

- The user stories in the sprint backlog should be estimated in story points, and these story points, with the creation of the sprint burndown chart, give the Agile project team visibility into whether the sprint goal will be achieved as the sprint progresses.

- The development team considers the velocity of its previous iterations (total story points of the user stories they completed in the previous sprint) when selecting the user stories to complete in the current sprint, and uses that number as a rule for determining how much work they can complete in the current sprint. If the development team has completed several sprints, they can use the average velocity of the previous sprints.

- The development team decomposes the user stories into tasks, which are usually between 4–16 hours of work. Having this level of detail enables the development team to understand exactly what work needs to be performed.

- The development team owns the sprint backlog; they are responsible for updating it on a daily basis throughout the sprint.

It's probably evident at this point that Agile user story backlogs are indispensable tools that are mandatory for the successful execution of any Agile project. They are the information repositories (user stories) for all Agile project requirements at every level of project planning, requirements decomposition, and project execution. By understanding Agile user story backlogs, their specific characteristics, and following the suggestions for their most effective use in terms of Agile best practices, you will help to ensure the success of your own Agile project.

Cross-Reference
See Chapter 16 - Using Communication Tools in the Initiating Process to learn more about the agile user story backlogs.

Introduction to the Business Case

The *business case* captures, documents, and communicates the purpose for starting the project. The business case is one of the first documents you create, and all projects should have a business case. The customer (not you) is responsible for creating a business case for the project. In some smaller projects, the project manager is responsible for creating it, but that is rare and not a best practice.

One of the goals for creating a business case is to convince the decision makers to go forward with the project. Without a business case, the proposed project lacks justification and purpose and may likely never get off the ground.

Note
The Project Management Institute's knowledge area for this tool is the scope management knowledge area. This tool is also associated with the integration knowledge area.

Tool Value
The business case document outlines the reasons, justifications, and problem statement for the proposed project. The project approver uses the information in this document to approve and proceed with the project.

Social Media Tools
The communication purposes for a business case are to inform and persuade. Communication from the business case can be posted on social media tools, such as Yammer, Socialcast, and Facebook (private group).

The business case and the benefits review plan document (covered in an earlier section) go hand and hand. Often, while your customer develops the business case, you are working with your project team and your customer to try to understand the benefits of the project. This is an ongoing project and everyone is learning the expected benefits along the way. While the business case is developing, so is the benefits' tracking information and the customer will store that particular information in the business review plan document.

Your customer updates the business case document during the initiation phase, and then reviews it at the end of every phase. If updates are needed, your customer makes them in the document. Regardless of the methodology you use, continually reviewing and updating the business case information is an important part of managing the project's benefits and keeping the business case as accurate as possible.

The business case must be well documented and completed thoroughly. Oftentimes, business case documents are incomplete or do not have all the required fields. Incomplete business case documents are ineffective communication tools and often provide little value. If the incomplete document is passed around, it can cause more harm than good to the project. You must ensure that the business case document is well written and useful by the decision makers and the project team. The business case is an important communication tool and something that you will want readily available. If there is an executive or a project sponsor who wants to review the business case document, that information should be easily accessible and available to them. Most project managers store the business case in the document control system for access by anyone who wants to review it.

Table 7.1 – Example of a Business Case Document Table of Contents shows a table of contents example for a business case document. The document contains all of the sections you need to capture and communicate the business case information. This example is generic enough to work for most industries, across most projects.

Table 7.1 – Example of a Business Case Document Table of Contents

#	Description
1	Introduction and Document Information
2	Executive Summary
3	Project Background
4	Current Problem Statement
5	Business Value Statements (Expected and Dis-Benefits)
6	Proposed Options
7	Proposed Project Solution
8	Proposed Costs
9	Proposed Resources
10	Proposed Time Frame
11	Major Risks
12	Document Sign-off & Approval

This is just one of the many examples of templates that are available to use on your project. Your project may need more sections. Some of the core sections in a business case document may differ depending on your company's standards or the approver's specific needs. Additions to the business case could include cost estimates, justifications, and so on. These extra sections must be researched and added to the project business case document so that you know the approver is getting the information they need to make a decision about the project going forward.

Planning to use a business case

When preparing a business case document, work with your customer representative or the individual who developed the document to ensure that it is complete. If you rush to get the document approved too quickly, you may end up updating it continually because the document doesn't include all of the information the approver needed to make a decision. Make sure the document is complete before sending it through the business case approval process.

During the startup phase, the business case document is important for scope management and helps you justify why the team is doing the project. The business case document helps in conversations where you need to justify the project's value.

Reporting from a business case

Usually, the customer representative, not the project manager creates the business case document for the project. It is the also the customer representative that communicates the business case to the project approvers and project team members so that everyone understands the goals and purpose of the project.

You do not regularly report from the business case document because it contains no project status information. It is not a status reporting tool; rather, it is valuable for communicating the purpose and justifying the case for doing the project.

During the project life cycle, you, the business representative, and the project team use the business case document as a reference guide to justify the project. The business case is created in document format and is stored as part of the document control system. That way, the document is available for interested project stakeholders.

Cross-Reference

See Chapter 16 - Using Communication Tools in the Initiating Process for additional information about how to create a business case document.

Introduction to the Customer Requirements

Customer requirements capture, document, and communicate your customer's wants and needs for the project. Projects should not start without some form of requirements document from your customer. The customer requirements document is the main repository for storing their requirements. There are many different customer requirements document formats, and each differs from industry to industry and from company to company. There are many different samples of customer requirements documents to choose from on the Internet. When you choose a customer requirements document, pick the template that will help you collect the requirements for your industry and project type. Even in the software world, for example, an application development project and a data warehouse project are two different types of projects; therefore, the methods in which you capture customer requirements would also be different.

Note
The Project Management Institute's knowledge area for customer requirements is the scope management area. This tool can be associated with the following knowledge areas: integration, time, cost, and stakeholder management.

Tool Value
Use the customer requirements to communicate and document to the project team the customer's wants and needs.

Social Media Tools
The communication purposes for customer requirements are to inform and instruct. Communication from customer requirements can be posted on social media tools, such as Yammer, Socialcast, and Facebook (private group).

No project can be successful without some form of documented customer requirements. The customer requirements document is the result of many communication sessions between your customer and the requirements analyst. Requirement gathering sessions can last for months, or years, depending on the complexity of the project. The time it takes to capture the customer's requirements is relatively short in comparison to the total duration of the project. Requirements gathering sessions occur during the project's planning phase when the project team is getting directions and your customers are deciding project goals.

The project requirements analyst captures and documents customer requirements and distributes them to the project team to help them understand the project. The customer requirements document includes detailed descriptions of the business needs, such as the scope, goals, and objectives for the project. One important concept to understand is that the customer requirements do not capture the technical areas of the project; those are captured in various technical documents. The customer requirements document contains only your customer's business needs. There is usually a series of back and forth discussions between the analyst and your customer to gather the customer requirements. This ensures that the analyst captures everything your customer wants for the project and that the two parties understand the project's scope. These discussions continue until all of the requirements are captured and approved in the document.

Table 7.2 — Example of a Customer Requirements Document Table of Contents shows a table of contents example for a customer requirements document. The document contains all of the sections that are required to capture and communicate the project's business needs. This table of contents example is generic and works for most industries and across most projects.

Table 7.2 — Example of a Customer Requirements Document Table of Contents

#	Description
1	Scope
2	Customer Needs (Goals and Objectives)
3	Policies and Procedures Definitions
4	Business Use Cases and Scenarios
5	Business Unit Interactions (if applicable)
6	Deployment Requirements
7	Output Reporting Requirements
8	Operational Requirements
9	Testing Requirements
10	User Documentation and Training Requirements
11	Requirements Priority Matrix
12	Assumptions, Risks, and Constraints
13	Participating Markets

This is just one of the many examples and templates that are available for your project. Additional sections may be needed for your specific project type. The project requirements analyst gathers and stores the customer requirements in a series of one or more documents. Although, customer requirements do not usually span more than one document, especially in software projects, but it depends on the project's size and complexity. It's confusing for people when you store customer requirements across multiple documents. Therefore, whoever creates the document is also responsible for ensuring that all documents are stored together and available to everyone. A document control system is perfect for storing multiple documents in a single location.

Capturing customer requirements is a special skill and difficult for most people to do. It takes many years for someone to master this skill, and even then, he or she may still struggle. Most project managers do not enjoy or feel comfortable capturing customer requirements—especially at a level that the project team needs to create the final product. Some project managers collect customer requirements, but most leave it to an expert who knows how to capture them properly and has the experience to do it. Usually, though, the requirements analyst captures project requirements. Requirements analysts specialize in this work and are trained and most qualified for the task. The requirements analyst communicates directly with your customer and is responsible for capturing and creating the customer requirements document.

A customer requirements document is a communication tool you use throughout the project life cycle. In the beginning of the project, the analyst collects and communicates the customer's requirements in the document. As the project progresses, team members reference the document to compare what they are building with what was originally requested. This document is especially important for scope changes and change requests. Scope changes include additions to the requirements originally captured in the document.

A change that is large enough to impact the project should go through the change control process. Some project managers don't require small change requests to go through the formal process as long as they don't impact the project. This is often a goodwill gesture and a smart political move for you. All large change requests go through the formal process. New functions or new reports are examples of change requests going through the formal change control process. You must define change requests as any additions to customer requirements after formal sign off and approval of the project. This makes the customer requirements document important and key to assessing and tracking project changes.

Capturing and collecting customer requirements are challenging tasks. In the following example, the first item in the list explains how to capture customer requirements.

- **Good customer requirements:** The customer wants a ten-story apartment building constructed in downtown Seattle on XX Main Street. **Assessment:** When the construction crew starts their work, they know exactly where to go and how big the building is going to be. When the team completes work on the fifth floor of the building, they know they have completed approximately half of the project.
- **Bad customer requirements:** The customer wants the team to build an apartment building in downtown Seattle. **Assessment:** The problem with this requirement is that the team has no idea how high to build it, or where to even start building it.

These are simple examples, but they show that you need to be specific when capturing customer requirements. If your customer does not clearly state the requirements, the project team will struggle. You play an important role in this process because you must be diligent in the requirements that you accept. You must constantly communicate to your customer the project's requirements to ensure that everyone agrees. Accepting incomplete requirements could have a negative effect on the project's schedule and budget—especially in the construction phase when your customer finds out that what the team is building is incomplete or worse, wrong. The project team might build one thing while your customer has something different in mind.

One skill you need is the ability to recognize when your customer requirements are complete, and if they are not complete, identifying what is missing. This skill enables you to go into projects with your eyes open and with less chance of problems. When you fully understand the project requirements, there is far less chance that you will run into requirements problems. This is because you know how to guide your project team to create the right product for your customer. This also allows you to be a valuable player in the requirements gathering process.

Planning to use customer requirements

During the planning process of a customer requirements document, your first and most important step is to ensure that you have a requirements analyst on the team. Without that resource, you and your team members will struggle if you do not know how to capture the requirements. Insist on hiring a resource who can capture your customer's requirements. When that person is on board, go over the customer requirements template. The goal of working together is to ensure that the template you use is acceptable for your project. Otherwise, you will need to change it or get a new version of it. You then ensure the customer is dedicated to working with the project requirements analyst to capture the requirements. Your customer must dedicate time and effort to provide project requirements or nothing can move forward, which wastes time and budget. When your customer commits to the time, set up requirement-gathering sessions and get started capturing the project requirements.

Note
Capturing customer requirements is critical to a successful project. Without this formal process, the project might be headed for disaster by not developing what the customer needs.

Reporting customer requirements

On large projects, a project requirements analyst usually creates the customer requirements document, not the project manager. When the requirements analyst finishes the document, he or she communicates the information. The analyst communicates the project requirements to you and your team so that everyone understands them. The project requirements analyst is the liaison between you and the project team throughout the project life cycle. The analyst who captured the original customer requirements is a great resource for the project team when they have questions and avoids randomizing the customer.

You don not report from the customer requirements document because it does not contain project status information. However, you do report the work progress defined in the customer requirements document. Use a status report to report progress against the customer's requirements defined in the document. For example, you report the progress of the various stages of the project, the scope completed, what is out of scope, and so on. The information in the status report is a direct reflection of the project work being completed.

The project requirements analyst creates the customer requirements document using a document format. The analyst should store your customer's requirements in the document control system so that the document is stored long-term, archived, and accessible by interested stakeholders.

Cross-Reference
See Chapter 16 - Using Communication Tools in the Initiating Process to learn more about creating and using customer requirements.

Introduction to the Design Specification Document

The *design specification document* describes the product's technical specifications. Every product has a design specification document that ranges from a scrap piece of paper to multiple, elaborate, computer-generated detailed documents. There is a good chance that your document will be somewhere between those two extremes. The design specification document contains enough information and specifics for the project team to create the product from the document directly. The design specification document includes design maps, design considerations, design methodology, and constraints. The analyst who creates the document is not limited to adding those areas only, though, they are common and found in most documents. You drive the document's development and use on every project. Having a project design specification document helps the design team and development team understand what they need to build for their customer.

Communicating the project's design specification document is challenging because it is a technical document that doesn't require everyone's approval. However, the people who create the document should also be part of the approval process. When the design specifications document is formally approved, the project team can start using the document. You must drive the communication and ensure the project team is receiving the documents, making comments on them, and approving or rejecting them where applicable.

Note
The Project Management Institute's knowledge area for this tool is the scope management area. The secondary areas that this tool could be associated with are risk and quality management.

Tool Value
The design specification document contains the detailed requirements to build a product.

Social Media Tools
The communication purposes for a design specifications document are to inform and instruct. Communication from the design specification document can be posted on social media tools, such as Yammer, Socialcast, and Facebook (private group).

Most industries use design specification documents, and software development projects have used these documents for years to record details about the project's design considerations. On software projects, for example, these documents describe screen layouts and report specifications and interface design. Without a design specification document, software developers would have to rely on their own opinions for screen and report designs. Additionally, making the design team completely responsible for screen or report layouts can be risky because they likely will not match your customer's expectations. The design specification document bridges the gap between your customer and the project team. In the construction industry, the architects and engineers create the design specification document for their customers.

Table 7.3 — Example of a Design Specifications Document Table of Contents shows an example of a table of contents for a design specification document. The document contains all of the sections that are required to capture and communicate the product design. This example is generic and works for most industries and across most projects.

Table 7.3 — Example of a Design Specifications Document Table of Contents

#	Description
1	Introduction
2	Project Overview
3	Project Scope and Purpose
4	Design Objectives
5	Design Constraints
6	Architecture • System • Server
7	System Design
8	Interfaces
9	Reporting
10	References

This is just one of the many examples and templates that are available to use on your project. Additional sections may be needed for your project. The process for using a design specification document starts with the design engineer or architect working with your customers to capture the product design details. For example, in a boat specification, a marine architect works with the boat designers and customers to decide how the boat will laid out—for example, location of bedrooms, bathroom, and galley. The designers document how the boat will be laid out in the design specification document. The designer continues until the boat specifications are fully documented in the document. Depending on the product you are making, the design specification capturing process can take months, or years, to complete. It can be a simple and quick process if you use an existing product's design specification. Reusing a design specification on an existing product is common and a great way to save time and costs.

To develop a design specifications document, the analyst goes through a formal requirements gathering process that includes many rounds of interviews, capturing requirements, and eventually compiling those requirements into a design specification document. The process is often long and involves many customers, developers, and team members providing feedback about the overall design. It is important for the analyst to work directly with your customers and ensure they are familiar with the design requirements. So much so, that they know what the final product would look like before the team starts to build anything. That is a perfect scenario, because if they don't like what they see, they can make changes immediately. This, in the end, will save time and money.

Before you start to gather design requirements, it is important to use the correct design specification template for your project type. The template is a great starting place for most projects because it saves time and frustration about where to start. Capturing a system's technical design can be complex, so starting with a template makes things much easier.

The design specification process can be challenging because it is difficult to capture all of the details around the final product's design and match those to your customer's expectations. Sometimes, customers have expectations that do not match what the analyst captured, which can be frustrating for everyone. Another challenge that analysts face when creating the design specifications document is capturing the information in a format your customers understand and the developers can use to build the product—keeping both groups happy can be difficult during this process. Sometimes, overcoming the different needs of the two parties is hard, and other times it is impossible. It becomes a big project issue when your customers are asking for something that the development team has no idea how to produce. If the development team can't build your customer's requirements, put the project on temporary hold. Then, your customers and project team can focus on creating a workable solution for the product design. This needs to happen quickly with as little impact to the project as possible. Fortunately, this does not happen very often, and project managers successfully make their way through these project scenarios when they occur.

Cross-Reference
See earlier in this chapter for more information about the customer requirements document tool. The customer requirements document contains the customer's specific design requirements and needs updating or referencing when design issues arise.

Tip
Design specifications span all industries. Ensure that the project team always focuses on the design specifications. The success of your project depends on it!

Planning to use a design specification document

When planning to use a design specification document, make sure there is an analyst assigned to the project. This is not work you will want to tackle on your own. Once you've hired an analyst, the work of collecting the design requirements from your customer begins. You play a big role in this process by supporting the analyst in getting the work done and rallying the team to come together and document the design requirements. This requires a time commitment from your customer. Your customer must be willing to dedicate the time that the analyst requires to collect the design requirements, which can slow down the project's progress. When your customers dedicate their time to the analyst, the analyst isn't guessing about design items or researching answers for questions from the project team, they are working hand in hand with the customers solving problems and getting answers immediately. Without your customer's time commitment, the analyst will have difficulty completing the document in a timely manner. The analyst could also run into situations where he or she is not capturing the information correctly the first time. This slows down the project and causes frustrations for everyone. After performing these planning steps, you will have completed the necessary steps to prepare adequately for the use of this tool.

Note
The two documents that capture customer requirements are the design specification document and the customer requirements document. The customer requirements document feeds the design specification document with specific scope and design information.

Reporting from the design specification document

The engineer or design analyst is responsible for creating the design specification document. This is a technical document, which limits who can produce it. The analyst leverages the work of the technical staff to help them complete the document from a design perspective.

The analyst, architect, or engineer who is creating the design specification document is also responsible for communicating it to everyone working on the project. You can help with the process, but it is up to the document creator to share the information with whomever they see fit. You are responsible for getting sign-off on the design specification document from the team and your customer. When you get formal approval for the document, you have permission to move forward with the project.

You are not required to regularly report from the design specification document. This document does not contain project status information, so there is nothing to report. The only time you would report from the document is when you are requesting approval and sign-off, which occurs during the project's final sign-off and approval stage of the design phase. All project deliverables need formal approval and signoff. The design specification document is expected to be signed off and approved before you move the project forward. The most popular format for the design specification is a document format. Sometimes, the analyst creates the material in a presentation tool for communicating the information to leadership and executives. The design specification document is stored as part of the document control system. This allows for the document to be stored long-term and anyone interested in it can easily access it.

Cross-Reference
See Chapter 18 - Using Communication Tools to Plan and Develop Project Deliverables to learn more about how to use a design specification document.

Introduction to the Executive Summary

The *executive summary* document provides an executive-level summary of the business case. Top executives are far too busy to wade through project documents and spend time understanding all of the details of the business case document. Instead, you and your customer produce an executive summary document so that a busy executive can consume and understand the project information quickly. The executive summary document contains project highlights and the important areas. However, since it is for executives, it also needs to be in a format that includes high-level details. This can be difficult to do; executives have a large variety of likes and dislikes when it comes to reviewing information. The executive summary is an important communication tool and used heavily in the project environment. The effectiveness of this communication tool is specifically built for busy executives and catered to the communication style they are most comfortable with. For example, every executive summary document has its own format and includes particular sections for capturing project information, but because you are working with executives, you will want to format the document to their specific learning style. For example, if you have an executive who is text oriented, you will likely add text-heavy data to the document because that is how he or she prefers to consume the information. In that case, you are directly creating the document in the style the executive wants to see the data and communicating to them in his or her preferred format. Because the executive summary document is closely associated with the business case document, the decisions the executive makes from the executive summary are generally the same as those he or she will make with the business case document.

The information in the document comes from the business customer or representative, so you likely will not create the executive summary document. On smaller projects, though, you may be responsible for creating the executive summary document. However, even in cases where you create the document, you will rely heavily on the business customer for information because, in the end, you are building the product for them, so they need to provide the information.

Note
The Project Management Institute's knowledge area for this tool is the integration area. The secondary area that this tool can be associated with is scope.

Tool Value
The executive summary document provides a brief and more condensed view of the business case document. This document specifically caters to the needs of the executive who will be using it.

Social Media Tools
The communication purpose for an executive summary document is to inform. Communication from this document can be posted on social media tools, such as Yammer, Socialcast, and Facebook (private group).

The executive summary document is a great communication tool for any project manager because it provides the details of the business case in a condensed and easy to consume format that is easily shared. You can offer the executive summary in place of the full business case for anyone who wants to quickly get some information about the project.

Executives love the executive summary document because it is one of the only documents that is developed just for them. It saves an executive's time by learning about project details from the executive summary document instead of sorting through too many documents to figure out what the project is all about.

Table 7.4 — Example of an Executive Summary Document's Table of Contents shows a table of contents example for an executive summary document. The document contains all of the sections that you need to communicate project information. This example is generic and can work for most industries and across most projects. This is one document where the document creator meets with executives to ensure that he or she is catering the information to the executives' learning and communication styles, as noted above. If your executive likes charts and graphs, the executive summary should include charts and graphs. Knowing your audience and communicating in a manner they like is an important part of communicating effectively with them.

Table 7.4 — Example of an Executive Summary Document's Table of Contents

#	Description
1	Introduction
2	Project Background
3	Current Problem Statement
4	Proposed Options
5	Proposed Costs
6	Proposed Timeframes

This is just one of the many examples and templates that are available for your project. Additional sections may be added for your specific project type. As you can see, this document is much smaller and more condensed with project information while still covering the important project areas. The document is not supposed to exactly match the business case document, but it will include some of the same information. That is one of the advantages of using a smaller, more condensed document; the executives can skim through the information to get what they need without having to spend time wading through a large document.

Planning to use an executive summary

When planning and preparing to use an executive summary, you and a user must consider the areas that the executive summary will be used. An executive summary helps you get approval for the project to move forward. Similar to approving the business case document, executives review and approve the executive summary document.

The business representative who created the executive summary and business case documents will use both documents to get project approval. Some executives prefer the smaller, more condensed executive summary document to review project information, and some executives like to review the full business case document. It is best practice to know your audience's preferred communication style.

Reporting from the executive summary

A user or business representative creates and communicates the executive summary. That individual works in the business area and leads creating the document. Reporting the executive summary officially occurs once, during the project approval meeting. In this meeting, your customers, executives, leadership, and project team gather to review the document, ask questions, and collect extra facts they need to make a go/no-go decision.

You do not have to report weekly from the executive summary document because it does not contain project status information. The executive summary document is stored as part of the document control system. Storing it in the document control system allows for long-term storage and is easily available to project stakeholders.

Cross-Reference

See Chapter 16 - Using Communication Tools in the Initiating Process to learn more about how to use the executive summary document.

Introduction to the Feasibility Study

The *feasibility study* identifies whether the project idea is viable for the company. Senior management or business owners decide whether to advance the project idea into a project. Most industries use feasibility studies to communicate the idea to senior management and owners of the proposed projects. A feasibility study documents whether the proposed project is viable, cost beneficial, and aligned with company goals. Feasibility studies range from small to complex and depend on the industry and project type. All projects should have a feasibility study that documents the proposed ideas and suggestions for the project. An example of a feasibility study is developing a new cancer-fighting drug. The feasibility study would include sections to create the drug, its side-effects, cost analysis, risk analysis, and research that supports combining those into a single drug.

Note
The Project Management Institute's knowledge area for this tool is the scope management area. The secondary associated knowledge area for this tool is integration.

Tool Value
A feasibility study lowers the risk of companies spending unnecessary time and money on a project that has minimal or no long-term benefits.

Social Media Tools
The communication purpose for the feasibility study is to inform. Communication from the feasibility study can be posted on social media tools, such as Yammer, Socialcast, and Facebook (private group).

A feasibility study is a great communication tool for any project manager. This section provides details for those who are deciding whether a project is worth continuing. No other document will do that on a project. This study can save a company time and money on an initiative that may not benefit the organization. As project manager, you are rarely involved in creating a feasibility study. This document is usually created by the customer because its sole purpose is project justification. However, you do use the document to assess the study's details and as a reference in delivering and controlling the project. For example, during project execution, if the feasibility study showed positive test results to justify the project, you will want to recreate those tests to prove those results. Ideally, you are looking for the same test scenarios and the results to match. The feasibility study, in this case, acts as reference for you and your project team. They use the feasibility study document to check and prove what the project team is testing by using the same parameters outlined in the study. You can also use the feasibility study to learn about and understand the decisions that led to the project's approval. The feasibility study helps you and your team understand why the owner approved the project, which is helpful when working on the project. This allows you to manage the project more efficiently while also being aligned with your customer or owner.

Table 7.5 — Example of Feasibility Study Tables of Contents shows a table of contents example for a feasibility study document. This document provides enough detail in each section so that the feasibility review board has enough information to make a go/no-go decision.

Table 7.5 — Example of Feasibility Study Tables of Contents

#	Description
1	Executive Summary
2	Background Information
3	Description of Current Situation/Problem
4	Description of Proposed Idea
5	Project Timelines
6	Feasibility Review Board
7	Go/No-Go Decision

The communication process for the feasibility study is two-fold. The first step would be your customer who created the document for the project is to run the idea and supportive documentation through the feasibility board for approval. When the feasibility board approves the idea and the project, the second step is your customers provides the documentation to you and your project team to review.

Feasibility studies come in all shapes and sizes and span across all industries. Some examples of feasibility studies include:

- **Upgrading a software/hardware system.** A company could create a feasibility study to develop a new system that would align various work groups. This could be a new system, such as a payroll system, an HR morale system, or a financial system.
- **Designing a new aircraft.** An aerospace company could launch a feasibility study that documents a new airplane design. This would include costs, lifespan, manufacturing time, market need, and safety considerations.
- **Planning to buy new software.** A company could conduct a feasibility study that documents a new software package. This study documents the software benefits, return on investment (ROI), costs, and the user impact. It could also include a make or buy decision.
- **Constructing a new building.** A development company could start a feasibility study that proposes a new building design. This would include costs, construction considerations, environmental concerns, and construction time frames.

There are many types of feasibility studies in the industry. Every industry, such as software, construction, and research has their own feasibility study template. The templates include different categories, such as business, government, technical, and so on. Here are some examples of feasibility studies used today:

- **Schedule feasibility study.** Analyzes how long it will take a project or process to complete and what the go/no-go decision point will be.
- **Organizational feasibility study.** Analyzes the impact on cost and resources if the company decides to reorganize their current resource base.
- **Legal feasibility study.** Analyzes whether it is worth pursuing a particular litigation.
- **Technical feasibility study.** Analyzes whether a technical idea will work within the current environment.

- **Cultural feasibility study.** Analyzes whether offshore teams and onshore teams can communicate and effectively deliver a project.
- **Construction feasibility study.** Analyzes whether it is cost effective to construct a building, based on height and location.
- **Environmental feasibility study.** Analyzes whether environmental conditions at a particular location are suitable.

Note

Projects need justification before they can be approved. Feasibility studies provide details and information that decision makers need to approve or reject a project.

Planning to use a feasibility study

In planning and preparing to use the feasibility study tool, make sure you read and understand the document, which may include reviewing the document with the requester or originator. In these discussions, you may want a team lead or two with you so everyone is clear about why the requestor is proposing the project. You should also include a technical resource in these discussions to answer technical questions that the requestor may have about the project. After performing these steps, you and your team members have adequately prepared for using the feasibility study on the project.

Reporting from the feasibility study

The project customers or owners are responsible for creating and reporting the feasibility study. The analyst who is working in the business, or for a particular owner, leads the document creation. Reporting from the feasibility study officially occurs once during the formal feasibility study review meeting. In this meeting, your customers, upper management, and staff gather to review the document, ask questions, communicate, and collect the extra facts they need to make a go/no-go decision. Upper management sits on the feasibility study review board and makes the final project approval decision.

You do not report weekly from the feasibility study because it does not contain status information. Your customer or requestor creates the feasibility study in a document format, and then stores it as part of the document control system. Storing the feasibility study in the document control system ensures it is stored long-term, archived, and always accessible.

Cross-Reference

See Chapter 16 - Using Communication Tools in the Initiating Process to learn more about how to create and a feasibility study.

Introduction to the System Requirements Document

The *system requirements document* captures the technical requirements for a project. The functional analyst creates the document mainly for software development projects. A software project contains technical information that must be described and documented. The purpose of the system requirements document is to map customer requests for a software system in technical terms that development teams can use to build the solution. Therefore, the functional analyst should only create the system requirements document after the customer requirements are approved. Creating the document before your customer locks on what they want could leave the system requirements document in a state of flux, which is never good for any project.

Note
The Project Management Institute's knowledge area for this tool is the scope management area. The secondary knowledge area associated with this tool is integration.

Tool Value
The value of a system requirements document is to document and describe, in detail, the technical areas of the project's solution for designers, developers, and the test team.

Social Media Tools
The communication purposes for a system requirements document are to inform and instruct. Communication from the document can be posted on social media tools, such as Yammer, Socialcast, and Facebook (private group).

The business requirements document feeds information to the system requirements document. Both documents work together to capture and report project information. On most projects, there is a one-to-one mapping table between technical requirements and business requirements. For example, when a customer needs a weekly report that shows the budget forecast, the technical requirement would entail creating a weekly budget forecast report. The mapping table ensures that every business requirement has a matching technical response. One of the most important tasks the functional analyst can perform when creating this document is to map the customer's business requests with the technical solutions. Without that mapping, you don't know whether you have technically provided a solution for each customer requirement.

Note
Some companies have different names for this document, such as "system requirements" or "technical requirements."

As project manager, you communicate the project's system requirements document for a couple of different reasons. First, you want to make sure that your customers see how the requests will be addressed technically, and second, you want the project team to understand what they need to build. The system requirements document meets both needs. You should communicate the same information to your customers and team members to ensure alignment. Usually, you communicate the information in separate meetings, which is a small price to pay to make sure everyone is on the same page and accepts the technical solution.

When presenting the system requirements document to your customers, focus on high-level and summary-level information only; skip the details. Your customers want summary-level information in the system requirements document, not all of the technical details; otherwise, the document becomes too complex. Some customers may want details, but that's rare. Providing details in the system requirements document is important to the project team because they are responsible for creating the product, so they need to know what to build.

During the project's design and development phases, project team members constantly refer to the system requirements document to understand the product's technical areas and to figure out what they have to build. Another reason for using the document is to map the technical requirements to your customer's business requirements and be able to speak to them. If the project team doesn't have an answer, they need access to the system requirements document. Occasionally, you may need to schedule meetings so that multiple team members can review the document. Or, you may have to email or add the document to the document control system to ensure that people can access it.

Table 7.6 — Example of System Requirements Table of Contents shows a table of contents template for a system requirements document. This template covers many areas of the project's technical details and is a comprehensive document for the project team to work from.

Table 7.6 — Example of System Requirements Table of Contents

#	Description
1	Document References
2	Sign-off Section
3	Document Conventions
4	Business Procedure Mapping
4.1	Business Requirements Identification
4.2	Business Process Analysis
4.3	Initial System Requirements Summary
5	System Description
5.1	System Overview
5.2	System Objectives
5.3	System Process Specifications
5.4	System Constraints
5.5	System Risk/Impacts/Assumptions
5.6	System Interfaces
6	User Interface Designs
7	Source System Model
8	Functional Processes
9	Functional Process Model
10	System Operational Requirements
11	System Deployment Requirements
12	Context Diagram
13	Conversion/Migration Needs
14	Data Communication Requirements
15	Inter-Project Dependencies
16	Testing Requirements

#	Description
17	Report Requirements

You should ensure team signoff on the system requirements document for all projects. Occasionally, your customer should also approve the document, but this is for your customer and you to decide. Teams in information technology have debated for years about needing customer approval. Some project managers want customers to sign off on the document so they are accountable for their own requirements. It is a best practice to get customer signoff, but it's up to you to decide.

The mapping between business requirements and system requirements is important because of the close ties that these documents have to each other. A missed business requirement in the system requirements document can lead to missed functionality, which could impact the final product. When you map each requirement (business and system), your customer is confident that nothing will be missed and they will see how the requirements will end up in the final product.

The following example shows a business requirement mapped to a system requirement:

- **Business requirement:** Capture customer contact information within a software application.
- **System requirement:** Develop a screen for users to enter personal contact information. The form should be web enabled and include relevant security features. The screen should be red and have the ability to add, delete, and edit entries.

While developing the system requirements document, the project team needs to understand if the customer is looking for minimum product requirements or recommended product requirements. This is important information for the team to know because you don't want them wasting time and effort capturing unnecessary information.

The following are definitions of minimum requirements and recommended requirements for a typical software or systems project:

- **Minimum requirements:** Documents the lowest requirements to make the software function. The minimum requirements are guidelines, not rules, to give the users the best possible experience with the application.
- **Recommended requirements:** Includes suggested hardware system requirements that the user should have for the software to run in an ideal state. When users have the recommended hardware to run the application, they should achieve the best possible software performance.

Planning to use a system requirements document

In planning and preparing to use the system requirements document, make sure there is a functional analyst on the team who is assigned to create the document. This is not an easy skill to find. Functional analysts are skilled, technical staff, and good ones are hard to find. The functional analyst is required to know the subject area well and be able to communicate effectively with your customer. The functional analyst should be working closely with the requirements analyst because their project deliverables are so closely linked. You and the functional analyst need to communicate while he or she is creating the system requirements document so that both of you can answer questions and support each other during this process. In most projects, the functional analyst and the requirements analyst are different people, so you have to keep them coordinated and working together on the project. If you and the functional analyst do not collaborate on the system requirements document, you could run into problems; this team dynamic is an important part of the project's success. The system requirements document is not considered finished

163

until all of the business requirements are mapped to the technical solutions—or at least addressed in the document. The system requirements document can start, but not finish, until the business requirements are complete and approved by the customer. If the system requirements are started and finished before your customer approves the business requirements, you may be in for some major rework on the project. After performing these steps, you would have adequately prepared for using the system requirements document on your project.

Finally, in planning and using the system requirements document, the functional analyst ensures that the project team has the right skills to build the product. Having the correct resources in place to build what your customer is expecting is critical to the success of the project.

Note
System requirements are critical to capture so that the team understands the project's technical areas.

Reporting from a system requirements document

The functional analyst assigned to the project develops the system requirements document. The functional analyst works with developers and designers to create the document so they understand the project and are not surprised by the document when they receive it. The system requirements document stores technical information about the project, not status information, so it is not reported on. There is a one-time approval and sign-off meeting with the project team when first creating the system requirements document. The approval and sign-off meeting enables the project team to approve the document, which allows the project to move to the next phase.

At the beginning of the project, after the functional analyst gets approval on the system requirements document, there is no reason to continue reporting from it. The system requirements document contains more reference and technical information about the project than any other document, but it does not contain status information. The system requirements document is stored in the document control system for long-term storage. Storing it in the document control system allows easy access by project stakeholders.

Cross-Reference
See Chapter 18 - Using Communication Tools to Plan and Develop Project Deliverables to learn more about how to create and use a system requirements document.

Introduction to the Work Breakdown Structure

The *work breakdown structure* (WBS) ensures that the project includes and identifies all of the work items needed to complete the project successfully, without adding any unnecessary work elements. The WBS breaks down the work into manageable work packages. You use the WBS to define the total project scope. It can include the description, cost, time, risks, quality, resources, and scope for each activity (work package). Within each work package, the WBS helps customers and team members identify the project deliverables.

Note
The Project Management Institute's knowledge area for the WBS is the scope management area. The scope management area is where the project team creates the WBS; however, everyone uses it throughout project.

Tool Value
The main value of the WBS is to identify and define all of the project work. It also displays the work in a graphic presentation, which is easy to read and understand.

Social Media Tools
The communication purpose for the WBS is to inform. Communication from the WBS can be posted on social media tools, such as Yammer, Socialcast, and Facebook (private group).

The WBS communicates all of the work on the project. It is a single repository that displays all of the information for every project deliverable. Having a single source saves time and effort from searching for project information, which potentially saves cost. The top level of a WBS shows the organization of work elements into larger categories of work deliverables. Every element in the WBS has a parent and child relationship that is easily identifiable.

Figure 7.2 — Project Level and Top Level of a WBS shows the top level (the project) and the major level (the phases). This is the first stage in developing and communicating a WBS. A "project management" element of the WBS should always appear on the left of the major project elements (Phase 1 in this example). In this project management element, project managers add their specific project management work items. The separate project management element ensures that you not only get credit for your project management activities, but running the project is included in the project's scope. Many project managers do not understand this and therefore don't create this separate element in their projects. That's a mistake, and a quick way of not getting the right exposure for all the work you do on a project. By having the project management element on its own, your project management deliverables can also be separated from the main project deliverables, which is valuable. The timeframe for producing project management deliverables can be outside the project timing so you don't end up pushing out the overall project finish date. For example, the time it takes to produce the project schedule does not have to push out the project finish date.

Figure 7.2 — Project Level and Top Level of a WBS

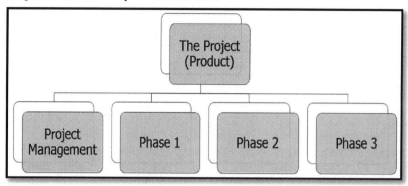

The WBS is helpful to all project team members. It graphically displays all of the project work items in a single chart. Each team member and stakeholder can refer to the WBS to understand what the project will deliver. It is also valuable to team members to help them understand what their work items are for the project.

The WBS provides details about each project activity, which may not be documented anywhere else in the project documentation. By developing a WBS dictionary, you and your team members identify work activities that belong to any part (category) of the project. The WBS dictionary contains all of the information about a work package (task). You communicate the WBS to the stakeholders and project team throughout the project life cycle. You will work continually to ensure that project activities complete on time and on budget. When project change requests occur, the new work items (tasks) become additions to the WBS.

The WBS should be a large part of defining, executing, and managing project changes. The WBS is the foundation for every project, regardless of size.

The following list identifies some of the benefits for using a WBS on your project. The WBS does the following:

- Identifies all project work
- Includes a project breakdown into specific work packages
- Includes a mechanism to roll-up items to a parent level
- Helps identify all project deliverables
- Supports activity estimates in time and cost

When developing a WBS, consider the following points:

- It is a systematic breakdown of the project objectives in a hierarchical format
- The project level is the project objective and the deliverable assigned to it
- The next level defines the major segments of the planned objective and deliverables
- Upper and mid-levels define a decomposition of the major segments into components
- Lower levels define the integration work to create each lower-level product
- By definition, the lowest level is the work package
- Each WBS element should represent a single tangible deliverable

- Each element should represent an aggregation of all subordinate WBS elements listed immediately below it
- Each subordinate WBS element must belong to only one single parent WBS element
- The deliverables should be logically decomposed to the level that represents how they will be produced
- Deliverables must be unique and distinct from their peers, and decomposed to the level of detail needed to plan and manage the work to obtain or create them
- Define deliverables clearly to eliminate duplication of effort within WBS elements, across organizations, or between individuals responsible for completing the work
- Deliverables should be limited in size and definition for effective control, but not so small as to make cost of control excessive, and not so large as to make them unmanageable or the risk unacceptable

The work package

A *work package* represents a work activity (task). Combining all of the work packages defines all of the work on the project. Only defined work falls in a work package. The work package description should always include a verb and a noun (for example, create the drawing, erect the steel, design module 6, and so on). Each work package communicates a deliverable to the project. A work package is the bottom level of the WBS.

Cross-Reference
For a detailed description of the work package tool, see Chapter 12 - Defining Communication Tools to Manage Project Communications.

WBS dictionary

A WBS dictionary is the document that defines and describes all of the work performed in each WBS element. The following list describes WBS dictionary characteristics:

- Sufficiently describes the project work, but does not need to be lengthy
- Includes forms or templates are helpful to all project stakeholders
- Uses formats at different WBS levels
- Contains enough description in each WBS element to produce a comprehensive statement of work
- Addresses all of the work that is scheduled to be performed
- Defines the entire project's scope

Usually, the project team works on a single project only. They may work on more than one project at different times. Each single project defines the project at the top level of the WBS. The next level down (major level) identifies the type of breakout the project will have. The major level starts the main categories of a project. Below this level, the subcategories start, and then are broken down into more detail. For example, the major level could be broken down by location, resources, phase, system, subcontractor, or by module. The bottom level is the work package.

WBS functional levels

When you develop a WBS, there are many levels of summary and detail elements. Below the top level, you can have many varying levels under each one of the elements. You could have four levels under one element and seven levels under another element. There are four *distinct* levels of a WBS. The top level is the project level. The next level is the major level, which defines all of the major areas of the project, such as project management, phase, and module. All levels below the major level, except the work package level, are considered mid-level and are parents of the level below them. The bottom level is the work package level that lists project deliverables. The level definitions are as follows:

- Project level: Charter and project scope

- Major level: Project management, components, assemblies, subprojects, or phases

- **Mid-level:** Subassemblies
- **Bottom level:** Work package (tasks or activities)

WBS in a project management office environment

When you work in a Project Management Office (PMO) environment, you work with multiple projects. A PMO oversees managing the company's or organization's projects. The PMO group is responsible for the coordination, support, and policies of the company's projects. In most PMOs, the reporting is the summary of the projects at the program level. WBS's in a PMO environment roll up to the summary level for reporting to senior management.

Figure 7.3 — Example of a Program WBS with Three Projects at the Top Level shows a sample of a PMO's WBS with the program at the project/program level and projects at the top level. Below the top (project) level in this example are various phases.

Figure 7.3 — Example of a Program WBS with Three Projects at the Top Level

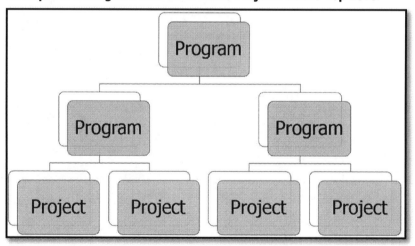

In the early stage of a project, it may be feasible to develop only a two- or three-level WBS. This is because the project details may not be available and there is not enough information to go any deeper. As the project planning process advances into the project definition phase, work details become clearer. The subdivisions of the WBS elements are developed at lower levels. These final sub elements, the lowest level of work packages, are the detailed descriptions of the work performed on the project. The product of this decomposition process is the completed WBS.

Figure 7.4 — Example of a WBS Integrated with the Planning Process shows an example where the WBS integrates into the scope planning process. It is important to note that scope definition development and the WBS development occur at the same time. As you learn more about the scope, you can apply that information to the WBS. The WBS will then help develop the scope. They work hand in hand.

Figure 7.4 — Example of a WBS Integrated with the Planning Process

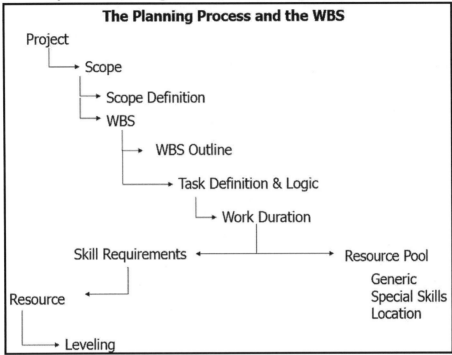

Figure 7.5 — Example of Work Packages in the Logic Network Diagram shows a sample of a WBS and the *work packages* that create the activities for a logic network diagram tool. Note the logic network diagram uses only the work packages, the bottom level of the WBS. The project schedule uses only the work packages to decide the start and finish dates for each activity that creates the project schedule. For example: *Work Package* "Design B1" in the WBS becomes *activity* "Design B1" in the logic network diagram.

Figure 7.5 — Example of Work Packages in the Logic Network Diagram

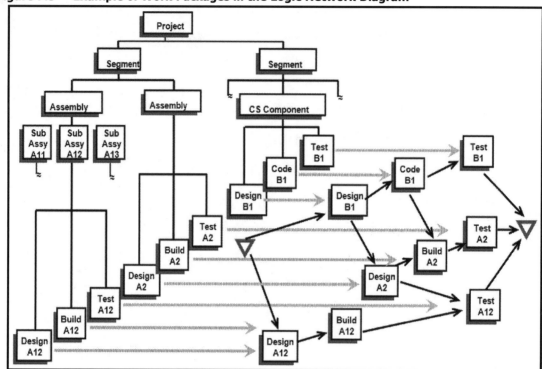

As you create the scope of your project, more detail is developed. These details become available to the WBS, and then are broken down to lower levels. In turn, the WBS supports developing the scope detail. If a team member starts creating or identifying work that is not in scope, it is important to remove those activities from the project. There should be no work included in a project that is not in the scope of work. If you do that extra work, you are adding value to the project that was not called for, and you are doing it for free. The owner will love it and you will not be happy because it takes unplanned time and budget away from the project.

Planning to use a WBS

Make sure the project team and stakeholders participate in WBS planning because the WBS is all encompassing in identifying and defining all of the project work. If possible, include the functional managers in the planning sessions too. Plan a short training class for those who have never used a WBS.

One best practice when working with the WBS is to set up some rules. These rules can include the maximum time (duration) or maximum cost a work package will incur, such as the work package duration lasting no more than one reporting cycle. Another rule could be that the cost is no more than a fixed amount and has a maximum amount of labor hours assigned to it.

Another best practice, as noted earlier, is to make sure that one of the elements on the second level is project management. This branch defines all of the project deliverables assigned to you.

Reporting from a WBS

The WBS is an important communication tool because, at one time or another, everyone who is working on the project will need information from the WBS because it describes all of the project work. Therefore, the

WBS must be in an area where everyone can access it. WBS charts can become quite large, especially horizontally. Because of this, you often will dedicate an entire wall to display the WBS information.

Another way to report the WBS is through the WBS dictionary. The WBS dictionary is stored near the WBS chart and is accessible within the document control system. The dictionary includes more details to supplement the WBS. These two tools support one another.

Tip
A WBS is one of the most important tools, if not the most important tool, on the project.

Figure 7.5 — Example of WBS with Four Levels represents a four-level WBS chart. This is a typical WBS where the top levels represent team leaders and the mid-levels represent senior staff representatives. The bottom level, in this example, shows the actual workers in each subarea of the project. Remember, the mid-levels can be many levels deep. The WBS identifies the level and the position that need reporting. For example, team leaders report from their top-level position, so there will be three reports. If a detail report is required, the team members at the mid-level (or possibly the bottom level) will produce the report. You will report (weekly status reports, budget report, performance report, and so on) from the project levels.

Figure 7.5 — Example of WBS with Four Levels

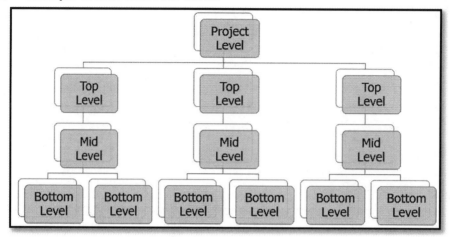

Because the WBS is on a wall displayed in the project office, it is updated only when the project work changes, which will become less frequent as the project matures. Change orders will most likely change the WBS because they add work, which adds work packages. You update the WBS on demand, only when it is not part of a regular periodic reporting cycle.

Cross-Reference

See Chapter 18 - Using Communication Tools to Plan and Develop Project Deliverables to learn more about how to create and use the WBS tool.

Summary

In summary, the tools described in the scope management knowledge area are specific to supporting project managers, team members, and customers in managing and controlling project scope. As you know, managing project scope is important and something not to be taken lightly by any project manager or the chance of project failure is high. Therefore, project managers and team members need to monitor and control scope management closely throughout the project life cycle. Scope management and control can be one of the quickest areas to get away from the project if not closely monitored.

This chapter explains tools such as the benefits review plan, business case, feasibility study, scope definition document, functional specifications, system requirements document, and the work breakdown structure. Each tool focuses on controlling the project's scope area. With these tools, project managers or team members are able to better control the project activities and drive the project team toward successful project completion.

Chapter 8

Communication Tools That Manage Project Time

IN THIS CHAPTER

- ◆ Introduction to the Baseline schedule
- ◆ Introduction to the Gantt chart
- ◆ Introduction to the Logic Network diagram
- ◆ Introduction to the Project schedule

The time management knowledge area consists of tasks that project managers perform to effectively manage a project's time. Time management is one of the top three areas (scope and budget being the other two) where project managers must be skillful to be successful in their role. Project customers (those who receive the finished product) do not want to hear about project delays or that the team missed a key milestone. Project managers must be effective communicators so as not to damage the customer relationship and time reporting is an important part of project reporting for any project manager.

Some projects are deadline-driven because they have an absolute end date that cannot slide. Coordinating the release of an operating system that will be on millions of desktops around the world is an example of a deadline-driven project. Because this software release is deadline-driven, the project manager's focus is on managing the project schedule as top priority. He won't focus as much on project's cost or scope, which is monitored by the executives and the leadership team. Cost and scope are important, but not as important as the schedule. In other words, money is no object, but hitting the date and meeting millions of people's expectations is when they will get the software is the ultimate priority for the project.

In this chapter, we explore project communications tools that you can use in the time management area. We present tools that you can use to manage activities that are specific to time spent on the project. The tools in this chapter will help you effectively communicate your project's time and schedule components, which will help you work more effectively with your customer.

Introduction to the Baseline Schedule

The purpose of the *baseline schedule* tool is to set up the first (original) project schedule. It is important that you create the baseline schedule before any work begins on the project. The baseline schedule is the original project schedule before the project team begins working on the project. Your customer usually approves the project's baseline schedule. For a project manager, the value of a baseline schedule is to track and report the project team's performance as work progresses. You can show executives and the project team how the project is progressing compared to the original baseline forecast. Reporting variances between the baseline schedule and the current schedule is called *performance reporting*, which is important in project management. You are responsible for communicating schedule variances to your customers and executives. You can use the baseline schedule to compare different project areas, such as the project's original schedule, costs, and resource assignments. Viewing the differences between the baseline schedule and the current progress is simple. The current schedule shows schedule slips and delays adjacent to the original baseline dates for each project task. When reviewing the project schedule, you can see which dates have changed at the task level. You can easily communicate project slips to your customer by using the baseline schedule tool. Without a baseline schedule, you and your customer would have a difficult time understanding where the project is slipping and causing delays. Using a baseline schedule is the best method to track and record current schedule slips.

Note
The Project Management Institute's knowledge area for the baseline schedule is the time management area. The secondary area for this tool is scope.

Tool Value
A baseline schedule lets you compare original project data to the current data. Over time, this project information will show trend analysis and variance analysis.

Social Media Tools
The communication purpose for a baseline schedule is to inform. Communication from the baseline schedule can be posted on social media tools, such as Yammer, Socialcast, and Facebook (private group).

The baseline schedule provides a simple comparison between two project schedules (the original and the current) so you can see whether the project is still on track or needs attention. You and the project team can use the baseline schedule throughout the project to communicate project schedule status and regularly compare the two schedules to help prevent project delays. The baseline schedule also uses cost data to track overage and insufficiencies. The baseline schedule communicates positive information if the project is hitting scheduled dates (no slips) and negative information if the project is not tracking to the original schedule (slips). In either case, the baseline schedule is valuable because it helps your customer and the project team communicate project schedule information to help keep the project on track and on budget. If you decide not to use a baseline schedule, you miss the opportunity to use a valuable communication tool that helps manage a project more effectively. Without the baseline schedule, it is more difficult to see where project delays and overruns occurred at the task level. Without a baseline schedule, you lose the ability to effectively communicate with your customer about project schedule delays and cost variances. It is much more difficult to show your customer the delays without a graphic representation of the slippages.

Note
In the project schedule examples, we used dates in the future to minimize any publishing changes. The schedules dated in the future should not impact the examples.

Figure 8.1 — Example of a Project Schedule and Baseline Schedule shows a project schedule and baseline schedule in a project scheduling tool. In this example, the project's original start date is December 26, 2019; however, it actually started one week late, on January 2, 2019. The original duration for Task 1 was three days, but the actual duration was five business days. Task 5, the last task of the project, is now tracking to finish eight days late.

Figure 8.1 — Example of a Project Schedule and Baseline Schedule

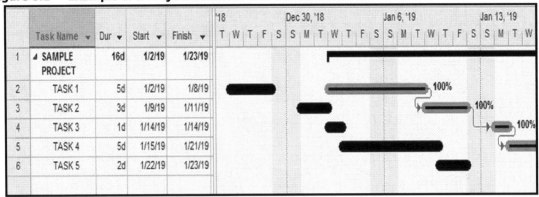

Tip

A baseline schedule is necessary to calculate performance measurements for your project.

When you record task work and create the baseline schedule with that work included, you are not setting up the baseline schedule correctly. When you try to perform performance reporting and run a schedule comparison between the baseline schedule and the current schedule, the results will be wrong. This is because the reported actuals (start and finish dates) are different from the original plan. For example, if you start the project one week late, and then create a baseline, all of the dates on your plan will represent that one-week slide, which is incorrect and throws off performance reporting throughout the project. Remember, for the most accurate reporting, no work can be performed on the project before you create the baseline schedule.

To capture project progress at different times during the project, you can create multiple versions of the baseline schedule. For example, at the start of the project you could create a baseline schedule, and then as the project progresses, you could create a new version of the baseline schedule at the beginning of each major phase. As the project progresses, you could then compare the new baseline schedule to the current schedule and quickly determine how well the project is moving forward. By creating baseline schedules at the beginning of each phase, you can compare the progress of one phase to the progress of another phase. Many project managers keep multiple copies of baseline schedules to view comparisons throughout the project.

The baseline schedule provides comparison data that you need to analyze project performance by using the *earned value technique*. This technique provides the performance s-curve report, schedule performance index, and cost performance index. You can use this information to analyze the rate at which the work is progressing and decide what to improve on the project based on the rate of progress. If the project is running behind, then corrective actions can be taken.

Tip

Always create a baseline schedule even if you don't think you need one, because you will in the future!

Planning to use a baseline schedule

When planning a baseline schedule, you must first complete and get approval on the project schedule with no progress on any of the activities. Next, you work with your customer to decide when to take baseline snapshots. By working with your customer to collect performance information, you are collecting your customers' reporting requirements. You can then determine whether your customer wants only one baseline (the original schedule with no progress reported) or a baseline recorded at the beginning of each month, or at the beginning of each phase. This is important because you take baseline snapshots in the scheduling tool, so you need to know your customers' expectations ahead of time. Remember, you can't go back after taking a baseline snapshot of your project schedule. After finding out the customers' requirements, you have adequately planned the project's baseline schedule.

Reporting from a baseline schedule

You are responsible for creating and reporting from the baseline schedule throughout the project. Reporting occurs at various times during the project, such as major project events, delivery date slips, or any other major project milestones.

You might, for example, use a weekly baseline schedule to compare work performed during a particular week with the baseline for that same week to see if the project is progressing as planned. A weekly reporting cadence provides customers and management with a constant checkpoint to see how well the project is progressing. You create the baseline schedule within a project-scheduling tool. Usually, you store the project files outside the project-scheduling tool and in the document control system for long-term archiving.

Cross-Reference
See Chapter 18 - Using Communication Tools to Plan and Develop Project Deliverables to learn more about how to create and use the baseline schedule tool.

Introduction to the Gantt chart

The *Gantt chart* communicates the project's activities to your customers, stakeholders, and team members. It is one of the most widely used tools in a project manager's toolbox and is valuable in communicating a wealth of project information. At a single glance, a Gantt chart helps you decide and communicate project status to anyone. You use the Gantt chart throughout the project life cycle to show project tasks, start and finish dates, task and project costs, resource assignments, and dependencies.

One of the most valuable uses of a Gantt chart is the "what if" scenario you can perform on your project. You can adjust project task dates, costs, or resource reassignments to see the various results for your project based on the different scenarios. Adjusting any of these data values can change the project dramatically, which gives you good insight into how those changes will look like without affecting the project. A Gantt chart lets you change, and change back, data values with little or no effort. There are few tools that can react "on the fly" to adjusted project data to immediately show you the possible impact. Just imagine the impact to your project schedule if a design task that was originally planned for 5 days took 30 days! A Gantt chart shows graphic and tabular information on a single page format.

Note
The Project Management Institute's knowledge area for a Gantt chart is the time management area. The secondary areas that this tool is associated with are scope, cost, human resources, communication, and risk.

Tool Value
A Gantt chart lets you display project information in a simple graphic and tabular format. Your customers, team members, and management will find this tool helpful when delivering and presenting project information.

Social Media Tools
The communication purposes for the Gantt chart are to inform and instruct. Communication from the Gantt chart can be posted on social media tools, such as Yammer, Socialcast, and Facebook (private group).

 Figure 8.2 — Example of a Gantt Chart shows an example Gantt chart. Gantt charts are easy to customize. You can add and delete items and move and size project columns however you choose. When you communicate project information using the Gantt chart, you don't need to report on extra columns of data that are irrelevant or do not provide value On the other hand, you can display cost fields, resource fields, or any other field within the tool. The choices are almost unlimited, sometimes leaving you with the challenge of which fields to exclude.

Figure 8.2 — Example of a Gantt Chart

	Task Name	Duration	Start	Finish	'18	Jan 6, '19
1	Sample Project	10 days	Wed 1/2/19	Tue 1/15/19		
2	Task 1	3 days	Wed 1/2/19	Fri 1/4/19		
3	Task 2	3 days	Mon 1/7/19	Wed 1/9/19		
4	Task 3	4 days	Thu 1/10/19	Tue 1/15/19		

In the example, the arrows in the graph view show you the sequence (order) of activities and the directions and connecting points of those arrows. In this example, Task 1 connects to Task 2, which connects to Task 3. This is a simple example, but one that effectively displays and communicates the project's task relationships. When creating a project schedule, project managers often miss these logical relationships between tasks. Usually, project managers create the project schedule by using the tabular view instead of the graphic view. This also happens when project managers are trying to troubleshoot issues with dates aligning correctly. They struggle to get the software-produced end date to match the required end date because they are using the tool's tabular view instead of the graphic view. It is far more difficult to see the problems when viewing a list of activities in the tabular view instead of looking at them in a bar graph. If you have problems with project dates, make sure the logical relationships between tasks are correct. Using the Gantt chart's graphic view shows valuable project information and relationships between tasks. It also enables you to work in a bar graph environment to move project dates around.

Project managers often use the Gantt chart to communicate with customers and team members. Customers often like to see the project's Gantt chart weekly to track the project's progress. However, your customer does not have to wait until the end of the week for a project report; instead, they can get this information on demand. If you store the project schedule in a document control system or a project scheduling tool, your customers have unlimited access to the project schedule. Knowing your customers have access to the schedule forces you to keep it up to date.

Usually, you should expect to report the Gantt chart formally once a week to your project team and your customers, but timing sometimes depends on the project's size and duration. For a project that spans multiple years, you may report monthly instead of weekly. The exact timing is something you and your customer decide for every project. On most projects, though, stakeholders and customers expect the Gantt chart (report) weekly once you begin that cadence with them. Your customer will also look forward to seeing project performance reports, which show what has changed and what has progressed since the last time you sent it.

A Gantt chart provides many advantages to you. You can use it to report cost and schedule data concurrently on the same chart. It's helpful to see tabular information on the left side of the chart and bar graph information on the right. Many project scheduling tools are set up this way. There are only a few tools, such as a tabular report and a spreadsheet report that can similarly report cost and schedules together. Another advantage of the Gantt chart is the ability to communicate the schedule in a bar graph showing bars for each project task over a timescale. Using the bar graph view, you can meet with customers to easily review project details and time lines.

A Gantt chart can also be a cost report, a schedule report, or a combination of both. The data in these charts includes work activities, cost data, resource assignments, time lines, and percent complete, to name a few. Choosing which columns of project information to communicate is unlimited within the scheduling tool. On most projects, you decide what information to communicate and what information not to expose to your customer.

The most popular project management scheduling packages include Gantt charts. The Gantt chart is a specific view that you select within the tool as you would any other view. Many project scheduling software packages, such as Microsoft Project® and Viewpath® include Gantt charts. For project managers who work for a company that uses the Earned Value technique, the Gantt chart can present earned value information.

Cross-Reference
For more earned value information, see Chapter 9 - Communication Tools That Manage Project Costs for more information.

Planning to use a Gantt chart

In planning to use a Gantt chart, you must first decide which fields and columns of data you want to use. To prepare, meet with your customer to decide what they want captured on the chart and how often they want it reported. Often, companies set standards for which columns and fields they want to use. In some case, you have limited choices about what you can choose to report using the Gantt chart. If a company is using an enterprise project server environment, the project server administrators may lock down the project's Gantt chart fields and only make a standard set available. Usually, you and your customer can choose the fields you want to use based on what makes the most sense for the project. Other activities you perform when preparing to use a Gantt chart include, identifying resources, time lines, and external dependencies.

Reporting from a Gantt chart

Usually, you are responsible for creating and reporting from the project's Gantt chart. The project information on the report will vary from project to project, depending on your customer's needs.

The following Gantt chart reports are popular for most projects:

- **Cost chart:** This report displays budgeted costs and actual costs.
- **Earned value chart:** This report displays cost and schedule performance indexes and variances.
- **Time chart:** This report displays tasks based on their scheduled start and end dates.
- **Labor hours chart:** This report displays planned and actual labor hours, over time.

It is easy to create any of these reports, but first you need to store some background information in the schedule before you display it on the Gantt chart. For example, entering relevant costs, time, and resource information into the scheduling tool makes creating these types of reports easy. Without that information, the reports would be difficult to produce.

Figure 8.3 — A More Robust Example of a Gantt Chart shows a more robust Gantt chart than that in Figure 8.2 — Example of a Gantt Chart. **Figure 8.3** includes resource names; the Gantt chart in **Figure 8.2** does not, although, both are from the same project.

Figure 8.3 — A More Robust Example of a Gantt Chart

	Task Name	Dur	Start	Finish	c 30, '18	Jan 13, '19	Jan 27, '19
					T S W	S T M	F T
1	SAMPLE PROJECT	18d	Wed 1/2/19	Fri 1/25/19			
2	TASK 1	3d	Wed 1/2/19	Fri 1/4/19	John		
3	TASK 2	3d	Tue 1/15/19	Thu 1/17/19		Bob	
4	TASK 3	1d	Fri 1/18/19	Fri 1/18/19		John,Bob	
5	TASK 4	5d	Tue 1/15/19	Wed 1/23/19		Linda	
6	TASK 5	2d	Thu 1/24/19	Fri 1/25/19		Fred	

Figure 8.4 — A Sample Gantt Chart for a Book-Publishing Project displays the roles assigned to the project and the associated costs assigned for each team member. The first line (line 1) in **Figure 8.4** displays a summary activity for the project. The summary line shows the project information rolled up (summarized) from the five detailed tasks associated with it. These tasks are connected (network logic), which provides the overall cost and time allocations for the project. In this example, the project duration is 18 days.

In **Figure 8.4**, project information includes durations, start and finish dates, and resource assignments. Your customer may be overwhelmed with all the data on the Gantt chart, so work with your customer to ensure they are getting the information they need to make project decisions. Do not simply provide information you need, focus on your customer's needs for showing data. Present the Gantt chart in a way that provides your customers the information they need without getting lost in all of the project details. For example, removing some of the columns can be a powerful way to communicate necessary information without overloading your customer with all of the data on the chart.

Figure 8.4 — A Sample Gantt Chart for a Book-Publishing Project

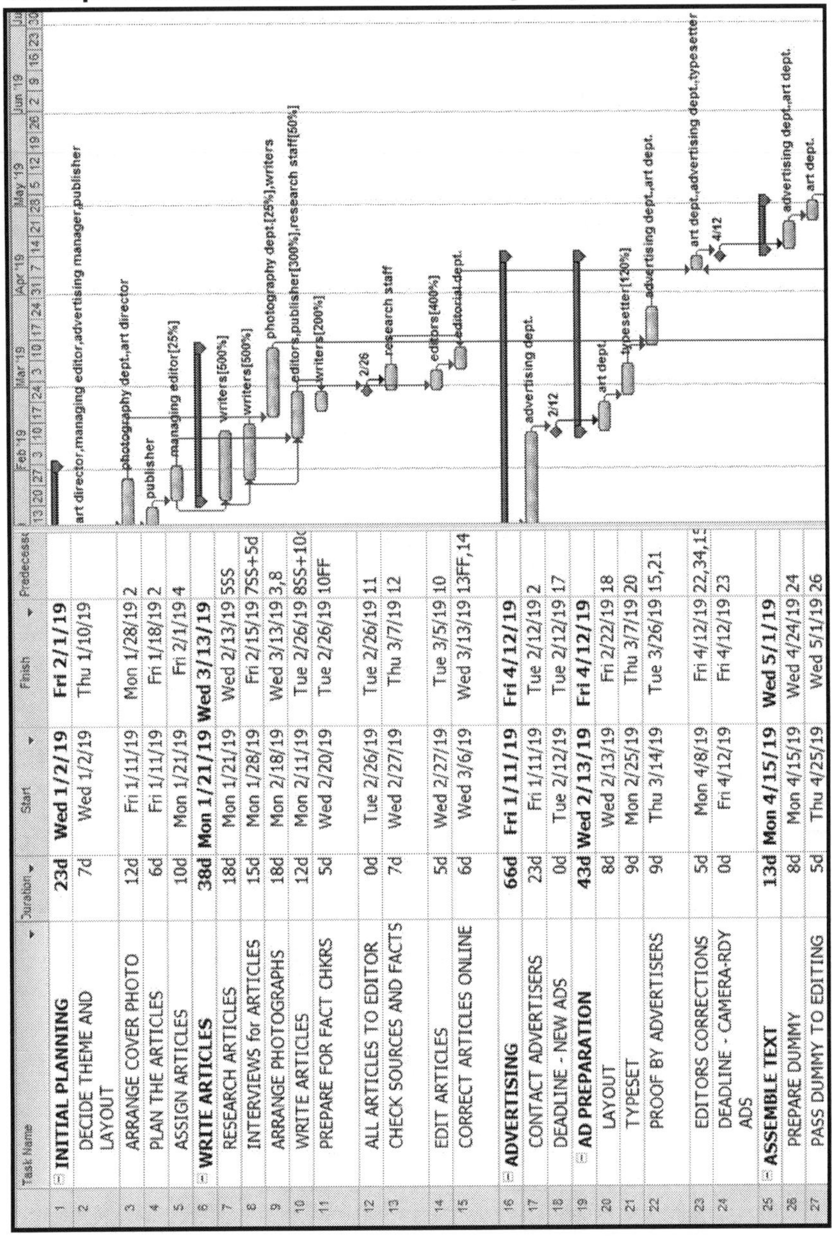

Most project managers use Gantt charts daily to manage and control projects. When the project schedule is up to date and accurate, those same project managers will use the Gantt chart as a communication tool for their customers. Team members, customers, management, or anyone else wanting detailed project information use the Gantt chart to view the project data they need.

You report from the Gantt chart weekly because of the valuable project information it contains. There are different formats for reporting Gantt charts, such as electronic and paper format. The Gantt chart lives in project-scheduling software. You will need to manually copy and store a weekly version of the project schedule in the document control system for long-term storage and archiving purposes.

Cross-Reference

See Chapter 22 - Using Communication Tools in Executing and Controlling Process to Report Project Information to learn more about how to create and use a Gantt chart.

Introduction to the Logic Network Diagram

A *logic network diagram* communicates predecessor and successor relationships for project activities. The diagram also shows the logical relationships between project activities. Project managers and project planners use logic network diagrams as visual aids to communicate and ensure the relationships between the project tasks are correct before finishing the project schedule. The diagram helps you determine the correct order for your project tasks. Medium to large projects use a logic network diagram because they often have complex task relationships. A diagram tool helps you select and logically order the tasks into a sequence that makes sense for the project. Occasionally, it is difficult to explain how project tasks relate to one another without using a diagram or a picture. When the project is so complex, you can use the logic network diagram to communicate the information. You also use the logic network diagram when the project goes awry or major logic changes occur. In these cases, the logic network diagram helps you re-plan your project. You and your team members can start with the existing diagram and re-order the existing tasks.

Note
The Project Management Institute's knowledge area for a logic network diagram is the time management area. The secondary area that this tool is associated with is scope.

Tool Value
Logic network diagrams allow for easy understanding and viewing of project tasks and their logical relationships to each other in a diagram.

Social Media Tools
The communication purpose for the logic network diagram is to inform. Communication from the logic network diagram can be posted on social media tools, such as Yammer, Socialcast, and Facebook (private group).

The logic network diagram communicates clearly and concisely the logical relationships between project tasks and activities. Using a project schedule's tabular view does not clearly show project tasks and does not lay out the tasks in a format that is easy to follow or understand. The logic network diagram also displays the project's critical path. Having critical path information mapped on a diagram early in the project will help you and your team members understand where to focus their attention to ensure a successful project.

The logic network diagram shows missing activities or relationships on the project schedule. When you review project tasks and lay them out across a logic network diagram, you can determine if there are major portions that have not yet been added to the project schedule. Project customers will be able to identify specific project areas assigned to them or whether you listed all of the tasks in their area. It is a great self-checking tool and only a handful of other tools can offer the same benefits; however, only the logic network diagram tool offers it graphically.

Figure 8.5 — Example of a Logic Network Diagram represents a typical logic network diagram. In this example, the project has six main activities, two milestones, and Start and Finish boxes. The diagram communicates the logical relationship between the activities. They are Start to A, A to B, B to C, C to Finish on one path, and the second path includes Start to D, D to E, and so on. An important relationship to watch on the logic network diagram is the D to C relationship, which shows that C cannot start until B and D are complete. From a project perspective, this is a finish-to-start relationship and something you should watch closely.

Figure 8.5 — Example of a Logic Network Diagram

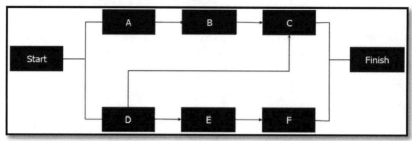

On complex projects, activity interdependencies can be challenging to understand. In **Figure 8.5**, the relationships between A to B, B to C, and so on are easy to understand and, therefore, easy to communicate. Interdependencies are the relationships between two project tasks. The logical relationships show the order in which to carry out the project tasks. This logic network diagram also shows the information that passes from activity to activity. For example, a pharmaceutical company performing drug research, per government rules, must pass several phases before being introduced to the public. In a logic network diagram, you can see the different phases of the research cycle and the relationship lines drawn between the phases that are required before the drug moves to the next phase. This example would show a single row in **Figure 8.5** (Start to A, B, and C, to Finish) where the letters A, B, C represent the actual phases of the drug research process.

The logic network diagram comes in two basic formats. The first is a pure logic diagram showing activities as boxes and the relationships between those activities noted by arrows. The second format is the timescale diagram that displays the activities as bars, similar to a Gantt chart.

Pure logic diagram

The pure logic diagram shown in **Figure 8.5** highlights the order and relationships between project activities. This chart is easy to follow because you can clearly see that the activities are represented by boxes, and the relationships are represented by the lines between the boxes. The boxes represent work activities, for example, in a software project you might have: Design, Dev, Test. The main benefit of a pure logic diagram is that it helps debug project logic. If there are complexities in the logic between the different tasks, the pure logic diagram must represent those logic paths. For example, the D to C relationship in **Figure 8.5** portrays complexity in the logic. On a pure logic diagram, activities follow one after the other.

Time scale diagram

The logic network diagram is a time-scaled chart. **Figure 8.9** shows a drawing that displays a time-scaled logic diagram drawn with bars instead of boxes. The bars are drawn on the chart in varying lengths because the bar lengths represent each project activity's duration. On a time scale diagram, the length of the bar is proportional to the duration of the activity and scaled to the project calendar. To understand how long a particular activity might be, you would scale it against the project calendar. Time scale diagrams look similar to the graphic portion of a Gantt chart, but many activities can be on a single row.

Figure 8.6 — Example of a Basic Network Diagram shows three activities and the logical relationships between those activities. The project planner decides how to create the links between the activities. **Figure 8.6** shows that a project planner to link the tasks had to indicate the relationships between Task A and Task B. In this example, the project planner has indicated that ID 1 is the predecessor, to ID 2 (Task B). Then, the project planner indicates ID 2 as the successor. This process is the same between Task B and Task C. The project planner would complete this process for the whole project.

Figure 8.6 — Example of a Basic Logic Network Diagram

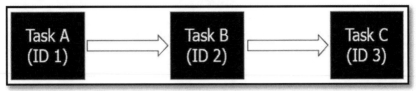

Now that you see how easy it is to link project activities together, the next step is to understand the four ways of defining those relationships (links). The following list explains the four types of relationships between activities:

- **Finish to start:** One activity must finish before the next activity can start (this is the default relationship between activities).
- **Start to start:** When one activity starts, the succeeding activity can also start.
- **Finish to finish:** When one activity finishes, the succeeding activity can finish.
- **Start to finish:** When one activity starts, the succeeding activity should finish.

Figure 8.7 — Example of Logic Network Diagram Task Dependencies graphically displays the four types of task dependencies in a logic network diagram. These are important for the project planner or project manager to note when creating and communicating the diagram in case questions come up about the relationships between tasks. The fifth dependency noted in **Figure 8.7** is "None" and is not considered a task dependency, but it is worth noting because "None" is a valid entry in logic network diagrams.

Figure 8.7 — Example of Logic Network Diagram Task Dependencies

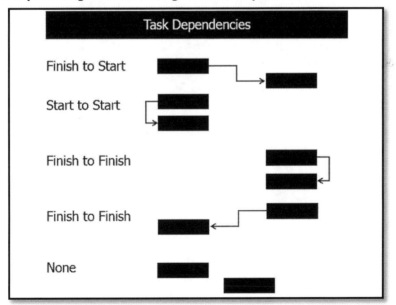

Cross-Reference

See Chapter 19 - Using Communication Tools for Project Reporting during the Planning Process for further details about creating these relationships for your project.

Planning to use a logic network diagram

In planning to use a logic network diagram, make sure you learn how to create one using your tool of choice. Typical project-scheduling tools include a logic network diagram view, but there are standalone tools available as well. In preparing to use this tool, you must add project tasks to the project schedule as a starting point for the diagram. It is a good idea to start with the project's current activities, and then lay them out on a logic network diagram. When the project tasks are loaded, you or the project planner can reorganize the tasks at will. After all of the tasks are organized in logical order, you can use the tool for your project.

There are times when you must draw the project activities by using pen and paper, even at a high-level, to get the process started. This is a good short-term solution to get the team thinking about project logic, but long-term, the information needs to be entered in a formal tool.

Reporting from a logic network diagram

You can report from the logic network diagrams throughout the project life cycle. Two methods for reporting the logic network diagram include a hand-drawn method (rarely used) and software. Usually software products, such as Microsoft Project, will draw a pure logic network diagram for the project, but not a timescale diagram. Using software ensures the diagrams are easy to follow and edit. You and your team members usually capture logic network diagrams on whiteboards or on paper. When you finish those discussions, you should immediately use software to clean up the diagrams and make them readable. When updating and moving project activities in a project scheduling tool, the software automatically changes the project schedule. When using a manual method, such as pen and paper, you lose the ability to easily move tasks around, discover the impact of those moves, and communicate that impact to your customers. Instead, you should complete the diagram in a software tool first, move the tasks around, and then figure out the impacts of those moves.

Figure 8.8 — Example of a Logic Network Diagram represents a time-scaled logic network diagram. This diagram clearly shows the critical path in darker bars: A, D, G, M, N, and R along the bottom of the chart. You can see on the chart that the bars are different lengths. The charts are different because these lengths represent the duration for each activity. Please note that activity "I" is a lighter color because it has more float than the other activities. A color diagram usually displays the critical path in red.

Cross-Reference
See Chapter 19 - Using Communication Tools for Project Reporting during the Planning Process for more information on this tool and definitions around lead and lag.

Figure 8.8 — Example of a Logic Network Diagram

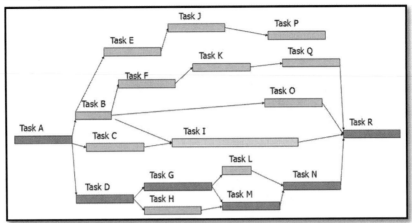

Figure 8.9 — A Sample Logic Network Diagram for a Book-Publishing Project represents a time-scaled logic diagram for a book-publishing project. It is a small portion of a total project and is a real-life example. The numbers at each end of the bar represent the start and finish dates, relative to the calendar above it. The numbers on the chart that are beneath each bar, roughly in the center, represent the duration of the activity. The number that is shown inside the bar is the activity's ID.

Figure 8.9 — Sample Logic Network Diagram for a Book-Publishing Project

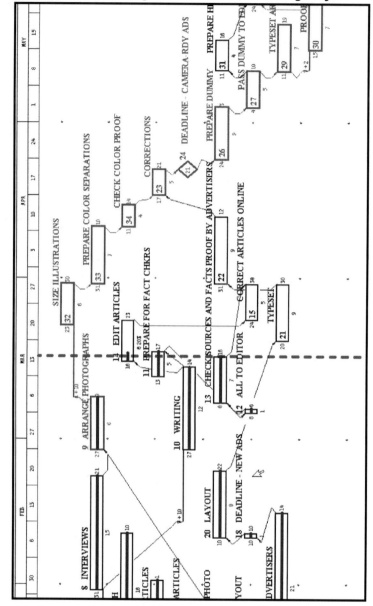

It is a best practice to report on the logic network diagram during the project life cycle. Because not only does it show the Gantt chart, it shows the relationships between the activities into the future.

Because the logic network diagram can be so large and difficult to draw on a standard piece of paper, the most suitable format for printing is a plotter. Using the diagram on a computer screen, or over a series of screens, is also possible, but may be challenging because the diagram can become large, complex, and hard to read on the screen.

Cross-Reference
See Chapter 19 - Using Communication Tools for Project Reporting during the Planning Process to learn more about how to use or create a network logic diagram.

Introduction to the Project Schedule

You use the *project schedule* to create, monitor, and control project activities. The project plan drives the project schedule. The project schedule acts as a central repository for all project task information and helps get the right information in the hands of those making project-level decisions. Project managers use project schedules almost daily for various reasons, such as reviewing current activities, seeing if cost information has changed, and reviewing the project's progress. The project schedule is your one-stop shop to communicate detailed project information. Your main goals for using the project schedule include: discovering what activities remain, activity start and finish dates, and what resources are required to complete the work. Without using a project schedule, even a small project can turn into a disaster because you have limited ability to control the tasks and people on the projects without seeing the information in a project schedule. Even project managers working on small projects should understand the order of the work, task dependencies, cost to perform the tasks, and who is responsible for each activity. This project information is critical regardless of project size to run a successful project.

Resource loading is an important part of project schedule management. When you load your project resources into the project schedule, and then add costs associated to those resources, you see the benefits and all of the functionality built into the project scheduling tool. With this information loaded in your project schedule, you can perform several types of project analysis. The analysis work includes understanding resource commitments, costs at a certain date, resource allocations, and so on. A fully loaded resource schedule is important for you when managing and controlling your project.

Note
The Project Management Institute's knowledge area for the project schedule is the time management area. The secondary concept area for this tool is scope.

Tool Value
A project schedule is the plan of record for the project. It displays where you have been, where you are, and where you are going on your project. Very few projects can be successful without this tool.

Social Media Tools
The communication purpose for the project schedule is to inform. Communication from the project schedule can be posted on social media tools, such as Yammer, Socialcast, and Facebook (private group).

The project schedule is one of the most important tools a project manager has to communicate project information. The wealth of data within this tool can help resolve complex problems. Project schedules include many fields of project information, such as project task activities, start and finish dates, resource assignments, costs per activity, activity dependencies, and earned value indexes. The complete list of fields and project information in the project schedule will help you decide which to include in your project schedule. You are responsible for building the project schedule from the project plan. The project plan consists of activities, durations, and logical relationships between the activities. These are all key items you need for building a project schedule. Once defined, you enter the information into a project scheduling tool and build the project schedule. The project schedule includes start and finish dates for each task and are calculated by the scheduling tool. The automated scheduling system does not have the ability to plan; its only job is to crunch the numbers and input from you or the project scheduler. Therefore, you must enter the following information into the tool before it can calculate the schedule. To calculate the project schedule, most scheduling tools need an activity description, duration, and logical relationships between activities, at a minimum. After entering even limited bits of information, the scheduling tool can complete the calculations and generate the project schedule. On most projects, you must constantly make a diligent effort to update and maintain the project schedule. Sometimes, on larger and more complex projects, you hand the scheduling responsibilities to a project scheduler to continue maintaining the project schedule. You are still actively involved, but you do not update the file or maintain it.

Project customers expect you to send the project schedule to them weekly. Seeing a week-to-week snapshot of how the project is progressing is important to most customers. Weekly is usually an acceptable time frame to send a snapshot because daily, for example, would be too much information. When communicating the project schedule weekly, your customers always remain in-sync and in touch with the project. If you send the project schedule less frequently, such as monthly, the project customer might feel out of touch. When communicating this information, start by going over the project milestone dates, and then drill into the specific tasks that occur during the time frame you are presenting on the schedule.

Figure 8.10 — A Sample Project Schedule for a Book-Publishing Project shows a typical project schedule in the Gantt chart view. This project schedule shows task duration, start and finish dates, and predecessor ID numbers. You can add many different columns of information to the project schedule, but depending on size, you may struggle with paper size for printing or screen size for presenting the information. Usually, it is up to you to decide which columns and fields you want to display as part of your schedule's default view. The choices are almost endless.

Figure 8.10 — A Sample Project Schedule for a Book-Publishing Project

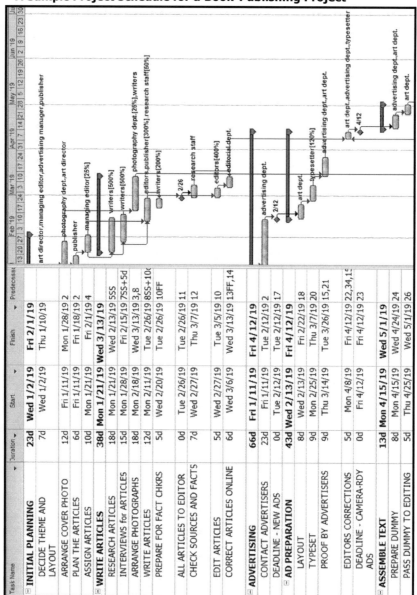

	Task Name	Duration	Start	Finish	Predecessors
1	**INITIAL PLANNING**	23d	Wed 1/2/19	Fri 2/1/19	
2	DECIDE THEME AND LAYOUT	7d	Wed 1/2/19	Thu 1/10/19	
3	ARRANGE COVER PHOTO	12d	Fri 1/11/19	Mon 1/28/19	2
4	PLAN THE ARTICLES	6d	Fri 1/11/19	Fri 1/18/19	2
5	ASSIGN ARTICLES	10d	Mon 1/21/19	Fri 2/1/19	4
6	**WRITE ARTICLES**	38d	Mon 1/21/19	Wed 3/13/19	
7	RESEARCH ARTICLES	18d	Mon 1/21/19	Wed 2/13/19	5SS
8	INTERVIEWS for ARTICLES	15d	Mon 1/28/19	Fri 2/15/19	7SS+5d
9	ARRANGE PHOTOGRAPHS	18d	Mon 2/18/19	Wed 3/13/19	3,8
10	WRITE ARTICLES	12d	Mon 2/11/19	Tue 2/26/19	8SS+10d
11	PREPARE FOR FACT CHKRS	5d	Wed 2/20/19	Tue 2/26/19	10FF
12	ALL ARTICLES TO EDITOR	0d	Tue 2/26/19	Tue 2/26/19	11
13	CHECK SOURCES AND FACTS	7d	Wed 2/27/19	Thu 3/7/19	12
14	EDIT ARTICLES	5d	Wed 2/27/19	Tue 3/5/19	10
15	CORRECT ARTICLES ONLINE	6d	Wed 3/6/19	Wed 3/13/19	13FF,14
16	**ADVERTISING**	66d	Fri 1/11/19	Fri 4/12/19	
17	CONTACT ADVERTISERS	23d	Fri 1/11/19	Tue 2/12/19	2
18	DEADLINE - NEW ADS	0d	Tue 2/12/19	Tue 2/12/19	17
19	**AD PREPARATION**	43d	Wed 2/13/19	Fri 4/12/19	
20	LAYOUT	8d	Wed 2/13/19	Fri 2/22/19	18
21	TYPESET	9d	Mon 2/25/19	Thu 3/7/19	20
22	PROOF BY ADVERTISERS	9d	Thu 3/14/19	Tue 3/26/19	15,21
23	EDITORS CORRECTIONS	5d	Mon 4/8/19	Fri 4/12/19	22,34,15
24	DEADLINE - CAMERA-RDY ADS	0d	Fri 4/12/19	Fri 4/12/19	23
25	**ASSEMBLE TEXT**	13d	Mon 4/15/19	Wed 5/1/19	
26	PREPARE DUMMY	8d	Mon 4/15/19	Wed 4/24/19	24
27	PASS DUMMY TO EDITING	5d	Thu 4/25/19	Wed 5/1/19	26

Tip

Make sure your activity durations are no longer than one reporting cycle. Anything longer and you will have a more difficult time estimating and reporting progress. When starting an activity in a reporting cycle, make sure that the activity finishes before the next reporting cycle.

The minimum information in a project schedule includes a task description, duration (in hours/days/weeks/months), and the logical relationships. A project-scheduling tool cannot plan. You must work with your team members to describe every activity, enter an estimate for each activity, and define the sequence for the activities. Your project schedule cannot be considered complete without at least these elements. You can add as many of the other fields as you want, but remember that the more fields you use, the more complicated and difficult the project schedule is to read. At a minimum, when creating the initial project schedule, you should have at least the aforementioned fields as a starting point. When communicating project schedule information, communicate at least the minimum number of fields to your customers, but plan to report many more fields to provide the complete picture of the project.

Note
Rarely can a project team complete a project schedule on the first try. It is a dynamic process that continues throughout the project and only ends when the project is complete.

When you communicate the project schedule to your project team, communicate at the task level, not summary task level. Team leads and team members will want to discuss individual tasks and issues or concerns they have at the task level. Rarely does a project team want to talk about the schedule in its entirety; they leave that up to you and the customer. You may want to discuss specifics with your team members at the task level so that you have a true understanding of the status. When you dive into the task details, and then report on those details, you are prepared to answer questions, which wouldn't be possible if you didn't spend the time to understand what was happening with the tasks. Identifying and discovering project schedule details is valuable to your role as project manager and critical for you to communicate project information.

Tip
Do not overload your project schedule with too many time constraints, such as "start no earlier than"," must finish on," "finish before." Keep time constraints to an absolute minimum and let the project-scheduling software do the work.

The project schedule can display hundreds of fields (columns) of information. Usually, it is best to keep the fields to a minimum so as not to overwhelm the project team with unnecessary details. Extra fields can cause confusion and may be unproductive while offering little extra value to the schedule. We recommend creating two separate reports with different fields rather than trying to crowd the fields onto one report. One could be a schedule report, and the other could be a cost report. Usually, they go to different people, one for schedule, and one for cost.

When reviewing and choosing a project-scheduling tool, look for features that you can use often on your projects. Some of the features these tools provide include:

- Reporting features, such as the ability to select, sort, summarize, and group information
- User friendliness, easy to read and create schedules with little to no training
- Resource capability assigning, leveling, and detailed reporting
- Cost analysis, budgeting, and tracking
- Earned value analysis

Note
Researching and selecting a project scheduling tool for your company is beyond the scope of this book.

Planning to use a project schedule

In planning and preparing to use a project schedule tool, you must first select the methodology you will use on the project. Once you know which methodology you are using, you can choose the scheduling tool. If you are unfamiliar with the project-scheduling tool, get some training on it before trying to create a project schedule. Sometimes, if the project is big enough and you have funds to hire a project scheduler or project planner, you don't need to learn the scheduling tool. On large construction projects, a project scheduler (or many) is on the project team and you don't own creating the project schedule. You work with the customer and stakeholders to understand what they want and need on the project schedule (cost or resources, both or neither). You decide how often to communicate the information to them based on their requirements. When these planning steps are in place, you or your project scheduler can create the project schedule.

Reporting from a project schedule

You rely heavily on your team members to help create the project schedule. On large projects, project schedulers create the project schedule because you don't have time to spend on it and still manage the project. Often, your company has project schedule templates to use as a starting point across different project types. No template works exactly for every project, so you will have to make changes and updates to the template. Project schedule templates are starting points for any project and contain the various project methodology tasks that your company's PMO wants completed for each project. Many large companies provide project schedule templates to use and expect changes and updates to the templates to occur based on the project's specific needs. If your customers or stakeholders have specific project tasks or requirements, add them to the project schedule to ensure the team completes these activities.

When reporting and communicating from the project schedule, you rarely use the project schedule alone because supporting details from the project status report help tell the whole project story.

Before you can do any project reporting, you must plan what types of reports you will communicate and how to create those reports. To create the reports, you need detailed information to sort, select, summarize, and group your tasks. For example, you may want to group project activities by phase or location. To do this, you must plan how to extract the activities that fit into the various groups. How you complete this depends solely on the software system you are using to manage your project schedule. Each software program has built-in reporting capabilities that you may want to use when communicating your project information to your customers and stakeholders.

Different formats are available for reporting the project schedule. The first and most commonly used format is on paper (document format) where the project schedule is printed and analyzed with your customers or stakeholders, in person, at a review meeting. This common method lets your customers ask you and the project team questions about various project schedule components.

The second method of reporting is publishing the project schedule electronically, via presentations, email, and posting to websites. This reporting technique is good because the information is instantly available to your customers, subcontractors, and vendors and lets them drill into task details at their convenience. Often, companies create project dashboards that contain project schedule information for communicating to interested project stakeholders. Dashboards provide real-time communication and are valuable to customers and stakeholders.

Cross-Reference
See Chapter 18 - Using Communication Tools to Plan and Develop Project Deliverables to learn more formation about project schedules.

Summary

In summary, the tools described in the time management knowledge area support you and the project team in controlling the areas related to time on your projects. Project schedule management is an important task and something to take seriously throughout the project. You need to watch and control time management closely because it is something that can quickly get away from you.

This chapter includes tools such as the schedule management plan, Gantt chart, logic network diagram, project schedule, project milestone list, and the baseline schedule. Each tool focuses on helping you and your team become more efficient in project communications in the time management knowledge area. With these tools, you and your team can control project activities and drive the team toward a successful project completion.

Chapter 9

Communication Tools that Manage Project Costs

IN THIS CHAPTER

- ◆ Introduction to the Budget Spreadsheet
- ◆ Introduction to Earned Value analysis
- ◆ Introduction to the Earned Value estimating tool

In this chapter, we explore project communication tools in the cost management knowledge area. Cost management includes the processes and procedures to manage and ensure that the project stays on budget. The tools described in this chapter are important for communicating your project's cost and budget. Project cost management is not business finance.

Much like time management, cost management is one of the areas that most customers watch closely, and the project's success can hinge on successful cost management. On a cost-driven project, you must be cost conscious and track the budget closely. Tasks such as running various budget reports, controlling contractor costs, closely watching forecasts, and closing out purchase orders are some of the critical areas of budget control.

The tools presented in this chapter can help you and your project team become better at communicating project cost information to customers and management. Each tool described in this chapter has its own unique purpose within the cost management knowledge area.

Introduction to the Budget Spreadsheet

The *budget spreadsheet* tracks, records, and communicates the project's budget and cost information. The budget spreadsheet is a critical tool for managing and controlling project costs; without it, you will struggle to stay on top of project finances. Project forecast management is another area in cost managing where using a budget spreadsheet helps you monitor and control the budget.

Communicating budget spreadsheet information can be challenging. When communicating budget information, choose your means of communication carefully and be mindful of the budget information and the message you are delivering. You can communicate the information in person, by email, or by other means. For example, sending an email to your customers stating that your project is millions of dollars over budget without first communicating that message in person or over the phone is probably not a suitable way to handle situation.

Note
The Project Management Institute's knowledge area for this tool is the cost management knowledge area. The secondary area that this tool is associated with is communications.

Tool Value
Budget spreadsheets provide the project's financial picture from an executive level down to the details, and give project managers total control over the project's financial data and reporting.

Social Media Tools
The communication purposes for the budget spreadsheet are to inform and persuade. Communication from budget spreadsheets can be posted on social media tools, such as Yammer, Socialcast, and Facebook (private group).

Some companies have formal applications that enable them to manipulate the budget, but the most common tool is the budget spreadsheet. Even if companies have software products that track costs and budgets, one of the most commonly used tool in that product will be the budget spreadsheets. The complexities and formulas in the spreadsheet differ from company to company and industry to industry. Some companies only track basic information, while other companies have complex formulas that enable you to watch every dollar spent. Some customers and leadership teams require strict budget tracking. Other projects are much looser and don't require the same rigorous budget tracking. Most companies have standard procedures and processes for you to track project budgets. On smaller to midsize projects, it is a best practice to track budget and spending once a week so you have a constant handle on your project's budget and can make changes quickly when budget issues arise. For example, project forecasts can change on a weekly basis, but project managers who track the budget weekly will see the forecast and will be able to respond quickly if there are issues. Knowing budget information can lead to solving potential issues much earlier.

Table 9.1 — Example of a Budget Spreadsheet (Cost by Group) represents a basic budget spreadsheet for a small project. This spreadsheet shows four separate groups with maximum dollar amounts assigned to each group, and the average dollars spent on similar projects. In this example, the project has up to $38,000 to spend, but will most likely come in around $23,000. (Note: Group A and D have not completed their portions of the project; therefore, this project is not yet complete.)

Table 9.1 — Example of a Budget Spreadsheet (Cost by Group)

Item#	Avg. Cost	Max Cost	Forecast Costs	Final Cost
Group A	$5,600	$10,000	$8,000	
Group B	$2,300	$5,000	$3,500	$3,805
Group C	$4,750	$8,000	$7,650	$5,654
Group D	$10,000	$15,000	$13,200	
Totals	$22,650	$38,000	$32,350	

Every company should have a budget spreadsheet template, but if one is not available, this example provides a good starting point.

Project budget spreadsheets differ from project to project, but they often contain some common items that are part of the budget management process. Most budget spreadsheets include categories such as average costs, maximum costs, forecast costs, actual costs, and final costs. There is no perfect format or number of columns to include on a budget spreadsheet because the information depends on many factors. As long as you get the information you need to manage and control your project's budget, use whatever works for you. If another project manager is tracking different fields and different information, it does not mean that your spreadsheet is wrong or ineffective; it simply means that your projects are different and he or she is tracking more or less information. Most customers don't care how you track the details, as long as you are tracking the budget correctly and not overspending.

Tip
Control your activities by setting a maximum cost amount. For example, set a limit that no activities can cost more than $10,000.

Management and customers hold you accountable for controlling project costs. As the project comes closer to finishing, their scrutiny about project spending heightens. The budget spreadsheet can help you respond to higher scrutiny from management or customers. For example, as the scrutiny becomes more intense, you can use the budget spreadsheet to understand project spending, forecast future spending, and predict overall project costs. These are the main areas in any budget spreadsheet, and you should watch them closely. Forecast information is one of the most examined areas on your project's budget. Forecast information provides the project's estimated costs at completion of the project. The forecast determines whether the project is projecting to complete over or under budget during the life of the project, so you can make adjustments along the way. The project forecast is complex and often an overused formula during the project budgeting process. Many project team members will over forecast to ensure that they receive the dollars assigned to their portion of the project without understanding or caring about the overall budget. It happens on projects all the time; be careful and continually monitor the forecast data. You need to know which resources are working on your project, so watch out for resources who charge your project without working on it. That happens when resources don't have a project to charge to, so they charge your project and hope you don't notice.

You must consider the importance of creating the data in the budget process. When team members don't enter their estimates consistently, the numbers on the budget spreadsheet can be all over the map. For example, if team members estimate differently, or do not have anyone controlling data entry, the forecasts and estimates can swing all over the place. Most companies control this swing by holding you and your finance department representative responsible for staying on top of and questioning team estimates by using reporting. Be diligent about staying on top of your project's budget. You are responsible for reporting your project budget, so you have a vested interest in making sure your team is following the process to enter financial data correctly.

Tip

When working on a foreign project, an unexpected exchange rate change can wreak havoc with the project's estimated cost. You can reduce the impact of this change by setting up a contract before the project starts so that if exchange rates change, the impact is accounted for in the budget.

Most budget spreadsheets display the dollars earmarked to the project by specific functional areas. For example, in a software project, the design, development, and testing teams each have a specific budget amount for their portions of the project. When the team leads for each area provide a budget estimate, you are responsible for holding the team leaders accountable to their budgets. Otherwise, budget overruns can occur in the different areas, which cause a negative impact to the overall budget. Tracking budget to the specific areas of the project is important because it increases the team leads' accountability for those areas. If you notice that a group is forecasting over their maximum amount, you can work directly with that team's lead to correct the situation immediately. You, as project manager, provide the maximum budget amount to each group and expect them to stay on budget throughout the project. This forces team leaders to look at their forecasts and maximum amounts to determine whether there is a delta (variance). If so, work closely with the team lead to resolve the delta. In the end, it will help bring that portion of the project's finances back in line, which course-corrects the overall project budget.

Note

A delta is the difference, or variance, of two amounts. If one amount is expected to be $10.00 and it ends up being $15.00, the delta is $5.00 dollars. "Delta" is a common term in project management when discussing variances between two terms.

One advantage of using a budget spreadsheet is the total control you have over the data. Some project managers like to use "what-if" scenarios by making a copy of the project's budget data and adjusting the budget amount or resource hour allocations to discover the impact those changes would have on the budget. These what-if scenarios become powerful communication tools when managing your project's budget. When you can move data around and play with it, you can answer difficult budget questions. Regular budget communications between you and your customer are important for any project. If your customer wants you to try different budget scenarios or resource assignments, you must be confident in your ability to adjust and play with budget data. You can easily create what-if scenarios in your budget spreadsheet and store them in a separate spreadsheet, leaving your original budget spreadsheet intact. Creating these scenarios helps you understand the impact of something occurring unexpectedly so you can make appropriate changes. The following are common what-if scenarios for managing project costs:

- How would changing employee rates affect the bottom-line project budget?
- What happens to the project's budget if resources mistakenly assign their hours?
- What happens to the budget if overtime is required?

Planning to use a budget spreadsheet

When planning to use a budget spreadsheet, you must understand the defined rules and processes for budget management within your company. Work with the finance or PMO teams to understand templates, timeframes, and other expectations for managing and controlling a project's budget. After you understand this information, you can develop the project's budget spreadsheet. The next step is to work with your customer to find out the budget reporting requirements. You should know when your customer wants to see financial data and make sure your customer's expectations are practical. Your customer might ask for something that is just not possible through the company processes. For example, a customer wants to see project actuals on a weekly basis. However, in this scenario, the company processes actuals on a monthly basis. Those timeframes do not match. Using this example, you would tell your customer that you can't get them that data weekly. There is little you can do in this scenario. Your customer may not be happy, but you cannot provide the data because it isn't available at the time they want. Set expectations up front expectations with your customer that weekly reporting is not possible. Without having these early conversations with your customer, you wouldn't know your customer's budget reporting expectations, which cause future communication issues around budget reporting. After completing these steps, you have adequately prepared for using a budget spreadsheet on your projects.

Reporting from a budget spreadsheet

On most projects, you are responsible for creating the project's budget spreadsheet. On larger projects, project managers often hire an administration team to be in charge of project reporting. This team is responsible for creating and reporting the project's budget spreadsheet. The budget spreadsheet is a regular project standard report that is delivered during the company's reporting cycle. Most companies use weekly forecast reporting and monthly actuals reporting.

A best practice is to constantly track your project's budget. Regardless of the company's formal reporting cycle, you should track, capture, and store the project's budget data once a week during the project life cycle. If the finance department accidentally performs a budget restatement or adjusts the project budget, you have a view of the data before the event occurred. You would then be in good shape to have the finance department correct the data by giving them the backup information. Having a weekly backup of your budget data is a best practice for any project manager.

During the project status meeting, you communicate budget information to your customers and address any concerns or issues they have about the budget. Communicating budget information in person adds accountability to you and ensures that team members are spending the budget wisely. Without a weekly checkpoint between you and your customers, project budgets can and will rise, and budgets can go over.

Table 9.2 — Example of Budget Spreadsheet (Hours/Project Costs) represents an advanced monthly tracking budget spreadsheet. In this example, the budget spreadsheet tracks two separate variances per month, one tracks labor hours, and the other tracks project costs. This information ensures that you and your team are accurately estimating their hours each month. At month end, you enter the actual hours for calculating total project costs. If you see that a team member's hours are inconsistent with the original estimate, it's time to take action. Work with that resource to find out how he or she developed the estimates. It may be that a particular resource simply needs training on the estimating process and there was no wrongdoing.

Table 9.2 — Example of Budget Spreadsheet (Hours/Project Costs)

Name	Emp Rate	Contactor Rate	Jan_ Act	Jan_ Est	Actual Total Costs per Month	Est. Total Costs per Month	Hour Var	Cost Var
Emp 1	$45		2	2	$90	$90	0	0
Contract 1		$96	5	5	$480	$480	0	0
Emp 2	$35		2	3	$70	$105	-1	-35
Emp 3	$25		5	1	$125	$25	4	100
Emp 4	$44		6	6	$264	$264	0	0
Contract 2		$100	10	6	$1,000	$600	4	400
Emp 5	$22		2	2	$44	$44	0	0
Emp 6	$45		10	15	$450	$675	-5	-225
Emp 7	$65		2	2	$130	$130	0	0
Emp 8	$45		15	5	$675	$225	10	450
Totals			59	47	$3,038	$2,638	12	690

This table is one of the thousands of budget spreadsheets available to use on your projects. As noted earlier, there is no right or wrong format; select the one that works for your project. Often, you pick a format that you like and have worked with before to use from project to project.

Cross-Reference

See Chapter 19 - Using Communication Tools for Project Reporting during the Planning Process to learn more about how to use a budget spreadsheet.

Introduction to Earned Value Analysis

The main purpose of *earned value analysis* is to measure continuous project performance and predict the final cost and schedule results. Earned value analysis displays project performance trends and allows project-level and detail-level calculations; it can also display different performance categories.

The earned value concept has been around for at least 40 years. Earned value is synonymous with performance measurement. Earned value analysis measures the actual effort being performed on the project and compares that effort with the original baseline plan. One of the major attributes of the earned value method is that it integrates time and cost to display project trends. Predicting future progress rate calculations are an advantage to using earned value analysis. Other advantages include schedule tracking and cost monitoring. This is one of few tools that integrate cost and schedule information. It also tracks cost and scheduling variances, which show you how far the project is ahead or delayed, as well as whether it is over or under budget. Earned value analysis compares the current budget to the original budget, and the current schedule to the original schedule.

Note
The Project Management Institute's knowledge area for this tool is cost management. The secondary areas that this tool can be associated with are time, human resources, and communications.

Tool Value
Earned value analysis lets you continuously track performance throughout the project life cycle. It displays the rate of performance in both time and cost.

Social Media Tools
The communication purposes for earned value analysis are to inform, persuade, and motivate. Communication from earned value analysis can be posted on social media tools, such as Yammer, Socialcast, and Facebook (private group).

Earned value analysis produces earned value S-curves, which are great for presenting your project's true performance. After the project work starts, earned value charts display the project's trending and performance information. These charts tell everyone how well the project is performing and how it is expected to perform. They call out any project anomalies from a cost or time perspective. If there are project anomalies, the project team can research them and decide how to resolve them.

Figure 9.1 — Planned Budget Sample for a Software Development Project shows a typical earned value trend chart. The chart shows the project's planned value (PV) before work begins. You create the PV (baseline) by adding the cost of each activity to the chart during the period in which it will be completed. Then, you total the costs from all of the activities in each period to see the value for that period. Plotting the values creates a cumulative curve like the one shown in **Figure 9.2.** This is an S-curve report because it resembles the shape of the letter S. It represents the projected rate the project should perform in the future. As the project continues, you calculate earned value (EV) and actual cost (AC) information on the project. By collecting this information, you have the project's performance trend information, which lets you perform course correction in the areas not performing as well. This is valuable information for you to track the project team's performance. **Figure 9.2** shows that the project is not performing as planned (PV versus EV) and is overspending its EV by about two times (PV versus AC).

Figure 9.1 — Planned Budget Sample for a Software Development Project

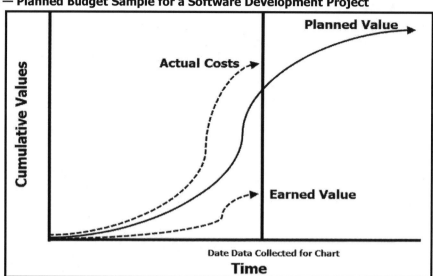

You benefit from earned value analysis because you can see the project's rate of progress and compare it to the original baseline plan to determine the differences. These results give you a better understanding of the project's performance and project team's status. Without performing earned value analysis, you don't have the same ability to see how well the project team is progressing. Earned value analysis provides a wealth of project data to discover how well the project is performing.

Government project managers have been using earned value analysis for many years. The construction industry mandates earned value for large projects, and the software industry has seen it become more popular. More recently, project management trends in the private sector are showing earned value becoming more prevalent across the industry. As you start to understand the value of using earned value analysis, it will become a standard report in your reporting process, especially when your customers are demanding performance analysis reports for their projects.

You may find that the best time to calculate earned value analysis is when you are working on medium to large projects because performance tracking is a fundamental customer request. If you are not tracking project costs or hours at the activity level, there is little sense to calculating earned value analysis and performance reporting. The tracking must be done on project activities for earned value analysis. As long as your project schedule is set up to track and report performance data, you can track cost and labor hours. When collecting this data, you open a large suite of available earned value analysis reports for your project.

Even when projects do not record costs or hours at the activity level, earned value analysis is still possible. The earned value would not encompass the full value as it would if it were implemented completely. You can create your own units to perform earned value calculations. You can still use earned value because you don't need a particular unit of measure or calculate performance. To calculate earned value analysis, you can create any unit type you want to track your project's performance by using that unit. Project managers commonly use the "duration" value to create earned value analysis reports.

Cross-Reference
Chapter 19 - Using Communication Tools for Project Reporting during the Planning Process to discover how to create an earned value analysis with your own unit of measure.

Measuring a project's earned value

Before measuring a project's earned value, make sure you understand the terminology for standard calculations, which is standard across the project management industry. There are three common earned value calculations: planned value (PV), actual costs (AC), and earned value (EV). These calculations compute the earned value parameters and reports.

Examples and definitions are provided below:

- **Planned value (PV):** This is the portion of the work that is planned on a task between the task's start date and the finish date. For example, the total planned budget for a four-day task is $1000. The PV is $1000.
- **Actual cost (AC):** This is the total actual cost incurred while performing work on a task during a given time period. For example, if a four-day task actually incurs a total cost of $350 on each of the first two days, the AC for this period (two days) is $700 (but the PV and EV are equal to $500 each, which is 50 percent of the value of the task).
- **Earned value (EV):** This is the value of the work accomplished, the portion of the work spent for a given percentage of work performed on a task. For example, if after two days, 50 percent of the work on a task is completed, you have earned $500 of the activity's $1000. In this case, you are performing right on schedule.

Tip

Earned value analysis is a great project performance measurement. Use earned value on your projects.

Calculating earned value analysis performance

There are a standard set of calculations for calculating earned value analysis, including:

- **Cost variance (CV):** The difference between a task's earned value and its actual cost. CV = EV − AC
- **Schedule variance (SV):** The difference between a task's earned value and its planned value. SV = EV − PV
- **Cost performance index (CPI):** The ratio of earned value to actual costs. CPI = EV / AC
- **Schedule performance index (SPI):** The ratio of earned value to planned value. SPI = EV / PV

Performing and interpreting earned value analysis

When performing a project's earned value analysis, the answers to some standard project questions become readily clear. How much money is needed to complete the project? Is there enough time to complete the project on schedule? When you have this project information, it gives you a whole new level of detail about the project. This information would not have been available if you did not perform an earned value analysis.

The earned value variance indicators for cost analysis can be either positive or negative. A positive variance indicates that the project is ahead of schedule and the cost is under budget. With a positive variance, you might be able to reallocate money and resources from your project to other projects that are in need.

A negative schedule and cost variance indicates that the project is behind schedule and over-running its budget. Immediate action needs to be taken to ensure the project gets back on track as soon as possible. If a task or project has a negative CV, the budget may need to be increased or the project scope revisited. If a project has a negative SV, another option is having team members work overtime to bring the project back on schedule.

Tip
Cost control is just as critical as time and scope management.

Earned value performance indicators that are ratios (such as CPI and SPI), can be equal to 1.0, greater than 1.0, or less than 1.0. A value greater than 1.0 using CPI communicates an under-running budget, and less than 1.0 indicates that you are running over budget. For SPI, if the value is less than 1.0, you are ahead of schedule, and if it is greater than 1.0, you are behind schedule. For example, an SPI of 0.84 means that you are working 16 percent faster than planned. It has taken you only 84 percent of the planned time to complete that portion of a task in a given time period, and a CPI of 0.8 means that you are running 20 percent over budget.

An activity's earned value (EV) is the percent complete of work on the activity multiplied by the budget (baseline) of the activity (EV = % complete X activity cost). When an activity is 100 percent complete, it has earned all of its value. When reporting progress on an activity, you only need a few percentage points. There are several methods for reporting an activity's progress. One method to report progress is to give an activity an agreed upon percent when it starts. For example, a project scheduler would automatically assign 25 percent complete when an activity starts. When an activity has reached 26 percent complete, but less than 50 percent, the activity would automatically receive 50 percent complete. The next progress step of an activity would automatically receive a 75 percent complete when the activity's percent complete was between 51 percent and 75 percent complete. An activity would only receive 100 percent complete upon completing the activity.

Some projects are set up where you only receive the value of the activity when it is complete. That is, it is either 0 percent or 100 percent complete. This earned value technique reporting provides two project benefits. The first is that it forces you to keep the activity durations short. The second benefit is that it eliminates arguments when team members are reporting progress because the activity is either finished or unfinished.

Performance values analyze the rate (speed) at which the project is being worked and estimates future progress.

Planning to use earned value analysis

When planning to use earned value analysis, review the company's process and procedures that are in place—learn them and follow them. If there are no procedures in place, make sure that a coding system is part of the scheduling program to select, group, and summarize the activities you want to use for an earned value analysis. Before developing earned value analysis, we recommend that you use the work breakdown structure (WBS) to make sure you have a fully defined scope of work for the project. The coding system for creating a WBS should be set up for each work package, and then you develop the cost for each work package (activity). Before you can run an earned value analysis report, you must first create a cost loaded baseline schedule so that you can perform project variance reporting.

Cross-Reference
See Chapter 8 - Communication Tools That Manage Project Time for more information about the baseline schedule.

Reporting from earned value analysis

On most projects, you are responsible for creating the project's earned value analysis reports. On larger projects, where you have an administration team, reporting is part of that group's responsibilities. The company's PMO manager will provide the processes for project managers to run earned value analysis on their projects. Earned value analysis reports are part of regular project reporting, and they are shared with project stakeholders weekly or monthly. Various earned value analysis reports include:

- Cost variance report
- Cost performance index report
- Schedule variance report
- Schedule performance index report
- S-curve report
- Schedule and cost forecasting report

Table 9.3 — Example of Earned Value Analysis Report shows a typical earned value table for a construction project. In this table, there are three values of an earned value analysis. The earned values calculations include the planned value (PV), the earned value (EV), and the actual costs (AC). In this example, the project is approximately halfway complete. The values in the Cost CPI and Schedule SPI fields indicate that this project is performing close to the original plan. As you review the project's activities performance, it is good to know how to read the data values in each column. This lets you see how a particular activity is performing on the project. The PV, EV, and AC fields have the values of 250, 210, and 210. The earned value formulas in this project calculate the cost variance as CV = EV − AC (210–210) = 0, the schedule variance calculates as SV = EV-PV (210–250) = -40. Then, to calculate the two indexes CPI and SPI, the formulas are CPI = EV/AC (210/210) = 1.0 and SPI = EV/PV (210/250) = 0.84. The results that show the activity performance as "Final Plan" indicate that you are working according to plan on the costs, and at a rate of 84 percent of the schedule. Overall, this project is performing well.

Table 9.3 — Example of Earned Value Analysis Report

Activity	Planned Value	Earned Value	Actual Cost	Cost Var.	Schedule Var.	Cost CPI	Schedule SPI
Preliminary Plan	100	95	110	-15	-5	0.86	0.95
Final Plan	250	210	210	0	-40	1	0.84
Move Out	300	280	265	15	-20	1.06	0.93
Remodel	1200	1200	1300	-100	0	0.92	1
Move In	250	250	240	10	0	1.04	1
Totals	2100	2035	2125	-90	-65	0.96	0.97

Figure 9.2 — Example of Typical Trending Curves for Earned Value Calculations represents an earned value chart that displays a project's performance trends. In this example, the project is behind schedule (EV–PV) by approximately two quarters and running over budget (EV–AC) by double (200%). To estimate how far behind the project is from the point where the EV touches the status date line, go horizontally back (left) to the PV curve. This imaginary line would touch the PV curve at the end of the third quarter of 2009. The project is running roughly a little over six months behind. When reviewing the project's costs, the project is spending about twice as much as it has earned (the difference between the point of AC on the status date line and the EV point on the status date line). If this trend continues, the project will deliver late (40% behind schedule) and be significantly (200%) over budget.

Figure 9.2 — Example of Typical Trending Curves for Earned Value Calculations

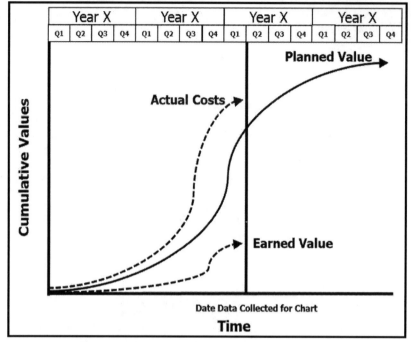

Each week during the standard reporting cycle, the earned value reports become part of the regular project reporting cycle. The earned value reports are important to project reporting and should be stored as part of the standard project reporting. The best format for reporting earned value analysis information is a spreadsheet, which is the most flexible and easiest to work with. That's not to say the earned value information will not show up in Microsoft PowerPoint® presentations or on internal websites, because they can. The earned value analysis reports are stored within the project document control system. This allows for the reports to be stored long-term and available for historical reference by your customer or project team members.

Cross-Reference

Chapter 19 - Using Communication Tools for Project Reporting during the Planning Process to learn more about how to use an earned value analysis.

Introduction to the Earned Value Estimating Tool

The purpose of the *earned value estimating* tool is to create accurate project estimates based on future trends and possible unknown events. When team members add their estimated working hours for a software project, the estimating tool uses those hours to calculate the estimate at completion (EAC). After the project starts, the EAC calculation requires that the project's actual costs as well as the forecast cost estimates are calculated properly. An estimating tool is helpful because you can decide, based on whether the project is running over or under budget, what to do and what corrective actions to take. In the construction industry, professional estimators create project estimates. In software, team members who work on the impacted systems provide project estimates.

When working with forecasters and estimators, it helps to have a clear understanding of the skills that each bring to the project. A forecaster provides future labor rates, equipment costs, and material costs. The estimator calculates the estimates by using future costs and rates. When a forecaster is involved on a project, it often causes projects to linger well into the future.

Note
The Project Management Institute's knowledge area for this tool is the cost management area. The secondary areas that this tool can be associated with are scope, time, and human resources.

Tool Value
An estimating tool lets you forecast the costs before starting the project. Management can then make a go/no-go decision before spending any money on a project.

Social Media Tools
The communication purposes for the earned value estimating tool are to inform, persuade, and motivate. Communication from estimating can be posted on social media tools, such as Yammer, Socialcast, and Facebook (private group).

A project estimate communicates future project costs. After the project's cost estimate is complete, you can share that information with your customers and stakeholders. Sometimes, the project estimate is higher than the assigned project budget. When that occurs, work with your customers and leadership team to decide whether there are changes that will bring the estimate within budget. If, at this point, the project estimate cannot come within budget, your only choice is to request more money. You could run hot in the budget for a while, but that is not always safe. Both choices are valid to consider as long as you have full management support. Occasionally, estimates come in as expected and the project's funding requires no further action.

A customer for a software project, for example, can benefit from using an estimating spreadsheet. Not only does the estimating spreadsheet provide a ballpark of the project's costs, it also shows the various roles working on the project. The life cycle process breakdown and other expected direct project costs (such as equipment) are also included. When customers have this information, they can course correct early in the project life cycle, which may prevent budget reallocations or overruns. By taking full advantage of the estimating process, you can look into the project's future from a funding perspective.

Tip
Project forecasting is challenging because you are estimating based on many unknown factors. Use experts and accurate data for the best forecasting results!

There are times when professional forecasters help create project estimates. Forecasters are usually involved in large projects with long durations. Professional forecasters are costly and larger efforts warrant bringing them in to perform this service. Long projects benefit the most from forecasters because they can provide insight into the labor rate and equipment costs—two, three, five and even ten years in the future.

The forecaster predicts future labor rates, material rates, and equipment costs and applies those costs to the project to determine a future cost estimate. The forecasts, which are broken down by time periods, allow you to use granular reporting. The further out the project forecasts, the less accurate they are. Making accurate predictions far into the future is almost impossible because the number of unknowns is too great.

Calculating formulas for estimating

Every project needs an estimate for both time and cost. Regardless of the project's size, forecasting and project estimating are required to decide the project's future costs. You, the cost manager, and customer use several different calculations to estimate the cost at the completion of a project; these are standard across all industries. The estimate at completion (EAC) formula follows:

- EAC using the remaining budget: calculated by using the actual costs (AC) to date, plus the budget at completion (BAC), minus the earned value (EV). The formula: $EAC = AC + BAC - EV$
- You use this estimate when the project team assumes they can meet the remaining activities' budget and ignores past performance.
- EAC using the cost performance index: calculated by using the actual costs (AC) and the budget at completion (BAC), minus the earned value (EV), divided by the cost performance index (CPI). The formula: $EAC = AC + ((BAC - EV)) / CPI$
- You use this estimate when the project team assumes the performance rate of completed work will continue throughout the rest of the project. Usually, this is the most accurate forecasting technique for proving EAC.
- EAC using cost performance index (CPI) and schedule performance index (SPI): calculated by using the actual costs (AC), plus total budget, minus earned value (EV), divided by cost performance index (CPI), times the schedule performance index (SPI). The formula: $EAC = AC + (total budget - EV) / (CPI * SPI)$
- You use this estimate when the project team assumes that this will most likely be the outcome for the project cost forecast. This formula takes into consideration both cost and schedule performance to date and uses them to estimate the future completion cost.
- EAC using forecast data: calculated by using the actuals plus the forecast (remaining estimate of work). The formula: $EAC = Actuals + Forecast$
- You use this estimate when the project team enters their forecast amounts toward the project and there are actuals already hitting the budget. The two values help determine the estimate of funds needed for completion.

There are three components to a standard EAC formula: the answer, the actual cost component, and the remaining portion of the formula. (This is a standard definition for all formulas.)

The following forecasting methods are the most popular in project management:

- Time series methods: uses historical data as the basis for estimating future outcomes
- Causal/econometric methods: take economic conditions to determine a forecast estimate
- Judgmental methods: expert knowledge
- Other methods include:
  - Simulation

- Prediction market
- Probabilistic forecasting

Planning to use an estimating tool

When planning to use an estimating tool, you must first decide the internal process and procedures to develop a project estimate. This might include working with the finance department or PMO to understand their cost estimating processes. From these processes, you then decide the best way to calculate a project estimate. After you understand the process from the various groups, you work with the estimating team and your customer to calculate the first project estimate.

Another method for project estimating when you and your team have limited experience is creating an estimate yourselves by using a WBS. Creating the WBS with small, detailed work packages helps estimate the cost of each work package. When all work packages have an estimated cost, roll up the cost to the project level to get an accurate project estimate. Transfer this cost into the master schedule activities for determining the earned value analysis.

Cross-Reference
See Chapters 7 - Defining Communication Tools that Manage Project Scope and Chapter 18 - Using Communication Tools to Plan and Develop Project Deliverables to learn more about how to create and use a WBS.

Reporting from the estimating tool

On small projects, project managers and their team members create project estimates. On large projects, the owner often hires professional estimators to create the project's estimates. Project estimates are valuable throughout the project life cycle, but they are frequently used when the project begins because it is important to determine the initial cost estimates during the budgeting process to ensure that you allocated enough budget to complete the project. The project estimator predicts the future project costs at the beginning of the project. That way, if the initial project costs are too high, it is much easier to cancel the project earlier in the process than later.

Note
Project teams try to estimate and forecast early in the project based on unknowns and never exactly hit the estimates!

The estimating report is an important part of the budgeting process and something that occurs at the beginning of the project. The estimating report is not part of the standard project reporting cycle and is only reported once or twice at the beginning of the project. The estimating report uses a spreadsheet format and is often found in other formats, such as PowerPoint or on internal websites. Estimating reports are stored within the project's document control system for long-term storage and historical reference.

Cross-Reference
Chapter 19 - Using Communication Tools for Project Reporting during the Planning Process to learn more about how to use and create the earned value estimating tool.

Summary

In summary, the tools described in this chapter help you and the project team control project costs. Managing project costs is one of the most important areas you are responsible for and need to be on top of. Because project cost is a third of the project triangle, you need to pay special attention to track and record all project costs.

As you review this chapter, the one tool that will help you control project costs is the earned value analysis tool. The different calculations and the ability to see project performance at a granular level are valuable for managing your project. This tool is relativity new, especially in software, but is catching on as one of the most effective and important cost management tools available. Project managers who use earned value analysis techniques have a better understanding of their project's performance and costs than project managers who do not.

The chapter also describes tools such as budget spreadsheets, the cost estimate report, and estimating tools. Each tool helps you manage and control project costs.

Chapter 10

Communication Tools That Manage Project Quality

IN THIS CHAPTER

- ◆ Introduction to the Comprehensive Test Plan
- ◆ Introduction to the Control chart
- ◆ Introduction to the Design Specification tool
- ◆ Introduction to the Quality Management Plan
- ◆ Introduction to the Quality Metrics tool
- ◆ Introduction to the Scatter chart

In this chapter, we explore project communications tools in the project quality management knowledge area. These communication tools are critical to controlling and managing the quality areas of your project. These tools can help you communicate project quality to your customers, management, and project team.

The quality management knowledge area includes project activities that relate to quality planning, quality control, and quality assurance. A project's quality level is subjective and not the same for everyone. Remember that an acceptable quality level for one customer may be unacceptable to another. Customer subjectivity is acceptable because you can implement project quality measurements that your customers agree on and that the project team is driven to meet.

The quality metric tool, explained in this chapter, can help you control quality management. Later in the chapter, you will learn about quality measurement, which is the quality level a customer is trying to achieve. On software projects, a common quality measurement is the number of errors or bugs in an application. A customer wants as few bugs as possible. They could demand zero bugs; however, that's not always possible. You and your team determine the project's quality bar and work with your customer for approval.

The tools in this chapter cover managing and controlling the project's quality. This chapter also covers how to communicate quality information to your customers and leadership team. Project managers must know how to control project quality and how to effectively communicate it to their customers and leadership team. If you cannot properly communicate quality information to your customer, the customer may not understand the quality level that the project team is delivering.

Introduction to the Comprehensive Test Plan

The *comprehensive test plan* documents and identifies a standard approach to planning, executing, and communicating the activities during a project's testing phase. A comprehensive test plan contains the processes and procedures to help project teams remove as many failures as possible before releasing the project to the users for testing purposes. The comprehensive test plan is often used in the software industry, but it's starting to gain popularity in construction, health, and pharmaceutical industries. For example, the comprehensive test plan is popular in the health industry to help ensure that project teams eliminate safety and health hazards in products prior to releasing them to consumers. In the construction industry, a comprehensive test plan is part of the commissioning process.

Note
The Project Management Institute's knowledge area for this tool is the quality management area. The secondary area that this tool could be associated with is risk.

Tool Value
The comprehensive test plan ensures quality control of the product. The test plan document defines the process to achieve quality control by testing processes using set limits.

Social Media Tools
The communication purposes for the comprehensive test plan are to inform and instruct. Communication from the comprehensive test plan can be posted on social media tools, such as Yammer, Socialcast, and Facebook (private group).

The goal of the comprehensive test plan is to ensure the highest-quality project standards at the level the project can afford. Unfortunately, the project's budget usually drives the quality level applied to the project. Because you manage the project's budget, you play a major role in deciding how much quality to apply to the project. Therefore, you will constantly work with the customer to ensure that the testing phase has enough budget to be successful. The cost of applying rigor to project testing is valuable. Not only does it take extra time to test that rigor, but it also takes budget. For example, if you are producing an application to launch a spacecraft, it's worth the extra time and budget to improve quality.

Communicating the comprehensive test plan is simple and straightforward. The test analyst who created the document (usually a tester or test lead) has the project team review the document together to ensure that everyone understands how testing will occur. The test analyst repeats this process a couple of times during the document creation process to make sure everyone on the project team is in agreement. When the document is complete, you send the final document to the relevant stakeholders for approval and sign-off.

The comprehensive test plan is an important communication tool for communicating testing information internally among the project team. The plan includes a lot of detail and contains many sections, such as testing scope, success criteria, quality test deliverables, environmental needs, schedule, safety, and associated testing risks. You communicate the comprehensive test plan to project team leaders by email and during formal meetings to ensure that everyone understands the testing processes. Project testing is key to any project, so it is important that everyone understands the comprehensive test plan and that the testing outlined in the document makes sense and is applicable for the project.

Table 10.1 — Example of a Comprehensive Test Plan Table of Contents represents a table of contents example for a comprehensive test plan. Different industries use this plan for their testing needs and change the contents to reflect their project's needs. The testing information in each section should fulfill the testing needs of most projects.

Table 10.1 — Example of a Comprehensive Test Plan Table of Contents

#	Description
1	Test Plan Identifier
2	References
3	Introduction of Testing
4	Test Items/Cases and Scripts
5	Risks and Issues
6	Features to Be Tested
7	Features Not to Be Tested
8	Approach
9	Item Pass/Fail Criteria
10	Entry and Exit Criteria
11	Suspension Criteria and Resumption Requirements
12	Test Deliverables
13	Remaining Test Tasks
14	Environment Needs
15	Staffing and Training Needs
16	Responsibilities
17	Schedule
18	Planning Risks and Contingencies
19	Approvals
20	Glossary

The comprehensive test plan benefits the entire project team because it contains the processes and procedures for each area of project testing. Project team members who are not on the testing team can use the plan to understand how testing occurs. Team members who help support project testing must understand the comprehensive test plan details, there are no exceptions. Everyone involved in testing needs to understand the comprehensive test plan details. On a software project, for example, the development team and the test team are tightly integrated; therefore, both groups need to understand the document.

The development team will find the comprehensive test plan document valuable. Developers will understand when to pass testing deliverables back and forth with the test team and where and how they interact in the testing process. Without a comprehensive test plan, the project's development and test teams would have no idea where or how to interact with each other to test the project. Thus, neither team would know how to properly test the project, which would negatively impact the overall project quality.

One of the areas that the comprehensive test plan *does not* cover is user acceptance testing. The comprehensive test plan does not describe your customer's testing because that information is in the user acceptance document. Your customer's user acceptance testing allows users to test product functionality before the product is officially released. When developers and test teams perform testing, they test the code behind the application. When business customers perform testing, they run tests on business functionality, and do not test the code like the developers. With this in mind, a best practice is to keep the developers' and testers' test cases in the comprehensive test plan, and the users' test cases in separate documents.

Tip
Make sure that stakeholders or customers sign off on the comprehensive test plan.

Planning to use a comprehensive test plan

When planning and preparing to use a comprehensive test plan, you should first connect with your test team to make sure that they are onboard to create the document. They usually are, but it's a good idea to check with the test lead to make sure he or she realizes that they are responsible for the document. Normally, a test lead can't create the document alone; they need other team members to work together to create the document. You can help the test lead line up the applicable team members needed to create the document. When you settle on who is going to help the test lead create the document, the next step is to ensure that the template has the sections you need. When the test plan is complete and ready to share, you can focus on communicating the test plan by working with the test lead to decide who needs the document. By performing this step, you both understand who is communicating test information before testing begins, which helps avoid future communication problems. After performing these planning tasks, you have adequately prepared to use the project's comprehensive test plan.

Reporting from a comprehensive test plan

The test team lead or a single tester is usually responsible for developing a comprehensive test plan and ensuring that everyone on the project accepts and approves it. That person also owns communicating the comprehensive test plan throughout the project.

Communicating the comprehensive test plan requires careful consideration. This plan is detailed and can be complex. It usually requires long sessions with the project team to discuss each section of the document to get clarification before being approved. Make sure that your test lead is communicating the comprehensive test plan among all project team members who need it for testing; otherwise, those who haven't seen it will be at a disadvantage if they have questions or concerns.

The comprehensive test plan is a one-time document that does not need weekly reporting because it does not contain project status. The test team members sign off on the document at the beginning of the testing phase and agree to perform the test process outlined in the document. The comprehensive test plan document is stored in the document control system, which is accessible to all team members and customers.

Cross-Reference
See Chapter 18 - Using Communication Tools to Plan and Develop Project Deliverables to learn more about the comprehensive test plan.

Introduction to the Control Chart

The *control chart* tracks data points relative to a particular controlled range's upper and lower limits. Test control ranges can vary dramatically and depend on the project type and data. Two examples of using control charts include tracking highway speeds and comparing the number of accidents that occur at specific speeds. Other control charts include tracking the cloudiness level in a water sample. The clearer the water, the less chemical content is exposed in the control chart. These are valid control chart tests and important to understand the quality level being tested.

A control chart provides a graphic view of test results, which is usually easier to understand than a tabular column of data. Some explanation may need to be offered about how to read it, but that usually doesn't last long—as people continue using it, reading and analyzing the data becomes much easier. Project control charts are popular with management, which is much better than forcing them to sift through pages and pages of test results. Meet regularly with executives to review the control chart and make sure they understand the control chart data. Depending on the results from control chart data, executives may decide that the project is too risky to continue or they may step in and prevent some of the risks from occurring. Either way, they would not have known about the issues without seeing the results documented on a control chart.

It's rare, but some projects, depending on the project type, will not have data to warrant a control chart.

Note
The Project Management Institute's knowledge area for this tool is the quality management area. The secondary area that this tool could be associated with is risk.

Tool Value
Control charts identify data that exceeds acceptable limits necessary for a quality product. It is easy to identify the data outside of the limits, and then decide the action plan to correct that data going forward.

Social Media Tools
The communication purpose for the control chart is to inform. Communication from the control chart can be posted on social media tools, such as Yammer, Socialcast, and Facebook (private group).

A control chart is a great tool for helping you manage and control the project's quality. Because a control chart is easy to create, maintain, and update, use it whenever possible and work with your test team to ensure that they use it to report test results.

Most team members also benefit from a project control chart. For example, when team members read a control chart, they can tell immediately if their roles have anything to do with the data represented on the chart. For example, a chemist can review a water cloudiness control chart and see that his or her role influences the data on the chart. Another example, a marketing representative on the same team can look at the same chart and see that his or her work has no impact on the chart data. This is important because both people have different roles on the project and potentially different abilities to influence the control chart. As project manager, it is important for you to ensure that all team members have access to the control chart regardless of role, and that you regularly communicate with everyone.

Figure 10.1 — Example of a Control Chart represents a typical control chart for a project. This example of a Water Cloudiness control chart represents the cloudiness conditions of the water. A value of 0.0 on the chart indicates no visibility and cloudy water, and a value of 7.0 represents a clear condition with complete visibility. In reviewing the chart, you can see that on Jan 5 the cloudiness condition hit a value of 6.0, which means it was almost clear and there was no or little cloudiness to the water. On Jan 12 the cloudiness value hit a 1.6 and the condition of the water was poor.

Figure 10.1 — Example of a Control Chart

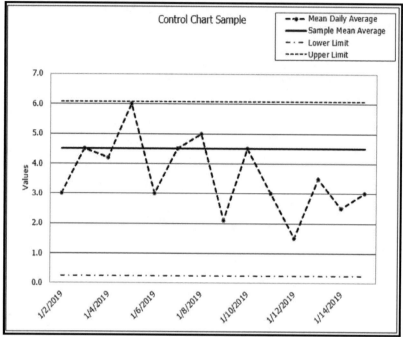

When creating or reviewing a control chart, consider the following areas:

- A central line (mean or average) of what you set for the test or gained from the data
- An upper control limit, the maximum acceptable limit for the data collected
- A lower control limit, the minimum acceptable limit for the data collected
- Process values plotted on the chart (data points)

During the planning process, the test team plans the various control charts that they will produce during the testing process. The project test team works directly with you and your customers to ensure that the different control charts they are creating capture the correct data points and help communicate the project's overall quality. During this session, make sure that your customers agree with the data that the test team collected. During these sessions, your customer and the test team jointly develop the upper and lower limits for the data test conditions. The test team can develop their own criteria for the upper and lower limits, but they need your customers, you, and the subject matter experts to approve the control chart conditions. Only your customer can state what they believe is an acceptable project quality level. Assuming what the acceptable project quality level is on your part or the project team's part can lead to disaster or disappointment.

Tip
Always let the owner or the customer select the quality limits. They are the only ones who can; after all, they are paying for the project.

One area often missed when communicating and working with a control chart is setting up the upper and lower limits for specific data points, also known as thresholds. When you discuss the control limits with your customer, it is important to ensure that everyone understands the acceptable quality level. It is also important that everyone agrees on what is unacceptable. Everyone must understand both conditions. Based on this communication, the data points for both limits (upper and lower) are set, and the test team has values that they can use as a guide in the testing process. For example, on a software project, a control chart might capture the number of bugs detected during the test phase. The threshold limits for the number of bugs detected at the upper end is five and the lower end is three. Therefore, if the project exceeds that threshold, and the project has six or more bugs, you, your customer, and the test lead must decide what to do about that many bugs. If the project receives six to ten bugs per test pass and only five are allowed before exceeding the maximum per the upper limit, your customer or stakeholders have a decision to make. They could decide to stop all testing and send the project back to the development team to correct the errors, or they could keep testing and hope the failure rate decreases. Other possible solutions to resolve this scenario include adding extra staff for testing or changing the test criteria. The project team would then react and adjust work activities based on the changes to ensure that the project gets back on track (acceptable quality) as soon as possible.

One challenge of developing a control chart is making sure everyone understands what the chart means from a quality perspective. Everyone needs to understand how the results impact the project quality. For example, if there are many data points over either an upper or a lower line, there could be real quality problems on the project. Every project has a quality level associated with it; therefore, every project manager should create control charts to track quality limits. Work closely with the test team to ensure there are quality levels tracked during the project and communicate control chart information whenever possible.

Planning to use a control chart

When planning and preparing to use a control chart, you must first work with the test team to decide suitable control charts for the project. After deciding the control charts, work with the test team to decide how they will produce the data for the control charts. Next, the test team works with you and the customer to decide how to report the control charts' results, including delivery method (in-person, email). After performing these planning steps, you have adequately prepared for the use of control charts on your project.

Reporting from a control chart

The test team creates the various control charts for the project. Occasionally, you are responsible for creating control charts. However, the test team provides you the data to create the control charts; you can't do it by yourself. A control chart contains specific project-level data and becomes part of the regular project reporting cycle on most projects. The test team and you should agree ahead of time when it makes sense to report the project's control charts. Usually, on software projects, you report the control charts during the development and testing phases.

There are many different types of control charts. Projects that focus on quality will likely include some of the following control charts:

- Balancing a building; temperature readings within various rooms in construction industry
- Deciding an acceptable limit; for example, five out of ten thousand parts are unusable
- Detecting software code defects or tracking bugs
- Discovering traffic flow volumes over a stretch of highway during different times each day
- Detecting particles per solution of runoff over time
- Analyzing the effect of a change on the design

- Counting the number of operating room delays per day
- Discovering the number of days ahead of schedule, behind schedule, or on schedule

Each week, you report using the control chart as part of your regular project reporting. If the test is continuing, the control chart report should be included as part of the standard project reporting and stored in the project's document control system.

Cross-Reference

See Chapter 20 - Using Communication Tools During the Executing and Controlling Processes to Administer the Project to learn more about how to use a control chart.

Introduction to the Design Specification Document

The *design specification document* includes detailed technical specifications of the product. Every product has a design specification document that ranges from a scrap of paper to an elaborate computer-generated detailed document. There is a good chance your document will probably be somewhere between. The design specification document provides enough information and contains enough details that the project team can use it to create the product. The design specification document covers many project areas, such as design maps, design considerations, assumptions, constraints, and design methodology. You drive the development and use of the design specification document on every project when developing a product. In doing so, the design team and developers have the information they need to develop the best possible solution for your customer.

Communicating the design specification document can be challenging because it requires coordination among several team members. Coordinating the project team can be challenging when you have so many people that need to be involved in the document. You are responsible for communicating the document to the project team and ensuring that everyone is adding their areas to the document and approving and rejecting sections of the document, when applicable.

Note
The Project Management Institute's knowledge area for this tool is the quality management area. The secondary area that this tool could be associated with is risk.

Tool Value
The design specification document communicates the detailed requirements to build the product.

Social Media Tools
The communication purposes for the design specification document are to inform and instruct. Communication from the design specification document can be posted on social media tools, such as Yammer, Socialcast, and Facebook (private group).

Most industries use design specification documents. Software development projects have been using these documents for years to record design details. For example, on software projects these documents describe screen layouts, report specifications, and user interface design. Without a design specification document, the software developers would have to rely on their own opinions for screen and report designs. Doing so and giving the design team complete responsibility for screen or report layouts is risky because the final product most likely will not match your customer's expectations. The design specification document bridges the gap between your customer and the project team. In the construction industry, architects and engineers create the design specification document.

To start creating the design specification document, the design engineer or analyst works with your customer to capture details about the product design. Developing the design specification document requires many rounds of interviews to capture requirements and compile them into the document. It is a long and tedious process due to how many customers and project team members it takes to provide input about the product design. The good news is that the more customers involved in creating the product design, the more they understand the final product design. This is great because if they know what the product is going to look like long before the project team creates it, you save time and budget during product development.

Before the design engineer or analyst can start interviewing customers and creating the document, you must ensure the design specification document template makes sense for the project type. Most design specification documents have a standard template to use as a starting point. There is a huge difference between a software design specification document and a construction design specification document. They won't even look remotely the same because they are two different documents. They have the same purpose, but they use different templates.

Using a design specification document can present challenges. Your biggest challenge is keeping your customer satisfied with the product design. Sometimes, your customer has expectations that do not match what the analyst captured in the document. When that happens, work with the customer and analyst to correct the situation and capture your customer's expectations. The biggest challenge for the analyst in capturing the customer's requirements is relaying those in the document so that they make sense to your customer and are workable by the development team. That is not always easy to do. Sometimes, overcoming the different needs of the two parties is difficult and other times it is impossible, which leads to project problems. These problems are especially challenging when your customer asks for something that the development team has no idea how to produce. Many projects go wrong when this happens. When this occurs, it is a best practice to put the project on hold until a resolution between your customer and development team occurs. Fortunately, this does not happen often and project teams move quickly through issues between the customer and the development team.

Cross-Reference
See Chapter 7 - Defining Communication Tools that Manage Project Scope for more information about the customer requirements document tool. The customer requirements document contains specific design requirements from your customer and need updating or referencing when there are design issues.

Note
Design specifications span all industries.

Planning to use a design specification document

When planning to use the design specification document, make sure that the design analyst is skilled and capable of developing the design specification document. You must have someone who is capable of collecting the requirements and working with customers to gather data. Review the template with the person responsible for writing the document. Rarely do design specification templates match the exact project needs; the design analyst who is developing the document can almost be guaranteed that he or she will have to adjust the template. After deciding the format and information to collect in the document, the design analyst is ready to start creating the document. You have an important role in setting up meetings, gathering individuals, and helping the design analyst through the process of creating the document. It is important to ensure that the people involved are willing and able to dedicate the necessary time to help the analyst create the design specification document. The analyst also needs help from team members and customers to complete the document so that the analyst isn't guessing or researching answers to questions that are readily available by team members who are more familiar with their own areas of the project. Without customers committing time to this process, it is difficult for the analyst to complete the document in a timely manner. There is also a risk that the design analyst may not capture the information correctly the first time and must go back to the customer for more information. Your customer will not like the added follow-up. After performing these planning steps, you will have completed the necessary steps to prepare adequately for using the design specification document.

Note
The design specification document and the requirements documentation are often used together. The requirements document feeds the design specification document.

Reporting from the design specification document

The engineer or design analyst is responsible for creating the design specification document. This is a technical document, which limits who can produce it. The analyst leverages the work of the technical staff to help complete the document from a design perspective.

The design analyst or engineer creating the design specification document is responsible for communicating it to anyone involved in the project. You can help with the process, but it is up to the document creator to share with whomever they see fit. You are responsible for getting sign-off on the design specification document from your team members and customer. Formal approval on the design specification document by your customer and team members means that everyone agrees with the content and the project can move on to the next phase.

Table 10.2 — Example of a Design Specification Document Table of Contents represents the table of contents for a software development design specification document. The document covers a wide range of topics, such as design considerations, architectural strategies, policies, and detailed system designs. Each area contains enough information to develop the final product, and you and your team members who work for a design company will use that company's design methodology to create all of the design specifications.

Table 10.2 — Example of a Design Specification Document Table of Contents

#	Description
1	Introduction
2	Document Outline
3	Introduction
4	System Overview
5	Design Considerations • Assumptions and Dependencies • General Constraints • Goals and Guidelines • Development Methods
6	Architectural Strategies
7	System Architecture • Subsystem Architecture
8	Policies and Tactics
9	Detailed System Design • Detailed Subsystem Design
10	Glossary

#	Description
11	Bibliography

Permission to reprint this design specification document is granted by Bradford D. Appleton. The full document template can be found at: *www.bradapp.com/docs/sdd.html*

The design specification document is not reported weekly as part of your weekly status reporting because it does not contain status information. The only time you report from the design specification document is during document development. You report from the design specification document throughout its development and one last time for final approval. Document format is the most popular format for creating the design specification document; however, you will often copy various sections of the document into presentations for executive reporting. The design specification document is stored as part of the document control system. This allows the document to be readily available for anyone on the project and archived and stored to long-term access.

Cross-Reference

See Chapter 18 - Using Communication Tools to Plan and Develop Project Deliverables to learn more about how to use a design specification document.

Introduction to the Quality Management Plan

The *quality management plan* includes the project's quality processes. Start using this plan early in the project life cycle and long before work activities or testing begins. The quality management plan helps you achieve the highest quality level possible. Projects managers who do not implement a quality management plan ignore an important area of project management and do a disservice to their customers

It is your responsibility to communicate the information in the quality management plan to the customer and your team members. Everyone involved in the project should know the contents of the quality management plan. . Some large projects have quality control managers who lead project quality and are responsible for the quality management plan. If you have quality managers on your project, they are responsible for communicating the quality management plan, not you. Whoever owns project management quality also owns driving project quality. This person's most important task is to ensure the team is hitting the quality levels that are documented in the quality management plan. One important area to consider in producing the quality management plan is the level of quality your customer is expecting. Some customers demand a quality level that they cannot afford or have assigned in the budget. Unfortunately, this happens regularly on projects where the customer asks for a higher product quality level than they can afford. Make sure that your customers understand that demanding a higher product quality level than they originally agreed upon costs more. Added budget costs to increase the project's quality level could mean hiring additional testers and longer test periods that extend the project's schedule.

Note
The Project Management Institute's knowledge area for this tool is the quality management area. The secondary area that this tool could be associated with is risk.

Tool Value
The value of using the quality management plan is the information it communicates about the project's quality to the customer and project team.

Social Media Tools
The communication purposes for the quality management plan are to inform and instruct. Communication from the quality management plan can be posted on social media tools, such as Yammer, Socialcast, and Facebook (private group).

The main benefit of implementing a quality management plan is the attention that the document brings to the project's quality level. Without a quality management plan, quality becomes a second thought and is often not considered or addressed. With an active quality management plan in place, your customer and project team consider quality a priority, which will contribute to a superior final product. The quality management plan outlines the process and procedures the team will follow to drive quality. That's it; that's the whole reason project teams use this document. The document also contains your customer's quality expectations and the desired quality level. As you work with your customer to ensure you document the acceptable quality level, your project team will use the document to ensure that they are meeting the specified quality level.

Table 10.3 — Example of a Quality Management Plan Table of Contents shows a table of contents for a quality management plan. Every project team should use a quality management plan to determine the level of quality to use when creating work products. Ideally, you should be ensuring that you are creating the highest quality work products possible for your project. . The quality management plan applies to multiple project types and is not industry specific. Depending on the project, like all other templates, the quality management plan requires updating to fit the specific needs of your project, and rarely does one plan fit the needs of every project.

Table 10.3 — Example of a Quality Management Plan Table of Contents

#	Description
1	Quality Management Approach
2	Project Overview
3	Quality Standards and Metrics
4	Quality Tools
5	Quality Planning
6	Quality Assurance
7	Quality Assurance Procedures
8	Quality Assurance Roles and Responsibilities
9	Quality Control
10	Quality Control Procedures
11	Quality Control Roles and Responsibilities

You are responsible for communicating the quality management plan to your team and customer so that everyone is aligned with the product's quality level. For example, the test team requires their work to align with the quality management plan through the Quality Control section of the document. Project testing is scheduled for two three-day periods, but because of complexities and time limits, the test team only completes one of the three-day period test cycles. As such, the customer will not think they are getting everything agreed upon for quality control. Even if no defects are found in the first test cycle, the customer will want the test team to perform that second cycle because they paid for a certain amount of testing to be done; therefore, they will expect that testing to occur. The customer may also feel like the test team is forcing decreased quality into the product by not performing the second test cycle. If the project ends and the test team never goes back and completes the extra testing, the team could potentially release a less quality product. The test team, by skipping the last test, could potentially miss errors or problems in the product that could have been found by extra testing. Completing the second round of testing would provide the customer the testing quality that they agreed to in the quality management plan. If the test team completed a third round of testing, they would have exceeded the quality level documented in the plan. Using this thought process, the customer would equate the product's quality level with the number of test passes. This could be right or wrong, but it would be the customer's opinion and you would need to deal with it. On the other hand, if the logic is that every test pass will find more errors, the project team may never stop testing, or may never get to a point where there are zero errors. In this case, work with the customer and stand behind what they agreed to as the quality level they were willing to accept and that they approved in the quality management plan.

The quality management plan does not provide a step-by-step process for quality testing and is not a detailed how-to-guide. The document provides the test team guidelines and procedures for testing each product quality area. When quality issues arise, refer to the quality management plan as a guide to decide how to resolve and correct testing failures. For example, if you have an issue in the quality control area, review the Quality Control section and the Quality Control Procedures section in the plan to find out how to resolve the issues. The plan is a reference guide to help you manage and control project quality.

There are only a couple of potential disadvantages for project teams implementing a quality management plan. One disadvantage is adding rigorous quality control for a project that does not warrant it, and another is adding time and money to perform quality testing where it is not cost-effective. Otherwise, you should implement a quality management plan on all projects. Few customers are not concerned with project quality. Individual team members who do not want to focus on quality, or don't care about quality, may not be a good fit for the team. Occasionally, you might need to reassign a team member. If a customer feels that other areas are more important than quality and they approve and document that expectation, respect those wishes and react where applicable.

The quality management plan covers many quality areas including:

- **Quality planning:** Identifies and enforces the expected quality level. Quality planning includes deciding how many test cases the test team runs for each test scenario. Discuss the quality level with stakeholders early in the project. Once you know the level your customer expects, he or she can work with the project team to ensure they meet that quality level. If the quality level drops due to bad test cases or product failures, quickly address those issues with the project team. Follow the procedures documented in the quality management plan to help regain the product's high quality level.
- **Quality assurance:** Focuses on the processes for managing and delivering solutions. The manager, project team, and other stakeholders perform various quality assurance processes throughout the project. An example of a quality assurance activity is user acceptance testing. Projects that have a phase built into the project methodology to let customers test the product early, increase their overall product acceptance. Without a User Acceptance phase, most customers will not see the product until it is officially released at the end of the project. This could be a major problem if your customers aren't happy with the results.
- **Quality control:** Ensures that quality control activities are continually performed throughout the project. These activities verify that project deliverables are high quality. Quality control activities include testing to ensure that tests pass at acceptable levels and that the customer approves the test results.
- **Quality standards:** Certifies the processes and systems of an organization and not the product or service. In 1987, the International Organization for Standardization (ISO) created a series of quality standards named ISO 9000-1987. These standards are applicable in many different industries based on the following categories: design, production, and service delivery. Many companies try to achieve the ISO 9000 quality standard to improve their operations. This standard is a benchmark used in industries around the world.
- **Quality tools:** The discipline of total quality control uses many quantitative methods and tools to identify problems and suggest avenues for continuous improvement. Quality experts have found that many quality-related problems can use the seven quantitative tools to resolve quality problems.

Planning to use a quality management plan

When planning and preparing to use a quality management plan, you must first decide when to start quality testing and how the team can improve project quality. After making those decisions, work with a test team member or a quality manager to develop the quality management plan. You own the project's quality management plan. After finding an owner, you and the owner work with the customer to decide where to focus quality testing. The next step is to gather the quality management reporting and communication requirements from your customer, which also includes the reporting requirements for the quality testing results. After adequately planning and documenting that information from your customers, you are prepared to use the project's quality management plan.

Reporting from a quality management plan

Any team member can create the project's quality management plan. Occasionally, you are responsible for creating the plan with the help and support of the test team. If the project is large enough, you and your customer could hire a quality manager to ensure that someone is dedicated full time to tracking and controlling project quality.

It is a best practice to review other projects' quality management plans as a starting point for your project. By reviewing those plans, you look for quality processes and procedures that other projects used that you can use for your project. The goal is to learn how quality was managed on other projects and use some of those best practices on your project. Most processes have been tested and proven to be successful, so use them for your project when applicable. Another technique you should take advantage of when trying to understand project quality is reviewing lessons-learned data related to quality testing and management best practices from prior projects. Information about special testing or quality levels is helpful to you and your team—specifically, what went right and what went wrong during the project's testing phase.

The quality management plan does not fall into the weekly status reporting cycle because it does not contain project status information. You are responsible for making sure the quality management plan is in a document format and stored in the document control system.

Understanding the Shewhart cycle

Walter Shewhart developed the Shewhart cycle in the 1920s. The Shewhart cycle chart helps improve the organization or product quality being built. As you learn about quality and its importance on your project, understanding the origin and history of the Shewhart cycle is important and sets context to how you will manage quality on your project. The Shewhart cycle process has been popular in quality management circles for years. You should practice this process on all your projects.

The Shewhart cycle chart is defined by four main areas:

1. Plan: Improve results by designing or revising the process components.

2. Do: Implement the plan and measure its performance.

3. Check: Evaluate and report results to stakeholders.

4. Action: Make a decision on possible process changes for improvement.

Apply the ideas from the Shewhart cycle chart to your project when quality is critical to the project's success. This process is important for controlling and communicating quality at each step. Communicate the progress and results as the project progresses through each step. The quality process is repeated throughout the testing process, which you communicate along the way.

The following figure represents an example of the Shewhart cycle chart. The chart starts at the Plan phase and runs continually until achieving quality on the project. This is a popular chart with many different versions on the Internet that incorporate the same format and information. This chart is standard in the quality management area.

Figure 10.2 — Example of the Shewhart Cycle represents a typical Shewhart cycle. The Shewhart cycle focuses on four main processes: plan, do, check, act.

Figure 10.2 — Example of the Shewhart Cycle

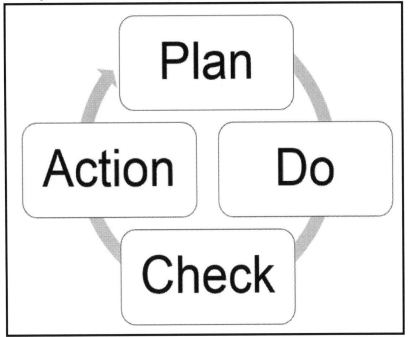

Cross-Reference

See Chapter 16 - Using Communication Tools During the Initiating Process to find out more about how to use a quality management plan.

Introduction to the Quality Metrics Tool

The *quality metrics* tool specifies your customer satisfaction level as it applies to product quality. A metric comprises one or more measures. It is a measurement of how satisfied your customer is with the results. Project quality metrics give you and your project team a project quality goal. By setting up quality metrics, your customers are on the same page as the project team so everyone is driving to the highest quality level.

Every project has a metric that measures the customer's satisfaction level for what they are receiving. For example, for every 1000 screws, a customer might accept 25 defective screws. This example represents the accepted satisfaction level, or the quality level. Other examples include the number of code defects in software, specific building codes in construction, or sample sizing in drug research. Regardless of the test applied, there is a customer metric that the project team needs to strive to achieve. If that is not possible, your customer may simply refuse the project and reject the product until they are satisfied. This could lead to lawsuits, civil cases, and project failure.

You should be aware of the difficulties in getting quality metrics from your customer and work with them to set up an acceptance level. This is difficult because your customer will demand the highest quality level possible, irrespective of the project's budget. Make sure to align the budget with your customer's demands. If there is not enough budget for the project team to attain the quality level that they were originally granted, you need to add more funds to the budget. The customer and management need to approve the extra funds, but in the end, the project needs additional budget to support the request for improved project quality.

Note
The Project Management Institute's knowledge area for this tool is the quality management area. The secondary areas that this tool could be associated with are integration and risk.

Tool Value
Quality metrics give you the ability to track and control project quality. Customer satisfaction is rated by how well the project team meets or falls short of individual quality metrics.

Social Media Tools
The communication purpose for quality metrics is to inform. Communication from quality metrics can be posted on social media tools, such as Yammer, Socialcast, and Facebook (private group).

Quality metrics are about satisfying your customer's expectations. However, meeting your customer's satisfaction does not always mean the quality has to be 100 percent; occasionally, they will accept a much lower percentage and still be satisfied. It is important that you or the quality manager ensure that your customer approves a range of project quality that they are comfortable with. This needs to happen before project activities start; the project team should focus on staying within the approved quality range. This is the best chance for your customer to be satisfied with the results. For example, if you are producing millions of screws every day, a failure rate of 25 per 10,000 could be significant, but small in comparison to manufacturing as a whole.

The following list shows some quality metric examples:

- **Software metric:** The number of reported bugs or software errors in an application. Severity level bugs are between one and three and each suggest the level of impact on the system. One is the most severe level.

- **Database metric:** The database must return results within 5 to 10 seconds, independent of the number of stored records or the number of users accessing the database.
- **Office metric:** Office cubicle units must be a minimum 6 feet high and V-shaped so they fit in a corner and have overhead storage units. There should be lighting under each overhead storage unit to provide enough desktop light. The desktop should be 2 feet by 6 feet, totaling 24-square feet of surface area. The units will have standard file drawers at each end of the V-shape and enough room for a file cabinet.
- **Cross border times metric:** When crossing the border between Canada and the United States, the maximum wait time should be 15 minutes. More than 15 minutes result in unhappy travelers.
- **Project cost and schedule metric:** It is best to set up metrics at the beginning of the project. The project should never be delayed more than one week and should never be more than 2 percent over budget.

Note

You must manage your customer's expectations as they relate to project quality.

When dealing with the challenges of quality metrics, "breakpoints" is a common term for exceeding your customer's level of satisfaction. *Breakpoints* are an unacceptable quality level that represents the dissatisfaction events that occur when a project reaches or exceeds a certain metrics level. The breakpoint is also just before the point where the quality level is still tolerable. In other words, breakpoints are levels that, if crossed over, the project has failed to meet your customer's expectations.

When developing quality metrics, one important part of metric development is deciding the breakpoints for each metric. Your customers should set their breakpoint expectations because the expectation is customer-specific. You are responsible deciding what steps to take when the project hits those points, and how to direct the team to respond to those issues. For example, if a project is constantly hitting 100 bad screws out of 10,000, your customer will direct the project manager to stop the manufacturing line. The customer and project manager would then walk through each process upstream of the failure point to find out where the failure rates occur. In performing upstream failure point analysis, the project manager and customer discover where the failure occurs. The project team can correct the failure point and move forward in the manufacturing cycle.

Planning to use a quality metrics tool

When planning and preparing to use quality metrics, you must first decide the various areas on the project where quality is essential. Some projects may have multiple areas where quality plays a role and other projects may have limited areas. When planning for project testing, decide where your customer wants the most focus and ensure the process and procedures are set up to apply that focus. After the project team decides what quality testing means for their respective areas, work with your customer to find out if they want to be involved in the testing cycle. In some project areas, there will be no customer involvement. Other areas, such as design, screen layout, or report testing, your customer will be heavily involved. Customers involved in this process can be sometimes challenging. Keep a handle on the challenges and manage your customer wisely. You can achieve this by something as simple as producing daily or weekly reports for your customer and keeping them in the loop during the testing process. How you handle customer engagement without derailing project progress is important during the planning process.

Reporting from quality metrics

Your role as project manager is to communicate quality metrics during the testing phase by comparing the results from the test team to your customer's expectations. If, during the planning process, your customer created multiple metrics, you must communicate all of them during testing. This visibility gives the test team exposure to your customer's metrics and ensures that everyone is aligned. As the testing process continues, communicate the results of each metric. Communication continues throughout the testing cycle.

Quality metrics fall into the weekly or daily status reporting cycle. Because the metrics do not contain project status information, but do contain information to judge quality, regular information reporting is essential. Information, such as the number of bugs found during software testing, wait times, or defective product amounts are examples of status reporting during weekly status meetings. Your customers and project team must ensure constant project quality and watch the quality metrics closely each week and react if the team does not meet those metrics. Whoever is responsible for creating quality metrics usually do so in a document or spreadsheet format and store them in the document control system, which provides long-term archiving and access to anyone interested.

Cross-Reference
Chapter 19 - Using Communication Tools for Project Reporting during the Planning Process to learn more about how to use quality metrics.

Introduction to the Scatter Chart

The *scatter chart,* or scatter diagrams, plots data points based on two sets of independent variables. Project teams use them to show relationships between two independent data points. Scatter charts display a pattern of data that lets customers and team members decipher what the patterns mean on the chart. Once you understand the data, you can make project-level decisions about what you see in those patterns. Project teams use scatter charts to test theories, try ideas, and look for possible relationships between two variables. The idea is that you can change one variable and watch what happens to the other. This is commonly called a cause-and-effect relationship chart and is used on many projects.

Note
The Project Management Institute's knowledge area for this tool is the quality management area. The secondary areas that this tool could be associated with are time, cost, and risk.

Tool Value
A scatter chart displays the relationship between two variables when you need to find out what happens to one variable when the other one changes. It communicates whether a relationship exists between two variables.

Social Media Tools
The communication purposes for the scatter chart are to inform and persuade. Communication from the scatter chart can be posted on social media tools, such as Yammer, Socialcast, and Facebook (private group).

A scatter chart can display large amounts of data that identify groups of information in a trending format. As project manager, you should watch this chart closely because it provides information that can increase project success. You can use the scatter chart to track project performance, such as earned value reporting. Monitor the scatter charts throughout your project and course correct along the way if you see a problem with the data. If the project data is trending in the wrong direction, use that data to jump into action and turn the team around.

When a scatter chart contains both project schedule and cost information, it is easy to communicate this information to your customers by going over the chart contents. This information keeps you informed about two of the most important project areas by using this communication tool.

The relationships on a scatter chart fall into various patterns or categories. **Figure 10.3 — Example of a Scatter Chart (No Correlation)** shows no correlation between the X and the Y variables. Y is not dependent on X or the other way around. The data points in **Figure 10.3** have no relational pattern and are scattered over the whole chart.

Figure 10.3 — Example of a Scatter Chart (No Correlation)

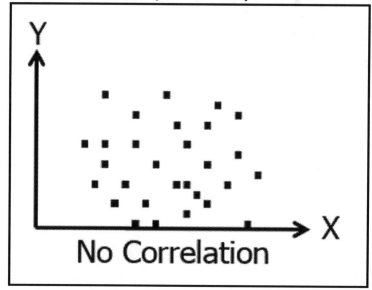

Figure 10.4 — Example of a Scatter Chart (Positive Correlation) shows a positive correlation between the X and the Y variables. An increase in Y may depend on an increase in X, or the other way around. The data points of Figure 10.4 have an upward slope. This signals a control in X may bring about a control in Y.

Figure 10.4 — Example of a Scatter Chart (Positive Correlation)

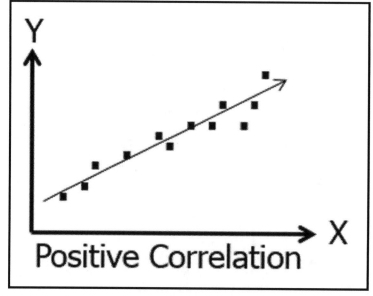

Figure 10.5 — Example of Scatter Chart (negative correlation) shows a negative correlation between the X and the Y variables. A decrease in Y may be dependent on an increase in X, or the other way

around. The data points in Figure 10.5 have a downward slope. This indicates a control in X may bring about a control in Y.

Figure 10.5 — Example of Scatter Chart (negative correlation)

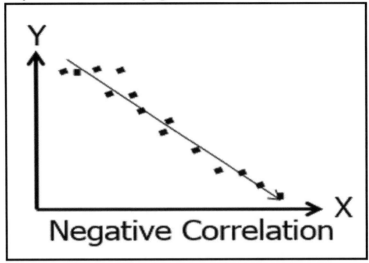

Figure 10.6 — Example of a Scatter Chart (Old Faithful Eruptions) represents a typical scatter chart. The chart shows the different wait times between eruptions (mins) and the eruption duration (mins). The Y-axis on the chart is the wait time between eruptions ranging from 40 to 100 minutes. The X-axis displays the duration of the eruption time ranging between 1.5 minutes to 5.5 minutes. Notice how the scatter chart forms a dumbbell pattern. Also, notice that if an eruption is short, the time between eruptions is also short. If eruptions are long, the time between eruptions is also long.

Figure 10.6 — Example of a Scatter Chart (Old Faithful Eruptions)

Old Faithful Eruptions

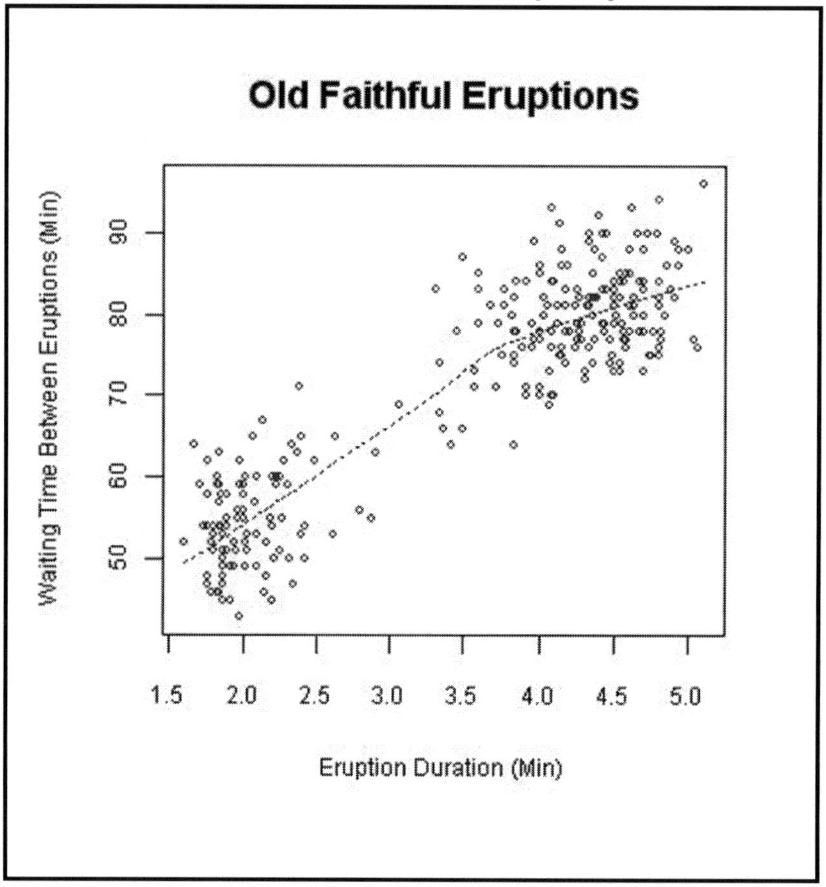

Project managers, team members, and customers (or stakeholders) can all benefit from using scatter charts. Project stakeholders benefit because scatter charts can graph specific product level data that, when placed on a chart, makes it much easier to make a product-level decision based on that data. You, as project manager, can also benefit from scatter charts, especially when you are charting schedule and cost information. After that information is on the chart, it's much easier to make project-level decisions, such as pushing out deadlines or adding more dollars to the budget.

The scatter chart plots data points based on two independent variables on an X-Y grid. The relationship between the two variables may form a pattern that reveals information not possible in any other way. Using the two-dimensional X-Y axes scatter chart you can see data patterns or trends by drawing an average curve through the data points. It is important to remember that time dimension in scatter charts plays a major role in data collection. For example, data can collect and be added to the chart at any time. The advantage of using the scatter chart is that it continues to chart data regardless of when it is acquired. Time is not a factor in data collection, unless it is one of the variables on the chart. Therefore, scatter charts can have data that is continually charting and plotting. This also holds true for sequential data and it does not matter the order the data is in, it is just a point on the scatter chart. The scatter chart is much different from a line graph even though it uses a line on the chart. It is not like a line graph because it does not matter which order the data is in, it just becomes a point on the scatter chart. On a line graph, the order of the data collection and charting is important.

A scatter chart can have multiple data point types. Each data point set has a unique identifier. It can be a symbol, number, color, size or any combination. If you want, you can average the data points as a line graph and not display the data points. However, if you want to, you can also show the line and the data points to display possible trends.

Planning to use a scatter chart

When planning and preparing to use a scatter chart, you must first plan and analyze the data to decide if it will match the scatter chart format. Usually, the data matches the format. You then work with the project team to discuss their role in gathering data to support creating a scatter chart. Usually, this is one or two team members who will be responsible for collecting and providing data throughout the project. You then work with your project customers and decide what types of scatter chart reports your customer wants. Talk to your customers so that they understand the format and can read and understand the scatter chart when it's delivered. Some customers may not initially understand the chart so you'll need to explain how to read it.

Reporting from a scatter chart

There is no single scatter chart creator. If the project is small, you or a project analyst creates the project reports. The scatter chart report falls into the category of predefined regular project reports. If the project is large enough, there is often a large administrative group responsible for creating various reports, and then someone in that group is responsible for creating the scatter chart.

Here are the possible chart types for scatter charts:

- Cost performance index and schedule performance index charts
- Average overtime hours worked to mistake count
- Activate ingredients in a product to its shelf life
- Experience versus salary
- Hours a light bulb burns versus room temperature

Figure 10.7 — Example of Scatter Chart (Schedule and Budget Tracking) shows budget and schedule information. This chart shows a project tracking ahead of schedule and under budget as the most dominate pattern on the chart. Each diamond (data point) on the chart represents a month's worth of progress based on the Schedule Performance Index (SPI) versus the Cost Performance Index (CPI) for the month. Considering the SPI, the axis is along the bottom and any diamond to the right of 1.0 is ahead of schedule. Diamonds to the left of 1.0 are behind schedule. The farther away from 1.0, the farther the schedule was either ahead or behind schedule.

The same holds true for the CPI. In this case, it would be the Y-axis or vertical axes. Any diamonds above 1.0 represent a performance under budget, and any diamond below the 1.0 mark is over budget.

Cross-Reference
See Chapters 9 - Communication Tools That Manage Project Costs and Chapter 19 - Using Communication Tools for Project Reporting during the Planning Process for more information on CPI and SPI calculations in the Earned Value sections of the chapters.

Figure 10.7 — Example of Scatter Chart (Schedule and Budget Tracking)

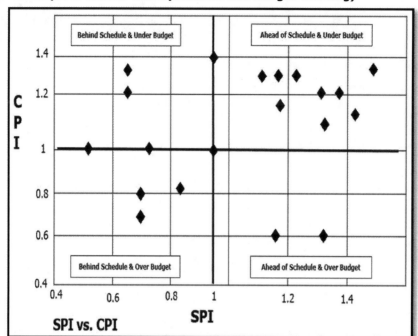

Scatter charts fall into the weekly status reporting cycle because they contain project status information that is relevant and applicable to the project. Scatter charts provide the best possible picture of the project to you, project team, or customers. A scatter chart uses the spreadsheet or charting format and is stored as part of the document control system.

Cross-Reference
Chapter 19 - Using Communication Tools for Project Reporting during the Planning Process to learn more about how to use a scatter chart.

Summary

In summary, this chapter touches on many tools to help project managers, customers, and team members manage and control the project's quality areas. You must instill the highest level of project quality practices into your team. The project team is also responsible for quality and should create everything at the highest quality level.

One tool that stands out in this chapter is the scatter chart. Take some time to learn about scatter chart capabilities. You will quickly see how effective it is and how to immediately use it on your projects. When you create scatter charts to help manage your projects, you mainly include schedule and cost information, but by combining earned value calculations, the tool becomes a valuable asset for any project.

Chapter 11

Communication Tools for Human Resource Management

IN THIS CHAPTER

- ◆ Introduction to the Circle-of-Communications chart
- ◆ Introduction to the Histogram report
- ◆ Introduction to the Project Organization chart
- ◆ Introduction to the Responsibility Matrix (RACI)

On most projects, managing project team members can be challenging because most of them are not your direct employees; they are often on loan to you from their functional manager(s). If they are contractors, they do not even work for your company. Usually, you have no authority to hire or fire them, nor are you even responsible for issuing their paychecks. You are simply a project manager with the resources that were available when the project started. It can be a struggle sometimes to motivate them to work late or perform extra tasks that may be over and above the actual duties. Another resource management challenge is planning so that resources have a balanced workload and are not overworked so as to avoid resource burnout. For example, a team member might have multiple assignments and your project is only one part of their total workload. Planning and balancing your team's workloads across multiple projects is complex for any project manager. It's wise for multiple project managers to communicate and plan the workload of shared resources.

One of your main responsibilities is obtaining resources for your team. You need to find the right project skills for the right roles. You must also ensure that your team understands their roles and specific project responsibilities. At the same time that the project is executing, you should be reviewing your resources. You will spend time deciding where you can improve team skills, work performance, and project contributions.

In this chapter, we explore project communication tools for the human resource management knowledge area. These tools help you communicate effectively and manage your project resources. Each tool can improve your overall project communications.

Introduction to the Circle-of-Communications Chart

The *circle-of-communications chart* identifies and documents the various project roles. The chart format is easy to follow and removes project politics of who reports to whom. Most project managers work in a team environment where they have a set of employees or vendors that do not formally report to them. Therefore, putting yourself in the top position on a formal organization chart and the team members beneath you is political suicide. Using a project organization chart to document team member relationships to you is problematic. Doing so puts yourself in a position where it appears that team members functionally report to you. On projects where you are functionally responsible for team members, a project organization chart may make sense, but even then, the focus is on reporting relationships and not communications, which is a problem. This is where the circle-of-communications chart is so valuable. The chart clearly shows the project manager as the center for all project communications. Because 90% of your job is communications, you should be the center of project communications. Another way to look at it is that all formal communications coming in and out of the project go by you, the project manager. There are no exceptions to this process; you own project communications.

Note
The Project Management Institute's knowledge area for this tool is the human resources management area. The secondary area that this tool could be associated with is communications.

Tool Value
The circle-of-communications chart provides a view of everyone involved on the project.

Social Media Tools
The communication purpose for the circle-of-communications chart is to inform. Communication from the chart can be posted on social media tools, such as Yammer, Socialcast, and Facebook (private group).

Figure 11.1 — Example of a Circle-of-Communications Chart shows an example of a circle-of-communications chart. The chart is simple and easy to follow. The project manager is located in the center of the chart, which clearly indicates that the project manager owns project communications. It does not mean, however, that communication cannot occur without the project manager, it only means that the project manager must be involved in formal and final communications.

Let's break down **Figure 11.1** to learn about the chart. As you can see, this example is for an IT software development project that has six project leads and individual team members who work for those leads. For example the development lead has two developers working for him or her, the Test Lead has two testers, and so on. Simple and easy to understand, right? What is unique about the chart are the lines that connect each project lead. The lines between the leads represent communication among the leads. Another unique part of this chart is the project manager circle. We already pointed out that you, the project manager, are the center of communications so you have the biggest circle on the chart. But, the project manager circle is also touching each of the leads' circles on the chart. The project manager constantly connects and communicates with the project leads in each smaller circle, which makes sense because projects that have team leads usually have a direct communication path to the project manager. Many companies create project teams with a project manager and team leads from each functional area needed on the project. Those team leads from the various functions would have team members that functionally report to them throughout the project. The concept of using core teams and extended teams is common in the project management industry to help people understand their roles. In this example, the leads in the six circles are part of the project's core team and the communication point between the project manager and the project's extended team members.

Figure 11.1 — Example of a Circle-of-Communications Chart

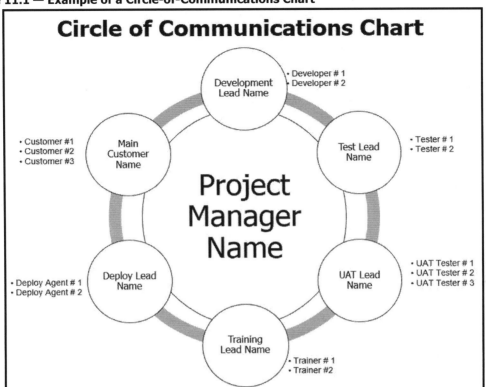

Circle of Communications Chart

- Customer #1
- Customer #2
- Customer #3

Main Customer Name

Development Lead Name

- Developer # 1
- Developer # 2

Test Lead Name

- Tester # 1
- Tester # 2

Project Manager Name

UAT Lead Name

- UAT Tester # 1
- UAT Tester # 2
- UAT Tester # 3

Deploy Lead Name

- Deploy Agent # 1
- Deploy Agent # 2

Training Lead Name

- Trainer # 1
- Trainer #2

Now that you understand the design and look and feel of the circle-of-communications chart, let's focus on using the chart as a communication tool.

To understand the communication side of the tool, there are a couple areas to cover. The first area is that all formal and final communications must go through you, the project manager. When team members or team leads want to informally communicate, they don't need to keep you fully informed, they can communicate without you to keep the project moving. Once there is formal communications between the team leads and something that needs to be shared to customers or leadership, you must be in the loop for those communications. The following example will help you understand how to use the chart for communication. The customer directly asked the User Acceptance Testing (UAT) tester for the UAT Test Pass #2 test results. In that project scenario, would the UAT tester go directly to the customer and provide the results? They could, there is nothing stopping someone from communicating with the customer, but it is not the official process and could cause problems if the customer reacts the wrong way to the results. If the UAT tester provides the direct results to the customer, bypassing you the project manager, that would not honor the golden rule that official communications goes though you the project manager. In this example, the UAT tester should follow the formal process and communicate only to his or her lead. The lead then shares applicable information with only the project manager. Finally, the project manager shares the information with the customer, if needed. You're probably thinking, "Wow, that's some overhead just to provide some test results." While that appears to be true to, but project managers realize that is far from the truth. In this example, the UAT tester had no idea that the project manager and another tester had not completed testing. The results from all of the testing have not been recorded. So, if someone provides test results to the customer at this point, the data would be wrong, creating even more problems for the project manager. The impact and politics of providing false data to a customer can be negative and long lasting. To avoid that, the communication process must be followed and all formal and final project communications must go through you, the project manager.

Another valuable and overlooked area of the circle-of-communications chart is remembering to add to the chart the names of everyone working on the project. By putting names on the chart, you indicate that only those individuals should receive project communications. This is often overlooked because it is so simple. If your name is not on the chart, you should not receive project updates and regular communications. By creating the circle-of-communications chart, you document and outline everyone involved on the project and who you are responsible for communicating with. The data you collect when creating the chart is data you will use in other communication tools, such as the communication requirements matrix and the role report matrix and therefore it is a best practice to create the circle-of-communications chart before creating any other communication tools. You won't be effective creating the other communication tools without creating the circle-of-communications chart first because you need to identify who you need to communicate with before you can complete the other tools.

Cross-reference
See Chapter 2 – Planning Project Communication for more information about the communication requirements matrix and the role report matrix.

Planning to use a circle-of-communications chart

When planning to use a circle-of-communications chart, you must first focus on its purpose, and then decide where and how to use it. You use the chart to collect the names and roles of project stakeholders, so how you use this data after it is collected is simple. You use this information to drive all project communications, such as setting up distribution lists, deciding who receives project status, deciding who should attend status meetings, and finally determining with whom to communicate with throughout the project.

You can use the circle-of-communications chart in several project documents. It is an effective project communication tool. The circle-of-communications chart is used in project communication charts, newsletters, status reports, and so on. For example, you use it to develop the project's stakeholder register and for the project's communication plan. The circle-of-communications chart won't include all the information that the other documents contain, but that is why it is such a quick and simple tool to create. Just add the roles and the names to start the process.

Reporting from the circle-of-communications chart

You will regularly use the circle-of-communications chart for reporting and communicating who is involved with the project. Reporting from the circle-of-communications chart is helpful when people ask you who is working on the project, who your customers are, who to send project information to, and so on—all of the information is on the chart. There will be many occasions where you will report from and communicate what is on the circle-of-communications chart; it is a best practice to add it directly to your project communications plan.

Cross-Reference
See Chapter 16 - Using Communication Tools During the Initiating Process to learn more about how to plan, create, and use a circle-of-communications chart.

Introduction to the Histogram Report

The *histogram report* displays project information using an easy-to-read graphic format. The histogram report consists of vertical bars across multiple categories along the horizontal axis. The report shows what proportion of data falls into each category and where the data can spread across those multiple categories. You use histogram reports for various reasons. Examples include cost and labor hours, percentage of time to a certain area, and number of used sick and vacation days per quarter. It is unbelievable the number of different reports that are possible using the histogram format. It is up to your imagination to decide which reports you want to create for your projects.

Note
The Project Management Institute's knowledge area for this tool is the human resources management area. The secondary area that this tool could be associated with is risk.

Tool Value
A histogram report is an instantly recognizable graph for your customers that shows variances in data categories. The chart displays simple variances between the horizontal data and the vertical values on the graph.

Social Media Tools
The communication purposes for the histogram report are to inform and instruct. Communication from the histogram report can be posted on social media tools, such as Yammer, Socialcast, and Facebook (private group).

You and your team will regularly communicate your project's histogram report throughout the project's life cycle. Some of your customers will expect multiple histogram reports so that they can continually monitor the project. Other customers may want only a few reports to ensure that they stay on top of the project but are not bogged down with too many reports. In either scenario, work with your customer to ensure that they are comfortable with the number of histogram reports they receive. If your customer wants more or less reports, adjust your communications accordingly.

Note
Histogram reports are also called stacked charts or skyline charts.

People commonly confuse histogram reports with bar charts (for example, the Gantt chart). Those outside the project management profession consider a histogram report and bar chart to be the same. Let's look at the differences to avoid any confusion.

Figure 11.2 — Example of a histogram report and bar chart shows a histogram report on the left and a bar chart on the right. You can easily see the differences between the two.

Figure 11.2 — Example of a histogram report and bar chart

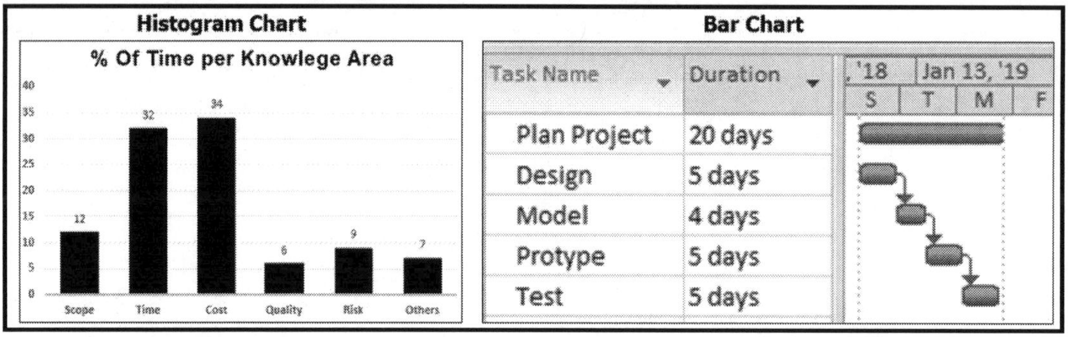

The process for creating histogram reports is project specific and often falls on you to decide the process and communicate it to the project team. You select the information that you want to show in the histogram report. You decide with whom to share the report based on the data captured in the report.

Cross-Reference

See Chapter 22- Using Communication Tools in Executing and Controlling Process to Report Project Information for more information about creating and using a histogram report.

As long as the data is available and refreshed for each reporting cycle, there are few challenges to creating a histogram report. The only challenge worth mentioning is ensuring the data is available and relevant—creating the report is simple. You cannot rely on a regular histogram reporting cycle if there are problems getting refreshed data for the report.

There are many project areas where histogram reports are useful for reporting, such as:

- **Cost management:** The histogram report displays information such as actuals, budget overtime (by week, month, quarter, and so on), and vendor cost comparisons over a stated period. The histogram report is a great choice for reports showing rental equipment costs, consultant hours, and other project costs where it is important to have visibility on ranges such as time. The possibilities and number of histogram reports are almost unlimited.

- **Resource management:** The histogram report displays resource availability over time. The chart shows budgeted and actual work hours, per week, for individual resources. In **Figure 11.3**, below, Bill is working the most hours in the group, which makes it is easy to determine who is working the least amount of hours. Histogram reports also show which resources have worked on project activities over their current workload. You will often use the histogram report to see the project's resource allocations. Use the report periodically (daily, weekly, monthly) to keep team members informed and accountable for the hours they are working and recording on the project. This resource hours per week data also helps you determine resource allocations for your project team members. Some resources might be over allocated, some might be under allocated. If the data shows either situation, adjust team members' assignments as necessary.

There are many benefits to using histogram reports: they display multiple levels of comparison data on a single chart. Multiple-level histogram reports, or stacked histogram reports, provide multiple data points on a single column of data. Another benefit is being able to drill down into a histogram report. You can select the highest level (summary level) of data, and then expand the data for additional details. Histogram reports are created by using a spreadsheet application and its chart wizards. The reports can be horizontal or vertical with two or three dimensions.

Because the histogram report is beneficial for many project areas, the data in the report determines who will benefit from using it. For example, if you create the histogram report with resource allocation data, the resources' functional managers will also want to use the report so they can see which projects resources are working on and how much time they are spending on each. If the finance department creates a histogram reports based on the project cost data, it becomes a key financial report for the finance team. The same report can be used in different project areas where project leads create their own histogram report versions. The histogram report is a robust and key communication tool for many members of the project team to use.

Planning to use a histogram report

When planning to use the histogram report, you must first decide which project areas will benefit the most from the report. Resource, cost, and scheduling areas are potentially best suited for this report type, but it can vary from project to project. Next, find out your customer's reporting needs, such as what type of data the customer wants to see and how often they expect them. Sometimes, customers have specific reporting requirements and the histogram will usually meet the needs of your customer. You also need to determine who will create the reports and ensure that he or she is scheduled enough time to perform work activities and create the histogram reports. After performing these planning steps, you have adequately planned for using histogram reports on your project.

Reporting from a histogram report

Usually, you are responsible for creating a histogram report on a project. On large projects, the administrative team is usually responsible for creating and communicating the histogram report.

The histogram report is a great communication tool for messaging specific project information to project customers. You will enjoy how quickly you can create a report and communicate it to your customers, and your customers will appreciate getting the information in a format that is easy to follow and that provides valuable project information.

Figure 11.3 — Example of a Histogram Report (Hours Worked per Resource) is an example of a histogram report. This example shows the hours per week for four project resources across a five-week period. Histogram reports are helpful for tracking project problems. Data, such as resource burnout, resource budgeting, or other project issues are all valuable to report with this tool. For example, the resource "Sam" on the chart is falling behind in his work because he had a short week in the third week and is now catching up, so his work may suffer.

Figure 11.3 — Example of a Histogram Report (Hours Worked per Resource)

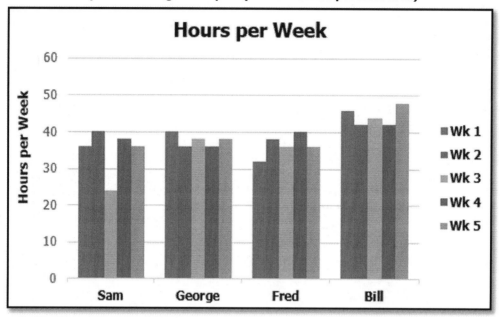

Figure 11.4 — Example of a Histogram Report (Work Hours per Resource) shows a second histogram report with a stacked histogram report in a 3-D format. In this example, it is difficult to find a particular resource's hours per week, but easy to see the cumulative hours per week for all resources. You can find out the number of hours worked in a chart like this better than most other reports. For details about an anomaly on this chart, you can create a detailed chart that shows what data is causing the issue.

Figure 11.4 — Example of a Histogram Report (Work Hours per Resource - Stacked)

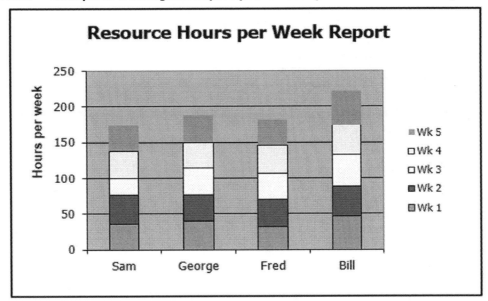

Add histogram reports to your standard reporting cycle on a weekly, bi-weekly, or monthly basis. The histogram report depends on the project's reporting cycle and the specific data required for the report. You create a histogram report by using the graphs included in a spreadsheet program. Then, you can make the report available in PowerPoint or on an internal website for anyone to access. It is a best practice to store the histogram report in the document control system for long-term archiving and availability to everyone.

Introduction to the Project Organization Chart

The *project organization chart* displays the project's organizational structure. Team members (especially new ones), customers, or management can use this chart to see who is working on the project and to understand their roles. The project organization chart helps team members decide with whom to communicate on the project. When reviewing each team member's assignment, you can cater your communications to them. For example, you would not send a plumber a work request for something electrical, or vice versa. The project organization chart also offers an at-a-glance view of missing roles (if applicable) and where the team might be short-staffed. Often, the project has a full team but may not have enough resources with a particular skill; for example, not enough testers in a software development project. The project organization chart may not specifically show staffing issues until you understand the project work needed. When you know the required project work, the organization chart may indirectly show that you need more resources for a particular role. A project organization chart for large projects let team members see across roles to discover contacts and team leads, which helps with team communications—especially team leads. On small projects, team dynamics are easier to manage, but a project organization chart still offers the same benefits as it does for large projects, just on a smaller scale. Either way, anyone can look at the project organization chart to see how big or small the project is.

Note
The Project Management Institute's knowledge area for this tool is the integration area. There are no other knowledge areas for this tool.

Tool Value
A project organization chart communicates project roles and their relationships to one another along the lines of authority. It shows the positions of all team members and is easy to follow.

Social Media Tools
The communication purposes for the project organization chart are to inform and instruct. Communication from the chart can be posted on social media tools, such as Yammer, Socialcast, and Facebook (private group).

The project organization chart provides several bits of information at a single glance. This chart shows a person's role and level on the project and each team member's reporting structure. The reporting structure, however, is one of the main issues that you can run into when using a project organization chart. The fact that you can see the team's reporting structure—with you on top of the reporting structure—can cause some major issues. On most projects, the project manager is not the functional manager of the project team's resources and is just assigned the people to work on the project; there is no formal reporting relationship. When you put yourself at the top of the organization chart, some team members get offended. Sadly, this happens all the time and you need to be aware of this potential political situation. If you hear resources complaining about the project organization chart, the easiest solution is to choose another tool. The politics and bad relationships this can cause with team members are not worth it. Instead, use the circle-of-communications chart covered earlier in this chapter. The circle-of-communications chart takes the politics out of who reports functionally to whom and lets you work more effectively with your team. However, if you can work through the team politics, the project organization chart is a great tool.

A project organization chart can also help you understand the communication links associated with the project. In *Chapter 3 - Working with Project Communications*, we discuss the various advantages and challenges of project links. When reviewing the project organization chart, you can decide how challenging your project will be from a communication link perspective. Total the number of resources on the organization chart to get the number to add to the link calculations as described in the formula in *Chapter 3 - Working with Project Communications*.

Cross-Reference

See Chapter 3 – Working with Project Communications for more information about communication links.

Figure 11.5 — Example of a Project Organization Chart shows a basic example of a project organization chart for a construction project. This project organization chart represents two levels of organizational structure. The first level shows the project manager and the second level shows the major project areas. The team leads are not necessarily individual contributors, they could be, but they are more like functional leaders for each group. Each team leader usually has team members under them who perform the work activities. In this example, the project manager may not know everyone's names, but he or she works directly with the lead for a particular area, and then that lead coordinates the team's work. In this example, the project manager works closely with Bill Johnson, the Foundation lead, but may never work with a single member in Bill's group.

Figure 11.5 — Example of a Project Organization Chart

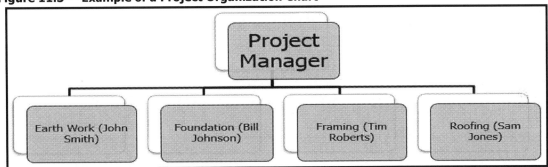

A project organization chart shows the project structure. The project organization chart is different from a *company* organization chart in that the project organization chart is valid only during the project. In defining this structure, the communication channels form indirectly from you. Referring back to **Figure 11.5** if there is a lead for a particular project area (Foundation, for example), the project manager would first communicate with that lead (Bill) to request approval to talk to Bill's team members, and only then would the project manager approach any of them. This is a respectful approach to project communications.

Usually, you are responsible for creating the project organization chart. Create the chart at the beginning of the project when there are just a few team members because it is easier to create with fewer resources, and then add to the chart as more team members arrive. As new members join the project, add them to the chart as soon as they sign on to the project. If you wait until later in the project, or when all assigned team members are on board before creating the organizational chart, it may never get finished. Usually, the organizational chart does not have the same priority level as your other project deliverables, so completing it early in the project is best so it gets done and is out of the way. Project managers or administrative support staff is usually responsible for capturing, compiling, and reporting the project organization chart on large projects.

Project organization charts are graphic and, therefore, a wonderful communication tool. The project organization chart may include color to communicate different work streams. The organization chart is used in various ways to communicate project information. Some project managers post the organization chart on a wall or in a central location, and others use it regularly in project presentations.

The project organization chart shows the managers and team members staffing the project. The chart shows the different relationships among staff members, such as:

- **Line:** Shows the direct relationship between superior and subordinate.
- **Lateral**: Shows the relationship among different departments on the same hierarchical level.
- **Team Member:** Shows the relationship among the project manager, leads, and team members. Most likely, you won't have authority over team members because they usually report to different functional managers.
- **Functional**: Supplies resources to the project and is not shown on the chart.

Planning to use the project organization chart

In preparing (planning) to create and use a project organization chart, you must first decide who the project team members are and which roles they are they filling. You need to know how to structure the project and decide who will assume team leadership roles. Different projects have different leadership roles; the project manager sets up the structure based on the roles. The project manager communicates the project structure to the various project leads to ensure those leads are accountable and responsible for their work areas. When working with the leads, you decide who the assigned team members are and who is missing. You can complete the organization chart when applicable, but if staff keep changing, it may be impossible to completely finish the chart.

Reporting from a project organization chart

The reporting process for the project organization chart is straightforward. When the first draft is complete, report it to the project team, customers, and management. Then, whenever a new team member joins or if someone leaves, update the project organization chart. At the start of the project, the chart is dynamic because you are adding staff. A weekly update is suitable during the beginning. Later, update the chart only when necessary, because it usually remains stable and people do not come and go that often. At the end of the project, when team members leave, adding a simple "X" through their boxes may be enough to keep the chart current if you don't have time to formally update the chart. Otherwise, update the chart as time permits and post a new copy to keep everyone on the project informed.

Figure 11.6 — Example of a Project Organization Chart shows a more advanced project organization chart than **Figure 11.5** because the chart includes more than one level. This example shows not only the team leaders, but their assigned staff. This is a great project organization chart for discussing staffing alternatives and deciding whether there is enough staff for the project workload.

Figure 11.6 — Example of a Project Organization Chart

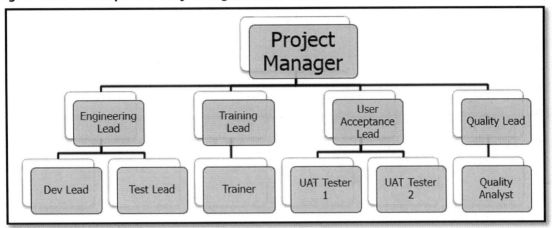

Other than the first draft, you will only produce a new chart when updating the project organization chart. You can use a presentation format, such as PowerPoint, to create the chart. The project organization chart is stored as part of the document control system, which allows for long-term archiving and availability to anyone interested in reviewing it.

Cross-Reference
See Chapter 16 - Using Communication Tools During the Initiating Process to learn more about how to create and use the project organization chart.

Introduction to the Responsibility Matrix

The *responsibility matrix* (RACI) document includes the accountabilities and responsibilities for each project role. The RACI defines the roles and responsibilities across the project. You lead your team by documenting each project role across the top of the RACI and each project activity down the side of the RACI. Where the role and the activity meet (intersection cell) is where you document the project accountabilities. The best time to create the RACI is at the beginning of the project when the project team jointly fills in the accountability levels for each role. For example, when the team looks at the designer role, they need to decide where the designer will be involved and at what level. So, the team would document in the intersection cell an "A" for accountable, an "R" for responsible, a "C" for consulted, and an "I" for informed. When you sit back and look at it, you will see exactly what that designer is going to do for each project activity. It is a simple and easy process to follow and a valuable tool for any project. At the end of this process, all of the project roles are documented. It is important that everyone agrees and signs off on the project RACI. That sign-off will be valuable to you as you run the project.

Note
The Project Management Institute's knowledge area for this tool is the human resources management area. There are no secondary areas for the RACI.

Tool Value
The RACI shows team members' assigned project tasks. Some RACIs further identify the level of authority assigned to a particular role.

Social Media Tools
The communication purposes for the RACI are to inform and instruct. Communication from the RACI can be posted on social media tools, such as Yammer, Socialcast, and Facebook (private group).

When creating the RACI, you should understand the four common accountability levels. There are different matrixes used in the industry, but there are only four main assignments in the RACI. The RACI diagram splits project deliverables into the following responsibility levels:

- **Accountable:** The resource who is ultimately accountable for completing the task, but may not complete the work themselves. Only one resource can be accountable for any project activity.
- **Responsible:** Those who complete the work tasks or develop deliverables to achieve the tasks. Multiple resources can be responsible for a project activity.
- **Consulted:** Those from whom you sought opinions from or consulted with, but who are not responsible or accountable for the work deliverable or task.
- **Informed:** Those who you are responsible for keeping informed and up to date about the project, but who are rarely involved in the project. This is usually a one-way communication only and tends to be leadership or management.

On software development projects focused on developing databases, there is a different RACI, called the CRUD Matrix. CRUD stands for create, read, update, and delete, which are specific levels of security access that are assigned to someone for controlling database data. Some users require more access than others to update data. Other users only need to read the data.

The following responsibility/security levels define the access level that various project roles can have to access data within the software application. These security levels include:

- **Create:** Ability to create database tables. The user would be able to add database tables to the system, change column names, change column sizes, and so on.
- **Read:** Ability to read database tables. The user would be able to read data from the tables that they have access to.
- **Update:** Ability to update database tables. The user would be able to update data in the tables that they have access to.
- **Delete:** Ability to delete database tables. The user would be able to delete data in the tables that they have access to.

In the construction industry, the project manager uses a RACI on most projects. There is a role for each person on the RACI. Communicating the RACI to stakeholders can be challenging due to its volatile nature. For example, a project manager asks a team member if he has completed a particular project activity. If the team member didn't know he was assigned to the activity, there's a good chance he wasn't working on it. The project manager would show the team member the RACI so he could see that he is assigned to the activity. During this interaction, the project manager could handle the situation in one of two ways. The first approach is to be demanding and tell the team member that he should have known that this was his assignment and to work only on tasks assigned to him. This approach usually doesn't work in the long run. Or, the project manager could take a more gentle approach and discuss the team member's outstanding tasks and ask him to complete the work. Either way, approach the matter carefully. Finally, a best practice is to go through the RACI with your team. That way, everyone knows their assignments and there are no surprises. The RACI is one of the more challenging communication tools for you to use on your project.

RACIs have many benefits, the most important being establishing accountability and responsibility for the project team. This benefit is by far the most valuable and the one tested throughout the project life cycle. For example, you refer to the RACI when assigning team members specific project tasks. On the other hand, when team members are assigned tasks, they check the RACI to confirm that they are responsible for completing the task. It is common to assign tasks to team members and have them check the RACI to confirm that the assignment is suitable. If not, you many need to find a more suitable resource.

Figure 11.7 — Example of a Responsibility Matrix Chart shows a RACI. In this example, you can clearly see the project roles across the top and the project activities down the side. The project's methodology, business requirements, system requirements, and design break into logical sections. In the intersecting cells between the roles and the project activities, there are a series of letters: A, R, C, and I. These letters represent the accountability level of the project role to that project task. The legend for this chart is located on the top-left corner of the chart and describes the accountability levels noted on the chart.

Figure 11.7 — Example of a Responsibility Matrix Chart

Responsibility Matrix Chart

Responsibility Codes:
Responsible: Performs the work
Accountable: Ultimately accountable for delivery; maximum one per task
Sign-Off: Approval must be gained for deliverable to be acceptable
Consult: Review & provide feedback
Informed
(blank) = not involved

	Proj Mgr	UAT Lead	Training Lead	Release Management	Sponsor 1 (TBD)	Lead Analyst	Designer	Dev Lead	Test Lead	Tier 1 Rep	Release Lead	Operations Lead
System Requirements												
Task C	I					R						
Work Product A		R,A					C					
Design												
Work Product A			I	I	C			R	C	I		
Work Product C							C					
Build												
Task F			I	I	C			R	C	I		
Task H							C					
Test												
Task I	R											
Work Product A			I	I	C				C	I		A
Task K							C				C	
User Acceptance Approval Phase												
Task L	R	R,A	R									
Work Product A	A											
Task N		A										
Production Phase												
Work Product A	I							R		R		
Task P				C	I			A				
Work Product B									A			
Post Production Support / Warranty Period (if Applicable)												
Task O	I							R		R		
Task Q									A			

The best time to create the RACI is at the beginning of the project, before any work activities begin. After selecting the project's team members, meet with the team to go through every role and item in the RACI chart. The meeting goal is to select the suitable accountability and responsibility for each project role. Often, team members are unclear about their roles, so reviewing the RACI as a team is one way to ensure everyone understands their roles. Even on small projects, it is important to understand who owns a task or deliverable at the beginning of the project.

Usually, you will find there are many project roles that have a combination of responsibilities for the project tasks. It is common to see a dual role of A/R for a single activity, meaning the project role (Customer) is both accountable and responsible to create the deliverable (requirements document). Another example is a project manager who is responsible for developing a project schedule and who is accountable for the project schedule.

Software projects are unique in that occasionally you might use a RACI and a CRUD matrix for a single software project. When software projects include databases, a large part of the project is focused on security. As noted earlier, the CRUD matrix enforces table security, so it is used on all software projects with databases. Every software project that includes databases and tables should include some form of security. Work with the database administrator to decide which roles need database access, and then create the CRUD matrix and grant proper access to those roles. Without a CRUD matrix, the tables would be completely available for anyone to randomly delete or change table data.

Table 11.1 — Example of a CRUD Responsibilities Matrix represents a basic CRUD matrix example. The CRUD matrix defines the application roles with the tables and responsibility levels. The report is easy to follow and easy to create. The chart in the example shows that the Administrator role has full access (CRUD) to all of the tables, and the Guest role has limited, read-only (R) access to the tables. As you review the chart and its various roles, you can see each role assignment for this software project. For communication purposes, you could easily share this chart with everyone on the project to ensure that it is correct.

In the CRUD matrix example, there is a role-to-table assignment for every table. Each role assignment has a C (Create), R (Read), U (Update), or D (Delete) in the intersecting cell to indicate the table security level. Software projects use this matrix for specific roles when those roles need to access or update the database.

Table 11.1 — Example of a CRUD Responsibilities Matrix

Task/Responsibility	Administrator	Power User	End User	Guest
Table A	CRUD	CR	U	R
Table B	CRUD	CRU	C	R
Table C	CRUD	R/A	C	R
Table D	CRUD	CRUD	C	R
Table E	CRUD	CRUD	D	R
Table F	CRUD	CRU	U	R

In some applications, there could also be a need to include roles such as Administrator, Power User, or Guest, and each role would be assigned at least C, R, U, or D in the table for the application. Often, the Administrator role is assigned CRUD for an application that indicates the Administrator role can do anything to the tables. Another example is a Guest role that is assigned an R role, indicating that they have Read access to the tables; they would be unable to create, update, or delete table data. Read access is perfect for a guest user on a system.

When completing a project RACI, it is a best practice to make sure that each project role has a minimum assignment of I (Informed). The I role is often used for team members or other interested parties regularly receiving project information and who want to access project details when needed. Providing an "Inform" assignment maintains constant communication and provides visibility for stakeholders to help them stay connected to the project.

In some projects, team members are assigned multiple roles for a project task, which are documented in the RACI. For example, team members might have both Accountable and Responsible roles for a project activity. Typically, however, when the role assignment is Accountable, the second role type is Responsible. We noted some of these examples earlier, but another example is a test lead on a software project who is "responsible" and "accountable" for developing and approving the software test plan. When a team member is assigned multiple roles, you might be able to reduce the project staff because resources are responsible for more of the project workload. However, in other cases, you may not be able to reduce the size of the team at all. Usually, team members are assigned multiple project roles because of specific project needs.

Planning to use the responsibility matrix

When planning to use a responsibility matrix, you first need to know your project's methodology. The project methodology drives the RACI framework and divides the project into manageable pieces. Then, you can focus on project roles for completing the tasks within the methodology. Next, you can fill those roles with project team members. Finally, review previous RACIs to understand where other projects used various roles. This gives you a better understanding of the roles and tasks that can help improve communications with the team. When planning a CRUD matrix, you must understand the various project's application roles and the databases and tables within the application. Next, document the security level access to each role. Security level access indicates which roles can change data in the application's tables. Work with the database administrator to complete the CRUD matrix.

Reporting from the responsibility matrix

You are responsible for creating the RACI. When the team approves the RACI, you can then store the responsibility matrix in the document control system for easy access. Approval should be straight-forward if you worked with the team to create the RACI because they would have approved it along the way. Work directly with anyone who rejects the RACI to find out their problems or concerns. Ensure that every team member signs and approves the RACI before starting project activities. When team members sign off on the RACI, they provide proof that they have seen the chart and accepted responsibilities and accountabilities in the chart. A lack of signatures can mean that the team hasn't acknowledged the RACI, allowing them to not be as engaged as they should be, claiming they didn't know about the chart or never approved their tasks. You can avoid this situation by ensuring that every team member signs and approves the RACI.

Database administrators start creating a CRUD matrix during the design phase for software database projects. Administrators wouldn't finalize the matrix until much later in the project. Starting the matrix creation early is fine, but it won't be finished until much later in the project.

You can include RACI details in an automated project scheduling tool. In doing so, you can update the matrix fields when you add new project activities. Thus, the effort to maintain the responsibility matrix is minimal and built in to the project schedule management. As each role is added to a project task, the nature of that role is documented. For example, when you add a tester to a test plan, you assign him or her as accountable and responsible within the schedule tool's resource assignment. You can easily do this by documenting Tester (A) and Tester (R) in the resource field. The A and R assignments are the same as using a separate responsibility matrix and assigning an A/R in the intersection cell.

The RACI does not contain project status; therefore, you do not report from it during regular project reporting. You should create the RACI in a spreadsheet tool or in a document table format. It is a best practice to store the RACI in the document control system to allow anyone interested in the tool the ability to review it any time.

Cross-Reference
See Chapter 17 - Using Communication Tools to Administer the Planning Process to learn more about how to plan, create, and use the RACI.

Summary

In summary, the tools described in this human resource management chapter help you manage and control your team. Managing a project team can be challenging and is something that takes practice and experience to be skillful at for most project managers. Project managers who are team focused and team driven are hard to find. Using these tools will help you become a better communicator and a better leader for your team.

This chapter introduces tools such as the circle-of-communications chart, responsibility matrix (RACI), and the project organization chart. Out of all the tools, the circle-of-communications chart is the most useful because it gives you the best chance of communicating effectively on your project.

With tools like these, project managers and team members have an easier time controlling project resources, driving successful projects, and keeping team members content

Chapter 12

Defining Communication Tools That Manage Project Communications

IN THIS CHAPTER

- ◆ Introduction to Agile Information Radiators
- ◆ Introduction to the Communication plan
- ◆ Introduction to the Change Readiness Assessment
- ◆ Introduction to the Daily Progress report
- ◆ Introduction to the Pareto chart
- ◆ Introduction to the Project Calendar
- ◆ Introduction to the Project Presentation
- ◆ Introduction to the Spider chart
- ◆ Introduction to the Stoplight report
- ◆ Introduction to the Work Package

Project communications is the most important area of project management. Communication management tools, such as the spider chart, daily progress report, and a stoplight report, all leverage best-practice techniques for performing project communications. You should continually try to improve how you communicate with your customers and team members. Using these communications tools can improve your communication efforts.

Some tools we mention in this chapter will be familiar to you. Keep an open mind and look at these tools from a pure communications perspective so that you can use these tools more effectively. Sometimes, the planning process for a tool will bring forth a new and better way to use the tool.

In this chapter, we also explore project communications tools that manage project information. These tools will help you communicate effectively while you manage and control the project. These tools will help you become a better communicator.

Introduction to Agile Information Radiators

Agile Information Radiators "radiate" information about different aspects of the project, product, project team, Scrum team, customer, and other project stakeholders. An information radiator is any tool that physically displays project information in the Scrum team's working space, or anywhere the project is being executed. There are two types of information radiators for an Agile project: low-tech, high-touch and high-tech, low-touch. Which type you use depends on where you are in the execution of your Agile project, as well as what your goals are for using the information radiator. . Low-tech, high-touch tools, such a sticky notes or cardboard cards are often used during the strategy meeting and release planning meeting at the beginning of the project. High-tech, low-touch tools can be added as the project progresses. The real question to ask is which tools will be the most beneficial to simplify the radiation of project information so that the project team can concentrate the majority of their efforts on performing the work. A major consideration in choosing the tools is how much time, money, effort, and training it would take to implement the tool. Additionally, you must consider the policies and procedures within your own organization that pertain to how to requisition the tools, as well as the time it takes to complete the process. As you complete the first few sprints on your Agile projects, you will start to identify processes that can be improved from sprint to sprint, which may include new tools. However, it is always best to start with very basic and inexpensive tools. If a request for additional tools stems from your Agile project team's continuous process improvement efforts, there is probably a better chance that your organization will provide high-tech tools such as dashboards if they see a short turnaround time on their investment.

Tip
Regardless of whether you are using low-tech, high-touch or high-tech, low-touch information radiators on your Agile project, try not to spend a lot of time making them look "pretty." Eliminate waste by creating "barely sufficient" information radiators. One of the basic tenets of Agile project management is to enable the project team to spend more time performing the work than making the information being radiated look perfect.

Tool Value
The main value of using information radiators, regardless of whether they are low-tech, high-touch or high-tech, low-touch is that they replace formal documents and meetings that are used in traditional project management. If you think about how much time you have spent on traditional project management projects updating status reports and project documentation, attending status meetings, and making presentations to senior management and other project stakeholders, you can appreciate how much time is involved performing these activities. On an Agile project, if a project stakeholder wants to know how the project team and the project is performing, all he or she has to do is walk into the team's working space (sometimes referred to as a "war room" or "combat information center") and look on the walls. In less than a minute, these interested stakeholders can get a snapshot of what is happening on the project. This is extremely valuable because the stakeholders get real-time project updates very quickly, and the project team does not have to stop what they are doing to provide the updates and can continue working without interruption.

Social Medial Tools
The communication purposes for the Agile information radiators is inform. The tool can be used in Yammer, Socialcast, and Facebook (private group).

Introducing low-tech, high-touch Agile information radiators
The first type of information radiators you can use on an Agile project are referred to as low-tech, high-touch. Team members create a physical project information radiator using a variety of simple tools. They

can use dry-erase white boards, easels and easel pads, multi-colored markers, blue painter's tape, multi-colored sticky notes, butcher paper, index cards, or user story cards. It is important when you first start planning an Agile project in the strategy meeting and release meeting that the tools used to radiate information be high-touch, and low-tech because the meetings are usually face-to-face; there is no need for formality to exchange ideas and information among attendees. Performing low-tech, high-touch planning activities helps ensure informality and allows the team members to feel comfortable making impromptu changes "on the fly" and to practice being innovative and creative when identifying the initial product characteristics. This also eliminates the time it would take to constantly update electronic documents every time a change is made. If a change is needed, team members get up and physically rearrange the information radiator by moving sticky notes or user story cards to new places that they believe to be a better fit in the overall project strategy.

Table 12.1 — low-tech, high-touch information radiator examples shows some low-tech, high-touch information radiator examples that are commonly used in Agile projects.

Table 12.1 — low-tech, high-touch information radiator examples

Tool	Description
Product Roadmap	A visual overview of a product's releases and the main components that provide project stakeholders a quick view of the primary release points and intended functionality at each release point.
User Story Map	A visual status display of a set of user stories that helps group user stories by product release, and indicates the progress of each user story throughout the project, release, or sprint.
Product Vision Box	A mock-up of a product on a physical box (often a cereal box) that contains graphic images and narrative content that conveys the product vision on an Agile project to interested stakeholders.
Kanban Board	A visual representation of the user stories in a specific sprint that illustrates the work on an Agile project that is currently in progress and identifies potential bottlenecks that may need to be cleared for successful sprint completion.
Risk Board	A visual display of the status and the severity of Agile project risks that have been documented and maintained by the Agile team, and the current status of project roadblocks that are brought to light as part of the daily standup meeting.

Introducing high-tech, low-touch Agile information radiators

The second type of information radiators used on an Agile project are referred to as high-tech, low-touch because no physical tools are used to create them; they are usually created and displayed electronically. Some of the tools include software applications, smart boards, electronic bulletin boards, and digital cameras. Although collocation is one of the basic tenets of Agile, we live in a virtual world and our team members are often geographically distributed around the globe. You'll want to strive to get as close to collocation as possible by using the myriad communication tools that are available. Most Agile project teams use a combination of high-touch, low-touch and high-tech, low-touch tools collaboratively. For example, if the majority of your team is located in the United States, but some team members are located in India, you can take pictures of the product roadmap and send them electronically to the team members in India. You can also use video conferencing software applications, webcams, instant messaging, web-based desktop-sharing and collaborative websites and document repositories.

Table 12.2 — high-tech, low-touch information radiator examples shows some examples of high-tech, low-touch information radiators that are commonly used for Agile projects.

Table 12.2 — high-tech, low-touch information radiator examples

Tool	Description
Burndown Charts	A graphical representation of the remaining work on an Agile project, release, or sprint that displays the development team's progress in terms of story points to determine if the current work is on track to be completed as planned.
Burnup Charts	A graphical representation of the work performed on an Agile project, release, or sprint that displays the development team's progress in terms of completed story points to determine if team is on track to complete work as planned.
Dashboards	A visual screen display of vital data about the progress and performance of both the development team and the overall project that is highly visible, easy to understand, and updated automatically with real-time data.
Cumulative Flow Diagrams	A graphical representation of workflow bottlenecks based on work-in-progress limits that plots both the total scope and the progress of individual features, user stories, and tasks to determine ways to eliminate waste and increase efficiency.
Velocity Tracking Charts	A graphical representation of an Agile project team's velocity over the course of multiple sprints to identify historical work performance trends for project team correction or adjustment, as well as future work performance forecasting.

Regardless of whether an Agile project team displays project performance or team performance using high-touch, low-tech or high-tech, low-touch information radiators, they are indispensable tools that should be part of the arsenal for any organization that is executing projects using Agile project management best practices. The most important thing to remember when choosing which type of information radiators to employ on your Agile projects is to only use the tools that maximize your team's effectiveness while minimizing waste in terms of cost, time, and effort.

Planning to Agile information radiators

When planning to use either the high touch or low touch radiators, Agile project teams need to consider how important both of these tools are for the project from a communication perspective. Information radiators can provides customers, leadership and any interested parties the latest project information. Agile project managers will use information radiators throughout the life of the project. Most Agile project managers take the time at the end of the sprint to ensure the radiators are updated and reflect how the project is progressing.

It takes time for Agile project managers to plan the use of these radiators on their project. The planning will entail what charts and dashboards to use at what stage of the project.

Many Agile project managers or Scrum Master will use these radiators throughout the duration of the sprint as well. Burndown Charts are a great example of a radiator that a Agile project manager would use during the sprint and report weekly how the team is progressing.

Reporting from Agile information radiators

On most Agile projects, there will be a series of information radiators that Agile project managers will use to report current status. Burndown charts, Burnup charts, Dashboard all at the fingertips of Agile project managers and common tools on these projects.

When thinking about reporting on information radiators, Agile project managers or Scrum Masters will have to ensure they are getting the project data they need from the team in a timely manner. Getting the data as the information becomes available makes the data more relevant and if there are issues (team not progressing like it should) the project team or leadership can make course corrections.

Most Agile project managers are familiar with information radiators and each tool is a common staple in their tools boxes.

Cross-Reference
See Chapter 22 - Using Communication Tools in Executing and Controlling Process to Report Project Information to learn more about Agile information radiators.

Introduction to the Communication Plan

The *communication plan* helps you decide, document, and plan the project's information needs. The communication plan helps ensure that the correct audience is receiving the project information on time and in an acceptable format. At a minimum, you will send a weekly project status report and a monthly newsletter. These two deliverables should contain enough information for your customers to understand the project and the overall status. You use the communication plan to document and set up a rhythm for the project's communications by using tools such as a status report, budget spreadsheet, issues logs, and so on. Customers and senior management will expect and rely on regular delivery of project information. As project manager, ensure that you use a communication plan for each project, regardless of its size or complexity.

Make sure your customers and team members approve the communication plan as early as possible in the project life cycle. By acquiring approval, you know that your customers approve the type of information they want to receive, the format they will receive it in, and the delivery time frames. Your customers should always feel that they have enough information and exposure to project information. The communication plan is one of the methods that you use to carry out this objective.

Note

The Project Management Institute's knowledge area for this tool is the communications management area. This tool can also be associated with the integration knowledge area.

Tool Value

The project communication plan documents and provides the processes and procedures for communicating project information. It is the road map the project team follows throughout the project.

Social Media Tools

The communication purposes for the communication plan are to inform and instruct. The tool can be used in Yammer, Socialcast, and Facebook (private group).

You should review and continually update the communication plan throughout the project life cycle. There are many reasons why, but at the top of the list is ensuring that you are create and deliver everything in the plan that you said you would produce. You may have documented that you will produce a risk matrix, but then never create it for the customer. You might have several reasons for not creating it. That's not the issue. The issue is that you promised something that you didn't deliver, which could be a problem. Your customer could be expecting the risk matrix because you agreed to it in the communication plan, but you didn't deliver it. They could be relying on that information for something on their part of the project. On some projects, customers will hold you directly accountable for delivering every item documented in the communication plan. A periodic checkpoint to review the current communication plan and status information you are sending could be helpful in preventing any confusion and ensuring that you are delivering what you said you would in the communication plan.

Table 12.3 — Example of a communication plan table of contents shows a table of contents from a sample communication plan. There are two new tools in the plan called, the communication requirements matrix and the role report matrix.

Table 12.3 — Example of a communication plan table of contents

#	Description
1	Communication Plan Overview
2	Circle-of-Communications Chart
3	Project Communication Requirements Matrix
4	Role Report Matrix
5	Method and Time Frames for Distribution
6	Lessons Learned (Previous Projects)
7	Historical Information (Examples/Samples)
8	Close Out

The most important parts of the communication plan are the communication matrixes noted in Sections 3 and 4 in the table above. These sections describe, in detail, the "who," "what," "where," "when," and "why" project status information you will deliver you your leadership and customers. The other sections in the communication plan table of contents example are also valuable, but make sure that you pay special attention to the two matrix sections #3 & #4.

When creating the communication plan, one of the most important areas to consider is the customer's involvement and approval of the document. Customers should agree to who, what, when, where, and how often you intend to communicate project information. That way, your customers understand when they will receive project information from you, and they can then establish their own rhythm for communicating or making project-level decisions based on that information.

Cross-Reference
See Chapter 2 – Planning Communications for more information about the circle-of-communications chart, communication requirements matrix, and the role report matrix.

One section in the communication plan outlines the time frame your customers will receive project reports throughout the project life cycle. When you set up the time frames for your project, you are also setting your project's rhythm. The rhythm includes the meeting cadence—the rhythm for how often meetings occur, such as daily or weekly—team members' delivery dates (final status reports), and the project status report delivery dates to the customer. If you don't understand your project's rhythm, you may struggle to communicate effectively; you must control your project's rhythm. Your customers will appreciate the continual and constant flow of project information, so ensure that they approve the project's communication rhythm. The following example shows rhythm cadence and accountability:

- Monday: Status collection day
- Tuesday: Weekly status meeting
- Wednesday: Status report submission and compilation
- Thursday: Customer project status review meeting
- Friday: Final project status report submission and distribution

This rhythm provides continuous weekly project communications to the project team and customers.

A communication plan helps anyone who is working on the project understand what type of project information will be sent throughout the project life cycle. It will document when the project team creates and delivers the report, the timing of the reports, who receives the information, and so on. For those who receive the communication plan, document the "who," "what," "where," "when," and "how" of project information within the communication plan. Knowing the answers to those five questions helps you and your team understand the information to obtain.

Planning to use a communication plan

When planning to use the communication plan, think about the five critical questions: "who," "what," "where," "when," and "how" to get the answer for each question. You will need to identify the various stakeholders and understand what information they need and in what format. Then, focus on when you want the information and where to send it. These are the main parts to any communication plan that you must focus on getting for your document. You should also decide if there are any available lessons-learned information from past projects around project communications and find, if possible, any helpful historical reports from previous projects. All of this information can help you communicate effectively. When collecting information and planning to create and use a communication plan, you will have the data to help you successfully communicate effectively about your project.

Reporting from the communication plan

On most projects, you and your team jointly create the communication plan. The communication plan is an extensive document that requires the project team's knowledge and expertise to complete the details in the document. Don't attempt to create this document on your own; it won't work out well and there is no way you alone will have all of the information you need for the document. You are going to need help. Your role on the project is to communicate and own the project information, so it also makes sense that you drive reporting the project communication plan.

One of the tools you can use to collect project communication requirements is the communication plan matrix. This tool displays the information for the customer about who is attending the meetings, and what types of meetings you will have on your project. The communication plan matrix also covers reporting frequency and how often reports or status will be sent to your leadership and customers. By creating the project matrix, you identify your customer's communication requirements and help yourself populate the various tools you need for the communication plan. Using the communication plan matrix is a win-win for everyone.

Communication plan matrix template

Table 12.4— Example of a communication plan matrix shows a summary of the customer information needs for a project. This matrix does not capture the scope of the project, just the customer's communication needs. Use the communication plan matrix as a cross-reference for populating the various tools you need for the communication plan. Don't confuse the communication plan matrix with the communication requirements matrix tool. It is easily done, but they are different tools. There are some similarities between the two tools, but they have different purposes all together. The communication plan matrix is a high-level gathering tool used to collect project communications information from your customers and team members. The communication requirements matrix stores detailed information about the roles. Let's look at a sample communication plan matrix.

Table 12.4 — Example of a communication plan matrix

Who	Information Needs	Types of Meetings	Frequency
Project Manager and Team Members	Action items, progress reports, change requests, and issues specifications	Team meetings, status meetings, staff meetings, design reviews, one-on-one contract negotiations	Daily, weekly, as-needed
Sponsor	Progress reports and financial reports	Financial meetings, major milestone(s), phase-end, go/no-go meetings, issue resolution	Monthly
Client	Status reports, ship dates, specifications change notices	Design reviews and change requests	As-scheduled

As you become familiar with using a project communication plan, you will have your favorite templates or examples that you follow. Luckily, the project management profession has hundreds of different communication plan examples for different project types, across different industries. There are plenty to choose from on the Internet.

Cross-Reference
See Chapter 16 - Using Communication Tools During the Initiating Process to learn more about how to create and use the communication plan.

Introduction to the Change Readiness Assessment Document

The *change readiness assessment document* helps you prepare and set up the organization for change. Usually, from a project perspective, change readiness means setting up the organization to receive what they requested while reducing the impact. The following example outlines an HR department needing a change readiness assessment. In this example, the HR department asked the IT department to develop a new payroll system to roll out globally. This is where the change readiness assessment document provides value to the HR department employees. This document outlines who will receive the new payroll system, what training they need, how they need to prepare their computers, and so on. Everything dealing with the change and what the employees need to do to prepare for the change are in the change readiness assessment document.

The change readiness assessment document helps you collect data and prepare the organization for any new changes. Most industries use a change readiness assessment process because every industry should be aware of how their customers or clients will handle change. Think about a construction company building of a new bridge. The construction company has to get the public ready for the new bridge. The company will show designs, talk about toll prices and project length, and so on. All of these activities are acts of change readiness, and each prepare the public for building a new bridge and what they can expect when the bridge is complete.

Another term for change readiness is "organizational change management." Organizational change management is a formal process. There are many different change management methodologies in the industry for you to learn and explore. We won't explore those methodologies in detail in this chapter; we will only cover the change readiness assessment report to ensure that you have what you need to use the tool.

Note
The Project Management Institute's knowledge area for this tool is the communications area. The secondary area that this tool could be associated with is stakeholder management.

Tool Value
The change readiness assessment tool prepares the organization for the change the project is going to deliver. Without a change readiness assessment tool, the organization may have no idea how the proposed product or service will impact them.

Social Media Tools
The communication purposes for the change readiness assessment are to inform, motivate, and instruct. The tool can be used in Yammer, Socialcast, and Facebook (private group).

All project managers should use the change readiness assessment tool because change readiness is not specific to a single methodology or project type; it applies to them all. For large projects that have a large customer base, such as a new bridge under construction, the change readiness assessment process is standard for all projects. As project manager, you must make sure you are focusing on this area of the project. Sadly, most project managers avoid or do not think about change readiness until much too late in the project. Often, project managers are busy with organizational change management work when the people are ready to accept the proposed change. It is so important to ensure that the people are ready for the proposed change and can get ready to work with you through this process. If you have an organization that won't accept changes, releasing anything new to them, such as a new application or product will be difficult. In those cases, the organization cannot handle the release of a new product at the same time so many other changes are going on.

Many organizations go through various changes all of the time, which adds to the complexity of change readiness for a project team. Organizations will go through reorganizations, major process changes, year-end planning, new-year fiscal planning, and quarterly planning. The common theme is that organizations are always changing. There is rarely a period when an organization is not changing something because of one reason or another. Remember the previous example about setting up a new HR payroll system? Can you imagine how difficult it would be to schedule the rollout of a new payroll system when there are so many other changes going on in an organization? The new payroll system will be regarded like any other change that people have to deal with and that they may not want to deal with. Well, this is exactly why a project change readiness assessment document is so useful and valuable on a project. The value of the change readiness document is that it outlines the steps an organization will take to get itself ready for a change. The organization accepting the change could be any organization, including HR, finance, or marketing.

Change readiness or organizational change management is not the same as project change management. Often, you will hear someone ask a project manager about how he or she handles project change management. Some project managers will mistakenly say, "I have a standard change control process for my project." However, the project manager is not thinking about organizational change management, he or she is thinking about project change management, such as, "How do I control scope changes, how do I handle budget changes, and so on?" When the project manager talks about scope management, you know he or she is not thinking about organizational change management. No, the focus is on the change management for areas like controlling scope, schedules, and budget, not organizational readiness. If you want to be sure what type of change management that is being discussed, clarify your questions and allow the project manager to respond with how he or she handles both levels of change management. It is common for project managers to initially think about project change control instead of organizational change management because project managers focus on delivering projects and what it takes to deliver them—who they deliver them to is usually secondary. Sadly, this is the case for most project managers. Project managers are so focused on controlling projects, they rarely think about what has to happen in the organization to get the individuals ready for the change they are about to experience. For example, installing new computers for everyone in an organization is a big change that people need to prepare for. In the IT industry, where project change control is much more relevant than organizational change readiness, project managers are much more focused on delivering the project and less focused on organizational changes.

Table 12.5 — Example of a change assessment readiness template provides an example of the top readiness factors to track to ensure the organization is ready for the change. The number of columns in the table can change based on your company or project considerations; however, these six columns are the most common.

Table 12.5 — Example of a change assessment readiness template

#	Change Readiness Factor	Readiness Status (G/Y/R)	Readiness Owner Name	Leadership Support Required (Y/N)	Impact of Change
1	Vision for Change				
2	Strategy and Plan Validated				
3	Benefits Understood				
4	Funding Secured				
5	Timelines Validated				
6	Resources Available to Execute				
7	Business/Customers Ready to Receive				
8	Security Set for Rollout				
9	Communications & Awareness				
10	Training Complete				

When the organizational change lead creates the change assessment readiness document, one of the major concerns is the number of change readiness factors the organization has to adopt. The more factors, the more work the organizational change lead will have to do to get the organization ready. Fewer factors should make it easier, but that is not always the case. There is no correct number of change readiness factors, and every organization and every project is different. Too many change readiness factors may make it difficult to get the organization ready to adopt the change. Too few factors, the organizational change lead may not be doing everything possible to get the organization ready. Project Managers should be watching how well the organizational change lead is getting everyone ready to accept the change and offer course corrections if this process is not moving along as quickly as it needs to. Only the organizational change lead should answer the questions about how many change readiness factors are needed for a project; it is not for anyone else to define. Most companies provide a common set of change readiness factors for projects that the organizational change lead needs to consider. The company-provided change factors are just a starting point for the organizational change lead to consider. The lead must review the company-level change factors and decide if they apply. Some of the change readiness factors at the organizational level may not make sense at the project level. As the organizational change readiness activities continue, the organizational change lead will continue to update the template, as needed.

Planning to use a change readiness assessment

When planning to use the change readiness assessment document, one of the first and important steps is discovering your customer's tolerance levels for handling change. The more comfortable your customers are with change, the easier it should be to roll out changes. This is a key step for the organizational change lead in the planning process because the less comfortable the customer is with change, the more work for the change lead. It happens that way all the time.

The other area to consider for planning to use the change readiness assessment template is the change readiness factors at the organizational level. Many organizations follow different processes and procedures for handling organizational-wide changes. The organizational change lead must be aware of these processes so he or she can navigate the project successfully through them. Project managers who ignore organizational-wide change readiness factors set up their project for some major issues.

Some organizations formally handle the change management processes, while others are informal. It is going to take the organizational change lead much longer to learn the organization's structured processes than unstructured processes. As project manager, consider that and allow for that time in your project schedule so you are not impacted.

Often, the customer's leadership team will pick a person in the organization to be on point for the upcoming change. Let's look at one example: The HR department asked the IT organization for a new payroll system. The vice president of the HR department assigns a senior-level HR employee to work with IT on the project. That person becomes the project's organizational change lead and takes on the duties of that role. It is unlikely that someone in IT could possibly work with everyone in HR, especially if it is a big department with many employees. Therefore, someone from the HR department must play the organizational change lead role. Selecting someone from IT to play the role of organizational change lead for a department they don't know could be a recipe for disaster. It happens, and sometimes it works out fine, but it is not a recommended best practice. A best practice is to have an HR person in the organizational change lead role to be on point to work with other HR employees for the new payroll system. Assigning someone from HR also helps in this example because that person knows the HR procedures and current systems and knows how to minimize impact to their fellow HR employees. Having the organizational change lead from the same organization also works well with product adoption because having a familiar face to work with while the employees learn and adopt a new payroll system is much easier for everyone.

Another area for the organizational change lead to address in planning to use the change readiness assessment template is the template itself. Specifically, review the default columns in the template and decide whether they are the correct columns for the product type that you are completing. The organizational change lead's key responsibilities are to work with the business customers (other HR employees in the example) and review the template to ensure that he or she understands the data needed for each column. The organizational change lead will cover the readiness factors in the template and add and delete factors as necessary. The next step is to review the columns of data for each change readiness factor. It is important to understand the change readiness factors and the data that is needed to support or track each factor. If the change readiness template needs any updates or changes, you and the organizational change lead must both agree. After you both agree, you can update the template to reflect the change readiness factors for the project. This is an important task for you and the organizational change lead to work together and drill down on the correct readiness factors for the project. Doing so will also help ensure the best chance of getting the organization ready for accepting the change (HR payroll system). Failure to complete the process by you or the organizational change lead will make it much more difficult to ready your customers (HR employees) for the change.

Cross-reference
*Organizational change management is a complex subject that takes years to master. See chapter 16 - Using Communication Tools During the Initiating Process of the book, "**The Tactical Guide for Building a PMO" written by William Dow, PMP** for much more information on this subject.*

Reporting from a change readiness assessment

Reporting from the change readiness assessment document is usually led by the organizational change lead, not the project manager. This is a major part of the organizational change lead's roles and responsibilities.

Reporting the change readiness assessment means providing continuous updates and status about how well the project is progressing through the change readiness factors. Reporting will also uncover areas that are struggling. Make a constant effort to ensure that everyone is aware of the details within the change readiness assessment document. That way, you or the leadership team will recognize roadblocks or concerns and jointly act quickly to resolve them.

The whole point to the organizational change management process is to keep everyone in the loop and ensure constant communication about how well it is going.

The change readiness assessment document will be communicated and reported on regularly throughout the project life cycle. You may want to take information from the assessment chart and add it to the status report, or you may want to just report status using the change readiness assessment report itself. Either way, regular and continual reporting of the change readiness assessment data is a critical part of the project's success and people will want to see this information throughout the project life cycle.

To create the change readiness assessment document, the organizational change lead will use either a table format in a spreadsheet or a table in a document. The most common format for this tool is a table format, which most project leadership and team members like. The change readiness assessment tool is stored in the document control system for long-term storage and retrieval.

Cross-Reference
See Chapter 17 - Using Communication Tools to Administer the Planning Process for additional about how to create and use the change readiness assessment document.

Introduction to the Daily Progress Report

The *daily progress report* documents the results of a daily progress meeting and helps you and your team understand the project's status, once a day. The software development industry uses daily progress reports as part of a development methodology called Agile/Scrum. The tool helps team members be more accountable for their work, share project status on their deliverables, and communicate with each other. The daily progress report is the documented results from that meeting. The term "Scrum" comes from the game of rugby. As in rugby, the Scrum uses a small, cross-functional team to produce the best project result. Although Scrum's main goal was to manage software development projects, it's useful for running software maintenance teams, or as a program management approach: Scrum of Scrums.

Note
The Project Management Institute's knowledge area for this tool is the communications management area. This tool can also be associated with all other knowledge areas.

Tool Value
Daily progress reports provide a current snapshot of the project, once a day. No other tools bring team members together every day to talk about the project and their own concerns and needs of the project.

Social Media Tools
The communication purpose for the daily progress report is to inform. The tool can be used in Yammer, Socialcast, and Facebook (private group).

Each day, after the team has the daily progress meeting, the project manager (or Scrum master) compiles the meeting results into a daily progress report. Scrum teams that avoid or do not document the updates from team members miss an excellent opportunity to communicate the information to a wider audience. We recommend that project managers, regardless of the industry and methodology they are using, use the daily meetings and document those meetings by using the daily progress report.

Communicating a daily progress report is valuable to you and the project team. Bringing the team together for 30 minutes at the beginning of each day allows the team to focus on the project and communicate project status, issues, concerns, highlights, and lowlights. It also provides an atmosphere of togetherness for team members.

Using the daily progress report benefits everyone on the team—not only project managers, team members, and upper management, but customers also can benefit from hearing project status and roadblocks the team is facing. The meeting is short, and the information from the meeting (the daily progress report) is provided directly by each team member. This ensures that everyone involved receives the information they need directly from those doing the work. You can work through roadblocks or issues with team members, and everyone can hear what everyone else is facing. Customers who sit in on the meeting, or read the daily progress report, can step in and help when needed. One important aspect of the daily progress report and the associated meeting is how simple the meeting is and how little time it takes. The process is as follows:

1. All team members gather in-person (or on a conference call).
2. You ask each team member the following questions:
   - What did you complete yesterday?
   - What do you plan to work on today?
   - What is stopping you from completing your activities?

3. A member of the team, or a scribe, captures the answers from each team member in the daily progress report.

4. At the end of the meeting, you receive the report from the scribe or team member who has cleaned up the formatting and send it to the team, management, and customers for review.

5. The process continues, daily, until the project is completed.

One of the benefits you receive from using a daily progress report is a higher commitment and accountability from each team member. When you address each team member directly, he or she is accountable to provide status and state what he or she is doing on the project. This provides an incentive for the team to make as much daily progress as possible so that individuals don't look bad in front of their peers, and to show that they are providing value to the project. It allows individuals to show you that they are not slacking off or letting other team members down by not pulling their own weight. It is a powerful tool for you to use. The daily progress report indirectly forces a friendly sense of competition among individual team members. Each team member competes against the other and listens and understands what everyone is working on.

Another important thing to remember when communicating project status using the daily progress report is the differences between this report and the checkpoint reports. The two are different. The daily progress report provides a current status of the project, each day, and the checkpoint report summarizes a week's worth of information. The issues and risks, for example, on a checkpoint report can be week's old, while the information coming directly from team members each day is real time.

Daily progress reporting is not new and you have probably been doing this for years. Daily reports are often used in situations when the project is in trouble and leadership is asking for daily status of the project. When troubling situations occur, or there is an upcoming milestone, the project team meets to discuss the problems or concerns until everything is resolved. If the team is focusing on a milestone, the team will continue to meet daily until they achieve the milestone. Most projects run into trouble at one time or another during the project life cycle, during difficult times, or times when the team needs to focus on a milestone. When the milestone is met, and the project goes back to normal, the project team can go back to having weekly status report meetings and reporting, or whatever their regular cadence is.

Planning to use a daily progress report

When planning and preparing to use a daily progress report, you must first align with team members about their participation and the value of these meetings. At first, team members might resist the idea of attending daily meetings. They will argue that it is a waste of time, just another meeting, or that it doesn't add any value. You should prepare for this resistance and insist that team members attend. After you set up the meeting, you can focus on who will collect status for the meeting. You need to select a minute taker for each meeting. The tool becomes irrelevant if nobody takes the minutes to capture the information. In cases when nobody collects the information that each team member reports during the meeting, you lose the ability to create the day's daily progress report. You would have to try to capture the minutes next time the team meets, but you lose action items, roadblocks, and potential ways of helping your team move forward. If you tell the team ahead of time to rotate taking the meeting minutes, they are usually more obliging and the team will step-up and collect the data.

Another area to consider when you have the data, is finding out whether leadership or customers want a copy of the daily progress report. It would give them a day-to-day recap of what is happening on the project. Some customers may think that this is too much information, while other customers will want the data. Sometimes, customers pass on receiving daily status and are satisfied with a weekly summary communication only. Those customers may feel that getting daily information while the project is

278

progressing may not be valuable and is too much data for them to process. However, you may think completely the opposite and value the reports even though your customers or leadership don't.

Reporting from a daily progress report

You are accountable for creating the daily progress report, but you are not responsible for going through the tasks to build the report. A team member collects the information at the meeting and sends it to you to compile and communicate the information every day.

The daily progress report allows you to hear the challenges and concerns about the project directly from each team member. It can be a big problem for you if the minute taker sends the information to you to compile and summarize, but does not capture who stated the information. You will be immediately aware that there is an issue, but you won't necessarily know who said it and who to help. On a large project team, when information is flying around from everyone, this could be an issue and it does happen. The minute-taker must capture the name of each team member who has an issue so that you can work with that individual to help resolve the issue. If the minute-taker summarizes all of the information captured by various team members, it lessens the value of the daily progress report and makes it more difficult for you to know who to help. It also lessens its value because it does not provide you with the details you need to help resolve the team's problems. For example, if the minute-taker documented that the project is $500,000 over budget, this statement does not tell you who raised the issue or where the project is over budget. You would need to start from square one find out who raised the issue. On the other hand, if the minute-taker documents that the finance manager stated that the design area is $500,000 over budget, you would know exactly who to work with to resolve the issue.

It is your responsibility to compile and send the daily progress reports to the team, customers, and, sometimes management. The value of getting this report each day provides immediate and constant updates to interested stakeholders and provides complete exposure about what is occurring on the project. The report should be in a document format, shared through email, and stored long-term in the document control system where it is accessible by anyone.

Cross-Reference
See Chapter 22 - Using Communication Tools in Executing and Controlling Process to Report Project Information to learn more about how to use and create the daily progress report.

Introduction to the Pareto Chart

The *Pareto chart* identifies the highest priority item, or items, in a data set. The Pareto chart is a unique form of a histogram and prioritizes which items to solve in what order. The chart helps you and your team focus attention and effort on the most important item on the chart. The chart provides the team a starting point to solve the first problem identified in the chart, and then the next, and the next, and so on.

Note

The Project Management Institute's knowledge area for this tool is the communications management area. This tool can also be associated with the following knowledge areas: integration, time, cost, quality, human resources, and procurement.

Tool Value

This tool identifies the predominate problem in a set of data elements. It ranks the items on the chart, allowing customers and team members to understand what to address first, second, and third.

Social Media Tools

The communication purposes for the Pareto chart are to inform and instruct. The tool can be used in Yammer, Socialcast, and Facebook (private group).

Because the Pareto chart is a graphic representation of the most important issues or items to address on the project, communicating the chart to customers or team members is easy. Customers can decide immediately where the largest problems or concerns are, and then focus attention on those areas to achieve resolution. You are responsible for communicating the problem areas to your customers and team members, as well as driving the resolution for each area.

Note

Vilfredo Federico Damaso Pareto invented the Pareto chart, and Joseph M. Juran and Kaoru Ishikawa made it popular. The popular Pareto's law states that 80 percent of the problems stem from 20 percent of the causes. The Pareto chart is a communication tool that helps prioritize the problems in an easy-to-read format. This law originated when Pareto was observing a connection between population and wealth and noticed that 80 percent of Italy's wealth was in the hands of 20 percent of the population. He then carried out surveys on various other countries and found that a similar distribution applied in those countries as well.

One of the benefits of the Pareto chart is that it helps you and your customers identify and rank the major problem areas to address. The chart has the capacity to graphically display the results of the analysis and focus the team on correcting the highest-ranked issue first, then second highest, third, and so on. Addressing the highest-ranked issues first provides the most benefit to the project with the least amount of work, thus following Pareto's law. If you take advantage of using Pareto charts, you can increase your project's chance of success because you identify, and then remove, the largest problem areas that your project faces. Without a Pareto chart, you might miss problems or issues, or not address them at all. This could have a negative effect on the project. Another situation where the Pareto chart is helpful is when the project team is working on lower-priority problems without realizing it. After creating the chart, the team may realize that they are focusing their attention on the wrong areas of the project and wasting time and effort on less important items. This could have a negative impact on the project. The team needs to focus on correcting the higher-priority items highlighted on the Pareto chart.

Figure 12.1 — Example of a Pareto chart (delivery problems) shows a Pareto chart where 60 percent of the project problems are in the first two categories. That percentage jumps to 80 percent when the third category is included in the analysis. Therefore, if the project team resolves the first two categories, they would solve 60 percent of the project problems. If they work on the first three categories, they resolve 80 percent of the project's problems. This process should continue until all problems are resolved.

Figure 12.1 — Example of a Pareto chart (delivery problems)

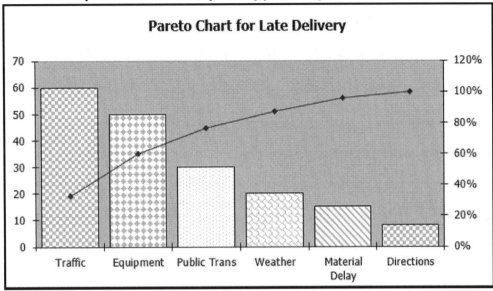

Figure 12.1 — Example of a Pareto chart (delivery problems) shows that traffic congestion is the major problem for a vendor's late delivery on the project. It is also clear that equipment issues (either lack of or availability) are a problem that needs resolution. To understand how the Pareto law works for this particular chart, review the cumulative percentage line. This line goes across the top of the chart, on a curve. The line indicates that the second point in the equipment bar column directly relates to roughly 65 percent of the problems, and the other problems represent the remaining 35 percent. Therefore, if the project team resolves the traffic and equipment problems, they would resolve 65 percent of the late deliveries. Imagine how easy it would be to create this chart for your project, and how valuable it would be to communicate the current project problems to your customers and management.

The following tips can help you read and understand a Pareto chart:

- Look for a breakpoint in the cumulative percentage line. This point occurs where the slope of the line begins to flatten. The project issues located under the steepest part of the curved line and on the left side of the chart are the most important.
- If there is not a clear breakpoint in the slope of the line, look for the issues that make up at least 60 percent of the problem. After you improve the predominate issues at the 60-percent level, recreate the Pareto analysis chart to find the new predominate issues. The project team needs to address the new issues.
- If the bars are similar in size, or more than half of the issues make up 60 percent, try a different breakdown of issues that might be more suitable, or consider the issues addressed. The project team has solved most of the issues with the least amount of effort. If you want to continue, recreate the Pareto chart with most of the issues removed from the analysis.

Planning to use a Pareto chart

In planning and preparing to use a Pareto chart, you must first define the major project problems that you want to track. The project problem defined in **Figure 12.1 — Example of a Pareto chart (delivery problems)** is the vendor's late delivery of material to the construction job site. The reasons for the problems are broken down into subcategories (equipment, traffic, weather, and so on). That same process occurs when deciding which areas you want to track for the project during the planning phase, so set up the Pareto chart as early as possible. This is not an easy task, and you must put some time and effort into thinking about what makes sense and what are the problems for the project that need tracking. After deciding the subcategories, work with the team to select someone who is responsible for creating the chart. That team member will own the Pareto chart and keep it throughout the project life cycle. If no one is available to take on this task, you should create the chart. This is often the case. After deciding the team member responsible for owning the chart, work with your customer to get the requirements for the Pareto chart. You may have to teach the customer about the Pareto chart by showing examples and explaining the value that the chart brings to the project. Customers may have their own unique requirements of what they want to see on the Pareto chart—unlikely if they have never used the chart before, but possible if they have used it on other projects and see its value. Your customers could have specific reporting requirements, such as time frames for when they want the report delivered to them, or other issues to specifically track on the report. After performing the specific planning activities, understanding the problems, and discovering the customer's requirements, you are adequately prepared to use the Pareto chart.

Reporting from the Pareto chart

You are usually responsible for creating a Pareto chart, but other team members may occasionally take on the responsibility as well. For example, the test manager is ideal for creating the Pareto chart because of his or her access to valuable test issues that can be charted for the project. The Pareto chart is an internal tool that focuses more on controlling how the project performs than delivering particular project status. Some other examples of how projects use a Pareto chart include:

- Safety violations charts (quality/human resources)
- Project issue charts
- Bug defects in testing, by bug categories charts (time)
- Cost estimating overrun charts

Every week you should report the project's Pareto chart(s) to your customers. The chart shows the project problems and, based on that information, you assign tasks to team members to resolve the problems. The Pareto chart is an important area of project monitoring and controlling, and therefore should be included as part of the standard project's reporting cycle. You should use a spreadsheet and its graphing capabilities to create and graph the project's Pareto chart. The Pareto chart is stored as part of the project's document control system for long-term archiving and accessibility.

Cross-Reference
See Chapter 22 - Using Communication Tools in Executing and Controlling Process to Report Project Information to learn more about how to use the Pareto chart.

Introduction to the Project Calendar

The *project calendar* displays major project tasks, milestones, and events on a formatted document that displays calendar days to allow for easy understanding of important and critical project dates. The project calendar is not a personal calendar. Project calendars store project information only, such as milestone dates, meeting events, current activities, and so on. The only personal information stored on a project calendar are vacations or known personal events that impact the project. Personal information applies to all team members, not individual team members, and only if it impacts the project.

Note
The Project Management Institute's knowledge area for this tool is the communications management area. This tool can also be associated with all knowledge areas.

Tool Value
The project calendar allows instant access to the project's schedule and is an excellent way to communicate schedule and project information. It is compact, portable, and easy to read and understand.

Social Media Tools
The communication purposes for the project calendar are to inform and instruct. The tool can be used in Yammer, Socialcast, and Facebook (private group).

After you load the project calendar with key dates and milestones, the calendar becomes a valuable tool for everyone on the project. The project manager, upper management, customers, and project team all use the project calendar to understand the project's time-based commitments. The project calendar provides a common understanding of the project dates and deliverables and raises awareness on scheduling conflicts that team members may have on one another. There are many benefits to using a project calendar, especially when you are looking at conflicts or scheduling for team members. For example, when a project has a major milestone delivery during the last two weeks of December, the project calendar displays the information for everyone so that they can discover the impact of this milestone during the holiday season. During the last week of December many people are off for the holidays, so having a project milestone during that time frame could be an issue for team members. If needed, team members can re-plan December's tasks for a time when they will be available to work. If team members re-plan project activities, the project calendar will highlight the impact and effect on the downstream tasks. When dates move for one task, and other tasks rely on that task, those dates also move. The project calendar highlights the tasks and dates that move and let everyone see the impact to the project schedule to make changes where necessary.

Yet another benefit of the project calendar is the ease of communicating project information to your customers or management. Carrying a fully loaded project calendar around with you enables you to access project dates at your fingertips, without having to fumble to get online, log on to a system, or go into the project's planning room. By having the information readily available, team members, customers, and management are reassured that you have everything under control.

The project calendar is a helpful tool for any project manager, team member, or stakeholder who is trying to understand the project's major milestones. In an instant, the project calendar provides high-level milestone dates to anyone, and if used correctly, it also tracks the high-level project status. As you monitor and control project execution, ensure that the project calendar is up to date for tracking status. As major milestones are completed, mark off the milestones on the calendar as complete and communicate that information to interested stakeholders.

Figure 12.2 — Example of a project calendar (software project) shows a typical project calendar from a project-scheduling tool. This project calendar represents a software project, showing both development and testing time frames. As you can see, the development work spans over a three-week period, and testing occurs over a two-week period. You will also notice the work flow, development and testing, respectively.

Figure 12.2 — Example of a project calendar (software project)

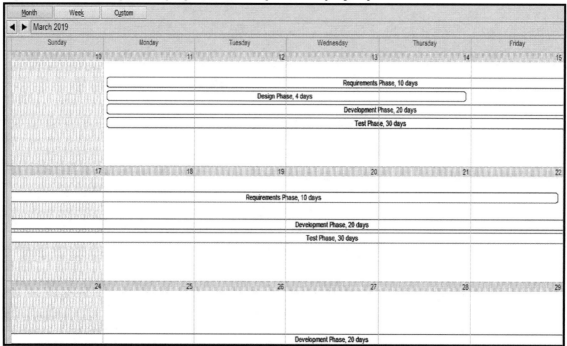

You can use the project calendar to communicate project timelines, costs, resources, and individual project activities. It is valuable to add weekly status meetings, key review meetings, and other major project events to the calendar when you first create it. The project calendar shows all of the project deliverables and it is a great asset during the planning process. During the planning process, the project calendar shows holiday schedules, vacation schedules, and time off for team members that could impact a project. For example, in December, many projects avoid the last two weeks of the month because of holiday season and vacations, so during the planning process, the project calendar has these dates blocked off as nonworking time. In doing so, your project will not calculate these dates as workable days.

You mainly use the project calendar as a guide to the project's time lines, milestones, and as a tool to ensure that the project is on schedule. You also use the project calendar to communicate with your team members about whether they are going to make the major milestone date on the project. Team members use the project calendar as a graphical representation of their milestones and plan their work and other activities around the calendar. If team members have a copy of the project calendar at their desks, they can quickly decide when they need to give time to the project. It becomes an individual planning tool for each team member.

Project calendars come in different views, depending on the needs of the project or organization. Here are some examples of available project calendars:

- **Long-range calendars:** 5 years, 10 years, 15 years, or longer
- Daily calendars: Daily events
- **Monthly calendars**: Monthly events
- **Multiple calendars:** One project is overlapping with another project's calendar
- **Hourly calendars**: Planning in 15-minute increments
- **Resource calendar:** An individual resource calendar that shows, for example, equipment such as cranes, trucks, bulldozers, concrete mixer, or people
- **Individual resource calendar:** For assigning human resources to a project

Planning to use a project calendar tool

When planning to use a project calendar, you must first decide where and how to use the project calendar. Large projects may have a project scheduling team to create a master project schedule. Most project managers want to create a project calendar using the information from the master project schedule. That way, you can see the project's major milestone events to monitor the project's progress. For example, in a software project, you add the major events of the development methodology, such as project requirements, design, development, and test directly onto the project calendar. Then, as your project team passes through each phase, you can track and mark off the progress on your project calendar. It is a great tracking tool for any project manager.

After you add the major phases to the project calendar, work with the various team leads to get them thinking about the duration of project phases. You need to add that data for each area on the project calendar. After receiving the initial dates from team members, add those dates into your project scheduling tool first, and then onto the physical project calendar. Getting dates from team members gives you the basis to start discussions with the customer about the proposed project finish dates. This leads to some great discussions with your customers and team members around project timing. This is the first time you will get the dates that the team proposes it will take for their project areas to align to the customer's expectations for a project end date. You drive those discussions among the parties to ensure there is agreement by everyone involved before the project dates are locked. After everyone agrees, you or the scheduler updates the project schedule with the agreed upon dates. After finishing these planning activities, you have adequately prepared to use the project calendar on your project.

Reporting from the project calendar tool

Your role is to create the project calendar tool for the project, but you will be doing so mainly as a tool for your own use. On large projects where there is a project planning and control group, someone is responsible for developing the project calendar tool.

The easiest method to create a project calendar is by using a word processing program or a project-scheduling tool. Most software applications can create a blank monthly project calendar. There are two schools of thought that project managers have about reporting from the project calendar. Some of your project manager peers do not report from it at all and only use it as a planning and executing tool. Other project managers use the project calendar as a reporting tool and incorporate it as part of the official project reporting processes. You and your customer can decide which method to use for reporting project information. Some customers prefer that the project calendar is officially reported from for the project, but treat the situation on a case-by-case basis. You may want to use the project calendar as an internal tool only and use other tools, such as the Gantt chart or project milestone list to report project status.

Figure 12.3 — Example of a project calendar shows a typical project calendar from Microsoft Word. This calendar is blank to allow for adding project-level milestones through the planning process. Depending on the planning process, a blank sheet is perfect for starting the discussions for a high-level project time frame.

Figure 12.3 — Example of a project calendar

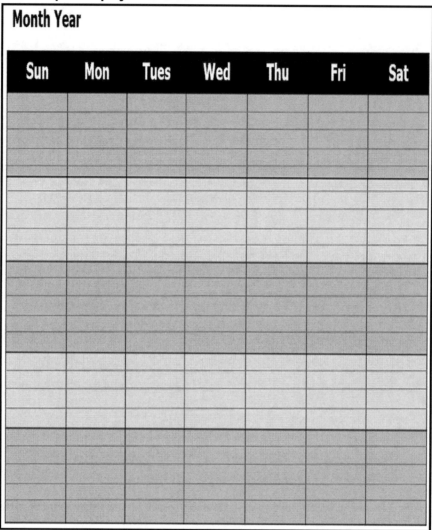

Note

Every project needs to have a graphical representation of its activities.

There is no formal reporting from the project calendar. If you decide that you want to report from the project calendar, you will have to prepare it once a week, or use the same reporting time frames as other project reports to ensure that it becomes part of the regular reporting.

There are two formats for the project calendar (printed and electronic) that you can use. The most useful part of this tool in a document format is that you can write on it, bring it with you, and have the information readily available for anyone to see. Using an electronic format also has benefits, such as continuous and automatic updating and providing real-time project status. When updating the project schedule, updating the project calendar is automatic.

Cross-Reference

See Chapter 18 - Using Communication Tools to Plan and Develop Project Deliverables to learn more about how to use the project calendar.

Introduction to the Project Presentation

The *project presentation* presents project information in a formal and structured manner to customers, executives, management, team members, and other stakeholders. You must be careful and consider the story that you want to present when creating a project presentation. If you do not put any consideration into your project presentation, and you just slap it together, your customers could walk away feeling that the project is out of control, unstructured, and they are wasting their money. This is not good and you could leave your customers with a lack of confidence in you. It happens when you rush into creating presentations to meet a deadline or you are put on the spot to present information about your project. If it happens early in the project and your customers have no creditability with you, it could be a long lasting issue. The customer may worry about the project if the presentation is confusing and you appear to have no idea what is going on.

Note
The Project Management Institute's knowledge area for this tool is the communications management area. This tool can also be associated with all knowledge areas.

Tool Value
Project presentations communicate plenty of project information. Presentations are given in a controlled environment in which you control the message delivery.

Social Media Tools
The communication purposes for the project presentation are to inform, motivate, and inspire. The tool can be used in Yammer, Socialcast, and Facebook (private group)

You own presenting your project's information, regardless of what it takes to get it done. You are responsible for calling the meeting, inviting participants, scheduling, message delivery, and all areas of putting together the presentation material. Project presentations let you show off your presentation skills and bring your project to the forefront for a project review with customers and management. There are thousands of project presentations on the Internet, and your company should have templates to get you started on the right foot. Regardless of the details in the project presentation, there are hundreds of templates available for use. The templates range from all types of messages, project types, milestone events (for example, project go-live decisions) to granular detail or high-level presentations.

The project presentation tool is valuable for presenting project information in a formal setting to customers and the project team. Project presentations give you an opportunity to collect project-level decisions during the meeting. This happens because the stakeholders are attending the meeting and are focused on the project material, so they can respond to questions or issues about the project moving forward. Formal project presentation meetings also give team members the chance to speak to your customers directly when they may not normally get a chance to do so. Make sure that team members capitalize on this and get the decisions they need from the meeting.

Figure 12.4 — Example of a one-page project presentation slide, specifically focused on project status shows a typical one-page project status slide. This project presentation example shows the required fields and phases for a typical data warehouse software project. The fields and information provide a page-at-a-glance view of project information.

Figure 12.4 — Example of a one-page project presentation slide, specifically focused on project status

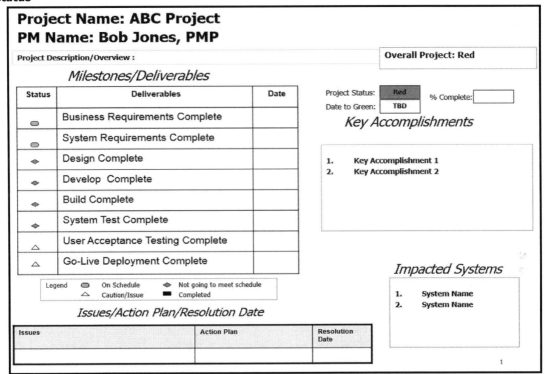

The project presentation should be clear, concise, and easy to read. When developing the project presentation, ensure that all project information is at a summary level to meet the audience's needs. Customers and management audiences are different, so creating the right balance of summary-level and detailed-level information can be tricky. Usually, project managers schedule a project presentation when the project team hits a major milestone, such as a software project's design complete, user acceptance testing (UAT) complete, or a go-live phase. Make sure the material you present is a true and current representation of your project. Milestone checkpoints give your customers confidence that the project is progressing either positively or negatively, but it does give them the ability to decide for themselves how it is progressing. This gives you a chance to shine by presenting the project in its best light and with the latest and most up-to-date information.

The project presentation is valuable to everyone on the project team, especially you. Team members who usually report through different department leads tend to do everything possible to ensure their area of the project is complete before presenting information to management and customers. This is helpful to you because it pulls all of the information together to represent the most current and accurate picture of the project at one time. You know exactly what is going on with the project and can present the data with confidence. During the day-to-day work activities of a project, pulling status information and compiling it into a formal presentation is not a typical activity. Project presentations force the team and project manager to come together to compile the information. It sets a stake in the ground to capture the most current status of the project.

Project presentations are different among industries. The presentation's format and information can vary, depending on project size, complexity, industry, and specific organizational requirements. The project presentation for a large construction project will be different than a presentation for a small software project. However, the core items of the presentation remain the same, but because the industries are so different, the project presentation is also different.

Planning to give a better project presentation

In planning to use a project presentation, you have several tasks to complete before the meeting can occur. These tasks include developing all project presentation materials, aligning customers and team members who are presenting at the meeting, inviting attendees, and booking the meeting room and equipment. The list goes on and on.

You should send reminders and follow-up prompts to key meeting invitees to ensure they are attending in case they forgot about the meeting or booked something else over the meeting. Key project members' double- and triple-book project meetings and have to miss meetings because of other conflicts. You could easily have a presenter forget or not attend your meeting if you don't follow up with them. By completing the planning activities to prepare the project presentation, you have taken most of the steps to adequately prepare for your presentation.

Reporting from project presentations

Usually, you are responsible for creating all project presentations. This is excellent news because you are responsible for the meeting and, therefore, own the responsibility of compiling all of the material. On large projects with a project administrator, often the administrator is responsible for developing the project presentation while working alongside you. Sometimes, this is simply a matter of compiling the information from various team members, so anyone can do it. Even in those cases, if someone else is compiling the project information for you, you still need to be active in the process. In the end, you own and have to present the information to your customer.

The following examples are various project presentations that you might make for a project:

- **Media presentation:** These presentations can occur when announcing and closing out a project or at major milestones.
- **Project kick-offs:** This initial meeting brings everyone together for the project.
- **Requests for funding:** You use this meeting to present to customers a request for additional funding.
- **End-of-phase presentation:** This meeting is scheduled when the project reaches the end of a particular phase (design complete) and you want to close out that phase.
- **Weekly status meeting presentations:** Weekly status meetings often have a presentation component to them that requires developing a project presentation and presenting to your customers.
- **Technical presentations:** Technical presentations are both discussions and presentations for management and contractors, for example.
- **Lessons learned:** This presentation covers lessons-learned information and addresses how future projects can benefit from lessons of the existing project.
- **Project closures:** A project closeout presentation is usually the last presentation where you gather stakeholders and get final approval on the team's efforts.

You are responsible for formally reporting project presentations during various times throughout the project life cycle. You are also responsible for creating the project presentations in software packages, such as

Microsoft PowerPoint or Apple Keynote® and storing them in the document control system for long-term storage and archiving. Project presentations often have controls on them around compliance. Sometimes, they require formal approval and sign-off from key stakeholders. We recommend storing project presentations in a document control system rather than on someone's hard drive or personal computer.

Cross-Reference
See Chapter 20 - Using Communication Tools During the Executing and Controlling Processes to Administer the Project to learn more about how to use a project presentation.

Introduction to the Spider Chart

The *spider chart* graphically presents comparisons of various types of information. Most team members use them to evaluate multiple alternatives based on multiple criteria. A spider chart, also known as a radar chart or star chart, is a two-dimensional chart of three or more quantitative variables represented on axes that start from the center of the chart. The relative position and angle of the axes varies and depends on the amount of data to compare. The chart resembles a spider web; thus, the name.

A spider chart is most useful when you need to see patterns in your data. It has multiple axes along which the data is plotted. On a spider chart, a point close to the center on any axis shows a low value, and a point near the edge is a high value. In some scenarios, you may want points near the center, or low values.

Note
The Project Management Institute's knowledge area for the spider chart is the communications management area. This tool can also be associated with the following knowledge areas: time, cost, quality, human resources, and risk.

Tool Value
A spider chart compares performance of different entities on the same set of axes.

Social Media Tools
The communication purposes for the spider chart are to inform and persuade. The tool can be used in Yammer, Socialcast, and Facebook (private group).

Figure 12.5 — Example of a spider chart shows a simple spider chart for the hours worked for five months (M) by Mr. Brown. **Note:** Months 1 through 3 are part-time, and months 4 and 5 are full-time. You can display several workers to quickly identify who worked the most and who worked the least. To keep the example simple, this spider chart only has one alternative. The spider chart is useful when you have relatively few alternatives (3-6) that you want to compare, based on a few different criteria (4-8). If you have more data to compare, a different tool may be more useful.

Figure 12.5 — Example of a spider chart

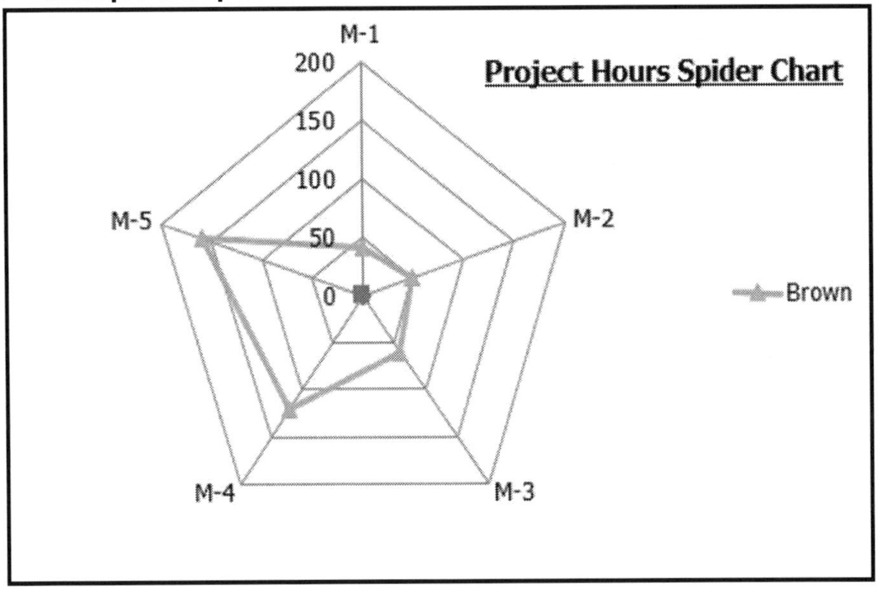

A spider chart is a great communication tool because it is visually compelling and easy to set up. It is also a quick and effective method for communicating project data to your customers. Projects have several different areas to report on by using a spider chart, including:

- Comparison reports
- Hours worked for team members
- Vendor comparison
- Cost and budget reports

Spider charts are quick and easy to create. Spider charts provide a great deal of project information for you and your team about the project. Your role is to communicate the project comparison data to stakeholders by using a spider chart, and then make project decisions based on what you find in the data. The chart compares project data, and the results of those comparisons help you make project decisions. When you use a spider chart, the chance of disclosing more information and potentially lessening issues is greater.

The spider chart graphically compares certain types of information about the project. The chart helps evaluate alternatives for the project depending on the data charted. A spider chart defines performance data and identifies strengths and weaknesses in that data. By using a spider chart, you no longer have to place data sets side by side to compare them. You can see variances or deviations in multiple types of information right in the chart. You can develop the chart by using a spreadsheet tool that has charting capabilities.

Planning to use a spider chart

In planning and preparing to use a spider chart, you must first decide if solving the problem by using the spider chart format will benefit the person or group receiving it. The data must meet the criteria of comparing different entities on the same set of axes. Most teams use a spider chart to evaluate multiple alternatives based on multiple criteria. When you understand these reasons, you will understand the criteria that you need to create the spider chart. You will analyze the chart first, and then work with your customer so that they understand what the spider chart is reporting about the variables. After preparing these steps, you are adequately prepared to use the spider chart on your project.

Reporting from a spider chart

You are responsible for creating the spider chart for your project unless you have administrative support to help you. If the project is large enough to have an administrative team, a member of that team may be responsible for creating the chart. Initially, the spider chart might be a little difficult to read and understand, but after you regularly use it, it will become a common tool that you use on all of your projects.

Figure 12.6 — Example of a spider chart (more complex example) shows a more complex example of a spider chart. In this example, two more team members have been added to the previous example (see **Figure 12.5**), Jones and Smith, to create a more realistic chart. The idea is to compare the monthly work of each team member. As you can see, Mr. Brown and Mrs. Smith work nearly the same amount of time each month, roughly half-time (there may be a reason both of them worked more in month 5). The chart shows that Mr. Jones worked full-time each month, except the fourth month, in which he hardly worked at all.

Figure 12.6 — Example of a spider chart (more complex example)

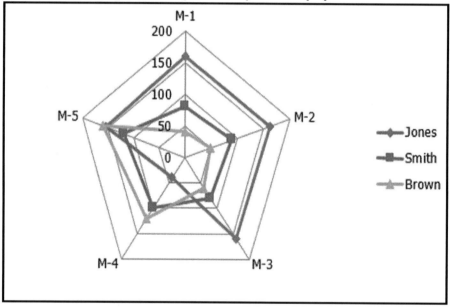

Figure 12.7 — Example of a weather spider chart shows an example of another spider chart. In this example, one of the unique areas is the low temperature readings of Ice Lands. The location is displayed by the small solid line with a circle on the chart. It is the small circle in the chart in the center. The data for this location is unique because of how little the variance in temperature is between summer and winter, especially when you compare it to the other two locations.

Notice the temperatures for Alice Springs. When you study the chart, you will see that Alice Springs is hot in January and cool in July. This data is opposite from the temperatures in the other two locations. This difference represents the northern and southern hemispheres. It appears Palm Springs and Alice Springs have the same temperatures during opposite times of the year. This type of chart shows the difference quickly and clearly.

Figure 12.7 — Example of a weather spider chart

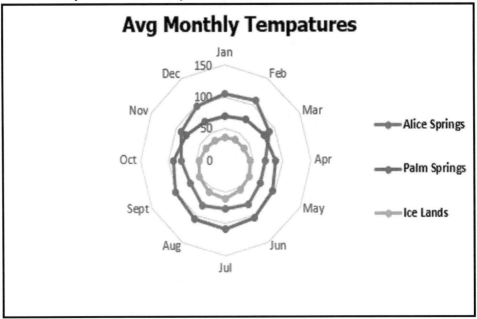

The spider report contains project-specific data that constantly changes, so it's important to report weekly or monthly, at a minimum. The spider chart is stored as part of the project's standard documentation and is always available to stakeholders and team members.

Cross-Reference

See Chapter 22 - Using Communication Tools in Executing and Controlling Process to Report Project Information to learn more about how to use a spider chart.

Introduction to the Stoplight Report

The *stoplight report* communicates simple project status information in a colored graphic format. Project schedules, mostly Gantt charts, use colored graphic symbols, mostly red, yellow, and green balls (stoplight colors) on each row of the project schedule to represent status (schedule, cost, or both) of an activity. Most automated project scheduling tools can create stoplight reports. These reports can become a common communication tool, without adding much cost or work to the project. The criteria for setting the initial parameters for each colored ball in the stoplight report belong to the company's Project Management Office (PMO). The PMO lead will expect all project managers to use the same parameters in their stoplight reports for consistency in cross-project reporting. When project managers randomly change the color parameters, you get inconsistent reporting. However, there are times when you need to change the parameters in the stoplight report. Different projects will have different tolerance levels for you and your customer; therefore, changes may be required. For example, a risk tolerance level could mean how many days a project manager would let a task become late before switching the color of the stoplight (ball) from green to yellow, or yellow to red. Alternatively, how much can a task go over budget before you change the color of the budget stoplight (ball) from green to yellow? Both examples represent you or your customer's risk tolerance level, and each example requires setting the limits before using the stoplight report. Some project managers are more tolerant than others, so the stoplight report's risk tolerance levels can vary among project managers.

Note
The Project Management Institute's knowledge area for this tool is the communications management area. This tool can also be associated with the following knowledge areas: time and cost.

Tool Value
The value of the stoplight report is to communicate project status at a glance by using a series of colored balls (stoplights: red, yellow, and green) to show the severity level of each report activity.

Social Media Tools
The communication purposes for the stoplight report are to inform and motivate. The tool can be used in Yammer, Socialcast, and Facebook (private group).

Using a stoplight report for your project shows that you are proactive about project communications by providing customers and team members' insight into the project. Sharing this valuable information by using a stoplight report requires little or no cost to the project. Most project scheduling tools include the stoplight report. The cost associated with using the tool equate to a small amount of time and effort to set up the criteria and making the stoplight report available to the project team and customers. Once the report is created, there is no added cost to use it, and updating it is easy. The stoplight report gets updated as the data changes in the project schedule. You are responsible for communicating the stoplight report in the same manner as you would communicate a project schedule or a Gantt chart. The functionality of the stoplight report is that it has an associated colored ball on each row of the project schedule, so everyone can see the status of each row. Customers value the stoplight report because the colored balls show the project status, at a glance, and by individual task and activity. If you choose to roll up the activity, your customers will be able to find out the status of the project, rolled up at the summary level.

There are many benefits to using stoplight reports on projects. One benefit is the low cost of creating them. Since the stoplight report is already available in the project's software-scheduling program, this is an easy sell for you. All you have to do is create the criteria for each colored ball, and then display the columns using the colored balls. It is that simple. The stoplight report is complete and ready for reporting purposes. As you update the project tasks, the colored balls change colors based on the criteria you set up.

Another benefit of using the stoplight report is seeing immediately the overall project status by reviewing the most dominate color on the project schedule. For example, if the project schedule shows most of project activities in red (critical), the project is considered in red status, meaning that it is either behind schedule, over budget, or both. There could be multiple conditions that produce a red status, budget and cost are just two big factors. If the majority of project activities are yellow, the project is in a yellow status, meaning it is in a potential problem state. Finally, if the majority of project activities are green, the project is in a green status, meaning it is advancing in the direction of the plan. There can be many variations when dealing with red, yellow, and green statuses that you need to consider when using the stoplight report. Every company handles how they process stoplight reports differently. However, no other tool provides a high-level status of the project by showing colored stoplights (balls) for each activity than the stoplight report. This is why it is such a valuable tool for you to use.

Figure 12.8 — Example of a stoplight report shows a typical stoplight report that was created by using an automated scheduling tool. In this example, Task 3 has a dark (red) indicator associated with the *Cost Variance* column, which indicates that the cost associated with the task is significantly over budget. Tasks with red (dark) balls in the *Schedule Variance* column indicate that the activity is running behind schedule. In either case, you, the customer, or management can grasp the status of each activity, at a glance, and discover the status of the overall project. It is the kind of report that is visually compelling to the most casual observer.

Figure 12.8 — Example of a stoplight report

	Cost Variance	Schedule Variance	Task Name	% Complete	Dur	Start	Finish				
1			⊟ SAMPLE PROJECT	41%	257d	Wed 1/2/19	Thu 12/26/19				
2	●	●	TASK 1	100%	5d	Wed 1/2/19	Tue 1/8/19				100%
3	○	●	TASK 2	0%	3d	Wed 1/9/19	Fri 1/11/19				0%
4	●	●	TASK 3	0%	1d	Mon 1/14/19	Mon 1/14/19				0%
5	●	●	TASK 4	40%	5d	Wed 1/2/19	Thu 1/17/19				40%
6	○	●	TASK 5	0%	2d	Fri 1/18/19	Mon 1/21/19				0%

When you set up the stoplight report for your project, you will quickly discover its value because of the instant project information you obtain. You, your customer, and leadership team will be able to see exactly where the project is having issues. Sometimes, your customers or leadership will start getting more heavily involved when they see that the project is having issues. Often, your customers get involved on an exception-only basis and let you run the project with limited interruptions, but when they see the stoplight report includes multiple red and yellow balls, you can almost guarantee that they will start getting more involved. Many executives on leadership teams prefer exception-based management as a way to stay involved, without having to get into the project details. By using the exception-based process, leadership can be involved in multiple projects without having to spend too much time on any one of them.

Tip
Managing by exception is fast and efficient.

There are usually only two main data points for using a stoplight report: scheduling data and cost data. Other data points are possible, but most project managers stick with the two basic project drivers because they are the most relevant and most popular for use with the stoplight report. They are also the most valuable to you for project management and control. Sometimes, a project manager also will use a quality or risk indicator in the schedule to make a very powerful project stoplight report.

Setting up and using a stoplight report is easy. You just set up the criteria for each indicator (red, yellow, and green), and then communicate with your customers what you set up and get their feedback. Your customers may have their own opinions about what they want the criteria to be for each color indicator, so be prepared to work with them closely and change the criteria, if needed. Make sure you and your customers agree on the red, yellow, and green indicators because you and your customers will use them throughout the project. Adding the stoplight report to a project brings huge benefits to everyone involved. Early reports, though, need communication and possible walkthroughs with customers to ensure that everyone correctly reads and understands the information.

Communicating with a stoplight report is easy, but some project managers do not take advantage of it. They may not see the value or maybe they simply do not know how to produce the criteria for the stoplight fields to create the report. It is simple, but it takes a couple of times working with the stoplight fields to get the hang of how they work. Usually, it takes a limited amount of time to learn how to set up and use this valuable communication tool.

Planning to use a stoplight report

When planning and preparing to use a stoplight report, you must first decide the performance criteria to use; most likely time or cost drives customer priority. When you understand the project's performance criteria, you then need to understand the customer's risk tolerance levels. The tolerance levels will make a difference for how the criteria are set for the stoplight report. Add the tolerance levels for each colored ball into the scheduling tool. For example, if the activity runs three days late, a yellow indicator is displayed, but if the activity is five days late or more, a red indicator is displayed. The customer's tolerance levels focus on those three and five days. They may want to trigger a yellow indicator on 1 day late and a red indicator on 2 days late if time is driving the schedule. You won't know their tolerance levels until you ask your customer and walk through the scenarios with them. Changing the criteria and tolerance levels for the colored balls in the scheduling tool is easy and something you can do. Configure the colored balls to whatever is appropriate for your customer's risk tolerance level.

You also need to understand during the project communication planning process what the customer wants to see in the stoplight report. Get this information during the planning process so you have time to set up the stoplight report to your customer's requirements long before project activities start.

Reporting from a stoplight report

On most projects, you are responsible for creating the stoplight report. Because you own developing and creating the project schedule, it makes sense that you also own the stoplight report. It would not be wise to pass this off to someone else because you need to stay on top of your project when the schedule goes off track. The only exception to this is on large projects where there is a scheduling team, and in those cases, stoplight report creation makes sense for someone else to complete. If any colored balls turn from green to red, or green to yellow, you will see it and be able to react. There will be times when a project activity shows red or yellow status, but you realize the activity is actually green. An example is an over-budget activity that shows red, and you already received customer approval for more funds, but you haven't received the money yet. In this case, the budget shows a red indicator, but it is actually green because the funds were approved, they just haven't arrived in the account. These types of scenarios happen on projects, but they don't impact the project as long as you are on top of the project and understand activity status.

When distributing project status, the stoplight report sends a loud and clear message one way or another about project status. A stoplight report full of green performance indicators shows a project that is under control from a cost and schedule perspective. A project that has mostly red and yellow indicators shows that it could be on the edge of trouble; people may need to pay close attention to it. Your customers and leadership should review the project to decide where they can help. There might be areas where they can turn around some of the project conditions that are causing the red and yellow indicators, especially if there are areas they can control. A project showing a stoplight report that is all red indicates there are serious project issues. Customer and leadership support is required immediately to get the project back on track. Be cautious when using and reporting on a stoplight report with an all-red status because of the high visibility it will bring to the project. Unless, of course, visibility is exactly what you want. Before you distribute an all-red stoplight report, you must understand the message you will portray about your project and what kind of reaction or support you are seeking from leadership or your customer. Sometimes, you might communicate one message, but the stoplight report will show another.

Each week's stoplight report is part of a regular project reporting process. The stoplight report contains project-specific data that is constantly changing, so reporting it weekly is important. Like all other documents in the project, it is a great idea to store copies of the stoplight report in the document control system for long-term storage and archiving.

Cross-Reference
See Chapter 22 - Using Communication Tools in Executing and Controlling Process to Report Project Information to learn more about how to create and use a stoplight report.

Introduction to the Work Package

The *work package* acquires project information at a detailed level that produces a document describing all of the project work. Work packages comprise most of the work breakdown structure (WBS) dictionary. This is often a hard-copy document that you create from a template, an electronic version of a document, or a combination of both. A work package also includes reporting progress for each work package as they are completed. A work package in a scheduling tool is a project activity or task where each (work package, activity, or task) is a specific deliverable. Each activity should define all of the effort, materials, equipment, risk, quality, cost, resources, duration, and scope for that single project deliverable. Because work packages are individual deliverables, by reporting progress on each one, as they complete, you can easily track overall project progress and performance. Work packages are usually short in duration, which helps you accurately estimate the remaining work. Each work package identifies and defines specific work and deliverables, and it helps control scope creep.

Note
The Project Management Institute's knowledge area for this tool is the communications management area. This tool can also be associated with all other knowledge areas.

Tool Value
The work package identifies and defines all of the work for each project deliverable.

Social Media Tools
The communication purposes for the work package are to inform and motivate. The tool can be used in Yammer, Socialcast, and Facebook (private group).

Each work package, at a minimum, should include a description, how long it will take to complete (duration) the work, and a predecessor and successor activity. They can also include the assigned resources—labor, material and equipment—as well as the scope of work, cost, risk factors, quality of work, and the WBS identification. When combined, the work package benefits most project stakeholders by formally documenting work progress and communicating the remaining work to be completed. Check off the various project components from the master list as they are completed, until the team delivers the entire project. If there are any questions about what was completed, who signed off on it, or the completion date, you can use the work package forms to communicate that information. Communicate the work package information at the individual level or summarize all of the work packages and reports for the customer information. By doing this, you let your customers know the latest work package and overall project status. Without the work package form, there is less documented proof that a work deliverable was completed.

Figure 12.9 — Example of WBS (highlighting work packages) shows a WBS and the associated work packages for each level. The work package is the lowest level of the WBS. When reporting work package status, you are reporting at the lowest project level.

Figure 12.9 — Example of WBS (highlighting work packages)

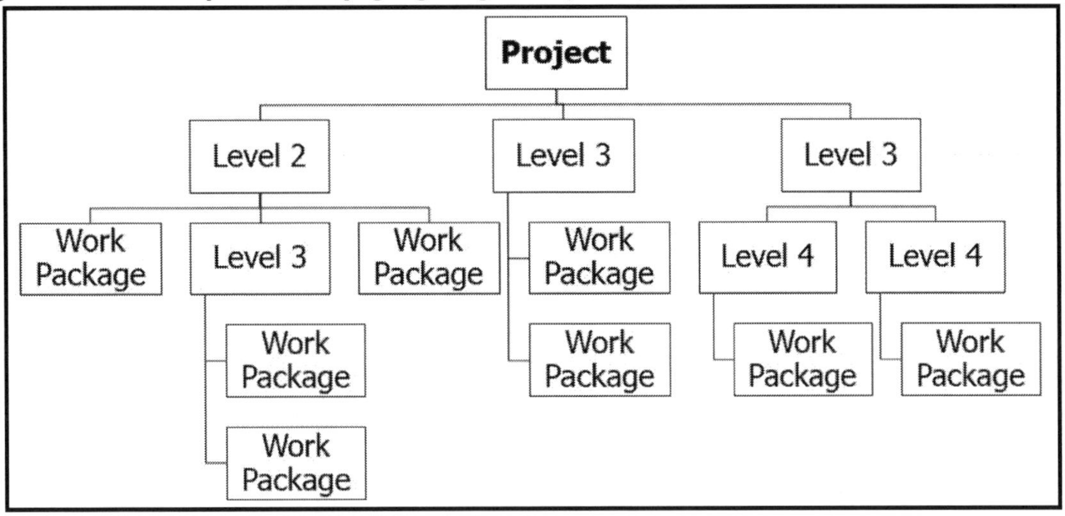

Be aware of the following work package characteristics:

- Any unnecessary project work should not have a corresponding work package; that work does not belong in the project.
- Every work package has a specific associated deliverable.
- Each work package should define all of the effort, materials, equipment, risk, quality, cost, duration, and scope for the deliverable.
- Work packages and WBS do not logically link; they are in a hierarchical format.
- Each work package has a unique ID.
- Work packages help control and identify change (scope creep).
- The work package description should have a verb and a noun, and optionally, a location.
- The work package is the lowest level of the WBS.

Tip
Always document a deliverable's completion.

Planning to use a work package

The main concern when planning to use a work package is making sure that you include all of the work that is required to complete the project. When developing work packages, you especially want to make sure that you don't include any work that is not required on the project. You should clearly understand the work that will and will not be included in the work packages. If any of the required work is missing from the WBS (summary of all work packages), your project schedule can be delayed or you may incur extra cost as well because project work is missing that needs to be completed and paid for.

Reporting from a work package

The work package is not a period report. It can contain project status information, but its main use is gathering and documenting information, not reporting on it. Work packages are included as part of a WBS dictionary and should be available to anyone who is interested in learning more.

There are probably as many ways to report project progress as there are projects. One way is to use the work package as the reporting document. When reporting progress using this method, as work completes, record it in a work package. Your role is to constantly determine what work is complete and what work remains. With this information, you can take the progress information and summarize it to communicate project status, usually on a weekly basis. The information documented in the work package describes the details about the work that was completed and the remaining work.

The following list of items can be included in a work package:

- Project name
- Project manager
- Description
- Finish date
- Responsible team members
- Cost variance
- Time variance
- Actual resource hours used
- Remaining hours
- Materials used
- Risk events that occurred
- Lessons learned

The individual who performed the work, or the lead person for that particular project area, is responsible for completing the work package results form. If there are major project areas led by different team leads or subcontractors, those individuals are responsible for compiling the information for their areas and reporting the results. When using the work package method to collect progress data, these forms are helpful in understanding what data to collect. Without the form, team members struggle with what information they should or should not collect. Because there are signatures on the forms, they could serve well in a court case where proof is required for formal acceptance. When presented in a legal dispute, it could sway an arbitration panel or court decision because there are signatures that indicate when a team member completed the work. When completing the project, each work package form should be part of the overall work documentation and included with the WBS for long-term storage and providing lessons-learned information.

Figure 12.10 — Example of a work package form shows a sample work package progress form from a construction project. The team lead (John MacDonald) completed the form when the work activity was finished. The information on this form provides documentation about the work in the work package. It also provides proof through the signatures that the customer approved and signed off on the work package. As noted earlier, if the work ever went to court or was disputed, having the signatures proving that your customer signed off and approved the work can be valuable in helping you win the court case. It is a best practice for you to collect customer signatures on work package forms.

Figure 12.10 — Example of a work package form

Work Package Progress Form — Construction Project

Project Name:	Project manager:	Date Required:
Construction Project	**Jack Smith**	**May 14th, 2019**
WBS Code:	Activity/Summary Description:	Actual Finish Date:
AJ.02.10.06	**Module 26 — North Wall Electrical box installation**	**May 7th, 2019**
Responsible Team Member:	Cost Variance :	Time Variance:
Charlie Wade	**-$645.00**	**+ 5 Days**

Completion Comments/Notes:

Wiring was installed with two circuits reversed and required an additional inspection. Task finished 5 days earlier, and under budget.

Approvals/Signoffs:	Team Lead Signature/Date:	Project manager Signature/Date:
Mary Jones	**John Macdonald**	**Bob Allen**
May 9th, 2019	**May 9th, 2019**	**May 10th, 2019**

You do not need to formally report individual work package forms to your customers based on the standard reporting process. The work package forms help you monitor and control project activities. The form also helps you report to the stakeholders, at a summary level. If the customer or any stakeholder wants to see work package details, they can review the work package form for all of the information they need.

There is usually no time frame associated with reporting a work package results form. Project work completes at various times and so does completing the work package form. Therefore, regular reporting can be challenging. Occasionally, you might have to gather the week's forms and report them at the end of day Friday, but that is uncommon. These forms do not lend themselves to formal reporting. Other tools do the reporting using the information from a work package. The work package document is stored in the project document control system.

Cross-Reference

See Chapter 21 - Using Communication Tools During the Executing and Controlling Process to learn more about how to create and use a work package.

Summary

In summary, the tools described in this chapter help you and the project team manage project communications. As we know, managing project communications is tricky, yet critical to the success of the project. You will spend 90% of your time on the project managing and controlling project communications, so you have to be ready and armed with the tools and processes to help you be successful.

One of the tools that can make an impact on your day-to-day project management responsibilities is the project calendar. The personal calendar has been around for many years for people to record their doctor and dentist appointments, but the project calendar is a relatively new concept that project managers should embrace. It is popular with its graphic format and easy-to-communicate characteristics for team members, customers, leadership, and other stakeholders.

This chapter includes tools, such as the change readiness assessment, checkpoint report, daily progress report, Pareto chart, spider chart, and so on. With so many tools at your disposal, you should have an easier time deciding how to manage your project communications more effectively.

Chapter 13

Defining Communication Tools to Manage Project Risk

IN THIS CHAPTER

- ◆ Introduction to the Expected Monetary value
- ◆ Introduction to the Issues list
- ◆ Introduction to the Risk Assessment
- ◆ Introduction to the Risk Matrix
- ◆ Introduction to the Risk Model
- ◆ Introduction to the Risk Register

Managing project risk is an important part of project management. You manage risks by regularly watching them to ensure that they do not negatively impact the project. Project risks include the project going over budget, missing key milestone dates, or resources leaving the project, in addition to other external dependencies. Risk events may or may not occur; therefore, project managers work more aggressively on risk management to prevent as many risks as possible from occurring and impacting the project.

You must be diligent in tracking and managing project risks to prevent them from becoming issues. Often, you will use a risk assessment form to track and oversee project risks because you can share the project risk information form with your customers, team members, and leadership. You must track risks on a weekly basis at least and communicate all risk items to the team. Many project managers review project risk events during weekly status meetings to ensure that everyone understands the risk events. It is important that the team actively closes risk items regularly.

In this chapter, we explore project communication tools in the project risk management knowledge area.

Introduction to the Expected Monetary Value

Expected monetary value (EMV) calculates a contingency value for a risk event. The EMV uses a mathematical technique to derive an average outcome of an uncertain event that could happen in the future. EMV is a mathematical formula that can help make comparisons between ranges of those uncertain outcomes.

If you could find out precisely what would happen if you chose one option or another, making project decisions would be easy. You could simply calculate the value for each contending option and select the one with the highest value. On real projects, decisions are not that simple. Someone making a decision tries to choose the most valuable option and the one with the highest EMV. When performing risk analysis on your project, you may choose modeling or model simulation over the EMV method. When choosing the modeling method, it allows people to apply their bias on the EMV method that they would not be able to on a risk simulation.

Note
The Project Management Institute's knowledge area for this tool is the risk management area.

Tool Value
The EMV supports decision analysis and calculates a contingency amount for a risk event or for the entire project.

Social Media Tools
The communication purposes for the expected monetary value tool are to inform, persuade, and instruct. The tool can be used in Yammer, Socialcast, and Facebook (private group).

Calculations from the expected monetary value provide great project cost communication. The calculations state exactly what contingency funds to assign for the project. Calculating the expected monetary value can be done by the total project or by each individual risk event to allow your customers and leadership to be fully aware of project calculations and contingency amounts. You will need to work with your customers to ensure that the extra funds are in the project for contingency purposes, as needed. By doing so, and after a risk event occurs, you can absorb the event's impact because you planned for it and had the money available in case the risk event occurred.

Table 13.1 — Example of expected monetary value (rain on new patio) below, which uses rain as the risk event, tracks the contingency value required based on the varying degrees of possible rainfall. This includes zero rainfall to a downpour. For each risk event outcome, you estimate a value and decide the probability of that outcome. In this example of rainfall on a new patio, you determine the probability by using factors such as time of year, weather reports, and historical information. The rain event's calculated value controls what actions to take if it rains. For example, if work stops when it rains, the expected monetary value could be the worker's wages and the cost from the damages to the concrete. If you bought tarps and covers to prevent the rain from hitting the concrete (tarps, for example, cost money and you would include the expense in the risk event). All of the expense examples are causes for calculating the value of the risk event.

Table 13.1 — Example of expected monetary value (rain on new patio) is an example of an expected monetary value calculation based on the possible five rain events occurring and the impact each event would have, should it occur. In this example, you can see that if a Gully Washer occurs, the project's expected monetary value equals 45.

Table 13.1 — Example of expected monetary value (rain on new patio)

Outcome	Probability		Value if Risk Occurs		Expected Monetary Value
Drizzle	15%	X	0	=	0
Avg. Rain	10%	X	50	=	5
Hard Rain	5%	X	200	=	10
Gully Washer	3%	X	1500	=	45
No Rain	67%	X	0	=	0
Total	100%		Expected Value	=	60

Calculating the total EMV provides the project with the amount of monies needed for emergency purposes (contingency). Your customers and leadership team will accept the EMV formula over guessing and not knowing what contingency funding to apply.

There are many different ways you can benefit from using the EMV method. Most importantly, it provides justification and reasoning behind the extra budget requested to cover unexpected risk events. The extra budget provides a buffer for managing not only the budget, but the various risk events as well.

Every risk event has an expected value. You create the risk event's value by using the EMV formula. The risk event's value is the estimated amount it takes to replace or fix the project should the risk event happen. Calculating the EMV is easy. You calculate the EMV by multiplying the event probability by the value if the risk occurs. You can see these two fields' event and value if risk occurs in **Table 13.2 — Example of the expected monetary value formula**, below. Every risk event has varying degrees of outcomes.

Estimating the value of a risk event outcome is better than estimating the probability. Probabilities are usually educated guesses, where the value is what it would cost to replace the item if the event outcome occurred. People are closer when they guess and calculate values than they are at probabilities.

Table 13.2 — Example of the expected monetary value formula shows an example of the EMV formula. This is the standard formula for multiple outcomes for a particular risk event.

Table 13.2 — Example of the expected monetary value formula

Outcome	Event		Value if Risk Occurs		Expected Monetary Value
Outcome Event 1	Probability 1	X	Value 1	=	Expected Monetary Value 1
Outcome Event 2	Probability 2	X	Value 2	=	Expected Monetary Value 2
Outcome Event 3	Probability 3	X	Value 3	=	Expected Monetary Value 3
					Total Expected Value

The main reason you would calculate the EMV is to determine the value of the risk event(s). When you know that value, you know how much budget you need to cover the events if they do occur. Projects must have an allocated contingency fund to cover known risk events; otherwise, if the event occurs and there is no budget for it, the project could fail. To get an accurate estimate of how much money the project needs to cover risk events, calculate the EMV.

Planning to use the expected monetary value

There are several steps you must complete when planning and preparing to calculate the expected monetary value (EVM) on your project. First, you must perform a risk analysis that identifies your project's risk events. You will need to create a risk matrix (risk matrix is covered in this chapter, *Chapter 13 - Defining Communication Tools to Manage Project Risk*, and *Chapter 19 - Chapter 19 - Using Communication Tools for Project Reporting during the Planning Phase*), and then identify the highest-priority risk events for which you want to apply the EMV analysis. Next, decide how far down the risk priority list you want to go to calculate the EMV. For every risk event, there is a trade-off for the value of knowing the EMV and the cost to get it. After setting the cut-off point for how far down the list to go, you and your team can start calculating the EMV by using the calculation from the previous section, for each risk event selected. This task is not difficult; it just takes time and effort from you and your team. How much time and effort it takes is up to you to decide. After all of the risk event EMVs are calculated, summarize them. The total you create is the contingency percentage for the project risk. Your last step is deciding what percentage of risk remains, and then estimating that value. Combining the two values, the calculated EMV and estimated EMV, will give you the project's total EMV (contingency). With this information, you can work with your customers and leadership team to put aside the funds in the budget in case the risk events occur.

Another acceptable method you can use to estimate the remaining EMV is the Pareto principal, the 80/20 rule. In this process, you assume that the portion of the identified risk is 20 percent of the risks and 80 percent of the contingency value. Therefore, the remaining contingency is 20/80 × the calculated value. Total the two contingencies and you have the project's total EMV.

Cross-Reference
See the Pareto chart tool in Chapters 12 - Defining Communication Tools That Manage Project Communications and Chapter 22 - Using Communication Tools in Executing and Controlling Process to Report Project Information for more information.

Reporting from expected monetary value

You are responsible for working with your team to calculate the risk events' EMV. Work alongside the project team, customers, and other interested parties, to develop the values and create the project's contingency needs. As noted, when you know the value of the risk events if they occur, you can work with your customers and leadership team to get that budget into your contingency funds. The expected monetary value is an excellent communication tool because it helps identify the project risks and their associated values, or costs, to correct the situation if the risk event occurs.

Table 13.3 — Example of expected monetary value (rolling dice) shows another example of calculating the expected monetary value by rolling dice. Each time you roll a dice, you have one-sixth (.1666) of a chance of rolling any one of the six numbers on the dice, which is *probability*. The number that you roll is the *value*. Therefore, multiplying the probability by the value you rolled gives the expected value. Remember, the expected value of each outcome provides no real value for this calculation. The total of all possible values is your EMV. In this case, every time you roll a dice, you average a 3.5 expected value. That means, if you were playing a board game, every time you rolled the dice, you would average 3.5 squares forward, and for every two rolls, you would average seven squares forward.

Table 13.3 — Example of expected monetary value (rolling dice)

Outcome	Event		Value if Risk Occurs		Expected Monetary Value
Roll Die 1	0.1666	X	1	=	0.1666
Roll Die 2	0.1666	X	2	=	0.3332
Roll Die 3	0.1666	X	3	=	0.4998
Roll Die 4	0.1666	X	4	=	0.6664
Roll Die 5	0.1666	X	5	=	0.833
Roll Die 6	0.1666	X	6	=	0.9996
				Total Expected Value	3.4986

Each week, you and your team should calculate the remaining EMVs for the project's risk events as part of the regular project management. Include reports from that process in the project's reporting. Use a spreadsheet to calculate the EMV for your project's risk events. After it is in a spreadsheet, it is easy to capture and report in other formats, such as Microsoft PowerPoint presentations or on internal websites. The EMV spreadsheets and presentations are stored as part of the document control system for long-term storage and archiving, and it is readily available for anyone interested.

Cross-Reference

See Chapter 18 - Using Communication Tools to Plan and Develop Project Deliverables to learn more about Expected Monetary Value (EMV).

Introduction to the Issues List

The *issues list* tracks project issues so that you can stay on top of those issues to prevent them from negatively affecting the project. The issues list is a central repository for storing project issues. The issues are stored, managed, and controlled by you throughout the project life cycle. You should check issues and risk events equally, although, you should focus a bit more on the issues because they already occurred and could be impacting progress. Sometimes, issues need immediate resolutions; other times, they can wait until the team has a chance to react to them, as required. Issues can quickly become risk events if they are not controlled, and they can easily start to have a negative impact on the project. Some issues may be large and important enough that you create related individual activities and tasks on the project schedule. This process is common where an issue actually becomes something the team has to resolve quickly and project activities are put on hold to focus on resolving the issue. Add the issue to the work activities so that team members can address and work on them immediately. When this occurs, and an issue becomes part of the project, create a new work package in the WBS. (See Work Packages in *Chapters 12 - Defining Communication Tools That Manage Project Communications* and *21 - Using Communication Tools while Executing and Controlling the Project.*)

Note
The Project Management Institute's knowledge area for this tool is the risk management area. The secondary area for this tool is quality.

Tool Value
The issues list is a central repository for storing and communicating the project's issues while continuing to track issues in a consistent format.

Social Media Tools
The communication purposes for the issue list are to inform and instruct. The tool can be used in Yammer, Socialcast, and Facebook (private group).

The issues list is one of the most widely used communication tools on a project. A project manager communicates the issues list at least once a week in order to drive resolution on each item. All projects have issues, some small, some large, and you must continually review and work on the issues list to increase your chance of a successful project. Without the issues list, you can have project problems, but have no idea what they are about and, in all likelihood, could be putting the project at risk and not even know it. Active issue management is one of your top responsibilities and priorities and something that can increase your chance of success.

The project issues list is valuable as a communications tool because it brings exposure to customers, team members, and leadership about project issues. One benefit you receive from using an issues list is a greater depth of knowledge about project issues and understanding how you can help resolve them. There is a big difference when you are engaged in issue tracking and resolution on your project, compared to being the person keeping a list up to date. It is a huge problem when you don't have any depth or knowledge about your project issues. Don't put yourself in that position on any project. You can handle issue management either way, but you benefit much more when you are fully engaged and actively working on your project issues. You also must ensure that all issue statuses go through you before updating or closing an issue on the issues list. Don't allow team members to randomly close issues without your knowledge. By having the issues status flow through you, you can better understand the issues and you may be able to prevent the same issue from occurring again in the future. One of your main responsibilities is to track, monitor, and control project issues, so it makes sense that you make this a top priority.

Table 13.4 — Example of project issues list shows an example of a typical project issues list. In this example, the columns represent a basic set of fields to actively report and resolve the issues. It is important you add as much detail as possible in the description field, so anyone reading the issue understands it and the impact it has on a project. This example is one of thousands available on the Internet, or as part of your company's PMO processes and procedures.

Table 13.4 — Example of project issues list

Issue Title	Type	Status	Description	Resolution
Project Funding	Budget	Open	Project is going to lose funding across fiscal years	Obtain dollars in second half of year
Resource Loss	Staff	Open	Project needs to hire two additional resources ASAP	Hire staff before fiscal year end

Is it an Issue or a Risk?

One important distinction that you need to be aware of is the difference between issues and risk events. The difference between a project issue and a risk event is that issues have already occurred and have been identified, and a risk event is a possibility that something may happen in the future. The main attribute of a risk event is that it is in the future (a risk event cannot be in the past); whereas, issues may be in the past, present, and future. An easy way to look at this is issues are more in the present; whereas, risk events are always in the future.

Another benefit of having an issues list is being able to communicate the consolidated list of issues to your customers and leadership. If you store issues in multiple places, such as email threads or in different spreadsheets, you may have trouble trying to remember where they all are, and who is working or trying to resolve them. This could be a real mess for you, and your customers could lose confidence in you if you let this happen. You must ensure that you have a good handle on your project's issues. The benefit of a consolidated list is that it not only forces you to engage in every project issue, but everyone has just one place to access the updated and current project issues. An old, outdated issues list is not an effective way to manage a project.

Tip
A best practice is to communicate issues to customers, stakeholders, and team members once a week.

Table 13.5 — Example of a comprehensive issues list provides more details about each project issue. Where the issues shown in Table 13.4 — Example of project issues list was more of a minimum set of fields to capture for an issues list. For a more **comprehensive issues list it is better to use Table 13.5 — Example of a comprehensive issues list.**

Table 13.5 — Example of a comprehensive issues list

ID	1	2
Issue	Weather problems, two weeks of rain has caused schedule delay.	Resource leaving paving team at EOD tomorrow.
Section Title	Construction	Staffing
Impact	High	Medium
Probability	2	4
Owner Name	Bob Smith	Mary Douglas
Date Open	12/4/2019	10/14/2019
Assigned to	Joe Jones	William James
Date Closed		11/28/2019
Status	Open	Closed
Resource	TBD	Hired a new Resource
Color	Red	Green, new resource hired and starts next week.

When entering issues in the issues list, it is important to enter as much data as you can. You don't have to know all of the information, but fill in what you do know; you can always come back and add more details later. One of the key fields in the issues list is the issue's color status. The color status is something you may know when you are entering the data, and it is a great way to share issue status. If the project has multiple issues, you will potentially have multiple colors, resulting in an informational dashboard and an effective communication tool.

Cross-reference
Follow the status definitions and guidelines outlined in the issue management plan about status colors.

Store your issues list in a central location, such as a document tracking system. The format can be a spreadsheet, a document, or any other application as long as everyone agrees on a single location. The location should always be available so that anyone can access it when they need to see the issues list. Team members may be working to resolve the issues, or customers may want to see what is happening on one issue or another, so setting up a central location that is open and available is the only way to manage risk. This will also satisfy everyone's requirements, as well as continue to keep project communications open and flowing.

If the project's issues are problematic, you may need to manage the issues once a day, compared to weekly. Because each issue varies, you must decide which issues to focus your time on resolving. At a minimum, you should review the issues list daily and decide which issues impact the project the most and focus your attention there. It is always best to work on the most impactful issue first. If the issue is large enough, you could instruct all of the team members to resolve the issue. If you do not review and work on the project's issues at least once a week, the project can be seriously affected.

Many methods are available to track issues. Several software packages are available to manage and maintain lists. The software packages are automated tools, such as word processors or spreadsheets, and there is the old-fashioned, manual method of using pen and paper. On a large project, it makes the most sense to invest in a software package so that multiple team members can access the issues simultaneously. You would still be able to control and monitor the project issues through the software, across a large group of team members. Software packages often let you create a knowledge base, based on the issues, that includes information about the issue and stores relevant information to allow further details to be associated to each issue. Other times, you use a document control system to create and store project issues. In either case, a software package or document control system (an automated tool) are the best methods for tracking and controlling project issues.

Planning to use an issues list

When planning and preparing to use an issues list, you must first decide how the structure of the list will look and how many fields you will use. You should use the same structure repeatedly, regardless of the size or complexity of the project. After you decide what the issues list will look like, work with your customer to ensure that the list is suitable for their purposes. The customer may suggest adding fields you haven't considered; therefore, adding a customer checkpoint during the planning phase and confirming what they want on the issues list makes good sense. During the customer conversations about how the issues list should look, address how often your customers want to receive the list and how often. Because the issues list is such an important communication tool that everyone relies on, it is important to ensure that the delivery time frames are set before the project starts. After performing these planning activities, you are adequately prepared to use the issues list on your project.

Reporting from an issues list

You are responsible for creating the issues list. Issue management is one of the main responsibilities of a project manager, so it makes sense that you own the list and treat managing issues as a top priority. Project managers who ignore or who do not actively manage project issues face project execution problems.

Communicating the issues list is one of your more important responsibilities. You should work on your project issues closely so that you can present them to you customer, if needed. If you can only speak to your project's issues at a high-level, you are not managing your project as effectively as you should. One best practice for communicating the issues list is reviewing it during your weekly project status meetings. By doing this, the project team gets full exposure to the issues list, and you can get updated information about how your team is resolving the issues. As you review the issues with team members during weekly status meetings, you are ensuring that the issues are being resolved as quickly as possible. Sometimes, issues remain open for most of the project, which is okay, as long as everyone agrees that the issue should remain open. However, you must ensure that you are continually readdressing that issue so it is not forgotten. An example of an issue that stays open for a while is a budget issue. The issue could be that the project is over budget and the issue remains open for the project's duration—or, until you find extra funding to add to the project budget to cover the overage.

Tip
Every issue should have a team member owner. If not, the issue defaults to you to own until you assign it to another team member.

You are responsible for regularly reporting the project issues list to both the project team and to customers. Creating the list in a document or a spreadsheet is very simple. The issues list is stored as part of the document control system for long-term archiving and access. Every team member, customer, or leadership member should be able to access the issues list; their visibility can often lead to quicker resolutions.

Cross-Reference

See Chapter 21 - Using Communication Tools During the Executing and Controlling Process to learn more about how to use and create an issues list.

Introduction to the Risk Assessment Form

The *risk assessment form* manages, assesses, and evaluates potential project risks. Project risks are events that could occur and potentially benefit or jeopardize the project. For example, the project does not have enough money in the budget to see it through to completion. If that risk event occurs, the project would have to stop until money becomes available or it could continue with management's support to go over budget. The risk assessment form provides a view of the potential project risks. The form also stores risk mitigation strategies in case the risk transpires. Risk assessment forms differ among projects and companies, but each assessment is valuable to the project team in helping to manage and control project risk events. By using the risk assessment form, you can see, on a single form, potential problems and how risk events could impact the project. The project team and customers can also use the risk assessment form to see how to help mitigate or reduce the risk from occurring.

Note
The Project Management Institute's knowledge area for this tool is the risk management area. There is no secondary area for this tool.

Tool Value
The risk assessment assesses and evaluates the potential impact of risk events occurring on the project. The assessment and mitigation information stored about each risk provides the mitigation steps for the team to follow if the risk event occurs.

Social Media Tools
The communication purpose for the risk assessment form is to inform. The tool can be used in Yammer, Socialcast, and Facebook (private group).

You communicate the risk assessment form as a regular part of project reporting. You are responsible for communicating the risk assessment information to impacted customers and team members. Reporting this information brings exposure to possible risk events and allows risk planning to occur to potentially avoid the risks from occurring. You document the time frames for reporting project risks in the communication plan. Reporting could be in a weekly report, a biweekly report, or even a monthly report. Work with your customers and leadership to understand time frames for reporting risks and document that cadence in the project's communication plan.

The most important benefit to using a risk assessment form is putting the project risks in a central repository for anyone to access. Storing the project's risks in a single location lets your customers and team members find the risks, evaluate the impact, and work to resolve or mitigate the risk before it occurs. It's difficult to manage potential project risks if they are stored in various locations. If risks are scattered on spreadsheets, websites, or in project status reports, it is more difficult to mitigate or eliminate the risks for one simple reason. If you and your team don't know about all of the project risks, you are not in the best position to resolve them.

Another benefit of using a risk assessment form is that you track all information about the risk on the form. The form includes data about risk probability, budget impact, scope impact, and schedule impact for every project risk. That is a wealth of project information for you and the project team to process. Tracking this information for each risk event puts each risk in perspective with the other risks and the project team can use the information to prioritize their important to the project. Occasionally, the risks are of little importance—it is good to track them—but the impact is minimal if the risk occurs. You and your team complete the risk assessment form by adding risk information weekly throughout the project life cycle.

Figure 13.1 — **Example of a risk assessment form** shows an example of a risk assessment form with one project risk event. In this example, the risk event describes a potential problem with an outside vendor on a construction project. The vendor is potentially going to deliver steel to the site one week late. The probability of that risk event occurring is low, about 10 percent, and the budget impact, if it does occur, is estimated to be $50,000. A contingency of $5,000 dollars has been set aside to cover the costs of the added activities that must occur if the steel is late. This leaves a shortfall of $45,000 between the impact of the steel delivered one week late and the $5,000 set aside to offset this event. If this event were to occur, you would set aside $50,000 from the contingency fund to ensure there is no loss to the project. If you calculate the contingency properly, there would be enough budget to cover this event. Further information about this example includes the schedule running one week late (if the event occurs) and the end date of the project pushing out one week later than planned. You then create a condition in the contract with the vendor company that stipulates that if the vendor company delivers the steel late, there is a penalty of $11,000 a day. You would also note in the contract that this late fee is payable immediately to offset the loss from the project budget if the steel is late.

Figure 13.1 — Example of a risk assessment form

Identification		IMPACTS								Mitigation
		Probability (%)				EMV (Contingency)				
WBS #	Description of Risk	Low 10	Medium 50	High 100	Budget Impact		Schedule Impact	Scope Impact	Penalty	Possible Solutions
1234A	Vendor delivers structural steel, 1 week late	X			50,000	5,000	1 week delay	N/A	Yes, 1 1,000 per day	Mitigate Avoid Transfer Accept

The process of completing the risk assessment form is simple. However, filling out the form is not your most important area of the work. The more important work for you and your team members is to consider the project impact that the risks could have on the project's success. When completing the form, you must understand the risk event details and the various impacts the risk events could cause if they occur. For example, deciding the probability and the budget impact of a risk event is rarely something you should tackle on your own. This is something that team members jointly decide with you. Both you and your team members need to decide on the chance that the risk event will occur at all. You also need to work together and decide on how much of the budget the risk event would use to ensure that the project stays on track after the event occurs. This same process continues for each column in the risk assessment form where you and your team members jointly evaluate the risk events together. One of the most important columns to complete in the risk assessment form is the contingency column and the dollar amount required for covering the project if the risk event occurs. This is the contingency amount that is put aside in the budget in case the risk event occurs while still keeping the project on track.

The risk assessment process is complex and challenging. Another challenge in completing the risk assessment form is the process of risk quantification. Risk quantification involves evaluating risks for possible project outcomes. It evaluates the probability of a risk and its effect on the project. The end-result of that calculation is the amount contained within the expected monetary value (EMV). This term is familiar in the project management industry. There are many formulas in the industry for calculating risk assessments and especially risk quantification.

The following example of a project scenario calculates the EMV. This scenario relates to risk assessment and quantification for rain fall. You are pouring a concrete patio in the backyard of your house. Your goal is to make it as smooth as possible and have it slope away from the house to limit any water problems. One of the risk events that might occur is the possibility of rain fall after pouring the concrete, which would ruin your patio's finish. The objective is to understand how much money to set aside in case it rains, allowing you to cover the costs of refinishing the patio.

Table 13.6 — Example of possible outcomes and outcome value chart shows the possible outcomes and expected values of this project. As you can see in the table, there are only three types of outcomes associated to this situation, and each has a calculated expected outcome value associated to it.

Table 13.6 — Example of possible outcomes and outcome value chart

Outcome	Risk Event Probability	Risk Event Value	Expected Outcome Value
Drizzle	0	0	0
Regular Rain Showers	5	$50.00	$2.50
Downpour	1	$1,500.00	$15.00
No Rain	94	0	0
Expect Monetary Value Total	100%		$17.50

After identifying a risk event, break the event down into the possible outcomes. In this example, first identify the types of rain (drizzle, regular rain, downpour, and no rain), and then estimate the probability of each outcome. For example, the likelihood of the rain occurring. The next step is to estimate the value of the outcome occurring. This can be difficult because understanding the value of a particular risk event is complex and not easy to calculate. To understand the complexity of the value of a risk event, consider the following factors:

- Type of project
- Resources used
- An associated billing rate
- Amount of time
- Materials used
- Quality requirements

When reviewing and considering the risk value factors in the list, you have the basis to estimate the value of the outcome of the risk event if it does occur. Then, use the formula noted above to calculate by multiplying the outcome probability × the outcome estimated value to calculate the expected outcome value. Repeat this process until you have all of the expected outcome value for each risk event. When you have the totals for each risk event, add the totals together to calculate the project's EMV. When you have the final total (the total from the individual totals), enter it into the risk assessment form's contingency column. The process is easy to follow once you create the formula for the first risk event because it is just a matter of copying that formula to the other risk events.

Note
Usually, there are varying degrees of an outcome for each risk event. For example, a snowstorm will cause a delay in the project. The varying outcome for a snowstorm is the amount of snow. It may snow 1 inch and cause no delay. It may snow 1 foot, 2 feet, or 3 feet, with the varying

outcomes producing a varying amount of project delay. There is also the probability that it will not snow at all, which is also one of the outcomes.

Planning to use the risk assessment form

When planning to use a risk assessment form, you should understand the process you are going to follow to complete the form. Project risk management is done in various ways. Some project managers are formal, while some are informal in how they process risks. If you are going to use the risk assessment form, you need to set up a process to use the form. You can't just send it to your team and expect them to know how to fill it out or know what to do with it. It is not going to happen. Take your time and walk the team through the risk assessment process for how to complete the risk assessment form so they know what to do. It is in your best interest to create a formal risk process and continue to use that process throughout the project.

There are other areas of planning to consider when preparing to use the risk assessment form, including:

- How you will get the risk information to enter on the form?

- Which team members need to be involved in this process?

- Where will the risk assessment forms be stored?

- How you will obtain the contingency budget for the risk outcomes in case they do occur?

- How is the contingency budget added to the project's budget?

These are some of the different areas you will need to consider when planning to use the risk assessment form. Few project managers can gather the team together and start filling out the information without having a plan in place.

After performing the planning activities for using the risk assessment form, you have prepared yourself and your project team to use it for your project.

Note
Research has shown financial benefits depend more on the frequency and how the assessment is performed than on the formula used to quantify the risk events.

Reporting from a risk assessment form

You are responsible for driving the project's risk assessment activities, usually called risk assessment sessions. These are meetings for entering risk event information into the risk assessment form and closing out risk events whenever possible. You will take your project team through using and reporting the risk assessment form throughout the project.

During risk assessment sessions, you should receive enough detail to communicate the issues to your customers and leadership. One best practice around the risk process is scheduling a separate customer-focused risk assessment meeting. In this meeting, you will go over the list of risks and the various assessments that the team has assigned to the risk events with the project's customers. The separate risk management meeting gives customers the details about project risks and the opportunity for them to help resolve the risks where they can. Unfortunately, when customers do not engage in this process, or attend the meetings, and leave the risk management completely up to you and your team to resolve, it hampers your chances of running a successful project. An important part of your role is to focus on ongoing communications around the project risks.

Most project managers use a spreadsheet to create and report their risk assessment form, which is acceptable because many project managers don't have a formal software application that contains the risk assessment form. Often, you may have to regenerate the project's risk assessment form into another format, such as a Microsoft PowerPoint presentation or on internal website for reporting purposes. Store the risk assessment form in the document control system for long-term archiving, storage, and accessibility.

Cross-Reference

See Chapter 21 - Using Communication Tools During the Executing and Controlling Process to learn more about how to use and create the risk assessment form.

Introduction to the Risk Matrix

The r*isk matrix* communicates the current project risks by prioritizing and categorizing project risk events into an easy-to-read chart for communicating. In this case, the risk matrix communicates the number of risks and the category (high, medium, low) where the risks sit on the project. When you color the risk matrix using red, yellow, and green, the tool becomes even more valuable in communicating project risk information. The risk matrix is also valuable without the color coding, but the colors make a world of difference. One of the advantages of using the risk matrix is that it is possible to produce multiple types of the charts using various project categories. For example, you can create a risk matrix that outlines all of the risks in a specific category, such as time, cost, or quality chart to get separate risk matrixes for the project. Multiple risk matrix charts let you and your customers prioritize how you approach risk management and let you compare how risky each category is to one another so that the team can focus on resolving the highest risk category first.

Note

The Project Management Institute's knowledge area for this tool is the risk management area. There is no secondary area for this tool.

Tool Value

The risk matrix is a simple and easy-to-read chart to assess the risk level of the project. No other tool can help someone decide, at a glance, how risky a project is to complete.

Social Media Tools

The communication purpose for the risk matrix tool is to inform. The tool can be used in Yammer, Socialcast, and Facebook (private group).

Team members and customers can use the risk matrix to decide the overall project's *risk level*. The risk level rates how risky a project is to complete against several known and unknown factors. The most common factors used in risk assessment include schedule, budget, or scope.

The most important benefit of using a risk matrix is the immediate ability to assess and understand the project's risk level when viewing the chart. The project's risk level is important to know because it lets project customers and leadership decide whether the project should continue or stop immediately. Often, when customers and leadership see a project with a high risk level they will cancel it because it could be too risky to the company. When you know your project's risk level, you can better focus your project team on helping reduce the possible risk events on the risk matrix.

When you continue to produce and report risks using the risk matrix, and week after week there are several high-level risk events, this will trigger customer and leadership involvement. It is common and expected that your customers and leadership will want to know what your project team is doing to reduce or resolve these events. The risk matrix is the perfect tool to drive these conversations because you are often in the best position to know whether you need help on the project.

The risk matrix tool can be beneficial on large or small projects because every project will have potential risk events, and every customer and leadership team will want to know where they fall on the chart. Is the project risky? Is the project not risky? These are questions your customers will ask all the time. It is guaranteed that project customers will want to know the potential risk events and where the project could fail and what they can do to prevent those failures. The more risks on the project, the more comprehensive the risk matrix tool.

Figure 13.2 — Example of a risk matrix shows a completed risk matrix. Before creating the risk matrix, the team identified 35 risk events and stack-ranked each risk with impact and probability, ranging from low to high. The team placed numbers from 1 to 35 (risk events) in the appropriate cells in the table. At a glance, customers, leadership, or team members can see the project has a high risk level. This is due to a majority of the risk events falling into the high-high columns and rows on the chart. The higher the count of risk events within a certain cell range (high-high, high-medium) determines the project's risk level.

Figure 13.2 — Example of a risk matrix

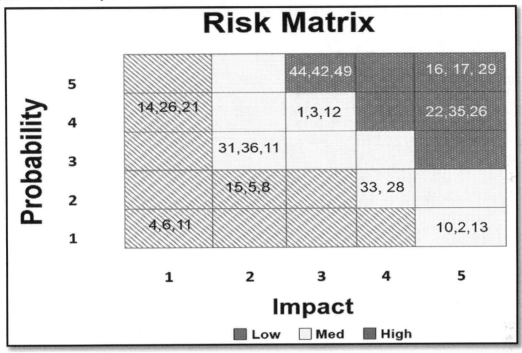

Earlier in the chapter, we covered color coding the risk matrix to add impact and effectiveness. As you can see in **Figure 13.3 — Example of a risk matrix (including expected monetary value)**, below, the tool is just as valuable in black and white, but not as much as when you add color coding or pattern fill. It is a best practice to add color coding or pattern fill to the following cells for your risk matrix. Reading the risk matrix from left to right, add background colors to these cells.

Red = high-medium, high-high, medium-high (top-right range of cells)

Yellow = high-low, medium-medium, low-high (middle range of cells)

Green = medium-low, low-low, medium-low (lower-left range of cells)

Color coding and pattern filling makes a big difference to your risk matrix and helps it become an even more effective communications tool, especially if you are using just black and white. Using a color coded version is much more effective.

When reviewing the risk matrix in **Figure 13.3 — Example of a risk matrix (including expected monetary value)**, it is clear to see how risky the project is by the number of risk events in the top-right corner of the chart. Also, by seeing how many risk events there are, in general, gives the project manager the impression there is some project risk that they will have to handle. In the example in **Figure 13.3— Example of a risk matrix (including expected monetary value)**, there are nine risk events assessed by the team as high-impact and high-probability. This example illustrates an extremely high-risk project. Anytime there are that many risks in the high area of the risk matrix, it lends itself to being a higher-risk project. The other risk events (noted by numbers) are scattered among the other cells, and while they should not be ignored, they are simply not as important as the top nine noted in the highest cell. When customers or leadership review this risk matrix chart, their focus will be at the top-right corner cells and on the nine risk events outlined by the team as the highest priority. Your customers and leadership will focus their attention on the higher risk events because, often, they are in the best position to help mitigate or eliminate them. When your customers and leadership are engaged in using the risk matrix, then you know that the right people are seeing the project's risks to resolve them where possible.

When reviewing the example in **Figure 13.2 — Example of a risk matrix**, it is clear that there are nine categories where a risk event can fall on a particular project. On the left side of the chart, there is a label called Risk Impact, which ranges from High to Low. The top of the chart has a Risk Probability label, which also ranges from High to Low. There may also be some variations to the chart. Some project managers like to expand the risk matrix and carry more values, such as Very High and Very Low. Regardless of the particular layout for the risk matrix, the process for filling out the chart remains the same. This process involves team members evaluating each risk event and how it will impact the project, by judging the risk impact against scope, schedule, and budget. The same risks are also evaluated on the probability of the risk event occurring. At the end of the process, after assessing all risk events, you and your team will have completed the risk matrix. You are now in a position where you can share and report the risk matrix to everyone on the project.

Cross-Reference

Chapter 19 - Using Communication Tools for Project Reporting during the Planning Process to learn more about how to create and use a risk matrix.

Tip

Calculate the expected monetary value of each risk event, per cell, to find out the cost of risk on your project.

As noted earlier in this chapter, the risk matrix tool can have different formats and use various data-points. The expected monetary value calculation, first introduced in the risk assessment form, lends itself nicely to plotting its data points on a risk matrix. **Figure 13.3 — Example of a risk matrix (including expected monetary value)** shows an example of the expected monetary values calculations for the risk events on the risk matrix. This project team decided previously that the project was high risk, and therefore it is expected to see high expected monetary value amounts in the upper-right corner of the matrix. In the example in **Figure 13.3 — Example of a risk matrix (including expected monetary value)**, the expected monetary value of the High-High cell is $92,425. This also happens to be the highest value of any of the other cells. When reviewing this risk matrix, notice the cells surrounding the $92,425 cell. Those cells also contain high values, which further justifies that this project is a high-risk project and a good portion of the project's budget will need to be earmarked and put aside in case the risk events occur.

Figure 13.3 — Example of a risk matrix (including expected monetary value)

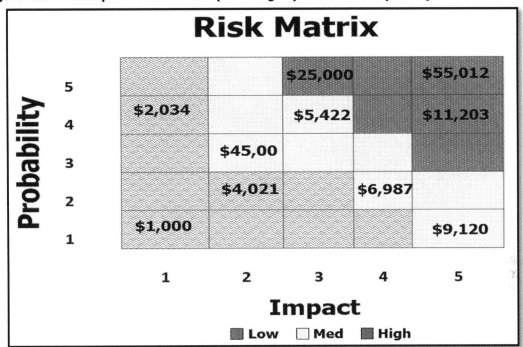

In this risk matrix, color coding and using pattern fill will help communicate this information to the customer and leadership. People will be especially interested in this risk matrix because there is budget involved and they will want to know what specific risk events cost if they occur. Use the same color definitions outlined above and add colors to this version of the risk matrix.

Planning to use a risk matrix tool

When planning and preparing to use a risk matrix, you must first decide how you will assign probability and impact to the project's risk. You will have to decide whether to schedule a separate meeting, assign only some and not all members of the team, and what process they will follow. Assigning probability and impact for each risk event is necessary before using the risk matrix. The reason for needing the data is because you can't complete the risk matrix without knowing where to place the risks onto the chart. This process of handling risk events and assigning impacts and probability happen at your discretion. Some of your project manager peers schedule extra meetings to focus on project risks, and others handle the risk management process during the team's regular status meeting.

After you decide the risk management assessment processes and you know what to capture and report, the next step is to capture the reporting requirements with your customers. Some customers will want the risk matrix color coded and some won't. Some will want it weekly, and some will want it monthly. Every customer will have unique requirements for reporting the risk matrix, so you need to be fully aware of those requirements. When meeting with the customer, there are three key areas to cover: what will be their involvement in the risk assessment process, what is their overall risk tolerance, and finally, what are their risk matrix report requirements. It is also a good idea to ask them their role in the resolution and closeout of the project's risks. After completing these planning activities and getting process answers from your customer, you are adequately prepared to use the tool on your project.

Reporting from the risk matrix tool

You are responsible for driving the risk assessment process and creating the project's risk matrix. By working alongside your project team, you add various risk events into different categories on the project's risk matrix. The risk assessment process is a negotiation process completed by you and your team members. Usually, your customers are not involved in the process, but there is nothing to say they could not be if they wanted to be. When your project team is stuck and can't decide where to put a risk event, they will leave it to you to decide. In almost all cases, you need to agree with your team and add the risk event where the team feels it should go. You do not often overrule the team's findings and recommendations. If you do, you could put yourself in a bad position with your team in the long run.

Communicating the risk matrix is your responsibility and something that should go no longer than one week or two, at most, between reporting. Risk events can prevent a project from succeeding, and you must stay on top of project risks to increase the chance of your project's success. Communicating the risk matrix past a two-week cycle is asking for trouble. You can quickly see one-time project risks become project issues that will negatively impact the project. Create a risk matrix using a presentation tool, such as Microsoft PowerPoint or Microsoft Word and store it in the document control system for long-term archiving purposes.

Cross-Reference
Chapter 19 - Using Communication Tools for Project Reporting during the Planning Process to learn more about how to use and create the risk matrix.

Introduction to the Risk Model

You use the *risk model* to create a project risk score. Risk assessment forms and risk scores relate to the overall sense the project team has on the project's risk level. By answering a series of risk questions in the risk model, where each question has a value associated to it, the project receives a total risk score. The risk scope can move up and down dramatically depending on how the project team jointly answers the risk questions in the risk model. Companies use risk scores to keep projects going and determine where to focus more resources and budget. Companies also use risk scores to keep the project under tight control. Using risk models allow companies to concentrate on higher-risk projects first, before getting involved in lower-risk projects that may or may not need any attention. The only way to tell the difference between the project types is using the risk scores. Higher risk scores mean a higher risk project that needs customer or leadership attention to help resolve project risks.

Note
The Project Management Institute's knowledge area for risk modeling is the risk management area. There is no secondary area for this tool.

Tool Value
The risk model provides a risk assessment of the project from the project team's perspective. No other tool asks team members and customers a series of questions that forms their thoughts on the risk level the way the risk model does.

Social Media Tools
The communication purposes for the risk model are to inform and motivate. The tool can be used in Yammer, Socialcast, and Facebook (private group).

The risk model is a good communication tool for communicating the project's risk score and the associated data about how the score is calculated. When communicating the risk model, you can show the customer the various questions applied to produce the risk score and the total risk score. The risk model holds valuable information about what the team thinks about the project's risk level by the answers they have provided to the risk questions. Communicate the risk model as often as possible to your customers and leadership to ensure that everyone is fully aware of how risky the team thinks the project is and what actions you or your team should take to mitigate or remove those risks.

Risk models give you the ability to create a project risk score to help you understand how risky the project is and provides exposure to the team's answers to various risk questions.

The unique area of the risk model is that the project team completes it together and the results don't come from an individual team member. Allowing the team to provide the risk score results, instead of an individual, is much more valuable to the project because one or two team members can skew the risk score based on what they personally think about the risks and the project in general.

You and your team can benefit from using the risk model because it drives creating a risk assessment score for the project. Knowing your project's assessment score compared to other similar projects helps you know how risky your project is and how much time and effort you should spend focusing on risk events. For example, if your project were a low-risk project you would spend only limited time watching risk events compared to a high-risk project. Creating a project risk score and an associated risk assessment spreadsheet provides you the direction you need to understand how much time you will spend on the risk events.

Many companies are starting to use risk models for project funding and resource commitments. These companies are compelling project managers to complete this risk modeling process with their team members to create a project risk score. When all projects have a risk score, leadership can look across projects to decide which are the high-risk projects. When all projects complete the same risk model and assessment, it levels the playing field and gives leadership the view of the risks across all projects. With risk score information, leadership can make business decisions, such as canceling projects, adding more budget, and pulling resources. Having project risk scores is a valuable process for any company and a best practice for you to consider using for your project.

Figure 13.4 — Example of a risk model shows a typical project risk model. The questions on the risk model are specific to the project type and the scores associated to each question are project-specific. Risk models can be adjusted according to project types, and in doing so, the project scores for each question would adjust as well.

Figure 13.4 — Example of a risk model

Project Risk Model Example

		Total Project Risk Score	Component Risk Assessments	
	Interim Score	0		
			Low Budget Risk	
	Low Risk 1 - 35	Score 0	Low External Dependencies Risk	
	Medium Risk 36 - 72	Score	Low Management Risk	
			Low Mission Critical Risk	
	High Risk > 72	Score	Low Failure Risk	
			Low Complexity Risk	
	Question Number	Project Risk Question	Answer Lists (Note—when you click in each answer cell, a drop down list arrow will appear)	
Budget Risk	1	What is the estimated total project cost?		
	2	What percentage of the agency budget does the project represent?		
	3	Have sufficient project funds been budgeted and allocated?		
	4	How much confidence is there in the expenditure and funding projections?		
	5	Is funding available for maintenance of the project deliverable after project closure?		
External Dependencies Risk	6	Is this project dependent on another projects deliverable?		
	7	Does this project require resources from other organizations?		
	8	Does this project require data from other sources?		
Management Risk	9	What is the level of management commitment?		
	10	Is the project sponsor resourcing the project?		
	11	What is the experience and training level of agency project managers?		

The risk model is a spreadsheet that contains a series of questions and scores associated with each question. When a user answers a question, the answer has an associated score. Totaling all answers (all single scores) produces one project risk score. The risk model has questions based on the project type and the associated industry. For example, it would be irrelevant to ask software questions in a risk model when assessing project risks on a construction project. The two projects are very different, so scoring from one of the projects would not be relevant with the other. Therefore, there is no a single risk model that applies to all types of projects. Updating the questions and answers is simple, but time-consuming, which is the only drawback to using the tool. Proactive planning and completing the risk model early in the project can prevent the tool's maintenance and use from becoming overwhelming. The time-consuming part of using this tool is really only a minor part of using the tool. Those of you who set it up early and only need to update it when new risks come to the project and new scores need calculating will benefit greatly from using it. If you do not create the risk model at the beginning of the project and leave it until later in the project or the end, you will think that the tool is more difficult to manage because you are behind the ball and late setting it up. Sometimes, your project manager peers don't use the tool because they don't see it as valuable as working on other project areas.

Tip

Projects need a new risk assessment score when adding new risk events to the project.

When using a risk model, one of the important areas is learning how to read and understand the results. Use the following score chart to understand a project's risk score. You can update **Table 13.7 — Risk Score and Description Chart** to reflect specific needs of your project; it is not meant to be a default table for every project.

Table 13.7 — Risk score and description chart shows a risk score description chart. Use this chart to discover the risk score for your project. Score ranges and descriptions vary among projects and it's up to you, your team, and your customers to decide the values. Customers' roles vary among projects, so consider that too.

Table 13.7 — Risk score and description chart

Risk Score	Description
1 – 35	Indicates your project has a low risk assessment score and your project is low risk.
36 – 72	Indicates your project has a medium risk assessment score and your project is medium risk.
72 or Higher	Indicates your project has a high risk assessment score and your project is high risk.

Note

You should know the specific project details to produce an effective risk model. Without knowing the details, you may answer the questions differently than if you had more information.

The risk model uses a series of categories; the project type and industry sets the specifics of the categories. The categories include budget risk, failure risk, and mission critical risks. The categories are unlimited, and you and your team decide which categories you will use to track in the risk model.

Planning to use a risk model

When planning and preparing to use the risk model, you must first find out if the company has a risk modeling process in place already. If so, you will use that process and associated risk model for your project. Occasionally, you may have to attend training on the company's process or team up with someone who knows it already. Assuming the company does not have a risk modeling process in place, the first step in the planning process is for you to adapt the risk model template for use on your project. This requires working with the template and understanding the complex calculations and formulas in the spreadsheet. It also requires knowing each area of the spreadsheet well enough to understand where specific risk events could occur. Without this knowledge, your ability to create an effective risk model is limited. After ramping up on the template, the next step is to decide how your project team will engage in the risk assessment process. This includes setting up various meetings to decide how team members are involved and what roles they will play. After finding out how team members will engage in the risk model processes, focus on the project's customer involvement. When discussing your customers' involvement level, ensure that you also capture their risk model reporting needs. Some customers may want to see the risk model completed and reported weekly, and some customers may find monthly is suitable. Ask the question around timing and capture your customers' reporting requirements.

If the company uses risk scores for securing project approvals, or funding requests, there is a good chance your customers will be heavily involved in the risk model process. You need to know this information and make sure that your customers are also aware because it may drive their involvement in the risk model process. After completing these planning activities, you have adequately prepared for using the risk model on your projects.

Reporting from a risk model

You are responsible for driving all risk management activities on the project. These activities include using risk models, risk assessment forms, funding toward risk spending, and all other areas involved in project risk. You are also responsible for driving the risk modeling process, which includes creating the risk model. You cannot do this alone, and therefore need the help of team members to complete the risk modeling process. When the project team is involved and active in the risk modeling process, it helps everyone get on the same page around the project's total risk score. Working together on this risk model also allows everyone to get involved and understand the project's risk assessment and risk score.

The risk model and associated results from the modeling process require regular reporting throughout the project life cycle. You may choose a week-to-week review of the project's risk scores to perform trending analysis on the risk items. You customers and leadership will also watch those trends closely and decide if progress against the risks is moving fast enough. If possible, report the risk model's contents within the regular status meeting, often held weekly. Otherwise, report the risk model information based on the time frames your customers want. The risk model is developed by using a spreadsheet and stored as part of the document control system for long-term archiving and accessibility.

Cross-Reference
See Chapter 17 - Using Communication Tools to Administer the Planning Process to learn more about how to use and create a risk model.

Introduction to the Risk Register

The *risk register* is the result of quantitative and qualitative risk analysis from risk response planning. It contains all of the identified project risk events and descriptions, causes, probabilities of occurring, impacts, mitigation plans, and updated status. The risk register is a section of the project management plan.

Note
The Project Management Institute's knowledge area for this tool is the risk management area. There is no secondary area for this tool.

Tool Value
This tool is a single repository for communicating the risk mitigation activities performed on the project's risks. It is the single location to find risk information. It documents how the team is working to reduce the impact or risk on the project.

Social Media Tools
The communication purposes for the risk register are to inform and instruct. The tool can be used in Yammer, Socialcast, and Facebook (private group).

One purpose of the risk register is to document the risk mitigation strategies for all project risk events. Risk mitigation includes the plans and actions to reduce or prevent harmful impact to the project. You can use two tools for risk mitigation planning. The first tool is a risk register, which is a list of the project's risk events with a detailed mitigation strategy documented for each risk item. The second tool is the risk assessment form, which we covered earlier in this chapter and includes a list of risk events. The tools are similar, but have different purposes. For example, there is no EMV in the risk register, but it is covered in the risk assessment form. The risk register carries data on risk mitigation steps; whereas, the risk assessment form recommends a strategy only and provides little details. There are other important differences to consider when working with these tools. One of the biggest and most important differences is that the risk events on the risk register have clear mitigation plans, which is unavailable on the risk assessment form. Risk assessment forms do not carry mitigation plans or strategies. You have to transfer the information from the risk register to the risk assessment form around risk mitigation. Another difference in the forms is that the risk register focuses on mitigation strategies; whereas, the risk assessment form uses calculations and impacts on schedule, scope, and budget. The two forms have similar characteristics, but they are different, and it is a best practice to handle them separately as two distinct tools. Risks without mitigation plans stay on the risk assessment form until plans are developed.

One method of working project risk mitigation is selecting one of the predefined strategies for resolving risk events. The project management profession has five major strategies for risks mitigation. They are acceptance, avoidance, transfer, mitigation, and retention. When working with strategies, you and your team members need to decide which strategy you will select for each risk event. Occasionally, you may choose avoidance as a valid mitigation type for handling risk events, which states that they will not try to mitigate risk. For example, a project team might decide to use the avoidance strategy on some risk events. If you have no authority or approval over project funding, you could choose risk avoidance as a valid and acceptable strategy.

Note
There is nothing stopping project managers or team members from combining the tools into a single comprehensive tool. That is possible, but not necessarily a best practice. Keep them separate for your best chance of success.

You should actively communicate your project's risk register so that team members stay involved and engaged with the risk management process. When team members think about risks while performing their work activities, they will remember to use the risk register to store potential risk events they encounter. The team will also use the risk register to perform steps to resolve the risk. For example, the risk register has mitigation steps documented for the risk events, and the team members need to see that information to know how to solve the risks. If you continually report from the risk register, team members and customers remain involved and active in the risk management process.

Often, those mitigation strategies can cause extra project work for the team. For example, if the project has four to five project risk events, and the team has chosen to mitigate each risk, they have extra work on the project. Capture all of the work inside the risk register, and then use it to track and monitor the work until it is complete. Some of this work is large to add to the project's schedule, but that is up to you to decide.

Communicating the risk register is also important for highlighting how the project team is addressing project risks. No matter which method the project team decides to use to handle risk mitigation, it is important to ensure your customers are aware and provide risk mitigation help whenever possible. Keeping your customers involved keeps them supportive of the team working the risk events. Constant communication and constant risk register updates are valuable to the project team, customers, and leadership.

There are many benefits of using a risk register on your project. The first benefit is that the tool is great for communicating with customers and leadership about how you are going to mitigate the project's risk events. The risk register displays the risk events and mitigation steps to give everyone the same information and to be on the same page to solve the risk event. As noted above, the risk register highlights the mitigation steps for the team and exposes their work activities for risk event items. You need to be aware of what you need to complete for closing out each risk event. Without the risk register, you would have no mechanism in place to track specific work tasks associated with the risk events. Therefore, you might struggle to keep a handle on what the team is doing to resolve the risks they are working on. If the team focuses on mitigation strategies only, and lets other work activities suffer, you can step in and help course-correct. The team can be resolving potential risk events, which in turn could waste time and money and impact the project deliverables. The risk event may never come to fruition and working to prevent a risk event that is a low probability could have a negative impact on the project.

Table 13.8 — Example of a risk register shows a risk register for a typical project. In this example, two risk events have established mitigation plans. The other project risk event does not have mitigation plan. The risk event without a mitigation plan won't be formally transferred from the risk assessment form to the risk register. This single risk event would transfer only if it had a mitigation plan. Two of the risk events on the sample risk register have specific mitigation steps or statements about the risk events. Depending on the strategy chosen for the risk event, the migration steps will differ from risk to risk. This risk register is easy to complete and, like the other risk communication tools, is excellent for communicating risk information to the project team and customers.

Table 13.8 — Example of a risk register

Risk #	Risk Category	Risk Description	Risk Probability (High/Medium /Low)	Risk Impact (High/Medium /Low)	Mitigation Plan	Risk Owner	Status
23	Budget	The Engineering group is 200K over budget on the project.	Medium	High	Project will receive special funding grant of 300K.	Fred	Active
13	Schedule	Phase 2 late by more than two weeks.	High	High	No known mitigation plan at this time.	George	Future
5	Economy	Interest rates become greater than 6%.	Low	High	Transfer risk to the Finance department who will absorb additional costs.	Sam	Past

In reviewing the risk register in the table, you can quickly see how valuable this tool is to anyone wanting to learn more about project risks. This table only shows a small sample of the columns of data that can be stored for every project risk. Columns like Risk Score are quite common in risk registers. The risk register is that one place to see all project risks and all of the information about the risk that either you or the project team has captured.

A project's risk mitigation plan requires a formal mitigation process. The two tools mentioned in this section (risk register and risk assessment form) are used as repositories for storing risk information and not necessarily for storing the mitigation process. The mitigation process is different and important for you to understand before you can use it successfully. The risk mitigation process is important for you and your team to know for completing the risk register information.

The risk mitigation process starts with understanding the project risk events and the different impact that each risk has on the project. After the team understands and lists the risk events in the risk assessment form, the team decides if there is a possible mitigation strategy for each risk event. If so, you move the risk event from the risk assessment form to the risk register, and then add the mitigation steps to the risk event.

After the project team decides which risks they can mitigate and which risks they can't, you add those events with clear strategies to the risk register. When you decide to do that and not put the risk events without strategies on the risk register, they stay on the risk assessment form only. When moving the risk event information between the two tools, the actual mitigation strategies do not have to be solidified at the same time. You and your team members only have to decide which ones could have a mitigation strategy, not a locked strategy. After the risks are added to the risk register, you and your team members decide on the mitigation strategy for each. That way, if the event occurs, the team is prepared to follow the documented strategy.

As the team starts the assessment process, they may find they have moved some risk events prematurely to the risk register when they still belong on the risk assessment form. Some risks may not have obvious mitigation strategies so would not move automatically to the risk register. Those risks are accepted as "as-is." An example of this would be the project having a drop-dead completion date. This is a non-mitigating risk event because completing the project is directly linked to a major opening of an international event. That drop-dead date would be an ongoing, unsolvable risk event that the project team would carry throughout the project life cycle.

As the assessment process continues, it is normal for the project team to accept risk events as a normal course of action. The risk acceptance process is normal and acceptable when the project team decides the risk is too low in probability, and the event does not warrant developing a formal mitigation plan. Most risk events only require observation and often do not amount to anything. By accepting a risk, the project team should document and justify that acceptance for future reference and continue to watch the risk until the end of the project or until it is removed from the risk register.

During the risk assessment process, the project team has five available mitigation strategies to choose from when deciding how to resolve or mitigate risk events. When selecting a strategy for each risk event, work with team members to implement a solution for each risk event. It is your responsibility to drive this process until each risk event is resolved and the project is complete.

Planning to use the risk register

When planning and preparing to use a risk register, you must first decide the steps and processes around mitigating risk events. You must plan how to direct your team members throughout the risk mitigation process, including determining the various project meetings to process risk events. You should also review the risk register template to ensure that it carries the information that applies to your project. If it doesn't, add the right columns of data to collect for your project risks. You can add additional columns like color coding, or scores, and so on. Anything you add has to match the process for collecting the information, that's important.

Your next step in the planning process is to work with your customers. You are going to want to know their involvement in the risk register, their reporting needs, and any other relevant information they want to know about the risk management process. Some customers will want to be actively engaged in this process by attending meetings and will want to be in on all strategy decisions for each risk event. In those planning discussions with your customers, make sure you also capture the reporting requirements. Find out how often they want to see the risk register and how they want the information sent to them. After preparing and following these steps, you are adequately prepared to use a risk register.

Reporting from the risk register

You are responsible for driving risk mitigation planning and own creating the risk register for most projects. Usually, you also own the risk assessment form, so it makes sense that you also own the risk register and are responsible for transferring project risk events from one tool to the other.

You will use the risk register to report status to your team members, customers, and leadership every week. The risk register contains the latest status of risk events and their mitigation strategies; therefore, regular reporting provides customers and leadership the information they need about project risks. Usually, you create the risk register in a spreadsheet, but it can also be created as a table in a document. The risk register is stored as part of the document control system for long-term and accessibility.

Cross-Reference
Chapter 19 - Using Communication Tools for Project Reporting during the Planning Process to learn more about how to use and create a risk register.

Summary

The tools described in this chapter help you monitor and control project risks and issues. Risk management is challenging so using tools to help you in this process will increase your chance of running a successful project. Issue management does not get the industry reorganization it deserves and we believe it is critical to a project manager's success. Therefore, we included tools about issue management in this chapter that are important for your project. The issues list and the issue management plan are critical for project managers to use.

As you read this chapter, the one tool that made the biggest impact on risk management is the risk matrix. The risk matrix is a simple and easy to use tool, but one of the most important communication tools you can use. Review and use that tool on your projects today. Add color coding to the table for the biggest effect and an easier way to communicate the tool. Your customers and leadership will love it.

This chapter included tools such as expected monetary value, issues list, issue management plan, risk assessment form, risk matrix, risk model, and the risk register. Each risk tool can help you control your project more effectively and help you bring your project to a successful conclusion.

Chapter 14

Defining Communication Tools to Manage Project Procurement

IN THIS CHAPTER

- ◆ Introduction to the Document Control system
- ◆ Introduction to the Formal Acceptance document
- ◆ Introduction to the Lessons-Learned document
- ◆ Introduction to the Project Proposal
- ◆ Introduction to the User Acceptance document

In this chapter, we explore project communication tools in the procurement management knowledge area. The tools included in this chapter will help you during the project's procurement process. Project procurement management is difficult for many project managers, such as managing a fixed-bid project and the customer continues to put in countless scope changes. That situation is difficult for any project manager to handle because the budget is fixed so there's no additional money to handle customer changes.

Another important part of procurement management is relationship management. Maintaining friendly relationships with your vendor company will be challenging on many of your projects. If the vendor company continually asks for more funding, but your customers don't want to pay the vendor company for the extra work, it's up to you to resolve the situation. On the other hand, if your vendor company continually seeks funds every time there is a project change, that's another problem for you to handle. Regardless of how big or small the project changes are, the constant battle for project funding becomes a full-time role for you. These types of project situations strain relations between companies so much so that some even dissolve relationships. Project managers are usually involved in these discussions, so don't underestimate how important the procurement process is for your project. Procurement management is a difficult process that takes years of practice to master.

In this chapter, we present tools you can use to manage project procurement activities. These tools are critical for communicating project procurement activities. Procurement is an important area for you to manage and be diligent about. Aside from purchasing products and services, you are also responsible for change control administration, contract knowledge, and legal awareness.

Introduction to the Document Control System

The *document control system* is a central repository and library for project information. This is an electronic filing system that stores all project files, documents, and other project artifacts. Document control systems have built-in security software that allows certain people access to varying levels of information, while locking out others. The document control system can hold any electronic file related to the project, with the only limit being file size. Often, companies put tight controls on how large the files can be, and how many files the document control system can hold, per project. Almost every project deliverable, such as project schedules, budget spreadsheets, requirements documents, and design drawings and specifications can be stored in the document control system.

Note
The Project Management Institute's knowledge area for the document control system is the procurement management area. Other areas this tool could be associated with are risk and cost.

Tool Value
The document control system stores all project documentation in a single repository and provides access to anyone involved in the project.

Social Media Tools
The communication purpose for the document control system is to inform. The tool can be used in Yammer, Socialcast, and Facebook (private group).

The document control system is not like other tools. One of the benefits of the document control system is that you can put all of your project documents into the document control system and anyone with access can pull the information. No more sending around emails or wondering which version of a document is the latest. The document control system is the one place to store all project files. The document control system does not have reporting functionality built into it; it is not used to report data, it only displays data. People come to the document control system and pull the information they need and often do so without asking you or your team members for help. It should be easy to find the project documents that you need. Project managers store every project deliverable, project list, or project presentation in this tool. Fortunately, you do not need to do anything special to communicate with the tool. Interestingly enough, the document control system is one of the best communication tools available to you because it stores all of the project files and provides unlimited access to anyone approved to look at the information.

The benefits for you, your team members, and any other stakeholders for using a document control system are many. To begin with, having all project documents in one place lets you control and monitor your project's documentation more effectively. You no longer need to worry about finding spreadsheets or looking for updated budget sheets, for example. Using a document control system helps you enforce storing all project files in one location.

Most document control systems have check-in and check-out capabilities that keep documents locked, which prevents unauthorized access and changes. Here are some additional benefits for using a document control system.

- Create documents faster and more efficiently.
- Access documents faster and more efficiently.
- Boost stakeholder or customer satisfaction by providing full access to project documents.
- Improve security by controlling access when checking in and checking out project files.

- Reduce document overload. No need for multiple versions of the same document.
- Become more productive because all team members are using the same repository.
- Provide immediate online access to project documentation from anywhere.
- Comply with auditing processes and procedures because internal auditors have full access to project documentation.
- Know immediately what is being checked in or checked out and by whom.

The document control system is an ideal tool for the multi-project environment where there you need to pass information from one project to another. For example, if one project manager wants to see a design drawing from another project, all he or she needs to do is access the drawing from the other project's document control system. Sharing files occurs instantly, and everyone gets the project information they need. Long gone are the days of trying to find files on email servers or personal hard drives when companies choose to use a document control system for their projects and document management purposes.

Note
Managing and controlling project documentation should be a top priority from the start of the project through completion and beyond.

Customers will find value in being able to access project information at any time (24/7) in the document control system. It is your job to ensure the project information in the document control system is the latest. It would not be good for you to provide out-of-date documents or reports to your customer. Customers can access project schedules, budget reports, status reports, or any other project document in the document control system. Deciding not to use a document control system can cause problems and confusion for anyone trying to find information. It will also portray a poor image to your customer that you cannot keep your documents and files straight, leading them to question how you could possibly run a successful project.

Increasingly, companies are starting to use document control systems for storing not only project information, but also all company documentation. Some of the more popular document control system packages include:

- Microsoft SharePoint®
- EMC Documentum®
- KnowledgeTree®

The biggest difference between the systems noted above is their functionality. When selecting a document control system, there are some key features that you should consider to help you manage and control your project's documentation, such as:

- Archival: Ability to archive documents
- Creation: Ability to create material, such as documents, spreadsheets, drawings
- Distribution: Ability to send and receive both technical and administrative reports
- Filing: Ability to file documents, manually or electronically
- Retention: Ability to hold documents for a specific period (sometimes long after project completion)
- Retrieval: Ability to retrieve documents and access the information quickly
- Security: Ability to lock documents and limit access
- Storage: Ability to easily store documents and get extra storage if needed
- Workflow: Ability to move documents among team members
- Risk: Ability to reproduce the entire system if necessary

Tip

All projects must have some form of document control. If you do not have a formal system, set up a manual workaround. A manual workaround, for example, would include putting a directory structure on a shared network drive and having all team members and customers save their files to this drive. This is a manual workaround because setting up the structures would be manual, setting up security would be manual, and nightly backups may need to be manual. It is not as robust as the full document control system solution, but it works for small projects.

All projects, regardless of size, can use a document control system, although, small projects do not have the same volume of documents that a medium or large project has. The importance of creating an organized structure for storing and controlling project documentation is still applicable. On medium and large projects, the documentation is so large, the only method for keeping files straight is adding them in a structured and organized manner to a document control system. Managing a large project without some automated mechanism for document control is almost impossible.

The document control system is a communication tool by itself. You, your team members, and customers can "communicate" with the document control system at any time by logging on to the tool and finding the information they need. Most document control systems have alert and messaging capabilities, which are useful for watching and monitoring folders, for example. When a file is added, changed, or deleted from a particular folder, the document control system can email or text you directly to let you know. Different document control systems come with many available communication alerts and messaging features. This brings a new level of communication for you, your team, and stakeholders.

You will use the document control system daily because this tool helps you manage and control your project's documentation. You are responsible for designing the structure of the document control system in a manner that you think will be the easiest way to find project information, which is the main point of the tool.

There are several key benefits for using a document control system, such as:

- Ease of use.

- Multiple access for several people.

- Mobile and Internet access to project information for project manager, team members, or customers.

- A repository for storing sign-offs and approvals.

- Security features for storing approvals you receive from customers or leadership. Team members often review project documents and the document control system is a perfect place to store those documents. You just put the document in a folder within the document control system and point your team members to its location. Without using a document control system, you and your team would waste valuable time searching through emails and hard drives to find documents that they may never locate.

Occasionally, companies don't have a formal document control system and project managers are forced to set up a manual solution for storing project information. To create a manual solution that simulates an automated tool, you will have to use tools such as email, personal hard drives, or network drives to create a project structure for storing files. Consider the manual solution as a short-term solution and escalate to your leadership and request a better long-term solution. With the cost of projects today, and the inexpensive document control systems that are available, companies have no excuse for making project teams deal with manual solutions. Manual solutions create risk that valuable project documentation could be deleted or stored on someone's laptop computer. Even the smallest companies running the smallest projects should have an automated document control system for storing important project-related documentation in a safe and secure environment.

Planning to use the document control system

When planning and preparing to use a document control system, you must decide how you want to manage and control the project's documentation. One of the most important steps in planning and preparing to use this tool is setting up the project's directory structures. Ideally, the first place to start when setting up the directory structure is the project's development and project management methodologies. Take the time and set up folders that match as closely as possible to those two methodologies. That way, when team members need to store their files, the directory structure matches the work they are doing. Developers on an IT project store their files in the development section, testers store their test plans in a tester section, and so on. On a construction project, the files could be set up by work type: electrical, plumbing, HVAC, and so on. After creating specific folders for project management and development methodologies, get your project team's opinions about the files and structure they want to use. Most team members will have suggestions for how you should set up the document control system. They may even ask for permission to set up their own sub-structures. Catering to team members when setting up your document control system is valuable because they are the main users of and need to know where to find and store project deliverables.

After working with your team members, ask your customers what their preferences are for the document control system. You can ask them what access they want, what alerts they want to receive, and how they will use the tool. These conversations can be interesting, especially with customers who are not familiar with all of the choices within the document control system and everything that is available to them. They often want full access to all of the project information in the document control system, which can cause confusion, concern, and extra work for you to explain the details because it's too much information for them to see. For example, most customers don't need to review detailed test scripts developed by the testers on a software development project. However, those files will be in the document control system and accessible by the customer. However, if you do not provide access to all of the project documents, your customers might think you are hiding something about the project. It is important that you review with the project team the security settings in the document control system on a continuing basis to ensure that everyone has the appropriate security access. If your customers or team members do not have the right security access, they could have problems trying to access project information.

Reporting from a document control system

The document control system stores project documentation and is not something you report project status from, nor do you store project status information in the tool. Rather, it stores electronic files that contain project information. The files could be project information, project budget, project issues and risks, and so on. Customers can access the latest status from the document control system. If they want the latest budget report, they find it in the document control system. All project information is stored in the document control system. As the project progresses, more and more files go into the document control system, which provides even more project information for your customers, team members, and leadership.

Cross-Reference
See Chapter 16 - Using Communication Tools During the Initiating Process to learn more about how to use and create a document control system.

Introduction to the Formal Acceptance Document

The *formal acceptance document* captures, records, and stores the customer's final approval and legal acceptance of the project. Usually, signing the formal acceptance document closes out the project and tells the team they have completed their work; in other cases, the document acts as the first task in starting the closeout process. You will find this document to be one of the tools you create and use most on your project. When your customers sign the formal acceptance document, they accept the work product(s), and the project team is free to move on to other projects. Without that signature, your customers have not accepted the project as delivered, and the project team may have to remain in place until the customer provides approval. This is an important distinction between the *formal acceptance document* and the *user acceptance document*. The formal acceptance document represents project approval, not a specific project deliverable as with the user acceptance document. When customers approve the formal acceptance document, they approve the completion of the entire project. At the end of the project, you can send a final report to your customer that summarizes all of the project's activities. The final version of the formal acceptance document should be stored in the document control system.

Note
The Project Management Institute's knowledge area for the formal acceptance document is the procurement management area. There is no secondary knowledge area for this tool.

Tool Value
The value of this tool is that it represents the formal acceptance and legal approval that the project team has delivered the project to the customers.

Social Media Tools
The communication purposes for the formal acceptance document are to inform and persuade. The tool can be used in Yammer, Socialcast, and Facebook (private group).

From a communications perspective, the formal acceptance document is one of the most rewarding documents that a project manager can have. When you send out this document, there are usually many cheers, best wishes, and "job well done" emails sent to your team members and other stakeholders. It is a great time for everybody involved.

There are many benefits to using a formal acceptance document. The first benefit is that it confirms that your customers have signed off and approved the project. These signatures are valuable if there are any questions or concerns regarding the evidence that the customer accepted the project. The evidence can be a signature on the document or an email acceptance. The legal nature of the acceptance document means that it will be subject to a more extensive approval process than other project documents.

Tip
Some project managers use a final report every time they complete a project. Consider using one for your projects.

The second benefit is to accepting that the project officially transfers ownership and responsibilities from you to the project owner. Make sure you get signatures from all of the stakeholders appointed to sign off on the project. You are responsible for getting the required signatures, not the stakeholders or owners. It is not beneficial for you if you cannot acquire approval from your customers mainly because you would need to hold onto the project and you wouldn't be able to officially transfer it to the customer to take over without that approval. Without the official sign-off and signature from the customer, you could own the project for longer than you ought to. This could be a problem if you delay giving a system to a customer, opening a building in construction, and so on.

The third benefit is that approval starts the point in time when many of the equipment and services warranties commence. This is an important time in the project for responsible vendors and subcontractors who could become involved in the maintenance contracts for a specified time period

Another benefit of using a formal acceptance document is that it can be critical if needed in a court of law. This document, once signed, is a legally binding agreement between two parties. You can imagine how important the customer's signature is for a multi-million dollar project—especially if you are in the middle of a major lawsuit with a customer who states that they never approved the project, but you have a signed document proving that they did.

Customers also benefit from using the formal acceptance document in legal actions; however, project managers must be aware of this double-edged sword. As the focus for the formal acceptance document is mainly for your customers to provide their approval and acceptance, the same holds true for you. When you sign the document, you are stating that the project team has delivered the scope of the project based on the customer's requirements. The document holds both parties accountable for the project, and if there is a legal case, you must ensure that you can stand behind the signed document.

Figure 14.1 — Example of formal acceptance document shows a typical formal acceptance document. When you and your customer sign, it represents both parties' acceptance of the project.

Figure 14.1 — Example of formal acceptance document

Formal Acceptance Document

Project ID/#: _____   Project Name: _____   Acceptance Date:
_____

Project Client/Owner Name: _____   Customer/ Owner Department Name:
_____

Project Manager Name: _____   Project Management Office Rep:
_____

Project Acceptance or Information:

    Acceptance or Reject Delivery of project: Accept: _____   Reject: _____ (*)

      * If rejected please explain the reason:

_____

_____

Further Comments:

_____

_____

Project Detail information:

Planned Start Date: _____   Actual Start Date: _____

Planned Finish Date: _____   Actual Finish Date: _____

Actual Budget ($): _____   Final Costs ($): _____   Over or Under Budget: _____

Signatures/Approvals Section:

Project Manager Approvals: _____

        Print Name

        _____

        Signature

Project Client/Owner Approvals: _____

        Print Name

        _____

        Signature

Note the **Project Client/Owner Approvals** line; no formal acceptance document is complete without that signature. In today's electronically driven society, the formal handwritten signature is going away, and email acceptance is now becoming the norm. Even when using the form above, you can capture the customer's approval when they send it by email—you simply copy the email directly into the document.

From a legal perspective, ensuring the customer's signature is on the formal acceptance document is critical. Because, if it isn't, it might be difficult to prove that the customer signed off on the formal acceptance document and not something else. Therefore, it is your responsibility to archive the document for future reference (legal cases, for example) or for internal company audits. Occasionally, legal departments step in and get acceptance signatures from the customer, relieving you from doing this task. The legal department stores customer acceptances with other project documentation, and they often have their own process for archiving project documentation so that they can retrieve it anytime they need it. You should request help from the legal department when you initially create the formal acceptance document. The legal department will confirm whether there are any issues that they can cover if the project gets into any legal trouble down the line.

Project managers often forget to use the formal acceptance document because they are too busy or preoccupied working on other projects. Some project managers consider the formal acceptance document unimportant or simply do not want to take the time to create it. Occasionally, if the project has not gone as planned, a project manager might feel that it is not right to request approval from an unhappy customer. In every project, regardless of how well it or how badly it went, getting sign-off is critical because, in most companies, the project cannot close out until the customer formally approves it. In some projects, customers may hold off providing their sign-off to delay the start of the project's warranty period. You should not allow this delay to happen. Sometimes project managers do not know how to continue when put in this position and, therefore, do not know what to do. For example, on a typical project, after the project team finishes their work activities, they start the warranty period and fix any issues that arise during that time. If the project team finishes their work and the project customer has not approved the project, you could be in a difficult situation. If that occurs, project managers have a few choices, each with pros and cons, and each needing the support of leadership before performing. These choices could include, but are not limited to, the following:

- Does the customer start the warranty period, even though the project is not accepted?
- Do you disperse the team to work on other projects?
- Does the project team sit idle or keep working and wait for the warranty period to start?

Regardless of the actions you take with your team, note that some customers will ride a situation, noted above, for as long as they can, which may prevent the warranty period from starting. You should have a back-up plan in place if this happens and engage leadership as soon as possible to help resolve it.

Planning to use a formal acceptance document

When planning and preparing to use a formal acceptance document, you must first find out if your company already has an acceptance process. Look for standard approval templates, processes, or methods. You should adhere to existing approval processes if they are in place. However, that does not mean that you cannot update it or improve it for your particular project, but you should not start from scratch and create your own versions. After discovering whether a formal acceptance document template is available, work with your customers to find out what they want to update or change on the template to suit their needs. It is important that the customer sees the formal acceptance document long before seeking their sign-off on the project. At this point, you are just looking for the customer's acceptance and approval of the proposed format, not the content in the document or the project itself. These conversations between you and the customer will help them be more willing to accept the document and sign off on it when the project finishes. After taking these steps, you are adequately prepared to use the formal acceptance document on your project.

Reporting from the formal acceptance document

You are responsible for developing and driving the project's formal acceptance document. These activities include developing the document and getting the customer signatures to close the project. You create the document during the planning phase, and then use the formal acceptance document at the end of the project to capture the customer's acceptance. This document is basic, providing the necessary space to capture acceptance and approval only. If the document is complex, it can be more difficult to get approval at the end of the project.

There is no weekly reporting from the formal acceptance document because it is a one-time document at the end of the project; it does not contain project status information, other than the project's completion. You create the formal acceptance document in a document format and store it in the document control system for archiving and long-term storage and accessibility.

Cross-Reference
See Chapter 23 - Using Communication Tools During the Closeout Process to learn more about how to use and create a formal acceptance document.

Introduction to the Lessons-Learned Document

The *lessons-learned document* captures and records the experiences and lessons you, your team members, and customers learn as they execute and deliver the project. Capturing and collecting lessons-learned information has one main purpose, which is to enable a project team to learn and grow from events in the past. The events can be positive and provide information you can use on future projects, or negative, and provide lessons to avoid in the future. You capture lessons-learned information based on everything that occurs on the project. Occasionally, you may want to focus the team's attention on just the main project areas, such as budget, schedule, quality, or scope. In other cases, you may decide to capture everything. Your customers must agree to capture valuable information and to provide lessons-learned information throughout the project.

Note
The Project Management Institute's knowledge area for the lessons-learned document is the procurement management area. There is no secondary knowledge area known for this tool.

Tool Value
Lessons-learned information could prevent you from wasting time and money. Taking the time to review lessons-learned materials before a project starts could save time and money on the current project.

Social Media Tools
The communication purposes for the lesson- learned document are to inform and motivate. The tool can be used in Yammer, Socialcast, and Facebook (private group).

You should communicate lessons-learned information throughout the project life cycle. This process starts at the beginning of the project and continues through the end of the project. Use the weekly status meeting to collect and discuss the lessons-learned information, and then add that information to the weekly status reports you share with the customer. At the end of the project, you will call a project-wide lessons-learned meeting and present all of the information that you collected each week and present it to your customers, team members, and leadership. The summarized lessons-learned information is documented regularly by capturing project happenings, as they occur.

When recording the project's daily events, don't forget to capture your team members' and customers' feelings or concerns. Those feelings and concerns emerge during the lessons-learned meetings when you ask people to share opinions, and the emotions often begin to flow during the meeting. A typical project daily event could be anything that is negative, or worth noting, to possibly prevent it from occurring again on this or any other project. There are also daily events that are positive, which need to be captured in the lessons-learned document. Typical examples include customers signing off on a key document before the deadline, or great levels of communications between the team leads, which causes team to have great morale and comradery.

During the project's weekly status meeting focus on what went right and what went wrong that week. It is that simple. You might choose to cover the main project areas, such as scope, budget, and schedule, or, you could open it to the whole project, it is your choice. Usually, you and your customer will agree on what to capture and cover in the lessons-learned meeting.

Future project teams can gain enormous benefits from learning how one project handled something, and then either repeat it or avoid it for your project. If project teams are aware of past projects mistakes, you can possibly prevent them from occurring on future projects. As long as future project teams continually learn from past projects' mistakes, capturing lessons-learned information is well worth it and will save time and money in the end.

Other benefits of collecting lessons-learned information include:

- Identifying experiences that have occurred on the project to pass on to future projects.
- Ensuring that teams are constantly identifying issues and risk events that occur on the project. In other words, the team is always looking for lessons-learned information instead of allowing those details to pass them by and not capturing them for historical reference.
- Learning about new processes and procedures, deciding how well those processes were performed on the project, and then using the data captured from lessons-learned information to increase your chance of success on the next project.
- Ensuring that the project immediately benefits by making mid-project decisions that are based on what you have learned from prior weeks. By waiting until the end of the project to capture information, you lose valuable information gained each week by your team.

Project managers can benefit significantly from using and implementing the various results from the lessons-learned information. Successful project managers learn the importance of this information quickly and whenever possible, try to implement the best practices from those teachings.

Table 14.1 — Example of a table of contents for a lessons-learned document shows a table of contents for a lessons-learned document or presentation material, and documents the four key questions you ask team members: Areas of Success, Areas of Improvement, General Lessons Learned, and Final Thoughts. When complete, the document is comprehensive and valuable for team members, customers, or future project managers.

Table 14.1 — Example of a table of contents for a lessons-learned document

#	Description
1	Areas of Success
	Project Budget
	Project Schedule
	Project Quality
	Other Areas
2	Areas of Improvement
	Project Budget
	Project Schedule
	Project Quality
	Safety
	Other areas
3	General Lessons-Learned Information
	Resource Assignments
	Working Conditions
	Overtime Issues
	Other Areas
4	Final Thoughts
	Failures
	Successes

The lessons learned process starts at the beginning of the project, not at the end. A common mistake project managers make is waiting for the project to complete, or being close to finishing before capturing lessons-learned information. Waiting until the end of the project is too late in the process to start collecting this data because most team members have moved on to other projects, so it becomes impossible to get this information. Even if it were possible, team members would have a hard time remembering most of the lessons-learned information from several months in the past. The lessons-learned information is critical to collect as soon as it occurs while it is fresh in the minds of the team members and customers working on the project.

Another advantage of collecting lessons-learned information during the project life cycle is being able to make project adjustments based on what the team learned from various project events. If an event is captured during the lessons-learned process, there is a high likelihood the team will not repeat the same event again? If it was a positive event, the team will learn from that event as well and may repeat it if the result was valuable to everyone.

Lessons Learned

A project manager decides at the beginning of the project to have biweekly team meetings that includes buying lunch for local team members and anyone who attends the meeting in person. Remote team members are welcome to attend, but they cannot charge the project travel budget to get to the meeting. Team members who live in a different country are never going to attend the lunch meeting, because they don't live locally and therefore can't make it to the meeting. After a couple of meetings, the local employees like the meeting's social aspect and are start to become a good team. The remote employees, who make up 40 percent of the project team, felt left out. As the project manager starts to collect the weekly lessons-learned information, the feedback from remote employees is that they are not happy about the bi-weekly meetings and feel like they are missing out. The remote team members feel like they are not part of the team because they do not get to be involved in the social aspect of the meeting. When the project manager reads the lessons-learned feedback, he sees that something needs to be fixed immediately. The project manager feels lucky to have collected weekly lessons-learned information because he may never have had a chance to get that feedback from the remote team members. How productive would the remote team members be if the project manager did not fix this immediately, or had waited until the end of the project to collect the lessons-learned feedback? The result would have been many lunches and many shunned team members who resented the project manager. In this example, the project manager started to authorize budget for the remote team members to go out and have their own lunch meeting. Even though, the remote team members were not meeting with the local team over lunch, they appreciated the project manager listening to their concerns and were much happier. This is one of many examples where collecting lessons-learned feedback paid off for the project manager and the team, and the project manager reacted and did something about the problem.

Collecting lessons-learned information is easy. Simply approach your team members and ask them what went right, what went wrong, and then document their responses. Capture the lessons-learned information each week during the weekly status meeting when everyone is together and thinking about the project. When you take the approach of asking what went well and what did not go well, you will collect more information than generic responses. Asking project team members for lessons-learned information from the beginning of the project puts them in an awkward position because they won't know what to provide, or have any idea where to start to answer. Rephrasing the question and asking them what when well this week, and where did we struggle, does the same thing, and they will certainly now how to answer that question.

Tip
Some team members struggle when you do not frame the questions for them, and may give random thoughts on lessons-learned information that makes no sense. When framing the two questions about what went right and what went wrong helps people focus their answers.

It is also valuable to get specific examples and details from team members or customers. For example, if a team member answers the "what went right" question with "budget," you don't get detailed and specific information. Good examples of responses from the "what went right" question might be, "the budget was managed correctly throughout the project," or "I could tell every week how much of the budget we were spending, and how much we were projecting to overrun." These kinds of responses provide real value as to what went right on the project. When you read the lessons-learned information for projects you didn't manage, you get detailed information about previous projects. You learn valuable information about what you should and should not do on your project. Often, the bits of information you pick up from reading someone else's lessons-learned document can change the way you execute your project. For example, if you see that another project's team members were inspired by something their project manager did, you may be inspired to do the same on your project. You take the same approach with the "what went wrong" question. You should accept only detailed and specific answers to the question so that you can use that information as a learning experience and possibly avoid repeating the same mistakes.

Tip
It is wise to reread the lessons-learned document roughly 25, 50, and 75 percent of the way through the project.

Read the lessons-learned documents for any similar projects to the project you are managing, or if there are other lessons-learned documents available, read and review them as well. If possible, after you read the lessons-learned materials, communicate with the author of those lessons learned to ask any follow-up or detailed questions. The goal would is to get as much information as possible from the author—especially for anything that is unclear or that you had more questions about.

Planning to use a lessons-learned document

When planning and preparing to use a lessons-learned document, you must first train team members and customers how to collect data throughout the project life cycle. The data collection process may be difficult for team members to adjust to during the project because most team members are accustomed to providing feedback one time, at the end of the project, and not throughout the project.

Collecting lessons-learned information from customers is usually easier than collecting it from team members because customers are usually quick to provide feedback about both their positive and negative project experiences. Team members, on the other hand, are busy, they move on to other projects, and forget about providing lessons-learned information. The next step is for you to plan what kind of information you will collect, when you will collect it, and what format you will use to collect it. Usually, you use the two-question format, but depending on the project, you may adjust that to suit the specific project needs. Some of your project manager peers may gather more information than others, so you should adjust your lessons-learned process to your project needs. Finally, you need to incorporate the lessons-learned information into a final report or presentation. You should choose to collect and store the data weekly and choose not to report it; whereas, some of your project managers peers choose to report information during the regular project status reporting cycle. After performing these planning steps, you are adequately prepared for using the lessons-learned document for your project.

Reporting from the lessons-learned document

You are responsible for capturing and collecting the project's lessons-learned information. Usually, this also means that you will capture the lessons-learned information during the project's weekly status meeting, and then compile the information into a consumable format for your project team or customers. The lessons-learned information becomes valuable feedback for how you are managing the project. This is valuable from a learning perspective because it can occasionally change how you manage the project going forward.

A good assignment for a project communications manager is compiling the lessons learned each week. This information could go into the monthly newsletter as "tips and tricks." Also, you could write articles about a particular lesson that would be of interest to the team and benefit the project and other stakeholders.

Reporting from lessons-learned information comes down to reporting from a weekly status report and a single meeting at the end of the project. A lessons-learned presentation and meeting occurs when the project finishes and closes out.

Tip

Schedule informal lessons-learned meetings with your customers so you can receive constructive and valuable feedback. Your customers may not want to give feedback in a large, project postmortem meeting where they may not be ready to give direct or negative feedback. It is important to capture your customer's real feelings and concerns while the project is in progress, not at the end.

Cross-Reference

See Chapter 23 – Using Communication Tools During the Closeout Process for more information about the lessons-learned process.

Introduction to the Project Proposal

The *project proposal* determines whether a proposed project is feasible, practical, and worth pursuing. The project proposal is usually developed from discussions among key stakeholders, and is generally written by marketing personnel, a project sponsor, or a project manager.

Also, if your company does not have the in-house expertise, or you use contractors for your project work, you can turn to outside companies to help fulfill that need. The project proposal should contain all of the details for assembling the project. The contracting company bids on the work based on that information. Communicating the project proposal is important because if you miss anything on the proposal, the companies that are bidding on the work are doing so without all the information. When you create the project proposal, look at the bidding document from a communications perspective and ensure that everything is included. If any portion is missing, the bidding companies might turn in a low bid, not realizing the project proposal is incomplete, which could cause future project problems—especially in the cost area. A perfect project proposal document equals a perfect bid process.

Note
The Project Management Institute's knowledge area for this tool is the integration area. There are no secondary knowledge areas for this tool.

Tool Value
Project proposals present ideas and project suggestions to create a project that senior management will accept or reject.

Social Media Tools
The communication purposes for the project proposal are to inform and persuade. The tool can be used in Yammer, Socialcast, and Facebook (private group).

The proposal document is valuable from a communications perspective because it communicates the proposed project to anyone involved with the project. When developing a complete and thorough project proposal, the contracting companies' estimates should closely match the project expectations. If they do not, you will most likely run into some project issues involving schedule, costs, scope, and quality, to name a few. Some companies that produce multiple proposals a year have templates that make this process automatic and much easier. A good proportion of the proposal document will already be complete with company information so that the person creating the project proposal will only have to add specific project information.

A well-written project proposal communicates project information in such detail that there is little need for extra information. To develop such a high quality proposal requires dedication and effort that saves time and cost on the project itself. A well-written proposal makes it easier for the bidders to define how they are going to do their work and provide an estimate on quality, costs and schedule. With a poorly written project proposals (meaning poor information is given to the bidders), the estimates will vary and ranges will be wide. If the bidding companies are not clear when they start the project, there will be many issues during the bidding process and throughout the project life cycle.

Table 14.2 — Example of a project proposal table of contents shows a typical project proposal table of contents. The document can vary slightly among industries; however, much of the information will be the same regardless of project type. The bidding process is often the same process across different industries. The only unique area of the project proposal process is what a particular industry needs. For example, a project proposal document for a construction project will have unique sections (for example, equipment) that a different project type wouldn't include.

Table 14.2 — Example of a project proposal table of contents

#	Description
1	Introduction
2	Proposal Submission Deadlines
3	Terms and Conditions
4	Pricing
5	Warranty Coverage
6	Mandatory Conditions
7	Mandatory Evaluations Criteria
8	Background and Current Practices
9	Project Description
10	Project Overview
11	Requirements Section
12	Project Structure
13	Technical Requirements
14	Critical Success Factors
15	Project Management Plan
16	Deliverables
17	Work Packages
18	Project Cost Control
19	Integration with Other Projects

The project proposal should represent the total scope of the project. Knowing the project's total scope allows bidding companies to correctly estimate their costs for completing the project because there are no unknowns.

One technique that helps both the bidding company's personnel and the proposal company's personnel is for you to hold a bid review meeting. During that meeting, you communicate the project proposal information to the bidding companies. You can address any questions or concerns that the bidding companies have about the project proposal document. This meeting allows full disclosure and communication of project details. The project proposal may not have had this information clearly described; therefore, bidding companies will have questions that they want addressed before starting the bidding process. The proposal team should also join the bid review sessions to ensure that they understand their roles and the bidding company's roles. You will have other opportunities to communicate the project proposal to the project team. However, it is a best practice for the project team to join the bid review meetings so they can hear the various questions and concerns that bidding companies have before the project starts. Often, the bidding company will put a few of its resources on the project when bidding the project work. This allows communication among those from the proposing company, and the team members from the bidding company during the early project stages.

The project proposal document is called many different names, such as statement of work, bid document, request for quotation, and request for proposal, to name a few. Different industries have other names for the project proposal document, but the core function of the document remains the same, which is to request outside services to perform the project's work activities. The service can be outside the company, or outside the department within the company, it does not matter. Project proposals can just as likely occur between departments as between companies.

Planning to use a project proposal

Long before considering a project proposal document, the company that has the skills to do the project may not have enough resources to work on the project. For example, a software development company may need a new time tracking system. They have resources with the skills to build it, but they may not be able to afford to take those resources off their current development projects. In this case, the company would go through a "make or buy" decision process to analyze whether it would be better to make the new time tracking system in-house (make), or contract the work (buy) to an outside company. If the company decides to contract the work outside the company, they must write a project proposal.

When preparing to create a project proposal, work with your procurement group to develop a project proposal template. By working with the procurement group, you will understand the procurement process and know what to do and not to do. The procurement process can be challenging because there is a legal side of the process that you may not be familiar with. It is also challenging because you may never be involved in the procurement process until you have to create your first project proposal document. Then, it may be too late, and you can slow down the project. Once you understand your company's procurement process, you can start creating the procurement document. If you do not know the process well enough, you are probably going to struggle creating the document.

Reporting from a project proposal

Reporting from the project proposal usually occurs during the initial procurement process and often as a one-time-only event. The document is mainly used to communicate project requirements during the early stages of the project and not throughout the project life cycle. You will rarely report from or use the project proposal outside of the procurement process.

You will not have to report from the project proposal document weekly or monthly because it doesn't contain project status information. Any reporting from the document occurs during the bidding process, which is between you and the bidding companies. The project proposal is stored as part of the document control system to allow for long-term archiving and accessibility.

Cross-Reference
See Chapter 16 - Using Communication Tools During the Initiating Process for more information about the project proposal document.

Introduction to the User Acceptance Document

The *user acceptance document* captures and stores customer sign-offs and approvals for various project deliverables. The user acceptance document represents specific project deliverable approvals, not approvals for the project phase, or the project itself. This is an important distinction for you to remember because the formal acceptance document, and the phase closeout document, both cover specific project areas, but do not cover project deliverables. The user acceptance document stores signatures and approvals for work deliverables. You must be diligent and ensure that your customers accept and approve the project deliverables, including requirement documents, design documents, test plans, and user acceptance documents. The user acceptance document and approvals are stored in the document control system for audit or litigation. You should keep of approval signature proof for every project deliverable. User acceptance documents are common across all industries. An important part of using the user acceptance document is your role in communicating and gaining approval from the customer. As project team members complete their deliverables, you work with the customer to sign off on the user acceptance document for that particular deliverable. You drive the user acceptance process and are responsible for ensuring the customer approves all project deliverables.

Note
The Project Management Institute's knowledge area for the user acceptance documents is the procurement management area. The secondary knowledge area for this tool is quality.

Tool Value
A user acceptance document is a single source that project managers can use to capture the customer's approval. It is a legal document on the customer's acceptance of the project's deliverables.

Social Media Tools
The communication purpose for the user acceptance document is to inform. The tool can be used in Yammer, Socialcast, and Facebook (private group).

A benefit of the user acceptance document is that it provides evidence that the customer accepted the project's deliverables. Without that approval, the project team could be heading down the wrong path and may never recover. For example, the customer is responsible for and develops the business requirements document for most projects. The project team owns and develops the technical requirements document. Because the technical requirements document translates business requirements into a technical solution, the customer may want to approve this document as well. When creating the user acceptance document in this case, the customer would be approving how the project team create the project's technical requirements document to ensure it matches to their requirements. Usually, the user acceptance document's author stores the project deliverables acceptance and approvals within the documents.

Tip
Use the acceptance document's table of contents as a checklist for all of the project deliverables.

Figure 14.2 is an example of a user acceptance document used in the software development industry. This example of the user acceptance document is usable by any industry on any project type. The most important part of this form is the customer signature at the bottom and the conditions and statements they are approving. Because this user acceptance document is project specific, the ability to update it and change it to the specific requirements of the project is valuable.

Figure 14.2 — Example of a user acceptance document

Date: _____

This acceptance form acts as a formal document of the _____ deliverable on the _____ project.

By signing off on this document, you agree to the following terms outlined below.

<u>Please approve each statement below:</u>

_____ The deliverable is of the highest quality the project can afford.

_____ I have fully tested the deliverable (if applicable) and it passes my tests and is ready from my perspective to be moved into a production environment. If the deliverable is a document, I have read it and agree to the contents of the document.

Signature: _____

Printed name: _____

Filling out the user acceptance document is simple. You update and change the user acceptance document based on the project team deliverables. You deliver the document and the deliverable to the approvers for signatures and approvals. A best practice is for the approval process to take no longer than one week. If it takes longer, people forget what happened on the project, or they think it is not important. You should continue to drive signatures and approvals until everyone required has signed off. After getting the signatures, hold the customers who accepted and approved the project deliverables accountable for any issues that arise. If there is any question about whether a customer accepted a deliverable or a particular project item, you have the signed document as proof. The user acceptance document is an official project document; a document that attorneys could potentially call into legal proceedings as evidence that a customer approved a project deliverable. You do not want your project to end in legal proceedings, but if it happens, the user acceptance document is evidence that supports customer sign off and approval of deliverables.

Tip
Make sure you get all of the required signatures in the user acceptance document. Remember, you may never see these people again, except in court.

You may want to seek legal advice when creating the user acceptance document to protect the project from court action. A legal team review provides you with confidence that, from a legal perspective, the signatures (approvals) you get on the document will hold up in court. If the legal team suggests updates or changes to the user acceptance document, you should carry out those changes immediately, and then send the updated document to the legal team for approval. Only after the legal team approves document do you over it with the customer for their approval.

User acceptance documents come in various formats and are created around the deliverables for the specific project. For example, the design document for a construction project looks different than a design document for a software project. The user acceptance documents for these projects will be different. You are responsible for creating a user acceptance document for your specific project and to make changes as needed.

Planning to use a user acceptance document

When planning and preparing a user acceptance document, you must first decide if there are existing processes that you must follow for obtaining user approvals. There may be standard templates, legal requirements, or PMO requirements to guide you through obtaining user acceptance. If not, and there is nothing in place, you must decide how you want to handle the process. This means planning which documents require sign off and setting up the document control system for storing and tracking approvals. It also means deciding on formal signatures or electronic approval and determining how long approvals need to be stored, and so on. There is time and effort you must spend to plan the user acceptance document.

The next step is for you to work with your team to decide how they will be involved in the user acceptance document process. This could mean aligning with them as they complete their project deliverables to ensure that your customers approve and sign off on the work deliverables. After performing these planning activities, you have adequately prepared to use the user acceptance document on your project.

Reporting from the user acceptance document

You will continually report from the user acceptance documents throughout the project life cycle. After the project team completes the project deliverable and the customer approves it, you will add the user acceptance document to the project's reporting for that period. The more deliverables you create, the more you report the user acceptance document. This is a process that will continue throughout the project life cycle.

Reporting from user acceptance documents occur after your customer accepts the work deliverables. This is not something that must occur at a specific time; it occurs regularly throughout the project life cycle. You should celebrate the sign-off for major project deliverables and report these accomplishments to your customers. The user acceptance document is stored as part of the document control system for long-term archiving and accessibility.

Cross-Reference
See Chapter 23 – Using Communication Tools During the Closeout Process to learn more about how to use and create the user acceptance document.

Summary

In this chapter, we explored the project communication tools in the project's procurement management knowledge area. Project procurement can be a difficult area to manage, especially when working with vendors and outside contracting companies. Most project managers know little about the procurement field. Occasionally, such as in contract negotiations, companies can be difficult to work with and require strict guidelines for both companies to follow. When working with outside contracting companies, it is important for you to get sign off and approval for project documents and contracts before any work begins.

The most important tool in the project procurement management area is the lessons-learned document. This document will have the biggest impact on your project, especially when you are starting a new project and there is historical lessons-learned information available from similar projects. The lessons-learned document is valuable to you and future projects so that project managers can learn and grow from project experiences.

In this chapter, we covered procurement-related tools such as the document management system, formal acceptance document, lessons-learned document, and user acceptance document. Each document focuses on procurement areas and is valuable for you and your team in executing a successful project.

Chapter 15

Defining Communication Tools for Working with Stakeholders

IN THIS CHAPTER

- ♦ Introduction to the Change Control Plan
- ♦ Introduction to the Change Request Form
- ♦ Introduction to the Dashboard Report
- ♦ Introduction to the Project Newsletter
- ♦ Introduction to the Stakeholder Register
- ♦ Introduction to the Stakeholder Management plan

In this chapter, we explore the communication tools you can use for the stakeholder management knowledge area to help you communicate more effectively with your stakeholders. Stakeholder communication is critical to a project's success, so you must take the time and effort to become a good communicator. For example, you will struggle if you don't communicate enough, or if you communicate too much with your customers. It's common for the customer to expect you to send a weekly status report, but you think sending a monthly status report and you think that is fine, that can cause serious communication problems with your customers who are expecting it week.

Another important part of stakeholder management is relationship building. You and your team members need to have effective relationships with your stakeholders in order for you to drive a successful project. You can send all the status reports you want, but if you don't have a good relationship with your stakeholders, the information might not be read. Or, even worse, it will be read, but they will nitpick and constantly look for problems. You need to spend time to form bonds and relationships with your customers and stakeholders to run a successful project.

Introducing to the Change Control Plan

The *change control plan* documents the processes and procedures for controlling project changes. When someone requests a change, you need to have a process to follow to adopt or reject the change. The change control plan helps a project stay in line with its goals, and requires that most change requests go through the process. The change control plan is *critical* to your project's success. You should create and share the change control plan before any work activity begins; otherwise, you will most likely have a difficult time controlling project scope. When value is added to or removed from a project, the scope change process includes following the processes within the change control plan. Most change requests add value to the project because they correct errors or improve other features. Other types of change remove value. Removing product features follows the same rigor as adding product feature. When you remove features, you also follow the processes outlined in the change control plan. For example, a software project has a looming deadline, and the project team is not confident that they are going to meet it. The customer may decide to remove some functionality that was originally in scope to meet the deadline. In this scenario, you would run "removing project scope" through the same change control process as adding project scope.

Note
The Project Management Institute's knowledge area for this tool is the integration area. The secondary areas that this tools could be associated with are scope and risk.

Tool Value
The change control plan helps you control project scope and costs by using an established process. It allows the project manager to identify scope creep by comparing the existing scope to the change requests.

Social Media Tools
The communication purposes for the change control plan are to inform and instruct. The tool can be used in Yammer, Socialcast, and Facebook (private group).

There are also project scenarios that are not change requests, but some project managers mistakenly call them change requests. For example, if a customer presents a request and it is within the scope of the project, it is not a change request. Make sure that the new request is a legitimate change request. The new request could already be included in the project's scope, but called something else. Before you call something a change request, compare the new request to the original project scope, and then decide if it actually is a change request.

Tip
Be reasonably flexible and do not make every request a formal change. In doing so, you create goodwill and positive relationships with your customers.

You may find that some change requests are small and take little time for the team to complete. It would take the team less time to make the change than to go through the change control process. This is where you, as project manager, step in and make the call about what to do with small change requests. Occasionally, it is valuable for you to consider doing the requested work to build a stronger relationship with your customer.

The change control plan helps ease conversations between your customer and the project team about how you will manage and control change requests. When you use a standard change control plan for your project, your customers may already be familiar with that process and, therefore, will readily accept it and use it. You are responsible for ensuring that the customer sign offs on the change control plan at the beginning of the project. The customer signing off on the change control plan makes the customer accountable for following the process every time they have a change. Customer sign-off limits miscommunication about the document or the change request process. After you introduce the change control plan, your customer may have questions or concerns that you need to address to ensure that everyone understands the document. Usually, customers accept the change control process and procedures and abide by them throughout the project, but some customers challenge the rules; therefore, their sign-off and approval is important.

It is important that your customer understands how to document change requests and that they are comfortable with the process as early as possible. If the customer is learning the change control process while also trying to request a project change, it will likely be disrupting and a bad experience for both of you. You want the change request process to run as smoothly as possible because you will implement it throughout the project life cycle.

Tip
Hold a short training session for your customers to explain how to complete a change request and how the change control process works.

Table 15.1 — Example of a change control plan table of contents shows an example of a change control plan's table of contents. In this document, the customers respond to a series of questions about the change impact to the project. The customer's answers and the details that they document for those questions are decision points for the change control board to approve or reject the change.

Table 15.1 — Example of a change control plan table of contents

#	Description
1	Change Control Board, Roles, and Responsibilities
2	Change Board Impact/Considerations Review
3	What Process Does Requestor Have to Follow to Initiate a Change? What Is the Flow?
4	Change Board Time Frames and Response Expectations
5	Change Request Documentation and Expectations
6	Any Additional Information about the Change Control Plan or Process
7	Mandatory Change Process Explained Here
8	Approvals and Responses from Change Control Board
9	Mandatory Change Process
10	Final Recommendation and Approval

Project stakeholders play a large role in the change control plan and procedures document, and can hurt a project if they request too many changes for the project team. If there are too many changes, the project team has little time to work on the project scope. Instead, the project team focuses on the change requests and not the project scope. Not every project change request is acceptable. Occasionally, the change requested is too great, and the schedule impact too large, or too costly. You may reject a large change or delay it until a later date in the project life cycle. On a software project, a large change request may wait until the next version. As project manager, you are must work closely with your stakeholders by using the change request process to ensure that suggested changes are necessary.

You are responsible for communicating to the customer how the team will react to being overwhelmed with change request work. When project teams are overwhelmed with change requests, and working an overloaded schedule, they are negatively impacted for the entire project. A change control plan communicates the processes and procedures to process project changes. It is likely project teams will have morale issues when they are processing multiple change requests while still trying to complete their project work. Managing and dealing with team morale issues is your responsibility, and in some cases, the team members' functional managers.

Here is an example of the steps you would take in processing a change request in the construction industry. The steps are similar for software and research projects.

1. Initiate the change request and log it into a change request system.

2. Analyze the specific change request and distribute a request for information.

3. Create and submit a change request form for analysis and cost estimating.

4. Submit the change request form, and cost and schedule impacts, to the change control board (or appropriate persons) for review.

5. Once reviewed, approve or deny the request.

6. Plan a time to do the work if it is approved.

Some change requests that are small and don't largely impact the project team won't need approval. Many government-mandated change requests also don't need formal approval. The change control board automatically accepts these changes and incorporates them into the project work. After the change control board tells you the approval decision, you are responsible for communicating the decision to the project team and customers.

Understanding change control plan

Every change control plan outlines the roles and responsibilities for every project member so that everyone understands their role in the process. The change control plan documents and describes the following roles:

*   **Change initiator:** Communicates the request and who confirms its completion.
*   **Project sponsor/owner/customer:** Communicates the approval of funds for the change request. The change owner assigns specific tasks to the task owners and communicates the progress on those tasks through completion.
*   **Change administrator:** Classifies, assesses, and monitors change request progress. Communicates progress throughout the process.
*   **Impact assessors:** Assesses the change impact by communicating change request impacts and risks.
*   **Change owner:** Communicates the required change and manages it through the process.
*   **Task owners:** Do the work to complete and deliver the change request.

- **Change manager:** Manages the overall change process, acts as a point of escalation for change requests, communicates change request information, exercises judgment in assessing requests, and escalates the change requests to a change board, if required.
- **Change board:** Reviews the change process and specific change requests, as needed. The change control board is comprised of the service delivery manager, customer representatives, and the change manager. The board makes the final acceptance or denial of the change request, and then you communicate it to the project team and the change initiator.

A limited number of projects have a solid scope, and something always happens that complicates project scope that needs your attention. Usually, you write change requests due to poorly written requirements and missed scope items. The more information in the project's requirements document, the less likely the customers will ask for many changes. If the project team communicates the requirements to the customer and gains approval, the customer is less likely to seek project changes. Without getting the customer's approval for the requirements document, you can almost guarantee that you will process many customer change requests.

When you use the change control plan, you are also responsible for reporting and communicating status from the change request process. You can communicate status during weekly status meetings or by sending a status report—any means that tracks and communicates change request information to your customer. Continuing to communicate status is great for providing full visibility to your customers about the status of proposed changes.

Planning to use a change control plan

When planning to use a change control plan, you must identify a standard change control process for your project. This process includes creating change control forms, identifying change control board members, holding weekly change control meetings, and setting up a change control repository or central website for tracking and storing changes. You must also plan the team members' time to handle and review changes outside the project activities on the project schedule. Usually, team members review and evaluate change requests as part of their day-to-day project activities, although, some team members think it is outside of day-to-day activities. That is for you to work out with each team member at the beginning of the project. Each team member should allow time to work on change requests in addition to their scheduled work. Earmark time to evaluate change requests for your team members and communicate that expectation at the beginning of the project. After performing these steps, you are adequately prepared for using the change control plan.

Note
Remember that the work activities for approved change requests should be included in the master schedule and the baseline schedule.

Reporting from the change control form

Make sure that you have a change control reporting process set up at the beginning of your project. That way, when the project starts working, the reporting method is in place to help you ensure that everyone is up to date on all of the change requests and status. There are many types of reports available for you to use during the change control process. Some of the common reports include:

- Outcome of the change control board (approve/reject).
- Communicating how to complete the change request form.
- Overall change control process (project manager and team members report this data)
- Total number of change requests, per month, and total, to date.

Although your most important task is running the project, reporting and staying ahead of change are also critical work activities for you. Reporting a change request's approval or rejection can be tricky. It is much easier to tell your customers the change request was approved than telling them it was rejected. A rejected change request could mean an unhappy customer; make sure that you communicate rejection sensitively.

Reporting can also include communicating the contents of the change request form. You and your team members may not develop the contents of the change request form, but you are responsible for driving the change through to completion. Usually, you report the change request form to different levels of management and the customers who are responsible for accepting or rejecting the change. The change request form is a valuable communication tool because it describes, in detail, the changes requested by the customer to ensure that everyone is on the same page.

You report the change request information throughout the project life cycle. You will continually report information from the first request to the last request. If team members did not correctly capture the scope, or the project has active and demanding customers, change requests can flow into the project daily. Change request reporting happens weekly at a minimum for most projects, but longer projects (two or more years) have monthly reporting cycles.

Cross-Reference
See Chapter 18 – Using Communication Tools to Plan and Develop Project Deliverables to learn more about how to use or create the change control plan.

Introducing to the Change Request Form

You use the *change request form* to monitor and control requested project changes. The customer or a team member completes the change request form to document and communicate a potential project change. You should review each change request form with the customer and show them how to fill it out. There must be enough information on the form for a project team to review and decide how to incorporate the change if it gets approved. The change request form must contain enough information for the change control board to approve or deny the change request. If there's not enough information, the board will send back the change request form and ask for more information.

Note
The Project Management Institute's knowledge area for this tool is the integration area. Secondary areas that this tool could be associated with are scope, quality, and risk.

Tool Value
The change request form identifies all changes to the project. It provides a common look and feel for capturing change request information.

Social Media Tools
The communication purposes for the change request form are to inform and instruct. The tool can be used in Yammer, Socialcast, and Facebook (private group).

You use the change request log to analyze change requests. The log stores the changes for historical purposes and helps you identify lessons-learned information. You should store the approval or rejection status of each change request in the log. The change request log is a central repository for all change requests.

You use the change request form and the change request log to store all project change requests. The change request log does not contain the same detail as the change request form. But, the change request log does carry enough detail that anyone who reviews the document can understand the change being requested. We include both tools in this section because they are highly dependent on each other and they align from a communication perspective. For example, there is no value to having a change request log unless there is at least one change request filed for the project. A change request does not need a change request log for reporting. It is a best practice, though, to enter the change request into the change request log to keep both tools synchronized. The change request log stores all change requests, while a change request form is for a single change request. For capturing data and reporting, the change request form stores all the information about a single change request. The change request log, on the other hand, stores high-level information about all requested project changes.

Change request forms provide formal documentation about the proposed or suggested project changes. The change request form should be simple for you, your team members, and customers to use. You use the change control plan, discussed earlier in this chapter, to set the standards and guidelines for processing change request forms. Some projects use many change request forms as the project progresses. Filing change requests does not derail a project, but it forces a project team to review and decide how to incorporate the change, if applicable. This process occurs repeatedly throughout the project. Your role is to closely supervise the change request process and communicate the information to everyone involved in the proposed project change.

You need to communicate with your customers when in the project life cycle you can perform the requested changes. The project team cannot complete every change once they are approved. The timing around release a change to a project is critical. It is rare that the project team can complete a change request as soon as it's approved. Trying to force a change request too soon can have a negative impact on the overall project. There should be strict timing guidelines for completing approved change requests. You must also have a point in the project's timeline where change requests are no longer accepted because the project is too far down the path or close to completing and the risk is too high to incorporate a new change. Be aware of timing and how the change could affect the project's completion.

Change request form

Many companies have their own version of a change request form based on the industry and project type. These forms capture the information you need to understand the proposed project changes. A construction company will have a different change request form from a software company because the industries are so different. Some of the core information captured in the change request form are standard, regardless of project type. Standard project areas that are impacted by change include scope changes, schedule changes, cost impact, and quality. Each of these project areas are the same, regardless of project type or industry.

Figure 15.1 — Example of a change request form shows an example of a standard change request form. This form is common among all industries and usable on any project. Without a doubt, forms are going to vary among companies and industries.

Figure 15.1 — Example of a change request form

Name of Project:	Project Manager:
Change Request #	Change Request Date:
Change Requested By Name:	Current Project Phase:

Description of Change:
Scope Impact:
Schedule Impact:
Cost Impact:
Quality Impact:
Possible Risks:
Reviewed By: Position: Date:
Recommended Action Approve or Reject

The change request form is a great communication tool for project managers. You can use the change request form as a communication tool to get customer approval for the requested change. You must ensure that no one on the project team is working on an unapproved change request until it has gone through the approval process. All change request forms need review and approval before any work occurs on the change request items. The time and effort spent on an unapproved change request takes time away from the project's current work activities, which can put the schedule and budget at risk. The change request form tracks a wealth of project data for easy communication to everyone involved in processing and approving or rejecting the change request.

- You can use a change request form in the following situations:

- To request scope additions or removal of changes.
- To communicate to customers or management a request to increase the project's budget.
- To communicate to leadership and request extra project staff.
- To communicate and request changes that are causing design errors. This includes reporting the discovery of problems that will change the project direction.
- To process a customer request for new functionality that differs from the original scope of work.

Change request log

You can use a change request log to keep a historical reference of the project's change requests. You will quickly discover the importance of change request logs and use them to communicate change requests at a summary level. You should create a change request log at the beginning of a project and add change request information (high-level) to the log as changes occur. Most projects need one change request log. Filters can select the closed and active change requests.

You will find great value in the change request log from a lessons-learned perspective. When storing project change information, the log provides a record of what project changes were accepted and rejected. Therefore, if the project goes over budget or becomes delayed, or has quality issues or staffing problems, you can review the change request log to understand why and what happened. As the project progresses, you should continue to store project change requests within the change request log, and then use this tool for gathering and collecting the project's lessons-learned information. A change request log communicates a running tally of the costs and the number of accepted and rejected change requests. This is valuable information if the project is cost or schedule driven.

Table 15.2 — Example of a change request log shows an example of a change request log. This is a basic example, but one that contains valuable change request information. This change request log stores only high-level information about the change requests—not the details. The change request log enables the viewer to see, at a high-level, all of the changes that were proposed for the project so he or she can understand which ones were accepted or rejected. The change request log is valuable for long-term storage of change request information.

Table 15.2 — Example of a change request log

CR#	Description	Date Req	Decision	Date Authorized	Approved by	Requested by	Implementation Date
A6-55	Modify main wall	2/3/2019	Y	4/14/2019	JSmith	MJones	5/14/2019
BJ-07	Add new baseboard	7/1/2019	N	N/A	Rejected	BThomas	N/A

You are responsible for reporting the information contained in the change request log. How often you report this information depends on the specific project needs, how often changes are requested, and overall project timing.

Planning to use a change request form

When preparing to use a change request form and a change request log, you must first find out if the company already has these two tools or if you're working from scratch. If the company has the tools, you can begin to use them immediately. Otherwise, if the two tools are not available, you must find some templates to use. On most projects, you will need to edit the change request form and change request log to meet your project and customer requirements. One best practice you should follow when customizing and working with the change request form and change request log is to find out whether your customers have are any special requirements for the change request process. If the customer does have special requirements, you should incorporate them into the forms. After performing these tasks, you will have adequately prepared for using the change request form on your project.

Reporting from a change request form

You are responsible for reporting the number of change requests associated with the project. You should use a document format for creating and sharing the change request form. After the customer or team members complete the change request form and send it to you, you email the project team members the same form for project impact assessment. When you have the impact information from the team, the next steps in the process is to go to the change request board for approval.

Display the change request log in a presentation format to customers or leadership as part of a larger presentation. It is a best practice for you to have supporting information about how the change requests are impacting project health. For example, it would be beneficial for you to present to your customers that the project is over budget by 50 percent, and there are 20 approved change requests that are causing that overage. Presenting that information together helps customers and leadership upon review. If you were to only present the 20 change requests and not point out budget impact, customers and leadership are not getting the full story. That many change requests require extra dollars. Those dollars may not be in the budget yet and, therefore, the project would be over budget. If the project is projecting to be over budget by 50 percent, and the customers do not know about the 20 extra change requests, they would have no context or explanation as to why the project is over budget.

Tip
Ensure that project managers properly document and log all project changes. Changes that come on the back of a scrap piece of paper are not acceptable and you must reject them.

Cross-Reference
See Chapter 20 - Using Communication Tools During the Executing and Controlling Processes to Administer the Project to learn more about how to use a change request.

Introducing the Dashboard Tool

The *Dashboard tool* provides customers and leadership staff a real-time graphical view of critical project information, such as project schedule, costs, issues, quality, and risks. Usually, project managers and their peers post dashboards on a company website where customers and leadership can view the latest information. Dashboards are popular with customers and senior management because they can see current project data, and then make decisions based on that data. Without a dashboard, those same groups would have to wait until the weekly status report to get the similar information. Communications from using a project dashboard are valuable. After you set up the process to ensure that the dashboard is updated daily, ongoing maintenance can be costly. When someone is interested in or needs project information, you direct them to the dashboard for the latest project status.

Note
The Project Management Institute's knowledge area for this tool is the communications management area. This tool can be associated with all knowledge areas.

Tool Value
Dashboards offer customers, upper and senior management, and team members real-time access to project information. Real-time access gives customers a feel for how well the project is progressing and whether they need to take action on any areas of concern.

Social Media Tools
The communication purposes for the dashboard tool are to inform and motivate. The tool can be used in Yammer, Socialcast, and Facebook (private group).

Dashboards are mainly used in multi-project environments because companies rarely want to spend the time and effort to develop them for a single project. The cost of continual maintenance and support rarely warrants a single project dashboard. They are expensive and often requires a team of people to maintain.

Dashboards are valuable when you need to roll up multiple projects into a consolidated view. Project dashboards are mostly used when customers and leadership need to see many different projects in their organization in one consolidated view.

Project dashboards have many benefits. The most important benefit is real-time access to project information in a graphical and chart format. For example, if the customer wants to track error count status during the testing phase, you can create an error tracking report format and add it to the dashboard. As testing progresses, the customer can see the latest error count information. Two other benefits of using a project dashboard is that it's easily accessible and always up to date.

Figure 15.2 — Example of a project dashboard shows a typical dashboard report. Companies use thousands of different dashboards. For example, the metrics in the following figure provide a graphical status of the project that focuses on six different areas. There is no correct number of project areas to add to a dashboard. Customer and leadership needs help you decide which project points to display.

Figure 15.2 — Example of a project dashboard

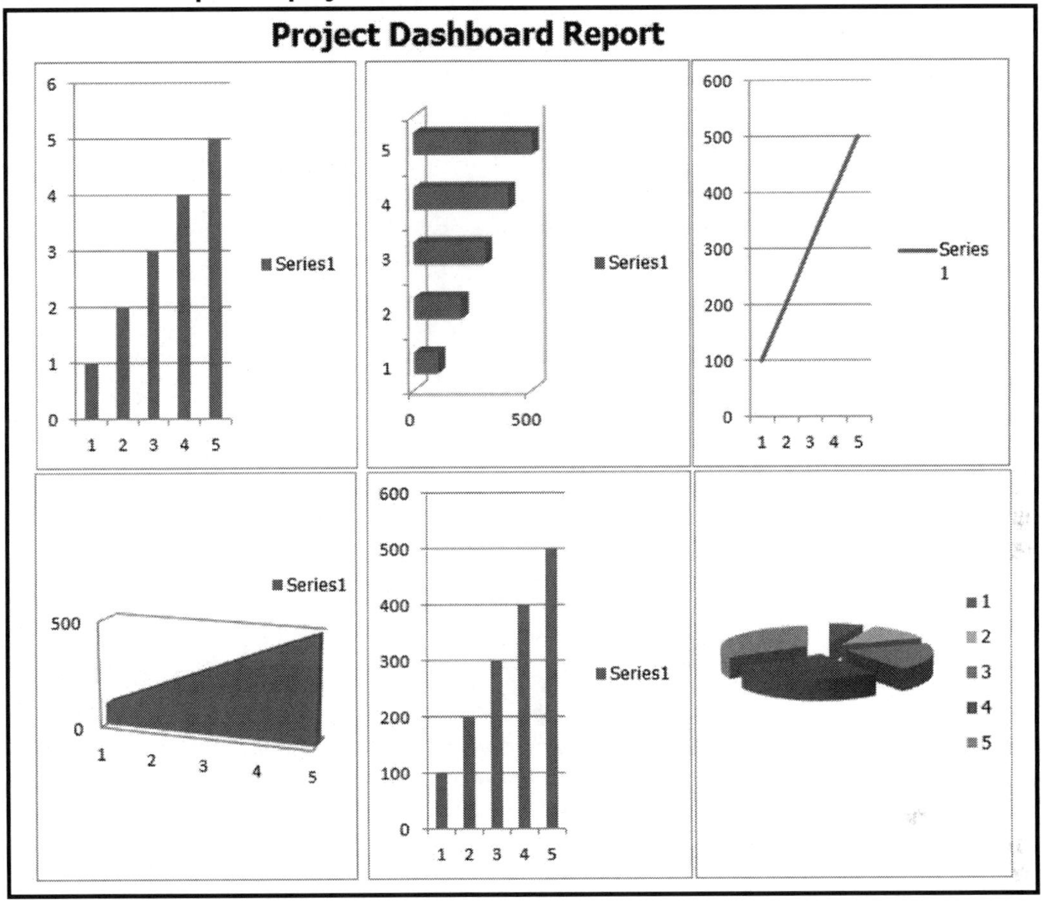

Project Dashboard Report

Tip
The best information to add to a dashboard report is summary-level information.

Project teams often create dashboards that pull out project details and drill in on capabilities. At first, creating a dashboard with high-level project information solves the need to communicate project information. But more often than not, customers or leadership will want to perform further data analysis and perhaps look at the data behind the data. These "drill-through capabilities" are common on project dashboards and are a real advantage to using this tool. Customers can often select the dashboard data that opens further dashboard pages to see finer details behind the dashboard data. Project managers and their peers use tools such as Microsoft Excel to develop and report project dashboards. These tools allow drill-through capability and ability to print information. Databases, such as Oracle® and Microsoft SQL Server® are also popular for storing and reviewing project dashboard data, and both have drill-through features available for further data analysis.

Dashboard reports commonly have many different project points, such as project costs, schedules, or other financial information. Other financial data can include the hours worked by team members, overtime costs, material costs, and so on. By creating these types of dashboards, you are catering to customers and leadership who focus on these limited but important project areas.

Dashboards do have their limits. Dashboards must have a meaningful value to the project, because keeping them current adds to team member workload. Other challenges or limits include adding too much information to the dashboard, which makes it difficult to read, confusing, and a huge overhead to preserve. The challenge that project teams have when creating a dashboard report is putting all of the project data points on a single screen that is easy to read and understand. Some companies use a dashboard that represents a view of their projects from a program perspective. A program-level dashboard report provides a summary of many company projects in a single view. It is valuable to see across all projects occurring in the company.

Program-level dashboards focus on specific areas of the company. Large companies have hundreds of projects, so adding all of them to a single dashboard is exactly the purpose of the project dashboard. Usually, companies with many projects divide the dashboards and show them in a single view with a range of 10 to 15 projects per grouping. Dividing the projects keeps the project list small and reduces the amount of data being produced, which makes it much faster to develop a report on an internal website. Having a program-level dashboard provides customers and leadership the view and pulse of projects in one summarized view.

Planning to use a dashboard report

When planning and preparing to use a dashboard report, you must first decide the role of dashboards in the company. Whether dashboards are common to all projects, or something new to the company, you must find out where and how they fit the project. Sometimes, there is no automated solution for creating a dashboard, so you will have to create it manually. If your company is capable of creating an automated dashboard, you need to determine the process for setting it up. After deciding the setup process and the types of dashboards that are available, you need to figure out who on the project team will gather the data and add it to the project dashboard. Usually, you need a couple of different team members to create the dashboard. Therefore, you need to figure out the balance between the team members' time working on the dashboard as well as on their project activities. You and the team members responsible for developing the dashboard meet with the customer to gather requirements for the dashboard. After taking these necessary planning steps, you are adequately prepared for using a project dashboard.

Reporting from a dashboard report

The dashboard is a complex and technical communication tool and is not a tool that most project managers can create by themselves. Because the dashboard is complex, you need a team of software developers to create and maintain the dashboard. Sometimes, the same development team will keep the dashboard for as long as the customer or leadership wants.

Manual dashboard report creation is either your or an assigned team member's responsibility. Either person must enter the project data by using a spreadsheet and manually creating data points or calculations. You or an analyst would continue the manual process monthly, if that is what you and the customer agreed upon. Alternatively, when you're able to automate the dashboard, the development team would take over the dashboard's maintenance tasks.

Cross-Reference
See Chapter 17 - Using Communication Tools to Administer the Planning Process to learn more about how to use a dashboard report.

Introducing to the Project Newsletter

Project newsletters provide a high-level project status and other project information in an informal format for customers, leadership, and the project team. You can use the format to deliver project information with colors and graphics in a relaxed manner. Project newsletters have high visibility and describe current activities for those working on the project. Many large projects create project newsletters to communicate project information. Newsletters are usually distributed monthly.

Note
The Project Management Institute's knowledge area for this tool is the communications management area. This tool can be associated with all knowledge areas.

Tool Value
A fun and light-hearted method for delivering project information. Although, the project newsletter usually contains the same content as a project status report, the communication method and the format and style for delivering the message are different.

Social Media Tools
The communication purposes for the project newsletter are to inform, inspire and motivate. The tool can be used in Yammer, Socialcast, and Facebook (private group).

Many project managers enjoy using project newsletters because they can deliver project information in an enjoyable and lighthearted format. Customers appreciate receiving information in this format because it breaks the monotony of the weekly status report. Even the most strict project manager can soften the news when presenting it in a project newsletter format. However, some information about team members or budget specifics may not be suitable to send in a newsletter. You must choose wisely what information to include in a newsletter.

You and your team may not have time to jazz up or add graphics or colors to project communications. Most send the information out as fast as they can and don't worry about color or data formatting. A project newsletter, however, allows you to add colors and jazzed-up graphics. Most team members will be actively engaged in the project newsletter process. Some customers receive it and offer praise for the good work the team is doing, while others will reuse this information and forward the information to their superiors for project exposure and intervention or support, if necessary. Often, customers send project newsletters to executives who are not usually part of the project reporting cycle or have anything to do with the project.

Figure 15.3 — Example of a project newsletter shows a project newsletter for a construction project. Note the graphics and easy-to-read format and layout.

Figure 15.3 — Example of a project newsletter

APPLE ROAD CONSTRUCTION PROJECT
MONTHLY NEWSLETTER

Volume 1 · Issue 5

What's Happening?
As of December 10th, 2019, the project is currently on track and progressing towards the August 10th finish date. There are no major issues or concerns, the project is on track and almost complete.

Highway Updates Related to Apple Road

- **ADA COUNTY**
  Interstate 84 Eagle westbound off-ramp rebuilding
  Construction started March 29 on a project to improve and widen the I-84 westbound off-ramp at Eagle Road. Improvements include a new off-ramp lane that will lengthen the ramp 1,600 feet.

- **Locust Grove Overpass construction**
  Work started in December 2019 on a new overpass that will connect Locust Grove Road and offer an extended route over Interstate 84 between Eagle Road and Meridian Road. Currently, Locust Grove Road south of Interstate 84 ends near the interstate.

Help Wanted!
- **Clean Up Crew wanted for open day clean-up**
- Jones Construction is hiring 10 – 15 clean-up workers for open day of Apple Road. If interested please contact Jones Construction @ 123-555-1212.

Links:
- **Gov Cal Highway Standards**
- **Highway Safety Reports - 2018 - 2019**

Key Contacts:
John Smith – Project Manager
Mary Jones, Communications and Media Contact
Jones Construction – Owners

To Unsubscribe:
If you do not wish to receive, further updates on the project contact Mary Jones.

Project Timeline

NEXT MILESTONE/DELIVERABLE	DATE
Project Finish	1/2/2019

For some reason, most small projects do not use project newsletters, maybe due to the size of the project, or because people may think that project newsletters are not valuable. Or, they could think that they know everything that is occurring on the project because it is small. In fact, by not using a project newsletter, the project teams are preventing themselves from communicating as effectively as possible to their customers. They are ignoring the importance of adding "fun" to project reporting that is often needed.

There are hundreds of newsletter formats, and each one caters to specific project needs. Most project newsletters include the same basic project information, such as current happenings, help wanted, time lines, contact information, a biographical write up on a team member, and other applicable information. Project newsletters should contain high-level project information only, and rarely should they contain the specific project details.

There are few disadvantages of creating project newsletters. Some consider the extra work to create a newsletter to be a disadvantage. However, after you create a newsletter template, the time involved is limited. Sometimes, customers want to be involved in the project newsletter process, which is a positive experience for everyone involved and allows the customers as well to add some fun items into the newsletter.

Planning to use a project newsletter

When planning and preparing to use a project newsletter, you must first find out if there is a company-wide standard format, style, or template available. A standard template will help you decide which newsletter components, such as content and format, to include. A template also provides a starting point for the information you need to collect to produce the newsletter. Then, you can work with the customer to find out their newsletter requirements. You should also track the customer's reporting requirements. Customers may have their own newsletter requirements, such as who should receive it. The customer might want to use some of the information in the project newsletter in their company's newsletter to gain exposure across the company. You might have to change your proposed newsletter to incorporate the customer's information. Another important area to consider when planning a newsletter is the customer's time frame for newsletter reporting. Understanding their newsletter reporting requirements at the project's planning phase is important because it enables you to set a communication rhythm with your customer and balance the team's workload. After preparing the format, content, time frame, and special customer requirements, you are adequately prepared to use this tool on your project.

Reporting from a project newsletter

You are responsible for creating and delivering the project newsletter. If the project is large enough to have an administrative team, the communications manager is typically responsible for creating the project newsletter. You can work with that team member to ensure that he or she understands the content and is comfortable with the newsletter information before sending it to customers.

You will report from the project newsletter once a month, not weekly, because it would be too much project overhead to create a weekly newsletter. Newsletters are created in a presentation format to focus on promoting project highlights and current happenings. Project newsletters are not detailed status reports and should never include the same details that are contained in a status report. Newsletters are created in a document format and stored in the document control system for long-term storage, archiving and accessibility.

Cross-Reference

See Chapter 20 - Using Communication Tools During the Executing and Controlling Processes to Administer the Project to learn more about how to use a project newsletter.

Introducing to the Stakeholder Register

The *stakeholder register* captures the names and information about project stakeholders. Project stakeholders consist of customers, leadership, team members, and others who are interested in the project. The stakeholder register is a popular project communication tool that has been around for many years. It is important to note that even though project team members are also stakeholders, they are seldom added to the stakeholder register. The stakeholder register contains names of the project customers, stakeholders, and individuals who have impact or influence on the project or the organization.

Note

The Project Management Institute's knowledge area for this tool is the stakeholder area. The secondary area that this tool could be associated with is communication.

Tool Value

Stakeholder registers contain a list of project stakeholders. The information in the stakeholder register will vary among project managers and does not need to be consistent. You are encouraged to capture the information you feel is suitable about your stakeholders.

Social Media Tools

The communication purpose for the stakeholder register is to inform. The tool can be used in Yammer, Socialcast, and Facebook (private group).

Stakeholder identification is one of the first important steps in the project management communication process. It is important for you to understand the importance of capturing the complete list of project stakeholders at the beginning of the project and continue to refine and update the list throughout the project life cycle. As project scope grows, so does the list of impacted stakeholders. It is wise to keep the stakeholder list current and accurate at all times during the project. Rarely, does the project stakeholder register get smaller, but it can happen if scope is reduced or groups drop off as you progress through the project life cycle.

Managing stakeholders correctly can be the difference between a successful or an unsuccessful project. There is no question about the impact stakeholders can have when they support you in delivering your project. If you have a good relationship with your customer, you will have a much better chance of running a successful project. If your stakeholder relationship struggles, your chance of running a successful project is limited. The key to successful stakeholder management begins with creating a solid stakeholder register and keeping it current. Sometimes, don't fall into the trap where your stakeholder register is simply a list of stakeholder names with some extra columns that offer limited value.

The stakeholder register is an important tool for communicating with your stakeholders. It is a best practice to capture your stakeholders' communication preferences so you understand how to communicate with them. If you don't know how to effectively communicate with your stakeholders, you can run into problems. Some stakeholders want status reports delivered in-person, while others want the reports emailed. Consider this valuable information to track and capture in the stakeholder register for each customer. If you have multiple stakeholders, across multiple projects, you will never remember their communication preferences. If you forget a customer preference, you might mistakenly communicate with them using the wrong medium or method.

Table 15.3 — Example of table of contents for a stakeholder register is a table of contents for a stakeholder register. Most project managers have a common set of columns they use in their stakeholder register from project to project. There is no right or wrong number of columns to carry in a stakeholder register, it is up to you to decide. That decision is yours because this tool is mostly for the project manager as a reminder for their customer's communication preferences.

Table 15.3 — Example of table of contents for a stakeholder register

#	Description
1	Name & Email
2	Project Role
3	Communication Preferences
4	Area of Project Impact
5	Project Expectations

There are some best practices that every project manager should consider when creating a stakeholder register, including:

- Identifying the people or organizations that are impacted by the project—no easy task. You will need to spend time with as many people as you can who are connected to the project to ensure they are in the register. Think about the project scope and the interdependencies of the various systems that are impacted by project scope.

- Identifying people or organizations as early as possible for a greater chance of success. The stakeholder register does not have to be complete at any stage of the project because you update the stakeholder register throughout the project life cycle. Continue to look for and add stakeholders to the register that you may have initially missed.

- For projects with many stakeholders, classify them according to their project interest, influence, and involvement. When project managers group or classify stakeholders into different areas, you have a much easier time working with them based on those classifications. For example, if you have a group of stakeholders who are interested in the project, but who have no impact or authority, you can send them a monthly status report, or they can attend a monthly meeting, which is different than working with a group of active and interested stakeholders who you work with weekly or daily.

Planning to use a stakeholder register

When planning to use the stakeholder register, you need to focus on a couple of main items to be successful. The first item is the columns or fields of information that you will capture in your stakeholder register. Ask yourself which fields you should include, which fields will get you the information easily, and how you will use the stakeholder register. Project managers have different opinions about using the stakeholder register. Some are open and share the stakeholder register, and some hold back and don't share it at all. The main reason why project managers have different opinions about sharing the stakeholder register is due to the information contained in it. For example, if you use a field on your stakeholder register called "Project Impact" and you name a stakeholder "low" without letting him or her know, it may upset the stakeholder and have a negative effect on you. In such cases, many project managers would rather just not show anyone the stakeholder register instead of having a conversation about it, which leads to its own problems.

The second item that you need to plan for is the lack of enough people on the list. Sadly, many project managers use the stakeholder register as a "check box tool" and don't spend the time or effort to thoroughly complete it. If you don't take the time or effort to complete the stakeholder register properly, you miss individuals or groups who should be included. And if you don't have everyone included, you might run into issues delivering your project. For example, it would be a huge problem if you miss a key group on the stakeholder register, and that group is fundamental in delivering part of your project's scope. Taking the time to complete the stakeholder register will help you run a successful project. When the stakeholder register is complete, send it to the team members and share it with your stakeholders to bring as much exposure to the document as you can. The more people who see the stakeholder register, the more people will have a chance of noticing that an individual or a group is missing. When that happens, reach out to the missing individual or group and add them to the stakeholder register.

Reporting from a stakeholder register

You are solely responsible for reporting the stakeholder register. The more you can expose the stakeholder register and share it with people, the better your chance of having the right resources and groups on the list. As noted, if you decide not to report or share the stakeholder, there is a good chance of missing stakeholders. If that happens, you are in a spot where you could be missing resources or groups and not communicating with everyone you need, which could be a huge issue for you and could impact you running a successful project.

There is no regular cadence for reporting from the stakeholder register because it does not contain regular project status information and the register should always be available for everyone to see. Therefore, there is no monthly or weekly reporting from the stakeholder register because it is always available. The stakeholder register is created in a table or spreadsheet format and stored as part of the document control system for long-term archiving and accessibility.

Cross-Reference
See Chapter 16 - Using Communication Tools During the Initiating Process for additional discussions about how to create and use a stakeholder register.

Introducing to the Stakeholder Management Plan

The *stakeholder management plan* documents how you will work with and manage your project stakeholders. You can send all the status reports, newsletters, and other project information you want, but if you don't have a plan to manage your stakeholders, none of those reports will matter. Stakeholder management is much more than creating a stakeholder register for yourself. Stakeholder management is a three-step process: listing your stakeholders, managing them, and monitoring and taking corrective actions. We cover these steps in more detail below. You must continually update and work with each stakeholder to ensure that you get the information you need.

Note
The Project Management Institute's knowledge area for this tool is the stakeholder area. The secondary area that this tool could be associated with is human resources.

Tool Value
The stakeholder management plan documents managing project stakeholders. The value the plan brings is having a single source to document how you will communicate and work with your stakeholders.

Social Media Tools
The communication purposes for the stakeholder management plan are to inform and instruct. The tool can be used in Yammer, Socialcast, and Facebook (private group).

You are responsible for managing stakeholders. You should use the stakeholder register in the stakeholder management plan. Add the stakeholder register to the first section of the stakeholder management plan named "List or identify your stakeholders." The two documents, however, are different and have unique purposes. The stakeholder management plan outlines how you will manage your stakeholders and the stakeholder register is a list of stakeholder names and detailed information.

When you think about the stakeholder management plan, focus on the following key steps for working with project stakeholders:

1. List or identify the stakeholders. Understand who your stakeholders are and create the stakeholder register.

2. Manage the stakeholders. Set up meetings, communicating and bucketing them into suitable groupings based on their project influence, interests, and impact or involvement.

3. Monitor and take corrective actions. As you communicate and work with your stakeholders, there has to be a process for continual improvements and course corrections. For example, if your customer wants you to email a status report weekly, and then suddenly decide they want the status report hand delivered, you have to react and adapt to the new request. You have to monitor and perform corrective actions throughout the project life cycle.

These are the three main activities that you will use to manage stakeholders. Different project managers may have their own steps or processes for managing stakeholders, but all project managers usually go through the same three steps.

Table 15.4 is a table of contents for a stakeholder management plan. There are many different versions of a stakeholder management plan that you can use on your projects. The sections described in the table would be the standard for most projects. It is a best practice for you to check with your PMO's or project management leads to see if there are specific sections that need adding to the template.

Table 15.4 — Example of a table of contents for a stakeholder management plan

#	Description
1	Document History & Approvals
2	Document Purpose
3	Identify Stakeholders
4	Manage Stakeholders
5	Monitor and take correct actions

Planning to use a stakeholder management plan

When planning to use a stakeholder management plan, focus on how you will use the document. The first step in the planning process is reviewing the template and ensuring that you are comfortable with the three main areas of stakeholder management. When you are comfortable with those areas, the planning process becomes much easier. Your focus turns to completing the template and working through the stakeholder management process. Within the template, there are specific tools that you will need to develop and some of the tools will take some planning and setup to create.

Cross-reference
See chapter 16 - Using Communication Tools During the Initiating Process for more information about how to create a stakeholder register.

The second tool that needs some extra planning and that you create in the stakeholder management plan is the power/interest grid. You use the power/interest grid to classify your stakeholders into categories of how you influence and impact the project. Sadly, most project managers do not use this valuable tool so they miss a key component in project communications. Some of the issues that you or your project manager peers could encounter when using the power/interest grid are the same as those you would encounter with the stakeholder register. Some project managers will fill in the grid but never share it with project stakeholders. Some project managers feel that if they put a stakeholder on the grid, he or she might not be happy with it and cause problems. The same logic applies to the power/interest grid as with the stakeholder register; create the tool and work with your stakeholders to adopt and accept it.

Cross-reference
Refer to the Project Management Institute PMBOK® Guide for more information about the power/interest grid.

Reporting from a stakeholder management plan

You are responsible for reporting the stakeholder management plan. However, because the stakeholder management plan does not include status information, there is no need for reporting it on a weekly or monthly basis. There is need, however, to report the stakeholder management plan at the beginning of the project when it's being created and you need approval and buy-in. Reporting from the stakeholder management plan happens throughout the document's creation. Work with your stakeholders to ensure that they receive the project information they need.

The stakeholder management plan is created in document format and stored as part of the document control system for long-term archiving and accessibility.

Cross-Reference
See Chapter 16 - Using Communication Tools During the Initiating Process for additional information about how to create and use a stakeholder management plan.

Summary

The communication tools described in this chapter are some of the best choices for project stakeholder management. The stakeholder management knowledge area is one of the most important areas when managing a project. The tools documented in this chapter will help you successfully manage and work with your stakeholders. Don't underestimate the importance of stakeholder communications and review each tool to decide if they will work for you.

One of the most important tools in stakeholder management is the stakeholder register. This document will have the biggest impact on your project, especially when you are starting a new project and there are new stakeholders you haven't worked with before. The stakeholder register is valuable for understanding who to communicate with and how.

In this chapter, we covered stakeholder management tools such as the change control plan, change request form, dashboard report, project newsletter, stakeholder register, and stakeholder management plan. Each tool focuses on stakeholder management and will help you run a successful project.

Part III – Project Communication Tools by Process Groups

Chapter 16

Using Communication Tools During the Initiating Process

IN THIS CHAPTER

- ♦ Mastering the Agile Project Vision Statement
- ♦ Mastering the Agile Estimating tools
- ♦ Mastering the Agile User story
- ♦ Mastering Agile User Story backlogs
- ♦ Mastering the Business Case
- ♦ Mastering the Circle-of-Communications chart
- ♦ Mastering the Communication plan
- ♦ Mastering the Customer Requirements tool
- ♦ Mastering the Document Control system
- ♦ Mastering the Executive Summary
- ♦ Mastering the Feasibility Study
- ♦ Mastering the Project Charter document
- ♦ Mastering the Project Kick-off meeting
- ♦ Mastering the Project Management plan
- ♦ Mastering the Project Organization chart
- ♦ Mastering the Project Proposal plan
- ♦ Mastering the Quality Management plan
- ♦ Mastering the Stakeholder Register
- ♦ Mastering the Stakeholder Management plan

In this chapter, we explore the communication tools that you can use to plan project initiation. Project initiation tools are simple to use and critical for starting your project correctly. We've included PMI-based tools and Agile-based tools in this chapter. Each tool in this chapter improves project information that customers, team members, and stakeholders receive by helping you become a better communicator when the project starts. During the project initiation process, you must identify the tools you will use to communicate information to your customers. Understand that even during the startup process, your customers will expect regular project status to ensure that everything is on track and progressing as planned. You are responsible for this communication, not only at the beginning of the project, but throughout the project life cycle. Therefore, it is important to get off to a good solid start and get these best practices in place.

Mastering the Agile Product Vision Statement

Before mastering the *Agile product vision statement,* you need to understand how it can assist and support your project. The following project scenario emphasizes the Agile product vision statement's importance and why it is critical to every Agile development project.

In this scenario, you are the product manager for an innovative mobile application software development company. Your company has successfully delivered several projects using Agile project management and product development techniques in the past. They were small projects with a budget under $100,000 and a delivery schedule under three months. Your vice president of product development told you that your fiercest competitor just released a personal journal mobile application and was first-to-market with this product type. Although your competitor's product has many valuable features, it only allows the user to upload personal journaling information to two types of social media. Because your company has years of expertise in developing different types of mobile apps, and has interfaced with all of the major social media tools, your vice president of product development wants you to develop an application similar to your competitor. The differentiating factor about your product is that it will be able to upload personal journaling information to any available social media apps, which is far more than the two your competitor's product can do. The launch of your product will help your organization gain a competitive advantage by being first-to-market with the ability to upload to any online social media apps and will increase your company's market share and profitability. Your vice president (who is your project sponsor) tells you to use Agile project management and product development techniques. You have also been designated as the project's product owner with an initial budget of $1,000,000 and an initial schedule of six months to complete the project. Armed with this early high-level information, you are ready to use the first tool for an Agile project: the product vision statement.

As the product owner, you are responsible for creating the product vision statement. Therefore, you must know as much information as possible about the product, about the goals, and about the product requirements. You document all of these in your product vision statement so that the completed document describes what the product and project will achieve and becomes the beacon that guides all project activities. The product vision statement is the first document you create for an Agile project, so it is the first communication tool to discover an Agile project's initial scope and requirements. Although it is your responsibility as the product owner to create the product vision statement, you will not have to do it alone. You will need feedback from your customers, management, and team members who have specific subject matter expertise, such as a Scrum master. This enables you to ensure that your product vision statement is clear, written in plain language, and as brief as possible while still stating the project and the product objectives.

Cross-Reference
We recommend that you review the Agile product vision statement in Chapter 6 - Communication Tools That Manage Project Integration for more information.

Creating an Agile product vision statement

To create an effective product vision statement, you need to follow some specific steps, in a specific order. The following steps are best practices for product owners when creating a product vision statement.

1. Determine the product's overall objective. To create a product vision statement, you must understand and effectively communicate the product's objective. This includes answering the following questions:

   - How will the product benefit the organization that is creating it?

- Will the benefits be realized by a specific department in the organization, or by the organization as a whole?

- What specific organizational strategic objectives will the product support?

- Who will use the product?

- Will internal customers or external customers use the product?

- Why does the customer need the product?

- What product features are crucial to the customer?

- How will the product compare with similar products?

- What makes the product different from similar products offered by the competition?

2. Create an initial product vision statement draft. After you possess a solid understanding of the product's objective, you need to create an initial product vision statement draft.

Figure 16.1 — Product Vision Statement Template shows a product vision statement template that is widely used and was adapted from Geoffrey Moore's Product Differentiation statement that he describes in his book, *Crossing the Chasm*. This template enables team members to explain the project to someone within two minutes, also known as an "elevator pitch." Your product vision statement provides clear direction at the beginning of an Agile project to the strategic objectives behind creating the product, and outlines the following:

- What specific product are you developing?

- Who are you building this product for?

- What differentiates this product from similar products on the market?

Figure 16.1 — Product Vision Statement Template

For (target customer)

Who (statement of need/opportunity)

The (product)

Is a (product category)

That (compelling benefit)

Unlike (primary competitive alternative)

Our Product (primary differentiation)

Let's take a more detailed look at the product vision statement template to understand the level of detail to include for each component in order to create an effective product vision statement.

- **Target customer** – Who you are trying to serve? You want your customers to clearly identify with your vision and not just your solution. These customers may be vastly different than customers you are targeting with other products.

- **Statement of need/opportunity** – Your product should solve a specific problem that your target customers are experiencing, so you must understand these problems from their perspective. Be careful not to fit the problem to your solution, but rather fit the solution to the problem.

- **Product** – Based on the target customers you identified and the problem you identified, determine the minimal product you can create to solve the target customers' problem.

- **Product category** – Describe the specific category, class, or product type that you created so that it can be compared to other products in the same category, class, or product type. This enables your target customers to compare "apples to apples" instead of "apples to oranges."

- **Compelling benefit** – Communicate the inherent benefit or value proposition for your product in the eyes of your target customers.

- **Primary competitive alternative** – This may not be something you are used to doing, but you should name your main competitor and their product so that your target customers will know what product to compare your product to in order to clearly understand the differences between them.

- **Primary differentiation** – And finally, specifically state what differentiates your product from your competitor's product so that it serves as an incentive to purchase your product rather than the competitor's product.

3. Perform a final quality check on the draft product vision statement. Before you review the draft product vision statement with the stakeholders, validate that you have followed best practices for creating it. Ask yourself the following questions and make changes to the draft product vision statement accordingly.

- Is the business objective described in your product vision statement specific enough to be attainable?

- Does your product vision statement adequately describe how the product meets the target customers' needs?

- Is your product vision statement clear and focused, and will it provide the Agile project team guidance throughout the project life cycle?

- Does your product vision statement outline the best possible solution to the target customers' needs?

- Is your product vision statement supporting the strategic objectives of the organization for which the Agile project is being executed?

- Does your product vision statement accurately communicate the inherent benefit or product's value proposition in your target customers' eyes?

4. Revise your product vision statement based on stakeholder feedback. When you have created and validated the initial draft per the guidelines above, you can review it with the other product and project stakeholders. This typically occurs during the initial strategy meeting where you (the product owner) and other stakeholders review the product vision statement. The stakeholders may include, but are not limited to:

- **Product stakeholders:** Customers and product users.

- **Project stakeholders:** Management from your own organization or the customer's organization, or other individuals working on other projects—basically, anyone who is affected by the project outcome.

- **Scrum master:** If you execute your project using the Agile framework, there's a good chance you will have a Scrum master on your team, so invite him or her for feedback.

- **Scrum team:** If you already have subject matter experts identified and engaged, or have pre-qualified certain members of your Scrum team to work on the project, include them for their technical feedback.

- **Agile facilitator:** It is often beneficial to include a facilitator who ensures that all of the Agile best practices are being followed as you review and make updates to the product vision statement.

5. Finalize your product vision statement. Similar to most of the other activities in Agile, creating, updating, and finalizing your product vision statement is an iterative process and may require several feedback cycles. You should repeat the process until everyone fully understands the product vision statement and agrees that it is sufficient. After you finalize the product vision statement, you are responsible for ensuring that all stakeholders can access it. Many companies print it on a poster board and post it conspicuously for all to see. This is a form of information radiator used in Agile because it "radiates information" about the product and project objectives. An Agile best practice is also to revisit your product vision statement at least once a year (if the project is greater than one year) to ensure that it is still valid and continues to take into consideration any organizational or market changes that may have occurred since its initial creation.

As is probably now very clear, you, as the product owner, are accountable and responsible for creating your product vision statement and supplying it to the other project stakeholders, both internal and external to your organization. An effective product vision statement clearly outlines the overall product and project objectives and helps increase the likelihood of a successful project.

Tip
Ensure that the product vision statement is very specific, avoids generalizations, and does not include phrases like "increase customer satisfaction," or "make our customers happy." On the other hand, be sure not to delve into too much technical detail and start naming specifics of the end product or product components. We are still at the 50,000-foot level here. And finally, always write your product vision statement in the present tense, as if it already exists. This is very powerful because it helps those who read the statement visualize it as if it's already in use.

Figure 16.2 — Product Vision Statement Example shows a typical product vision statement, using the Geoffrey Moore's template and based on the scenario outlined at the beginning of this chapter for the product vision statement.

Figure 16.2 — Product Vision Statement Example

For (Smart Phone users)

Who (want to journal their daily activities)

The (Life Journal App)

Is a (mobile journaling application)

That (that allows them to track all of their daily activities)

Unlike (the EZ Personal Log mobile journaling application)

Our Product (allows users to upload journaling information to ALL current social media, not just the top two most popular forms of social media)

Product Vision Statement

The product vision statement example below shows a typical product vision statement, using Geoffrey Moore's template and based on the scenario outlined at the beginning of the chapter. This is what is referred to as an elevator pitch, which displays the product vison statement in normal text, as a literal statement, in order to make it more readable.

Product Vision Statement Example

"For Smart Phone users who want to journal their daily activities, the Life Journal App is a mobile journaling application that allows them to track all of their daily activities. Unlike the EZ Personal Log mobile journaling application, our product allows users to upload journaling information to ALL current social media, not just the top two most popular forms of social media."

As you prepare to create your project's product vision statement, make sure to follow this simple and easy-to-follow format for your best chance of success. As you develop additional statements across the various projects you work on, they become easier to create and your customers and leadership become more comfortable with the format.

Using Agile product vision statement

The Product Owner should consider the Agile product vision statement as the "elevator pitch" for their project. The product vision statement should clear, succinct, and follow the template outlined above.

There will be many opportunities to use the product vision statement in the early stages and throughout the life of the project, especially when leadership or customers ask general questions about it. Project Managers will also use the product vision statement as the guide to all project activities. Since the product vision statement is the first document created, the Project Manager will ensure the project is delivering according to the statement, its scope, and its requirements.

Mastering Agile Estimating Tools

Before mastering *Agile estimating tools,* you need to understand how they can assist and support you and your team on your Agile project. The following project scenario emphasizes the importance of these tools, and why Agile estimating tools are critical to every Agile project.

In this scenario, you are the product manager for an innovative mobile application software development company. Your company has successfully delivered several projects using Agile project management and product development techniques in the past. They were small projects with a budget under $100,000 and a delivery schedule under three months. Your vice president of product development told you that your fiercest competitor just released a personal journal mobile application and was first-to-market with this product type. Although your competitor's product has many valuable features, it only allows the user to upload personal journaling information to two types of social media. Because your company has years of expertise in developing different types of mobile apps, and has interfaced with all of the major social media tools, your vice president of product development wants you to develop an application similar to your competitor. The differentiating factor about your product is that it will be able to upload personal journaling information to any available social media apps, which is far more than the two your competitor's product can do. The launch of your product will help your organization gain a competitive advantage by being first-to-market with the ability to upload to any online social media apps and will increase your company's market share and profitability. Your vice president (who is your project sponsor) tells you to use Agile project management and product development techniques. You have also been designated as the project's product owner with an initial budget of $1,000,000 and an initial schedule of six months to complete the project. Armed with this early high-level information, you are ready to use the first tool for an Agile project: the product vision statement.

You already held several strategy meetings with your vice president (who is also your project sponsor) and some additional members of your organization's senior management who are interested stakeholders. Even though your project customer is your vice president of product development, he asked several individuals from the business side of the organization to provide input about end-user requirements, which are critical to the project's success. In addition, you have assigned a Scrum master who you have worked with on previous Agile projects that were successful, as well as several development team members with previous Agile and Scrum experience. All of these individuals were instrumental in creating the following product vision statement, which guides all future project activities and sets the stage for all future scope and development. *"For Smart Phone users who want to journal their daily activities, the Life Journal App is a mobile journaling application that allows them to track all of their daily activities. Unlike the EZ Personal Log mobile journaling application, our product allows users to upload journaling information to ALL current social media apps, not just the two most popular forms of social media."* You can now start decomposing the high-level requirements represented by your product vision statement into themes, features, epic user stories, detailed user stories, and specific tasks to fulfill these requirements.

Cross-Reference
We recommend that you review the Agile estimating tools in Chapter 7 - Defining Communication Tools that Manage Project Scope for more information.

Creating Agile relative sizing

Before we talk specifically about relative sizing, it is important to understand that Agile estimating is part of an overall adaptive planning process in Agile project management. This allows your Agile project to be flexible, which is mainly performed through the incremental delivery of requirements to the customer in the form of user stories. It is also important to understand that estimates are uncertain by definition, and the further out you try to estimate something, the more inaccurate your estimates will be. This is illustrated by a concept known as The "cone of uncertainty." This concept indicates that at the beginning of a project, very little is known about the product or the work required, so your estimates are likely to be inaccurate. However, as you proceed through the project and gain knowledge, your estimates will become progressively more accurate. At the beginning of your Agile project, your best estimates on the level of effort to complete each Agile project requirement can only be relatively sized in comparison to each other. One method of determining the "relative size" is to initially estimate the requirements in terms of T-shirt sizes, from small to extra-large and everything in between. At this point in your Agile project, you just don't have enough information about the requirements to make a definitive estimate. The more knowledge you gain about the requirements as you progress through the Agile project and the creation and decomposition of user stories into estimated story points, the better you understand them, and progressively the more accurate your estimates to completion will become. By continually decomposing user stories down to the lowest level possible, your Agile project team will eventually be able to attach tasks and specific hourly estimates to complete each task within the user stories. This reduces the "uncertainty" of your requirements and narrows the "cone of uncertainty" as you get a better understanding of the Agile project requirements, all the way down to the task level.

Figure 16.3 — The Cone of Uncertainty shows a "cone of uncertainty" example. As you can see, T-shirt sizing is used first, and then story point values are assigned to each T-shirt size, which are then used to further decompose user stories all the way down to the task level, where actual hourly estimates can be made in terms of work effort.

Figure 16.3 — The Cone of Uncertainty

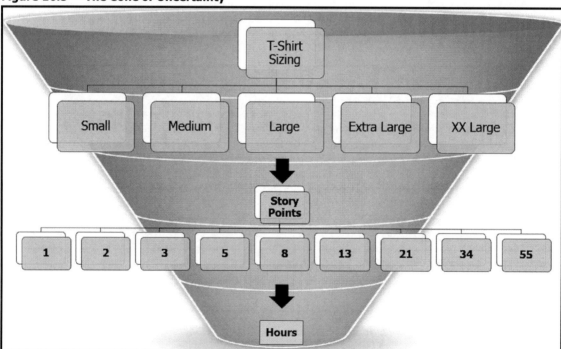

To estimate the requirements on your Agile projects, use relative sizing for the requirements' size estimation. Relative sizing allows you to estimate the "level of effort" a user story will take to complete, relative to the other user stories you perform on your Agile project. In other words, how much effort a requirement (or "user story") will take compared to the effort it will take to complete the other requirements (or "user stories") on your Agile project. It is also very important to understand that relative sizing does not equate to a specific unit of time. It does not equate to minutes, hours, days, months, or years. It simply compares the effort required to complete each user story "relative" to the other user stories on your Agile project, and then determines which will take more time and effort and which will take less time and effort. Relative sizing helps provide a "high-level" estimate of project difficulty throughout the project life cycle and, therefore, how much time and effort the project will take to complete. The unit of measure for relative sizing is typically defined by story points, a unit of measure that describes the amount of effort it will take to complete a user story without equating it to a specific unit of time.

Relative sizing is based on a technique called affinity estimating. This is a consensus-based technique that is quickly and easily estimates the effort required for a large number of user stories. This technique is very helpful when you start a new project and you need to estimate a large product backlog. When using the affinity estimating technique, you need to complete some specific steps, in a specific order, to create effective estimates. Complete the following steps as best practices for affinity estimating and relative estimating.

1. A facilitator reviews the user stories with the project team. First, a facilitator reviews all of the user stories with the entire project team. This is quite often the product owner.

2. Without talking to each other, the team works together to arrange the stories in size order. When the team's questions about user stories have been answered, the team silently works together to arrange the user stories by the amount of effort to complete them. You can use T-shirt sizes, such as small, medium, large, extra-large, or some other unit of measure if you like. On Agile projects, many teams arrange "sticky notes" on a white board or index cards on a table. However you do it, it's important that no one talks while arranging the user stories.

3. The facilitator leads a discussion of the initial estimate. When the team is done arranging the user stories into appropriate size categories, the facilitator leads a discussion based on everyone's initial sizing estimate. Everyone gets a chance to question the estimates and a chance to state their case for why they believe an estimate to be inaccurate, as well as offer additional comments.

4. The team has additional opportunities to silently make adjustments until they reach a consensus for all user stories. When everyone's cases have been stated and opinions have been voiced, the team has a second opportunity to silently make adjustments to initial estimates. Following the adjustments, the facilitator opens the floor for further discussion and adjustments and the process continues until a consensus is reached and all of the user stories have an estimate.

Figure 16.4 — T-shirt Sizing Example shows an example that uses T-shirt sizing (small, medium, large, and extra-large) for relative estimating of user stories on an Agile project.

Figure 16.4 — T-shirt Sizing Example

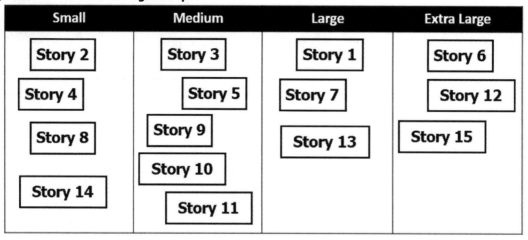

Using Agile relative sizing

The project team uses the Agile relative sizing information in determining the size of each user story. The size of each user story is stated in story points. Once that information is known and story points are determined, the Agile project team can slot the story points into each sprint to determine the length of the project. Based on the size of the team and the length of the sprint, the project team often has to spread the story points across multiple sprints of the project.

The Agile team will continue to use the relative sizing process throughout the project, as well as when new items are added to the Product Backlog. The User Stories at the top of the Product Backlog should be estimated more precisely than those of lower priority.

Creating Agile story points

Story points can help you make more accurate estimates during the relative sizing process to estimate the level of effort to complete your Agile project's requirements. Story points are an Agile best practice because they are the most effective unit of measure for estimating the level of effort to complete user stories. However, it is important to remember that story points do not represent a specific unit of time. During release planning meetings and subsequent meetings with the customer and the Agile project team, story points determine the relative level of effort for each user story compared to the other user stories. You may be wondering how these values are determined for story points. Following are recommended steps that are best practice for an Agile project team to determine story point values for a specific Agile project's requirements.

1. Select a requirement that the team considers a medium level of effort. First, your team selects one theme, feature, or user story from your product roadmap that they are fairly confident of the level of effort it will take to complete. This may be a user story that team members have previous experience developing and a fairly good idea how much time and effort it will take to complete. That user story then becomes the team's benchmark.

2. Use the Fibonacci sequence to establish story point values. After the team determines the medium-sized benchmark user story, they start the estimating process by using story points to assign a benchmark numeric value. The Fibonacci sequence is very effective in helping to estimate user stories on your project. The Fibonacci sequence is a number sequence for Agile estimating that

helps establish story point values on your Agile projects. The mathematical equation for the Fibonacci sequence is Fn = Fn-1 + Fn-2, where "F" is the next number in the sequence, and "n" represents the previous numbers in the sequence. In plain language, each number in the sequence is determined by adding the previous two numbers. Therefore, the Fibonacci sequence starts with one, then one plus one equals two, then two plus one equals three, then three plus two equals five, and so on. For example, let's say your project team reaches a consensus that a medium-sized requirement is assigned the Fibonacci sequence number 55. You will then evaluate your project's other user stories by comparing them with the benchmark of 55 story points. If a user story takes about the same time and effort as your benchmark, you can assign it 55 story points as well. Anything considered smaller than medium is scored as 1, 2, 3, 5, 8, 13, 21, or 34. Anything larger than medium is scored as 89, 144, and so on, based on the Fibonacci sequence.

Using Agile story points

Agile project teams will use the results of the user story process to determine how many user stories they are able to complete in a sprint. The results of this process will also allow the team to understand exactly how many story points the project will entail. If using the 55-story point baseline for medium size projects, teams will quickly understand the breakdown of requirements into small, medium, large and extra-large buckets. Project teams will continue to use the story point estimates for determining how many Sprints the project will contain.

Creating Agile Planning Poker

Agile *Planning Poker* is a variation of the Wideband Delphi technique that makes the most accurate estimates as possible and helps you avoid the risk of having one influential or overly persuasive team member controlling the estimates. Team members make their estimates individually and without any undue influence from other team members. When using the Planning Poker technique, it is an Agile best practice and strongly recommended that you use story points as the unit of work effort.

Note
Anchoring occurs when one team member exerts an undue influence on the rest of the team. If each individual on an Agile project team simply "makes a case" for why his or her estimate is the "best," "most correct," or "most accurate," the first person who speaks up sometimes has a greater influence than anyone else. Whatever he or she says influences everyone else. Teams can also be influenced by strong-willed or dominant team members who may or may not have an agenda, but who argue forcefully. Planning Poker for Agile estimating helps prevent this from happening.

Planning Poker is a consensus-based technique, meaning everyone works together to come up with the most accurate estimate. An estimate calculated by the Agile project team is much more accurate than an individual team member's estimate. The following steps are recommended best practices to conduct a Planning Poker session.

1. Give each project team member a deck of Planning Poker cards. Each team member receives a deck of Planning Poker cards that have the Fibonacci sequence numbers 1 to 144 on them. The deck also includes a Question Mark card, which means you need more information; an Infinity or Googol card, which means the user story is so large that you cannot possibly estimate it; and the all-important Coffee Cup card, which literally means that it's time to take a break. The cards can be pre-printed, created manually on index cards, or even found as an app on a mobile device. In addition to the Planning Poker cards that you can create or buy, there are also collaborative

software products that enable you to play Planning Poker when your team members are not located in the same geographic region.

2. The facilitator reads each user story and team members ask questions. As with Wideband Delphi and affinity estimating, Agile best practices dictate that Planning Poker be chaired by a facilitator, who does not participate. The facilitator reads each user story that needs estimating, and team members ask questions to clarify specific requirements in the user story and discuss any constraints or assumptions they have about a particular user story.

3. Project team members estimate the value of the user story. Following each user story discussion, each team member places his or her card face down to represent the estimate. After the facilitator counts to three, each team member simultaneously shows his or her Planning Poker card for that user story. If the majority of team members are centered on the "median" then there is not much more to discuss. However, if there are outliers—anyone who thinks that the estimated effort on a user story is much less or much more work than the median—they make a case for their reasoning and further discussion continues about the user story. This process continues until a consensus is reached or until a pre-arranged number of rounds have been completed. An Agile best practice is to complete a maximum of three rounds of Planning Poker estimation for each user story. If a consensus cannot be reached, the facilitator decides the story point value for that particular user story, and the team moves on to estimate the next user story.

Figure 16.5 — Planning Poker Deck Using a Fibonacci Sequence Example shows an example of a typical Planning Poker card deck using the Fibonacci sequence.

Figure 16.5 — Planning Poker Deck Using a Fibonacci Sequence Example

Using Agile Planning Poker

Agile project teams will use the results of the Agile Planning Poker process to estimate how much work each requirement or user story will require. After going through the planning poker process once to create a baseline, the project team members will use that baseline number to create the remaining estimates during the planning poker process. Once all iterations are complete and all requirements estimated, the project team can determine the scope of each sprint. By refining these estimates, the project team will have a better understanding of the project and its timeline.

After jointly reviewing the results of the planning poker process, the Agile team will work with the Product Owner to update the Product Backlog. The Agile team will continue to use the planning poker process as new requirements come into the backlog and have not been estimated or assigned to an iteration.

Creating Agile team velocity

On Agile projects, teams use velocity to plan how much future work the development team can accomplish for upcoming sprints. Velocity is also used to make commitments for the amount of work the development team expects to perform in the next sprint. Therefore, in order to estimate more efficiently and confidently, long-term at the release level and overall project level, it is important to know the development team's velocity. Velocity is simply the number of story points that can be completed within a specific Agile project time frame, such as a sprint. It is the rate that the development team can deliver value to the customer. In other words, velocity tells you how much work can be done in a given time frame. This is the Agile team's measure of the throughput, per sprint, and the rate at which the development team delivers value. Velocity is one of the most common Agile metrics. Following are some important velocity characteristics for an Agile development team.

- The principal concept behind velocity is to help Agile development teams with the estimated work to implement a requirement for user stories in a given time period. Velocity measures how quickly work was performed, and how much work was performed during a specific sprint, compared to how quickly work was performed and how much work was performed during previous sprints.

- For the Agile development team, velocity is an essential component of iterative planning because it helps the team make commitments up front, with confidence, and is based on empirical data gathered from velocity performance of previous sprints.

- Velocity cannot be calculated until after the first sprint is complete, at which time velocity can be computed and the result can be used as a benchmark for subsequent sprints. After each sprint, the project team's velocity changes, requiring the average velocity to be recalculated to produce a more accurate estimate for future work performance. Average velocity is calculated after each sprint, becoming more accurate over time, and normally stabilizing after three to six sprints, eventually plateauing and becoming fairly constant and predictable.

- For accurate average velocity measurements, each sprint should be the same length throughout the project life cycle. It may take a few sprints to determine the optimal length, but once the length is determined, it shouldn't change. If sprints have different lengths throughout the project, the amount of work the team can perform in each sprint will be different, and it will be impossible to determine the team's average velocity per sprint. It would be like comparing apples to oranges.

- Each development team member should work the same number of hours during each sprint, and the entire development team's total number of hours worked during each sprint should also be consistent throughout the entire project.

- It is important, but not always possible, that the same development team members remain on the team throughout the project life cycle.

- When sprint lengths, work hours, and team members remain consistent throughout a project, velocity can be effectively used as a measurement to determine if the development team's work performance speed is increasing or decreasing. This helps to accurately estimate the remaining time to complete the project at any point during the project life cycle.

Note

Forecasted velocity is an estimate of team velocity when it is either impossible or impractical for the team to execute a series of sprints to determine average velocity, or when you do not yet possess enough empirical data to determine velocity. This normally occurs at the beginning of a new Agile project that has no similarity to previous Agile projects. In this case, it is truly a "guestimate" for the starting point of a team's velocity that is updated and becomes much more accurate after the first few sprints because it will be based on empirical data.

Agile estimating tools are an integral part of the adaptive planning process that you must perform on your Agile projects. For Agile project teams, you must continuously re-estimate after each successive sprint and release so that you can eventually determine your development team's average velocity, which you can use as an empirical measure of project performance in terms of cost and schedule throughout your Agile project.

Using Agile team velocity

The Agile team will use velocity to measure the team's per-sprint performance. Velocity is defined as the number of story points a team can commit to and successfully complete during a sprint. The more sprints the team completes, the more information that is provided to refine the team's estimates for each sprint.

Project or Scrum masters typically often produce and express team velocity data in charts and graphics. Management and leadership are often interested in evaluating the performance of each team, including whether they are met the goals they set. Most Agile teams require a number of sprints before reaching maximum capacity, with normal velocity typically stabilizing after 5-6 sprints. The reason for the slow start for most project teams is unfamiliarity with their teammates; project team members tend to produce greater results once they develop a rhythm over time.

Mastering Agile User Stories

Before exploring *Agile user stories,* you need to understand how they can assist and support you on your Agile project. The following project scenario emphasizes the importance of user stories and how they are critical to every Agile project.

In this scenario, you are the product manager for an innovative mobile application software development company. Your company has successfully delivered several projects using Agile project management and product development techniques in the past. They were small projects with a budget under $100,000 and a delivery schedule under three months. Your vice president of product development told you that your fiercest competitor just released a personal journal mobile application and was first-to-market with this product type. Although your competitor's product has many valuable features, it only allows the user to upload personal journaling information to two types of social media. Because your company has years of expertise in developing different types of mobile apps, and has interfaced with all of the major social media tools, your vice president of product development wants you to develop an application similar to your competitor. The differentiating factor about your product is that it will be able to upload personal journaling information to any available social media apps, which is far more than the two your competitor's product can do. The launch of your product will help your organization gain a competitive advantage by being first-to-market with the ability to upload to any online social media apps and will increase your company's market share and profitability. Your vice president (who is your project sponsor) tells you to use Agile project management and product development techniques. You have also been designated as the project's product owner with an initial budget of $1,000,000 and an initial schedule of six months to complete the project.

You already held several strategy meetings with your vice president (who is also your project sponsor) and some additional members of your organization's senior management who are interested stakeholders. Even though your project customer is your vice president of product development, he has included several individuals from the business side of the organization to provide input about end-user requirements, which are critical to the project's success. In addition, you have assigned a Scrum master who you have worked with on previous Agile projects that were successful, as well as several development team members with previous Agile and Scrum experience. All of these individuals were instrumental in creating the following product vision statement, which guides all future project activities and sets the stage for all future scope and development. *"For Smart Phone users who want to journal their daily activities, the Life Journal App is a mobile journaling application that allows them to track all of their daily activities. Unlike the EZ Personal Log mobile journaling application, our product allows users to upload journaling information to ALL current social media, not just the top two most popular forms of social media."*

Cross-Reference
We recommend that you review the Agile user stories in Chapter 7 - Defining Communication Tools that Manage Project Scope for more information.

Creating Agile epic user stories

After creating your initial product vision statement from your strategy meetings, you will continue decomposing project and product requirements by creating epic user stories that further define the requirements. Epic user stories are created during Agile release planning meetings and are based on the initial list of product features that were identified as part of the strategy meeting to create the initial product roadmap. When creating an epic user story, complete the following steps to ensure that you create an effective story statement.

Note

Agile project management incorporates two different types of user stories. At the beginning of the project, usually during the release planning meetings in the planning phase, very high-level requirements are captured in epic user stories. These are basically the 50,000-foot view of project and product requirements. Be careful not to delve into too much detail here, but rather concentrate on capturing only high-level requirements at the product feature level.

1. Identify specific project stakeholders. You most likely have a good idea about who your project stakeholders are, which is probably anyone involved with your project or who will be positively or negatively affected by your project's outcome. Naturally, these also include those individuals who helped you create the product vision statement. Other stakeholders may include, but are not limited to, the following:

    -   Individuals with technical expertise who work with the final applications and systems that will be integrated with the product.

    -   Compliance personnel from federal agencies, such as the Federal Communications Commission (FCC).

    -   Individuals in a support position who may need to interact with end users to answer questions and solve problems.

    -   Marketing personnel in your organization who need training on specific product functionality in order to effectively market and sell the product.

    -   Scrum team members who may already have specific expertise in developing these types of products for previous Agile products.

2. Identify specific product customers and end users. After you have identified your project stakeholders, you need to identify your customers and end users. Minimally, a representative from your business partners should be included when writing epic user stories. When writing epic user stories, another Agile best practice is to include a cross-section of end users who will actually be using the product. Personas are also useful when creating epic user stories. For more information about personas, see Introducing the Agile User Story in Chapter 7 - Defining Communication Tools that Manage Project Scope.

3. Create an initial epic user story. After you determine your stakeholders, customers, and end users, you can start creating epic stories on your Agile project. Bring everyone together in a release planning meeting and develop the 50,000-foot level requirements that you want to deliver in the first product release. Epic user stories represent product features and high-level functionality.

Figure 16.6 — Agile Epic User Story Example shows an example of an epic user story in a template that Agile project management teams often use. This specific template is generally accepted as a best practice for creating user stories on Agile projects. This template is usually created as a 3" × 5" or 4" × 6" printed card that has the user story information on the front and the acceptance criteria on the back.

Figure 16.6 — Agile Epic User Story Example

User Story (front)

ID # : 1
Title: Life Journal App Login
As a Registered Life Journal App user
I want to log in to the Life Journal App on my cell phone
so that I can access the journaling history that I have previously entered into the app.

Value =	Priority =
Estimate =	Owner =

Acceptance Criteria (back)

When I do this:	This happens:
Log in with my registered 4-8 character ID and registered 4-8 character password	my previously entered journaling history is displayed
Try to log in with an unregistered ID	an error that explains my ID and/or password is incorrect is displayed

Let's take a more detailed look at the components on the front of the epic user story card so you understand what you need for each component.

- **ID #:** A number assigned to each user story for future reference and sorting. When the first user story is created on an Agile project, it is assigned a value of 1, and each successive user story is numbered in succession as 2, 3, and so on for each user story. The product owner can sort user stories by ID # in the document repository, such as Microsoft Excel.

- **Title:** The user story title should be descriptive enough to describe the user story requirements, and unique enough that it can be distinguished from other project user stories.

- **As a:** The main user for your product who you distinguish from other types of users. Here is where using personas is especially useful because you can identify different types of users who have similar product functionality requirements.

- **I want to:** A specific action that an end user will perform when using the product in order to bring about an expected result.

- **So that:** The specific result that the end user expects to happen when using the product and performing the action described under **I want to**.

Now, let's look at the back of the epic user story card. The back of the card is extremely important because each user story must have acceptance criteria that specifically indicate whether the user story will be accepted by the end user based on the criteria outlined here. This acceptance criteria will eventually be added as acceptance tests when the development team delivers the specific functionality to the customer at the end of an Agile project sprint.

- **When I do this:** A subset of actions that the end user will perform that are contained under **I want to** component on the front of the user story card. These are specific actions that the user will perform after a user story has been completed that validates the user story's completion.

- **This happens:** A statement of expected functionality that the customer must approve after the development team has delivered the user story functionality to the customer to help ensure that the user story meets all of the customer requirements. The customer won't sign off on a user story until the user story acceptance criteria have been met. This statement (**this happens**) is the expected result when the user performs the action of the user story functionality.

  - Revise the epic user story based on stakeholder, customer, and end-user feedback. After you initially create an epic user story, you review it with other stakeholders, customers, and end users. The review also occurs during the release planning meeting. The customer or end user writes an initial epic user story and presents it to the product owner. The product owner will then ask the customer specific questions so that both the product owner and the customer fully understand the customer needs for this specific epic user story. This is usually an iterative process and continues until both parties feel they have fully captured that specific epic user story requirement, which they then mutually approve.

  - Finalize the epic user story. Similar to other activities in Agile, creating, updating, and finalizing epic user stories is an iterative process and may require several feedback cycles. You should repeat this process until everyone fully understands the epic user story that has been created and agrees that it is sufficient. After you finalize the epic user story and everyone feels that the specific epic user story requirement has been captured, the epic user story is considered mutually approved and you can move on to create the next epic user story. This process continues until all product functionality for this release is captured at the feature level in the form of epic user stories.

Using Agile epic user stories

At the beginning of an Agile project, the project team knows very little about the customer's specific requirements. User stories are created at a very high level, or epic level, during the release planning meeting. There is not much detail at this stage in the project, but it is important to create these statements as a starting point for requirements or feature definitions and initial estimating. The epic user stories will be decomposed throughout the project until they are detailed enough to assign the necessary tasks to complete them. In addition, at the beginning of an Agile project, it makes no sense for a project team to spend an inordinate amount of time creating detailed user stories and attempting to determine definitive estimates to complete them. There just isn't enough information up front to spend this time wisely. Only when the team is ready to assign a definitive hourly estimate to a user story (which only occurs in the "current" sprint) is it worth spending time to go into the lowest level of detail (the "task" level) on each user story.

It is also important to note that you don't need to create all epic user stories at the beginning of the project. Both Agile project management and Agile product development are, by their very nature, flexible and iterative. This means that before each major product functionality release, the product owner meets with the customer, development team, Scrum master, and other important stakeholders in a release planning meeting. This ensures that specific epic user stories are created and then decomposed into smaller user stories on a release-by-release basis, instead of decomposing all of them at the beginning of the project.

Creating detailed Agile user stories

After the epic user stories are created for an upcoming release, you and customer work together to continue decomposing project and product requirements by breaking down the epic user stories into smaller user stories that further define the requirements. Decomposition is a technique that is not exclusively implemented on Agile projects, but is also used extensively on waterfall projects. (Does the work breakdown structure (WBS) come to mind?) It consists of breaking down large sets of customer requirements into smaller and smaller pieces until they can be understood and implemented by the development team. For Agile projects, this means breaking down Agile project requirements (such as features represented at the release level as epic user stories) into smaller, more defined project requirements (such as user stories), and also into even smaller project requirements (such as the associated tasks within each user story that need to be performed in order to complete the user stories during each sprint).

You must work continuously with the customer to break down requirements from the epic level to the detailed user story level, based on when the requirements need to be completed in the project life cycle. Meanwhile, the development team works on the specific requirements that have been broken down to the detailed user story level so that they can assign specific tasks, hourly estimates, and resources to complete the user stories and to satisfy the lowest level of customer requirements. As a metaphor, think about highway construction through the center of a mountain, where the mountainside is broken down into boulders, which are broken down into rocks, which are broken down into stones, which are eventually broken down into gravel, and ultimately broken down into dirt or sand.

The format and the tasks you perform to create detailed user stories are the same as those used to create epic user stories. You may be wondering when you know that a detailed user story is broken down into its lowest form. The answer is that 1) if you can decompose a user story to the level where you can identify specific project tasks to assign to specific resources, time estimates, and cost estimates; 2) and if you can list the tasks in the user story; 3) and if you can use the acceptance criteria as a checklist to indicate that the user story is 100% complete and accepted, then you have properly decomposed that detailed user story. Bill Wake created a specific Agile approach to help those creating detailed user stories to help determine when they have successfully decomposed a user story to the lowest level by using the mnemonic, "INVEST" approach. The INVEST approach is a common Agile best practice for determining when a user story has been completely decomposed, and ready to have tasks, resources, hourly estimates, and cost estimates assigned to it. The INVEST mnemonic is a very useful reminder of the major characteristics of effective user stories on your Agile projects. Following is a description of the components of this mnemonic:

- **Independent:** The user story should stand on its own and be independent of any other user stories to implement the product function that the user story describes.

- **Negotiable:** The user story should not be overly detailed, but should leave room for discussion and expansion of details.

- **Valuable:** The user story should demonstrate product value to the customer.

- **Estimable**: The user story should be descriptive, accurate, and concise so that those who are completing the user story can accurately estimate the necessary work to create the desired functionality.

- **Small:** The effort to complete the user story should not take a team member more than half an iteration to complete.

- **Testable:** The user story results should be definitive so that you can easily validate that they match the acceptance criteria.

Figure 16.7 — Detailed Agile User Story Example shows an example of a more detailed user story than an epic user story. Notice that the format and template is the same for any type of user story. This example contains more specific requirements' functionality, as well as more detailed acceptance criteria than the previous epic user story example.

Figure 16.7 — Detailed Agile User Story Example

User Story (front)
ID # : 1013
Title: Newly Registered Life Journal App Initial Customer Access
As a Newly Registered Life Journal App Customer
I want to successfully log in to the Life Journal App for the first time
so that I can start using the New Life Journal App functionality.

Value =	34 Story Points	**Priority =**	97
Estimate =	68 Hours	**Owner =**	Kevin Reilly

Acceptance Criteria (back)

When I do this:	This happens:
Connect to the Life Journal App web site for the first time	a prompt is displayed asking whether I am a new or existing user.
A prompt is displayed asking whether I am a new or existing user and I select the 'New User' button	a prompt is displayed that allows me to enter my user information.
Finish entering my new user information	a prompt is displayed indicating that an email has be sent to me with final instructions on how to access my newly-created New Life Journal App Customer Login.

Let's take a look at the remaining sections on the front of the user story card that weren't covered in the previous example.

- **Value:** The value of a user story in terms of story points. Story points are the preferred method to estimate the level of effort for specific user stories on an Agile project. During release planning meetings and subsequent meetings with the customer and Agile project team, you use story points to determine the relative level of effort for each user story compared to the other user stories.

- **Estimate:** The hours that the development team estimates a user story will take to complete 100% of the tasks. The estimate is determined at the beginning of each sprint during the sprint planning meeting.

- **Priority:** The priority that the user story is assigned at any point during the project. One of the product owner's main responsibilities is to constantly reprioritize the user stories with the customer throughout the course of the project, based on the highest value to the customer and/or the highest risk to the project at any particular time; this represents that priority.

- **Owner:** The development team member who is responsible for completing the user story. Although this individual may not personally complete all of the user story tasks, he or she is responsible for 100% of the tasks contained in this specific user story and is accountable for ensuring that the functionality is delivered, as specified, to the customer.

Using detailed Agile user stories

Detailed user stories are the required project features and functionality in the product backlog that have been decomposed to the lowest level. This means that specific tasks can be attached to these user stories, with hourly estimates to perform each task and specific resources assigned to perform each task. Agile project teams employ user stories to quickly address customer requirements without creating detailed and formal requirements documents, as is common in traditional product development. The user story enables you to respond quicker and with less overhead to fluid real-world environments. In essence, the user story follows the concept of "adapting." The user story is also written from the user's perspective and always includes acceptance criteria, which is also written by the user. This ensures that when the development team completes the tasks for each user story, the user will "accept" the user story based on these criteria.

User stories go through various stages of the development process, and those stages are tracked on a storyboard. A storyboard is typically a whiteboard divided into sections that represent the product delivery process. The storyboard provides a clear view of the overall status of the user stories as they travel through the development process. It is also important to note that user stories are not contractual agreements. After you create epic user stories for an upcoming release, the product owner and customer continue decomposing the project and product requirements by breaking down the epic user stories into smaller user stories that further define the requirements. The decomposition process continues until the final product is delivered to the customer.

Hopefully, we indicated the important role that user stories play in an Agile project. It is one of your primary responsibilities to work with the customer, end users, development team, and any other stakeholders who have valuable input about the requirements to effectively create user stories throughout the Agile project life cycle. It is also crucial that the product owner and the customer understand and become proficient at properly creating user stories at the release level and the sprint level. Understanding specific customer requirements by properly creating user stories will help you ensure that the customer receives the requested functionality as determined by the requirements, and that 100% of the functionality is delivered according to the acceptance criteria outlined in the user stories that represent the requirements.

Mastering Agile User Story Backlogs

Before mastering *Agile user story backlogs,* you need to understand how they can assist and support you on your Agile project. The following project scenario emphasizes the importance of Agile user story backlogs, and why they are critical to every Agile project.

You are the owner and principal consultant for a project management training company. You have been offering classes for project management certification for many years now, but have been concentrating on one specific certification based on traditional/waterfall project management. Although Agile project management has been around for over a decade, and was originally specific to software development, it is now becoming extremely popular in all types of industries, especially in construction, information technology, and healthcare management. As a matter of fact, it is so popular that it is becoming a prerequisite for many existing project managers to learn before being promoted, obtaining a new position, or consulting on projects that need to be executed quickly and efficiently. To take advantage of the new demand for Agile project management, you decide to create an Agile Project Management certification course that you can offer to existing customers who have attended your previous traditional project management courses, as well as those with no previous experience in traditional project management. This course will be offered in a live, two-day, boot camp format and online as a self-study course. Because you already have experience creating the curriculum for these types of courses, the tasks to create the new courses will be fairly straightforward, and you can do the majority of the wok yourself. However, to gain a competitive advantage, you decide to create a third course to combine live study with online homework and exam preparation for your Agile project management students. This will be a synchronous course where students will dial in for 90 minutes each week for 11 weeks, and you will coach them on the best way to prepare for the new Agile project management certification exam. Because you don't have any experience creating this type of course, you hired a consultant to work with you throughout the project. You decide that this project is a good candidate for using Agile best practices because you have been executing projects using Agile best practices for a while. You are currently in the eighth sprint of a total of 10 sprints in the current release and you developed a product vision statement, a product backlog, a release backlog, and sprint backlogs for each sprint.

Cross-Reference
We recommend that you review the Agile user story product backlog in Chapter 7 - Defining Communication Tools that Manage Project Scope for more information.

Creating the Agile user story product backlog

After creating the initial product vision statement from your strategy meetings and continuing to decompose project and product requirements, you will have created some epic user stories that further define the requirements. The Agile product backlog is the first Agile user story backlog that is created for an Agile project. After the product owner creates the product roadmap and the release plan, some high-level features will have been identified. These are the first entries when initially creating the product backlog. Even though these are still at the feature level, and may not have even been decomposed yet at the epic user story level, this is where user stories are first documented. The artifact to be the user story repository is the product backlog.

Figure 16.8 — Agile Product Backlog Example shows a product backlog example using a template in a format that is often used by Agile project management teams.

Figure 16.8 — Agile Product Backlog Example

ID#	User Story Title	User Story	Relative Estimate	Story Points	Priority	Owner	When I do this	This happens
6	Slide Design	As a product owner I want our course presentation slides for all calls to have the same design so that we have consistency in "look and feel" in the presentations	Medium	4	1	Kevin	When I open any of the call PPTX files	They have the same design
12	Sales Page Draft	As product owner I want a draft of the "Live" product page to be available as soon as possible so that we can continue to tweak it	Medium	12	2	Roberto	When I go to the KRPM website	I can see the draft page and tweak it
13	Waiting List Process	As a product owner I want a defined process that explains how we will handle the waiting list for the Pilot Class	Small	2	3	Kevin	When I read the process	I know how we handle the waiting list
1	Early Bird List	As a product owner I want people to be able to sign up to a announcement mailing list as soon as possible, so that they can be informed about news of the pilot class	Medium	16	4	Kevin	When I go to the KRPM website	I can sign up for a "Live" announcement newsletter
7	Agenda Draft	As a product owner I want a draft of the course agenda to be available so that it can be expanded	Medium	8	5	Kevin/Roberto	When I open the course agenda	I can see the draft agenda for all calls
9	Budget	As a product owner I want to know how much profit/loss the product will likely be making so that I am aware of any losses	Medium	8	6	Roberto	When I look at the budget for the class	I can see profit/loss
10	Pilot Price	As a product owner I want the price for the Pilot Class to be published as soon as possible to that we can market the heck out of this thing.	X-Small	1	7	Roberto	When I look at the budget for the pilot class	I can see the price each student has to pay
18	Online Forum	As a student, I want to access an online location to get additional questions answered so that I don't hog the time available to other students during the live calls.	Large	32	8	Kevin	Why I enter a question in the Online Forum	I receive an answer within 24 hours
8	Coaching Platform	As a coach, I want the live coaching calls to be done via a stable platform so that I don't have to worry about technical details	Large	32	9	Kevin	When I am being told which system to use for the calls	I will trust that the system is a good one
15	Admin Assistant	As a product owner I want to have the role of KRPM Admin Assistant assigned early on so that this person can be brought up to speed	X-Small	1	10	Roberto	When I ask Roberto who it is	He can give me 2 names (primary and backup)

Let's look at the components of the product backlog to understand what is needed for each component.

- **ID #:** A number assigned to each user story for future reference and sorting. When the first user story is created on an Agile project, it is assigned a value of 1, and each successive user story is numbered in succession as 2, 3, and so on for each user story. The product owner can sort user stories by ID # in the document repository, such as Microsoft Excel.

Note

Although you can use any software application as a user story repository, many Agile project managers and product owners use Microsoft Excel because of its built-in sorting features.

- **User Story Title:** The user story title should be descriptive enough to describe the user story requirements, and unique enough that it can be distinguished from other project user stories.

- **User Story:** This is the actual user story text written by the customer, which is the main vehicle used to capture the customer's requirements. All user stories should follow a specific template throughout the project in order to ensure consistency.

- **Relative Estimate:** During the initial strategy meetings, features, themes, and epic user stories are created, but there is not yet sufficient information to decompose them down to the detailed user story level. The project team can only rank them according to their level of effort "relative" to the other epic user stories that have been created. T-shirt sizing is often used for relative sizing. In this example, user story #6, "Slide Design" was assigned the medium level of effort, and the other user stories in the product backlog were sized relative to this specific user story.

- **Story Points:** This is the value of the user story in story points. Story points are the preferred method for estimating the level of effort to complete specific user stories on an Agile project. During release planning meetings, and subsequent meetings with the customer and the Agile project team, you will use story points to determine the relative level of effort for each user story compared to the other user stories.

- **Priority:** The priority that the user story was assigned at any point during the project. One of the product owner's main responsibilities is to constantly re-prioritize the user stories with the customer throughout the course of the project, based on the highest value to the customer and/or highest risk to the project at any particular time. This represents that priority.

- **Owner:** The development team member who is responsible for completing the user story. Although this individual may not personally complete all of the user story tasks, he or she is responsible for all of the tasks in this specific user story and is accountable for ensuring that the functionality is delivered, as specified, to the customer.

- **When I do this:** This is the specific result that the end user expects to occur when using the product and performing the action described above, in terms of what the product will do when they perform this action.

- **This happens:** A statement of expected functionality that the customer must approve after the development team has delivered the user story functionality to the customer to help ensure that the user story meets all of the customer requirements. The customer won't sign off on a user story until the user story acceptance criteria have been met. This statement is the expected result when the user performs the action of the user story functionality.

Using the Agile user story product backlog

The product backlog is the ordered list of all product requirements on an Agile project and serves as the single source for all of the requirements. It is a dynamic document and evolves as the product evolves. It contains the features to build, functions, requirements, non-functional requirements, and acceptance criteria for each requirement. Higher-ranked user stories are usually more detailed because they need to be estimated by the project team for upcoming sprints. Lower-ranked user stories may not even get developed, or they may be deferred if user story priorities change during the project. The product owner is ultimately responsible for creating and maintaining the product backlog. Maintenance is also referred to as product backlog "grooming" when the product owner constantly adds more detail and order to the user stories. As the project progresses, the product owner works with the customer to decompose epic user stories into more detailed user stories, and reprioritizes them in anticipation of the next product release and the next sprint. While the development team is completing the detailed user stories in the current sprint, the product owner is continually grooming the product backlog to determine which user stories should be queued up to be completed in upcoming sprints.

Creating the Agile user story release backlog

After you create the initial product vision statement and the initial product backlog (during the Agile strategy meeting), as well as creating the product roadmap and release plan (during the Agile release planning meeting), you will need to determine which user stories will be contained within the sprints of the project's first release. The specific order in which the project user stories need to be completed (based on their value to the customer, risk to the project, and dependencies on each other) is outlined in the release plan. The release plan subdivides the user stories in the product roadmap into specific releases, and you will need to create a separate release backlog for each release. During the initial release planning meeting, the length of each sprint is determined, as well as the number of sprints in each release. You will also create a release goal, which describes the overall release goals and which features you expect to deliver at the end of the release. At this point, the product owner takes all of the initial product backlog user stories that have been identified for the first release and adds them to the release backlog. The release backlog is a subset of the overall product backlog and represents the user stories that the development team plans to develop and deliver as part of this release.

Figure 16.9 — Agile Release Backlog Example shows an example of a release backlog in a format that is often used by Agile project management teams.

Figure 16.9 — Agile Release Backlog Example

Release Title: Life Journel App Project
Release Dates: May 30, 2019 - August 1, 2019

Release Goal

As a <instructor>,
I want to <ensure all materials are finalized>
So I can <conduct the first class with
confidence>.

Release Hour Information — Working Hrs/day

Release Hour Information	Working Hrs/day	
Number of working days		100
Kevin (40 hrs wk)	8	800
Roberto (40 hrs wk)	8	800
Sprint Length = 2 Weeks	Total:	1600
Number of Sprints = 10	Total per Sprint:	160

User Story List and Estimated Hours Remaining

User Story	Story Points	Status	Owner	PO Approved/User Story Complete?	5-30	6-06	6-13	6-20	6-27	7-04	7-	7-18	7-25	8-01
Release Planning Meeting	4	Complete	Kevin/Roberto	Yes	3	0	0	0	0	0	0	0	0	0
User Story # 6 - Slide Design	12	Complete	Roberto	Yes	40	24	6	0	0	0	0	0	0	0
User Story # 12 - Sales Page Draft	2	Complete	Kevin	Yes	10	10	10	0	0	0	0	0	0	0
User Story # 13 - Waiting List Process	16	Complete	Roberto	Yes	40	40	40	34	26	18	10	8	0	0
User Story # 1 - Early Bird List	8	Complete	Kevin	Yes	10	10	10	10	10	10	6	4	2	0
User Story # 7 - Agenda Draft	8	Complete	Kevin	Yes	28	20	16	8	0	0	0	0	0	0
User Story # 9 - Budget	1	Complete	Kevin	Yes	10	10	10	10	8	4	2	0	0	0
User Story # 10 - Pilot Price	32	Complete	Kevin	Yes	10	10	10	10	10	5	5	5	5	0
User Story # 18 - Online Forum	32	Complete	Roberto	Yes	3	3	3	3	3	3	3	3	2	0
User Story # 8 - Coaching Platform	1	Complete	Roberto	Yes	3	3	3	3	3	3	3	3	3	0
Product Demonstration Meeting	1.5	Complete	Kevin/Roberto	Yes	1	1	1	1	1	1	1	1	1	0
Release Retrospective Meeting	1.5	Complete	Kevin/Roberto	Yes	2	2	2	2	2	2	2	2	2	0
Actual Hours Remaining					1600	1400	1220	1040	960	800	600	440	140	0
Scheduled Hours Remaining					1600	1440	1280	1120	960	800	640	480	320	0
				Sprint:	1	2	3	4	5	6	7	8	9	10

Let's take a look at the four main sections of the release backlog.

- **Release Title & Dates:** This section contains information about the overall release, including the project name, the release name, and the release development and delivery date range.

- **Release Goal:** Describes the overall release goals and which features are expected to be delivered at the end of the release to support the overall business objective for the product features. The goal is based on business priorities as well as the development team's speed and experience.

- **Release Hour Information:** Contains hourly information for each team member and formulas to calculate the total hourly information to determine how much work the development team performed at the release level. This total becomes input for creating the release burndown chart. The release burndown chart is an Agile information radiator that displays the development team's progress throughout each release.

  - **Number of working days:** The number of working days during the release. Remember to include holidays, vacations, and other non-working days when adding the actual number of working days.

  - **Working hours per day:** The number of "productive" hours each development team member is expected to work each day. Although this example shows that both employees are working 8 hours per day and 40 hours per week, this is not typical of a real-life Agile project. It is the product owner's responsibility to determine the actual number of productive hours per week that each development team member is available to work on the user stories, uninterrupted. The product owner must also remember that hours spent in Agile project meetings take away from productive time.

  - **Sprint length:** The length of each sprint in the release (two weeks, in this example).

  - **Number of sprints in the release:** The number of sprints in the release, (10 sprints, in this example).

  - **Total hours in release:** The total number of hours in the release, calculated by aggregating the total hours for each development team member.

  - **Total hours in each sprint:** The total number of hours in each sprint, calculated by dividing the total number of hours in the release by the total number of sprints.

  - **User Story List and Estimated Hours Remaining:** This section contains information about each user story in a release. The product owner enters the scheduled and actual work hours performed by the development team in this release. The hourly information in this section is also used as input for creating the release burndown chart.

    - **User Story:** The user story title and ID # from the product backlog.

    - **Story Points:** The value of the user story, in story points, from the product backlog.

    - **Status:** The current status of the user story. Although there are no best practices for using this field, it often combines the status description and a specific background color that radiates additional information about the user story's status. Some examples include: Pending (light blue background), In Progress (yellow background), Blocked (red background), and Complete (green background).

    - **Owner:** The development team member who is responsible for completing the user story. Although this individual may not personally complete all of the user story tasks, he or she is responsible for all of the tasks in the user story and is accountable for ensuring that the functionality is delivered, as specified, to the customer.

- **PO Approved/User Story Complete?** This entry indicates whether the product owner has approved the completed user story: Yes (green background), No (red background).

- **Sprint End Date:** The last day of each sprint, including the month and day. In this example, there are 10 sprints in the release.

- **Actual Hours Remaining:** The actual remaining work hours in the entire release. The product owner enters the hours at the end of each sprint for each user story in the release. The hours are taken from the sprint backlog total for each sprint in the release. Usually, these hours will not match the scheduled hours remaining per sprint, but they should eventually (hopefully) burn down to zero when the release is complete.

- **Scheduled Hours Remaining:** The scheduled remaining work hours in the entire release, which burn down after each successive sprint until eventually reaching zero at the end of the release. The hours are calculated by populating the first sprint cell with the total release hours (1600 in this example), and then subtracting the total hours per sprint (160 in this example) for each successive sprint. The calculation assumes that the development team will work 160 hours per sprint for the duration of the release.

- **Sprint #:** This is the number of each sprint within the release. In this example, there are 10 sprints in the release.

Note

Although this example does not display a release backlog section to document issues and roadblocks that are encountered during a release. It is a good idea to always document issues and roadblocks when you have them on your project. Many Agile project managers maintain a separate worksheet in the release backlog that includes a cross reference to the user story ID to track issues and project roadblocks. It is much easier to include all of the information about user stories in a specific release (including issues or roadblocks) in a single document.

Using the Agile user story release backlog

The release backlog contains a limited set of user stories that are derived from the product backlog and the product roadmap and selected for a specific release. The release backlog repository must be updated diligently by the product owner at the end of each sprint within the release. This ensures that the data being represented about the development team's work performance during the release can be used to properly report the amount of work performed so far in the release. The data is then used as an input when creating the release burndown chart and provides visibility to the project team and stakeholders as to whether the development team is meeting, and will continue to meet, the release goal. The product owner inputs the development team's actual velocity during each sprint to track their progress better, provide feedback about their estimates, and to help make scope decisions about future releases.

Creating the Agile user story sprint backlog

After creating your initial Agile release backlog (as part of the Agile release planning meeting), you need to determine which user stories to include within the current sprint. The specific order in which the user stories need to be completed (based on their value to the customer, risk to the project, and dependencies on each other) is outlined in the release backlog. At the beginning of each sprint, the Scrum team holds a sprint planning meeting to decompose each user story in the release backlog into specific tasks. The purpose of the sprint planning meeting is for the development team to commit to completing a set of user stories in the release backlog that are currently the highest priority. This commitment defines the specific user stories that will be contained in the sprint backlog, which is a subset of the release backlog. The product owner works with the development team to create a sprint goal that represents a product component that can be demonstrated to the customer at the end of the sprint. The product owner enters the sprint goal and the specific user stories into the sprint backlog. The product owner then presents the stories being considered for this sprint to the development team and answers their questions. Each development team member offers input about each task they think should be performed for that specific user story. They also offer estimated hours for each task. After all of the tasks have been finalized and estimated for every user story, individual team members select the tasks they would like to perform. The Scrum master will assign any remaining tasks after everyone has made their selections. At this point, the development team conducts a final workload review to determine the feasibility of the work being successfully performed in the sprint. Any user stories that cannot be completed in the iteration are removed from the sprint backlog. At the end of the sprint planning meeting, the development team members give a verbal commitment to the product owner that all their assigned tasks in each user story will be successfully completed by the end of the sprint.

Note
A key to every successful Agile sprint is based on a "reciprocal commitment" among the development team, the product owner, and the customer, which enables the development team to get all of the work done in the sprint backlog during each sprint. A reciprocal commitment means that the development team commits to completing all of the work in the sprint backlog according to the "definition of done," and everyone else commits to leaving the development team alone to do the work and not changing user story priorities during the sprint.

Figure 16.10 — Agile Sprint Backlog Example shows a sprint backlog example in a format that is often used by Agile project management teams. You will notice that this template is almost identical to the release backlog template. The only difference being that the lowest level of decomposition in the release backlog is the user story, while the lowest level of decomposition in the Sprint backlog is the user story task.

Figure 16.10 — Agile Sprint Backlog Example

Release Title: Life Journel App Project
Sprint Dates: July 7, 2019 - July 18, 2019

Sprint Goal
As a <instructor>
I want to <ensure all PowerPoints and Weekly Self Assessment Question initial drafts are completed>
So I can <perform a final review of these materials before scheduling the pilot class>.

Sprint Hour Information	Working Hrs/day	
Number of working days		10
Kevin (40 hrs wk)	8	80
Roberto (40 hrs wk)	8	80
Sprint Length = 2 Weeks	Total:	160
	Total per day:	16

User Story Task List and Estimated Hours Remaining

User Story / Tasks	Story Points	Status	Owner	PO Approved/User Story Complete?	M 7	Tu 8	W 9	Th 10	F 11	M 14	Tu 15	W 16	Th 17	F 18
Sprint Planning Meeting	1.5	Complete	Kevin/Roberto	Yes	3	0	0	0	0	0	0	0	0	0
User Story # 25 - PowerPoint Presentations	50	Complete		Yes										
Create PPTX from Agenda for week 1-6 calls		Complete	Roberto	Yes	40	24	6	0	0	0	0	0	0	0
Finalize PPTX for week 1-6 calls		Complete	Kevin	Yes	10	10	10	0	0	0	0	0	0	0
Create PPTX from Agenda for week 7-11 calls		Complete	Roberto	Yes	40	40	40	34	26	18	10	8	0	0
Finalize PPTX for week 7-11 calls		Complete	Kevin	Yes	10	10	10	10	10	10	6	4	2	0
User Story # 17 - Weekly Self Assessment Questions	27	Complete		Yes										
Create 11 sets of 15 questions		Complete	Kevin	Yes	28	20	16	8	0	0	0	0	0	0
Verify spelling, grammar, format, accuracy of question content		Complete	Kevin	Yes	10	10	10	10	8	4	2	0	0	0
Perform final proofreading of questions		Complete	Kevin	Yes	10	10	10	10	10	5	5	5	3	0
Publish questions		Complete	Roberto	Yes	3	3	3	3	3	3	3	3	2	0
Distribute questions		Complete	Roberto	Yes	3	3	3	3	3	3	3	3	3	0
Sprint Review Meeting	0.5	Complete	Kevin/Roberto	Yes	1	1	1	1	1	1	1	1	1	0
Sprint Retrospective Meeting	1	Complete	Kevin/Roberto	Yes	2	2	2	2	2	2	2	2	2	0
Actual Hours Remaining					160	140	122	104	96	80	60	44	14	0
Scheduled Hours Remaining					160	144	128	112	96	80	64	48	32	0
				Day:	1	2	3	4	5	6	7	8	9	10

Let's take a look at the four main sections of the sprint backlog.

- **Sprint Title & Dates:** This section contains information about the overall sprint, including the project name, the sprint name, and the sprint development and delivery date range.

- **Sprint Goal:** Describes the overall sprint goals and which product components are expected to be delivered at the end of the sprint to support the overall release goal. The goal is based on business priorities as well as the development team's speed and experience.

- **Sprint Hour Information:** Contains hourly information for each team member and formulas to calculate the total hourly information to determine how much work the development team performed at the sprint level. This total becomes input for creating the sprint burndown chart. The sprint burndown chart is an Agile information radiator that displays the development team's progress during each sprint.

- **Number of working days:** The number of working days during the sprint. Remember to incorporate holidays, vacations, and other non-working days when adding the actual number of working days.

- **Working hours per day:** The number of "productive" hours each development team member is expected to work each day. Although this example shows that both employees on the project are working 8 hours per day, and 40 hours per week, this is not typical of a real-life Agile project. It is the product owner's responsibility to determine the actual number of productive hours per day and per week that each development team member is available to work on the user stories, uninterrupted. The product owner must also remember that hours spent in Agile project meetings take away from productive time.

- **Sprint Length:** The length of each sprint in the release (two weeks, in this example).

- **Total hours in sprint:** The total number of hours in the sprint, calculated by aggregating the total hours for each development team member.

- **Total hours per day:** The total number of hours in each day, calculated by dividing the total number of hours in the sprint by the total number of days.

- **User Story Task List and Estimated Hours Remaining:** This section contains information about each user story in a sprint, and the specific tasks to complete the user story. The development team enters the scheduled and actual work hours they performed during this sprint. The hourly information in this section is also used as input for creating the sprint burndown chart.

- **User Story/Task:** The user story title and ID # from the release backlog, and the associated tasks to complete the user story.

- **Story Points:** The value of the user story, in story points, from the release backlog.

- **Status:** The current status and the associated tasks to complete the user story. Although there are no best practices for using this field, it often combines the status description and a specific background color that radiates additional information about the user story and task status. Some examples include: Pending (light blue background), In Progress (yellow background), Blocked (red background), and Complete (green Background).

- **Owner:** The development team member who is responsible for completing the user story and its associated tasks. Although this individual may not personally complete all of the user story tasks, he or she is responsible for all of the tasks in the user story and is accountable for ensuring that the functionality is delivered, as specified, to the customer.

- **PO Approved/User Story Complete?** This entry indicates whether the product owner has approved the completed user story and its associated tasks: Yes (green background), No (red background).

- **Sprint Day:** This is the column header for each day in the sprint, including the abbreviation for the day of the week and the day of the month. In this example, there are 10 days in the sprint.

- **Actual Hours Remaining:** The actual remaining work hours in the entire sprint. Development team members enter the hours daily. Usually, these hours will not match the scheduled hours remaining per sprint, but they should eventually (hopefully) burn down to zero when the sprint is complete.

- **Scheduled Hours Remaining:** The scheduled remaining work hours in the entire sprint, which burn down after each successive day until eventually reaching zero at the end of the sprint. The hours are calculated by populating the first day cell with the total sprint hours (160 in this example), and then subtracting the total hours per day (16 in this example) for each successive day. The calculation assumes that the development team will work 160 hours during this sprint.

- **Day #:** This is the number of each day within the sprint. In this example, there are 10 days in the sprint.

Note

Although this example does not display a sprint backlog section to document issues and roadblocks that are encountered during a sprint. Many Agile project managers maintain a separate worksheet in the sprint backlog that includes a cross reference to the user story ID to track issues and project roadblocks. It is much easier to include all of the information about user stories in a specific sprint (including issues or roadblocks) in a single document.

Using the Agile user story sprint backlog

The sprint backlog is the set of user stories from the release backlog that the product owner selected for completion during the current sprint. The sprint backlog is the development team's forecast for functionality to develop during the current sprint. It is the main document that guides the development team's work during any given sprint. This user story and task repository is created as a result of the sprint planning meeting and represents a commitment by the development team to complete all of the user stories in the sprint backlog according to the "definition of done," by the end of the sprint. And just like the product owner must diligently update the release backlog with the actual work performed during each release, the development team must diligently update the sprint backlog with their daily work. Updating the spring backlog ensures that the development team's work performance data during the sprint can be used to accurately report the amount of work performed so far in the sprint, but also in the release and in the overall project. This data is then used as an input for creating the sprint burndown chart and provides visibility to the project team and project stakeholders as to whether the development team is meeting, and will continue to meet, the sprint goal, the release goal, and the overall project goals. Each team member enters his or her hours daily for each assigned user story and the associated tasks to complete the user story to determine whether they are meeting the specific sprint goal, and if not, determining what specific adjustments must be made to get back on track.

After reading this in-depth discussion of Agile user story backlogs, we hope you understand how your Agile project's success depends on the different levels of requirements decomposition that occurs throughout the project's different stages. And of equal importance is that Agile user story backlogs represent specific documents that are repositories for the requirements at all levels and stages of Agile project planning. The power of using Agile user story backlogs is predicated on the effective creation and use of Agile user stories to help the customer and the product owner continually communicate and document the customer's wants and needs to the development team. From creating the initial product backlog and release backlog at the very beginning of the project, to creating executing the last sprint backlog at the end of the project, Agile user story backlogs are the main tools for organizing, updating, prioritizing, and re-prioritizing Agile user stories throughout the project life cycle. From the recorded data at all of the backlog update levels, you can continually monitor the development team's ongoing performance for the work performed, as well as the ongoing performance and accurate forecasting of the whole project for budget, schedule, and all other competing project constraints.

Mastering the Business Case

Before mastering the *business case*, you need to understand how it can help and support you on your project. Most project managers use the business case to justify and explain their project. No other document outlines exactly why the project is valuable than the business case. Therefore, it makes sense that it is the first resource you or the customer refers to when explaining the project's importance.

For example, a small antique shop in Iowa is running out of space to store their antiques. The buyers are on the road daily and send merchandise back to the store to sell, so the shop keeper continues to struggle with where to put everything. The business owner's frustration grows daily and there appears to be no end in sight. Something has to be done because the business can't keep collecting more inventory than sales, and they simply need more space. The shop keeper knows that the only solution is to expand the current location by adding another building on the lot. The shop clerk wants to add a new building on the same lot, 100 yards from the existing building. That way, the two buildings are close enough to look like the same store front and customers can easily move between both buildings. The shop clerk cannot make the decision to add the new building herself; she must convince the business owner of her idea. The shop clerk has complained for years that the current building is too small, so the ask is out there, but there is no convincing the business owner, and sadly, the antiques keep coming in and there's no place to put anything. Day in and day out, the shop clerk can barely move around the shop and her frustrations grow. She also knows that the renovation is going to cost money and the owner is not going to approve it without asking a lot of questions.

The business owner's questions will include:

- How much will the renovation cost?

- How long will it take to build?

- Where will the new building go?

- How long until we see a payoff between putting the building up and getting a return on our investment?

- What is the justification?

- What is the value of doing this? Will we see real payoffs quickly if we go forward?

Knowing the owner, the questions could go on and on; the shop clerk knows that she needs to do her homework or the renovation request would never fly. She also needs a spot where she can store the answers to these questions, and the first place she thought of was the business case. She knows the business case is the perfect place to store answers to these questions. If she can fill in the document, she can present it to the business owner and hopefully answer all of his questions.

A business case describes, in detail, the answers to these questions and justifies the project's existence and importance.

Cross-Reference
We recommend that you review the business case in Chapter 7 - Defining Communication Tools that Manage Project Scope for more information.

Creating the business case

When thinking about creating a business case, the first and most important consideration is the information needed for the project approver. It makes no sense to put a document in front of a project approver if the information needed to approve the business case is not complete. Most project approvers have a hot spot or two about what they want to see before they decide on approving the project. Consequently, when you think about creating a business case, you will often start with a business case template, and then work with the project approver to find out the information he or she needs in the document.

The steps for creating a business case vary among customer representatives.

The following steps outline how to create a business case:

1. Find the business case template and meet with the project owner to go over the project information. The goal of this meeting is to ensure that the project owner questions have a spot for you to complete in the template. If you have worked with the project owner before, or if you have worked with other project managers who have worked with this project owner before, look for other project business cases documents. This will give you a feel for the information the project owner needs.
2. When the project owner completes and approves the document template, your work as the project's business representative begins.
3. Complete the sections of the business case. Make sure you add and complete the extra sections that the project owner requested.
4. While completing the document, it is a best practice to continually meet with the project owner to provide updates about project status. Doing so builds a strong relationship while keeping the project owner informed.
5. When the document is complete, meet with the project owner to review the business case. This is the project approval meeting, so you should leave the meeting with the project's go/no-go decision.
6. Send the business case to your project team, and then store it in the document control system for long-term storage and retrieval.

Using the business case

As you think about using the business case, remember that it will be used for limited areas and only at the beginning of the project. Although rare, you, your customer representatives, and team members might use the business case throughout the project to review the project's justification and ensure that it's on course to meet the original goal.

During the beginning stages of the project, you and your business representatives will use the business case during project approval meeting with the project owner, the project kickoff meeting, and early team meetings. These early and initial meetings between you and your customer representative and your team members are optimal for using the business case to ensure that everyone is on the same page and aligned with the project's objective.

As the project moves into the executing phase, there are rarely any updates or changes to the business case. Changes should be for exceptions only.

Mastering the Circle-of-Communications Chart

Before mastering the *circle-of-communications chart,* you need to understand how it can help and support you on your project. The circle-of-communications chart's main benefit is that it documents who's who on the project. The circle-of-communications chart outlines and documents who should receive project communications and shows everyone on the project team. It is a simple tool to use on your projects. Regardless of the project type, you need to know who to communicate with on the project; this tool provides that information. The tool also lets you see the relationships among team members and yourself, the project manager. You are in the center of the chart and, therefore, the center of project communications. You are in the center because you are responsible for all formal and final communications. Showing the project manager in the center of circle-of-communications chart rather than in a simple list shows the communication value. Seeing a list of names and trying to connect how everyone works together is much more difficult than viewing a circle-of-communications chart. The following project scenario highlights the reasons why the circle-of-communications chart is important to every project.

A large software company in Toronto, Ontario decided to create a large multi-organization time-tracking system. The project owner approved the project and assigned a project manager. One of the first duties of the project manager is project communications. The project manager starts filling out the company's project communication plan template and quickly discovers that the document is not well structured and lacks any real substance. The project communication plan is not valuable at all. He starts filling in the information about the project team, starting with his name, the developer lead's name, the developers, and so on. He completes the table and the document and sends it to the team for approval. In the project manager's mind, the document is complete, so he feels like he has completed the communications as well. As the project progresses, it runs into its first issue around testing. The project manager, tester, and customer work to resolve the issue. Communications are flying back and forth and nobody is paying attention to what is happening. The tester sends an email directly to the customer with a status update. The tester states in his email that the test team is overworked, tired, and ready to give up on the project unless they get help. The tester goes on to say that they have worked around the clock, canceled vacations, and everyone is working overtime. The customer is upset by this email and escalates the information to the project manager and the project manager's manager. Management is now involved in the project because the tester randomly sent an email to the customer complaining about the test team's working conditions.

Could this scenario have been avoided? Yes. If the project manager used the circle-of-communications chart from the beginning of the project, the project team would have seen that all formal communications go through the project manager first, no exceptions. This is not to say that the circle-of-communications chart can prevent mistakes from happening. But had the project manager implemented the chart, the tester may have thought twice about emailing the customer directly. In this scenario, the project manager ends up in an awkward position with the customer, and the test team member is removed from the project.

Cross-Reference
We recommend that you review the circle-of-communications chart in Chapter 11 - Communication Tools for Human Resource Management for more information.

Creating the circle-of-communications chart

You can use Microsoft PowerPoint SmartArt functionality to easily create the circle-of-communications chart. Specifically, you use the Radial Circle to start creating the circle-of-communications chart. There are probably many tools that you can use to create the circle-of-communications chart, but Microsoft PowerPoint is a good starting point. The default graphic requires some changes, such as adding names instead of titles within the circles, but they are simple to do, and when it is ready, the Radical Circle becomes the circle-of-communications chart.

Here are the steps to create a circle-of-communications chart for your project.

How to create the circle-of-communications chart

1. Create the default circle from a presentation tool, such as Microsoft PowerPoint.

2. Add extra circles to the ring to represent your project team leads. The default amount is four circles, but each project has a specific number of immediate team leads.

Note
There is no limit to how many circles you can add; the more circles, the less readable the graphic becomes. Keep the circles to a manageable number and remember to only note your leads.

3. When adding the team lead circles to your chart, increase the size of the middle circle so there is a section of the circle touching each outer circle. This represents the project manager role as being involved in project communications. The large circle does not imply all communications; it just represents a connection point.

4. Add team lead names to the circles in the outer ring of the circle-of-communications chart. You can also add your name to the main circle in the middle.

5. After the team leads are identified and named, the team leads add their direct team members. Create a text box in the chart and add a bulleted list of names who work for each lead. So, the development lead names the developers, and the test lead names the testers, and so on. After all of the names are added, the circle-of-communications chart is complete.

Using the circle-of-communications chart

Before using the circle-of-communications chart, you must identify who will use it. The circle-of-communications chart is typically used during the project initiation phase. However, you should update the circle-of-communications chart as team members' change. Multi-year projects undergo many team member and customer changes and, therefore, you must be diligent about regularly updating the circle-of-communications chart. Regular updating gives you the latest information about project stakeholders and helps ensure that you are communicating with them.

Mastering the Communication Plan

Before mastering the *communication plan*, you need to understand how this tool can help and support you. The following scenario stresses the tool's importance and why the communication plan is critical to every project.

A medium-sized pharmaceutical company wants to develop a new application that tracks the testing status of their drugs at various locations around the world. The medical technicians compile the drug testing information into one central location where everyone can access the test results. Each location has a project manager assigned to the project. The unique part about this project is that each location that needs to review the data is in a different location around the world. The application is being developed in the United States, but the application will need to be customized for the different locations around the world. Customizations include supporting different languages in the user interface and reports, and keyboard mapping changes that could affect the application. These localization changes make this project complex and communication among the different locations adds to the complexity. Here is your challenge:

- How can you manage and control your communications with the different locations?
- How do you set up and control effective communication with the project managers around the world?
- How can you communicate project information over the various time zones?
- Do you expect all project managers to travel to the United States or will you go to them?

You need to answer these critical questions before the project kicks off. If the questions are not answered in the communication plan, it will be difficult to gather project information from the different locations. You must have a communication plan in place—especially in global scenarios such as this one.

The solution is to develop and use a communication plan. A communication plan documents and describes, in detail, how project information will flow. The communication plan documents status meetings, status reports, reporting frequency, and all other areas of project communication. A project of this size requires a robust communication plan that requires buy-in from all locations and all project managers to be successful.

Cross-Reference
We recommend that you review the communication plan in Chapter 12 - Defining Communication Tools That Manage Project Communications for more information.

Creating the communication plan

Project communication is critical on every project, but an up-to-the minute status on most projects provides little to no value and costs a tremendous amount of time and effort to collect the information. Setting expectations, such as daily reports or a continuing up-to-the minute status, only sets you up to fail in meeting those expectations.

The steps to create a communication plan vary among project managers. Instead of providing step-by-step instructions to create a communication plan, we've included a project communication plan template. You can use this template if your company does not already have one.

Table 16.1 — Example of a Project Communication Plan

#	Section Title	Description
1	Project Communication Plan Overview	Write a communication plan executive summary. Include the plan's purpose, goal, and the "who, what, where, why, and how."
2	Project Communication Requirements Matrix	Document and develop the document's communications requirements matrix to control who receives what kind of project information.
3	Role Report Matrix	For those receiving the report, document their roles, how often they receive it, and the report type. This matrix is a valuable tool for understanding how project information will flow. Developing this matrix with your project stakeholders early on in the project prevents stakeholders from missing valuable project information as your project progresses.
4	Time Frame	Document when each report will be distributed.
5	Lessons Learned	Document how you are going to get the lessons learned. It is important to document the lessons learned during the weekly status meeting.
6	Historical Information	Identify and document the plan for keeping historical information about the project.
7	Closeout	Document the plan for the final report, the formal acceptance document, lessons-learned document, project archives, and the user acceptance document.

Using the communication plan

Before using the communication plan, it is important to identify who will use it. Knowing who will use the communication plan helps decide the report's level of detail, distribution frequency, style, and format. Be careful not to communicate project information at the wrong level to an executive or a stakeholder. For example, giving the vice president a ten-page project status report would be communicating the wrong level of detail. Before using a communication plan, review the materials in *Chapter 12 - Defining Communication Tools to Manage Project Communications* and familiarize yourself with the activities and tasks for preparing to use this tool, and then complete the following steps:

1. Ensure that your communication plan covers all of the project's areas that you want to communicate. Are the right reports listed, are the time frames reasonable, are your customers satisfied with the proposed reports, and so on. In this step, think about the communication plan recipients. Recipients should include leadership, vendors, and customers; adjust the communication plan according to their specific needs.

2. Review lessons-learned information from past projects and update the communication plan with best practices. There could be valuable information in another project manager's lessons-learned document, so take advantage of that information if it is available.

3. Work with the customer to get approval on the communication plan. This step includes sending the communication plan and the user acceptance document to the customer for approval and sign-off. You may have to meet with team members and customers together to go over the plan and walk through the document. If the customer engages with you while you are building the communication plan, an extra walk through may not be required. After you receive approvals from everyone you requested sign-off from, make sure to store the document and the approvals in the document control system for long-term storage and retrieval.

4. As the project moves from planning to executing, continue to review and update the communication plan based on the customer's continuing and often changing communication requirements. This is also the point in the project where you start sending all of the reports that are outlined in the communication plan. This is the implementation point for the communication plan and the best time to find out if your customers are getting what they need from the information.

5. Update and improve the communication plan throughout the project life cycle. Even near the end of the project, the customer might request a new report that you will need to document in the communication plan. Your role is to make sure that your customers and team members approve and sign-off on the plan, when applicable.

After completing these five steps, you should fully understand and be able to use the communication plan tool on your projects.

Mastering the Customer Requirements Document

Before mastering the *customer requirements document*, it is important to understand how it can help and support you on your project. The following project scenario highlights the benefits that you, the project manager, can gain by using the customer requirements tool.

A company's finance department wants a new financial system developed to replace their old, legacy, 20-year-old system. The staff wants the ability to track people's actuals, their monthly forecasts, budget data, estimate to complete data, and any variances. They want the new application developed in four months, and the project's budget is unknown. You work in the finance department, and you are a senior project manager in the department, so management asks you to manage this project. The project resources are still in question, but you, as project manager, understand that this is a top-priority project, so finding resources to work on your project will not be an issue. As you start the project, you quickly discover that there are no requirements anywhere and nobody has documented anything. You ask the project analysts and customers and determine that no one has written anything down. The fact that there is no project documentation worries you. You also wonder why nobody on the project has a clue about what they are supposed to be working on, and yet they continue to work every day and don't ask questions. This is a mess, so one of the first tasks you do is schedule a formal customer requirements gathering session. This is a chance for you to document the customer's wants and needs for the project. In the requirements gathering sessions, you have several questions for the customer, including:

- What are you trying to accomplish?
- What are the project goals?
- What are your business needs?
- What do you like about the existing system?
- What do you dislike about the existing system?
- What are your critical success factors for this project?

To record the answers to these questions, you use a customer requirements document. The document covers all of the customer's wants and needs. Often, these documents cover business-specific requirements; however, that is usually not covered in a single session. It is common for you to have multiple discussions and requirements gathering sessions to understand the customer's requirements. All projects, regardless of size or complexity, need some form of requirements from the customer.

Cross-Reference
We recommend that you review the customer requirements document's in Chapter 7 - Defining Communication Tools that Manage Project Scope for more information.

Creating a customer requirements document

Creating a project's customer requirements document is an important activity for every project. All team members must understand the customer's requirements because they are building the project deliverables based on the captured requirements.

Creating and capturing customer requirements provides the opportunity for you and the team to understand exactly what your customers want from the project. For example, what are the scope, goals, and objectives that they want the project to fulfill? What are their specific business needs? When everyone on the team is involved in capturing customer requirements, it's less confusing for everyone.

Customer requirements gathering sessions are complex, and you must manage them effectively or they can be a waste of time for everyone. Some customers have unreasonable requirements expectations and try to force the project team into an awkward position to deliver something unreasonable, which may not be possible. Therefore, managing customer requirement sessions are sometimes tricky; try not to promise the world to your customers.

You should be active from the very beginning in the customer requirements gathering sessions. It is important that you understand what your customers want so that you can make project decisions based on those expectations. If you only oversee the requirements gathering sessions, you may not understand the project requirements, which can hurt you while you run the project. You might run into difficult project situations where you are asked to make tough decisions, but you don't have the background you need. Spend the time to understand your customer's requirements from the start.

Project customers play a big part during the requirement sessions and, in the end, are responsible for ensuring that you and the team understand their requirements. The customer's requirements drive the project, so everyone must understand them and there should be no confusion. If you make sure that early in the project everyone is on board and understands the customer's requirements, there likely won't be any confusion during the project. If people are not clear about the customer's requirements, then the project team might be thinking one thing and the customer is thinking something else, which leads to project issues.

The steps for creating a customer requirements plan vary among project managers. Instead of providing step-by-step instructions for creating a customer's requirements document, use the template in **Table 16.2 — Example of a Customer Requirements Table of Contents**, below.

Table 16.2 — Example of a Customer Requirements Table of Contents

#	Section Title	Description
1	Scope	Document the scope of the project, including items that are clearly out of scope.
2	Customer Needs (Goals and Objectives)	Document the project's goals and objectives. Include detailed project goals or objectives.
3	Policies and Procedures Definitions	Document customer-specific procedures or definitions, such as internal policies within the customer or client area that may impact the project. It is important to add the procedures to the document, as they will impact the final product of the project.
4	Business Use Cases and Scenarios	Document use cases and user scenarios. This is one of the main areas of the document; capturing this information is critical to the project's success.
5	Business Unit Interactions (if applicable)	Document interactions the customer groups have with other areas of the company or, if applicable, outside the company. Recognize those interactions in this document to ensure that you consider them when designing the system.

#	Section Title	Description
6	Deployment Requirements	Document the project's deployment requirements. If there is anything special about deploying the final product, use this section to capture that information.
7	Output Reporting Requirements	Document reporting requirements. Reporting requirements can range from the data type needed (for example, software development projects) to a specific report that is created when the product goes live.
8	Operational Requirements	Document specific operational requirements, such as ongoing support, backup and recovery options—anything required for ongoing product support and maintenance. Operation requirements are software-focused, but they also apply to other industries.
9	Testing Requirements	Document specific testing requirements that customers will want to be involved in for the project. The requirements can vary among projects or industries, but this section provides the opportunity to capture specific testing needs.
10	User Documentation and Training Requirements	Document specific user documentation or training requirements. Projects vary, but users may have specific project training requirements that need to be captured and documented in the requirements document, such as training global users or using a "train the trainer" model.
11	Requirements Priority Matrix	Document the customer's requirements in priority order. Requirements can be based on High, Medium, or Low. Some project manager's set priorities based on Value, Cost and Risk as well. The goal is to ensure the requirements each have a defined priority.
12	Assumptions, Risks, and Constraints	Document project assumptions, risks, and constraints. Tracking this information is important so that team members understand project assumptions and constraints.

Using a customer requirements document

Before using a customer requirements document, identify who will benefit from it. Understanding who on the project team needs to use the document helps you determine the detail required, distribution frequency, style, and format of the report. This ensures that you are communicating the correct amount of detail to team members, customers, or clients.

Before using a customer requirements document, review *Chapter 7 - Defining Communication Tools that Manage Project Scope* and familiarize yourself with the activities and tasks for preparing the customer requirements document. Then, complete the following steps:

1. Ensure that the document is complete and correctly captures the customer requirements. Set up a meeting with the customer and the analyst together to ensure that they both approve the document's contents. With their approval, getting customer approval should be easy.

2. Seek approval from the downstream users of the customer requirements document. For example, on a software project, downstream users could include testers, developers, and designers. Each group must be able to use the document for their portion of the project; if not, you must add information to the document so they can use it.

3. Distribute the customer requirements document and the user acceptance document for project approval.

4. After the project is approved, store the document in the document control system for long-term storage, archiving, and retrieval purposes.

5. Compile the project's technical components in the customer requirements document.

6. As the project moves into the planning process, the team will become clearer on the business requirements. Team members need to start translating customer requirements into technical requirements. When the technical requirements are complete, the customer requirements document becomes a supporting document for the project and won't be used very often.

As the project moves into the executing phase, there are rarely any updates or changes to the customer requirements document. The only exception is when the customer introduces scope changes. When the customer introduces change requests into the project, it forces changes to the customer requirements document. Those changes need to be made in the associated technical requirements as well.

Mastering the Document Control System

Before mastering and using a *document control system*, you must understand how it can help and support you on your project. The following project scenario stresses the tool's importance and why it is so critical to every project.

There is a large construction project under way in Toronto, Ontario. You have managed the project for the last couple of months and everything is progressing well. The project is on track and is expected to finish on time and within budget. The project team is developing reports, documents, charts, graphs, and several other documents. The floor plans are also progressing well and project information is flowing. Suddenly, the project hits a point and is now in trouble. There are questions coming from all directions and people want to find project documents, reports, and key decisions that were made. Customers are asking questions, the project team is scrambling to find answers, and everyone is demanding information from you. There is a general theme to the questions; they want information such as status reports, budget reports, and cost spreadsheets. People want to find project information. Questions you ask yourself include:

- How can I get the information to everyone in a timely and controlled manner?
- How can I provide the information quickly without overwhelming everyone?
- Where is the information stored?
- What system should we use to meet all these requests?

Enforcing the use of a document control system to store all project documentation helps prevent a scenario such as this one from occurring. The document control system stores project information. Most tools offer a structured and organized approach to storing files and locating project information. The document control system can save time and effort finding and recovering project information. Smaller projects do not require an automated document control system; a manual filing system may be acceptable. However, you must create the same project structure in a manual system as you would for an automated system to ensure that team members and customers can find the information when they need it.

On medium and large projects, there are often many documents and vast amounts of information that need storing in the document control system. In these situations, the only solution is to keep project documents in an organized and structured location for future reference.

There are many automated solutions (software packages) you can purchase. There is a host of other storage and retrieval products on the market and it grows all the time. Software packages are almost useless, though, unless someone (usually the project manager) sets them up and creates an organized structure for storing project documents.

Cross-Reference
We recommend that you review the document control system in Chapter 14 - Defining Communication Tools to Manage Project Procurement for more information.

Creating the document control system

It is common for small companies that do not have an automated document control system to set up directory structures on their internal networks. The directory structures are usually set up by the project manager and used as the document control system. When controlling and organizing project documents, rarely does a manual solution work as well as an automated application. If possible, use the more robust applications for your projects and see if your company will invest in a company-wide solution. If purchased at the company level, all projects can share the cost and everyone benefits from the features of these powerful tools.

You should use a document control system for all projects whenever possible. Software applications help you share project information and offer a location for long-term and secure file storage.

Tip

As project managers face stricter internal audit requirements, they need to have better control over their documents. Project managers are encouraged to put documents in a controlled environment where project information is available for quick and easy access by project teams or anyone auditing the project.

A document control system also stores project approvals and formal signoffs in a safe and secure location. If you ever need to recover approval evidence, it should be easy to find.

Customers should also be able to access project details and other information about the project within the document control system. They should be able to add and update project documents that they own and are responsible for. However, if your customers have access to too much information, they might get derailed or sidetracked by digging into project documents that aren't their business to read or see. For example, if a customer reads a design document and disagrees with the design, in some companies, they would have no right to question that design. A customer could cause problems on the project with something he or she "found" when looking at the documents in the document control system. On the other hand, if team members and customers cannot access information, you will need to continually provide regular updates, which wastes time and effort that could be spent managing the project.

When the document control system is software-based, information technology staff in large companies should be available to install and configure the tool, depending on the software package, because installation steps vary. Individual project managers rarely have to do more than create a project instance and start storing project files.

The following steps outline how to create a manual document control system for companies that do not have an automated system, but still want to take advantage of this valuable communication tool. To create a manual document control system, complete the following steps:

1. Find a shared network drive where your team has read and write access. Most companies have a common drive, or a network drive, that everyone can access across multiple groups. Create the manual document control system in this shared network location. Worst-case scenario is that you will use your own hard drive or a portable hard drive for the team to access.
2. Set up a file format and structure based on your project's established work breakdown structure (WBS). This includes developing and publishing a standard naming convention for files, and setting processes and procedures for the document format structure.
3. Create the top-level directory using your project's name.
4. Create subdirectories based on major project categories. This will vary among projects, but they are relatively the same across the different industries. Suggestions for subcategories include:
   - Administrative documents
   - Financial documents
   - Drawings
   - Project schedules
     - Project costs
     - Issues and risks documents
     - Project management documents

5. After you set up each directory, set up the security rights for each folder. You may need your security team's help.

6. Finally, communicate the new directory structure to your team and customers and train them how to use it.

Figure 16.11 — Example of a Document Control System shows the directory structure for a document control system. The directory structure shows folders for a single project, but the folders will vary depending on the project type you are managing.

Figure 16.11 — Example of a Document Control System

Manually Created Document Control System

1. Administrative Files

New Hire Files

Payroll

Project Startup Files

2. Finance Files

Project Budget

3. Project Schedule

Project Schedule & Management Plan

4. Risks & Issues

Risk Register

Issue List

Risk & Issue Management Plan

5. Technical Files

Technical Project Information

Design Specifications

Using the document control system

Before using a document control system, you must identify who on your project team will use it so you can decide the level of detail, style, and how you will store the information. This tool ensures that you can communicate project information to your customers, and project documents are accessible, when applicable.

Before using the document control system, review the materials in *Chapter 14 - Defining Communication Tools to Manage Project Procurement*, and then complete the following steps:

1. Make sure that team members and your customer are fully engaged and know how to store project documentation. You might need to set up extra training sessions or one-on-one sessions to ensure that they know where to store project files. Unlike most tools, the document control system is not something that requires approval or sign-off because it is an internal project management tool that the team uses and that has no bearing on the project outcome.

2. After you confirm that the project team and customers are properly storing project documentation, make sure that they continue to do so. Everyone on the project should always store all the project deliverables in the document control system. As project manager, you should continually check and remind everyone to use the document control system.

3. As the project moves to the executing process, spot-check the document control system to ensure that everyone is using it. Look in the document control system for project deliverables, such as sign-offs and approvals for each key document. The reason for storing the customer requirements in the document control system is mainly for internal audits or anyone looking for important project documents. Make sure your project documents are stored in the document control system or you could fail an audit and suffer the consequences.

Mastering the Executive Summary

Before mastering the *executive summary*, you need to understand how it can help and support you on your project. The first and most important area where the executive summary can help you is with your executives. Executives use the executive summary and the business case (if needed) to approve the project to go forward. The executive summary is a valuable tool to help executives decide whether they're going to approve a project. The following project scenario explains the use and importance of this tool.

The Human Resources (HR) department wants to introduce a new rewards system—a system that most companies only dream of offering. The HR staff led by a senior user has had this rewards system in mind for many years; however, has not had the executive support to make it happen. The current HR executive was busy, always out of the office, and never available to sit down and listen to her staff and explore new ideas. The tide was turning and the CIO wasn't as impressed with the current HR executive because she was always away from the office. There was change in the air, and the CIO fired the HR executive. Meanwhile, the CIO needed someone to take charge and told another executive to work two jobs for a while: VP of R&D *and* VP of HR. The new VP, as you can imagine, was busy working two roles and spending the day bouncing back and forth between offices. During the time of change, the new VP was excited to hear from the HR staff and the senior user took the time to present her idea about the new rewards system. During the meeting, the senior user was prepared. She presented the materials, sold the idea, and had a 45-page business case ready and available for the VP. It appeared she had all the answers for the VP and he was impressed. He was also way too busy to read a 45-page document. The senior user had a problem, she needed to get the business case data in the hands of the VP of HR, but in a smaller, more condensed document.

To capture the business case data in a format that is easy to consume by the VP of HR, the senior user created an executive summary document. This document summarizes the key items of the business case in a format that the executive could easily follow and digest. The senior user knew how the VP liked to digest project information, so she catered the document to his specific learning style.

Cross-Reference
We recommend that you review the executive summary in Chapter 7 - Defining Communication Tools that Manage Project Scope for more information.

Creating the executive summary

When creating the executive summary document, it is important to get approval from the busy executive who either won't or doesn't have time to comb through huge project documents. Executives are busy and spread their time across many different projects, so it is understandable that they can't review and grasp large project documents. When this happens, a senior user, business representative, or project manager must put project information in a format that is easier to digest so that executives can quickly decide about moving a project forward.

An executive summary document provides project information to the executive in a small and condensed package.

Steps for creating an executive summary document vary from project to project and depend on the tool being used. However, the creation process should be the same for every project starting with the template outlined in *Chapter 7 - Defining Communication Tools that Manage Project Scope*. Think about the following items when considering your executives and creating the executive summary document:

- **Get a blank copy of the template.** Grab a copy of the executive summary template from *Chapter 7 - Defining Communication Tools that Manage Project Scope* and go over the blank template with executive(s). Make sure they understand what will be in it and whether it contains the information they need to make a decision.

- **Identify the communication style.** Find out the format that executives want the executive summary in. Some will prefer a document format, while some might prefer a formal presentation format. Either way, you need to know the format to deliver the information. Make sure you also find out whether they prefer graphics or text. If you create an executive summary document filled with text and data, and then find out that the executive prefers graphics, you will struggle communicating with them.

- **Identify the key items from the business case**. The executive summary document and the business case go hand-in-hand; therefore, taking information from the business case and putting it in the executive summary document is common. You won't put the whole document in there, but you will add main sections of the document to the executive summary.

Note

Check with executives before adding items from the business case to the executive summary document so you don't add sections that they may or may not care about.

Using the executive summary

Before using the executive summary, make sure that the document is in the format and style for presenting it to the executive. As you may recall, the executive summary document is used to get buyoff and approval from executives; therefore, it is extremely important to ensure that the document is in the correct format.

Using the executive summary document is straight forward and should be considered a part of the approval process. The executive summary document, as well as the business case, support documentation around the proposed project's startup and approval. This document is not an exact replica of the business case, but it does include much of the same information. The documents are companion documents and are often used together.

Before using the executive summary document, review the materials in *Chapter 7 - Defining Communication Tools that Manage Project Scope*, and then complete the following steps:

1. Create the project's executive summary document.
2. Set aside time with the project team to review and approve the document. Make sure that the team knows what they are signing up for and collect any information from the team that they think may not be possible.
3. Schedule time with the executive to review the executive summary document.
4. Present the materials in the agreed format to executives, and then help them understand the project information.
5. After receiving project approval, the executive summary document is stored in the document control system.

After everything is complete and the executives approve the project, the next step is moving the project into the planning process. When the project moves into the planning process, there are no more steps for you to work through and you won't need the executive summary document.

Mastering the Feasibility Study

Before mastering the *feasibility study*, you must understand how it can help and support you on your project. The following project scenario highlights the importance of this tool.

The staff in the marketing department wants a new system that scans computers to discover the company's most popular and most used software application. The marketing department thinks that if employees are using a particular software application, the rest of the world would likely use that same application. It's just a hunch, but they believe it would pay off. After the marketing department collects the information from employee computers, they will develop various worldwide marketing campaigns to promote the "most used" software application. The marketing group contacted you to manage the effort to build the scanning software. The immediate problem you thought of when approached with this project is how to get the data from everyone's computers, and how likely is this idea in general. You realize that this is going to be a tough project to manage. But before you send your team down the path of trying to create scanning software, you ask the marketing department some questions about the project.

Your questions include:

- What is the long-term value of knowing this data?
- What kinds of marketing plans do you have after you receive the data?
- How often do we scan employee computers?

To get the answers to these questions, you refer to the marketing department's feasibility study that they created to get the project approved. The feasibility study captures the answers to these questions and gives executives the information they need to decide on whether to go forward with the project. As the project manager looking for some information about the project, the feasibility study is a great place for you to start.

Cross-Reference
We recommend that you review the Feasibility Study in Chapter 7 - Defining Communication Tools that Manage Project Scope for more information.

Creating a feasibility study

There are two main reasons for customers to create a feasibility study document. The first reason is to justify why a company or organization should begin a project, and the second reason is to show how the project will positively impact the bottom line. After the customer creates the feasibility study, executives can approve the document before officially agreeing to the project. The process for completing the feasibility study document allows for insights and early discussions about the project. It also provides a better understanding of the proposed project for those who will be doing the project work. In turn, it gives the project team something to estimate the project size and to figure out whether the project is possible. Companies also use the feasibility study to shut down projects before spending large sums of money. If the feasibility study results show that the project will not impact the company's profits, shutting down the project before it even starts is the right decision. The feasibility study is more of a scapegoat for executives to use for ideas or proposals that they may not be comfortable turning into projects. Usually, if a company has a business group work on an idea and create a feasibility study, it is likely the project will be approved and proceed. There are times, however, when ideas are bad—some proposed projects are just not feasible. These projects usually don't make it past the early stages to become projects. The feasibility study and associated process saves a company time and resources from starting work on a project that may never get off the ground.

The steps to create a feasibility study can vary among project managers and depend on which tools are used. Instead of providing step-by-step instructions on how to create a feasibility study, a better choice is for you to complete the template. You can use the following sample feasibility study template for your projects.

Table 16.3 — Example of a Feasibility Study Table of Contents

#	Section Title	Description
1	Executive Summary	Document the project's executive summary. Document the project's high-level value.
2	Background Information	Document background information about why the company is requesting the project and what value it will offer if it goes forward.
3	Description of Current Situation/Problem	Document the current problem that the project will address or resolve. Occasionally, the problem may not be bad enough and may not warrant creating a new project. This is where the document's author will have to "sell" executives on the project's feasibility.
4	Description of Proposed Idea	Document the proposed project idea to help sell the idea and tell what the project is.
5	Project Timelines/Schedule	Document the project's proposed time lines. Add hard dependencies or deadlines into this section of the document. Create a rough schedule.
6	Feasibility Review Board	Document the Feasibility Review Board's roles and responsibilities. What will they do? How long will it take to provide an approval? Who are they? Document the project's approval process for it to get in front of the Feasibility Review Board.
7	Go/No-Go Decision	Document the go/no-go decision and associated criteria of the document. This section captures the project's approvals.

Using a feasibility study

Before implementing the feasibility study, identify who will use it so you can determine what kind of details you need, the style, and format of the study. This information ensures that you communicate enough detail for the project team and customers.

Before using the feasibility study, review the feasibility materials in *Chapter 7 - Defining Communication Tools that Manage Project Scope*, and then complete the following steps:

1. Read the feasibility study to understand the proposed project. Meet with the requestor or the study's author to review the suggested project. Understanding the project before it starts will be valuable.

2. Work with the feasibility study's author and your project customer for approval. The customer is usually responsible for getting approval for the study; however, you may be involved in the approval and signoff process as well. After getting approval for the feasibility study, the customer directs you to start the project.

3. Store the feasibility study and approvals in the document control system for long-term storage, archiving, and availability. You probably won't use the feasibility study very often after the project moves into the planning process.

There are rarely feasibility study updates or changes when the project moves into the executing phase. Exceptions might happen when the customer reviews the feasibility study as the project nears completion to ensure it closely matches as the original request. But even then, the feasibility study document is rarely updated.

Mastering the Project Charter

Before learning how to use the *project charter*, you should understand how it can help and support you on your project. The following project scenario highlights the importance of using the project charter and why the project charter is critical to every project.

The sales department has asked the information technology (IT) group to create a new application that can be used worldwide. The IT group says they can create the application in about six months and provided a project estimate of $1,000,000. They have no idea what the actual project cost will be because it is so early in the requirements phase, so they guessed at this estimate. The IT group also has no idea about the project's scope, goals, or objectives. They also have not asked about critical success factors, start or finish dates, or resource requirements. The sales team has not yet documented any of the key project start-up information. As project manager, you know how important this documentation can be and you need it to start your project and kick it off. Because you are the most senior project manager in the department, management decided it would be best for you to manage the project. The problem is, without the startup information, you have some catching up to do, and you need the information before you can get much further into the project. You have some questions about how you are going to get the information you need, such as:

- How will I get the information?
- Where do I start?
- Do I already have contacts in the business who can provide the information?

You should be able to find the answers to your questions in the project charter document. The project charter includes the main project areas that most people will need to know. These areas include the project's purpose, scope, goals, budget, timelines, resources, critical success factors, and expected benefits. This is not a complete list, but they are some of the key items in the project charter document. This information will provide the project team with the information they need to start the project. Without a project charter, you and your team won't know why you are involved in the project or what objective you are trying to achieve.

Cross-Reference
We recommend that you review the project charter in Chapter 6 - Communication Tools That Manage Project Integration for more information.

Creating the project charter

Usually, the project customer or sponsors create the project charter document. You and your team can support document creation, if asked, but usually you wouldn't be involved in the process. The project charter starts as the customer's responsibility, but ends with the project team responsible for using it to execute the project. The project charter describes many project areas and is the single information source for the project team to use to understand the project, including customer goals.

One of the project charter benefits is its flexibility and how useful it is for any size project. Each section in the project charter applies to any project, across most industries. All project charter documents have the same basic sections, including the project's purpose, scope, budget, schedule, deliverables, critical success factors, and resources. You should make sure that the main project areas are also, in one form or another, covered in the project charter document. Budget, for example, is one key area of the project charter that you will watch closely throughout the project.

Your project customer should be active in creating the project charter. Customers are responsible for many sections of the project charter and should drive this document to ensure it captures what they want and expect from the project. A project scope item that is captured incorrectly, or is simply wrong, can send a project in the wrong direction, and the customer will not be happy with the results. Because the project charter captures the wants and needs of the customer, their role in creating, accepting, and document reporting is critical to the project's success.

The steps to create a project charter vary among project managers. To create the project charter, complete the project charter template. Use the following project charter table of contents for your project if your company does not already have one.

Table 16.4 — Project Charter Table of Contents

#	Section Title	Description
1	Introduction	Introduce the document's purpose, revisions, and general information about the document's contents.
2	Overview of the Project	Document the project's overview, customers, and business reasons.
3	Purpose of the Project	Document the project's purpose, why it is important, and who is involved.
4	Objective and Goals	Document the project's objectives. What are you trying to achieve?
5	Business Need and Opportunity	Document the business need or opportunity that the project will offer the company.
6	Financial Benefits of the Project	Document the financial benefits for completing the project. Include both hard and soft financial benefits that the project will offer the company.
7	Expected Benefits	Document any other expected project benefits that don't fall under financial, but are still important to document.
8	Scope	Document the project's scope, including both in-scope and out-of-scope items.
9	Project Budget	Document the project's current budget allocations. Document all constraints and assumptions.
10	Project Start and Finish Dates (Timelines)	Document the project's proposed start and finish dates. Make sure that you document all of the constraints, assumptions, and any other major milestones.
11	Major Deliverables	Document major project deliverables that are in line with your project's methodology. Each methodology has its own set of project deliverables.

#	Section Title	Description
12	Resources	Document the project's resource requirements. Make sure you include skill sets, time frames, training, and all other project resources.
13	Critical Success Factors of the Project	Document the project's critical success factors and what your customers feel the project should include to be successful.
14	Assumptions and Constraints	Document project assumptions or constraints that are worth noting in the charter document.
15	Sign-offs	Document your customers and project team members who signed off on the project charter document.

Using a project charter

Before using a project charter, identify who on your project team will use it. When you know who will use the project charter, you will understand the details you need from them, distribution frequency, style, and document format they want. Now that you have this information, you can be assured that you are communicating the right amount of detail for your project team, customers, and leadership.

Before using the project charter tool, review the project charter material in *Chapter 6 - Communication Tools That Manage Project Integration*, and then complete the following steps:

1. Work with your customers to review the project charter together so you can ensure that the document includes everything necessary to start the project. If so, you accept project responsibility and can begin project initiation activities.
2. Send your project's charter document for final customer and leadership sign-off. Send a copy of the project charter and the user acceptance document to your customers for approval. After getting approval, add it to the document control system for long-term storage, archiving, and retrieval.
3. Start the hiring process to build your project team. The hiring process includes working with functional managers to get external resources, when needed.
4. Hold your project's kick-off meeting and present the project charter to your team. This meeting is the first time they get to review the project charter. A follow-up meeting with the team may be necessary.

As the project moves into the planning process, you or your team will use the project charter document as a general guide only; you will rarely use it to drive team activities. There are little to no updates to the project charter document in the project's executing phase.

Mastering the Project Kick-Off Meeting

Before mastering the *project kick-off meeting*, you should understand how it can help and support you on your project. The following project scenario stresses the tool's importance and why the project kick-off meeting is critical to every project.

The design of a new tennis stadium is complete and a large construction firm has landed the contract to build the tennis stadium in time for summer. The construction firm decides to take some shortcuts to save costs and starts immediately into the construction phase. There are no meetings, little communication, yet the construction firm decides to go full steam ahead. The firm doesn't include anyone else in their decision to immediately start building the tennis courts and player facilities. The construction firm's project manager believes that bringing all of the subcontractors together at the beginning of the project is a waste of time and money, and would only cause delays in project construction. Therefore, the construction firm decides to forgo the project kick-off meeting and figures the project team can meet any time. As the project progresses, there is little communication between the construction firm and any of the other subcontractors. Suddenly, the construction firm hits a major roadblock during the construction phase. They cannot continue without requesting help from the project's subcontractors. The construction firm needs the other subcontractors to help them get over a design hurdle on the tennis courts. Because the construction firm initially left the subcontractors out of the loop, it will be difficult for them to jump in now and be able to immediately help with the problem. Because the construction firm left the subcontractors out of the loop and didn't communicate with them, the subcontractors have little understanding about their role and responsibilities or how they can help. At this point, the subcontractors do not even feel like they are part of the project.

Think about this situation from the project manager's perspective. What would you have done differently? Then, ask yourself the following questions:

- How important would a project kick-off meeting have been in this situation?
- How could the various subcontractors and the construction firm have learned the design requirements for the tennis courts?
- What about contacting the Tennis Association, do they have requirements for court sizes, locker rooms, balls, and nets?
- What would have helped each group form better relationships and start the project with high morale?

To answer these questions, the project manager should have called a project kick-off meeting. A project kick-off meeting helps prevent that type of situation from occurring and would have kept the various subcontractors and construction firm communicating effectively. The customer and leadership team should have insisted that the project manager held a project kick-off meeting and not use the excuse of cost to prevent the meeting from occurring. A project kick-off meeting would have saved two to three months of lost work, and thousands in cost to the project budget. Because nobody planned this work, it affects the project costs immediately, which may risk the whole project. Project kick-off meetings are critical communication tools for every project and helps drive toward a successful project.

Cross-Reference
We recommend that you review the project kickoff meeting in Chapter 6 - Communication Tools That Manage Project Integration for more information.

Creating the project kick-off meeting

A project kick-off meeting can motivate a team like no other meeting. Kicking off a project, forming a project team, and coming together to perform a goal is exciting. Bringing everyone together at the start of the project and providing them with the scope, goals, objectives, and project background is priceless. The team will know all about the project from the start. You should not take on the meeting responsibilities yourself; make sure that the customer is involved in driving parts of the meeting. It is important for the project team to hear directly from the customers what their thoughts and perspectives are about the project and what they expect at the end. When the project team gains inside knowledge directly from the customer, they feel connected to the customer and quickly engage with the project.

There are plenty of topics to cover in a typical project kick-off meeting. The project kick-off meeting provides an opportunity to share project information with your customers and team members at the same time, and is often a charged and energetic meeting for everyone involved.

Project kick-off meetings vary in length and usually last a full business day because there are always several agenda items to cover. Therefore, it is important to have the right agenda to ensure that you deliver the message correctly and that the right people attend the meeting to receive and understand your message.

You and the customers who co-host the meeting need to spend time creating an agenda that will energize and excite the team. The agenda must have a project message and a management message; both messages are important to get across at this early stage of the project.

Stakeholders or customers should attend the project kick-off meeting to give their perspective about the project. Their attendance provides a level of enthusiasm to the meeting that the team will embrace. The fact that the team can hear directly from the customers about their thoughts regarding project scope, goals, and objectives is priceless.

Think about the following information and requirements for stakeholders who attend the project kick-off meeting:

- **Identify and define stakeholders.** Find out who the key stakeholders are and ensure they are invited to the meeting. Prior to the meeting, it is valuable to explain what their roles will be during the meeting and what materials they will cover.
- **Conduct a stakeholder analysis**. There are two levels of stakeholders on every project: first are your customers, clients, owners, or leadership team; and second are the project team members. A stakeholder analysis discovers what the stakeholders want and need from the project.
- **Identify the stakeholders' information needs.** Communicate the stakeholders' needs during the project kick-off meeting so that everyone knows how to keep the stakeholders informed of the project status.
- **Decide team member roles.** If team members are unclear about their roles, they need to work directly with you to address their concerns or issues. You might be able to identify a team member's assigned tasks or you can point the team member to a team lead for direction.
- **Include company-specific tasks**. Include specific activities outlined by the company for the kick-off meeting.

At the end of every project kick-off meeting, it is a best practice for you, as the project manager, to ensure that proper documentation of the meeting occurred and that everyone achieved what they need to from the meeting. These tasks include:

- **Document agreements and share them with the team.** Someone from the administrative team usually takes the meeting minutes and documents the minutes and sends them to the meeting attendees within two days of the kick-off meeting.
- **Clearly identify action items**. You should highlight and identify assignments or action items during the meeting, and then follow up in the meeting notes.
- **Establish clear expectations**. The meeting minutes will capture expectations that were identified during the meeting and you will ensure that the project team members met customers' expectations during the project life cycle.
- **Communicate requirements and deadlines.** Communicate specific communication or associated deadlines that the customer may have.
- **Answer questions that were brought up during the meeting.** Often, there are questions you cannot answer during the meeting and you'll need to respond later. You are responsible for answering outstanding questions by sending the answers to meeting attendees.
- **Provide additional information.** If anything comes up during the project kick-off meeting that needs tracking or more research, you are either responsible for performing that work or delegating it to a team member for resolution.

The steps for creating a project kick-off meeting vary from project manager to project manager and depend on your favorite tools. Instead of providing step-by-step instructions for creating a project kick-off meeting agenda, you can use the following project kick-off meeting agenda template to get started.

Table 16.5 — Table of Contents for a Project Kick-Off Meeting Agenda

#	Section Title	Description
1	Project Goals and Objectives	Document the project's goals and objectives. Your customers or project owners may provide specific goals and objectives, in addition to adding the project team's goals, in this section.
2	Project Scope	Document the project's scope
3	Project Out-of-Scope	Document the project's out-of-scope items. It is important to call out what items the project will not complete so that your customers and team members are clear from the beginning of the project.
4	Risks & Issues	Document the project's risks and issues. At this point, the project may not have many risks and issues, but it is important to track and note any at this time.
5	Budget Estimates	Document the project's budget estimate. During the project kick-off process, the estimate will be at a tolerance level and a fixed variance level only. It is too early in the process to have a refined estimate at this stage of the project.
6	Project Schedule (Timelines)	Document the project schedule. The schedule will reflect milestone-level only, which matches the project's major deliverables. The methodology you selected will drive the deliverables.
7	Methodology Deliverables	Document the methodology deliverables. Depending on the project type and the methodology you chose, this section will include the relevant project deliverables.
8	Requirements Deep Dive	Document the project's detailed requirements. Go over the list of the customer's requirements. Ensure you explain each requirement thoroughly so everyone understands.
9	Design Deep Dive	Document the project's detailed design information. Go over the specific design requirements and any special design considerations.
10	Development Deep Dive	Document the project's development details. Go over the specifics around development that may be special or unique to the project. If the project requires special technology, in this development section would be a good time to cover those specifics.
11	Test Deep Dive	Document the project's detail testing information. Go over the specifics around testing for the effort. If there is any special testing software or testing requirements

#	Section Title	Description
		unique to the project, cover these details in this portion of the meeting.
12	User Acceptance Criteria Deep Dive	Document the project's specific user acceptance-type testing. Go over the specific requirements from the user that they may have for the project. Cover as much detail as possible so everyone is aware of the acceptance criteria.

Using a project kick-off meeting

Before scheduling a project kick-off meeting, identify who on your project team will not only be invited, but who will be involved in the meeting. You need to understand the details that need to be covered during the meeting and the meeting style and format. It is also important to know the meeting length, location, and which stakeholders to invite before setting up the meeting.

Before scheduling the project kick-off meeting, review the materials in *Chapter 6 - Communication Tools That Manage Project Integration*, and then compete the following steps:

1. Work with your customer to schedule the project kick-off meeting. This may need some coordination and time to ensure that remote team members (if applicable) are planning on attending the meeting in person. It takes time to schedule stakeholders who are involved in the project because they usually have plenty of meetings to attend and limited free time. Coordinating the room, food, presentation equipment, and giveaway prizes requires plenty of time to complete before the meeting. Book the meeting early!

2. Meet with your team members and your customer to complete the kick-off meeting presentation material. It is important that long before the meeting event, your presentation materials are ready to present. Some projects have pre-scrub meetings where you present the meeting material to leadership early to allow them time to scrub the material to their liking before everyone else sees it. After pre-scrub meetings, change or update the meeting materials based on their feedback. Doing so is a best practice to ensure that leadership approves the presentation materials before presenting them to customers and leadership. Another best practice is for you to have a pre-scrub meeting with your customer to review the materials before the official meeting. If problems arise from the customer side, you can resolve them before the meeting. In taking this extra step, leadership and customers are prepared, and the official meeting becomes a "rubber stamp" meeting. We recommend the processes outlined in this step as they have proven to be successful.

3. Conduct the project kick-off meeting. Present the materials to team members, customers, leadership, and sometimes executives. This is normally a joint effort between you, your customers, and team members who provided supporting materials for the meeting. Each customer and project will be different, so you will have to adjust accordingly.

4. Complete the meeting follow-up activities. You should store all project kick-off meeting materials within the document control system for long-term storage, archiving, and retrieval purposes.

After the project kick-off meeting, the project moves into the planning process and there are no additional steps for you to complete for the project kick-off meeting.

Mastering the Project Management Plan

Before mastering the *project management plan*, you must understand how it can help and support you on your project. The following project scenario highlights the tool's importance and why the project management plan is critical to every project.

A large construction company is building a bridge over an expansive river. The bridge is two-and-a-half miles long and is expected to take three years to build. The schedule is not yet final, and is not expected to be ready for a few more months. This is a large project, and to be successful, the project requires that the state government, local government, and environmental groups work together. As project manager, you understand that this is going to be a large project and that you will need many control documents to ensure the project is successful. You have never completed such a large project, and your firm is giving you the chance to prove yourself on this project. You know this has to go right, and you struggle with several questions about what to do next. These questions include:

- Where do you start on the project?

- What should you do to add some rigor to your project?

- Who will work with you on the project?

- How will you manage the budget?

- How will you manage the time?

To answer these questions, you will use a project management plan. The project management plan contains the various management plans needed to manage and control the project. A project management plan is a great starting point for any project. Most large projects include a project management plan. A standard project management plan includes the following documents:

- Scope management plan

- Schedule management plan

- Cost management plan

- Quality management plan

- Process improvement plan

- Staffing management plan

- Communications management plan

- Risk management plan

- Procurement plan

These management plans include specific processes and procedures.

Cross-Reference
We recommend that you review the project management plan in Chapter 6 - Communication Tools That Manage Project Integration for more information.

Creating a project management plan

Creating the project management plan is a best practice for all projects, regardless of industry or type—the only condition being the project's size. A small, one-month-or-less project would not necessarily need a project management plan because the time and cost to produce the various documents for a short project outweigh the value of the documents. You must decide when to use a project management plan for a short project and have it be cost effective for the project. For medium to large projects, though, you will use a project management plan.

Note
It is important to add the same rigor and process on all projects; however, not to the same degree on smaller projects.

The project management plan is the overall master document that guides the execution and control of project deliverables. The project management plan is a series of other management documents that help you manage and control your projects. Without a project management plan in place, you wouldn't have the controls or procedures to help guide you in running your project. Without planning documents in place, various issues such as scope, budget, and schedule can negatively impact the project.

Often, the project manager authors the project management plan and is responsible for its continuing maintenance and upkeep. You will have an invested interest in developing and completing project management plans for your projects.

Customers should be active and engaged when you create the project management plan. Customers need to be aware of the project's processes and procedures so they know how to handle certain situations. A good example of what customers need to know is the processes and procedures for risk and issue management. The project management plan includes processes and procedures for the project manager to create and track issues and risks. Customers need to understand these processes well in order to track project risks and issues. By following the process, your customers are less likely to derail or disrupt those who are working on project activities. Customers who think they have identified an important risk and stop the project team from working on tasks to address these risks are not dealing with the process properly. These situations are not good for any project and do not follow any standard risk and issue processes.

The steps for creating a project management plan vary among project managers and depend on which tools you use. Instead of providing step-by-step instructions for creating a project management plan, we've provided the following template for you to use.

Table 16.6 — Project Management Plan Table of Contents

#	Section Title	Description
1	Introduction	Document introductory information for the project management plan. Include information that is specific to the document itself.
2	Project Description	Document the project description; specifically, what the project will achieve, and what the project team will perform.
3	Application	Document how you will apply and use the project for the company.
4	Scope	Document the project scope.
5	Constraints and Assumptions	Document project constraints and assumptions.
6	Risks	Document the project's risks.
7	Issues	Document the project's issues.
8	Relationship to Other Projects	Document the project's relationships or interdependencies on other projects. This is important to capture, especially if the project is dependent on other projects before proceeding.
9	Mission Statement	Document the project's mission statement for customers and the project team. This should be a one- or two-line statement about the project's overall mission.
10	Project Objectives	Document project objectives. You can include the project owners' or clients' objectives and those of the project team.
11	Project Team Members	Document the project team members, including names and contact information.
12	Project Roles and Responsibilities	Document team members' roles and responsibilities. Include customers, clients, and active team members.
13	Project Plan Management	Document how you will manage and control the project.
14	Project Approach	Document your approach to managing and controlling the project. There are many different project management styles and approaches and it is important to document the approach you want to use, including your project expectations. Documenting your project approach ensures that everyone is in line at the beginning of the project.

#	Section Title	Description
15	Conflict Management	Document how you will manage and control project conflicts.
16	Project Administration	Document administrative activities for the project.
17	Project Tasks, Deliverables, and Milestones	Document the major tasks, deliverables, and milestones at the highest level. Document lower-level details in the project schedule, not in the project management plan.
18	Planning Approaches/Methodologies	Document the project methodology, including why you selected the methodology.
19	Key Deliverables	Document the major deliverables for the project. Lower level or sub-deliverables will be included in the project schedule.
20	Major Milestone Dates	Document major milestone dates for the project. These dates will depend on the methodology used, and if there are any additional milestones selected for the project.
21	Scope Management	Document how you will manage and control project scope, such as strategy, planning, definition, verification, and change control.
22	Issue Management	Document how you will manage and control project issues, such as purpose, strategies, and processes and procedures.
23	Risk Management	Document how you will manage and control project risks, such as purpose, strategies, and processes and procedures.
24	Problem Management	Document how you will manage and control problems or concerns, such as purpose, strategies, and processes and procedures.
25	Financial Management	Document how you will manage and control project finances, such as purpose, strategies, and processes and procedures.
26	Communication Management	Document how you will manage and control project communications, such as purpose, strategies, and processes and procedures.
27	Summary	Document the summary project information that is not covered in the other sections. Approvals and signatures are important items to include.

Using the project management plan

Before using the project management plan, you must identify who on your project team will use the document so that you can determine the details you need to include, distribution frequency, style, and document format. Doing so, helps ensure that you are communicating the right details to the project team, customers, and leadership.

Before using the project management plan, review the project management plans in *Chapter 6 - Communication Tools That Manage Project Integration*, and then complete the following steps:

1. Make sure the project management plan is complete. Review the document with your project team and customers to ensure that it correctly captures all areas of the project. This step also entails ensuring that the various project management documents such as the project's communication plan are included in this document, or there are pointers (or links) to the documents if they are stored as separate documents. For example, when reviewing the project management plan, you will know whether the risk management plan is included in the document or whether there is a link in that section that points to the document.

2. Distribute the project management plan to your team and customers for acceptance and approval. Also, send the user acceptance document for official project approval.

3. Store the project management plan and acceptance documents in the document control system for long-term storage, archiving, and retrieval purposes.

4. Enforce the use of the project management plan and associated processes for your project. This step includes using management plans when a project situation happens. For example, use the issue management plan when the first issue occurs. Use the procurement management plan when you hire the first vendor. As the project moves into the executing phase, you and your team use different management plans for different project events.

After completing each step, you should fully understand and be able to use the project management plan for your projects.

Mastering the Project Organization Chart

Before mastering the *project organization chart*, you must understand how it can help and support you on your project. The following project scenario highlights why project organization is critical to your projects.

A large software company wants to replace its in-house accounting system with one of the larger software applications on the market. The in-house system has been around for many years and has many subsystems that send and receive data. To replace the system with an off-the-shelf version is going to require a large team. A team member from each subsystem needs to be part of the core project team to ensure that they continue to receive the data they need after the off-the-shelf version goes into production. There are fifteen subsystems involved in the implementation, so this is going to be a complex project to manage. You are going to need at least fifteen people on the project team, not counting the implementation team. With a team this large, you are going to need a process to manage the various resources. You have many questions about resource management and control, as any project manager would with a project this size. Your questions include:

- How will you gather everyone together?
- How can you tell who is working on which system?
- Are there any open positions you need to fill?
- Who is going to report to whom?
- What will the organizational structure look like?

This scenario is a perfect example for needing a project organization chart to help you control and understand your project team. A project organization chart is also valuable for the project team so that they can see the organizational structure and where other team members are working. An organization chart provides valuable information to you and your team by letting everyone see who reports to whom, which reduces confusion.

Cross-Reference
We recommend that you review the project organization chart in Chapter 11 - Communication Tools for Human Resource Management for more information.

Creating a project organization chart

Creating an organization chart is an important step on every project. Mapping project roles to the person performing the task is essential to your understanding of whether you have the right roles for your project. Project organization charts take little time to produce, but they make a huge difference to project communications and overall project structure.

An advantage to using an organization chart is being able to recognize project staffing and shortfalls. The ability to view, at a glance, how large or small a team is that is working on an area of the project is valuable. When you keep project organization charts current, you can find out exactly where the project staff is grouped, and which job openings are available. When a team member leaves the project, update the project organization chart to reflect the change and highlight job openings that need to be filled. Those openings could be critical and affect the project's critical path. When that information is available from the project organization chart, you can drive the message home and highlight the risk to the project. In addition, project organization charts show a level of risk based on the team size. For example, when the project loses team members over a short duration, there is a resource risk on the project, which is made clear to your customers and leadership by highlighting job openings on the project organization chart.

The steps to create a project organization chart vary for each project manager. The following steps can help you start a project organization chart if you've never created one before. We have also provided a template as a starting point for your projects. You will need to update the template based on your specific project needs and requirements, but it is an excellent guide to get you going.

1. Create a blank organization chart for your project in one of the popular software packages. Doing so provides you with a starting point for creating the project organization chart. Add your name and your customer's name to get the project organization chart started.

2. List the various roles and team member names. If you've already created a project role and responsibility matrix, use it to find names and roles to add to the organization chart. This can be a time-consuming task, but it's important to include all of the project roles on the project organization chart.

3. Send the organization chart to your project team for review. You can also send it to your customers for feedback, but you do not need their approval.

4. Save the organization chart in the document control system for long-term archiving, storage, and retrieval. You should also post the organization chart on the project communication board or your project website to bring exposure to who is working on the project.

5. Continue to refine the project organization chart and update it as various team members roll on and off the project.

Using a project organization chart

Before using the project organization chart, identify who on your project team will use the chart so that you can cater it to their communication needs. When you've identified the main users of the chart, you can decide on the level of detail, distribution frequency, style, and the project organization chart format.

Review the project organization chart in *Chapter 11 - Communication Tools for Human Resource Management*, and then complete the following steps:

1. Use your project organization chart ("org chart") as extra material for the human resources plan. Ensure that the project's roles and current openings on the project organization chart and the human resources plan match. For example, if the project organization chart shows a need for ten developers, the human resources plan should also indicate the need for ten developers. If you see that you don't have the developers you need on the project, you may, at a minimum, add "To be hired" in the name boxes for those developer roles. It is important that the project organization chart and the human resources plan always match. If a customer questions the need for ten developers, for example, you have written justification and details in the human resources plan that you can show your customers to help answer their questions.

2. Present the project organization chart to your customers and leadership. This presentation allows team members to receive exposure at a management level that they may not normally receive and helps them recognize that they are part of a team.

As the project moves through its life cycle, post and present the project organization chart on websites, newsletters, and status reports so that everyone knows who is working on the project. Provide exposure to team members as much as possible and highlight the good work they are doing on the project. This allows team members and outside individuals who are not working on the project to understand who is working on what area of the project and who can provide information about different areas when there are questions. If any team members or customers have questions, they can go directly to the person in charge of that area for answers.

Mastering the Project Proposal

Before mastering the *project proposal*, you need to understand how this tool can help and support you on your project. The following project scenario stresses the importance of the project proposal and why it is critical to every project. Project proposals are typically relevant for construction projects where they are continuously used.

The Alaska State's Highway Engineering Department needs to build a new railway crossing over one of the major state highways. The railway crossing is due by October 10 before winter storms hit and shut down the project for weeks or months. The engineering department has twelve employees who work in the railway department and can perform the work. The problem is that they are already working on many other projects and they are unable to make the tight deadline for this new project. The engineering department must install the crossing as soon as possible and before the cold weather comes. The engineering department has asked you to be the project manager for this project. You have worked on railroad projects for many years and you jump at the chance to manage this effort. You need to get this project started as soon as possible, and you have several questions that need answering before you can get started. These questions include:

- How do you get this project started?
- How do you write a contract for this work?
- How much money is in the budget?

To answer these questions, you should use a project proposal to document the project requirements. The project proposal document contains all of the relevant project information that you can present to outside companies and bid the work to them for this project. Because the engineering department does not have enough staff to install the crossing in time, you have no choice but to develop a project proposal document and send it to various construction companies for bidding purposes. If the company matches the conditions of the contract and meets all the criteria, they usually win the project.

Cross-reference
We recommend that you review the project proposal in Chapter 14 - Defining Communication Tools to Manage Project Procurement for more information.

Creating a project proposal

Creating a project proposal is more than likely a large undertaking for any project team. The legal sections of these proposals are important, especially for projects that are going through the bidding process. Most project proposals are for bidding purposes only, and some companies rarely use them internally for projects because the focus is hiring outside contractors. Therefore, the legal side of project proposals can be difficult, and if you don't have much legal experience or legal training, you could get the company into some trouble without even knowing it. You and your contract manager's first job is to ensure that every company bidding on the work is handled the same way. There can be no special considerations for any company. For example, you cannot provide key project information to one company without offering the same information to all of them, which can cause legal issues and even lawsuits for unfair business practices. Can you imagine a company offering insider information to one company for a multimillion dollar contract and leaving the other companies out in the cold? When a project is in the bidding process, hire a legal representative, if possible, to support you—especially if there are any concerns or confusion about the bidding process. Otherwise, if you mess up and don't have a lawyer to help you, you could put your company and the project in jeopardy.

When you create the project proposal document, it is critical that you add everything possible about the project to ensure that the bidding companies aren't missing anything. It is unfair to any company to leave out known issues or concerns about a project that might affect the work delivery. Companies that intentionally leave out work are setting up the project to fail. A common practice that bidding companies take advantage of is adding a certain level of contingency (or padding) into their bid estimates to allow for any doubt or unknowns on the project. Most companies expect those added costs to be included and factored into the project proposal submissions and usually allow for that in the budget.

Project proposals act as the basis for contracts between two companies, so they need to be ironclad. Missing information may result in a series of change requests, which can derail a project if not managed correctly, making it run over budget, late, or miss part of the project schedule.

The steps for creating a project proposal can vary among project managers. Instead of providing step-by-step instructions for creating a project proposal, you can complete a project proposal template. Note that there are sections specifically for the bidding companies to complete, noted in the table below, which can vary among project types.

Table 16.7 —Project Proposal Table of Contents

#	Section Title	Description
1	Introduction	Document the project proposal specifics, such as prepared by, revisions by, and document purpose.
2	Proposal Submissions Deadline	Document the project's submissions deadlines. It is important to call out this information so bidding companies do not miss important deadline information.
3	Terms and Conditions	Document the contract's terms and conditions. The terms of a condition can vary among projects, so it is important to add the appropriate information in the document.
4	Pricing	Document the project's pricing information. If there are specific pricing information about the project, include it in this section of the document.
5	Warranty Coverage	Document warranty information about the project. Warranty information doesn't apply to all projects, but when it does, document it completely.
6	Mandatory Conditions	Document the project's mandatory conditions. It is critical that the requirements are documented. For example, "the project must finish on a *specific date*" or, "the project must finish under budget."
7	Mandatory Evaluation Criteria	Document the project's mandatory criteria based on the conditions outlined in the previous section.
8	Background and Current Practice	Document and provide a description of the background and current enterprise practices.
9	Project Description	Document the project's description.

#	Section Title	Description
10	Project Overview	Document and provide a description of the proposed project and outline the expected results. Create a brief outline of what the project aims to achieve and list the main project targets. Identify the project's success criteria.
11	Requirements Section	Document and provide a description of the project requirements. This section includes details for the bidding company to successfully bid on the project.
12	Project Structure - Roles & Responsibilities	*Note: This section is for the bidding company to complete.* Document the organization structure of the existing project, including roles and responsibilities for each role. If possible, include a project organization chart. This allows the bidding company to understand how large the project team is and where the groups could interaction.
13	Technical Requirements	Document technical information about the project. Capture technical areas that bidding companies need to be aware of, or may need to staff.
14	Critical Success Factors	Document the project's critical success factors and what your customers think are critical, allowing the bidding companies insight into how they can succeed on the project.
15	Project Plan Management	*Note: This section is for the bidding company to complete.* Document and provide an overall project management plan and a detailed work breakdown structure (WBS).
16	Deliverables	Document and provide a list and a brief description of all tangible project deliverables. Ensure that you capture the deliverables in the WBS at the work package level.
17	Work Packages, Tasks, Activities, and Milestones	*Note: This section is for the bidding company to complete.* Document and develop a brief description for all work packages with durations for each package. Provide a list and brief description of all project milestones and when they are expected to finish. A milestone is a task with no duration (zero time). A milestone identifies a significant event in your schedule. For example completing a major deliverable is a milestone event.

Using a project proposal

Before implementing the project proposal, identify who on your project team will use it so that you can cater your communications and focus on the distribution, style, and format details of the document. The main users of the project proposal document are outside vendor or contracting companies, the document details will be the same for everyone. Remember, you can get into serious legal trouble if you do not provide the same information to all companies, at the same time, throughout the bidding process.

Review the project proposal in *Chapter 14 - Defining Communication Tools to Manage Project Procurement*, and then complete the following steps:

1. After creating the project proposal document, schedule a review meeting with your customers to ensure that the proposal is correct and matches their needs. You also need to schedule a review meeting with your legal department. After you receive agreement from everyone involved the document is ready for approval, sent it along with the user acceptance document for approval by customers and leadership.

2. After you receiving approval, store the project proposal and the user acceptance document in the document control system for long-term storage, archiving, and retrieval purposes.

3. Start project discussions with outside vendors and contracting companies. Companies that are heavily project-focused typically engage in the request for proposal (RFP) process. Your procurement group should have guidelines for you to follow for contacting several companies to bid on project work.

4. After starting the project proposal process, work with the project team, customers, and leadership to respond to various vendor companies. Keep the bidding process going until you select a winning company.

5. After completing the bidding process, use the project proposal document as a basis for developing the project's contract. Much of the same information from the project proposal will go directly into the contract as the legal agreement between the two companies.

6. Begin the project with the winning company by creating the contract and having both parties sign off and agree on it.

7. As the project moves into the later phases of the project, you will use the project's contract more often than the project proposal because the contract is the legal document and the winning company should be working to satisfy it and not the project proposal.

Mastering the Quality Management Plan

Before mastering the *quality management plan*, you must understand how it can help and support you on your project. The following project scenario highlights the tool's importance and why the quality management plan is critical to every project.

A medium-sized pharmaceutical company is planning to put a new drug on the market in the next few months, but the tests continue to fail. In clinical testing, the new drug is causing allergic reactions in eight out of ten patients, so it is unsafe for general release to the public. Most of the company's resources are focused on this one drug, and they are focused on getting the failing results resolved as quickly as possible. The failure has had a negative impact on the company, and the problem must be resolved as soon as possible. As the most senior project manager on the project, you were chosen to run the SWAT team to resolve this issue. Your mission is to cut out the allergic reactions, get the drug retested, receive approval from leadership, and get it out the door for final approval from the Federal Drug Administration. You have one month to do this or the company will miss the launch date due to manufacturing backups. Missing the launch date means the loss of hundreds of thousands of dollars in lost sales.

As leader of the SWAT team, you first investigate testing and quality levels applied to the drug throughout its development cycle. You have many questions, such as locating the test results, finding out the quality level, and finding the quality metrics or quality management plan. You are concerned that these documents are either missing or unavailable for one reason or another. After further investigation, you figure out why people are having allergic reactions to the drug and you are relieved that the end is in sight. You determine that the allergic reaction is due to an additional new drug that is being added at the last minute to the drug formula. This new drug is a pain reliever, but it does not mix well with the other drugs. Early tests showed some abnormal results, but the test team ignored them and the drug continued to the clinical-testing process. You have several questions before you move forward. These questions include:

- What do you know?
- Whom should you tell the problem to?
- Where was the quality level for this project?
- What testing occurred?

To answer these questions, you need a quality management plan. When you reviewed the project materials, you never found a quality management plan and no one mentioned how quality was going to be measured. The quality management plan covers areas such as quality planning, assurance, control, and standards. The quality management plan is critical to all projects by ensuring that there are quality checks in place and that the labs are getting the best possible results with the highest quality level.

Cross-Reference
We recommend that you review the quality management plan in Chapter 10 - Communication Tools That Manage Project Quality for more information.

Creating a quality management plan

You are responsible for creating and developing the quality management plan. Regardless of the project size, every project must have some quality checks in place to ensure the highest quality possible. You need to keep your team focused on quality for all project areas. It is your job to always ensure the highest quality possible on the project.

Project customers should expect to use a quality management plan for their projects; otherwise, quality is likely not a high priority for them. Your customers need to be involved in setting the project's various quality levels and determining what quality means to the project. The project team may have one definition of quality and your customers may have another definition. It is important that they both agree on the project's quality level, and that the quality management plan reflects that agreement. There should be no surprises during the project life cycle and as different quality scenarios or concerns arise, the customer and the project team should be in complete agreement.

The steps for creating a quality management plan can vary among project managers. Instead of providing step-by-step instructions for creating a quality management plan, you can complete the quality management plan template.

Table 16.8 — Quality Management Plan Table of Contents

#	Section Title	Description
1	Quality Management Approach	Most quality management approaches base their work on the International Organization for Standardization (ISO). This general approach uses tools such as Continuous Improvement, Design Reviews, Six Sigma, TQM, and Effect Analysis.
2	Project Overview	Write a short, descriptive project overview.
3	Quality Standards	Define the quality level you want to set as a standard. State the metrics needed to preserve the quality standard.
4	Quality Tools	Choose the tools you will need to support the quality standard. You can use many tools, such as control charts, cause-and-effect diagrams, Pareto charts, scatter diagrams, statistical sampling, fishbone diagrams, and risk simulation. There are also quality audits and inspections to consider when developing this section.
5	Quality Planning	Identify and enforce the project's expected quality level. To ensure that everyone preserves a quality level throughout the project life cycle, discuss and plan the quality level with your customers and stakeholders early in the project.
6	Quality Assurance	Document the tasks that the project team must follow to meet quality assurance. Document how you will set up and determine quality assurance.
7	Quality Assurance Procedures	Document the process that implements quality assurance during the project life cycle. Do not forget continuous process improvement.
8	Quality Assurance Roles and Responsibilities	Identify the team members who will be assigned to quality assurance and document their roles and responsibilities.
9	Quality Control	Document the plan to monitor and control project task results and decide if the results meet the quality standards set up by the project.

#	Section Title	Description
10	Quality Control Procedures	Document the process that implements quality procedures during the project life cycle.
11	Quality Control Roles and Responsibilities	Identify the team members who will be assigned to quality control and document their roles and responsibilities. Create a quality roles and responsibility matrix for the team.

Note

Please note, in the defining portion of the quality management plan, Chapter 10 - Communication Tools That Manage Project Quality, there are several quality tools that are worth considering for your project. Tools such as the Pareto chart, control chart, risk simulation, and histograms are all excellent communication tools for managing quality level on your project.

Using a quality management plan

Before implementing a quality management plan, you must identify who on your project team will use it so you can determine the plan's level of details, distribution frequency, style, and format.

Before using the quality management plan, we recommend that you review the quality management plan in *Chapter 10 - Communication Tools That Manage Project Quality*, and then complete the following steps to use the plan:

1. Schedule a meeting for the team to review and verbally approve the plan.
2. After receiving verbal approval, deliver the quality management plan and the user acceptance document for approval by your customers and leadership.
3. After receiving approval on the quality management plan, store the quality management plan and the user acceptance document in the document control system for long-term archiving and retrieval.
4. Implement the quality process created and documented in the quality management plan.

As the project moves from the planning phase into the executing phase, you are responsible for continually updating the quality processes based on project results. Updates and adjustments occur throughout the project life cycle. You should seek approval and sign-offs on the quality management plan every time you change it.

Mastering the Stakeholder Register

Before mastering the *stakeholder register*, you need to understand how it can help and support you on your project. The following project scenario highlights the tool's importance and why the stakeholder register is critical to every project.

A large software development company in San Francisco, California has decided to create a new mobile phone application. The mobile application is going to change the way we use our phones and will be like no other application on the market. As the project begins, the project manager starts developing his typical documentation that he uses for every project. He develops the project repository, creates a project schedule, lines up the project's finances, and so on. The project manager feels like he is going to run a successful project. As the project progresses, everything is running smoothly and as expected. The project is using the waterfall methodology, and the project manager has moved through the requirements phase and into the development stage. The next stage of the project is development and the developers are ready. The project manager organizes a hand-off meeting between the project designers and the project developers to share information and make sure the developers have what they need. The meeting occurs with the project manager, designers, and developers and suddenly the lead developer asks about the database design and why it is missing in the design specifications. The lead developer goes on to say that there is no way that an application can be developed without a back-end database. The project manager and designers quickly realize that they forgot to include the database management people from the beginning of the project. At this point, the project will have to go back to the design table and will lose months of work.

How could this have been avoided? What could the project manager have done to ensure the right people were listed and part of the project from the start?

The answers to these questions come from a stakeholder register. The stakeholder register includes all of the individuals and groups (in this case, the database team) who are involved with a project.

Cross-Reference
We recommend that you review the stakeholder register in Chapter 15 - Defining Communication Tools to work with Stakeholders for more information.

Creating the stakeholder register

You are responsible for creating your project's stakeholder register. Your team members can help you build the stakeholder register, but you are responsible for creating it. One of your key responsibilities during this process is to constantly communicate the stakeholder register to help ensure that nobody is left off and nobody misses any communications. You might need to set up a series of 1:1 meetings with the customers to discuss the stakeholder register at status meetings and send it to everyone on the team to review. The more you share the stakeholder register, the better chance you have of keeping the list as accurate as possible and ensuring the right people are included. This is one communication tool you should over communicate and continue to update and keep current.

The steps for creating a stakeholder register can vary among project managers. Instead of providing step-by-step instructions for creating a stakeholder register, you can complete the following stakeholder register template with your stakeholder information.

Table 16.9 — Stakeholder Register Template

ID	Name & Email Address	Project Role	Contact Prefs	Area of Project Impacted	Project Expectations
1	Bob Jones -- bobjones@test.com	CIO	In-Person	Whole project	Budget & Schedule to come in on time
2	Mary Smith -- Marysmith@test.com	VP	Email	Reporting	Mary wants to make sure her reports are developed as soon as possible.
3	Kath Holt -- Kathholt@test.com	VP	In-Person	Budget	Kath is the VP of Finance and therefore wants to ensure we stay on track and on budget.
4	John Patrick -- Johnpatrick@test.com	Customer	In-Person	Whole Project	John will play the role of the project customer and will be the main point of contact.
5	Douglas Olive -- DouglasOlive@test.com	Customer – SAP	In-Person	SAP Reporting	Douglas owns the SAP platform and will be on the project to drive that portion of the project.

Using the stakeholder register

You use the stakeholder register to identify and capture information about the project stakeholders. Depending on the columns of data you want to capture, you enter information for each stakeholder, and then work with individual stakeholders to ensure the information is correct. You should constantly communicate the information stored in the stakeholder register to your stakeholders.

Before implementing the stakeholder register, review the stakeholder register section in *Chapter 15 - Defining Communication Tools to work with Stakeholders*, and then complete the following steps to use the plan:

1. Complete the stakeholder register template for your project. Work alongside your customers and project team to capture information about all of the relevant stakeholders.
2. When the document is complete, share the document with your customers and project team for feedback. Share it with your peers and management in case they know individuals or groups that you may have missed.
3. When the document is complete, send it out for review to everyone listed and on the project, which might be a different list of people, so make sure you cover everyone.
4. Store the stakeholder register in the document control system for long-term storage.

As the project moves through the various lifecycle process (design, development, testing), reintroduce the stakeholder register during status meetings and other project events. You want to make sure that this document does not become a check-box activity and it's something you keep up to date. Consider the importance of the stakeholder register for your project and you will be a much better communicator for your stakeholders, leadership, and project team.

Mastering the Stakeholder Management Plan

Before mastering the *stakeholder management plan*, you need to understand how it can help and support you on your project. The following project scenario stresses the tool's importance and why the stakeholder management plan is critical to every project.

A large lumber company in Vancouver, Washington plans to replace its telephone system. The system has been in place for twenty years and is long overdue for replacement. The project manager kicks off the project and gathers all of the key stakeholders for a meeting. The stakeholders attend the meeting and understand the project's scope, goals, and objectives. Every stakeholder is thrilled about replacing the aging telephone system. As the project progresses, it runs into some issues and starts taking longer than expected. Not a single group can be blamed for the project running behind; the whole team is to blame. While the project continues to struggle, the company is starting to see some turnover in key staff. One of the staff members who is leaving and will be replaced is Bob, the lead stakeholder on the project from the finance department. Bob has been on the project from the beginning, but has found a new opportunity and is leaving the company. Sally, also from the finance department, will take over for Bob on the project. Sally's is a vice president and Bob is a requirements analyst—these are different roles and each has different expectations from a communication perspective. The project manager meets with Bob and Sally and brings Sally up to speed on the project. The next step for the project manager is to update the stakeholder register and remove Bob's information and add Sally's. The project manager makes the update and feels good about Sally being on the project. However, just by adding Sally to the stakeholder register, the project manager is not fully set up for success when communicating with Sally. The next step for the project manager is to understand Sally's communication preferences. The project manager needs to work with Sally individually and ask her a series of questions about her role, impact, and communication preferences. These questions include:

- How do you like project communications delivered? For example, in-person, email, a dashboard?
- What influence will you have on the project?
- What is your impact on the project?
- Are you a key decision maker?

To answer these questions, you must follow the stakeholder management strategy. Identify and manage your stakeholders and take corrective actions when needed. A project manager will struggle to be successful if he or she does not use a stakeholder management plan. In scenarios like the one noted above, if the project manager is not communicating properly with the vice president, the project may have some issues. The project manager will especially have problems if the vice president is a key stakeholder and active on the project.

Cross-Reference
We recommend that you review the stakeholder management plan in Chapter 15 - Defining Communication Tools to work with Stakeholders for more information.

Creating the stakeholder management plan

You must take full responsibility for creating a stakeholder management plan. A stakeholder management plan does not take a lot of effort to create. You should create the stakeholder management plan during the project's planning phase.

The steps for creating a stakeholder register can vary from project manager to project manager. Instead of providing step-by-step instructions for creating a stakeholder register, you can complete the following stakeholder register template.

Table 16.10 — Stakeholder Management Plan Table of Contents

#	Section Title	Description
1	Document History & Approvals	Document the specifics of the document including prepared by and approval information.
2	Document Purpose	Document the stakeholder management plan's purpose.
3	Identify Stakeholders	Document the project stakeholders. Understand who your project stakeholders are so that you can create the stakeholder register. Most project managers insert the stakeholder register into the stakeholder management plan at this point.
4	Manage Stakeholders	Document the steps for managing your stakeholders.
5	Monitor and Take Corrective Action	Document the steps for performing corrective action. As you communicate and work with your customers, there must be a process for continual improvements and course corrections. For example, if your customer wants you to email a status report weekly, and then suddenly wants the status report delivered in person, you will have to react and adapt to the new request.

Using the Stakeholder Management Plan

When planning to implement the stakeholder management plan, you must first consider how you are going to use the document for your project. You can use the stakeholder management plan to understand how to communicate with project stakeholders. The stakeholder management plan's value is that it contains the stakeholders' reporting requirements. There is no other project document that contains stakeholder communication strategy information. The stakeholder management plan is an important document for delivering a project. You must understand the critical nature of the document and keep it up to date.

Before using the stakeholder management plan, we recommend that you review the stakeholder management plan section in *Chapter 15 - Defining Communication Tools to work with Stakeholders*, and then complete the following steps to use the plan:

1. Complete the stakeholder register template. Work alongside your customers and project team to capture relevant stakeholder information.
2. When the document is complete, you will have the information and names of the people you need to talk to about their communication preferences. You must have the list of people to start with before you can know your strategy.
3. Interview and work with each stakeholder to capture communication requirements. If there are a large number of stakeholders, group them into categories. For example, "these stakeholders need

face-to-face communications," "these stakeholders want weekly emails," and so on. The process is not difficult, you just need to buckle down and understand your stakeholders.

4. When the interviews are complete, start documenting your communication strategy in the communication plan. For example, if every stakeholder comes back and says he or she is okay with a weekly email, document in your plan that you will email a weekly status report on Friday's before end of day. Documenting the strategy is easy; you just need to hear what your stakeholders want.

5. When the stakeholder management plan is complete, and you documented your strategies in the plan, send it out to your stakeholders for review. You don't need to get their approval on the document, but it would not hurt if you had it and it is a best practice for you to try and capture.

6. Store the stakeholder management plan in the document control system for long-term storage.

Summary

The communication tools that we described in this chapter are some of the best choices for the project's initiation process. The initiation process is the first process in a project's life cycle. Project managers need to set up a communication rhythm and understand how to create and use the tools in this chapter before any work begins. The initiation process is also one of the most important processes that must be done correctly or the project will suffer. The initiation process also has the most communication tools available. You will not use all the tools outlined in the initiation process, but you should at least consider using some of them.

The tools in this chapter include some of the popular tools used by many project managers. These tools include the business case, circle-of-communications chart, communication plan, customer requirements, document control system, feasibility study, project charter, project kick-off meeting, project management plan, project organization chart, project proposal, quality management plan, stakeholder register, stakeholder management plan.

Each of these tools will help you be successful in managing and executing your project.

Chapter 17

Using Communication Tools to Administer the Planning Process

IN THIS CHAPTER

- ♦ Mastering the Change Readiness Assessment
- ♦ Mastering the Dashboard report
- ♦ Mastering the Responsibility Matrix
- ♦ Mastering the Risk Model

In this chapter, we explore project communication tools for administrating the project planning process. Project managers should spend most of their time planning projects, so they need a series of communication tools to help them along the way. The tools in this chapter help the project manager with this task.

The planning process for large projects often go on for several months and during that time, the project manager is expected to communicate status. The tools that we outline in this chapter will help you manage the planning process and will help you communicate more effectively.

Let's explore the communication tools necessary to help you plan your project.

Mastering the Change Readiness Assessment

Before you can master the *change readiness assessment,* you need to understand how this tool can help and support you on your project. The following project scenario highlights the tool's importance, and why the change readiness assessment document is important to every project.

A large hospital in western New York was struggling with their payroll system for many years. They hit a problem when the system that sends the paychecks started sending them to employees two weeks late. The employees, as you can imagine, were furious, some were so mad at the company that they were thinking about quitting. The hospital administrators called emergency meetings and the human resources payroll supervisor was working day and night to resolve the issue. This issue impacted all of the hospital's locations and something had to be done immediately. The project kicks off and the project manager and key customers are assigned to it. The key customer was at the headquarters location and had counterparts in all other locations on the project. As the project manager and key customers worked through the problem to pick out software, connecting the software to the other locations was a key requirement of the software they needed to buy because the payroll issue was happening at all locations. As the project progressed, the project manager and customer decided on the software package to purchase and hired an implementation team to install it. The software was installed at the main hospital first, and then rolled out to the other hospitals, one installation at a time. As the project progressed, the main hospital had no problems and the implementation was a success. When the project manager went to the first location outside the main hospital and approached the IT support person, that person has no idea about the upcoming release. The project manager contacted the second location, and they had no idea either. None of the locations had any idea about the new software installation. The project manager and key customer did not prepare the locations for the new payroll software installation, and none of the locations could take the new software. The project was a failure because each location needed to have the payroll system at the same time, so one location having the software and not the others was unacceptable.

To have prevented this scenario from occurring, the project manager should have used a change readiness assessment document for the project. The change readiness assessment document describes, in detail, the information that people need to accept and adopt the upcoming change. Using a change readiness assessment document in this scenario would have prepared the different locations for the upcoming change.

Cross-Reference
We recommend that you review the change readiness assessment tool in Chapter 12 - Defining Communication Tools That Manage Project Communications for more information.

Creating the change readiness assessment

When creating the change readiness assessment document, your first step is to ensure that the template includes the information needed for the organization that is about to experience the change. The key section of the template is the *readiness factors* section. You should closely consider readiness factors for your project. Every company will have a set of their own readiness factors, so they will be different from place to place. As the person responsible for driving change in the organization, you must ensure that the readiness factors for your project are completed and follow the company's standards. Readiness factors are important to address when preparing the organization for a change. The process for deciding the project's organization factors depends on many items. The first item is the project type and what are you implementing in the project. The project type will play a big role in understanding the change readiness of an organization. The second item is discovering special considerations for the individuals who are going to be impacted by the change. Do they need training? Do they have the right skills? Part of your role in the change readiness assessment process is meeting with the individuals who are about to experience the change and understanding what can be done to avoid any problems. You should understand what is important to each individual that is about to experience the change. For example, if the organization experiencing the change is using a particular operating system on their computers, and that operating system is going to be replaced with a different one, those users will need training on the new software. In this example, you would add training as a change readiness assessment factor in the change readiness assessment document. Identifying the readiness factors is a key part of creating a change readiness assessment document and is project and organization specific. If you don't consider the importance of these factors, or you don't completely capture the factors in the change readiness assessment document, you will have a tough time getting the organization to adopt the change whether it's a new system, new leadership, etc.

There is no special process for creating a readiness template besides sitting down and filling it out. Instead of going into details about completing the template, review the template below as a starting point for your project.

Table 17.1 — Example of a change assessment readiness template shows an example of a change readiness assessment template. This template was introduced earlier in the book (*Chapter 12 - Defining Communication Tools That Manage Project Communications for more information*); however, this example has been filled in to help you understand how to use it for your project. In this example, you will quickly see how valuable a change readiness assessment template is. For example, focus on #4: Funding Secured, which is in a Red status and has a big impact to the organization. Focus on resolving the Red issues as soon as possible.

Table 17.1 — Example of a change assessment readiness template

#	Readiness Factor	Readiness Status (G/Y/R)	Readiness Owner Name	Leadership Support Required (Y/N)	Impact of Change
1	Vision for Change	Green	To be identified	Y	Big Impact
2	Strategy and Plan Validated	Yellow	Kath Holt	Y	Medium Impact
3	Benefits Understood	Red	Dean Jones	Y	Medium Impact
4	Funding Secured	Red	Kath Holt	N	Big Impact
5	Timelines Validated	Yellow	Kath Holt	N	Big Impact if not scheduled with key staff
6	Resources Available to Execute	Green	Kath Holt	Y	Low Impact
7	Business/Customers Ready to Receive	Red	Kath Holt	N	Medium Impact
8	Security Set for Rollout	Green	Dean Irene	Y	Medium Impact

#	Readiness Factor	Readiness Status (G/Y/R)	Readiness Owner Name	Leadership Support Required (Y/N)	Impact of Change
9	Communications & Awareness	Green	Dean Irene	Y	Low Impact
10	Training Complete	Yellow	Dean Irene	N	Low Impact

Using the change readiness assessment

Before you can use the change readiness assessment report, you must identify who will use this tool. In most projects, you're not responsible for creating the change readiness assessment document. On large projects, you hire a person solely for managing and preparing the organization for the upcoming change. In the project management industry, these roles are known as "readiness project manager," or "organizational change lead," or similar. The titles might be different, but each is responsible for preparing the organization to receive the project's product.

Before using a change readiness template, review the document to determine whether the format will work for your organization. If not, revise the template as early into the project as possible. Add necessary columns and complete the information for each column within the template. When the document is filled out, complete the following steps:

1. If you are driving the change for the organization, you will work with the individuals across the organization to determine their change readiness areas—also known as "change readiness factors." Each change readiness factor will have a single owner, and you will work with them to collect the needed information to ensure that the organization is ready for the change. For example, in the table above, Readiness Factor #7: Business/Customers Ready to Receive, your responsibility would be to work with Kath Holt and her customers to make sure they are ready to receive the project's product. For example, a new payroll system is being created for the finance department and Kath Holt is the finance manager who is responsible for the department. Your role would be to work with Kath to ensure her employees are ready and trained to adopt the new payroll system. You would continue to work with Kath and her employees throughout the project life cycle.

2. During the weekly status meetings, update the organization change readiness document based on the project's updated status. Pay close attention to the change readiness factors you collected and decide if they are impacted by the project's status. If the project status alters one of the project's change readiness factors, work directly with the owner and update the readiness documentation based on what is occurring on the project.

3. Continue to manage each change readiness factor for the project. Also, work closely with the owners of the change readiness factors to ensure that everyone is ready for the upcoming change. By the end of the project, you or the change readiness lead would have completed the work of each change readiness factor and the organization would be ready to accept the change.

4. Once approved, store the change readiness assessment in the document control system for long-term archiving and accessibility.

Mastering the Dashboard Report

Before you can master the *dashboard report*, you must understand how this tool can help and support you on your project. The following project scenario highlights the importance of the tool and why the dashboard report is important to every project.

A large software company is interested in consolidating their project reporting. Every year, the company works on 20 to 25 different projects and employs hundreds of staff. The projects span multiple project types, including software development, hardware upgrades, implementation, and package solution evaluations. Each project uses a standard project management methodology. In the project management methodology there is a set of project characteristics that are common across projects. These characteristics include, but are not limited to, quality, status, risks, issues, and finish dates. It is important to note that even though the projects are different, they each have the same basic characteristics. You, as the project manager, need to consolidate the information from each project into a format that is easy to read and understand by your leadership team. The information must be ready for them to review by 8:00 am each day, and you are responsible for providing it.

The challenge is that the leadership team demands a dynamically created status; they no longer want to wait for you to compile and send a manual report. You know that anything that is automatically created can have problems, and because it is for leadership, you must be extra careful. You are concerned and have some questions about how to move forward with an automated solution. Your questions are:

- How do you consolidate this information?
- What information is standard across all projects for grouping and reporting?
- How will you automate this so it does not become a support nightmare?
- What tools are available for this process?

To get the answers to these questions, you can use a dashboard report for all of leadership's consolidated reporting. Project dashboard reports are quickly becoming a favorite management reporting tool and are becoming standard in most large companies' enterprise project management. A project dashboard combines data from multiple projects into a single view, which is usually stored on a company's intranet site. When you combine multiple project data sets into a single dashboard, leadership can see the status of all of your projects, not just a single project. Comparing one project against another is one of the biggest advantages a dashboard produces. Leadership and customers will benefit from using the project dashboard across multiple projects because of the information it presents and the summary view of the project information it displays.

Cross-Reference
We recommend that you review the dashboard report tool in Chapter 15 - Defining Communication Tools for Working with Stakeholders for more information.

Creating a dashboard report

Creating a dashboard report is a common method of communicating project information throughout the organization, at every level. Dashboard reports are becoming common for today's projects, providing leadership a consolidated view for each project's status and issues. One of the factors to consider when creating a dashboard report is the long-term expense and the cost of maintenance to the company. Creating a dashboard report is not a one-time activity. They take time and effort to produce and you should view them as tools that supply project information. Project dashboards need regular updating and improving. As more projects start and more project information is available, consider adding the data to the project dashboard. This provides visibility to leadership and gives project customers a view into extra project data. Some dashboard reports report data real-time, which requires a support mechanism to produce the data.

Sometimes, you may want to provide a dashboard report, but cannot create an automated version so your only choice is a manual solution. Producing a manual dashboard report, with a consolidated view of the project status is better than not producing one at all. The simplest dashboard report available is a series of charts created in a spreadsheet tool, such as Microsoft Excel. Excel has charting capabilities, so you could create a series of six or more charts, side by side, as the purest, most basic form of a dashboard report. For example, the project dashboard in *Chapter 15 - Defining Communication Tools for Working with Stakeholders,* in Excel, shows a large amount of project information to the customer.

Your customer should be involved in deciding what information to include in the dashboard report. The data should provide real value to the customer, which allows them to make project decisions. The customer should be diligent about selecting the right data for the project dashboard. The customer should work with the project team to determine when the data gets updated. A dashboard report is almost useless if you do not regularly update the data, or if the data becomes stale. At a minimum, the dashboard requires weekly, if not daily, updates.

The steps for creating a dashboard report tool vary. Complete the following steps to manually create a dashboard:

1. Choose a tool that has charting and spreadsheet capabilities, such as Excel. The goal is to create the dashboard structure, and then move to automating the data entry. It is important for the customer to find value in the data you are presenting on the dashboard. Get customer approval so that you do not waste time creating charts that nobody wants. You can always create more complex charts later, if the customer approves.

2. Select the most relevant and important project data for your charts, such as cost charts, resource hours charts, change request charts, performance charts, and estimating and forecasting charts. Some of the more technically savvy project customers will already have favorite chart types to use for the dashboard display.

Tip
Make sure that you can produce the chart that your customer wants. Do not promise the customer that you can produce a report when you have no idea how. It is possible you may not be able to produce it.

3. Create the table of data for each chart in the spreadsheet. Remember, the data must be valuable and relevant to the customer or they won't use the dashboard. Your customers only want to see data they care about; anything else will seem irrelevant to them.

4. Continue this process and create data tables for each chart type and add them to your project's dashboard report. It is common for only six charts to represent a dashboard, especially when using a spreadsheet. You can use up to nine separate charts, but depending on the charts, that might be too much information, making it difficult to read.

Tip
Remember, you are creating a single chart for a single row of data. Therefore, if you have cost data in one table and resource hours in a second table, you must create two separate charts. Do not combine the charts; it would defeat the purpose because each chart should be focused on a single item.

5. Align the charts together, three across and two down on the spreadsheet. You can use **Figure 17.1 — Example of a dashboard report (using Microsoft Project)** as a guide for placing the charts in the dashboard report.

6. When you finish aligning the dashboard charts, you are ready to use the dashboard report.

Figure 17.1 shows a spreadsheet version of a project dashboard report. Dashboard reports come in all shapes and sizes and are specific to project type and customer needs.

Figure 17.1 — Example of a dashboard report (using Microsoft Project)

Using a dashboard report

Before you can use the dashboard report, identify who will use it so that you can determine how much detail to include, distribution frequency, style, and dashboard format. Usually, customers, leadership, and executives in the organization are the main users of the dashboard. Therefore, the dashboard information is at a high level and consolidated to show all of the projects in the organization. The customers or leadership who guide you in creating the various reports to be used on the dashboards.

Before using a dashboard report, review the dashboard report in Chapter 15 - Defining Communication Tools for Working with Stakeholders for more information.

Then complete the following steps:

1. Make sure your project customer values the project dashboard and that it delivers the information that the customer needs to make project decisions. The customer might want to learn more about the project, which is also a good reason for using a project dashboard. The first mistake you can make is to add a dashboard report that provides no value to the customer. It wastes their time and sets a bad impression.

2. After receiving approval of the dashboard format, enforce using the dashboard report. Work with the customer to understand what project information to add or tweak on the dashboard. Other activities for working with the dashboard include changing the timing for receiving data files, or adding more users, and so on. For manual dashboard reports, there are many areas you can work with to ensure the dashboard is suitable for the customer, such as moving it to an automated format or introducing new data and chart types.

3. Throughout the project's executing process, the dashboard report will contain up-to-date project information. The dashboard will be always available to your customers and leadership who want to see the latest happenings on the project. If the dashboard is manual, you will need to deliver it to your customers once a week. It is important that you communicate with your customers regularly and ensure they are receiving the dashboard data they expect. There are many methods for sharing dashboard reports, such as sending the dashboard as a spreadsheet, in email, or in a formal presentation.

4. After you create the project dashboard report, store the document in the project's document control system for long-term storage, archiving, and retrieval purposes.

A printed dashboard report can be the first step toward a full-blown, automated, enterprise-wide dashboard on every manager's computer. An automated dashboard allows any manager to view project information on their screen in any way they want. If they want, they can drill down to the lowest detail. Many consulting companies create enterprise dashboards.

Mastering the Responsibility Matrix

Before you can master the *responsibility matrix*, you must understand how it can help support you on your project. The following project scenario highlights the importance of a responsibility matrix and why it is so important to the project.

A midsized insurance company in Dallas, Texas has decided to develop a new payroll system to replace its current manual application. Management assigns you the role of scheduler and cost control manager. The project is already three months into the planning process, so you are a little behind when you start, but you are confident that you can catch up quickly and start to add value to the project. You do not know the other team members, so the project manager introduces you to 11 team members on your scheduling team, and 5 members of your cost team. After a week on the project, you are finding it difficult to get information you need about who does what on the project. You have requested a project organization chart, but the project is so large it only shows group titles, so it does not give you the information you need. You need answers to many questions to find out who is responsible for what area of the project. Your questions include:

- Do team members understand their project responsibilities?
- Which groups are involved in the project?
- Who is the consultant that decides project deliverables?
- Who is accountable for producing what on the project?

To get the answers to these questions, you can use a responsibility matrix. The responsibility matrix shows who is responsible for performing project activities. For project deliverables, it documents who creates the project deliverables. New team members can immediately use the responsibility matrix to understand who works on what, and which groups are involved in the project. The responsibility matrix is sometimes called "RACI," which stands for responsible, accountable, consult, and inform. Other names include "responsibility assignment matrix," or "RAM."

Cross-Reference
We recommend that you review the responsibility matrix in Chapter 11 - Communication Tools for Human Resource Management for more information.

Creating a responsibility matrix

When creating a responsibility matrix, make sure the project team understands immediately who is responsible for what on the project. The responsibility matrix is especially important on projects where team members are located in different organizations. Projects with a large vendor presence also use responsibility matrixes. Make sure that no one is working on a task that they shouldn't be working on.

In software development projects, such as database technology projects, there is a different responsibility matrix type called the CRUD matrix. The CRUD matrix stands for create, read, update, and delete. These represent different security access levels, which are granted to particular roles in a software application. For example, one role in the software could have only an "R" access assigned to it. In that case, it would mean it could only "read" data from the tables, it could not "create," "update," or "delete" records from that table.

Make sure there is a responsibility matrix on every project, regardless of how large or small. The responsibility matrix should also be developed and approved before any work activities begin. Get approval on the responsibility matrix to avoid confusion or possible conflicts with team members. Implementing a responsibility matrix helps ensure that the project team understands the project activities they are responsible for. Using the responsibility matrix also prevents team members from overlapping or duplicating work activities.

Developing a responsibility matrix can be a long process, but it is important that team members agree on their roles and responsibilities before work begins. You cannot execute a project, and then decide to put a responsibility matrix in place and expect people to follow it. It is not going to happen. The responsibility matrix eliminates confusion and miscommunications between team members by stating who is responsible for each project deliverable.

You must be diligent about getting sign-off and approvals for the responsibility matrix from the project team and management. It is a best practice to engage team members before revising the responsibilities matrix or CRUD. This can't be done with half the team or with only limited people involved. You must drive everyone's involvement when creating the responsibility matrix. You will also use the formal acceptance document to get responsibility matrix sign-off, and then store both documents in the document control system.

The project customer might play a small role in creating the responsibility matrix and might want to be involved in assigning project resources to the project. When customers are assigned project tasks, they need to understand and agree to their roles while you are creating the responsibility matrix. If the customer cannot take on a role or task, you are responsible for working with them to assign it to someone else. It is the customer's responsibility to account for and ensure completion of assigned activities.

The steps for creating a responsibility matrix vary. If you have never created a responsibility matrix, the following steps can help you get started.

1. Define the responsibility matrix template. Find out if your company has one because it will include company-specific fields that will be unique to your company.
2. Go over the template with your team. Explain to each team member the legend and what each letter stands for and the chart's layout and format.
3. Show your team how to add deliverables to the template, by major project milestone. Include deliverables in the project initiation phase, design phase, and test phase. Add deliverables directly to the template.
4. Add all the project roles in the columns across the top, forming a matrix.
5. As a team, add the responsibility code for each role to each deliverable on the project. These discussions can be challenging, and as project manager, you will need to drive these discussions for what makes sense for the project. This step includes adding the letter "R" to you for the task of creating an end-to-end project schedule. This can be a long process and may cause the team members concern. The biggest problems the team members will have is taking on tasks they do not believe are theirs, or a task that another team member is working on in their area of the project. The responsibility matrix discussion can be uncomfortable and requires a strong project manager to ensure that everyone is on board and ready to complete the tasks assigned to them. Include your customers in this discussion early, and don't leave it until after you and your team have completed the matrix and presented it to the customer. That could be a recipe for a disaster. Continue the process until you and your team members are satisfied with the results.
6. Send the completed RACI to the project team and your customers for approval. This is a critical step in the process because your team members and customers approve what they will be accountable for on the project.
7. Update the matrix when changes occur. Keep it current.

Figure 17.2 — **Example of a responsibility matrix** shows an example of a responsibility matrix template. This blank template is ready and available for you to complete. Updates to the template are project-specific and include particular project roles and project phases that differ among projects. It is your responsibility to update the matrix accordingly.

Figure 17.2 — Example of a responsibility matrix

Responsibility Matrix Chart Example

Responsibility Codes:
Responsible: Performs the work
Accountable: Ultimately accountable for delivery; maximum one per task
Sign-Off: Approval must be gained for deliverable to be acceptable
Consult: Review & provide feedback
Informed
(blank) = not involved

	Proj Mgr	UAT Lead	Training Lead	Management	Sponsor1 (TBD)	Lead Analyst	Designer	Dev Lead	Test Lead	Tier 1 Rep	Release Lead	Operations Lead
Project Initiation/Kickoff												
Task A	R											
Work Product A												
Task C												
Business Requirements												
Task C	R											
Work Product A			I	I	C				C	I		
Work Product B							C					
System Requirements												
Task C	I					R						
Task D			I	I	C			R	C	I		
Work Product A		R,A					C					
Design												
Work Product A			I	I	C			R	C	I		
Work Product B		R,A					C					
Work Product C							C					
Build												
Task F			I	I	C			R	C	I		
Task G		R,A					C					
Task H							C					
Test												
Task I	R											
Work Product A			I	I	C				C	I		A
Task K							C			C		
User Acceptance Approval Phase												
Task L	R	R,A	R									
Work Product A	A											
Task N		A										
Production Phase												
Work Product A	I							R			R	
Task P					C	I		A				
Work Product B									A			
Post Production Support / Warranty Period (if Applicable)												
Task O	I							R			R	
Task P					C	I		A				
Task Q									A			

Using the responsibility matrix

Before you can use a responsibility matrix, identify who on your project team will use it. This is important information because you need to know the level of detail to include, distribution frequency, style, and the responsibility matrix format. A responsibility matrix stores detailed project activities and project assignments. Before using the responsibility matrix, review the responsibility matrix section in *Chapter 11 - Communication Tools for Human Resource Management*, and then complete the following steps:

1. Work with your team members to review the contents of the responsibility matrix. The goal is to ensure that everyone agrees with how the responsibility codes are allocated to them. Work with everyone involved in the project and discuss, as a team, each role and responsibility.

2. After everyone agrees, approves, and signs off on the contents of the responsibility matrix, the document is locked unless major project changes occur. Use the responsibility matrix as a checklist at the beginning of each project phase and go over it with your team members to ensure everyone is in agreement. Make sure they review it and are comfortable with producing the deliverables they agreed to for that particular phase.

3. As the project moves into the executing process, you should continually review the responsibility matrix with your team. The goal is to ensure that they create the deliverables they agreed to when they signed off on the document. As the project continues through its lifecycle, continually check progress of the deliverables assigned to your team members until everything is complete and the project closes out.

Mastering the Risk Modeling Process

Before you can master the *risk models and modeling*, you must understand how it can help and support you on your project. The following project scenario highlights the tool's importance.

A small design and construction company in Tacoma, Washington, has hired a risk management consulting company to analyze the risk events among five software projects. The owner of the design and construction company, who also owns the five software projects, is risk adverse. When it comes to project risk, she is fidgety and likes to be well aware of all the possible risk events. She wants to know which of the five projects has the most risk and what she can do to prevent those risk events. Because of a poor business cycle, she needs to postpone one of the projects because there is not enough budget for all projects. She feels that if she assesses all the projects, and then decides which is the riskiest, she may be able to postpone just one. As the most senior project manager at your risk consulting company, you have offered to take on and manage the task of finding out which project(s) to postpone. You start your activities by running a risk analysis and creating a risk matrix for each one of the five projects. You discover a pattern for each project, but three of the matrixes were so similar it is hard to tell which one has the highest risk. The owner is not pleased. She was looking for a more definitive answer because she must cut at least one project from the five. She wants to see from you a method with simple and understandable justification. You try to explain the matrix values, but this makes the owner even more confused and angry.

- You understand what the owner wants, but do not have the correct tools to create the results.
- How could you have avoided this situation?
- How can you solve this dilemma?

You should use a risk model to get the answers to these questions. There are many types of project risk models, but most of them are in-house and customized using a spreadsheet, and some are computer programs designed for a specific task. The risk model tool is perfect for this scenario. In creating a risk model, you create a project risk score wherein the elements, which you can measure and compare, are consistent across all other projects. This gives you reliable metrics for comparing one project to another. You create the metrics for the model and have total control over them and their associated scores. However, the owner or customer must approve the metrics before you run the model.

Cross-Reference
We recommend that you review the risk model tool in Chapter 13 - Defining Communication Tools to Manage Project Risk for more information.

Creating a risk model

Creating and updating a risk model for each project is one of your primary responsibilities. As the project changes, the risk score will also change. Therefore, you need to update the risk model to produce a new risk score and a new risk assessment for the project. It is important for every project manager to understand the project risks, the overall assessment of those risks, and the level of severity associated to them. The risk score concept for many project managers is fairly new, but it helps uncover a project's real risk assessment. Without it, you may not know your risk impacts and how relative they are in scale to other projects. Some project managers and team members assess risks as low risk, medium risk, or high risk, and make the assessments based on their personal feelings, not facts or data. Rarely does high, medium, or low ever have enough detail to explain the meaning behind an assessment, and often project managers or owners lean on their experiences from past projects to clarify what they mean. A risk score removes this situation and forces projects through the same assessment ratings to produce a score based on the same criteria applied to the same types of projects. In the end, the higher risk score project is the riskier project.

You can create a risk score on all of your projects by using a project risk modeling spreadsheet. After doing so, you will quickly become accustom to using risk scores on your projects and rely on that information to help you decide on project items. Some decisions you make by using risk score information include how much contingency is needed in forecasting, staffing allocations, and schedule adjustments. These decisions include anything related to the project and the overall risk assessment.

Project customers should be active in the risk modeling process. In project situations where you are risk adverse and the project client is more of a risk taker, the project's overall risk score should reflect both parties' opinions in how they answer the questions. It is critical the project does not report a risk score skewed by the dominant opinions of one or two people. This process must have agreement from the whole team for it to be reliable and successful.

Figure 17.3 — Example of a risk model

Project Risk Model Example

		Total Project Risk Score		Component Risk Assessments	
	Interim Score	0			
				Low Budget Risk	
	Low Risk 1 - 35	Score 0			
				Low External Dependencies Risk	
				Low Management Risk	
	Medium Risk 36 - 72	Score			
				Low Mission Critical Risk	
				Low Failure Risk	
	High Risk > 72	Score			
				Low Complexity Risk	
	Question Number	Project Risk Question		Answer Lists (Note--when you click in each answer cell, a drop down list arrow will appear)	
Budget Risk	1	What is the estimated total project cost?			
	2	What percentage of the agency budget does the project represent?			
	3	Have sufficient project funds been budgeted and allocated?			
	4	How much confidence is there in the expenditure and funding projections?			
	5	Is funding available for maintenance of the project deliverable after project closure?			
External Dependencies Risk	6	Is this project dependent on another project's deliverable?			
	7	Does this project require resources from other organizations?			
	8	Does this project require data from other sources?			
Management Risk	9	What is the level of management commitment?			
	10	Is the project sponsor resourcing the project?			
	11	What is the experience and training level of agency project managers?			

To ensure all projects calculate their risks using the same methodology, organizations should adopt the risk model template on all projects. Using the risk model template ensures the criteria for assessing risks are identical for all projects. Using this risk model also helps you make assessments between projects. The risk scores reflect the true risk scores of the project and help everyone understand which projects have the most risk.

Using a risk model

Before using the risk model, identify who on your project team will use it so that you can determine the level of detail to include, distribution frequency, style, and report format. Risk models are detailed in nature and allow anyone trying to understand how risky a project is a much easier process.

Before using a risk model, review the risk model section in *Chapter 13 - Defining Communication Tools to Manage Project Risk*, and then complete the following steps:

1. Open your project's risk model spreadsheet.

Note
The developer created the template in Microsoft Excel, so using Excel or a software package that can read Excel files is desirable.

2. Change each risk question to make it more applicable to your project. The risk model spreadsheet comes with various standard risk questions that apply to most projects; however, because the questions are generic, they may not fully apply to your project. Work with your team members and customer to develop the questions and adapt them to your project. In doing so, you create the true project risk score, which is a much better representation of the project's risk level.

3. Adjust, if applicable, your risk scores after answering the risk questions. In the same way you changed the risk questions, there is a good chance you will need to change the score ranges as well. At the end of this step, the risk model should be ready to use.

4. As the project moves into the planning process, enforce the use of the risk model on your project. Have project team members answer the risk questions and periodically calculate new project risk scores.

5. Report the results of the risk model, specifically the risk score, to your customer and leadership. Store a copy of the project's risk model in the document control system for long-term storage, archiving, and retrieval purposes. Depending on the results and the discussions from customers or leadership, you may need to make project adjustments.

6. As the project moves into the executing process, meet with your project team monthly and re-run the risk model to produce a new risk score.

7. After every run, a new risk score is created. Present the results to your customer and leadership for review. If applicable, make project changes or adjustments based on your customer's review of the risk score.

8. At the end of the project, after running your last risk model, provide the last version to your customer. Store the risk model in the document control system.

Summary

The tools described in this chapter are some of the more common communication tools for project managers to use for project planning. The planning process is one of the most important processes for project managers to complete correctly. Proper project planning sets up team members to complete projects deliverables. Without good and thorough planning, your project may suffer.

The tools in this chapter include some of the popular tools, such as the change readiness assessment, project dashboard, responsibility matrix, risk model, and the project approach. These tools are common to project managers and are used in almost every industry. Using the reporting communications tools identified in this chapter will benefit both the stakeholders and the project team and improve project communications. The tools and reports are simple, easy to create, and informative for presenting information to various parties.

Chapter 18

Using Communication Tools to Plan and Develop Project Deliverables

IN THIS CHAPTER

- ◆ Mastering the Baseline Schedule
- ◆ Mastering the Change Control plan
- ◆ Mastering the Comprehensive Test plan
- ◆ Mastering the Design Specifications
- ◆ Mastering the Expected Monetary Value
- ◆ Mastering the Project Calendar
- ◆ Mastering the Project Schedule
- ◆ Mastering the System Requirements
- ◆ Mastering the Work Breakdown Structure (WBS)

In this chapter, we explore project communication tools to help you during the project planning process. When project managers start planning a project, they rarely consider the tools they will use because their focus is elsewhere, such as the project's budget, schedule, scope, and resources.

The tools in this chapter will guide you as you think about how you will manage the project's planning and executing processes. These tools give you a head start when managing and administrating the planning process and make you aware of tools that you can start using immediately.

Mastering the Baseline Schedule

Before you can master the baseline schedule, you must understand how this tool can help and support you on your project. The following project scenario highlights the baseline schedule's importance.

Your company is working on a prestigious subcontract for a skyscraper in Dubai, United Arab Emirates. The skyscraper is the tallest building in the world. Your company has completed about 25 percent of the job, and it is on time and within budget. The BD project manager scheduled a meeting with your company to get a progress update. He wants a comparison report between the original planned finish dates and the actual finish dates for the activities that your company has completed, or is working on. He also wants to see a performance chart to evaluate your progress against what you had planned to do. You show the BD project manager the schedule and explain that your team is two days early. He understands, but patiently repeats his request for a variance report on the project's finish dates. The BD project manager stands up, says that producing variance reports are in the contract, and wants the two variance reports (cost and schedule) on his desk first thing in the morning. You tell him the task usually takes three days to complete and, therefore, it may not be possible to get it to him in two days. Unfortunately, you did not create a baseline schedule when you started the project because you simply never thought you would need it. You neglected to read the part of the contract that defined the scheduling requirements. The current schedule has had five changes, so creating a baseline schedule from it will be difficult. You ask yourself the following questions:

- How can I go back in time and recreate the original schedule without compromising the current schedule, and have the requested reports ready by morning?
- Is there a saved schedule that does not include progress?
- Is that schedule accurate? How will we know if it is accurate?

To answer these questions, you should have used a baseline schedule tool. However, the answers to this scenario are two-fold. You must first recreate the original schedule by removing all progress and changes from the current schedule. Then, use the original schedule to create a baseline schedule. When you have a baseline schedule, the cost and schedule variance reports will be relatively easy to produce using any automated scheduling tool.

Cross-Reference
We recommend that you review the baseline schedule's document planning questions in Chapter 8 - Communication Tools That Manage Project Time.

Creating a baseline schedule

Creating a baseline schedule is a best-practice technique for all projects. Even if you do not plan on using one, it is so simple to create, that you should create one just in case you need it. More than likely, there will be several occasions during the project where you will refer to a baseline schedule, so having it will be valuable. Some examples of needing a baseline schedule include reviewing date and cost variances, analyzing schedule and cost performance indexes, monitoring estimates at completion, and reporting the remaining estimate to complete. These scenarios would not be possible without creating the baseline schedule.

You should create a baseline schedule as soon as you receive approval of the original schedule. The original schedule establishes the baseline. Every time there is an approved change request, update the baseline to keep it synchronized with the current schedule. Otherwise, there will be a false variance between the current schedule and the baseline schedule.

Project customers quickly learn how valuable the baseline schedule is when they see the project's performance information. Your customer can compare the current budget and the baseline budget, current schedule to the baseline schedule, and so on. When you create a baseline schedule, many performance reports are available.

Creating a baseline schedule is straightforward; however, it does depend heavily on the project-scheduling tool you use. Each product will have a slightly different process for creating a baseline. To create a baseline for your project, follow the instructions for your project management software system.

Tip
Ensure there is no progress reported on any tasks when creating a baseline schedule.

Using a baseline schedule

Before using a baseline schedule, identify who on your project team will use it so you can determine the level of detail, distribution frequency, style, and baseline schedule format. Review the baseline schedule section in *Chapter 8 - Communication Tools That Manage Project Time*, and then complete the following steps:

1. Compare the baseline dates to the current project dates by using a scheduling tool to refer to the graphic time line. Or, you can use the tool's reporting capabilities. In this step, you review, analyze, determine where the project currently stands, and compare the actual dates to the planned dates for each project activity. Report and act on those variances, where applicable.

2. Compare the project's current costs to the baseline costs and report the information to your customer and upper management. Use the series of reports in the project scheduling tool.

3. Compare the project's labor hours to the baseline labor hours and report the variances. Use the series of reports in the project scheduling tool.

4. Report the total project variance to your customer and upper management. Depending on the impact and different variances, your customer may require you to make course corrections to the project.

Mastering the Change Control Plan

Before you master the *change control plan*, you must understand how it can help and support you on your project. The following project scenario highlights why a change control plan is critical to every project.

A large telephone company has decided to replace the human resource system with a new off-the-shelf application. The new application will need to capture and store employee data, and therefore certain precautions must be taken to protect that data from getting into the wrong hands. These precautions need the project manager to collect input from different groups in the company responsible for securing data. The project manager will work to understand how to collect the data in the new application and how it can be displayed while still protecting the employee's personal data. The legal department and the employees' union representatives will want to ensure they understand who has access to what data, and who is controlling that access. You, as the top project manager for the company, are now leading this effort, and one of your first tasks is to create the customer requirements for the project. You assign an analyst to work with each group to collect their system requirements. After your analyst completes the business requirements document and receives approval, the project manager puts the document under change control. No changes are allowed without formal approval. The project manager and the analyst believe that everyone's requirements are documented, and because they all signed off, the next phase of the project can begin. As the project moves into the design phase, the leadership team reviews some of the screen designs, and they notice examples of screens and reports that display personal information. The leadership teams are not happy with what they see. Your analyst thought he was clear when he wrote in the specifications document to show only limited personnel information fields on screens or reports. However, because he said "limited" in the document, and did not specify exactly what "limited" meant, the development team wants a change request to remove personnel information fields on the screens. It appears the analyst didn't correctly capture the specific requirements around what type of information can be displayed on the screen, and it will cost the project time and budget to correct. The development team made wrong assumptions in their coding, but they are standing behind their decision to code what they saw in the document. You have several questions, including:

- How can I control this project change?
- What process or procedures should I follow?
- How do I control costs and schedule changes associated to this change?
- What happens if we get 25 to 50 change requests in one week?

To answer the questions, you should use a change control plan. A change control plan documents the process and procedures to control project changes. Project changes occur all the time, and projects that have clearly defined and an established change control process can usually prevent changes from negatively influencing the project.

Cross-Reference
We recommend that you review the change control plan in Chapter 15 - Defining Communication Tools for Working with Stakeholders for more information.

Creating a change control plan

Creating a change control plan is critical to every project, regardless of size or industry. Scope changes can easily derail projects and possibly shut them down. Change control is a serious part of project management and something that you should closely manage and control throughout the project.

Establish a project change control process as early as possible in the project to ensure that all parties, team members, and customers agree to use the process. The best time to create a change control process is before any work activities begin. By creating the change control process early, the chance of random change requests are reduced. The project will face far fewer random change requests because your customers understand the cost of asking for a project change, and the process team members will have to follow to incorporate the change. Customers understand that when the team is processing a change, they are not working on project deliverables. This can cause a delay in the project and a rise in project costs.

Stay on top of change requests; otherwise, you can easily run into major project issues. The costs and schedule impacts from a large change request are sometimes too much for the project to absorb. Therefore, you may need to go back to your customer to get more time or more money to include the extra work. When you manage projects that employ contractors and vendors, you must be aware of their contracts. The change control process can play a large part in what project work the "hired" vendors or contractors can perform. The contract could stipulate that the contractor or vendor was hired to do one task, and you want them to do something completely different. When that happens, you may have difficulty getting vendors to do more than is stated in the contract.

For fixed-bid projects where both companies agreed on a single cost to perform the work, project changes will likely result in a change request for the added work, and involve added project costs. You must drive all change requests through the project's formal change request process.

Tip

If a project manager handles change requests in any other way than a rigid change control process, they are asking for trouble, and this could hurt the project.

Steps for creating a change control plan can vary. Use the following template to create a change control plan for your project. This table of contents template provides the major sections and will be helpful when the document is completed and you are looking for particular information around processing project changes.

Table 18.1 — Example of a change control plan table of contents

#	Section Title	Description
1	Change Control Board, Roles and Responsibilities	Document the roles and responsibilities of the Change Control Board, such as: the board's purpose and direction, what they are responsible for, what they can and cannot approve, and so on.
2	Change Board Impact/Considerations Review	Document the impacts and considerations that are different about this Change Control Board that may not be the same as on other projects. Some projects handle Change Control Boards differently; this section documents those differences.
3	Change Process	Document how change requests are initiated and flow through the change control process. Include the Change Control Board presentation, the change request documentation to complete, time frames, and approvals.

#	Section Title	Description
4	Change Board Time frames and Response Expectations	Document the time frames and expectations the Change Control Board has on their responses. For example, if they need to decide on the change request in one week, document the time frame here. If there are expectations on timing, document those exceptions here as well.
5	Change Request Documentation and Expectations	Document the change request form and any additional documentation based on the special needs of the project.
6	Additional Information About the Change Control Process	Document additional information about the change control plan or process here. Any special considerations, such as the process for emergency change requests go in this section. Change Control Boards are usually standard, but is important to capture any different processes in this section.
7	Mandatory Change Process	Document how the Change Control Board will handle mandatory changes. This includes internal audit findings, government laws or regulations changes, or any company processes that are forcing project changes.
8	Approvals and Responses from Change Control Board	Document approval expectations and possible responses from the Change Control Board. These include "canned" responses, such as: denied for being too costly, outside the project scope, having significant schedule impact, approved with cost impact that needs understanding and acceptance by the executive team.

Using a change control plan

Before using a change control plan, identify who on your project team will use it so you can determine the level of detail, distribution frequency, style, and format of the report. Review the change control plan in *Chapter 15 - Defining Communication Tools for Working with Stakeholders,* and then complete the following steps:

1. Ensure that your customer is aware of the change control process, including the project's change control plan. Review the change control plan with your customer early in the planning process to ensure they understand the process. You might conduct a training session, a lunch-time meeting, a one-on-one meeting, or whatever it takes to ensure your customer knows how to submit change requests.

2. Request formal sign-off and approval from your customers and team members when they are comfortable with the project and the associated change control plan. Gain approval by sending the change control plan and formal acceptance document to your customers and team members.

3. After receiving approval from your customers and team members, store the change control plan and formal acceptance document in the document control system for long-term storage, archiving, and retrieval purposes.

4. Enforce the use of the change control plan. This requires that you work with your team members and customers and, as they suggest changes, ensure they follow the change control process.

5. As your project moves into the planning process, set up a Change Control Board, selecting members from leadership, your customer group, and executives. When setting up board members, review the change control plan to ensure they are comfortable with it. You may need to make changes to the plan based on the board's input and feedback along the way. If the plan changes, you will need to get customer and team approval again. Also, you should set up weekly change control board meetings to review the change requests.

6. As the project moves into the executing process, ensure all project changes go through the formal change control process. No exceptions are allowed to this process. This includes helping your customers develop change requests, scheduling the Change Control Board meeting, and walking your customers through the process. You continue running the change request process throughout the project.

Mastering the Comprehensive Test Plan

Before you master the *comprehensive test plan*, you must understand how it can help and support you on your project. The following project scenario stresses the importance of the comprehensive test plan and why it is critical to every project.

A large software company has developed a new telephone device that some say will change the world. The company has promoted the new telephone device for months and is ready to launch it in the United States and Canada. Thousands of customers are excited about the new phone and many have been standing in line for days to buy it. Clearly, advertising works and the worldwide hype about this new product is enormous. Management has asked you to be the project manager for the launch of this incredible new device. You gladly accept, as this is the type of project that can help your career if you succeed. The expectations are great and the product is sure to be a success, or is it? Being the project manager, you are afraid that the phone's success is riding solely on your back, so the pressure is on. Your upper management team has several questions for you:

- How will you ensure the device will work out of the box?
- Will customers be able to make their first, second, and one hundredth calls?
- What will you do to ensure product reliability?
- What tests are required to ensure the phone's successful launch?

To answer these questions, you need a comprehensive test plan. You use a comprehensive test plan to ensure the right rigor and structure for the testing process to all but guarantee a successful project launch.

Note
It is important to understand that simply having a test plan does not guarantee that nothing will go wrong. However, having a test plan will significantly reduce the chances of major problems occurring on the project, and that alone is worth the effort to produce this valuable tool for your project.

Cross-Reference
We recommend that you review the comprehensive test plan's planning questions in Chapter 10 - Communication Tools That Manage Project Quality for more information.

Creating a comprehensive test plan

Creating a comprehensive test plan is critical for every project, regardless of the project type or industry. Some form of testing must be completed on every product. The testing performed on a project sets the project quality. Limited product testing often leads to major quality problems. You must be active in creating the comprehensive test plan and work closely with the test team to ensure that the plan is high quality and that the test cases are as complete as possible. As the project moves into the testing phase, ensure that the testers complete each test case thoroughly, and the results are as expected. Otherwise, you will continue the process of fixing bugs, retesting, fixing, and retesting until everything is resolved and the project is ready to launch; a process that often takes months. Depending on the problems, the only way that this process finishes is when the comprehensive test plan specifically states, "The project can launch when there are a specific number of errors at certain severity levels." For example, a project can launch if there are only two severity-level bugs, but cannot launch if there are four or more.

A project customer demands high-level quality applications and stability in the products they are buying. From cars rolling out of auto plants to denim jeans coming off the assembly line, each product has its own quality level and testing applied to it before being released to the public. Today, consumers are less tolerant of cheap toys and expect better durability than they once did.

The steps for creating a comprehensive test plan vary. Use the template we provided to create a comprehensive test plan for your project.

Table 18.2 — Example of a comprehensive test plan table of contents

#	Section Title	Description
1	Test Plan Identifier	Document identification information about the document, such as naming conventions, revision history, and so on.
2	Introduction of Testing	Document the testing required for the project. Document high-level requirements, expectations, and the goals of the testing for the project.
3	Test Items/Test Cases and Scripts	Document the items required for testing; usually, this is a high-level list of items. Make sure to add the test cases and test scripts to run during the testing phase.
4	Testing Risk & Issues	Document specific issues and risks associated with testing. Often, there are risks and issues associated to testing activities only, not the total project issues or risks.
5	Features to Test	Document the application features that are required to test.
6	Features Not to Test	Document features that will not be tested.
7	Approach	Document the testing approach, such as special circumstances, including how testing will occur, methodology used, and other applicable information.
8	Item Pass/Fail Criteria	Document the pass/fail criteria for testing. Often, a customer has specific testing criteria they want applied to the testing.
9	Entry & Exit Criteria	Document the entry and exit criteria for testing. Often, test teams have set up a criterion they want applied to the project. An example of a common exit criteria is the number of bugs remaining before the project goes live. The criterion is that, if there are less than three bugs remaining in testing, the project can still go live with those bugs.
10	Test Deliverables	Document various testing deliverables for the project, including who is responsible for which testing deliverable, and the times frames for each task.
11	Environmental Needs	Document environmental needs for the project. Document the space, security, hardware, and any other environmental factors.
12	Staffing and Training Needs	Document the project's staffing needs. Document the roles required and special training requirements for the testers assigned to the effort.
13	Responsibilities	Document the testing team members' specific responsibilities, such as the test lead and, if applicable, test manager. This section should include

#	Section Title	Description
		details about each member, such as work responsibilities and other relevant information. It is important to understand what each role performs on the project.
14	Schedule	Document the test schedule associated to the testing portion of the project. The project's testing deliverables, staff assignments, and time frames are documented in this section. It is best practice to copy the testing schedule into this section directly, providing the most current project testing information.
15	Contingencies Plans	Document test contingency plans and ensure the plan has all relevant items, time frames, and other relevant information in this area. It is important to document this in case there are problems and the project needs to draw on these contingencies.
16	Approvals	Document the approvals and staff members who have signed off on the test document.

Using a comprehensive test plan

Before you can use a comprehensive test plan, identify who on your project team will use it. This information is important so you can determine the level of detail, distribution frequency, style, and test plan format. Usually, the test lead and the project tester will be the main users of this document.

Review the comprehensive test plan section in *Chapter 10 - Communication Tools That Manage Project Quality* and then complete the following steps:

1. As the project moves into the latter stages of the planning process, sign-off and approval of this document is critical. This needs to be done long before the team needs to use the comprehensive test plan. It is essential that your customers also sign off and approve the test plan long before testing begins because the team needs to know the level of product quality they are striving for as early as possible. Otherwise, if the quality level is unknown, the project team could spend time getting the product to a higher quality level than needed.

2. After receiving approval and sign-off from your customer and team members, store the document in the document control system for long-term storage, archiving, and retrieval purposes.

3. As the project moves into the executing process, make sure that your project teams use the comprehensive test plan. Make sure the test lead enforces the testing processes using the details outlined in the test plan. You may need to step in and help the test lead if you see they need it. However, you are not responsible for driving this process; that is the test lead's responsibility. You should offer help and support when needed.

4. You will help your test lead execute and enforce the use of the comprehensive test plan throughout the testing phase. Your help may include updating and changing the comprehensive test plan (requires re-sign-off), or getting involved with items as testing occurs on the project.

Mastering the Design Specifications

Before mastering *design specifications*, you must understand how they can help and support you on your project. The following project scenario highlights their importance.

A large building construction project is just getting underway. The foundations are complete, and the framing has just begun. The project has 52 instances of unclear, missing, or just plain wrong drawings and specifications. These errors have resulted in requests for information (RFIs) from the architects. The architects need more clarification, revisions, or changes to the drawings and specifications they are using. Each error has caused a delay in the schedule and increased costs. These errors in the drawings and specifications have also resulted in change requests and schedule extension requests, which will add more costs to the project. The team is expecting errors 53 and 54 soon because a third-party provider is going to perform an independent audit, and early results show there are more problems. As the project manager on this construction job, you need to understand how to approach this problem. There are many questions that you need to answer immediately, such as:

- How could you have prevented this from happening?
- How are you going to get the project back on schedule?
- How will you make up the cost overruns?

To answer these questions, you can use design specifications. Design specifications are clear and complete specifications of a product with the intent of building that product. On construction projects, the design specifications are the plans (drawings) by the engineering and architectural groups who are working on the project. In software, design specifications show how the user interface, screen shots, and reports will look.

Cross-Reference
We recommend that you review the design specifications planning questions in Chapter 7 - Defining Communication Tools that Manage Project Scope for more information.

Creating design specifications

The design team creates design specifications for most projects, regardless of the industry. For example, in software, construction, and research industries, there are design teams who design the product items. On construction projects, the design team consists of architects, engineers, and analysts. On software projects, the design team consists of lead developers, lead designers, and lead testers. Design specifications are complex documents that require technical knowledge and expertise to complete. These individuals need to be able to understand and articulate technical information into a usable format for the whole project team to use. Developing clear, accurate, and complete design specifications documents is important to the success of creating any product. It is one of the success criteria for a project.

To be successful, you must communicate the information in the design specifications document to your customer. Your customer can review the document, suggest changes, and understand the fundamental details behind the product design. Usually, design specifications include visual representations, drawings, and layouts of the product so that team members can visualize the final result. Don't prevent your customers from accessing design specifications documents or ignore their input about requirements. If you ignore your customers, they will only become frustrated and unhappy. However, seeking their advice and suggestions early in the project is a smart tactic for project managers. Share the design specifications document with your customers for early and long-term product acceptance.

You must ensure the design specifications document has been approved by your customer before considering it final. If you are waiting for approval, your customer might have some issues with the design which is preventing them from accepting the document. To help with customer acceptance, the design details should always be available for them to review, and the project team should be available to answer questions or address concerns. You should host a series of design specifications review meetings with your customer to analyze the document so they understand what the team is developing. During these meetings, your customer will have access to team members so they can discuss product details directly with a specific team member. When you have open communication among everyone on the project—especially your customer—it gives your customers confidence that you are guiding the project in the right direction to satisfy their needs.

Design specifications are often so broad in content that it would be impossible to create a valid sample for the multiple industries we mention in this book. In *Chapter 7 - Communication Tools That Manage Project Scope*, we used a software design specification template that you would use as the basis of developing a design specification for a project. Complete the following basic steps to create a design specifications document.

1. After your customer approves the customer requirements document, use that document to create the preliminary design specification document. Preliminary design work requires enough engineering resources to develop a conceptual layout, a primary specification list, a work breakdown structure (WBS), a conceptual budget, and a schedule. The specification evolves from the creation process.

2. Have the project team review the preliminary design concept specifications developed by the design team. A preliminary review is compulsory to ensure that the design addresses the scope of work. During that review, more ideas are likely to develop, and the project designer will add these to the design specifications document.

3. Lead your project team, specifically the designers, in developing a draft design specifications document.

4. After creating the draft document, your project's lead design analyst will share it with other team members and the customers for early review and input.

5. After the team members and customers have given their input and feedback about the document, incorporate the feedback into the final document.

6. Enforce the use of the design specification document on your projects.

Using design specifications

Before you can use design specifications, you must identify who on your project team will use them. This information will help you determine the level of detail, distribution frequency, style, and the design specification document format. Usually, this document contains detailed requirements for the product being designed.

Before using the design specifications document, review the design specifications section in *Chapter 7 - Defining Communication Tools that Manage Project Scope,* and then complete the following steps:

1. Send the design specifications document to customers and team members for sign off and approval.

2. Store the design specifications document in the document control system for long-term storage, archiving, and retrieval purposes.

3. Continue to use the document to update the final product design. Schedule design sessions for the document, answering team members' questions, and ensure the team uses the document to create the design for the final product.

Mastering the Expected Monetary Value

Before mastering the *expected monetary value (EMV)*, you must understand how it can help and support you on your project. The following project scenario highlights its importance.

For the project you are working on, you are trying to choose between two vendor companies. The stakeholders for each vendor have narrowed the bidding competition and are close on their bids. One bid is $400,000 and the competing bid is $380,000. Your team has done some research and found that both vendors are equally qualified; however, you also found out that neither vendor always delivers on time. Five percent of the time, the first vendor delivered 10 days late. The other vendor has a record of being late 25 percent of the time, and by 60 days. You know that for every day there is a delay, your company will spend an extra $2,000 on operating costs. Your team chose the second bidder because they bid the lowest, but you are unsure about this decision and have many questions you need answered, such as:

- What if the vendor is 60 days late?
- If the project is delayed, will the outcome change?
- How much money will you have to set aside if the vendor is late?

To get answer these questions, you should use the expected monetary value. The EMV calculates a contingency value for the project's risk events should they occur. By calculating the expected monetary value, the lowest bidder in this scenario turns out to be the most expensive.

Cross-Reference
We recommend that you review the expected monetary value's planning questions in Chapter 13 - Defining Communication Tools to Manage Project Risk for more information.

Creating an expected monetary value

You play a part in creating the project's expected monetary value (EMV). By creating the EMV, you get a better understanding of the project's value. You learn more about percentages and probabilities for some of the project's risk events, which is great information to know. It is easy to determine the EMV; all you have to know is the value of a risk event if it did occur and the probability of it occurring. Usually, you can estimate how much it would cost to replace a part of the project, or how many days delay a risk event would cause. However, trying to determine the probability of the risk event occurring is more difficult. For example, say that a wire shorts out in one room of a new building that your team is constructing and a fire starts. The fire only consumes the room and part of the hallway. You estimate it will cost about $122,500 to repair the damage, but what were the odds (probability) of the wire starting a fire in that room at all? When you are working with risks, and especially EMV, you must be able to accurately estimate the probability of the risk event occurring. If you cannot, someone else can, such as your insurance company. The probability of a wire starting a fire in a new building is less than 0.0001 of a percent. The point is it takes a lot more effort than simply multiplying two numbers. You must know what those two numbers represent in the calculations.

Many large construction projects use as standard procedures for managing and controlling project risks. The time and effort you and team members spend to calculate the EMV pays off in the end. The communications side of using an EMV are remarkable and something that project teams and customers can use throughout the project.

Calculating the EMV formula provides a dollar amount for emergency purposes. Calculating this formula is a more accepted method than guessing and not knowing what to apply.

The steps for creating an EMV vary. The following steps can help you start the process for creating an EMV for your project.

1. Before you calculate an EMV, work with team members, perform a risk analysis, and identify possible risk events.
2. Give each risk event a probability of occurring and its impact if it did occur.
3. Create a risk event matrix and identify the project's top risks, which will identify low, medium, and high risks.
4. Calculate an EMV (contingency) for each top risk event.
5. Estimate the remaining contingency value needed for the project. To do this, you may want to use Pareto's rule. See C*hapter 12 - Defining Communication Tools That Manage Project Communications for more information* on the Pareto Chart..
6. Add the values from step 4 and step 5 to create the project's EMV.
7. Create a contingency report and deliver it to your customers, team members, and upper management. The report should describe how you calculated the project's total EMV.

Tip
Do some research and find out what the average contingency is for the project type you are working on in your location. If there is a large difference between your contingency value and the average, you may want to re-evaluate how you calculated yours. If your contingency is correct, explain the difference in the report.

Using an expected monetary value

Before you can use the EMV, identify who on your project team will use it. This information is important to know so that you can determine the level of detail, distribution frequency, style, and report format. Review the EMV section in *Chapter 13 - Defining Communication Tools to Manage Project Risk*, and then compete the following steps:

1. Monitor and control the EMV throughout the project. You will need to know how much contingency has been used and how much remains. You will need to identify outstanding risks and estimate the remaining contingency values. As the project executes, monitor the value of the risk events that occur and compare them with the estimated values you calculated and make corrections as necessary.
2. When risk events occur, estimate the cost of the risk event and apply it to the contingency money to cover the risk events. You continue this process throughout the project.
3. As the project closes, evaluate the remaining funds in the contingency fund (if there is any) and move them into the project's main funding bucket for distribution.
4. Start the lessons-learned process to track how the project managed the contingency funds against the associated risk events.
5. As the project closes out, store the EMV estimates and associated documentation in the document control system for long-term storage, archiving, and retrieval purposes.

Mastering the Project Calendar

Before you can use a *project calendar*, you must understand how it can help and support you on your project. The following project scenario highlights its importance.

A large manufacturing company in Denver, Colorado has decided to implement a new human resource management system to replace their current system. The current system can no longer keep up with the demands from the personnel department. Management assigned you to be the project manager, and you have already started to delve into the details. Your customer in the personnel department is demanding and wants to ensure that you stay on top of the project's schedule and communicate it to them weekly. Unfortunately, the personnel department's staff is not especially computer literate and you're worried that if you send them a weekly project schedule, it would be meaningless to them because they would not know how to read it. You could develop various helpful reports from the scheduling tool, but it may be difficult for the staff to grasp the project time frames. You are frustrated and do not know what to do. As the project progresses, management is hearing complaints that the customer is not getting the status about the project schedule they have been asking for, and that you have not found a way to provide it to them. Management wants to know what you are doing to provide the project schedule to the customer because they too are hearing complaints from the customers. Management asks you the following questions:

- What are you doing to report the project's schedule?
- How does the customer currently access the project schedule?
- Is there a manual way to provide a project schedule to the customer?

To answers these questions, you should use a project calendar. The project calendar communicates the project's high-level time frames directly to your customer and is a valuable communication tool for every project manager. You can print the calendar and hand write the project time frames or produce an electronic version using the built-in calendar view in most scheduling tools. This provides your customer with a high-level picture of the project's timelines. Using a project calendar allows you to meet with your customer and plan the project schedule and key milestones together. With the dates in front of your customers, you can negotiate and talk to them about what the project will look like from a scheduling perspective. For example, if there is a scenario where the project schedule shows the project's development phase occurring over a major holiday, you and the customer may agree to move those dates to a more suitable time frame. However, if you leave the development phase over the holiday, you add a level of risk to the project. By moving a major project milestone date, you and your customer can look on the calendar and find out the downstream effects of moving the date. The project calendar provides a great picture of the project's major milestone dates and is one of the best tools you can use for your projects.

Cross-Reference
We recommend that you review the project calendar tool in Chapter 12 - Defining Communication Tools That Manage Project Communications for more information.

Creating a project calendar

Having a project calendar at your side is always helpful for providing on-the-spot answers about the project schedule. Another benefit of the project calendar is that it shows the high-level schedule of the project's deliverables across the months of the year so you can see the project in graphical format, making project planning the much easier. When reviewing the different project milestone dates, your customer may see overlaps or impacts to their business processes, such as month-end reporting, quarterly reports, or year-end reporting. If this is the case, work with the team members to adjust the project schedule as needed.

Tip

Add multiple projects to a single calendar to get a multiple project schedule view. You can quickly see time frame overlaps.

The easiest way to create a project calendar is to print out a blank copy of a project calendar template (month-by-month view). Write down the project's major deliverable dates on the calendar. If you manage multiple projects, create a project calendar for each project you manage, and potentially an overall project calendar to track project overlap. After the team approves the timelines, create multiple paper copies of the calendar. That way, you can give them to your team members and customers to refer to throughout the project.

You can also use a project-scheduling tool, such as Microsoft Project, to create a project calendar. After entering the tasks on the project schedule, you can change the view to Calendar to create a project calendar. Print the results for a paper copy of the electronic calendar and you will be ready for those on-the-spot questions about project time frames.

Figure 18.2 — Example of a project calendar shows a project calendar generated from a project-scheduling tool. The calendar in this example shows high-level phases only, but is enough to plan and communicate project activities to anyone interested.

Figure 18.2 — Example of a project calendar

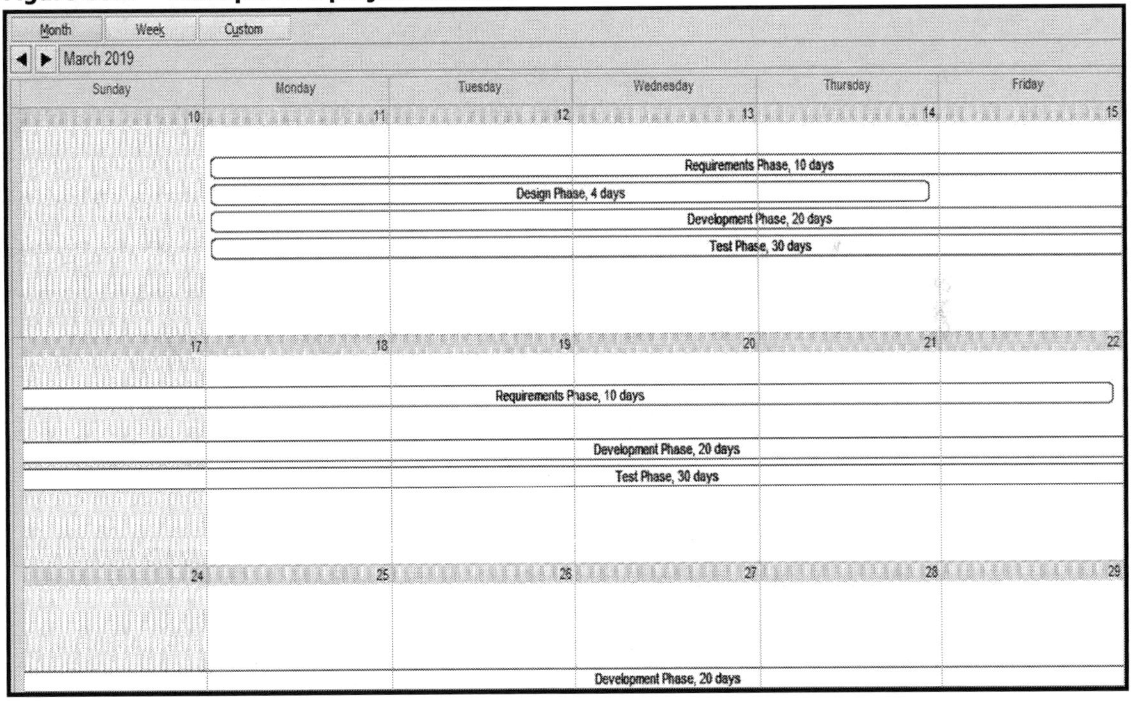

Using a project calendar

Before you can use a project calendar, identify who on your project team will use it. This information is important so you can determine the level of detail, distribution frequency, style, and calendar format. In this case, the project calendar will be used by many project members, starting with you and the project team.

On most projects, you are the main user of the project calendar because you are the sole person who understands the project dates.

Review the project calendar section in *Chapter 12 - Defining Communication Tools That Manage Project Communications*, and then complete the following steps:

1. Create a project calendar by using one of the many available templates.
2. Add all relevant project milestone dates on the calendar. A best practice is having a paper copy of the project calendar with you at all times. The dates on the calendar should be milestone dates from the official project schedule.

Tip

Having a paper copy of your project calendar gives you the project dates at your fingertips. There is no substitute for having these dates available when your leadership or customers ask and want an immediate answer. No logging into systems, no waiting for sites to come up, the dates are there and available for you.

3. Create the automated version of your project calendar in your company's document control system. Having an automated version of the calendar will allow leadership, customers, and team members to have access to the project dates at all times.
4. Store project calendars in the document control system for long-term storage, archiving, and availability.

Mastering the Project Schedule

Before you can master the *project schedule*, you must understand how it can help and support you on your project. The following project scenario highlights its importance.

A large software company is developing and implementing a large payroll system. The present off-the-shelf system is not keeping up with the current employee needs or demands. After some research, the company tried a decision-tree diagram that they ended up rejecting the decision to buy. Instead, they decided to develop the software in-house. As the company's most senior project manager, you are excited to start and get underway. You feel the project will be challenging, with many different groups in the company involved. As you start the project, one of your first tasks is to gather work activities from each department and any dependencies they may have. As you work with each of the groups and start to document and capture this information, you quickly become overwhelmed. Capturing and recording this information on paper and trying to discover the different dependencies between all the activities are almost impossible for one person. You realize there is no way to capture all of the information and understand how to link it without some help. As you ponder what to do next, management is starting to ask questions, such as:

- What tasks are required to complete the project?
- What tasks are related?
- Who is working on what task?
- Are there any dependencies between groups?
- What date does the project expect to finish?
- What are the costs associated to the design phase of the project?

To answer these questions, you should use a project schedule. A project schedule records project tasks in a single location, with time frames and resources assigned to each project task. On most projects, you load associated costs into the schedule for each activity. When costs, resources, and time frames are contained in the project schedule, it becomes valuable to you and your customer. Few projects are successfully completed without using a project schedule.

Cross-Reference
We recommend that you review the project schedule tool in Chapter 8 - Communication Tools That Manage Project Time for more information.

Creating a project schedule

A project schedule is one of the most popular tools in a project manager's toolbox. Creating a project schedule can be complex—especially when project managers' resource load and cost load their schedules and add dependencies between the activities. Creating schedules is a technical skill that you need on today's projects. Figuring out dependencies between tasks can be challenging and time consuming. Maintaining and monitoring the project schedule is one of your major responsibilities throughout the project. Whether you are physically responsible for updating the project schedule or not, it is your responsibility to ensure that the schedule is complete and always up-to-date. For large projects, many project schedulers may be assigned to a project. In those cases, you directly work with the project schedulers to ensure the plan is accurate.

You should use the power of the project schedule and use the information it provides for project status and updates. You shouldn't use the project schedule as a task list only, which provides limited value to your customers and to yourself. The project schedule is a lot more than a simple task list.

Tip

If you are going to create a project schedule, create it properly and enter the resources, costs, and dependencies. In doing so, you get an accurate picture of the exact status of the project.

The project customer is involved in creating and using the project schedule. The customer will often examine the contents of the plan to ensure they are getting what they need from it. If you decide the project schedule is nothing more than a task list, you may have difficulty answering customer questions when they demand more information.

The steps for creating a project schedule vary. Complete the following steps to get started:

1. Create your project activities in the project scheduling tool. A best practice for naming activity descriptions (not the summary activities, but work package lowest level) is ensuring that they each have a verb and noun. It is important to make sure that all bottom level activities have a verb and noun combination in their name so that readers reviewing the schedule will understand the exact description and information about the activities. For example, an activity named "cover photo" could mean a million different activities or tasks to a photographer. Instead, naming the activity, "Arrange Cover Photo for Final Take" makes sense and provides a description that allows anyone reviewing the schedule more information about the task.

2. Work with your team members to estimate the duration of the activity. This is a critical task because estimating durations is a difficult process and a task that almost everyone struggles with. Estimating project task durations is a process where team members use their expertise to tell you how long they think it will take to do the task. You guide your team members through the estimation process to ensure that each activity includes a best-guess duration.

3. Identify the predecessors and successors (logical relationships). This is a challenging process and requires careful consideration. When linking project tasks, team members must think about what they need to do to complete a task, in addition to thinking about how tasks depend on one another. When the project schedule activities are linked, it is important to remember that any change to any date will adjust the other dates. Project team members must be involved when setting up predecessors and successors for project tasks. Team members must also understand how dependencies rely on each other to complete project work.

4. At this point, you should have a basic project schedule at best, but it offers a starting point. Take this starting point schedule and work with your team members to ensure that they correctly captured the tasks and assignments. Correct improper dependency links immediately. This is a good time to review the linking among all the areas of the project created in step 3.

5. As the project progresses, update and keep the project schedule as current as possible. You will continue to update the project schedule as one of your regular activities. Your team members must keep you aware of their task status and when they finish actual work tasks. You update the project schedule weekly or monthly depending on the project's size and length.

Note

The following steps are optional, but recommended for every project schedule. The two steps (resource and cost loading) are important for using the full benefits of the project scheduling tool.

6. Assign people and materials or equipment to the project's activities (resource loaded). Resource loading can be complex, but it is important because it ensures that someone is directly responsible for each individual activity on the project schedule. Project resource loading is important for team workload management and discovering how many activities an individual team member can work on.

7. Apply costs to project activities (cost loaded). Cost loading schedules is also a difficult task, but once it is completed, it pays off. The ability to discover exactly what individual activities will cost and what the overall project is going to cost is valuable for project planning and execution. Cost loading involves loading resource costs and other costs into the schedule. When assigning resources to a task, the associated costs apply directly to the task itself. The difficulty of associating costs to an activity is finding all the information you need to do this task. For each activity, you need to capture the hours, the rate for various skill sets, the costs for materials per task, and finally equipment costs for every task on the schedule. For a one hundred or two hundred line schedule, this is a time-consuming process. For 1,000 activities or more, it takes a team of schedulers. Equipment costs are also difficult to estimate when applied across the project schedule activities. Project schedulers must spread the larger equipment costs (such as a crane for a construction project) across all the activities involving the crane. This can be challenging because the costs and the work may not spread easily among the activities. To simplify this, construction projects create a single activity called "crane," and apply all the tasks and time frames to that single activity. This allows the relationship of one activity to one cost unit to remain intact.

Using a project schedule

Before you can use a project schedule, identify who on your project team will use it. This information is valuable for determining the level of detail, distribution frequency, style, and project schedule format. In this case, the project schedule can be used at the highest level of the project and the lowest level of the project. The lower the level, the more detailed information the individual task will need. Deciding the amount of detail to display is up to you. Review the project schedule section in *Chapter 8 - Communication Tools That Manage Project Time,* and then complete the following steps:

1. As the project progresses into the executing process, ensure that your project team and customers have approved and signed- off on the project schedule. This may require several meetings with team members and customer to ensure everyone agrees.
2. Store sign-offs and approvals in the document control system for long-term storage, archiving, and retrieval purposes.
3. Enforce the use of the project schedule. You should track and monitor the project regularly using the project schedule, either daily, weekly, or another specific time frame. You decide how often you want to report progress for your project. There is no right or wrong way to decide when to update the project schedule as long as you update it in time for the company's cutoff (usually weekly). It is a best practice for you to go no longer than a week to update the project schedule.
4. As the project progresses into the executing phases, you should be adding tasks, adding and removing resources, changing dependencies, and adjusting costs.
5. As the project completes, store your project's final project schedule in the document control system for long-term storage, archiving, and accessibility.

Mastering the System Requirements Document

Before using a *systems requirement document*, you must understand how it can help and support you on your project. The following project scenario highlights its importance. ⋅

A large log home manufacturer, in Seattle, Washington, has decided to replace their payroll system with an updated application developed internally by its IT department. As fast as the company is expanding, and with the number of new employees recently hired, the existing system has quickly become outdated and can no longer serve its original purpose. Management selects you to be the project manager for this effort. As the project progresses, the project's analysts collect business requirements from the customer. After collecting those requirements and getting approval from the customer, the project team focuses on the project's technical requirements. The challenge is deciding where to create and store the technical requirements. The analysts are concerned about what information to collect, and where to document the project's technical requirements. The analysts ask you some tough technical questions, such as:

- Which legacy systems will feed this new application?
- Which conversion activities are required?
- What will the user interface look like?
- Will the new application be enough for the company's future growth?

To answer these questions, you will enforce the use of a system requirements document. A system requirements document contains the project's technical details that provide the development and design teams' information they need to develop the product. The software industry uses the system requirements document as a standard deliverable on almost every project. A system requirements document is an excellent communication tool because of the technical information it contains and the detailed information it provides about how to develop the product.

Cross-Reference
We recommend that you review the system requirements document tool in Chapter 7 - Defining Communication Tools that Manage Project Scope for more information.

Creating a system requirements document

Creating a system requirements document on any software development project is often complex and is an analyst's responsibility. Analysts have the training and technical background to turn the business requirements into technical requirements, which can be challenging in their own right. You are seldom involved in the details of developing the system requirements document due to the technical nature of the document.

System requirements documents vary among industries and have a multitude of different names that all basically mean the same. The idea behind the document is to map the business requirements or customer requirements to a technical solution. For example, if your customer has a need to store large amounts of data every hour, the system requirements might be a database.

You must ensure the system requirements document is complete and accurate for the downstream users of the document. If the downstream users can't understand it, then they will have difficulty building the product from the document. For example, the designers and developers of the project are the two main users of the system requirements document, and therefore must be active in creating this document so they understand what is needed in the project. You must ensure these two groups are actively engaged in creating the document and approve it before the project begins. If you do not manage and control this process, there could be problems. The main problem that could occur if the groups were not involved in creating the document is that they may not like what is in it. In that case, they could create deliverables based on what they think should be in the document, not what is in the document. If this happens, it can be disrupting to the project team and have a negative impact on the project.

In some projects, you might encourage your customers to be involved in creating the system requirements document. A technically inclined customer can review and be part of the process. Other customers will have little interest in creating the system requirements document and therefore don't get involved in this process. You will need to manage this process closely. If your customer asks technical questions or wants to review the system requirements document, you should let them. You can support this process by providing technical resources for your customer and being available to answer questions. When your customer becomes involved, you must add more time and possibly cost to the schedule for the extra work.

You can use the following system requirements document template for your project. The table of contents provides the major sections of the document and will be handy when the document is completed and you are looking for some particular information.

Table 18.3 — Example of a system requirements table of contents

#	Section Title	Description
1	Document References	Document all initial document items, such as author, contact name, date, and revision history.
2	Sign-off Section	Document the staff who signed off on the project. This includes the sign-off signatures or copies of emails containing signatures.
3	Document Conventions	Document conventions associated to the document, such as Business Processes (BP##) or Operational Requirements (OPR##).
4	Business Procedure Mapping	Document business procedure mapping, such as procedures the business uses that are relevant to project activities or deliverables.
4.1	Business Requirements Identification	Document the project's business requirements.
4.2	Business Process Analysis	Document the specific business processes and business process descriptions. Map the business processes to the business requirements document. The mapping is easier to create in a table format, and easier to read.
4.3	Initial System Requirements Summary	Document the mapping among the system requirements and the business requirements. The project analyst creates a mapping table to provide traceability among system and business requirements.
5	System Description	Document the system description. This can be a high-level description that includes system functionality.

#	Section Title	Description
5.1	System Overview	Document the system overview. This is usually a high-level system overview that is under development.
5.2	System Objectives	Document the system objectives from a technical perspective. This will clearly state what the objectives are for the new application.
5.3	System Process Specifications	Document the mapping among process names and descriptions, and their mapping back to system requirements. This provides traceability among system processes mapping to system requirements.
5.4	System Constraints	Document system constraints, such as applications that need to work together, database space, availability, and so on.
5.5	System Risk/Impacts/Assumptions	Document risk, impacts, or assumptions. It is important to document system risks associated to the project. Also document impacts to risk events or assumptions.
5.6	System Interfaces	Document the interfaces your system will have with other systems so that technical team members can look at both systems to find out impacts or changes for either system. If you miss the new application, you could have major problems.
6	User Interface Designs	Document the details for the user interface design, such as the look and feel, sample screen shots, usability expectations, and so on.
7	Source System Model	Document the details of the source systems, if applicable. If the project has a source system or is reading information from a source system, include those details.
8	Functional Processes	Document the system's step-by-step functional processes. Document as much detail as possible for the technical staff. The project analyst completes this process using a table that includes process names, process descriptions, and process steps, and describing each in detail.
9	Functional Process Model	Document the step-by-step functional process in a series of diagrams, allowing the technical staff consuming the information to understand the processes from a series of diagrams. These diagrams may help team members understand the processes, which could make coding or the development cycle easier.

#	Section Title	Description
10	System Operational Requirements	Document the operational procedures (step-by-step process) to move a system into a production environment in the company.
11	System Deployment Requirements	Document the deployment requirements for production, and then the steps after production implementation, such as communications to the application's users that it is ready for use.
12	Context Diagram	Document the application's context diagram. Usually, this includes a picture of the diagrams, tables, databases, and so on.
13	Conversion/Migration Needs	Document conversion or migration needs. It is important to cover all details of the conversion or data migration work in this section. This information is for the project team involved in the process to understand exactly what they must do for the application.
14	Data Communication Requirements	Document data communication requirements for the application, such as notifying the users of data changes, data availability times, and other data-related items.
15	Inter-Project Dependencies	Document project dependencies with other projects. Dependencies include other projects launching, data dependencies, or anything else that connects the projects.
16	Testing Requirements	Document the project's various testing requirements. This can be as high level as the steps to perform the testing, to the details of specifics around test cases. This will depend on the needs and requirements of the project.
17	Report Requirements	Document the project's report requirements. If the project requires special reports, the project analyst documents the details here for everyone to review.
18	Summary	Finalize and summarize the information in the document.

Using a system requirements document

Before using a system requirements document, you must identify who on your project team will use it. This is important so you can determine the level of detail, distribution frequency, style, and format of the system requirements document. This document is detailed and complex. It provides the details for designers and developers to create their portions of the project, this document should not contain high-level content.

Review the system requirements document section in *Chapter 7 - Defining Communication Tools that Manage Project Scope*, and then compete the following steps:

1. After the project analyst completes the system requirements document, it is a best practice to arrange for a team review of the document to ensure that everyone is onboard and understands it.

The project should not go further until the project team reviews and approves the document. The system requirements document is the basis for what the project team will produce, so it is important that team members review the document and understand what they need to deliver. You need to engage the team in these discussions and ensure they approve the document.

2. Store the document approvals in the document control system for long-term storage, archiving, and retrieval purposes.

3. As the project moves into the executing process, make sure your team members are using the system requirements document. Your project's team leads should refer to the system requirements document to create the deliverables described in the document. Your project team will use the document throughout the project life cycle until they have completed their deliverables.

Mastering the Work Breakdown Structure (WBS)

Before mastering the work breakdown structure (WBS), you must understand how it can assist and support you on your project. The following project scenario emphasizes its importance.

A midsize design and engineering company in Fairbanks, Alaska has just won the contract for a small project supporting the mega Panama Canal expansion effort. The entire project schedule for this enormous effort is scheduled continuously from 2005 to 2025, but your portion of the project is targeted to last two years. The overall project has a $5 billion dollar budget. You are the project manager, and your budget is $3 million. When you arrive in Panama City and begin to start work on the project, you find yourself busy with initial project startup activities. One of your first activities is hiring and building a project team, which you complete in two weeks. As the team engages, and the project progresses into the requirements phase, your team members have more and more questions, such as:

- In which zone is dock No. 2?
- What is the budget for module 6?
- Who is responsible for the layout of the West Bank survey?
- What are the project risks?

To answer these questions, you should use a WBS. A WBS breaks down a project's work activities in a hierarchal order to reach a manageable level of activities. A WBS identifies all of the work on a project. A component of the WBS is the WBS dictionary. The WBS dictionary catalogs information for easy access. In the scenario above, had you created a WBS to address the team members' questions, you could have directed them to the WBS dictionary for answers. This would have eliminated a lot of confusion and team member questions.

Cross-Reference
We recommend that you review the work breakdown structure tool in Chapter 7 - Defining Communication Tools that Manage Project Scope for more information.

Creating a work breakdown structure

Project managers, design teams, project controls staff, and construction managers should all be involved in developing the WBS. The WBS must reflect all necessary tasks to complete any given project, including everything from inception to completion. The tasks and subsequent subtasks should be in a descending order, with groupings by work type. The tasks should have an associated coding structure and should use work codes, schedule activity codes, budget/cost, and contract codes. The codes sort, select, group, and summarize project tasks. The WBS is the ultimate reference point and tool for managing project details. It has an associated dictionary wherein lies the descriptions for particular WBS elements and associated codes.

Creating a WBS, especially for large projects, takes days or weeks and includes multiple meetings with various stakeholders; even the project owner should be involved with this process. Remember, the WBS includes all of the work that needs to be completed on the project, in detail. It is extremely beneficial for all of the stakeholders to create the WBS, for two reasons: it creates a detailed understanding of the project work, and it bonds and motivates the team.

You can also use an automated scheduling system, such as Microsoft Project, to create a WBS. By indenting the schedule activities, you automatically create the WBS without even realizing it. Microsoft was the first to present this feature in a scheduling system, and now all scheduling products include this much-needed capability.

You use the WBS throughout the entire project life cycle, from initialization to closeout, and beyond. The WBS is involved in every project aspect. After it's approved, the WBS changes very little. Occasionally, though, there are change requests that require the WBS to be updated.

Because the WBS is graphical, it is best practice to use a plotter to draw it and hang the print in the project office. That way, everyone can review it and provide feedback. The other half of the WBS is the WBS dictionary. The dictionary is the detailed presentation of the WBS, and it documents every element of the WBS in written terms.

The project customer should be involved in developing and approving the WBS, including subsequent revisions, and may wish to have input into the elemental breakdowns, coding structure, retrieval process, and specific requirements from their operations and/or financial groups.

The steps for creating a WBS vary among project managers and greatly depend on their favorite tools of choice. Make sure of the following before you get started creating the WBS:

- The project team and other stakeholders participate in developing the WBS.
- The functional leads and managers are involved.
- The WBS must make sense from the point of view of how the organization does business.
- The descriptions of each element are obvious.
- All products are identified and all deliverables are in the WBS.
- The sum of the work is represented by the level 2 elements, which must add up to 100 percent of the work (i.e., 100 percent of the scope).
- The sum of the work represented by the child elements under each parent element must equal 100 percent of the work of the parent.
- The integrative elements, where necessary, are assembly-type work.
- The work packages are reasonable in size (the amount of work).
- The WBS element numbering is in a logical manner and, if possible, related to other projects and organization numbering schemes.
- The description of each element is understandable in terms of what it represents.

Basic rules or guidelines to follow when you are creating a WBS

There are rules you should follow in order to create a WBS. These rules or guidelines are standard throughout the project management profession. Use the following guidelines to create your WBS.

- Each WBS element should represent a single tangible deliverable.
- Each element should represent an aggregation of all subordinate WBS elements listed immediately below it.
- Each subordinate WBS element must belong to only one single parent WBS element.
- The deliverables require decomposing to the level that represents how they are produced.
- Deliverables must be unique and distinct from their peers, and decomposed to the level of detail needed to plan and manage the work to obtain or create them.
- Deliverables require clear definition to eliminate duplication of effort within WBS elements, across organizations, or between individuals responsible for completing the work.
- Deliverables should be limited in size and definition for effective control, but not so small as to make the cost of controlling them excessive, and not so large as to make the item unmanageable or the risk unacceptable.

Identifying functional levels of the WBS

When you create a WBS, there will be many summary levels (parents) above one level of detail elements. Below the top level, you can have many varying levels under each one of the elements. That is, you can have four levels under one top-level element and seven levels under another top-level element. There are four main levels of a WBS:

- **Project level:** Charter and project scope
- **Major level:** Major components, assemblies, subprojects, or phases
- **Mid-levels:** Subassemblies
- **Bottom level:** Work package, task, activity

There are many different ways to create a WBS: you can use the top-down method, the bottom-up method, or build it a piece at a time.

Tip

When creating the WBS, it is important to include all of the work on the project and not work that is not on the project.

One of the most popular ways to develop a WBS is to get the project team and stakeholders involved in the process. Before the group meets, everyone should read the preliminary scope and understand the project's objective. You will need a roll of butcher paper or plotter paper, several packages of sticky note pads, and some pens or pencils. The following steps apply to the *top-down method to create your WBS*:

1. Schedule a large room (conference room) with a long table for a WBS meeting.
2. Explain what everyone will do, and hand out the sticky note pads and pens to everyone in the room.
3. Roll out the paper and put the project description in an element (box) at the center-top.
4. Facilitate the group in creating the next (major) level, which will be the major project categories. Make sure there is an element (category) for project management, usually drawn on the far left.
5. Identify the elements under each element on the major level. You are now starting the mid-level elements for your project.
6. Continue working this process until the project team breaks the work into smaller elements.
7. Break the work down to the work package level. Make sure each work package description includes a verb and a noun for clarity.
8. Fill in the appropriate information into that work package: cost, start and finish dates, resources, risk, and quality.
9. Store your WBS materials in the document control system for long-term storage, archiving, and retrieval purposes.

WBS Bottom-Up Method

Another method for creating a WBS is the bottom-up method. Start out the same as the top-down method (above) with a roll of butcher paper and sticky note pads. Each stakeholder writes a description (at least a verb and a noun) of a work package on a sticky note and places it on the table. When everybody thinks they have written enough descriptions, and the ideas are exhausted, gather the work packages. Identify with the group members all the identical work packages and keep only one of the duplicates. Gather the remaining work packages and place them into groups based on the most applicable categories. For example, if you were a construction project, these categories would include mobilizations, earthwork, and foundations. You will find during the grouping process that the project team members will order these categories from left to right, in the order of accomplishing the work. You will find mobilization and earthwork starting at the left side of the butcher paper, and the ending group (far right) as closeout activities. The team members in the grouping process set the order of the tasks automatically. You will find that the project management activities such as scope, planning, cost estimating, and so on will be placed in its category in the far left. These work packages fall into the project's administration category.

Using a work breakdown structure

Before you can use a WBS, you must identify who on your project team will use it so that you can determine the level of detail, distribution frequency, style, and format of the report.

Review the WBS section in *Chapter 7 - Defining Communication Tools that Manage Project Scope*, and then complete the following steps:

1. Post a graphic representation of the WBS on the wall in the project war room, on a central project website, and in the document control system for easy access by team members.

2. Describe to your customers the overall work breakdown of the entire project using the WBS graph. Only go to the lowest level your customer wants. This allows your customer to understand the project's structure and overall work activities.

3. Work with your team members and describe their project tasks using the WBS. Go over the specifics of the team members' tasks, interdependencies, and where the task fits in the project.

4. Use your project's WBS to gather information dealing with schedule, costs, resources, risks, issues, purchasing, and quality aspects of the project. This step includes all aspects of managing the project when using the WBS. While the project is in progress, identify completed tasks by each work package and report progress on the project.

5. Store the WBS in the document control system for long-term storage, archiving, and retrieval purposes.

Summary

The tools we described in this chapter are the best choices for managing and administering your project in the project's planning process. Without proper project administration, you will quickly lose control and not carry out the needed goals and objectives the customers are expecting.

The tools in this chapter include some popular tools, such as the baseline schedule, change control plan, comprehensive test plan, design specifications, expected monetary value, functional specifications, project calendar, project schedule, system requirements document, and work breakdown structure. These tools are common to project managers and used across most industries. Project managers and team members must understand how important administering a project is to ensure successful completion. Developing and ongoing maintenance of the communication tools covered in this chapter may seem time-consuming, but the value you will receive from using them is priceless. For example, without a change control plan and procedures document in place, a simple change request could send team members scrambling and could derail the project, yet that one tool could prevent this from occurring. Other tools, such as the risk register, comprehensive test plan, and the critical chain tool are all valuable to your project in the planning and executing processes

Chapter 19

Using Communication Tools for Project Reporting during the Planning Process

IN THIS CHAPTER

- ♦ Mastering the Budget Spreadsheet
- ♦ Mastering Earned Value Analysis
- ♦ Mastering the Earned Value Estimating tool
- ♦ Mastering the Logic Network diagram
- ♦ Mastering Quality Metrics
- ♦ Mastering Risk Register
- ♦ Mastering the Risk Matrix tool
- ♦ Mastering the Scatter chart

In this chapter, we explore project communication tools used during the project's planning process. The tools specifically focus on reporting and communicating with customers, team members, and leadership during the project planning process.

There are many different tools in this chapter. Some of the tools will help you create information that drives the project deliverables. For example, you use the baseline schedule and the logic network diagram to manage and control project planning. There are other tools that you and your team members will use for reporting purposes, such as the project milestone list and scatter charts. These are an excellent mix of tools that should help you become an effective communicator during the planning process.

Mastering the Budget Spreadsheet

Before using the *budget spreadsheet*, you must understand how it can help and support you on your project. The following project scenario highlights why the budget spreadsheet is critical to every project, especially those that are cost-driven.

A large real estate firm has decided to overhaul its computer sales application to bring it into the 21st century. The current system has been in use in every sales office all over the country for many years. Replacing the sales application is not going to be easy and will take a lot of coordination with the sales offices to ensure success. You, the most senior project manager at the company, are stepping up to lead this project. You understand the project is going to be big and realize there are several different areas for you to work in. You also realize that working on such a large project is going to be expensive, but you do not know just how expensive. You have many questions, such as:

- How do you track the costs and budget for such a large project?
- What mechanisms will you use to control and monitor costs?
- What is your budget?

By using a budget spreadsheet, you can answer these questions. The budget spreadsheet captures and tracks project costs. You use the budget spreadsheet estimates that were provided by the various groups to request funding from the customer to continue with the project.

Cross-Reference
We recommend that you review the budget spreadsheet in Chapter 9 - Communication Tools That Manage Project Costs for more information.

Creating a budget spreadsheet

A budget spreadsheet is an important tool for any project. You must ensure that you have complete control over the project dollars at all times. There are hundreds of different types of budget spreadsheets available, and most companies have templates or examples you can use. In addition, most experienced project managers also have a version of a budget spreadsheet they like to use on their projects.

You must understand how to closely track the dollars on your project. If you are uncomfortable with the calculations, or unfamiliar with how to assign dollars across the project, work with the finance department to clear up any confusion. On most projects, you are responsible for the dollars assigned to a project, and without detailed and weekly tracking, the project can quickly get out of control.

One of the most complicated parts of budget spreadsheets, and budgets in general, is handling project forecasts. When you create a budget spreadsheet, you create forecast columns to track project forecasts. Budget forecasts are the expected rate of spending project funds; you must closely watch forecasts to understand how close the project is tracking to the budget. For example, if the forecasts come in at $500,000 for a $700,000 dollar project, you quickly discover, at a glance, whether the project is tracking correctly. This is just a high-level glance from the cost part of the project and does not influence any other parts of the project. It is important to understand that funds alone do not provide the current project status; they are only one part of it.

The challenging part of the budgeting process is watching the forecasts swing weekly, because on some projects this does happen. Forecasts can move significantly every week, throwing the project budgeting process into emergency planning to understand what happened and why it changed. Emergency planning is an important part of the budget management customer review process because as forecasts shift each week, the shift in dollars requires explanation. Customers want to understand why the amounts change weekly, and if you only track budgets monthly, you could miss the week-to-week swings and the budget and forecast amounts could alarm you or customer. Project budgeting is best captured and reviewed on a weekly basis, with the project customer. The customer should be active and accountable in creating the budget spreadsheet and know how their funds are expected to be spent. The customer must hold you and team accountable to the project budget to ensure they are spending it wisely.

The steps for creating a budget spreadsheet can vary among project managers and depend on their favorite tools. **Table 19.1 — Example of a budget spreadsheet (hours/project costs)** shows an advanced monthly tracking budget spreadsheet. This is a good spreadsheet to use when tracking monthly hours (actuals and estimates) for individual team members.

Table 19.1 — Example of a budget spreadsheet (hours/project costs)

Name	Emp Rate	Contactor Rate	Jan Act	Jan Est	Actual Total Costs per Month	Est. Total Costs per Month	Hour Var	Cost Var
Emp 1	$45		2	2	$90	$90	0	0
Contract 1		$96	5	5	$480	$480	0	0
Emp 2	$35		2	3	$70	$105	-1	-35
Emp 3	$25		5	1	$125	$25	4	100
Emp 4	$44		6	6	$264	$264	0	0
Contract 2		$100	10	6	$1,000	$600	4	400
Emp 5	$22		2	2	$44	$44	0	0
Emp 6	$45		10	15	$450	$675	-5	-225
Emp 7	$65		2	2	$130	$130	0	0
Emp 8	$45		15	5	$675	$225	10	450
			==	==	==========	===========	=====	===
Totals			59	47	$3,328	$2,638	12	690

This budget spreadsheet is easy to create and is something any project manager should be able to do. Complete the following steps to create your own budget spreadsheet.

1. Enter each team member's name in the Name column. Regardless of how many people are on the project, you should document everyone's first and last name in this column.

2. Enter each team member's burn rate (burn rate is the standard cost of employees, per year) to the EMP Rate column. You should be able to get these rates from the finance department. Enter the rates for each employee into the budget spreadsheet. The rates might be different for each

employee and the roles they play. Be careful when working with and reporting team member rates because this information can be sensitive and not to be shared broadly.

3. Complete the same process for the contractors and vendors that are on your project team. The rates will differ depending on the contract and vendor's costs, but again, should be easily obtainable.

4. Fill in the Actual Hours column and the Estimated Hours column (in the table, these columns are noted as Jan Act and Jan Est columns). There are two different methods for getting this data. First, you can work with your team members and get both values from them, or you can get this data from your company's financial system. Because this process is completed monthly, it does not take much time and it is fairly easy to get team member's monthly hours.

Tip

Estimates and forecasts often change from week to week, so you should go into the financial system weekly to find out if there are any changes to the team members' monthly estimates.

Note

An important note to consider, the table shows only one month. The project manager will enter two columns for each month of the project, Actuals and Estimates, and depending on how long the project is projecting, there could be up to twelve additional months, or twenty four different columns. When creating a budget spreadsheet like this, the only available data a team member can provide early in the project is the estimates per month. Although the information may be rough, those estimates should be enough to clarify the expected project costs.

5. After entering your team members' actuals and monthly estimates on the budget spreadsheet, the template formulas will automatically calculate your spreadsheet totals.

6. Review the data and adjust as needed. The budget spreadsheet is now complete and ready to use. You will continue this process through the project life cycle.

Using a budget spreadsheet

Before using a budget spreadsheet, you must identify who on your project team will use it so that you can determine the level of detail, distribution frequency, style, and format of the report.

Review the budget spreadsheet section in Chapter 9 - Communication Tools That Manage Project Costs.

1. Always ensure your budget spreadsheet data is as accurate as possible. To do this, you may need to set up a process to compile and report information, and then review the tasks your team members are performing and enter their estimates once a month. When developing these processes, work closely with your team members to ensure they know what to expect.

2. After setting up the process for data entry and updating your budget spreadsheet, work with your customer to discover their reporting requirements for the budget spreadsheet. Understanding how often they want to see the budget spreadsheet is important for setting up a good communication rhythm with them.

3. As your project moves into the executing process, you will continue to constantly update the budget spreadsheet. You do this by gathering the actuals from the financial systems each month, and then adding those values into the budget spreadsheet by updating each team member's estimates. After each monthly update, copy the budget spreadsheet into the document control system for long-term storage, archiving and availability.

4. As the project finishes, store your final budget spreadsheet in the document control system.

Mastering the Earned Value Analysis Tool

Before you can use the *earned value analysis* tool, you must understand how it can help and support you on your project. The following project scenario highlights the tool's importance.

A large research company, in Dallas, Texas is working on a new bio-energy product that will transform water into a form of gas. Management has asked you to be the project manager. The project has a planned schedule of 25 months. The management team has reviewed and approved the $2,000,000 budget. You have received approval to spend $120,000 per month until the project is complete, and everyone agrees that this is a reasonable expense rate for this project type. The owner and the project team fully expect to stay within the cost limits of $120,000 per month for the life of the project, and everyone is excited to get the project under way.

At the end of the first month, you present a glowing performance report to the management team that shows the actual costs for the first month were only $90,000. This was under the planned budget by $30,000, or 25 percent. The stakeholders are happy until one of the financial officers asks if the project is on schedule and *performing* according to the $120,000 budget rate, and not the $90,000 cost. You quickly assure the financial officer the project is on schedule, and just as quickly the financial officer shoots back several questions, including, how you know whether the performance equals the spending rate. No one in the room can answer the question. The last statement in the meeting came from the financial officer, "I want the performance answers by the next progress meeting." No one said a word. The financial officer speaks up again asking some tough, but fair questions, such as:

- Have you performed according to your schedule?
- How much of the $90,000 have you actually earned?
- What is your cost performance index?

To answer these questions, you should use the earned value analysis techniques. Without using the earned value analysis techniques, it is difficult to integrate cost and schedule data to create a performance report. Without those performance reports, you or your executives would have a difficult time understanding the project team's true performance. In today's project environment, especially large projects, it is common for one group to create the project schedule, and a different group to estimate and track the project costs. Therefore, the cost and the schedule are rarely integrated, making it difficult to find out the project's performance rate.

Cross-Reference
We recommend that you review the earned value analysis tool in Chapter 9 - Communication Tools That Manage Project Costs for more information.

Creating the earned value analysis performance tool

Creating the earned value analysis process is becoming more popular because it integrates scheduling and costs into a single view. Earned value analysis creates both a tabular and graphical presentation of reports for customers and team members to use. When creating earned value analysis reports, you must ensure there is an existing project schedule that is being maintained. The second step is to ensure you cost load (funds or labor hours) the original project schedule. Finally, you create a baseline schedule from the original schedule. When the project starts, it is ready for performance reporting.

Before creating earned value reports, you should be comfortable with the terms and calculations. We previously covered some of the terms (see *Chapters 6 - Communication Tools That Manage Project*

Integration and *7 - Defining Communication Tools that Manage Project Scope* for more information about the terms), but it is valuable to review them before creating earned value reports.

The earned value calculations consist of the following:

Cost formulas for measuring cost performance

Table 19.2 — Cost calculations for earned value reports

Name	Calculation
Cost Variance (CV)	$CV = EV - AC$
Cost Performance Index (CPI)	$CPI = EV / AC$

Schedule formulas for measuring schedule performance

The following items are the schedule calculations for the earned value reports. Here are the two calculations.

Table 19.3 – Schedule calculations for earned value reports

Name	Calculation
Schedule Variance (SV)	$SV = EV - PV$
Schedule Performance Index (SPI)	$SPI = EV / PV$

Note
The first variable in each calculation is the earned value (EV) variable. In the schedule variance calculation, EV is the earned value variable.

Earned Value Analysis Terms

Earned Value: At the time of calculating the report, earned value is 2, or 2 percent complete for the task, multiplied by 5 percent that is expected to be complete for the task.

Planned Value: At the time of calculating the report, the planned value represents how much work was expected to be completed at this time; however, the task should have been 5 percent complete, and was only 2 percent complete.

Cost Variance: At the time of calculating the report, the task was 2 percent complete, showing the task is −$108 over what it was estimated to have cost at 2 percent complete.

Schedule Variance: At time of calculating the report, planned value was 5 percent, the task was 2 percent complete; therefore, it shows the task as behind schedule.

Cost CPI: At the time of calculating the report, cost CPI is 0.02 for this task, which indicates from a cost perspective the task is over-running due to over spending and is actually completed at this time.

Schedule SPI: At the time of calculating the report, SPI is 0.40, which means the work rate is performing at 40 percent of what was expected.

Table 19.4 — Example of an earned value performance report shows an extensive earned value performance report that displays various performance data values for each activity in your project schedule. As you can see, the chart shows not only the three earned value fields: planned value, earned value, and actual cost, but also the cost and schedule variance fields, and the performance field's cost and schedule performance indexes. This report and the S-curve graphics report, provide all the information you need for performing performance analysis on your project.

Table 19.4 — Example of an earned value performance report

Activity Description	% Complete	Planned Value (Budget)	Earned Value	Actual Cost	Cost Variance	Schedule Variance	Cost CPI	Schedule SPI
Preliminary Plan	2%	100	2	110	-108	-98	0.02	0.02
Final Plan	100%	250	250	210	40	0	1.19	1.00
Move Out	100%	300	300	265	35	0	1.13	1.00
Remodel	70%	1200	840	1300	-460	-360	0.65	0.70
Move Back In	1%	250	2.5	10	-7.5	-248	0.25	0.01
Total	55%	2100	1394.5	1895	-500.5	-706	0.74	0.66

Figure 19.1 — Example of an S-Curve chart shows an earned value S-Curve chart that displays your project's up-to-date trend, such as actual values, planned values, and finally, earned values. This chart shows a project's condition that can be trended to display an estimate at completion. It is clear from this example that the project is performing behind schedule and is significantly over budget.

Figure 19.1 — Example of an S-Curve chart (performance reporting)

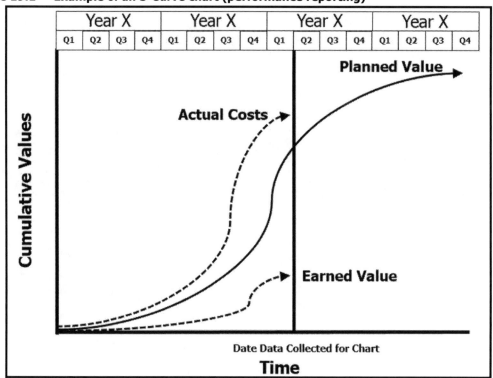

When you decide to use the earned value analysis (EVA) technique to report your project's progress and performance, there is a lot of thought and planning that goes into running a project using EVA, but the benefits will significantly outweigh the time and effort to create and maintain it. Use the WBS to help you plan and develop your project schedule; the process works best when the entire team and customers are involved. Your customers will provide ideas and buy-in, and their involvement is important for creating a better product. While planning the earned value analysis, assign specific team members to be responsible for the status and performance of each project activity.

Complete the following steps to get started creating an earned value analysis report.

1. Decide how your team members will estimate each activity and how to collect actuals. The easiest way to do this is to use labor time sheets because they are efficient at keeping track of the hours that team members work on each activity. It is hard to get a project's actual costs because they may not be available for a least a month after the company's billing cycle has been posted to the books.

2. Create you original project schedule.

3. Cost load (using funds or labor hours) your project schedule. This is not an easy task. Each activity requires an estimated cost applied to it, which can represent funds, labor hours, or both. If you have trouble estimating an activity's cost, you may be more comfortable breaking it down into several smaller more manageable pieces. Do this before recording any progress because otherwise it is much harder to do later. Using the project's WBS can significantly help with the cost loading process.

Cross-Reference
Turn to Chapter 7 - Defining Communication Tools that Manage Project Scope to learn more about the WBS.

4. Forward your original schedule to your customer and your team members for approval. This includes sending the original project schedule and the user acceptance document to your team members and customers to gain their approval. Usually, you will have a project schedule review meeting with team members and customers to review the schedule, ensuring everyone understands it and providing them the confidence to sign off on it.

5. After getting the sign-off and approval, create your baseline schedule.

6. After the first reporting cycle begins, the earned value analysis carries throughout the project life cycle. There are different pieces of information needed to create the performance reports, such as the activity's actual start date, the percentage complete, or the activity's actual finish date if it is 100 percent complete. Update every activity on your project schedule that is in progress, and enter actual finish dates for activities that have completed since the last reporting cycle.

7. Gather actual costs for each project activity that reported progress. This calculation can be determined in many ways. For example, actual costs could be labor hours to date, per activity, hours times ($\times$) labor rate, or gather actual costs by funds, totaling the expenses for each activity. Each calculation will depend on how you created the original estimate.

8. You now have all the information you need to create the earned value reports, by updating the performance report, applying the new progress information to your scheduling system, and creating the performance reports. The performance reports can be tabular or graphical by using the plan value (PV), earned value (EV), and actual cost (AC) curves. The report should automatically be created each month during the reporting cycle. The reports should consist of the following data:

   - S-Curves showing the plan value (PV), earned value (EV), and actual cost (AC) curve

   - Cost and schedule variance reports

   - Cost performance index (CPI) and the schedule performance index (SPI)

9. The earned value reports are now ready for distribution.

10. Maintain your baseline schedule and keep it current with approved change requests each reporting cycle. Every time you add value or remove value from a project, you must include it in the baseline schedule. If an approved change order adds 1,000 hours to the current schedule, you should add the 1,000 hours to the baseline schedule. Without the baseline change, the performance reports will be undervalued or overvalued, which can give an appearance that the team is either underperforming or over performing.

Using the earned value analysis performance tool

Before you use the earned value analysis performance tool, you must identify who on your project team will use it so you can determine the level of detail, distribution frequency, style, and format of the earned value reports.

Review the earned value analysis performance section in *Chapter 9 - Communication Tools That Manage Project Costs*, and then complete the following steps:

1. Share your earned value reports after each reporting cycle, or on-demand, when applicable. Send the reports to the project owner, customer, team members, subcontractors, and occasionally, the media.

2. Host several status meetings to review the earned value reports with everyone involved in the project. Your first meeting is strictly for team members to become current on the project's performance, the second meeting is for the customer to become current on the project's performance. In each meeting, action items could result for either you or your team members from reviewing and discussing the project performance. If that is the case, adjust your project where applicable.

3. Ensure that you continue to focus your team members' work efforts on the results from the performance report meetings. They may need to switch focus to various areas on the project that need updating to improve the project's performance. Examples include adding staff, reducing scope, and moving activity time frames.

Mastering the Earned Value Estimating Tool

Before you can use the *earned value estimating* tool, you must understand how it can help and support you on your project. The following project scenario highlights the tool's importance.

A project team has been working on an estimate for over six months. The project entails constructing a natural gas pipeline from the northwest shelf off the coast of Australia, coming ashore at Port Hedland, and then down to Perth, over seven-years. Just north of Perth, there are plans to build a large, natural gas refinery at Wanneroo, Western Australia. The estimating team is having difficulty justifying the project's estimated cost to the natural gas board. The previous review of the estimate resulted in criticism toward the estimators who had not considered all project areas and future labor costs. The board members consider the estimates inadequate. The team has broken down the work to a detailed level they feel comfortable with for developing their estimate. As you lead the estimating team in this effort, you have several questions that you want answered, including:

- How can we scrub this estimate to reveal shortages? What is the estimate variance?
- Does the team have other saving techniques to reduce the costs?
- Should we create the WBS now and estimate at the work package level?

To answer these questions, you should use a forecasting tool to address future labor, material, and equipment costs. Forecasting is a technique for discovering future project costs. On large projects, such as the one in this scenario, a professional forecaster is hired to help in this process. With the forecaster's findings, you can predict project costs based on future industry trends. In this scenario, a professional forecaster would have been valuable in producing a true estimate for the pipeline. Due to the seven-year duration of this project, it is not too late to hire a forecaster.

Cross-Reference
We recommend that you review the earned value estimating tool in Chapter 9 - Communication Tools That Manage Project Costs for more information.

Creating an earned value estimating tool

A professional forecaster is trained to read future conditions and can create project forecasts. Forecasters can look at trends, figure out how they will affect the project, and report the impacts to you, your team members, and customers. A forecaster can gather information about a project or a subject area that requires a forecast, such as labor rates, materials, and equipment. For example, a forecaster will know which union contracts to include for increases in labor rates for the local area. The forecaster will also know working conditions to extrapolate those effects on future rates. The end-result of a forecaster's work is to provide the forecast information to you or the project team for creating a project estimate. The project team should rely on the forecaster to provide this data when applicable. You need to be involved in the estimating process and ensure that the estimate includes rate changes and inflation, especially if the project is more than two or three years in duration. You expect the estimate to come as close as possible to the real project costs. When there are changes or updates to the project's budget or schedule, you will provide updated information based on the changes and adjust it as necessary.

Although the estimating process is complex, the results of the project are a projection of the real project costs. The projection is important for the customer so they can determine whether to proceed with the project or shut it down.

Creating a Project Forecast

The following steps explain what a forecaster performs to create a forecast.

1. The forecaster identifies what to forecast and why to forecast it; this usually includes material, labor rates, and equipment.

2. The forecaster gathers information and data to complete the forecast.

3. The forecaster analyzes data and information and confirms all informational resources.

4. The forecaster derives the project forecast and any impacts via the project cash flow.

5. The forecaster delivers the forecast information and estimates.

6. Finally, the forecaster gathers information to make the forecasts as accurate as possible for labor rates, material, and equipment costs.

As project manager, you should understand these steps and how you can help the forecaster do his or her work. You need to know how long the process will take, the cost impacts of doing the work, and the impact to the project. We recommend that you work closely with your forecaster. Doing so will give you a much better understanding of future industry trends.

Creating a Project Estimate Tool

The following steps explain how a forecaster creates a project estimate.

1. Assign a forecaster to your project. This could be you or a separate team member focused solely on estimating.

2. Ensure the forecaster understands the scope of work and what to base the estimate on.

3. Work with the forecaster when they are reviewing the design specifications (i.e., construction industry drawings), and identify areas that need an estimate. Answer questions as needed.

4. Work with the forecaster as they perform the project's estimate.

5. Present the estimate to your customer or leadership team. In construction, for example, the estimate becomes a bid.

6. Store the project's estimate and associated documents in the document control system for long-term storage, archiving, and retrieval purposes.

Using the earned value estimating tool

Before using the earned value estimating tool, you must identify who will use it. This information is important so you can determine the level of detail, distribution frequency, style, and format of the earned value estimating tool. Project estimates are detailed so that there is no confusion about the expected costs for each project area.

Before using the estimating tool, review the estimating tool section in Chapter 9 - Communication Tools That Manage Project Costs for more information, and then complete the following steps:

1. Apply the cost estimate or labor hours to the budget creation process. For example, if you have an estimate from a vendor or contracting company, they can use that estimated value to discover how close it is to the project budget.

2. Depending on whether it is over or under budget, react as applicable. This means that you may have to ask for more money from your customer, or ask the customer to reduce scope and costs.

3. At the end of this process, store the relevant documents in the document control system for long-term storage, archiving, and accessibility.

Mastering the Logic Network Diagram

Before you can use the *logic network diagram*, you must understand how it can help and support you on your project. The following project scenario highlights the tool's importance.

A large aerospace company has just announced the design of a new plane to be added to their commercial airplane division. This is an exciting announcement for the company and the aerospace industry, and it is expected to become number one in commercial airplane sales. The company is buzzing with excitement, and everyone is thrilled with the new plane's design. As the most senior project manager in the company, leadership asks you to be the new project manager. As you start the project, your first order of business is to find out the different groups involved in this effort. The second area to tackle is the order in which the different groups have to perform their work. Once you determine who the various groups are, you can start gathering the list of tasks each group is required to perform to design and build the airplane. For a large commercial airplane, you realize that this is going to be an enormous list, and the dependencies among the various groups will be complex. Each group quickly replies to your request for tasks. You receive thousands of tasks and have no idea how they will all work together. You also have no idea how they will fit together to build a plane. The number of tasks you receive quickly overwhelms you, and you have no idea where to start. You have many questions about where to start, including:

- What are you going to do?
- Where do you start?
- Is there a logical starting point anywhere among the tasks?
- What are the predecessors for each task?
- What are the successors?
- How much staff will be needed?

To answer these questions, you should use a logic network diagram. The logic network diagram sequentially and logically orders all of the project tasks. The tool is easy to use and graphically shows the logic of each project activity. In a complex scenario, such as building an airplane, a logic network diagram makes perfect sense and allows the project team to group and move tasks around to get them in the correct order. When you begin a project, the ability to see the logical dependencies among project activities is priceless. The logic network diagram is one of the only tools that enable you to do this.

Cross-Reference
We recommend that you review the logic network diagram tool in Chapter 8 - Communication Tools That Manage Project Time for more information.

Creating a logic network diagram

Creating a logic network diagram at the beginning of a project provides many benefits that you may not fully understand. It provides, or visually displays, the project's logical sequence of events. By doing so, it produces the various relationships and outlines the main contact points for each area. It easily displays activity convergence. This is where many activities converge into a single milestone activity. Convergent activities tend to be at a higher risk. Anyone creating the diagram can update the task sequence using the tool. Sequencing project tasks is a project manager activity; however, project team members should also be part of the process. They can help you review, update, and sometimes delete the sequencing, if necessary.

Tip

Project managers should be diligent and active when sequencing tasks while creating the logic network diagram. It is important to ensure communications and the relationship among dependent groups. It is also important to encourage the various groups to discuss the order of tasks and dependencies.

The project owner or customer may be active in creating and understanding the project's logic network diagram. The diagram allows them to understand the order of each task and where they are involved in the project. Often, due to other project consideration constraints, the customer may need to reorder tasks where they see a conflict; the logic network diagram will show project impacts for that reordering.

The steps for creating a logic network diagram can vary. Complete the following steps to get started:

1. Open the project scheduling tool.
2. Enter the tasks for project. For this example, create activities called Test 1 through Test 20 on your project schedule.
3. For example, if you are using Microsoft Project, select **Views**, and then select **Network Diagram**. The tool auto produces the project's logic network diagram. Other tools may have different approaches to getting to a Network diagram within their software.
4. Connect and link the project activities with predecessors and successors. Every task must have a predecessor or successor, except the first and last tasks in the project schedule. It is also not advised to add links on project summary tasks.

After working with the various groups involved with the project, the project's logic network diagram is complete.

Figure 19.2 — Example of a logic network diagram shows a logic network diagram using a project scheduling tool. This is a simple example created by scheduling software.

Figure 19.2 — Example of a logic network diagram

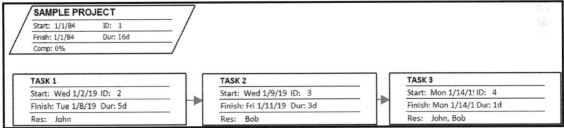

Using a logic network diagram

Before using a tool such as a logic network diagram, you must identify who on your project team will use it so you can determine the level of detail, distribution frequency, style, and format of the logic network diagram. Review the logic network diagram section in Chapter 6, and then complete the following steps:

1. As your project moves out of the initiation process and into the planning process, make sure your team members and customer sign-off and approve the logic network diagram. Because the diagram is so important to the logical order of work activities, it is important that they sign off and approve it before work begins. Send the logic network diagram and the user acceptance document to your customer and team members for sign off and approval.

2. After getting approval and sign-off from both groups, store the documents in the document control system for long-term storage, archiving, and retrieval purposes.

3. As the project moves into the executing process, enforce the use of the logic network diagram. As your project team organizes the project's layout, they will use the diagram to help them with the planning process. Communicate the use of the tool externally as well, so that external groups who have critical pieces on the project are aware of the logic network diagram.

4. One of the advantages of using the logic network diagram is displaying the order in which your team will complete project tasks, and it allows you to create a straw man schedule. In this process, you first create task boxes in the tool and add project tasks in their own boxes. Then, using the tool, work with team members to arrange the task boxes in logical order. Once complete, you can create a master project schedule based on the logic and order within the diagram. This process is easier to complete in the logic network diagram than in a project scheduling tool.

5. Continue this process until the project close-out process where you store the final version of the logic network diagram in the document control system for long-term storage, archiving, and accessibility by everyone on the project.

Mastering Quality Metrics

Before you can use *quality metrics*, you must understand how they can help and support you on your project. The following project scenario stresses the importance of using quality metrics.

A large manufacturing company has developed nuts and screws for years. The company has been so successful in the marketplace that they have decided to expand their product line to include a new type of screw. The company is excited about the new screw, and market tests have proven that it will be successful. The company president was approached by a large space agency CIO who has shown interest the screw. The large space agency CIO asked if the manufacturing company could perform "special" tests on the screw for them. This is exciting for the company who is hoping to secure a long-term contract with the large space agency, so they happily accept their request. Your assignment, as the most respected project manager at the company, is to work with the large space agency's test team to ensure they are getting everything they need for testing. This is your moment to shine, but as the testing progresses, results come in that are unfavorable and the large space agency test team is not happy. They are about to give up on the project and you do not know what to do. The large space agency's team asks some specific questions about quality, including:

- What quality level is acceptable for the screw?
- What area of testing is failing?
- What is an acceptable failure level, per thousand screws?

To answer these questions, you should use quality metrics. Quality metrics ensure that projects are striving for the highest quality level. Quality metrics force team members to hit a specific quality level that is determined by the project metrics. In this scenario, is it acceptable if two screws out of 200 fail? It is unlikely, but possible, based on the rigor that large space agency applies to testing. You should leverage the quality metrics defined at the beginning of the project to ensure that testing meets or exceeds the pre-determined level—in this case, two failures. If it does not, then in this scenario, the large space agency team was correct and justified to end the project unless something immediately changes.

Cross-Reference
We recommend that you review the quality metrics tool in Chapter 10 - Communication Tools That Manage Project Quality for more information.

Creating quality metrics

Quality metrics are levels of rigor and controls that are applied to testing. These metrics determine the quality level of the end product. The testing results for each quality metric come from a series of testing limits, upper and lower,. When testing completes, the company can determine the quality level of product based on the number of pass and fail results.

You need to understand how the project's quality will be determined and judged. Quality metrics ensure that the project team is adding rigor and process to their testing and work results to achieve the highest possible project quality. Quality metrics are applied to various parts of the project. For example, in the software industry, a popular quality metric includes code drops. Code drops indicate how often the development team had to drop new code for the test team to re-test. Another software quality metric shows how many bugs were found in the code. The list goes on for software quality metrics used on most projects.

When developing quality metrics, it is important to use a standard process each time to ensure the metrics are consistent across tests. The industry has a well-known process called the Shewhart Cycle. The Shewhart Cycle chart has four main areas:

1. **Plan:** Improve results by designing or revising the process components.
2. **Do:** Implement the plan and measure its performance.
3. **Check:** Evaluate and report results to stakeholders.
4. **Act:** Make a decision about possible process changes for improvement.

Using the Shewhart Cycle requires an ongoing circular process through the four main areas of the cycle. It is critical to complete these areas in a circular motion, starting from the "plan" and moving through to the "act" area, and when you finish the "act" area you move back to the "plan" area. It is a continuous cycle. Using the Shewhart Cycle provides a standard method for creating quality metrics for any given project area.

Your customer must be active in understanding and defining the quality level that is acceptable to them. For example, some customer may have a higher tolerance for accepting risk and will agree to a higher number of product failures than more conservative customers might. You must be aware of your customer's tolerance level and ensure the project is driving toward that level. The eventual goal is making sure the customer is satisfied with the released product.

The steps for creating quality metrics can vary. We have provided some guidelines for creating your own quality metrics, below.

To start learning how to create quality metrics, we have a simple scenario for you to follow. You can adjust or adapt this scenario for your own project.

Scenario: We want to track the number of software errors by severity level for every release that goes into the user acceptance environment. There are five release cycles from which to produce metrics. The metrics the team is judged on would be the last metric. This metric is as follows: zero severity 1 bugs, less than 3 severity 2 bugs, and less than 5 severity 3 bugs. If the project team members can hit the quality metrics on bug counts, the project is at an acceptable quality level.

1. Work with your project's test lead to make sure they understand and define the metrics they are testing and tracking. The metrics should be based on the overall quality metrics defined for the project. The test lead tells their testers the metrics, and you tell your customers. Work with the test lead to develop the quality metrics tracking table to store the metrics when the testing process starts. See **Table 19.5** for a sample of this table. The test lead will take ownership of capturing and reporting this information going forward and throughout the testing process.
2. As the project releases its first round into the user acceptance environment, you will then work with your test lead to track the results. Your test lead count the software errors based in the different severity categories (Severity 1, Severity 2) after the first round. Once complete, enter those results into the new created quality metrics table for reporting purposes.

Table 19.5 — Example of quality metrics results in a user acceptance environment shows a sample of quality metric from the first round of testing in the user acceptance environment. Because this is the first round of testing, the project team has time in the schedule to recode and retest to bring the error counts down. This chart is good for tracking toward the overall project metrics.

Table 19.5 — Example of quality metrics results in a user acceptance environment

Bugs By Status and Severity Levels					
Status	Sev 1	Sev 2	Sev 3	Sev 4	Total
Active	5	22	5	0	32
Resolved	0	0	0	0	0
Closed	0	55	22	5	82
Total	0	77	34	34	145

3. After the values are in the quality metrics table, compare the results from testing to the quality metrics defined for your project. Remember, those metrics were zero severity 1 bugs, less than 3 severity 2 bugs, and less than 5 severity 3 bugs. In table 19.5, it is clear the development team has some work to do to hit the metrics they need to achieve.

4. Continue this process until the project testing phase is complete and the project testing team has achieved the quality metrics set up for the project. The project should not be considered complete or at an acceptable quality level until the level of quality agreed to has been reached.

Using quality metrics

Before using quality metrics, you must identify who on your project team will use them so you can determine the level of detail, distribution frequency, style, and format of the quality metrics report. Quality metrics are often described and reported with detailed information. It is important to capture the details so team members can create the metrics they are trying to achieve. Quality metrics documented at a summary level would not be valuable to the project.

Review the quality metrics section in *Chapter 10 - Communication Tools That Manage Project Quality*, and then complete the following steps:

1. As the project moves into the planning process, the first step is to get approval and sign-off from team members and customers. The project team works hard to get a quality level outlined by quality metrics, and before the team spends the time and effort to achieve those goals, you must ensure everyone signs off and approves the metrics. You may need to meet with the customer and team members to ensure everyone agrees on the metrics and are comfortable signing-off on them. After everyone consents to the quality metrics, share them for approval and sign-off. This includes combining the user acceptance document with the quality metrics the customer has previously approved and agreed to sign.

2. After approvals and sign-offs are received from your customer and team members, store the information in the document control system for long-term storage, archiving, and availability to anyone interested in reviewing them.

3. As the project moves into the execution process, you must ensure your test team is working towards those quality metrics within the testing phase. Make sure that your test lead is capturing the test results, reporting and communicating those results, and driving the test team toward hitting those defined quality metrics.

Mastering the Risk Register

Before you can use the *risk register*, you must understand how it can back and support you on your project. The following project scenario highlights its importance and why the risk register is critical to every project.

A large, world-renowned health agency has decided to set up a new health care program in several impoverished countries around the world. The new health system will provide sorely needed medicines to people in these countries, saving many lives; this application is long overdue. Drug and prescription information will be readily available to doctors when the system goes live. You are a lead project manager in the health care industry and want to manage this new system project. You are excited and ready to get going, but you also realize that many risks are surfacing that need immediate attention. Your management team asks you several questions about the different risks—and risks are starting to appear from everywhere. The questions that management asks include:

- How do you manage project risks?
- What strategies did you develop for risk events?
- What mitigation plans do you have in place for each risk?
- What risks are current on the project?

To answer these questions, you should use a risk register. The risk register provides a tracking and status mechanism for controlling and reporting project risks. The risk register is often identified as a risk list. The risk register should provide everything you need to effectively manage and control project risks.

Cross-Reference
We recommend that you review the risk register in Chapter 13 - Defining Communication Tools to Manage Project Risk for more information.

Creating a risk register

Risk mitigation is one of the most important categories in the risk register. Risk mitigation is the method of trying to ensure that project risk events do not stop or derail a project, also known as risk response planning. When you perform early analysis and decide strategies for project risk events, you can prevent or reduce harm to the project. Sometimes, this work avoids the risk event completely. Developing alternate courses of action, or workarounds for each risk event, provides a better mechanism for handling them if they do occur. Discuss the risk mitigation process early with the customers so they are on board and approve the process.

One risk mitigation technique is to bring the customer and team members together to examine the project's risk events and document how to react to the risks should they occur. The time taken in selecting a strategy for risk events can save the project team time if risk events do occur.

Note
It is important that you continue to re-address risk events throughout the project and suggest strategies for those events as they arise.

The risk register is relatively new for many of you and your project manager peers and one that will help in the risk mitigation of any project. You should create the risk register at the beginning of the project and enter the project risks into the risk register as soon as possible. You can use the risk register and the risk assessment tools to help manage and control risks. The risk register is an important tool for reporting project risks. The customer and project team should review it at least once a week. Often, risks are resolved in the background as part of the project work, which you may not find out until later; reviewing the risk register once a week prevents that from occurring. You will learn and understand which project risks are completed at the next meeting.

You should actively create risk mitigation strategies for the project, and should work closely with the customer to ensure they are in the loop and suggest ways to resolve project risks with the project team. Project teams may have one idea for how to resolve risks, and the customer may have a different idea. Communication issues between the project team and customer requires immediate resolution. You should drive this to a conclusion.

The steps for creating a risk register vary; however, the following steps provide a great starting point.

1. Add the risk events that have a risk response plan in the risk register spreadsheet. There may be several risk events listed on your project that might be candidates for creating a mitigation strategy. You should only add the events that have mitigation strategies to the risk register.

2. Next, work with your team members to identify a strategy for mitigating the risk events. Risk mitigation includes risk strategies to use on your project:

   - Risk acceptance
   - Risk avoidance
   - Risk transfer
   - Risk mitigate
   - Risk exploit
   - Risk enhance
   - Risk share

3. At this point, work with your team members to select a risk mitigation strategy for every risk event that warrants it. When selecting the risk event mitigation strategy, make sure everyone understands why the strategy makes sense for that risk. The first strategy selected may not make sense, but as a group, you should come to a consensus on which strategy is correct for the risk event.

4. Finally, communicate the completed risk register to your customer, leadership, and team members.

Using a risk register

Before using a risk register, you must identify who on your project team will use it so you can determine the level of detail, distribution frequency, style, and format of the risk register report.

Review the risk register section in *Chapter 13 - Defining Communication Tools to Manage Project Risk*, and then complete the following steps:

1. As the project moves into the planning process, it is important that the customers and team members sign-off on the risk mitigation strategies. Their sign-off confirms agreement with the strategies selected for mitigating the various project risk events.

2. Share the risk register and the user acceptance document with your customers and team members for approval. Once approved, store both documents in the document control system for long-term storage, archiving, and retrieval purposes.

3. As the project moves into the executing phase, you need to actively monitor the project risk events. If a risk occurs, activate the risk mitigation strategies when needed. This includes weekly risk register reviews, driving the mitigation strategies selected, and ensuring the team focuses on the high-level risk events.

4. Drive the risk mitigation process and risk strategy throughout the project life cycle. When the project reaches the close-out phase, and all risk events are resolved, store the final risk register in the document control system for long-term storage, archiving, and availability to anyone interested in reviewing it.

Mastering the Risk Matrix

Before using the *risk matrix*, you must understand how it can help and support you on your project. The following project scenario stresses its importance.

A large manufacturing plant has decided to update one of its most important and critical machines with a newer and faster model. The current machine, though it has been successful for many years, cannot process the steel fast enough, which is slowing down production in the plant. You, as the lead manufacturing project manager for all plant-related projects, have decided to lead the machine replacement project. You are excited about the plant producing steel much faster with the new machine, but you are worried about replacing a machine that has been so reliable for so long. One of the first activities you perform on the project is gathering the team together to come up with list of risk events. In that process, you find out quickly that there are many risks, but struggle to understand how important each is to the project. You also have no idea of the likelihood or the impacts to these risks, which makes it difficult to prove how risky this project is. You have several key questions that need addressing immediately, including:

- What is the risk level for this project?
- How many risks does the project have?
- What is the general impact of the risks?
- How does one estimate the likelihood of a risk occurring?

To answer these questions, you should use a risk matrix. A risk matrix is a table that documents the probability and the impact of each risk event. When mapping the risk events to the risk matrix table, you and your team identify and decide immediately how important and critical the risk events are to the project. Based on the impact and probability determination of each risk, the risk falls into the right cells on the chart (table). The result is a risk matrix for your project. At a glance, anyone should be able to see the project's risk level. After you start using the matrix and get your project team members involved in the risk assessment process, everyone who uses the tool will quickly learn to adopt it as one of their favorite tools.

Cross-Reference
We recommend that you review the risk matrix in Chapter 13 - Defining Communication Tools to Manage Project Risk for more information.

Creating a risk matrix

Creating a risk matrix is a great way to bring the team together and focus on one part of the project. In doing this, the team, as a group, decides the probability and impacts of every important risk event. This exercise also has a bonding effect on the team. After creating the list of risks, and their probability and impacts, plot the risks in the matrix. If you use a risk matrix, you will be able to monitor and control your risks more effectively. You will have a much better understanding of impact and probabilities of your project risk events by using the risk matrix. The risk matrix provides the information you need to help team members focus on resolving risk events much sooner than later because you and the team members can clearly see where the risks fall on the chart and will know which ones to pay the closest attention to.

Your project customer should be involved in creating and assessing the project's risks. Each customer has a different tolerance for risk events; therefore, the probability and impact decisions will differ from customer to customer. In addition, project team members might assess a risk differently. Bringing the two groups together and deciding on one assessment for the risk event is valuable and makes creating the risk matrix much easier for you and team members.

Many large construction projects use the risk matrix as a standard procedure for managing and controlling project risks. The time and effort that you and team members spend to produce the matrix has an incredible payoff in the end. Providing the customer and leadership the project's risk level at a glance is valuable.

The steps for creating a risk matrix vary. Complete the following steps to get started.

1. Open a new risk assessment matrix template for your project.
2. Meet with your team members and document the project risk events. This process is the same for every project.
3. Number each of your project's risk events 1, 2, 3, and so on. When the risks are determined, assign each risk a numerical value. There is no significance in the number assigned to each risk event. Assigning a risk event a number (1, 2, 3, and so on) is for tracking purposes, and the number represents the risk event within the risk matrix.
4. Decide both the impact and probability for one of your project's risk events and add it to the appropriate box.
5. After assigning the risks in the right cells on the risk matrix, the process is complete. As noted earlier, it is important that your customers and team members are involved in this process. Having everyone involved in deciding the probability and impacts of each risk event and where they are placed in the risk matrix chart is important. It is vital that everyone is in full agreement about where risks are placed in the chart. The customer's involvement in this process means that they can see the assessment assigned to the risk event and can either agree or disagree at that time. The risk matrix creation process brings everyone together and provides an opportunity for everyone to set the tolerance levels for handling project risk events. It is important for you to manage your project and understand your customer's tolerance level and ability to assess the risk events with the information in the risk matrix.

Using a risk matrix

Before you can use a risk matrix, you must identify who on your project team will use it so that you can determine the level of detail, distribution frequency, style, and format of the risk matrix report.

Review the risk matrix section in *Chapter 13 - Defining Communication Tools to Manage Project Risk*, and then complete the following steps:

1. Ensure your project team members and your customers agree on the risk events and where they were assigned in the risk matrix. This includes understanding how the team makes assessments and where each risk event fell on the risk matrix. To gain approval, you may need to gather everyone and go over the risk matrix together to make sure everyone is on board and comfortable with the results.
2. After you gain everyone's approval on the risk events assignments in the matrix, the next step is creating the risk mitigation steps. Project managers often start working risk events in the high-probability, high-impact cells. For example, if there are several risk events in the high/high cell of the matrix, the project team will need to work on mitigation steps for those areas first. The project team does not create risk mitigation steps for every risk; it is not worth it and sometimes too expensive (both in time and cost). They should only produce them for high-priority risk events. It would be a risk to the project schedule if the project team impacted and tried to mitigate every project risk event.
3. After your project team decides the high-level project risks, drive the mitigation step activities and procedures to reduce those project risks. This includes anything from removing the risk, to

transferring it to another area of the company or a third-party, to ignoring the risk altogether. Whatever strategy the team selects for the risk event, you need to drive that resolution through your project team members.

4. Throughout this process, you will continually present the risk matrix to your customers and leadership. This is an important step because it keeps everyone involved with the project's risk events. It is also important to understand how your team members resolve risk events. When presenting the risk matrix to your customer, it is important that you understand the background of each risk event. It is also important for you to know why your team members placed the risk event in one box (cell) compared to another. If your customers were not involved in the risk assigning process, you can expect that they are going to want to know why risk events were placed where they were on the risk matrix. Be prepared to answer those questions.

5. The risk matrix and assignment process continues through the project life cycle. Remember that the risk matrix assignment process is ongoing and you will continue regular risk assessment processes throughout the project. It is a best practice to review the risks once a week.

6. When the project closes out, and all risk events are resolved, store the final risk matrix in the document control system for long-term storage, archiving, and availability.

Mastering the Scatter Chart

Before you can use the *scatter chart*, you must understand how it can help and support you on your project. The following project scenario highlights its importance.

You are nearing the end of a three-year project, which has had its difficulties. The project customers think the project has always been behind schedule and over budget. You know this is not the case. In fact, most of the time, the project has been on schedule and close to staying on budget. You have shown the customers the schedule and budget reports each month. Try as you may, the reports have too much detail to identify a trend, and the customers become frustrated trying to figure it out. You ask yourself the following questions in the hope of trying to find a way to get the information to your customers:

- What can you do to convince the customers that the project was on time and within budget?
- Can you create a report or chart that displays the project being on time and within budget most of the time throughout the project?

To answer these questions, you should use a scatter chart. A scatter chart displays both schedule and cost performance on the same chart. A scatter chart plots the schedule performance index (SPI), and the cost performance index (CPI), for each month of the project.

Figure 19.3 — Example of a scatter chart diagram shows a scatter chart that displays most of the time that the project was on schedule and within budget.

Figure 19.3 — Example of a scatter chart diagram

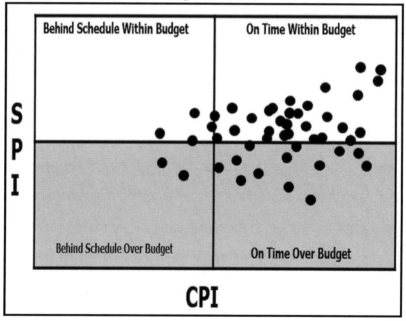

544

Cross-Reference

We recommend that you review the scatter chart in Chapter 10 - Communication Tools That Manage Project Quality for more information.

Creating a scatter chart

When you have two variables and want to evaluate whether there is a relationship between them, the best tool to use is a scatter chart. As one variable goes up, the other goes down, or vice versa; the scatter chart will identify this for you. Alternatively, as with the scenario, you can show a grouping of data to prove an assumption or make a point. You usually use a scatter chart in preference to a line chart when you have two variables that are independent of each other. A scatter chart has two value axes showing one set of numerical data along the x-axis and another along the y-axis. It combines these values into single data points and displays them in uneven intervals, or clusters.

With a scatter chart, you use an independent variable plotted on the x-axis and a dependent variable plotted on the y-axis. When you add a trend line, you see the relationship between the variables. For example, you might see a linear relationship between the concentration of a compound in a solution and its reflective color. To be successful with certain sets of data, you should consider creating a scatter chart. When you arrange your data for a scatter chart, place X values in one row or column, and then enter corresponding Y values in the next row or column. The x-axis and the y-axis of a scatter chart can only be a value axis. This means the chart only displays numeric data on each axis. To display numeric data with greater flexibility, change the scaling choices on the axes.

The types of information you may want to display are various group comparisons. The groups usually have some relationship with each other. If you want to show project performance trends, you can compare the SPI against the CPI, similar to what we did in the scenario.

A project customer may request scatter charts from you, but they are rarely involved in creating them. These reports are more project manager or project team focused, and the customer does not get too involved in creating them. The customer will find them of great value, though, when you create and use them.

The steps for creating a scatter chart vary. Complete the following steps to get started.

1. Collect the data for your project's scatter chart.
2. Open a spreadsheet tool that has a scatter chart graphing functionality.
3. Pick two of your project's variables to plot on the scatter chart. For this example, select and enter the same values as represented in **Table 19.6**. This step includes entering of all the data in the spreadsheet to match the chart.

Table 19.6 — Example of data for creating a scatter chart diagram shows two variables for creating a scatter chart. This example shows the variables to create a weight-versus-height scatter chart.

Table 19.6 — Example of data for creating a scatter chart diagram

Weight	250	145	176	199	320
Height	6.1	5.5	6.9	6.2	6.9

4. Select the data for your scatter chart. On the spreadsheet, highlight all of the data you just entered, including the weight and height labels.

5. Select *insert a new chart*, and then select scatter chart as the chart type. The spreadsheet produces a complete and ready-to-use chart.

Figure 19.4 — Example of a height and weight scatter chart shows an example of a weight and height scatter chart built from the data in step 3. This is a good example of how this chart could be used in a doctor's office to review patient height and weight data.

Figure 19.4 — Example of a height and weight scatter chart

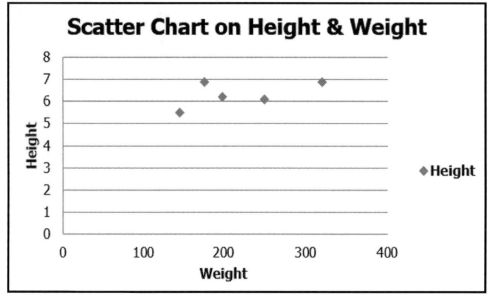

Using a scatter chart

Before you can use a scatter chart, you must identify who on your project team will use is so you can determine the level of detail, distribution frequency, style, and format of the scatter chart report. Scatter charts have more detail level data that allows anyone analyzing the data to have the details they need for analysis.

Review the scatter chart section in *Chapter 10 - Communication Tools That Manage Project Quality*, and then complete the following steps:

1. Analyze the scatter chart and decide if patterns in the data look like they need attention; if they do, react where applicable. There can be up to five correlations (positive, negative, possible positive, possible negative, and no correlation) on any scatter chart that you need to be aware of and understand how they define the data. As you review the scatter chart, look for those conditions and determine whether there is any correlation between the two variables. There may be situations where you can easily adjust the data on the chart that would positively impact the project. There are also situations where the data is much more challenging to adjust, which may have a negative impact the project.

2. Continually gather and monitor your project's data and add it to the scatter chart. As you complete that process, move to step 1 to re-analyze the data. You will continue this process through the project life cycle.

3. As the project completes, store the scatter charts in the document control system for long-term storage, archiving, and retrieval purposes.

Tip

Scatter charts can also help you identify trends in the project's performance.

Summary

The tools that we described in this chapter are the best choices for creating, disseminating, and reporting project status during the planning process. Most tools you use control the project, but the tools covered in this chapter are specifically for project planning.

This chapter includes some of the popular tools such as the budget spreadsheet, earned value analysis, earned value estimating, logic network diagram, quality metrics, risk register plan, risk matrix, and scatter chart. The cost estimate and the logic network diagram are two more tools that make sense in the planning process to help everyone involved in project planning.

Using the reporting communications tools outlined in this chapter benefit you, your customer, and the project team. The reports are simple, easy to create, and informative for presenting information to the various parties.

Chapter 20

Using Communication Tools During the Executing and Controlling Processes to Administer the Project

IN THIS CHAPTER

♦ Mastering Agile Project Meetings
♦ Mastering the Change Request form
♦ Mastering the Control chart
♦ Mastering the Project Newsletter
♦ Mastering the Project Presentation
♦ Mastering Project Status meetings

In this chapter, we explore the project communication tools you use during a project's executing and controlling process. During these processes, you focus on project management and administration.

Managing and administrating some projects can be challenging, and without communication tools, you have limited ability to successfully deliver your projects. Your top priority while executing a project is to report status and provide customers, leadership, and other stakeholders the information they need to make project decisions. Project stakeholders need project information to make key decisions, and you are responsible for providing that data. If you don't communicate project status throughout the project, stakeholders will not be informed and won't be in the best position to help you succeed. Consider the tools in this chapter critical for managing and driving your projects.

Mastering Agile Project Meetings

Before mastering *Agile project meetings,* you need to understand how they can assist and support you on your Agile project. The following project scenario emphasizes their importance and why Agile project meetings are critical to every Agile project.

You are the product manager for an innovative mobile application software development company. Your company has successfully executed several projects using Agile project management and Agile product development techniques in the past. The past projects were fairly small with a budget of under $100,000, and a delivery schedule under three months. Your vice president of product development approached you and indicated that your fiercest competitor has just released a personal journal mobile application and was first to market with this type of product. Although your competitor's product has many valuable features, it only allows the user to upload personal journaling information to the top two types of online social media. Because your company has years of expertise developing different types of mobile apps, and has interfaced to not only the top two types of social media, but to all of the other major types of social media, your vice president of product development wants you to develop an application similar to your competitor. Your new product's differentiating factor is that that the users will be able to upload personal journaling information to any of the currently available social media apps. The product's launch will help your organization gain a competitive advantage by being first to market with the additional online social media interfaces, which will ultimately increase your company's market share and profitability. Your vice president of product development (who is your project sponsor and project customer) told you to once again use Agile project management and product development techniques. You have also been designated the product owner and have been given an initial budget of $1,000,000 with an initial schedule of six months to complete the project and deliver the product to market.

You have already held several strategy meetings with your vice president of product development and some additional members of your organization's senior management, who are interested stakeholders, and created a product vision statement. With the help of your Scrum master, the customer, and other key stakeholders, you have held the release planning meeting for the first product release and created a product roadmap and product backlog, which contains several epic user stories for the first release. In addition, you have decomposed the epic user stories into detailed user stories at the lowest level of decomposition using the Agile INVEST approach. Having laid the groundwork in both the project strategy meeting and project release meetings, you have prioritized the detailed user stories you want the Scrum team to work on during the project's first sprint and created a sprint backlog that contains the detailed user stories. You are now ready to plan and execute your project's first sprint using the best practices outlined for Agile project meetings.

Cross-reference
See Chapter 6 - Communication Tools That Manage Project Integration, Agile Product Vision Statement to learn more about the activities performed during the Agile project strategy meeting, and Chapter 7 - Defining Communication Tools that Manage Project Scope, Agile User Stories to learn more about the activities performed during the Agile project release planning meeting.

Note
Although Agile project strategy meetings and Agile project release meetings lay the foundation for the Agile project sprint meetings, this section focuses on Agile project sprint meetings.

Agile project meetings overview

Agile project meetings provide ways in which the Agile project team can periodically assemble to communicate the different aspects of an Agile project throughout the project life cycle. The end result of each meeting is gaining more specific information about the Agile project's requirements and performance throughout its life cycle. Here, we will review specific information about Agile project sprint meetings, which occur iteratively throughout the entire project, during each successive sprint. This meeting centers on the Scrum team and occurs during each sprint of an Agile project. The Scrum team usually consists of the product owner, the Scrum master, and the development team. A sprint is a short, fixed-length subset of releases and represents the executing portion of the project. Agile project sprint meetings help guide the Scrum team through planning estimation at the beginning of each sprint (sprint planning), the daily status of project activities during each sprint (daily standup), the demonstration of the product components that have been developed during the sprint (sprint review), and the lessons-learned activities that are identified at the end of each sprint so that process improvements can be implemented during the next sprint (sprint retrospective).

Each Agile project sprint meeting is critical to the success of any Agile project, and each meeting has some common guidelines for execution, information gathering, information reporting, and meeting follow-up tasks. These can be broken down into the following five categories, which we will use to delve into further detail for each type of meeting:

- **Meeting Overview:** Provides some general information about the type of Agile project sprint meeting and its importance for an Agile project.

- **Recommended Meeting Attendees:** It is extremely important to identify the minimum recommended attendees who need to be present in order to run the meeting effectively. You should also identify other attendees to invite and the rules of engagement for the recommended and optional attendees.

- **Potential Meeting Roadblocks:** You should understand the roadblocks others have encountered while running Agile project meetings, which is critical to an Agile project sprint meeting's success. This will prevent you from making the same mistakes during your meetings.

- **Meeting Guidelines:** These guidelines have been gleaned from the experiences of countless other "Agilists" who've held Agile project sprint meetings and learned how to improve the execution of these meetings each time they've been held.

- **Meeting Steps:** There are specific steps that you should follow as best practices during each Agile project sprint meeting in order to ensure maximum results and maximum success.

Agile sprint planning meeting

- **Overview:** This meeting occurs on the first day of each sprint. Scrum team members plan and agree on user stories or backlog items that they can complete during the sprint. They also identify the detailed tasks and acceptance criteria (tests) for delivery, according to the "definition of done." The "definition of done" is created by the Scrum team. It is a description of the mandatory steps that must be completed for a user story to indicate that the particular product component's functionality is ready to be delivered to the customer by the end of the sprint.

- **Recommended Attendees:** The recommended attendees for the sprint planning meeting are the product owner, Scrum master, and the development team, collectively known as the "Scrum team." This is the core team that actually performs the work on the user stories for the sprint. These are the only individuals who are permitted to attend this meeting so that the focus remains on discussing, estimating, and assigning resources to the user stories to be completed during the sprint.

- **Potential Roadblocks:** Try to avoid the following roadblocks:

- Drilling down into too much detail. Try to stay at a high level when talking about the user stories without specifying each feature in full. Concentrate on what the user story is describing and do not "gold plate."

    - Not identifying the tasks necessary to implement specific features. When you drill down into each user story and determine the specific tasks necessary to get the work done, do not add anything extra. Stick to the necessary tasks for that user story.

    - Lack of understanding that the plan is not frozen and will change. Understand that Scrum is an Agile method of development and that scope and requirements are expected to change. Embrace the change and make adjustments as your team sees fit.

    - Lack of participation from required attendees. It is imperative that everyone on the Scrum team be active in all discussions. The overall team is responsible for the outcomes of each sprint, so all members must make their voice known if they don't agree with something. It is also crucial that each Scrum team member provides personal estimates for each user story and the accompanying tasks.

- **Guidelines: Follow these guidelines:**

    - Conducted at the beginning of each sprint (4-8 hours). A sprint planning meeting is conducted once at beginning of each sprint and can last between 4–8 hours. A good rule of thumb is to dedicate two hours for each week of the sprint for the sprint planning meeting.

    - Product owner creates the agenda. The product owner creates an agenda that outlines the guidelines, inputs, tasks, and outputs of the sprint planning meeting. It also "time boxes" the review of each item to keep the sprint planning meeting focused and on schedule.

    - Product owner leads the planning session. The product owner leads the planning session and is the main facilitator.

    - Product owner establishes ground rules. The product owner establishes and enforces the ground rules for the planning session.

    - Product owner documents outputs. The product owner documents all outputs from the planning session, which include, but are not limited to, sprint backlog and product backlog updates.

- **Steps: Complete the following steps:**

    1. Discuss the sprint goal. Create a sprint goal. Before sprint planning, the product owner has selected an initial sprint goal that is usually dictated by the overall release theme for that specific release. This is usually included in the sprint backlog.

    2. Present user stories. The product owner presents each user story on the sprint backlog to the scrum team. These user stories will have already been prioritized by the product owner prior to sprint planning.

    3. Ask questions to understand the user stories. As the product owner presents each user story, the Scrum master and the development team ask questions about the user story to determine

as much information as possible and to clarify the individual feature requirements. This will help them better estimate the level of effort and list specific tasks necessary to complete the user story.

4. Perform user story estimation. After the user story Q&A session, story points are assigned to each user story, usually using a method called Planning Poker. This method assigns a number that corresponds to a specific level of effort to each user story, after the number of a "base" user story has been initially defined. Planning Poker uses a modified Fibonnaci Sequence to help identify the number of story points for each user story. Planning Poker is an excellent tool for estimating a more specific level of effort than the relative estimate calculated for the user story during the release planning meeting.

5. Finalize the sprint backlog. Update the user stories and their corresponding estimates on the sprint backlog, which is the official list for sprint planning.

Agile daily standup meeting

- **Overview:** This meeting is held every day during the sprint, at the exact same time and location. Recommended attendees include the Scrum team. This meeting helps facilitate daily team communication and synchronization and ensures that everyone is working towards the same priorities and end goals, on a daily basis. Anyone interested in the project or the specific functionality from the sprint can attend the daily standup meeting. However, only the Scrum team members are allowed to speak during the meeting so that each team member's status can be quickly reviewed and that the focus is solely on your team and the status of their current activities.

- **Recommended Attendees:** Anyone interested in the project or the specific functionality from the sprint can attend the daily standup meeting. However, only the product owner, the Scrum master, and the development team are allowed to speak during this meeting so that each team member's status can be quickly reviewed and that the focus is on your team and the status of their current activities.

- **Potential Roadblocks:** Try to avoid the following:

  - Individuals who are not part of the core team interjecting their thoughts. Only Scrum team members are allowed to speak at these meetings, but sometimes individuals who are not part of the core team interject their thoughts. This detracts from the focus of the meeting.

  - Discussion moves to general questions or other tangents that are not specific to team task progress. Three specific questions (***What did I accomplish since our last meeting, What will I be working on today, What roadblocks are impeding my progress?***) need to be answered by each Scrum team member during this meeting. However, sometimes the discussion moves to general questions or other tangents that are not specific to team task progress.

  - "Parking lot" issues are discussed in detail. Any issues that cannot be immediately resolved should be put into the "parking lot" and discussed in more detail offline, after the meeting.

  - Product owner or Scrum master acts as a facilitator and runs the meeting. The meeting is run by the entire team and the product owner or Scrum master must not insist on being a facilitator, unless requested by team consensus.

  - Same location is unavailable at the same time every day. Valuable work time is wasted when scrambling to find another meeting place if the same location is not available each day.

- **Guidelines: Follow these guidelines:**

- Conduct the daily standup meeting every day during the sprint.

- The daily standup meeting runs no longer than 15 minutes.

- The daily standup meeting should be held at the same time and place every day, if possible.

- The product owner, Scrum master, and development team must be must be present so as to display team unity, and to ensure that every team member knows what everyone else is working on that day. If a team member cannot attend, be sure to appoint a proxy to fill in for them so that their update information is properly communicated.

- Anyone can attend, but only the product owner, Scrum master, and development team may talk.

- **Steps: Complete the following steps:**

  - Every team member shares input and answers the following three questions:

    1. **What did I accomplish since our last meeting?** The individual will state the specific tasks they completed since the last meeting.

    2. **What will I be working on today?** The individual will state the specific tasks he or she will work on for the rest of the day—such as continuing work on an existing task, starting a new task, or both.

    3. **What roadblocks are impeding my progress?** Individuals will state any issues that are preventing them from completing their work.

  - Log "parking lot" issues and discuss them offline after the meeting. As the three questions are being answered, the product owner will log the items in what is referred to as a "parking lot." The "parking lot" is usually a white board or easel pad in the daily standup room where a short description of the issue is listed. After each team member has answered the three questions, anyone that has an issue listed in the "parking lot" will stay after the meeting and work with the product owner and any other pertinent Scrum team members to determine the steps to overcome the roadblocks and resolve the issues.

Note

You may be wondering why this meeting is called a daily "standup" meeting. The answer is actually quite simple. All attendees are supposed to stand—not sit—during these meetings so they feel uncomfortable and want to go back to their desks to work. Many Agile teams dedicate a specific location called a daily standup room for these meetings, where there are no chairs or tables, but simply a white board, easel pad or big screen monitor to capture parking lot items.

Agile sprint review meeting

- **Overview:** This meeting is held on the last day of each sprint. Any project stakeholder can attend this meeting, but the minimum recommended attendees are the Scrum team members and the customer. Usually, all of the Scrum team members will participate in this meeting. The Scrum team ensures that all of the product acceptance criteria have been met and that the product's working functionality is demonstrated to interested stakeholders. After functionality is demonstrated, interested stakeholders can ask questions and provide feedback to the Scrum team.

- **Recommended Attendees:** Anyone who is interested in the project or the specific functionality from the sprint can attend the sprint review meeting. The Scrum team looks forward to having a large number of attendees to show off what they have completed, and to generate excitement about the project and the product.

- **Potential Roadblocks:** Try to avoid the following:

- Not showing the actual functionality. Make sure to show the actual functionality that you have currently developed, and don't try to fudge anything. It will be very obvious and could be embarrassing.

- Showing a PowerPoint mockup of the functionality. In some cases, it is okay to show a PowerPoint mockup of functionality, as long as you indicate beforehand that it is a mockup of the user story functionality, and that it will be fully functional by the next Sprint review meeting.

- Attempting to include last-minute functionality. Never try to include last-minute functionality that did not meet the criteria of "done" for this sprint. This almost always ends in disaster and usually breaks something that is working.

- Functionality that previously worked, no longer works. If there is functionality that was previously complete and worked, but no longer works during the Sprint review meeting, explain this to stakeholders and move on to the next product feature demonstration. They will understand.

- Product owner may not accept certain functionality. Even after everything you've done, the product owner may not accept the demonstrated functionality. If this occurs, during the Sprint retrospective event, find out why and ensure that the same thing does not occur again in the future.

- **Guidelines: Follow these guidelines:**

  - Conducted on the last day of each sprint (1-2 hours). A sprint review is conducted once, at end of each sprint, and can last between 1–2 hours. A good rule of thumb is to dedicate one hour for each week of the sprint for the sprint review.

  - Invite stakeholders who are interested in attending the demonstration.

  - Ensure all Scrum team members are present or have a proxy. It is imperative that all Scrum team members attend the meeting so as to display team unity and show that the demonstrated functionality was a team effort. If a team member cannot attend, be sure to appoint a proxy to demonstrate the functionality that person worked on.

  - Demonstrate the features on the actual equipment on which it will function. If possible, demonstrate specific features in the actual environment where it will function. If you can't, make sure to explain to stakeholders why not and when they can expect to see it demonstrated in the actual environment.

  - Do not try to embellish the actual working functionality in any way. Never try to embellish the actual working functionality to make it seem like you have accomplished more than you actually have. This will always backfire.

- **Steps: Complete the following steps:**

  1. Present release goal, sprint goal, and new features. The product owner will present to attendees the release goal, the sprint goal, and the feature user stories. This serves as an introduction to what will be reviewed during the meeting.

  2. Perform a product feature walk through. The development team will demonstrate the functionality for each feature that has been completed for the sprint. Usually, each development team member demonstrates the specific functionality that he or she completed, as well as any integration work that they performed on the current feature set.

3. Answer questions from interested stakeholders. The Scrum team answers all questions posed by the stakeholders present at the meeting.

4. Accept functionality and close out the sprint. After all questions have been answered, the product owner formally accepts the functionality and closes out the sprint.

5. Introduce expected features to demonstrate during the next sprint. The product owner may also choose to briefly mention the feature user stories expected to be demonstrated at the next sprint review.

Agile sprint retrospective meeting

- **Overview:** This meeting occurs on the last day of each sprint, immediately after the sprint review meeting has ended. The only individuals allowed to attend this meeting are the Scrum team members. This is the core team that actually performed the work on the user stories during the sprint. The Scrum team will delve into the specifics of what can be improved to make your team stronger and to make the next sprint more successful. This is one of the most important meetings because it allows your team to evaluate what was done correctly, and what can be improved for the next sprint. It also allows your team to create plans to implement these improvements, and to identify potential roadblocks that may surface during the next sprint. Although the sprint retrospective is one of the most important meetings in Agile, it is sometimes the most contentious. Team members are asked to look at themselves and others, as well as processes, and to jointly develop solutions to problems that surfaced during the sprint

- **Recommended Attendees:** The sprint retrospective is usually limited to the Scrum team because they will be delving into the specifics of what can be improved to make the team stronger and to make the next sprint more successful.

- **Potential Roadblocks.** Try to avoid the following:

  - Focus is shifted from process improvement to "ganging up" on individual team members. This must be avoided as much as possible; the discussion should always focus on the process, not the Individual.

  - Not all team members may want to participate. Teams are composed of individuals with different personalities, backgrounds, and often different cultures. Some individuals may not feel comfortable sharing in this situation. It is up to your team, as a whole, to welcome input and create a safe haven for input without fear of ridicule or repercussion.

  - Individuals or processes external to your team are blamed for failures within the team. Team members should not look outside your team for things that did not go well during the current sprint. It may be that some things are external to your team and out of their control, but those issues should be escalated to the proper organizational authorities. Your team should look for solutions to problems inside the team before escalating them to outside entities.

  - If there is contention on your team, you may need a meeting facilitator. In some cases, especially if your team is still in the "forming" stage, it may be necessary to have an objective facilitator attend the meeting to resolve conflicts and to ensure that the meeting stays focused and productive. This role is often filled by an Agile coach who is practiced in the principles of Agile and Scrum, but is also external to your team and possibly even the organization.

- **Guidelines: Follow these guidelines:**

- Conducted on the last day of each sprint (1–3 hours). A sprint retrospective meeting is conducted once, at the end of each sprint, and can last between 1–3 hours. A good rule of thumb is to dedicate one and a half hours for each week of the sprint for the sprint retrospective meeting.

- Everyone must participate. Ensure that all attendees are involved in the conversation and offer their opinions because this is a team effort and everyone's opinion and input is important.

- Discussion should not be limited to process improvements. This meeting should not only focus on process improvements, but should also include discussion about stakeholder communication, team collaboration, whether the Scrum team has the correct tools to perform their tasks, and recurring issues that kept surfacing over and over during the current sprint.

- Use an external facilitator if necessary. Many Agile project teams ask someone from outside the team to act as the sprint retrospective meeting facilitator. This could be another project manager, product owner, a Scrum master from a different project, or an Agile coach from an outside consulting firm. This person has no stake in the meeting's outcome other than to ensure that all attendees follow the agreed upon rules of engagement. An external facilitator is also beneficial because he or she can record meeting notes and perform follow-up activities, allowing attendees to fully participate, including the product owner and the Scrum master.

- **Steps: Complete the following steps:**

    1. Every team member shares their input and answers the following three questions:

        - **What went well with the Sprint?** Discuss the positive activities and events that occurred during the sprint so that your team can take note of these and continue to perform these positive activities in future sprints.

        - **What did not go well with the Sprint?** Discuss the negative activities and events that occurred during the sprint and try to determine the cause of these.

        - **How can we improve what did not go well with the Sprint?** Identify areas that need improvement as a result of discussing the negative activities and events that occurred on the current sprint. Determine what improvements can be implemented in the very next sprint.

    2. While these three questions are being asked of each team member, create specific plans of action to improve these areas in future sprints to ensure the negative activities and events do not occur again.

    3. Identify any roadblocks that could potentially occur in the next sprint that may prevent your team from implementing the plans of action for the identified areas of improvement.

One of the common myths about Agile project management is that there are no meetings and that the few meetings that are held are unstructured and disorganized, as compared to traditional project management. Hopefully we have proven that this cannot be further from the truth, especially when implementing Agile using Scrum. Each meeting is critical to the project's success, especially those at the sprint level. The truth is that there are actually more meetings and they are more structured and organized in Agile project management than in traditional project management; they are simply held at different times and with different frequency. The key to the success of these meetings is to hold them regularly, invite the recommended attendees, avoid potential roadblocks, follow the recommended guidelines, and complete the steps that are considered best practices to ensure maximum meeting results and maximum project success.

Mastering the Change Request Form

Before you use a *change request form*, you must understand how it can help and support you on your project. The following project scenario stresses the tool's importance and why the change request form is critical to every project.

A large mattress company in Jefferson City, Missouri recently designed a new king-sized mattress they call the "King Plus," because it is the largest and most luxurious mattress on the market. The company is receiving more and more requests for something larger than the California King mattress, so they decided to step up and meet the demands of their customers. As the senior project manager at the plant, management asked you to lead this project. You accept and are excited about getting started immediately. A couple of months pass, and the project is moving along nicely. You complete the design phase and begin the prototyping phase. Upper management has seen some of the results from the prototyping. They are commenting about the size, feel, and comfort of the mattress; this is exactly what prototyping is all about, so you are glad they are providing their input. As testing continues, leadership is starting to complain and becoming more negative about the mattress. You begin to think this whole idea was a big mistake. Some of the customers who are testing the prototype mattress are calling and complaining as well. Those customers want many changes, and the only part that people like about the mattress is its size. Upper management knows they must get the mattress design correct before it hits the market because it will be widely scrutinized, and any bad press will hurt the company. As the prototype phase completes, leadership requests a series of changes to the mattress that are outside what they originally wanted for the King Plus mattress. You must get a handle on and control everything they are seeking to make sure the mattress, in the end, meets management's needs. You are quickly becoming overwhelmed with all the changes that everyone is requesting and must get a handle on the situation fast or your project will spin out of control. You have a series of questions to find out how to get the project under control, but you have no one to ask. These questions include:

- How do I track and control the changes?
- How do I report and keep a handle on the changes?
- What process can I set up?
- How does leadership or the customer document a change for this project?

To answer these questions, you will use a change request form and a change request log for tracking and controlling project change requests. A change request form is the official paperwork to introduce changes into a project. Change request forms contain the information on the change being requested on the project. The change request form should contain enough details for you and team members to explore the impact of making the change to the project or product. To store the list of project change requests, you use a change request log. A change request log is a central repository for all change requests. It serves as the central location where anyone can go to report the number of changes, capture descriptions, or any other information about the project changes. Both approved and rejected change requests are stored in the project's change request log. This ensures the changes are stored long-term and are available from a historical perspective.

Cross-Reference
We recommend that you review the change request tool in Chapter 15 -Defining Communication Tools for Working with Stakeholders for more information.

Creating a change request

You are responsible for creating project change requests. Change requests can come from any customer, leadership or team member, but there should only be one person entering the data into the change control process. Having a single person responsible for the change control process gives the project the rigor and control it needs.

To be successful, you must be diligent about processing change requests correctly. Not every small change requires a change request because there is a level of good will between the customer and the project team that should include "extra" work. On the other hand, that extra work must be small and not affect project delivery. If it does, the extra work becomes a formal change request and your team should process it accordingly. You define what extra work means and decide what should and should not become a change request. When managing fixed-price projects, for example, work items that arise while executing the project that are not part of the original contract (scope) usually become project change requests. Watch this closely to ensure the project does not run over budget. On fixed-price contracts, it is easy to overrun budgets with the extra change requests from your customers. The costs quickly add up as change requests pile up on a typical project. The cost of change requests are added to the baseline costs.

Project customers need to be active in the change request process, especially when changing or updating the project schedule or project costs. Customers should use the change request process when requesting project changes. Customers, like everyone else, need to ensure they are providing enough information to your team to evaluate their change request. All change requests need approval from the change control board before being worked on. There can be no work completed on a change request without approval. When you approve the change request, the project team can perform the work of the change. Without the change control board's approval, if the project team cannot do the change request work, it must be approved.

A change request log is the formal tracking and reporting of the project's change requests. The items captured on the change request form go directly into the change request log spreadsheet for formal tracking and reporting. The change request log does not contain the same details that are in the change control form. What the change control log does provide is an excellent summary of all the project change requests in an easy to consume format for viewing or reporting.

The steps of creating a change request can vary among project managers. **Figure 20.1 — Example of a change request form** shows an example of a change request form. There are many different versions of change request forms; this is one version you can use on your project. Most companies have their own unique versions of the change request form available for use by their project managers.

Figure 20.1 — Example of a change request form

Name of Project:	Project Manager:
Change Request #	Change Request Date:
Change Requested By Name:	Current Project Phase:

Description of Change:
Scope Impact:
Schedule Impact:
Cost Impact:
Quality Impact:
Possible Risks:
Review By: Position:
Date:
Recommendation (Approve or Reject):

The following guidelines will help you create a change request process.

1. Establish a change control board.
2. Identify the project change and complete a change request form.
3. Submit the completed form to the change control board.
4. If approved, assess project impacts and include the project in work activities. Update the project schedule, project costs, and work assignments.
5. If the change request is rejected, your customers should be able to find out the reason why. Occasionally, your customers may want to update or change the change request form and resubmit for consideration. The change control board reviews the change request once your team makes the changes based on why it was cancelled originally.

Using a change request

Before using a change request, you must identify who on your project team will use it so you can determine the details needed, distribution frequency, style, and format of the change request form. The change request form includes the details so that people reviewing the form can understand what the change request is all about.

Before using the change request, review the material in *Chapter 15 - Defining Communication Tools for Working with Stakeholders*, and then complete the following steps:

1. As the project moves from the planning phase to the executing phase, make sure your team members have approved the change request form. Your team members need to know what information they will receive about the change request and that the information is enough for them to assess the change. Meet with your team members to go over the change request form and ensure it meets their requirements. If the form doesn't meet their requirements, you need to consider changing the form to provide the information needed. If your team members request a change to the form, you should make the change so that it is acceptable for everyone and ready to use.

2. After your team agrees that the form is correct and functional, the next step is for you to meet with the customer and find out whether they want any more changes to the form. This is a quick conversation because the customer will have completed the form when requesting a change. Therefore, they will be less likely to want to add extra fields to it. However, they may want to delete unnecessary fields; this is where working with the customer ahead of time pays off. You can explain to your customer why the fields are important and why your team members need them. You should then explain to your customer that they must provide this information or your team members cannot properly assess the change request and they will have to wait until the necessary information is provided on the form. After discussing this with your customer, get their approval that the form is acceptable, and make sure they will use it for creating a project change request.

3. Most project changes occur when the project moves into the executing and controlling process. This is when you send the change request form to your customer or whoever is requesting a project change. If you send them the form too early, they might lose the form and not have a copy when needed.

4. After receiving the approved change request form from the customer, follow the steps outlined in the change control process created in the project planning phase.

5. Process change requests as they come into the project using the change request form.

Mastering the Control Chart

Before mastering the *control chart*, you must understand how it can assist and support you on your project. The following project scenario emphasizes its importance and why the control chart can be helpful on every project.

A transportation department has decided to implement a safety project that determines the average highway speeds on a major highway over a 72-hour period. The goal for this project is to determine how to lower the accident rate on a particular stretch of the highway that had eight fatalities the previous year. The transport department needs to make this a priority to prevent additional casualties. As the lead project manager for the department of transportation, you ask to manage this effort. Management agrees, and you start working on the project. As the project begins, the first things you do are establish a team, collect traffic data, and find the reasons behind the fatalities. You realize you need to go out to the site so you can see what is happening first hand. You gather the survey equipment and take your crew to the site for data collection. As you begin the collection process, the data starts pouring in and your upper management starts to ask questions about the data. They too are interested in getting this resolved as soon as possible, so they are anxious to get answers from you. Their questions include:

- What is the upper speed limit in your sampling data?
- What was the lower speed limit in your sampling data?
- What is the average speed limit in your sampling data?
- What time frame recorded the highest speeds for that portion of the highway?

To answer these questions, you should use a control chart to present the data findings from the test results in a usable format. A control chart is a graphical report that displays the upper and lower control limits on a sample of data. The chart uses a sample mean line that sets the average, or middle points, for the control limits. The objective of the control chart is to determine how many data points are above the upper limit, how many are under the lower limit, and the percentage of the total outside the limits, both high and low. For example, in this scenario, we could have 100 cars of which two cars exceeded the upper limit, and one car was below the lower limit. This indicates three percent of cars were outside the test limits.

Cross-Reference
We recommend that you review the control chart in Chapter 10 - Communication Tools That Manage Project Quality for more information.

Creating a control chart

Creating a control chart report is simple. Each chart must have some common elements. Those elements include a central line, an upper control limit, a lower control limit, and process values plotted on the chart. A control chart is not applicable on all projects, but when data points are available, they are great communication tools.

Use control charts as often as possible to control your project's quality aspects. There are many examples in which control charts are used, such as counting the number of failures in a batch during product manufacturing, or counting the different severity-level bugs approaching a software release. To enhance project quality, look for areas where you can map data points onto a control chart.

To ensure project success, you and your customers need to continuously promote and manage quality. Using a control chart to graph the different data points ensures that your team is focusing on quality and they are continually working to improve results. A control chart provides an excellent view of the project's quality issues and evidence for where your team needs to focus.

The steps for creating a control chart vary. The following steps can help you get started if you have never created a control chart.

The following steps will walk you through creating an initial control chart that you can update with your own project information.

1. Open a spreadsheet tool. (We used Microsoft Excel.)

2. Create your time-related data and title it "Date." For this example, we took a sampling of three days. Enter the following three days into three separate vertical cells in the spreadsheet.

   - 3/1/2019

   - 3/2/2019

   - 3/3/2019

3. Create the sample (Sample 1)-related data; create the following samples for this example. Enter the three samples vertically on the spreadsheet, and in the same row as each date.

   - Sample 1-1 (Row 1) = 2

   - Sample 1-2 (Row 2) = 6

   - Sample 1-3 (Row 3) = 5

4. Create a second sample (Sample 2) column of data; create the following samples for this example. Enter the three samples vertically on the spreadsheet, and in the same row as each date.

   - Sample 2-1 (Row 1) = 4

   - Sample 2-2 (Row 2) = 3

   - Sample 2-3 (Row 3) = 4

5. Create the Mean Data (daily average); create the following samples for this example. The mean data is the average data for your sampling. Again, simply use three rows of data to get familiar with creating these charts. Enter the following three samples vertically on the spreadsheet, and in the same row as each date.

   - Mean (Row 1) = 1.2

   - Mean (Row 2) = 1.8

   - Mean (Row 3) = 1.8

6. Create the Sample Mean data (average of all means). Create the following samples for this example. The Sample Mean data is your zero-point data for the chart. Enter the following three samples vertically on the spreadsheet, and in the same row as each date.

- Sample Mean (Row 1) = 4.50

- Sample Mean (Row 2) = 4.50

- Sample Mean (Row 3) = 4.50

7. Create the Lower Control Limit of 0.24 by entering the three samples vertically on the spreadsheet, and in the same row as each date.

8. Create the Upper Control Limit of 6.08 by entering three samples vertically on the spreadsheet, and in the same row as each date.

9. Chart the data. Control charts are line charts. Select Line as the best option for this chart type, and then select the data in the spreadsheet for charting purposes.

- Select the Time Sheet data. In the spreadsheet, select the data in the Date column.
- Select the Mean data. In **Figure 20.2 — Sample control chart**, select the data in the Mean (Daily Average) column.
- Select the Sample Mean data. In **Figure 20.2— Sample control chart**, select the data in the Sample Mean (Average of All Means) column.
- Select the Lower Limit data. In **Figure 20.2— Sample control chart**, select the data in the Lower Control Limit column.
- Select the Upper Limit data. In **Figure 20.2— Sample control chart**, select the data in the Upper Control Limit column.

Your control chart is complete.

Figure 20.2 — Sample control chart represents the sample data selected for the control chart. The data represents 14 days with an average mean of 4.50. The lower and upper limits have a large range. To calculate the average means, add the mean daily average data and divide it by the number of data points, or rows.

Figure 20.2 — Sample control chart

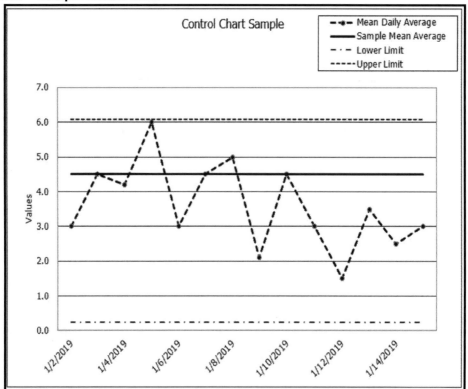

Using the control chart

Before using the control chart, you must identify who on your project team will use it so that you can determine the level of detail required, distribution frequency, style, and format of the chart.

Complete the following steps:

1. Analyze the control chart data and determine how it affects the test results. When you review the data, determine the initial steps to take and then, with your team members, dive into the test result details for further actions about what you can do to address them. You may need to call a series of meetings to get through all the data points and determine the best course of action.

Tip
When reviewing the chart, you and team members must understand the upper and lower limits.

2. Analyze the chart's test results and determine if they are acceptable. If the data is acceptable, decide if further testing is required, or potentially stop testing at this point.

If the results are unacceptable, you will need to perform further data analysis. This could result in further testing or modifying parameters (upper and lower limits), or simply re-running the tests.

After completing all of the test cases, the test manager documents the test results and distributes them to you, your team members, and your customers.

After testing is complete, store all of the testing materials in the document control system for long-term storage, archiving, and retrieval purposes.

Mastering the Project Newsletter

Before you begin to develop and master the *project newsletter*, you must understand how it can help and support you on your project. The following project scenario highlights its importance and why the project newsletter is important to every project.

A large insurance company in downtown Sidney, Australia has decided to replace their main insurance software program in the next six months. The software has simply outlived its usefulness and needs replacing as soon as possible. As the most senior project manager in the company, you have elected to take on the role and manage the replacement project. You are excited about this project because you were the project manager on the original project many years ago. As you get started, you quickly realize that your customers and leadership will need high-level project information rather than status report details. The information should give your customers and leadership status information, but not overwhelm them with project details. As project manager, you need to come up with a way to disseminate the data to your customers and leadership. Some of the questions you have for this scenario include:

- How do I get regular project updates?
- How do I make the information interesting and informative?
- What is an effective communications tool for providing a project summary?
- How do I communicate high-level project information only?

To answer these questions, you should use a project newsletter. A project newsletter is excellent for communicating project information in a presentation format. It is easy to read and, if created correctly, can generate enthusiasm for the project. Project newsletters are most valuable once a month, but some projects create them weekly when warranted. However, more often than once a month can become just a fancy status report, which defeats the project newsletter's purpose.

Cross-Reference
We recommend that you review the project newsletter tool in Chapter 15- Defining Communication Tools for Working with Stakeholders for more information.

Creating a project newsletter

Project newsletters are useful, especially for leadership and your customers, because the reader does not have to sift through detailed project information to get project status. Project newsletters create enthusiasm and a lightheartedness about a project that a project status report does not. Project managers often overlook project newsletters because they do not have time, do not see the value, or do not want to bother. This is a huge mistake because project newsletters are one of the easiest communication tools available. The newsletter is a great tool for sharing high-level project information. Updating the newsletter each month comes down to simply making a few updates and continuing to share it until the project is completed. The minimal effort it takes to produce the project newsletter pays off throughout the project life cycle. The project newsletter provides customers and leadership continuing project information, in an easy-to-read, lighthearted format that offers a level of fun to the project.

Quite often, project customers drive the use of a project newsletter for their own status reporting. Occasionally, project customers use project newsletters to report up through the management chain so that upper management can get project information. This is a great way for your customer's management to get involved in the project. They can pull project information out of the project newsletter that they may never have been able to find in a regular project status report.

Although the steps can vary, the following guidelines can help you create a newsletter.

1. Create or define the newsletter template by using desktop publishing software or one of the Microsoft Office tools for creating your newsletter template. Look at internal company policies regarding templates and work with the customer for approval about what they want in the newsletter. Your customers may have distinct requirements they want in a project newsletter.

2. Work out the administrative areas of the project newsletter long before sending out the first version. These areas include identifying who will develop the newsletter going forward, where the content will come from, how often the newsletter will be produced, identifying newsletter recipients, selecting a template, and so on.

3. Create the first version (template) for the project newsletter.

Using the project newsletter

Before using a project newsletter, identify who on your project team will use it so that you can determine the level of detail needed, distribution frequency, style, and newsletter format. Usually, project newsletters provide high-level project information, highlights, and positive project information.

Before using a project newsletter, review the material in *Chapter 15 - Defining Communication Tools for Working with Stakeholders*, and then complete the following steps:

1. Set up a rhythm for the project team and customers to provide data for the project newsletter. Schedule time to compile the newsletter and decide a time frame for distribution. Monthly newsletters are usually sufficient, but should be driven by customer needs. Make sure to find out if other newsletters are going out that share the same time frame as your newsletter so that you can check for duplicate project information.

2. Collect and compile project information, and then send the project newsletter.

3. Incorporate any feedback or issues you receive after sending the project newsletter to your customers, leadership, and relevant stakeholders. Use the feedback to update and improve the newsletter where applicable. This process continues throughout the project life cycle.

Mastering Project Presentations

Before you can begin to develop and master a *project presentation*, you must understand how it can help and support you on your project. The following project scenario highlights its importance.

A large software company has decided to set up a software project in a new area of the company. The company has been around for many years and has a strong software development methodology in place. As an experienced project manager, with a 15-year work history with the company, you decide to take on the project for this new area of the company. This area has new executives and new customers that nobody in your group has worked with yet, so nobody can provide you any history or background about the customer. You are both excited and nervous because you have a big job ahead of you. In this role, you will be teaching the new customers how projects are ran. As you start on the project, your best course of action is to work with the new group leaders and teach them the project methodology you will use. The methodology you use is simple and straightforward if you have used it before, but it is complex and overwhelming if you are new to it. As you start teaching the methodology to the group leaders, they have many questions about getting status and status reports. They also have questions about where and how to get project information. Questions from the group leaders include:

- How can I get a feel for the project status?
- What phase of the project just finished?
- How is the project budget tracking?
- How is the project schedule tracking?
- What are the current project risks and issues?

To help answers these questions, you should create a project presentation to show the latest project status to include in the training. Project presentations are formal presentations to the project team, all the way up to senior management and the customer or project status owner. Project presentations can be a simple one-page document, or multiple-page documents, where you compile as much information about the project as possible.

Cross-Reference
We recommend that you review the project presentations tool in Chapter 12 - Defining Communication Tools That Manage Project Communications for more information.

Creating project presentations

On most projects, there are two main project presentations types. One presentation type is a one or two-page presentation where you summarize the major parts of the project for review by leadership and your customers. You can email the simple project presentation to your customers for review. This is an informal way to present project presentation information. This presentation contains high-level summary information only. Customers can review and understand what is occurring on the project at a high-level, without getting unnecessary details. Another method of presenting a project presentation is in a more formal manner and consists of a large presentation and a team meeting to go over the presentation in detail. Project managers use formal project presentation meetings for many reasons, such as phase close-outs, major project milestone reviews, and budget, risk, issue, and schedule reviews. Usually, project managers schedule this type of project presentation when they need formal approval from the customer on a deliverable or project phase. When creating these presentations, get your team leads involved and ensure that they are actively engaged in developing content for the presentation, and that they will attend the meeting to answer questions or concerns from your customers. You do not want to put the information from your team in a project presentation, and then be on the spot to answer customer questions about that content.

A project presentation is a representation of your project at a major milestone, and it is critical for representing the current project status. Open risks, issues, or roadblocks should be included in the presentation material for resolution by customers or leadership. These presentations provide an opportunity to get support and approval from leadership and customers for project-level decisions that need immediate resolution.

Tip

You should schedule a "preview" meeting for both the team members and the customers before the presentation. These meetings provide both parties a sneak preview of the materials before the formal meeting. If there are any issues or concerns, you can address them with a smaller audience and usually take care of them before the presentation.

Rather than providing step-by-step instructions on how to create a project presentation, you can complete the template applicable to your presentation. Complete the following steps to fill out a project presentation template:

1. Decide on the correct template to use. Find out if there are company templates to use. If so, work with the customer to change it to meet their needs. Your customers should approve the template before you officially present it. The project presentation template you use will depend on what you are presenting at the current stage of the project. It may sound simple, but many project managers do not realize that for every stage of the project, you use a different project presentation template. For example, a project kickoff presentation is different from a lessons-learned presentation. Project managers must select the right template for the presentation type they are going to present.

2. Work with your team members to gather the information you need to populate the presentation material. Usually, your team members will provide information to populate the project presentation template. Your team members are doing the project work and, therefore, are much closer to the project. They are the best choice for providing the latest and most accurate status.

3. Keep the audience in mind when you create the project presentation. Add the information to the template you selected for this presentation type. At this point, you are ready to present your project presentation.

Using project presentations

Before using a project presentation, identify who on your project team will be involved creating and delivering them. This way, you can work closely with them and jointly develop the presentation. By creating the presentation together, you also maintain a consistent message that you want to present to your customer.

Before using a project presentation, review the project presentation section in *Chapter 12 - Defining Communication Tools That Manage Project Communications*, and then complete the following steps:

1. Find out if there are company standards that you must follow before spending any time or effort creating and presenting a project presentation to your customers. For example, the budget has to be a certain percentage of accuracy to present, the project has to pass internal audit, the project has to have a budget over $1 million. You must be aware of company policies and adjust the presentation where applicable.

2. Focus your team members on preparing the content for the project presentation. This includes arranging the meeting, hosting preparatory meetings, if there are any, and creating the project presentation content itself.

3. Schedule the meeting and present the materials.

4. After the meeting, send action items and meeting minutes to the presentation attendees.

5. Store the project presentation materials in the document control system for long-term storage, archiving, and retrieval purposes.

Mastering the Project Status Meeting

Before you can master the *project status meeting*, you must understand how it can help and support you on your project. The following project scenario highlights why project status meetings are critical to every project.

A large automobile company in Niagara Falls, Ontario, Canada is in the beginning phase of its next new SUV production, and the project manager is bringing your team together to kick off the project. This project will consist of many different groups, and each group has their own roles and responsibilities. The groups are made up of designers, engineers, and quality inspectors, to name a few. One of the project's challenges is that the new SUV will have parts created all over the world, but shipped to the main manufacturing plant for final assembly. One of the challenges for the project manager is to ensure that the different locations constantly communicate throughout the project life cycle. The project manager must make sure that no one group is holding up another group, preventing them from completing their work. The project manager is depending on the groups to effectively communicate with one another throughout the project. The project manager's main concern is keeping the groups effectively communicating. The project manager is considering ways to solve or manage the project's communication issues and has some immediate questions, such as:

- How will I gather status from each team member?
- What will each group cover during status meetings and how will that information help other groups?
- Who needs to attend the meetings?
- What information should be included in the report, and will each group have different information to share? If so, what will it be?
- How often does this meeting occur?

A project status meeting is an excellent way to bring the project team together to discuss project status and work out project issues and risks. You can use the project status meeting in several ways, such as ensuring your team is tracking to the schedule, budget, and project scope. Other ways include encouraging and praising team members for good work and holding cross-group discussions so everyone can share information.

Cross-Reference
We recommend that you review the project status report tool in Chapter 6 - Communication Tools That Manage Project Integration for more information.

Planning the project status meeting

The project status meeting provides the opportunity for you to bring together team members, and sometimes customers, to discuss project status and to address issues or concerns your team is facing. This may be the only time the project team gets together, either in a room or on a conference call, and focuses their attention on the project. During the rest of the week, team members focus on their own project activities and tend not to interact with anyone else unless they have to. If the project has many issues or problems, we recommend the best practice of creating a daily project status meeting. This situation is usually temporary until the project is back on track, and then status meetings return to a weekly cadence. In some projects, a daily status meeting is an excellent way of keeping the project on track and marching forward. It can be an informal checkpoint, but provides enough opportunity for you to meet with team members and discuss high-level issues that they are having.

Cross-Reference

Refer to Chapter 12- Defining Communication Tools That Manage Project Communications for more information about the daily progress report.

When planning project status meetings, we recommend that you hold two separate meetings: one with team members and another with customers (owners). Holding two meetings allows team members to get into deeper project details that would be irrelevant to customers and leadership. At the customer-focused project status meeting, the project customer can dive into details around budgets, time lines, and resources that would not be applicable or relevant to most team members. Project status meetings are the one opportunity where a customer can discuss details that are unclear or where they need more information than is available in a status report or other project emails from day-to-day project operations. Customers should use status meetings to ensure that they are happy with the progress, and they should be available for removing roadblocks or other concerns the project team may have.

We suggest you use the following template to create a project status meeting agenda and meeting.

Table 20.1 — Example of a project status meeting agenda

#	Section Title	Description
1	Review Last Week's Minutes and Action Items	Cover action items from the last meeting as well as any relevant meeting minutes.
2	Review Current Action Items	Covers current action items that team members are working on. Each team member will speak about his or her respective action items.
3	Review Project Schedule	Review the project schedule and ensure the team is tracking to it. Each team member will speak about his or her respective area of the project schedule.
4	Major Area Updates	Get particular project status updates from project leads. Depending on the project type, a design lead, engineer lead, test lead, and so on would provide status. Each team lead will speak about his or her respective areas and provide updates about issues, risks, or other concerns they are facing.
5	Review Current Budget Information	Cover the project budget and cost review.
6	Review Project Risks	Review project risks. Each team member will speak about project risks they are encountering.
7	Review Project Issues	Review project issues. Each team member will speak about the project issues they are encountering.
8	Review Lessons Learned	Gain lessons-learned information during the last reporting period from team members. Capture what went well, what went wrong, and any other important lessons-learned information.

#	Section Title	Description
9	Walk-on's	Covers any extra items you or the team wants to call to your attention or that of other team members.

Facilitating the project status meeting

Before you facilitate the project status meeting, you must identify who on your project team will be involved in the meeting. You need to understand what role they will play, what materials they will present, and how they will be involved in the meeting. Knowing this information will help you run a more effective meeting because you will understand exactly how to use your team members.

Before planning the project status meeting, review the material in *Chapter 6 - Communication Tools That Manage Project Integration*, and then complete the following steps:

- Set up a regular cadence for project status meetings. The cadence will depend on when the company requires project managers to report their respective projects status. Project status meetings are an excellent way to collect project information to add to the project status report.

- Set up internal status meetings. Establish internal team meetings and customer status meetings on everyone's professional calendars. A best practice for project managers to consider is scheduling status meetings as separate meetings. One meeting is for the internal team meeting, and the other meeting is for your customers. It is important to set a day's lag between each meeting to allow information to be updated from one meeting before presenting the information to recipients at a different meeting. For example, if the project status for the company is due on Friday, team members' meetings should be held on Tuesdays and customer meetings should be held on Thursdays. You can then send the project status report on Friday, the day it is due. This gives you a day between the internal meeting and the customer meeting, and a day between the customer meeting and submitting the final report.

- Drive the project status meetings. You facilitate the meeting by promoting conversations and going through agenda items.

Tip
Collect lessons-learned information from team members during this meeting.

- Send the minutes to the attendees, and then store them in the document control system for long-term storage, archiving, and retrieval purposes.

Summary

The tools we described in this chapter are the best choices for managing the project's administration component during the execution and controlling process. As you know, this is the process where the project is in full swing, so managing the project at this time is critical.

The tools outlined in this chapter can help you manage your project more effectively and regularly communicate project information. The tools included the change request, project newsletter, project presentation, and project status meetings.

Chapter 21

Using Communication Tools During the Executing and Controlling Process

IN THIS CHAPTER

♦ Mastering the Issues list
♦ Mastering the Project Meeting Minutes
♦ Mastering the Risk Assessment form
♦ Mastering the Work Package

In this chapter, we explore project communication tools that can help you monitor and control your projects during the executing and controlling process. These tools will help you keep tighter control over the project as it moves through the various life cycle processes.

One of the most widely used project tools in this chapter is the issues list. If you don't regularly track and monitor issues, those issues can negatively affect the project's progress. The issues list is one of your main project communication tools; it will engage team members, customers, and occasionally leadership in helping to resolve project issues.

Mastering the Issues List

Before mastering the *issues list*, you must understand how it can help and support you on your project. The following project scenario highlights why the issues list tool is critical to every project.

A large aerospace company has just announced that it is developing a new airplane for military use. The plane will take five to seven years to produce, with a planned release of 2021. The plane will be one of the largest and able to fly around the world with just two refueling stops. As a project manager, your assignment is managing the cockpit construction and design. You have previously been involved in producing many planes, so this is just another construction project to you. Because of your plane design background and knowledge, you are familiar with the various risks and issues associated with building planes, and you share your concerns with the project team. You know the cockpit has many dependencies with the other sections of the airplane construction project and you will be responsible for driving each dependency to resolution. Without a cockpit, the plane cannot fly. Therefore, your portion of the project is critical. The challenge you face is how to expose project issues so that other team members, customers, or leadership can review them. Questions you have about your project area include:

- How do I capture and track issues?
- What information should I capture about issues?
- How can I give management exposure to my particular issues?
- Which tool should I use to discuss issues during project status meetings?

To answer these questions, you should use an issues list. The issues list is a critical communication tool, and one that every project should include, regardless of size or complexity. In the previous scenario, you would create and display an issues list that includes your specific area's issues, which is accessible by anyone. Often, issues in one project area are related to or resolved by other areas. Therefore, increasing issue exposure to everyone can help drive quicker resolutions.

Cross-Reference
We recommend that you review the issue list tool in Chapter 13- Defining Communication Tools to Manage Project Risk for more information.

Creating the issues list

An issues list is one of the easiest tools available. A basic issues list contains six columns: issue ID, title, status, priority, owner, and due date. Large, complex projects have intricate issue tracking systems to capture details around each issue and to ensure that you or the issue owner diligently tracks each issue. Large projects require sharing issues across multiple groups, so issue tracking systems become more relevant for those projects.

You must be diligent about tracking and managing project issues. Occasionally, issues can halt a project until they are resolved. Issues can range from simple to complex, and you need to manage and monitor them to resolution. Review project issues with team members and customers each week until they are resolved. After they are resolved, move the issue to the closed issues list for historical purposes. If there are lessons learned from the issue, document them in the lessons-learned document.

Project customers might be active in resolving project issues; the more active they are in issue management, the less likely those issues will negatively affect the project. Customers have the ability to lessen a project issue from something the team feels is large to something small and workable.

Steps for creating an issues list vary among project managers and depend on their tool of choice. Instead of providing step-by-step instructions for creating an issues list, you can complete the template provided below. Use this template if another one isn't available. You may have to update this list for your project.

Figure 21.1 shows the issues list for use on a project. This list provides the relevant fields for issue tracking, and you can use them for most projects. Project managers can update and improve the issues list according to the needs of their projects.

Figure 21.1 — Example of an issues list

ID	Issue Description	Impact	Severity	Originator	Date Opened	Assigned to	Target Resolution Date	Status	Resolution
1	Platform problems	High	2	Bob Smith	12/4/2019	Joe Jones		Open	TBD
2	Resource left paving team	Medium	4	May Douglas	10/14/2019	Fred Brown	11/28/2019	Closed	Hired new resource
3	Lost $100K of budget from the project	High	1	Bill Jones	11/12/2019	Bill Jones		Open	ASAP

Using an issues list

Before using an issues list, identify who on your project team will use it so you can determine the level of detail needed, distribution frequency, style, and format. Issues lists often contain many details so that the project team can understand and help resolve the issue. Make sure the fields on the issues list are complete and that team members understand the issues on the list. Team members can't be sure if they can resolve an issue when an issues list is incomplete.

Review the issues list in *Chapter 13 - Defining Communication Tools to Manage Project Risk*, and then complete the following steps:

1. Ensure that your project team or your customers have correctly filled out issues list form. You are responsible for filling in missing information. You and your team members may struggle to resolve an issue with limited information or missing pieces; therefore, it is important to have all relevant information entered on the issues list.

2. Arrange weekly review sessions with your project team to ensure that they are responding to issues. This usually occurs during the project's weekly status meetings, but some project managers schedule separate issue review meetings.

3. At a minimum, schedule a weekly status meeting with your customers so they have the opportunity to examine the issues list and ask questions. This usually occurs during the customer status meeting, but you can schedule a separate status meeting to cover just issues.

4. Manage and force the use of the issues list. Add and remove issues, perform issues reporting, and manage overall project issues.

Mastering Project Meeting Minutes

Before you use *project meeting minutes*, you should understand the value that they bring to your project. The following project scenario highlights how project meeting minutes are critical to every project.

A large lumber company in Vancouver, BC, Canada plans to replace their inventory system. The company's inventory system keeps track of each lumber mill's daily production volumes, inventory levels, and purchasing information. As you can imagine, this is an important system, and a replacement project like this requires full support from both management and team leaders at each mill. There are 55 mills located around the world, and each will use the new inventory system. Because the company headquarters will be the staging area for the project, it is critical that communication between headquarters and the mill locations are constant; otherwise, there could be project problems. As one of the most senior project managers in the company, management asks you to lead the project. You accept, and then call the core team together and ask everyone to provide project updates and status. Your first challenge is finding a time during the week when 55 people are available for a one-hour meeting, and to add to that challenge, you must factor in time zones from around the world. This is a feat in itself, but you finally find a time that everyone agrees to attend. As the project progresses, all 55 locations attend each week, and everyone gets the latest project status. What surprises you is how well the project is going. Then, as the project moves into week 12, something happens and only 36 locations dial in for the status meetings. The next week, attendance drops from 36 locations to 28 locations. You email everyone to ask them to attend, which works temporarily and attendance increases to 40 locations. The project that was going so well, with high participation, has suddenly lost support of the project team. For some reason, the project managers in the different locations can no longer attend those critical status meetings and, therefore, are no longer as committed to the project. Because many team members are missing the meetings, they are not privy to the discussions, action items, and decisions made about the project, which is critical to the project's success. You have no idea how to get the teams to interact. You also don't know how meeting decisions are going to impact the different locations. You need each project manager from each location on the status call for you to be successful. People are getting frustrated and asking many questions about what happened at the meetings because they were not able to attend. Their questions include:

- What happened on the project last week?
- What are the action items from the meeting?
- Who made the decisions and what decisions did they make?
- What is the project status?
- How is the yellow issue for costs tracking?
- What lessons-learned information was captured?

Project meeting minutes would answer all of these questions and keep each project manager up to date. In the previous scenario, if you had captured and shared meeting minutes, team members at each mill would have an update on the status, decisions, and action items each week. You would have used meeting minutes to capture project status information, and anyone interested could review them and understand what is happening on the project.

Cross-Reference
We recommend that you review the project meeting minutes section in Chapter 6 - Communication Tools That Manage Project Integration for more information.

Creating project meeting minutes

You should assign someone to capture meeting minutes because it is difficult to run a meeting and capture the minutes. You can rotate the responsibilities of taking minutes among all team members, or if possible, assign an administrative staff member to take the meeting minutes at every meeting.

Ensure that project meeting minutes capture all discussion areas and action items from the meeting. Some projects have agendas that focus on capturing project information and status; whereas, other agendas are much looser and not designed with that in mind. Either way, make sure that whoever is taking the minutes captures the right information so that the project meeting minutes are usable by anyone needing them after the meeting adjourns.

A best practice technique is to use action items within the meeting minute's template and discuss the project's action items at every meeting until team members complete each item. As the project status meeting begins, read the action items from last week's minutes and ensure that each item from the previous week is complete or has been addressed. If an action item is incomplete, it remains on the list and you review it with the responsible team member to find out why it was not completed and how long it will take to complete.

Tip
No action items should go longer than a week's duration if the cadence for project status meetings is weekly. Anything longer than a week should become a task on the project schedule and not an action item for weekly project tracking. For example, hiring a resource could come up as an action item for a team lead at a project status meeting, but usually takes longer than a week to complete. This would no longer be an action item, but would be added to the project schedule as a separate project activity.

Project customers actively review and receive project information from project meeting minutes. They review project decisions, action items, next steps, and the project's progress that's captured in the project meeting minutes. Some customers will be involved in project meetings, while others won't. If your customer does not join the meeting or does not want to be involved, you should still provide them access to project information that they need to see, which also strengthens communication between the two groups. This gives your customers the information from which to ask questions, dive into details, and get information they need to be successful.

The steps for creating project meeting minutes vary. We recommend that you use a project meeting minutes template.

Using project meeting minutes

Before using project meeting minutes, identify who on your project team will benefit from them so you can determine the level of detail needed, distribution frequency, style, and format of the project meetings minutes. Usually, project meeting minutes are detail-oriented, so there is an expectation to add as many details as possible to the project meeting minutes document.

Review the material in *Chapter 6 - Communication Tools That Manage Project Integration* about meeting minutes, and then complete the following steps:

1. Create a place in the document control system to store meeting minutes. There, you can add the meeting minute's template.
2. Identify a team member or administrative assistant to capture the meeting minutes. Secure this position long before the meeting so that the person knows, going into the meeting, that he or she is accountable for taking the minutes. Make sure you have a backup in case the first team member

cannot attend a meeting. You are responsible for ensuring that the minute's taker has the template for each meeting.

3. After the meeting, store the meeting minutes in the document control system for long-term archiving and availability for anyone interested in reviewing them.

4. Use the project meeting minutes to manage various project areas. The information covered at project meetings is valuable to you and the team for running the project. For example, action items help drive project deliverables.

Mastering the Risk Assessment Form

Before you use the *risk assessment form*, you must understand how it can help and support you on your project. The following project scenario highlights how the risk assessment form is critical to every project.

A famous real estate tycoon has just announced his newest project in Nashville, Tennessee to build a new 18-hole golf course, hotel, and casino. The project will take three years to complete and will be the largest casino in the Nashville area. The budget for this project is $400 million. As a trusted adviser and leading project manager for this tycoon, he has chosen you to manage this massive project. As the project progresses through the various stages of the life cycle, project issues and risks start pouring in. Because you are leading all three projects and managing over 900 risks, you start to feel overwhelmed, and you have no idea how to handle all the risks. You don't know how the risks might affect the project. You are also struggling with how to effectively track them, as there are just too many to handle. Upper management—especially the tycoon—are asking many tough questions about the risks and they expect you to have a better handle on them. Their questions include:

- How risky is each project?
- What is the expected monetary value of each risk event?
- What is the probability of each risk event occurring?
- What is the risk score for each project?
- What is the total budget impact to all risk events, across all three projects?

To answer these questions, you should use a risk assessment form to track and manage project risks. The risk assessment form captures and assesses project risk events. As you complete the form, it calculates an overall risk score for the project. Many project managers do not calculate a risk score or perform proper risk assessments and, therefore, run into project problems. If you choose to ignore, or simply not complete a risk score, leadership has difficulty looking at a wide range of projects and deciding which one is riskier and one requires their attention. Companies that capture risk scores and assess risks properly allow leadership to focus on the high-risk projects and not worry as much about the less risky ones.

Cross-Reference
We recommend that you review the risk assessment form section in Chapter 13 - Defining Communication Tools to Manage Project Risk for more information.

Creating a risk assessment form

Creating a risk assessment form is critical for every project, regardless of the project's size or complexity. Every project has risks, and project team members need to track and assess the risks throughout the project. By adding the risks to a risk assessment form, team members have the knowledge and information they need about a potential risk event. You and the project team are responsible for controlling project risks; you are responsible for ensuring that risk events do not negatively affect the project. The risk assessment form provides you and your team an overall assessment of each project risk, and from there you can decide how to properly mitigate the risk.

Project customers use risk assessment forms and are often main contributors for adding project risks. Often, customers have risks directly associated to them, so keeping them actively engaged in the risk assessment process ensures that they are aware of and responsible for resolving their risks.

The steps for creating a risk assessment form vary. The following steps will get you started if you have never created this form. You will need to update the template based on your specific project needs and requirements.

1. Create a risk assessment template for your project. You can use an existing company template or start from scratch. Add the project risks to the template. It is a best practice to enter project risks in categories. The project type often dictates the risk categories. There are already some sample categories in the template that you can use immediately. Categories are also industry specific, so you can update the categories as needed, depending on your industry.
2. After entering the risks in the risk assessment form, meet with your team members to assign three values to each risk event. The values are: probability, impact, and exposure. The form's legend from the template will guide you in determining the value for each risk, but you may need to update the legend for your project.
3. After adding values for each risk event, the form will generate a project risk score. This is an automated number calculated from the numbers entered each field. If it doesn't create a risk score, your company's template may have its own calculations or you may have to copy the formulas into the template. The most important part of this process is to ensure your project has a risk score, regardless of the template you used to produce the number.

Figure 21.2 — Example of a risk assessment form shows an example of a risk assessment form. This form produces the project's risk score when you enter the three values for probability, impact, and exposure. The risk assessment form is simple to use and a powerful communication tool for your project.

Figure 21.2 — Example of a Risk Assessment Form

Risk Assessment Form

Risk Category		Risk Owner	Probabilty	Impact	Exposure	Risk Score	Mitigation Plan	Action Item
Application								
			0	0	0	0		
Communications								
			0	0	0	0		
Functionality/ Usability/Performance/Controllability								
			0	0	0	0		
Environment								
			0	0	0	0		
Legal								
			0	0	0	0		
Process								
			0	0	0	0		
Technology								
			0	0	0	0		
Work Breakdown Structure								
			0	0	0	0		
RISK SCORE TOTAL						0		

Other Risk Categories to Consider:
Requirements
Staffing
Costs/Resources
Quality/Features
Management
Customers
Time/Schedules
Staffing
Environmental including legal
Regulatory etc

Risk Scoring Chart

Probability %	ative Project Im	Exposure: How many aspects of	project are impa
Chances of risk occurring in %	3: High	5: All activities (80 -100%)	
	2: Medium	4: Most Activities (60-80%)	
	1: Low	3: Many activities (40-60%)	
		2: Some activities(20-40%)	
		1: Few activities(1-20%)	

Using a risk assessment form

Before using a risk assessment form, you must identify who on your project team will use it so you can determine the level of detail needed, distribution frequency, style, and format of the risk assessment form. Make sure you add as much detail as possible in the risk assessment form so that anyone reviewing it will understand the risk event and decide whether they can help or offer support to mitigate the risk event. Capturing risks at a high-level usually provides little value and often produces more questions than had you or your team entered as much detail as possible.

Before using a risk assessment form, review the material in *Chapter 13 - Defining Communication Tools to Manage Project Risk*, and then complete the following steps:

1. Communicate the project risk score to your customers, leadership, and executive staff, as applicable. Share the risk assessment form with everyone involved, scheduling risk meetings to go over the risks, and storing the risk assessment form in the document control system.

2. Continue to update and assess project risk events throughout the project, including constant communication of the risk score to everyone involved with the project. You must also continue to manage the risk events for your project. Review all project risks during the weekly status meeting so that everyone is fully aware of the potential risk items and can add and remove risks when needed.

3. At the end of the project, store the final risk assessment form in the document control system for long-term storage, archiving, and retrieval purposes.

Mastering the Work Package

Before you can use a *work package*, you must understand how it can assist and support you on your project. The following project scenario emphasizes why the work package is critical to every project.

As the senior scheduling manager, you have been working on the construction of a luxury hotel in Belize on the Gulf of Honduras for the last two years. The project is approaching completion and everyone on the project is excited because the president of the hotel chain is coming next week to dedicate the hotel at the grand opening. There will be much celebrating. You and the cost manager are gathering documentation to calculate the final building cost and the amount of remaining work. You are busy planning and scheduling the remaining work that you must complete in order to turn the hotel over to the owners. The project manager comes to you and wants to know how many labor hours it took to complete the electrical work in the theater. He specifically asks for the hours broken out by standard electrical construction work and the specialized electrical work for the theater system. You only have the work breakdown structure (WBS), which identifies the standard electrical work, and now you must subdivide the electrical work into the two categories. You have all sorts of questions, including:

- How am I going to meet the owner's request, while completing my own work?
- What could I have done or should I have done, when?
- When was the best time to develop the WBS to meet not only this request, but also others that may arise?

To answer these questions, you should create a work package. It would have been simple at the beginning of the project to have the WBS work packages identify the two different types of electrical work; after all, they are two individual subcontractors, and you could have easily separated them. Now, you have to go back and break the electrical work packages into the two subcontractors and report the results. This will now take a bit of time.

Cross-Reference
We recommend that you review the work package section in Chapter 12 - Defining Communication Tools That Manage Project Communications for more information.

Creating a work package

Before you can gain any value from a work package, you should have created a WBS at a detailed level necessary to track all of the project work. The work package identifies the resources, cost, schedule, and other information you want to track during the project life cycle. The work package results are the actual labor hours, start and finish dates, actual cost, lessons learned, and so on that occur as the work package progresses toward completion.

To use and take advantage of the work package, you should create a WBS with the information you want to track, control, and report. You must first set up various structures to break out the work to report on schedules, costs, and labor hours. After the project starts, you can collect actual project data. Each work package has planned information, and that information will have actuals as the work accomplished on the work package is completed.

Project customers and owners should understand how important this tool is for reporting. Without planning and tracking the information in each work package, it would be difficult, if not impossible, to know the real status of the project.

The steps for creating a work package vary, but the following steps can help you get started.

1. Create the WBS during the planning process. By creating the WBS, you create the work packages at the lowest level of the WBS. See *Chapter 7 Defining Communication Tools that Manage Project Scope* for more details about the WBS.

2. After the final WBS is approved and operational, establish a baseline project schedule. The baseline schedule creates all the information the project will need to make a comparison after the project has started. With a baseline schedule, you can compare the original start and finish dates with the project's current start and finish dates. Doing so, you and your team will know exactly how far ahead or behind schedule you are on the project. It is difficult to create a baseline after you have started the project because you would have to remove all the changes made to the project and all the reported progress.

3. After the project starts, you can track the actual project work and report the progress of each work package, reporting actual start dates and actual finish dates. If a work package has started, but has not finished, report the start date and the percentage complete. Also, report actual costs and the actual number of hours worked on each work package. This information creates the reports produced for each reporting cycle.

4. Create reports from the work package. After you have included the project's progress information for a single reporting cycle, you can create the reports for your customers and leadership to analyze. The work packages should include a description of work package, scope, scheduling data, cost, resources, quality, risk, procurement, contract requirements, constraints, and assumptions. Reporting on the work package with relevant project information will give your customers and leadership plenty of project areas to review.

At this point, the work package is created and ready for you to use on the project.

Using a work package

Before using a work package, you must identify who on your project team will use it so you can determine the level of detail needed, distribution frequency, style, and format of the work package report. We recommend that you add as many details as possible when creating the work package so that everyone fully understands what each work item includes. Work packages are your activities on the Gantt chart.

Before using a work package, review the work package in *Chapter 12 - Defining Communication Tools That Manage Project Communications*, and then complete the following steps:

1. Identify when to perform the work, including deciding the dates, equipment, and materials to complete the work and identifying whether there are any limits to completing the work. For example, noise restrictions on construction projects that prevent work from starting before 8:00 a.m. or ending after 7:00 p.m.

2. Prepare for the work activities. Acquire equipment and materials, permits, resources, evaluate risks and issues, and review the project schedule to ensure tasks are on track.

3. Instruct the team members to complete the work activities.

4. Check and inspect the work completed. This process requires you or the team leads of the respective areas to review completed work deliverables to ensure they were on time and created with high quality. Construction projects, for example, would use building inspectors, plumbing inspectors, electrical inspectors, and safety inspectors.

5. Approve the work completed by team members and report progress about the various work packages that are completed or in progress.

6. Store all relevant documents in the document control system for long-term storage, archiving, and retrieval purposes.

Summary

The tools we presented in this chapter are the best choices for monitoring the project though the executing and controlling processes. When the project is in the executing process, you will find that the tools in this chapter are invaluable in helping you effectively communicate project information to customers and leadership.

The tools outlined in this chapter, such as issues list, risk assessment form, and work package, can help communicate the key project components. For example, the issues list and the risk assessment form are tools that help you stay on top of your project throughout the project's life cycle, and the project meeting minutes help you drive action items and monitor the project's processes.

Using the reporting communication tools outlined in this chapter will benefit project managers, customers, and project team members. The reports are uncomplicated, easy to create, and informative for presenting information to the various parties.

Chapter 22

Using Communication Tools During the Executing and Controlling Process to Report Project Information

IN THIS CHAPTER

♦ Mastering Agile Information Radiators
♦ Mastering Daily Progress reports
♦ Mastering the Gantt chart report
♦ Mastering the Histogram report
♦ Mastering the Pareto chart
♦ Mastering the Project Status report
♦ Mastering the Spider chart
♦ Mastering the Stoplight report

In this chapter, we explore project communication tools you can use during the project's executing and controlling process; specifically, the tools in this chapter focus on reporting project status.

It is important for project managers to provide continued project reporting during the execution and controlling process to ensure that the project is on schedule and within budget. The tools in this chapter focus on status and are best used for the entire project execution. During this time, there is plenty of project information flowing for you to track how your team is performing. As you review the tools in this chapter, such as the daily progress report and the status report, you will see how they are used heavily during the execution phase of the project.

Mastering Agile Information Radiators

Before mastering *Agile information radiators,* you need to understand how they can assist and support you on your Agile project. The following project scenario emphasizes their importance and how Agile information radiators are critical to every Agile project.

You are the owner and principal consultant for a project management training company. You have been offering classes for project management certification for many years now, but have been concentrating on one specific certification based on traditional/waterfall project management. Although Agile project management has been around for over a decade, and was originally specific to software development, it is now becoming extremely popular in all types of industries, especially in construction, information technology, and healthcare management. As a matter of fact, it is so popular that it is becoming a prerequisite for many existing project managers to learn before being promoted, obtaining a new position, or consulting on projects that need to be executed quickly and efficiently. To take advantage of the new demand for Agile project management, you decide to create an Agile Project Management certification course that you can offer to existing customers who have attended your previous traditional project management courses, as well as those with no previous experience in traditional project management. This course will be offered in a live, two-day, boot camp format and online as a self-study course. Because you already have experience creating the curriculum for these types of courses, the tasks to create the new courses will be fairly straightforward, and you can do the majority of the wok yourself. However, to gain a competitive advantage, you decide to create a third course to combine live study with online homework and exam preparation for your Agile project management students. This will be a synchronous course where students will dial in for 90 minutes each week for 11 weeks, and you will coach them on the best way to prepare for the new Agile project management certification exam. Because you don't have any experience creating this type of course, you hired a consultant to work with you throughout the project. You decide that this project is a good candidate for using Agile best practices because you have been executing projects using Agile best practices for a while. You are currently in the eighth sprint of a total of 10 sprints in the current release and you developed a product vision statement, a product backlog, a release backlog, and sprint backlogs for each sprint. At this point, you decide to begin a similar project for a risk management certification course that you want to create with the same Agile and Scrum tools that you used for your Agile certification project. You hired a different consultant for that project, and you now want the consultant to transfer the knowledge gained from the previous project to the new consultant—specifically the knowledge for using the major Agile information radiators that you created and used extensively on the current project, including the product roadmap, Kanban board, burndown chart, and burnup chart.

Cross-Reference
See Chapter 12 - Defining Communication Tools That Manage Project Communications for more information on Information Radiators.

Creating the Agile product roadmap

Before the development team performs any work on an Agile project, there are a series of initial project planning meetings called "strategy meetings." Strategy meetings lay the foundation for the project before any actual product development begins. During the initial strategy meeting, the product owner acts as the facilitator and works with the customer to create the product vision statement. The product vision statement is the first artifact (and first information radiator) created on an Agile project. It sets the stage for all future scope and development. The next strategy meeting centers on creating the initial product roadmap, which is the second information radiator created on an Agile project. This meeting is usually held in the project war room where the product owner again acts as the facilitator and helps the customer continue further project decomposition and product requirements from the overall product level to the feature and epic user story levels. Because the product roadmap is a low-tech, high-touch information radiator, it will only require some basic tools, which include a white board, an easel chart with pads to write on, multi-colored permanent and dry-erase markers, multi-colored sticky notes, and blue painter's tape. When you create a product roadmap, you need to complete some specific steps, in a specific order, to ensure that an effective representation of the product's high-level features is created. You use the low-tech, high-touch tools during this type of brainstorming session because making updates to the product roadmap is as easy as moving a sticky note from one part of the white board to another as feature priorities change. The following steps are recommended best practices for product owners to follow when creating a product roadmap.

1. **Determine the Product Requirements.** The first step in creating a product roadmap is to define the product that will be the result of your Agile project execution. These requirements begin as themes, which are logical groups of features and represent a requirement at its highest level. Features are components of product themes that have been decomposed and represent a new capability that the customer will have once the feature has been developed. This normally occurs during the strategy meeting where the product owner, development team, and customer brainstorm as many features as they can identify. Meeting participants write down the features on index cards or large sticky notes so that they can be moved around and re-prioritized throughout the brainstorming session. As the features are placed on a white board or wall in the project war room, they become the physical representation of the product roadmap, and they also represent the first entries in the product backlog.

2. **Organize the Product Features.** After you have identified your initial product features, the product owner works with the development team to group the features into themes. The themes can be based on a variety of classifications, such as flow of use, technical similarities, or business need, among many others. Certain questions will help guide the product feature organization into themes, such as: 1) How would customers actually use the product? 2) If the product is delivered, what else would the customer want to do or need to do? 3) Are there any technical aspects of the features that can be identified by the development team in order to ensure that the features' non-functional requirements are also included? When all of the features have been group logically, this second version of your product roadmap will usually look quite different than the initial one where participants randomly posted sticky notes on the wall. Now, there is a certain order to the features.

3. **Estimate and Order the Product Features.** After you have arranged your features on the product roadmap into logical groups, you need to estimate, order, and prioritize them, in terms of highest customer value and highest project risk. You will also need to determine dependencies on other features, meaning that one requirement must be completed (predecessor) before another can be started or completed (successor). To estimate the features, the product owner works with the customer to determine each feature's business value, and will then work with the development team to determine the level of effort to completely develop the feature. Here is where you can use relative sizing to determine the level of effort for each requirement relative to the other requirements that have been identified. Relative sizing is a form of affinity estimating, which is a consensus-based technique that is very useful to quickly and easily estimate the required effort for a large number of user stories. A common method of relative sizing and affinity estimating is called "T-shirt" sizing. Participants determine which product backlog features represent a "medium" size (relative to the size of the other features being reviewed), and then assign a corresponding T-shirt size to the other features, such as extra small (XS), small (S), medium (M), large (L), extra-large (XL), or even double extra-large (2XL). Each feature will then be assigned a story point value using the Fibonacci Sequence, indicating a score that pertains to the level of effort to complete the feature.

When you have determined and documented each feature's relative size, the participants need to determine each feature's priority in the product roadmap. To accomplish this, the participants must first determine each feature's relative priority, and then each feature's priority in terms of the overall Agile project. Relative priority enables the participants to understand how one feature relates to other features in terms of business value. Many Agile project teams assign a business value to the features in a product roadmap on a scale of 1 to 100, assigning those with higher business value a higher numerical value. When each feature's relative priority has been determined, you order them by priority in your product roadmap. An Agile best practice is to calculate relative priority by dividing the business value (1 to 100) by the score (Fibonacci Sequence score in story points). A feature with a high value and low effort will have a higher relative priority than a feature with low value and high effort.

After you have determined each feature's relative priority, document the values for each in the product roadmap. Determine each feature's overall priority by analyzing the following aspects of each feature relative to the other features in your product roadmap:

- **Relative priority:** Analyze the feature's relative priority by dividing the business value by the story point score.

- **Dependencies:** Identify the feature's dependencies or prerequisites. Are there other features that must be completed before starting or completing this feature?

- **Feature grouping:** Identify logical groupings of features in your product roadmap. Logical groupings are extremely important because they will help you determine the logical product releases.

After you have completed the analysis, you can prioritize and sort the features in your product roadmap. The goal here is to place your highest priority features first so that you can decompose and more accurately estimate the level of effort to develop the requirements. The product owner will add the prioritized feature's list to the product backlog, and then the requirements to develop during the project's first release and first sprints can be scheduled.

4. Map out high-level feature development time frames. When you are done prioritizing the features in the product roadmap, you need to determine specific timelines for the release of the product requirements because, at this point, they are at a very high level. First, select a logical time increment, such as days, months, weeks, quarters, and so on. Next, break up the product roadmap into logical increments by determining the length of a release. A simple example is identifying, at a high level, that it would take one year to fully develop the product and you plan on releasing a major product feature each quarter, or every three months. Your team would then use the blue painter's tape to physically indicate on the product roadmap where the releases begin and end. The end result of this exercise is your Agile project's initial release plan.

Figure 22.1 — Agile product roadmap example shows an example of a product roadmap as a low-tech, high-touch information radiator that was created using a white board and sticky notes.

Figure 22.1 — Agile product roadmap example

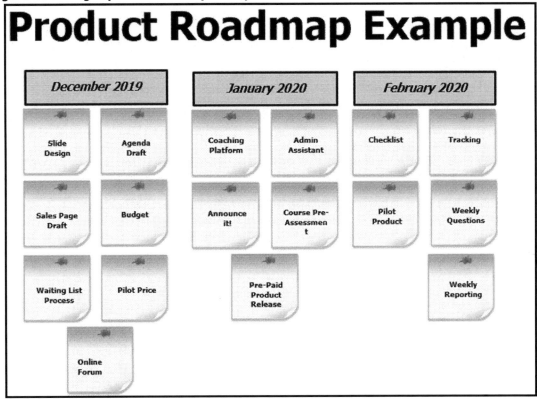

Using the Agile product roadmap

The product roadmap is a dynamic document that evolves as the product evolves. Similar to most of the other activities in Agile, creating, updating, and finalizing the product roadmap is an iterative process that may require several feedback cycles. Actually, the only time the product roadmap is considered truly final is when the project has been completely executed. One of the product owner's major responsibilities is to update the product roadmap as priorities change, which they inevitably do on any project. Although the product roadmap is a low-tech, high-touch information radiator, it is an extremely important to any Agile project. The product owner will most likely need to document all of the information in a high-tech, low-touch format, especially if the Agile project team is virtual and/or geographically distributed. Most Agile project teams capture the roadmap by taking a digital photograph of it, entering the information into an electronic document, or a combination of both. The product owner is ultimately responsible for the creating and maintaining the product roadmap. As the project progresses, the product owner will work with the customer to decompose epic user stories into more detailed user stories, and reprioritize them in anticipation of the next product release and the next sprint. While the development team is working on completing the detailed user stories in the current sprint, the product owner is continually reprioritizing the product roadmap to determine which user stories should be queued up to be completed in upcoming releases and upcoming sprints.

Creating the Agile Kanban board

Another type of low-tech, high-touch information radiator that many Agile project teams use is the Kanban board. Kanban is a just-in-time methodology that was born from manufacturing and was eventually perfected by Toyota. Kanban boards help control production. Kanban is Japanese for "signal" or "visual signal." Hanging on the factory wall for everyone to see is the Kanban board, which visually display each physical product component that needs to be developed. Slots in the board contain physical cards that are different colors. If you ever punched a time card, then think about the Kanban board as the rack on the wall where you kept your time card when you punched in and punched for work. With the Kanban board, as work progresses, the workers add, move, and remove cards, depending on the status of the particular work being performed.

Kanban boards are a good fit for Agile teams because just-in-time processing allows workers to make choices, solve problems, and improve processes, which represent some of the key benefits of employing Agile on your projects. Similar to the product roadmap, updating a Kanban board is as easy as moving a user story sticky note from one part of the white board to another when the status changes as it makes its journey through the sprint. The following steps are recommended best practices for creating a Kanban board.

1. Create the physical board. The first step for creating a Kanban board is physically "framing" it on your white board or a wall in the war room. To do this, the product owner and development team decide which columns will be on the Kanban board. The first column usually represents the user stories backlog that will be completed during the current sprint. Subsequent columns will include the status of each user story as it makes its way through the sprint. This is up to the team itself, but some basic status columns could include "kickoff," "progress," and "review." After you decide the column names, the team uses blue painter's tape to create the blank Kanban board. Many teams also include the maximum number of user stories in any one of the queues by placing the "work in progress limit number" at the top of the specific column.

2. Initial load of the Kanban board. The product owner places the user story sticky notes that are completed during the current sprint in the "backlog" column, which is usually the first column moving left to right on the board. During the sprint planning meeting, each individual team member selects user stories to work on, based upon a maximum number of user stories established in the work in progress (WIP) limits. The user story sticky notes will not yet have colored dots (described below) on them because no work has been performed on them yet.

3. Kanban board updates. Each development team member physically moves the sticky notes that represent the user stories they have chosen to complete to the "kickoff" column and puts a yellow dot on the sticky note to indicate that the work for a particular user story has been started. When the preliminary work for a user story has been completed, the development team member puts a green dot on the user story to indicate that the user story is ready to "pull" into the "in progress" queue. The next development team member will see the green dot and move the sticky note to the "in progress" queue and will place a yellow dot on it, indicating he or she is starting work on the next set of tasks. This process continues until the user stories go through all phases of the sprint. Many teams also include a red dot to indicate a roadblock or bottleneck on a user story. This is a signal that there is something wrong with the user story so that all development team members can stop their work and resolve the issues causing the roadblock.

Figure 22.2 — Agile Kanban board example shows an example of a Kanban board as a low-tech, high-touch information radiator that was created using a white board and sticky notes.

Figure 22.2 — Agile Kanban board example

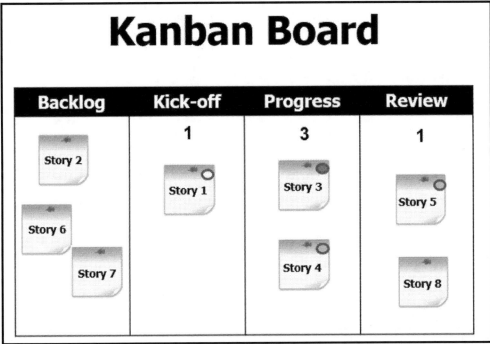

Note
There is another low-tech, high-touch information radiator used by Agile project teams called a task board. The task board is similar to a Kanban board, but it displays the progress of individual tasks within each user story, rather than just the user story as a whole. Task boards are used sometimes because daily Agile project work involves more than planning and tracking progress, and sometimes needs to be tracked at the task level.

Using the Agile Kanban board

A Kanban board displays the work in progress for an Agile project at the user-story level. The work-in-progress concept is crucial because one of its purposes is to help the development team limit the work in progress as much as possible using WIP limits. One such limit is the maximum amount of user stories being actively worked on by the development team at any particular moment during a sprint. By limiting the number of user stories being actively worked on, the team can focus on correctly completing only a few user stories instead of working on many activities for many different user stories simultaneously. This also helps prevent bottlenecks by discouraging too much work in the queue at any given time. Kanban boards are usually reserved for very mature Agile development teams with extensive experience in Agile and the Kanban Agile method. Usually, the length of a sprint for a Kanban project is no more than five consecutive working days, or one week. The ultimate goal of using the Kanban board is to help the development team manage their work and immediately respond to project changes as the project progresses.

Creating the Agile burndown chart

By the time your Agile project team is ready to start its first sprint, you will have already created a product vision statement, a product roadmap, a release plan, a product backlog, and a release backlog. You are now at the point in your Agile project where the product owner needs to communicate with the Scrum master and development team about which specific user stories must be completed during the project's first sprint. An important tool that helps document this information is the sprint backlog, which is a subset of the release backlog. Most Agile project teams use Microsoft Excel to create the sprint backlog because it not only allows them to document all the work progress that is being performed during the sprint, but you can also use it to automatically create a high-tech, low-touch information radiator called the sprint burndown chart. You can do this by creating a macro in Excel based on the data from the sprint backlog to automatically create a visual display of the sprint progress using the macro. There are many templates available that already have the macro programmed into Excel, so there is no reason to reinvent the wheel and create a new one from scratch.

Figure 22.3 — Agile sprint backlog example shows an example of a sprint backlog using a template in a specific format often used by Agile project management teams.

Figure 22.3 — Agile sprint backlog example

Sprint Dates: July 7, 2019 - July 18, 2019

Sprint Goal
As a <instructor>
I want to <ensure all PowerPoints and Weekly Self Assessment Question initial drafts are completed>
So I can <perform a final review of these materials before scheduling the pilot class>.

Sprint Hour Information — Working Hrs/day

Number of working days		10
Kevin (40 hrs wk)	8	80
Roberto (40 hrs wk)	8	80
Sprint Length = 2 Weeks	Total:	160
	Total per day:	16

User Story Task List and Estimated Hours Remaining

User Story / Tasks	Story Points	Status	Owner	PO Approved/User Story Complete?	M 7	Tu 8	W 9	Th 10	F 11	M 14	Tu 15	W 16	Th 17	F 18
Sprint Planning Meeting	1.5	Complete	Kevin/Roberto	Yes	3	0	0	0	0	0	0	0	0	0
User Story # 25 – PowerPoint Presentations	50	Complete		Yes										
Create PPTX from Agenda for week 1-6 calls		Complete	Roberto	Yes	40	24	6	0	0	0	0	0	0	0
Finalize PPTX for week 1-6 calls		Complete	Kevin	Yes	10	10	10	0	0	0	0	0	0	0
Create PPTX from Agenda for week 7-11 calls		Complete	Roberto	Yes	40	40	40	34	26	18	10	8	0	0
Finalize PPTX for week 7-11 calls		Complete	Kevin	Yes	10	10	10	10	10	10	6	4	2	0
User Story # 17 - Weekly Self Assessment Questions	27	Complete		Yes										
Create 11 sets of 15 questions		Complete	Kevin	Yes	28	20	16	8	0	0	0	0	0	0
Verify spelling, grammar, format, accuracy of question content		Complete	Kevin	Yes	10	10	10	10	8	4	2	0	0	0
Perform final proofreading of questions		Complete	Kevin	Yes	10	10	10	10	10	5	5	5	3	0
Publish questions		Complete	Roberto	Yes	3	3	3	3	3	3	3	3	2	0
Distribute questions		Complete	Roberto	Yes	3	3	3	3	3	3	3	3	3	0
Sprint Review Meeting	0.5	Complete	Kevin/Roberto	Yes	1	1	1	1	1	1	1	1	1	0
Sprint Retrospective Meeting	1	Complete	Kevin/Roberto	Yes	2	2	2	2	2	2	2	2	2	0
Actual Hours Remaining					160	140	122	104	96	80	60	44	14	0
Scheduled Hours Remaining					160	144	128	112	96	80	64	48	32	0
				Day:	1	2	3	4	5	6	7	8	9	10

To ensure that you get an accurate depiction of the team's progress throughout the sprint, it is critical that you accurately record certain components when you initially create the sprint backlog, as well as capturing progress on a daily basis throughout the sprint. Let's take a more detailed look at some of the sprint backlog sections and the specific components that are present in each section.

Cross-reference

See Chapter 16 - Using Communication Tools During the Initiating Process for more information on the completing the Sprint Hour Information & User Story Task List and Estimated Hours Remaining fields.

The sprint burndown chart shows the development team's "remaining" hours of work in the sprint. It is more important for the development team's Scrum master to be aware of remaining work rather than performed work because the remaining work provides a better gauge of adjustments needed in order to complete the work and finish the sprint. Using the data from the sprint backlog at the beginning of the sprint, and the data entered daily by the development team during the sprint enables you to create the sprint burndown chart based on the most up-to-date data about the team's progress.

Figure 22.4 - Agile sprint burndown chart example represents an example of sprint burndown chart using the data from the sprint Backlog in the example above.

Figure 22.4 — Agile sprint burndown chart example

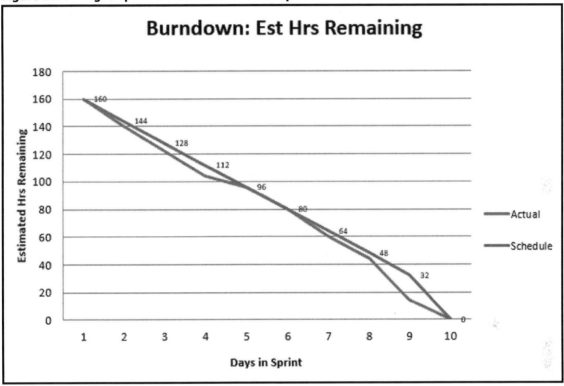

In this example, the vertical axis corresponds to the estimated hours that remain in the sprint. The horizontal axis represents each day in the sprint. In the example, on the first day, there are a total of 160 hours of remaining work in the sprint. The straight line represents the scheduled hours that remain in the sprint backlog, which are expected to "burn down" at the rate of 16 hours per day and eventually reach 0 scheduled hours remaining at the end of the sprint. The erratic line in this chart represents the actual hours in the sprint backlog, which are dependent on the actual number of work hours completed and entered by each development team member for each task.

Using the Agile sprint burndown chart

The sprint burndown chart is a very powerful high-tech, low-touch information radiator used by Agile development teams to gauge their progress throughout a sprint. Burndown charts can be created to gauge the progress of not only a sprint, but a release and an entire project by using the same type of tool. The Agile burndown chart makes it easy for anyone interested in the project's progress at any level to obtain a quick update just by glancing at the information radiator. It is typical that the line that represents the development team's actual progress does not match the scheduled progress—they rarely match exactly. The burndown chart is also very powerful because it visually indicates certain things about the hours entered or not entered by the development team, so it's important to understand how to interpret certain burndown chart images and trends and know what they mean. You can look for the following burndown chart trends on your Agile projects to understand what they mean.

- **Normal:** It is normal for the team to be behind, and then catch up on a subsequent day, and vice-versa. Knowing the actual hours that remain to burn down both above and below the scheduled hours that remain is expected.

- **Add user stories:** If the actual hours remaining are consistently below the scheduled hours remaining, the sprint is running ahead of schedule. This could be caused by inaccurate over-estimates, or the team is becoming more proficient. The development team may choose to add user stories to the current sprint.

- **Remove user stories:** If the scheduled hours remaining are consistently below what is expected, the sprint is running behind schedule, which could be caused by inaccurate under-estimates, or the team is working on becoming more efficient and seeking to increase their velocity. The development team may choose to remove user stories from the current sprint.

- **Not reporting hours:** If the actual hours remaining display as a straight horizontal line, the team is not reporting the hours worked on a daily basis.

- **Fudging:** If the actual hours remaining and the scheduled hours remaining are exactly the same, as displayed by both lines on the chart overlaying each other, the team is lying. Some new Agile development teams are afraid to honestly report their actual hours worked. They usually overcome this fear after the first couple of sprints.

- **Failing:** If the first few days of a burndown chart show a straight horizontal line, and then suddenly a straight vertical line, this indicates that not only have the hours not been reported, but no actual work is being done. This indicates a failed sprint and the product owner, Scrum master, and development team should terminate the sprint, determine the problems, and then begin a new sprint.

Creating the Agile release burnup chart

Another type of high-tech, low-touch information radiator is the Agile burnup chart. The burnup chart is the opposite of the burndown chart. The burnup chart is also a visual representation of the project's progress over time, similar to the burndown chart. However, it accomplishes this by displaying the actual amount of work 'completed' so far on the project, rather than the amount of work 'remaining'. The concept is that that the amount of completed work will 'burn up' as time goes by. Using the data entered into the release backlog at the end of each release, the Release burnup chart will be created based on the most up-to-date data available on the team's progress at the release level.

Figure 22.5 – Agile Release burnup chart is a high-tech low-touch information radiator that was created using a Microsoft Excel spreadsheet.

Figure 22.5 – Agile Release burnup chart Example

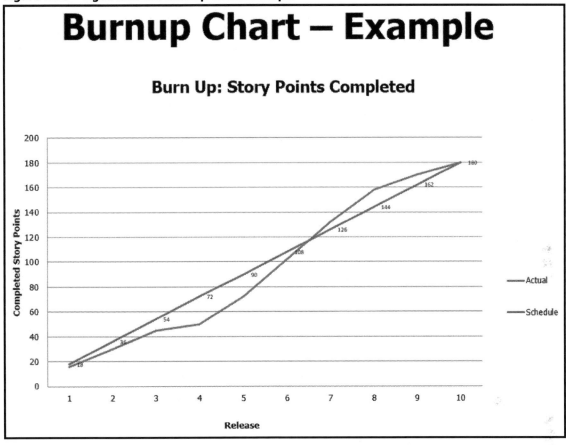

Burnup Chart – Example

Burn Up: Story Points Completed

In this example, the vertical axis corresponds to the number of story points remaining in the sprint. The horizontal access represents each sprint in the release. At the beginning of the first sprint in this release, there were a total of 0 hours of work completed in the sprint. The straight line in this chart represents the scheduled story points to be completed in the release backlog, which are expected to "burn up" at the rate of 18 story points per sprint, and eventually reach 180 story points completed at the end of the release. The erratic line in this chart represents the actual story points in the release backlog, which are dependent on the actual number of story points completed by each development team member on each user story. The product owner enters the hours at the end of each sprint into the release backlog.

Using the Agile sprint burnup chart

Burnup charts are most often used to display a release's progress and illustrate its progress over the course of the project. Burnup charts are usually updated on either a weekly or sprint basis by the product owner. It can also indicate whether the team is progressing according to release planning, ahead of release planning, or behind release planning. You can store the release burnup chart in the same spreadsheet as the release backlog. Progress will display in an upward trend as more work is accomplished during the release. There are also other types of burnup charts; for example, the sprint burnup chart, which displays the remaining amount of work in order to complete the target commitment for a sprint. However, burnup charts are best used to display release progress because most senior management stakeholders are used to viewing the performance of project teams in terms of the work they have performed rather than the work they have remaining.

After reading this in-depth discussion of Agile information radiators, we hope it is clear how your Agile project success is dependent on the use of these, whether they are low-tech, high-touch or high-tech, low-touch, or a combination of both. The purpose of Agile information radiators is literally to radiate information about the different aspects of the project, the product, or project team to the Scrum team, the customer, and any other stakeholders who are interested in the project. Both types of information radiators are best displayed in the Agile project team's war room so that anyone can stop by and get a glimpse of the status at the sprint, release, or overall product level without interrupting the development team. Remember, only the Agile team members who actually create and use the tools can decide which information radiators are most appropriate, as well as when to introduce them on their projects.

Mastering the Daily Progress Report

Before you can use the *daily progress report*, it is important to understand how it can help and support you on your project. The following project scenario highlights its importance.

A large software company has decided to start using the Scrum software methodology in their development cycle. Although this methodology is new to the company, the software industry has used it for many years. As a senior and experienced project manager, you want to learn the new methodology and you decide to manage the project. Using the Scrum methodology, you see immediately how much work the project team will complete by each sprint cycle. This is one of the major benefits to using this methodology. You believe this is a win-win for everyone involved, especially for the project's team members. You are excited to get started. Management, on the other hand, is not so excited because they are unfamiliar with the new methodology. Their biggest worry, other than assuming there will no longer be any structure or process, is getting status from the projects that use the methodology. Some of management's main questions include:

- How will we get status using the new methodology?
- Who is working on which items?
- What roadblocks could prevent the team from moving forward?
- How can we help move the project forward?

To answer these questions, you use a daily progress report, which includes answers to the following questions from each team member. The questions are:

- What did you complete yesterday?
- What do you plan to work on today?
- What is preventing you from completing today's activities?

After answering these questions, you and your customers complete the project status. At the daily progress report meeting, each team member states what they have completed, what they plan to work on, and any issues they may have. This allows team members to hear from one another and offer support where they can. The software industry and the construction industry both use the Scrum methodology for daily progress reports, and it is rapidly spanning across other industries.

Cross-Reference
We recommend that you review the daily progress report in Chapter 12 - Defining Communication Tools That Manage Project Communications, for more information.

Creating a daily progress report

By capturing status information once a day, you can find out how much progress the team members are making on the project. Once you hear the progress, or lack of progress, you can directly follow up with team members who have outstanding items, and you can remove roadblocks where applicable. Capturing status information also helps you hold team members accountable for status reporting. It can be a problem when a team member plans to do something one day, and then reports the next day that the task is not done. You can address the issue by reviewing the previous day's information and ask the team member why he or she never finished the task. Without capturing status information every day, team members' progress is lost and unrecoverable.

Project customers should encourage their project managers to use a daily progress report for all of their projects. The time it takes to pull the team together and hear the latest project status is valuable to everyone, especially the customers and leadership team. The report provides a first-hand view from the project team about issues and concerns they have with the project, and where they need help. Daily progress reports and associated standup meetings provide customers with levels of detail they don't normally see from the project team. It also ensures greater communications between all parties.

The steps for creating a daily progress report vary, but you can follow these steps to get started:

1. Set up a daily progress report meeting with your team members. Customers can also attend the meeting, but the focus is to get information directly from team members.

2. Elect a member of your project team to capture information from other team members and store the information direct in the daily progress report. This is an important task, but can be time-consuming, so we recommend rotating this responsibility among all team members.

3. Hold daily progress report meetings and have each team member answer the three standard questions about their work activities. The minutes taker captures the information in the daily progress report.

4. At the end of each meeting, the minutes taker sends you the daily progress report for your review and to make updates or corrections. When you have the daily progress report, forward the report to everyone involved in the project. Store the latest copy in the document control system for long-term storage, archival, and availability to anyone wanting to review it. This creation process continues throughout the project life cycle.

Using a daily progress report

Before you can use a daily progress report, you must identify who on your project team will use it. This is important so that you can determine the level of detail needed, distribution frequency, style, and format of the daily progress report.

Before you start using the daily progress report, review the materials in *Chapter 12 - Defining Communication Tools That Manage Project Communications*, and then complete the following steps:

1. Ensure that you capture and store project information from each team member in the daily progress report. If a team member has no updates or misses the meeting, the minutes taker must capture the information from those individuals after the meeting. It is important to hear and track what each team member is doing, even if they are ill, regardless of how much or how little work they have performed, or if they attended or missed the meeting.

2. Review the daily progress report and act on any action items that your team members provided at the meeting. If you hear that a team member cannot move forward, work directly with that person to help him or her resolve the issues. If you learn that a team member is not working on anything, assign them work or have them work on tasks with another team member. Make sure that people who have some spare time help others on the team if they can. It is acceptable to let employees have some spare time on the project, if there is nothing for them to work on or they cannot help another team member. The daily progress report provides daily project information that helps you make these kinds of decisions, keeping you on top of the project.

3. Store the daily progress report in the document control system for long-term storage, archiving, and retrieval purposes.

Mastering the Gantt chart

Before mastering the Gantt chart, you must understand how it can help and support you on your project. The following project scenario highlights its importance.

A large moving company just won a major contract to move music equipment for a large band during their international tour of Canada, the United States, and the United Kingdom. The band will tour for ten months. The moving company will move all stage equipment, music equipment, and other materials, from city to city, and country to country. As the most senior project manager at the moving company, and a music lover, you decide that this will be a perfect project for you. As you start working on the project, you begin by meeting with the band and manager to ask several questions that need addressing immediately, such as:

- When does the tour start?
- Which cities are we traveling to and on which dates?
- What equipment needs moving?
- In what order do you set up the equipment?
- What is the budget for moving expenses?
- How many resources are working on the tour?
- When does the tour end?

To answer these questions, you should use a Gantt chart to track the project activities and costs. A Gantt chart documents the project tasks and time lines and is the main repository for the, project schedule, resources, and task-related information. All project managers should use a Gantt chart to track project activities, or you will have a difficult time controlling the project.

Cross-Reference
We recommend that you review the Gantt chart tool in Chapter 8 - Communication Tools That Manage Project Time for more information.

Creating a Gantt chart

Creating a Gantt chart is easy to do and is something that every project manager should have some knowledge about how to create. A Gantt chart helps you stay on track with your project and the project's time line. The Gantt chart may be the only project communication tool you use on a project, especially a small project.

When creating a Gantt chart, make sure to use the correct fields for reporting purposes. Popular fields to display in the Gantt chart include: description, resource name, percent complete, total float, duration, start and finish dates, predecessor and successors. You choose the fields you want to display in the Gantt chart, but those are the most common.

The steps for creating a Gantt chart vary among project managers because of the versatility of the tool and the project manager's favorite tool of choice.

Complete the following steps to get started creating a Gantt chart:

1. Identify the information you want on the Gantt chart. This information includes project activities—rolled up or summary levels—resource names, and percent complete. This step defines the look and feel of the Gantt chart on the tabular section, or left side of the report.

Note

There are two sides to the Gantt chart, a tabular side where the tabular columns display data, and a graphic side where the timescale and calendar information displays.

2. Create a baseline schedule, if you have not already done so.

3. Add extra information in the right side of the Gantt chart. The graphic, or timeline side, has many available valuable data fields for reporting.

Caution

Never connect logic relationships to summary tasks, only to detail tasks. Let the detail tasks drive the summary tasks.

4. The Gantt chart is now complete and ready for reporting.

Figure 22.6 — Example of a basic Gantt chart shows a basic Gantt chart. This example is simple, but provides a great starting point for creating project activities. The project dependencies and summarized view in the Gantt chart provide an excellent representation of the project's time frames.

Figure 22.6 — Example of a basic Gantt chart

	Task Name	Duration	Start	Finish
1	Sample Project	10 days	Wed 1/2/19	Tue 1/15/19
2	Task 1	3 days	Wed 1/2/19	Fri 1/4/19
3	Task 2	3 days	Mon 1/7/19	Wed 1/9/19
4	Task 3	4 days	Thu 1/10/19	Tue 1/15/19

Using a Gantt chart report

Before you can use a Gantt chart, you must identify who on your project team will use it so you can determine the level of detail needed, distribution frequency, style, and format of the Gantt chart. The Gantt chart can be detailed, although, project managers can always summarize the Gantt chart for reporting or printing purposes. The real value of the Gantt chart is tracking the details and being aware of project activities.

Before you starting using the Gantt chart report, review the material in Chapter 8 - Communication Tools That Manage Project Time, and then complete the following steps:

1. Identify the information that your customer wants to see on the Gantt chart. Because the Gantt chart is so powerful, you must determine which characteristics—such as cost, schedule, resources, WBS, and performance—that your customer wants you to display.

2. Update the Gantt chart to satisfy the customer's requirements, and then present it to them for review. When your customer is happy with the chart's look and feel and the key milestone dates, get their approval and sign-off by sending the Gantt chart and the user acceptance document to the customer for approval.

3. As the project starts, tell your team members to use the Gantt chart to report progress. They will need to enter the actual start date, actual finish date, actual work hours, actual cost, and remaining duration for each activity they have begun working on.

Mastering the Histogram Report

Before you can use the *Histogram report*, you must understand how it can help and support you on your project. The following project scenario highlights its importance.

A large furniture plant in Little Rock, Arkansas decides to replace its ten-year-old inventory system with the most recent version. You are the project manager, and as the project progresses, you realize the large number of staff working on the project is causing the budget to explode. You start asking questions about who is working on the project and why the costs are so high. You must find the underlying cause or you will never complete the project on budget. Upper management is watching the budget closely and wants detailed reports based on the project's resource hours and allocations. Upper management's questions include:

- How many hours this week did the staff work on the project?
- What are the cumulative hours of the office staff?
- Who worked the most hours last month? Who worked the least?

To answer these questions, you can use the Histogram report. Histogram reports have the ability to report both cost and resource data because the Histogram report displays information using stacked bars, which strengthens the data and makes reporting easier. In this scenario, you should use a histogram report to report on the project resource issues. Management would us the report to understand what is happening with the resources.

Cross-Reference
We recommend that you review the histogram report in Chapter 11 - Communication Tools for Human Resource Management for more information.

Creating a histogram report

Creating a histogram report is easy to do and valuable for communicating project information. You will find histogram reports helpful as you execute and control your projects because of the richness the reports provide about project data—especially when you use the histogram report from a resource management perspective. The histogram report with resource data is valuable and provides a good view into project resources.

When your customers start using the histogram report, they will find great value in what the report provides. Your customers will come to expect the histogram report on a continual basis because of how much information it displays and how easy it is to read and understand.

The steps for creating a histogram report vary among project managers, depending on their favorite tools of choice. If you have never created histogram report before, here are some simple steps to help you get started. We also created a template for you to use as a starting point for your projects. You will need to update the template based on your specific project needs and requirements.

1. Open a spreadsheet tool. We used Microsoft Excel, but any tool with graphic capabilities will work.
2. Create the first row of data as the title row. In this basic example, we used Resource Name, Wk1, Wk2.
3. Create the second through fifth rows of data as represented in Table 22.1. This data represents hours worked per resource across the various weeks. Table 22.1 displays an example of what the hours would look like for this work group across five weeks.

Table 22.1 — Example of histogram data represents the data for this simple histogram report. The sample data shows how to develop the report so it will be immediately helpful for your own project.

Table 22.1 — Example of the histogram data

Resource	Wk. 1	Wk. 2	Wk. 3	Wk. 4	Wk. 5
Sam	36	40	30	21	70
George	40	33	44	60	38
Fred	32	38	36	40	36
Bill	22	55	20	75	40

1. Highlight all rows of data to create the chart.
2. In Excel, with the highlighted data, click **Insert**, select **Chart**, select **Column**, and then select the **Stacked Bar** chart for your chart type. The **Stacked Bar** chart creates the histogram report because it adds multiple values of data into one column (each week).

Figure 22.7 — Histogram report example shows an example of a histogram report based on the data you have entered so far in the example.

Figure 22.7 — Histogram report example

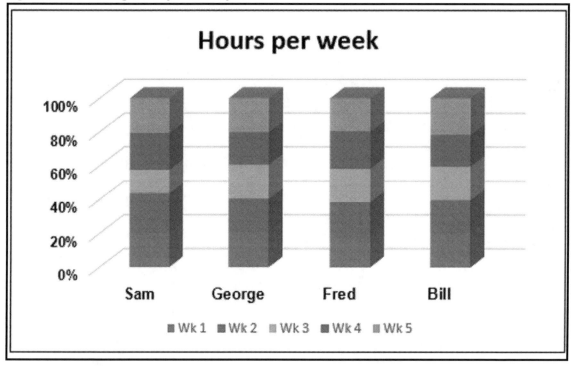

608

Using a histogram report

Before using a histogram report, you must identify who on your project team will use it so that you can determine the level of detail needed, distribution frequency, style, and format of the histogram report. The histogram report is a chart that displays data at a summary level. Anyone looking at the chart who needs further details can look at the source data that built the report for more information.

Before using the histogram report, review the materials *in Chapter 11 - Communication Tools for Human Resource Management,* and then complete the following steps:

1. Decide an internal process within your project team to get the histogram data. This step may affect when you can produce the report. Depending on the report type, you may choose to collect this information automatically from an internal system while others may collect the data manually. The one thing to consider when thinking about producing the histogram report on an ongoing bases is where you will get the data.

2. Ensure your customers are comfortable with the report and can understand it. This is usually not a problem, but is something you should confirm. This step ensures that your customers know you are not creating reports for the sake of reporting, and that you want them to get real value from the reports. Discuss the histogram's reporting periods, and the frequency they want to receive the report. Usually, customers want weekly reporting.

3. Enforce the use of the histogram on the project. This includes creating the report, delivering it to your customers, and potentially setting up separate review meetings to discuss the information. Depending on the histogram report type, your customers or leadership may have several questions for you about the data behind the report. Resource histograms can be valuable for providing team members' work hours, either on a weekly or month basis. Depending on the results, you can make or update the reports when needed.

4. Store the histogram in the document control system for long-term storage, archiving, and retrieval purposes.

Mastering the Pareto Chart

Before you can use the *Pareto chart*, you must understand how it can help and support you on your project. The following project scenario highlights its importance.

A large construction firm has won the contract to erect two large skyscrapers in downtown Buffalo, New York, during the summer. They decide to use the just-in-time inventory method—a method that reduces the load of carrying too much inventory—to save costs. During the building phase, the crew notices that the delivery for materials is expected by 7:00 a.m. each workday is arriving later and later each day. It is getting so bad that at times, the crew must stop work due to lack of materials. As project manager, you need to get control of this situation as soon as possible. Waiting for materials not only affects your budget, but it also affects the morale of the crew members who are sitting or playing around—someone could get hurt. As you start delving into why the materials are late each morning, you turn up more questions than answers, such as:

- How many categories or possible reasons could we have for the late deliveries?
- What is the percentage of issues across the categories?
- What percentage could we lower the issues, working on two, three, or four categories?
- What is the number one reason for the late deliveries?

To answer these questions, you should use a Pareto chart to better understand how the materials are being handled. A Pareto chart is a histogram chart with the data arranged in ascending order (from the largest number of occurrences to the lowest number of occurrences). The Pareto chart is popular for helping project managers focus and resolve project issues in order of priority. Without a Pareto chart, determining the order of importance and the impact each issue has on the project would be almost impossible.

Cross-Reference
We recommend that you review the Pareto chart in Chapter 12 - Defining Communication Tools That Manage Project Communications for more information.

Creating a Pareto chart

A Pareto chart is priceless for discovering the most dominant project issue in a set of issues, and it allows project team members to focus on those areas of concern. You often use Pareto charts for charting the number of occurrences of a particular issue, number of bugs, types of risk events or safety occurrences.

When you realize how powerful this tool is and how much it will benefit you, you may want to use Pareto charts on all your projects. For example, in a software development project, Pareto charts based on bug types are a great benefit because they allow the team to discover the specific category in which most of the bugs are occurring, and focus their attention there. This is valuable project information. Without it, the project team might randomly fixing bugs with little or no idea how those bugs affect the project overall.

Project customers like Pareto charts because they are graphical, so they are easy to read and understand. Customers appreciate seeing the project's dominant issues and how the team is reacting to them.

To capture and control project risks, we suggest creating both a Pareto chart and a risk matrix. Each tool provides the most project risk coverage and management. Creating a risk matrix breaks out the highest risk events into the most predominate categories for charting purposes. For example, the process for creating a risk matrix includes team members working together and adding risk events to the matrix and assigning categories of high-high, high-medium, and so on. After this process is complete, you can use the results to create a Pareto chart.

Cross-Reference
We recommend that you review the risk matrix in Chapter 13 - Defining Communication Tools to Manage Project Risk for more information.

The steps for creating a Pareto chart tool vary. To get started, complete the following steps:

1. Select and analyze the issue or problem you are trying to resolve and compare to identify the risk categories for charting.
2. Open any spreadsheet application to create the Pareto chart. You can use any spreadsheet tool; we used Microsoft Excel in this example.
3. Decide the unit of measure for your project's Pareto chart. In this example, we used the number of occurrences of the percentage of change requests by category type.
4. Create the first row of data as title data. In this example, we used the titles: Change Request Category, # of Occurrences, % of Change Requests, and Cumulative.
5. Create four columns of data under each title you just created. The data will fall under the categories: Change Request Category, # of Occurrences, % of Change Requests, and Cumulative. When creating the categories, the information is dependent on the project type you are managing. Occasionally, categories can be difficult to discover; in other cases, they are easy to discover, such as the number of software bugs across different areas of the application. For example, the Pareto chart would display the number of bugs (problems in software code) by different sections within the application. For instance, number of reporting bugs, number of data entry bugs, number of interface bugs.
6. Enter data into the spreadsheet using the three different categories. In **Table 22.2 - Example of data used to create a Pareto chart**, the data shows that the project team has filed 50 change requests for this project. The two new columns, % of Change Requests and Cumulative %, are automatically calculated in the table and, therefore, do not need data entry. It is important to understand what each column means. The % of Change Requests column is a calculated field based on the number of occurrences divided by the total number of requests. Therefore, in this example, 50/167 is 30 percent. The Cumulative % column is also automatically calculated by adding together the % of Change Request column and the Cumulative % Column. In every chart, the first row of data will carry the same value in the Cumulative % as the % of Change Requests column because there is no preceding Cumulative %. The first row acts as a starting point for the rest of the data. However, for additional rows, use the Preceding Cumulate % amount plus the current % of Change Request amount to calculate that row's Cumulative %.
7. **Table 22.2 - Example of data used to create a Pareto chart** shows the project team's Cumulative % of 30 percent to the engineering's value of 26 percent for % of Change Requests to total the Cumulative % value of 56%. Enter 56% in the Cumulative % column on the Engineering row. Continue this calculation for all rows of data.

Table 22.2 — Example of data used to create a Pareto chart represents the data to create a sample Pareto chart. This example provides a great starting point for creating a Pareto char for your project.

Table 22.2 — Example of data used to create a Pareto chart

Change Request Category	# of Occurrences	% of Change Requests	Cumulative %
Project Team	50	30%	30%
Engineering	43	26%	56%
Construction Errors	32	19%	75%
Customer	30	18%	93%
Wrong Equipment	12	7%	100%
Total # of Requests	167		

8. Create your project's Pareto chart by selecting all the data in the table, and then (in Microsoft Excel), click **Insert**, select **Chart**, and then select **Column** for the chart type. Once created, the chart is ready for use.

9. Create your chart's percentage line (originally, this was a column type) and convert it to a line chart by selecting the column of data that represents the cumulative percent of defect on the spreadsheet. Then, change the chart type to represent a line chart. The results will change the cumulative percent into a line and display across all categories.

10. Once complete, assign a name to your chart, and your Pareto chart is ready for project reporting and presentation. Store the Pareto chart in the document control system for long-term storage, archiving, and retrieval purposes.

Figure 22.8 — Example of a Pareto chart shows a Pareto chart for a project. In this example, the chart covers the various reasons and percentages as to why a project contractor is always late delivering materials.

Figure 22.8 — Example of a Pareto chart

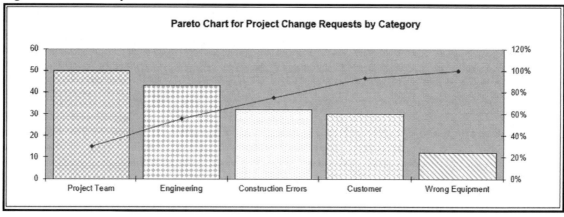

Using a Pareto chart

Before using a Pareto chart, you must identify who on your project team will use it so you can determine the level of detail needed, distribution frequency, style, and format of the Pareto chart. The Pareto chart displays high level and/or summary level data. If there are any questions about the chart, you will have the background data to support how it was developed.

Before using the Pareto chart, review the materials in *Chapter 12 - Defining Communication Tools That Manage Project Communications*, and then complete the following steps:

1. Ensure that your customers and team members are comfortable reading and understanding the Pareto chart. You may need to schedule a series of review meetings to ensure that everyone understands the chart. Occasionally, you may need to work directly with anyone who is struggling to understand the chart until they are comfortable with the data.

2. Encourage the use of the Pareto chart on your project. Find out how to get the chart data, and then set up ongoing team meetings to create the chart and deliver it to your customers. Internal meetings with team members can occur during weekly status meetings where team members go over risks and issues; separate meetings also work where you focus on just creating the Pareto chart.

3. Schedule customer meetings to review the Pareto chart. You can update or change existing meeting agendas to discuss the Pareto chart.

4. Store all versions of the Pareto chart in the document control system for long-term storage, archiving, and retrieval purposes.

Mastering the Project Status Report

Before you can use the *project status report*, you must understand how it can help and support you on your project. The following project scenario highlights its importance.

A tourism coordinator in a small town in Ontario, Canada has come up with a new idea to celebrate this year's Canada Day holiday that is going to make the whole country stand up and take notice. The goal is to place a Canadian flag on the lawn of every home in the small town, making this small town the most patriotic by flying more flags than any other city or town per capita in Canada. The tourism coordinator, who is a project manager, decides to take on the challenge and lead this project. The mayor of the town is a little unsure about the idea, but has decided to earmark a small budget for the project to be used for television advertising, radio, and print media to communicate the idea and help the town achieve its goal. "Fly your Flag, Fly you're Flag" is the town's new motto. The tourism coordinator is excited that the mayor and the townspeople like the idea. But she is also fully aware that she will be under pressure to perform well on this project and that the city council members will expect continual project status. The one area she struggles with is understanding which project details that the city council members will want to see each week. She has several questions about how to provide status, and the city council members have their own questions as well, including:

- What did the project team accomplish last week?
- What are the current issues and risks?
- How is the project progressing?
- What is the progress on the project?
- How many flags are in front yards out of the total number of front yards?

To answer these questions, the tourism coordinator should use a project status report. The project status report provides the latest project information. The tourism coordinator will add a summary of details for each major project area to her status report. The time frame for project status reporting is usually weekly for most midsize to smaller projects and goes until the project is complete. Large projects usually report monthly because weekly reporting would be too much overhead with little return. There are many examples of project status reports across many industries and even more projects. Companies usually have a standard template for projects. In the previous example, the city council members would benefit from a project status report created by the tourism coordinator once a week.

Cross-Reference
We recommend that you review the project status report in Chapter 6 - Communication Tools That Manage Project Integration for more information.

Creating a project status report

Creating a project status report is critical for all projects, and most companies expect you to create a project status report weekly for each project. The project status report is the most common communication tool for projects. The status report is also one of the only communication tools that you will create willingly because of its value and the continuing pressure you will receive from customers and leadership to provide one regularly.

Note

On large projects where an administrative team is in place, it may not be necessary for the project manager to create a status report themselves, but have another member of the team create them. Even if the project manager does not create the status report, it is best practice for him or her to understand the project status reports and speak to the details.

Create a status report and work with your customer to decide the reporting cadence early in the planning process. Some customers will want daily status reports, but most will want weekly reports for small to midsize projects. Weekly status reports work best for small to midsize projects because enough time will have passed between reports that team members will have completed some of the project activities. On large projects that span years, a weekly status report, as noted, would be overhead and not valuable because it can take months for progress to show, so producing status reports with little to no project movement would be a waste of your time and effort.

Creating a project status report is a straightforward and common task for you. However, creating a project status report that provides value to your customer is much more challenging. Usually, a project manager creates a generic project status report based on the company's template and sends it to your customer with no regard for how it will serve the customer's needs. You will often not even know whether your customer reads the project status reports. Therefore, it is critical that you work with your customer to create a report that offers information they need about the project. Otherwise, you could waste time producing a report that no one but you will have read.

You and your customer are both responsible for the contents of the project status report. The customer should be involved in the project status report process to ensure they receive the project information they need. A report that does not contain the information your customer wants is of no value to them. Work with your customer to make sure they receive the information they need.

The steps for creating a project status report vary, but you can get started by completing the following steps:

1. Work with your customer to decide whether the project status report template contains the fields they want to include. Some customers are particular about the fields they want included. This information sets the foundation for all status reports you will send to the customer. You must also find out how often your customer wants to receive the project status report: weekly, monthly, or daily. The project status report is typically a weekly report, but some customers may have different requirements. Some may want to receive it more often than weekly; whereas, others would prefer to receive it monthly.
2. Develop an internal process where your team members help you collect and compile project information to include in the project status report.
3. Create the project status report, including compiling the information, completing the template, and creating the report.
4. Distribute the project status report via email and create a location in the document control system to store it.

Using a project status report

Before you can use a project status report, you must identify who on your project team will use it so you can determine the level of detail, distribution frequency, style, and format of the status report.

Before using the project status report, review the materials in *Chapter 6 - Communication Tools That Manage Project Integration*, and then complete the following steps:

1. Enforce the use of the project status report on your project. You can refer to it for project information, to manage project deliverables, and respond to customer and team member concerns about project status. Always have a hard and soft copy of the project status report available to refer to if needed. You should also have a copy of the project calendar available to answer any questions about the project schedule.

2. Use the project status report to provide project information to your project customer, and schedule meetings with your customer to review the project status report. Set up this meeting at the same time you determine the project status report delivery cadence. We recommend that you have copies of the project status report available for your customer to refer to and make notes on during the meeting.

Tip

Send the project status report the day before the project status customer review meeting. Your customer will appreciate you being proactive and they will be able to review the materials ahead of the meeting.

3. Work with your team members and drive the project deliverables based on the status of the report. This includes checking on status, resolving issues or risks, and removing roadblocks. You should drive much of your project work from the project status report.

4. Store the project status report in the document control system for long-term storage, archiving, and retrieval purposes.

Mastering the Spider Chart

Before you can use the *spider chart*, you must understand how this tool can help and support you on your project. The following project scenario highlights its importance.

A large computer manufacturing company has announced the latest in laptop design and is planning a fall delivery to customers across North America. The company is excited about the new laptop because of its advanced features and extended battery life. It has tested at an unbelievable four days without needing a charge. This laptop and battery will change mobile computing. You are the project manager on this project and as you review the project details, you discover that several resources are charging to your project. The problem with that is you do not know who they are, or what they do for your project. This information is worrisome because the largest part of the project's expenses is associated to labor dollars, and without correcting or getting control immediately, the project will not stay within budget. Leadership is watching closely and wants to make sure the new laptop gets out to the market on time and on budget. Upper management sees the hours and associated resource dollars rising each month and they want to step in to help resolve the situation. Leadership is asking a series of questions that you cannot answer, including:

- How many hours did Mary work last month?
- How many hours did Alice work last month, considering she is part time?
- What are the total hours worked for all resources?
- Who worked the least amount of hours, and are they still contributing to the project?

To answer these questions, you should use a spider chart. The spider chart provides a graphic method of presenting and comparing project information. At first, the spider chart appears difficult to read, but after building and using them a couple of times, you will quickly become familiar with them and find them valuable for comparing project data. You will also have to teach your customer how to read and use the spider chart; they too will come to appreciate this tool.

Cross-Reference
We recommend that you review the spider chart in Chapter 12 - Defining Communication Tools That Manage Project Communications for more information.

Creating a spider chart

Creating a spider chart is valuable for making project data comparisons. For example, resource hours or project costs per group are areas where you want to compare data points and graph them; the spider chart is the perfect tool for this.

You will quickly learn how valuable a spider chart can be in helping to manage and control various project areas. For example, spider charts are valuable for comparing project areas and their associated costs. The spider chart is excellent for answering questions, such as the monthly analyst group cost compared to the design group cost. Alternatively, you can see how many hours a week one team member is working compared to another. This is all valuable information for managing and controlling your project.

The steps for creating a spider chart vary, but you can complete the following steps to get started.

1. Open any spreadsheet tool to create your project's spider chart. In this example, we used Microsoft Excel.
2. Create the first row of data as your title row and enter data such as hours and resource names.

The data for a particular project resource will go down a column instead of across the columns. The goal is to have multiple values of data in the spider chart across various months.

3. Enter the data for each column.

Table 22.3 — Example of spider chart data shows sample data in the spreadsheet columns. The data represents hours worked for various staff members, across the month.

Table 22.3 — Example of spider chart data

Hours	Jones	Smith	Brown
M-1	110	80	40
M-2	162	110	50
M-3	120	80	60
M-4	40	100	120
M-5	154	120	160

4. Select the data in the cells, click **Insert**, and then select **Chart.**
5. In the Charts area, click Other Charts, and then select Radar with Markers (in Microsoft Excel).
6. The spider chart is now complete. If desired, you can apply formatting or chart titles to improve the look of the report.
7. Store your spider chart in the document control system for long-term storage, archiving, and retrieval purposes.

Figure 22.9 — Example of a spider chart shows a spider chart of employees' working hours using the data above.

Figure 22.9 — Example of a spider chart

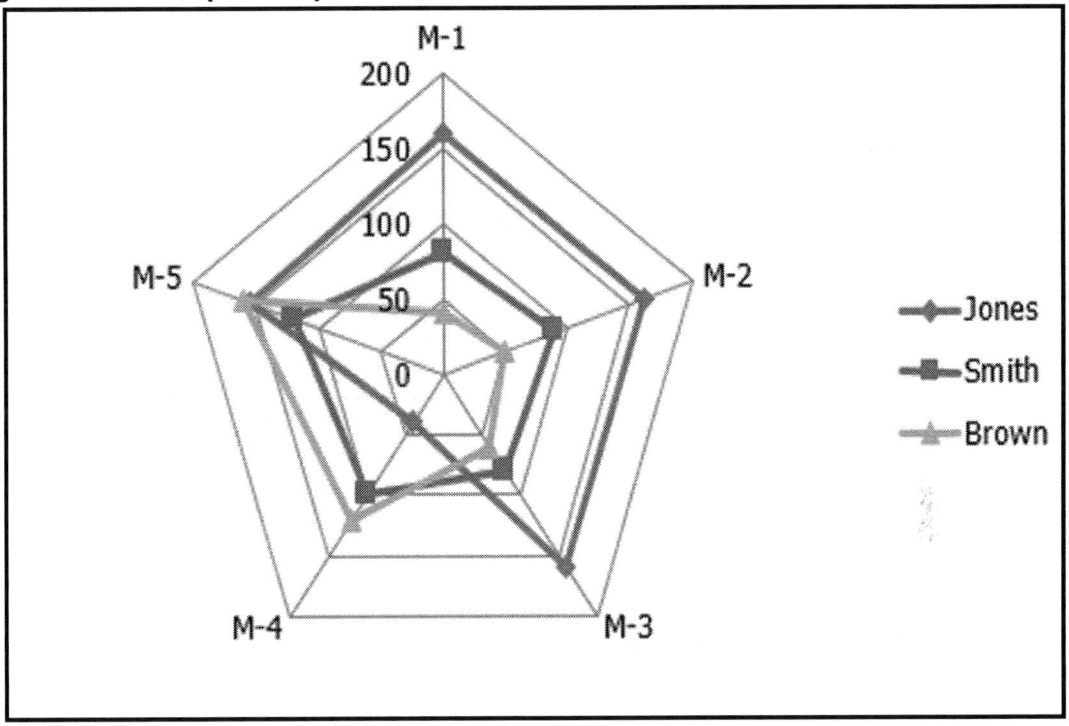

Using a spider chart

Before you can use a spider chart, you must identify who on your project team will use it so that you can determine the level of detail needed, distribution frequency, style, and format of the spider chart. The spider chart shows summarized data and provides high-level project information. However, if a customer, team members, or management have questions or concerns about the report, you can turn to the data that produces the report for answers.

Before starting to use the spider chart, review the material in *Chapter 12 - Defining Communication Tools That Manage Project Communications*, and then complete the following steps:

1. Analyze your project's spider chart to determine the state of the project. This includes breaking down data, checking for boundaries, anomalies, data spikes, and so on.
2. After completing the project data analysis, you can make project level decisions based on your findings.
3. Present the spider chart findings to your customer and leadership for review and feedback.
4. Depending on your customer's or leadership's decisions, update the information on the spider chart where necessary. You might need to add extra time data points (months, years) or extra categories to the chart.
5. Store all versions of the spider chart in the document control system for long-term storage, archiving, and retrieval purposes.

Mastering the Stoplight Report

Before you can use the *stoplight report*, you must understand how it can help and support you on your project. The following project scenario highlights its importance.

A large automobile framing plant in Barrie, Ontario, Canada has just announced their latest truck frame design, which they expect will change truck design for years to come. The automobile frame, developed by using a new combination of steel and aluminum, will lighten the overall weight of the vehicle by almost 300 pounds. For the auto industry, a lighter truck means higher gas mileage, and therefore the frame will be important to every automaker around the world. As the plant's leading project manager, you decide to take on the project. Management agrees, and you start working on the project's activities immediately.

As you start working on the project, you discover early on that because of its importance to the industry, this project has a high level of management overhead that includes ongoing project status reporting. Senior management is focused on the schedule and cost status. However, because there is such a high demand for the new truck frame, the project must hit both its schedule and budget targets. There can be no exceptions. Many automobile companies are lined up to buy the new frame and the automobile companies will not tolerate delays. The downstream impacts of a delay would hurt their own production lines, and the negative press it would create only adds to the problem. As project manager, you need a way to effectively control all components of time and cost, by task, and ensure at-a-glance that you can see the project's trouble areas. Specifically, you are focused on areas that keep the project progressing on time and on budget. You struggle to find the best way to report information that allows for tight management and control of project activities, as well as upper-level dashboard reporting to satisfy management and the project's customers. As the project continues, leadership asks questions about the project's schedule and cost. Leadership adds some increased pressure to provide a report that answers their questions at a high level. The questions leadership asks include:

- What is the project's current schedule status?
- Is the design phase on time and on budget?
- What is the project's current cost status?

To answer these questions, you should use a stoplight report. A stoplight report provides an updated project status by using color indicators to represent each task's progress. At a glance, leadership and customers gain an understanding of the overall project status by the most dominant color on the report. For example, an all red report suggests a project in serious trouble. A report that shows all green suggests the project is on track. A stoplight report takes little time to create and set up on the project schedule and is popular and useful for project reporting.

Cross-Reference
We recommend that you review the stoplight report in Chapter 12 - Defining Communication Tools That Manage Project Communications for more information.

Creating a stoplight report

You are responsible for creating the project stoplight report. A stoplight report is one of the easiest reports to create in all the communication tools. You can spend just minutes determining the calculations and associating indicators to create the report. The stoplight report offers huge benefits in communicating project status, especially when someone quickly glances at the project schedule and focuses on the color indicators only. Anyone looking at the project schedule can tell if the project is in a red, yellow, or green status with a single glance. All project managers should report their project schedules using color indicators.

Before you can benefit from a stoplight report, you must complete the following items on the project schedule:

- Baseline project schedule
- Project must be currently under way with active tasks
- Project schedule must have reported progress

These three activities, at a minimum, must occur on the project schedule before using a stoplight report.

Note

If you are unfamiliar with how to create a baseline schedule, refer to Chapter 18 - Using Communication Tools to Plan and Develop Project Deliverables for more information.

The stoplight report is a variance report; variance reports calculate the difference in project information. The schedule variance shown on a stoplight report calculates the difference between the current finish date and the baseline finish date. In this case, it takes the actual finish date of a task and subtracts the original finish date (baseline finish date). For the cost variance calculations, the color indicators represent the actual costs minus the baseline costs (budget). When tracking the project's schedule or the cost variance, the color indicators on each activity row allow you to focus directly on where the project is in trouble. It then prompts you and your team members to focus on that area to get the project back on track.

A project customer will use the stoplight report, but will rarely be involved in creating the report, which is your responsibility. Your customer will be able to see, at-a-glance, the project's schedule and cost status within each major area. If more details are needed, such as why one section shows yellow or red, the customer can work with you for more information.

The steps for creating a stoplight report vary based on the software tool you use to create the report. Complete the following steps to get started:

Note

You must set a baseline schedule for this formula to work. Make sure no progress has been recorded before setting the baseline.

1. Open your project's scheduling tool. Usually, you add the stoplight report conditions to your existing project schedule, but it can also be set up with a blank schedule. For this example, we used Microsoft Project® to create the stoplight report.

Note

You must have tasks in the schedule to display the stoplight indicators. Enter one or two temporary tasks to test that the stoplight indicators will display the correct color when you create the formulas.

2. Create a field that will store the two stoplight report calculations. Right-click the **Task Name** column, and then select **Create Custom Fields**. Each scheduling tool should have its own version of creating custom fields.

3. Click the drop-down box in top right corner. Change the Field type from Text to Number. Be sure to name and note the custom fields you create. For this example, use SV for schedule variance and CV for cost variance as your new custom field names.

4. Click the Formula button, and then create a new formula for schedule variance. In the Formula box, click the Field drop-down arrow, select Date, select **Baseline Finish**, and then in the **[Finish]** field, type a minus (-) sign. Repeat the same steps, select the Field drop-down arrow, select **Date**, and then select the **[Baseline Finish]** field. After completing the formula, click **OK**. If a box appears that asks to overwrite the field, click **OK**. Here is the formula:

[Finish] - [Baseline Finish]

5. Click the **Graphical Indicators** button for ranges of variances. Use the graphical indicator, and then select the indicator color based on the tolerance range. Select the first box in the first row and enter the following tolerance ranges for schedule variance (days). Refer to the online Help if you are unclear about this section.

    *   If schedule variance is less than 1, the indicator is green. If you are on schedule or ahead of schedule, your indicator will be green.

    *   If schedule variance is within 1 and 5, the indicator is yellow, meaning the activity is within five days of the original schedule (baseline).

    *   If schedule variance is greater than 5, the indicator is red. In this case, the activity is more than one week behind schedule.

Continue this process until you have completed all three rows. Click the **OK** button to save your work. **Figure 22.10 — Example of values to use for graphical indicators (Microsoft Project)** shows the Microsoft Project version of what the graphical indicators look like when complete.

Figure 22.10 — Example of values to use for graphical indicators (Microsoft Project)

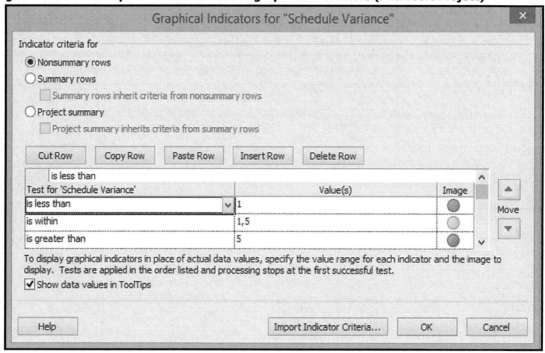

6. Repeat the process for the cost variance formula. Select the **Cost Variance** field. Select the **Formula** box. In the **Formula** box, click the **Field** drop-down arrow, select **Costs**, select **Baseline Costs**, and then select the **Baseline Costs** field. Type a minus (-) sign, and then click the **Field** drop-down arrow again. Select **Costs**, and then select **Actual Costs**. Click **OK**, and then click **OK** again when asked to overwrite the field. If a box does not appear asking you to overwrite the field, continue. The formula should look like the following:

[Baseline Costs] – [Actual Costs]

Note
*Name the custom field **Cost Variance** and note the name because you will need to use it in the following steps.*

7. Select **Graphical Indicators** for your range of variances. In this step, use the graphical indicator and select the indicator color based on the tolerance range. Enter the following criteria as you did in step 5 in the Cost Variance field. The typical tolerance ranges for cost variance (days) include:

- If cost variance is less than or equal to 1, the indicator is green.
- If cost variance is within 2 and 99, the indicator is yellow.
- If cost variance is greater than 100, the indicator is red.

Note
You can create your own ranges. The ranges shown here are just examples.

After entering all three rows, click **OK**, and then click **OK** again to go back to the project scheduling tool.

8. Insert both new custom fields into the project schedule by clicking the **Add New Column** drop-down arrow and finding the columns you just created. In this case, select **Schedule Variance** first, and repeat the process for **Cost Variance**.

9. The report is complete, and as long as there are one or two tasks in the project schedule, the indicators will display the stoplight colors. If you use existing indicators on your project, it will represent the latest status of those activities. Tasks must be in the schedule for the stoplight indicators to show. Enter one or two temporary tasks to test.

Note
The cost variance indicator will not appear until costs are added to the project schedule.

Figure 22.11 — Example of a stoplight report (using a single schedule variance indicator) represents a project schedule that shows the schedule variance stoplight indicators only.

Figure 22.11 — Example of a stoplight report (using a single schedule variance indicator)

To create a cost variance report, add the cost variance custom field (CV) you created.

Figure 22.12 represents a project schedule showing the cost variance stoplight indicators only.

Figure 22.12 — Example of a stoplight report (using a single cost variance indicator)

When creating both the cost variance and schedule variance report, add both fields in the report.

Figure 22.13 represents a project schedule showing the cost and schedule variance stoplight indicators. Most project manager wants this view showing both indicators on their projects.

Figure 22.13 — Example of a stoplight report (using schedule and cost variance indicators)

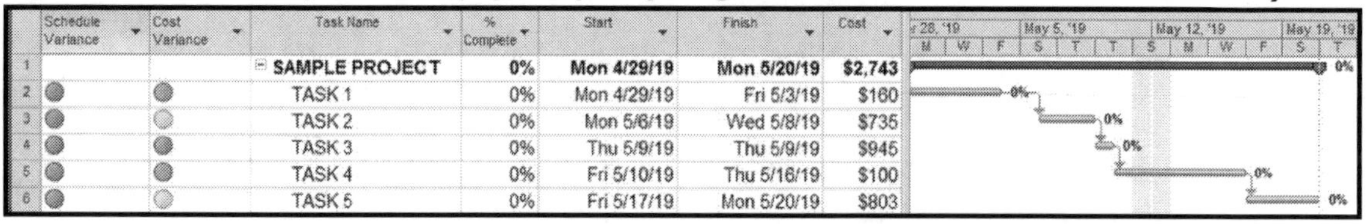

	Schedule Variance	Cost Variance	Task Name	% Complete	Start	Finish	Cost
1			SAMPLE PROJECT	0%	Mon 4/29/19	Mon 5/20/19	$2,743
2			TASK 1	0%	Mon 4/29/19	Fri 5/3/19	$160
3			TASK 2	0%	Mon 5/6/19	Wed 5/8/19	$735
4			TASK 3	0%	Thu 5/9/19	Thu 5/9/19	$945
5			TASK 4	0%	Fri 5/10/19	Thu 5/16/19	$100
6			TASK 5	0%	Fri 5/17/19	Mon 5/20/19	$803

One of the most powerful features of this tool is the multiple levels of stoplight indicators on your schedule to represent the true project status (shown in **Figure 22.12 – Example of a stoplight report (using schedule ad cost variance indicators).** Using a single indicator, such as cost variance, is good, but provides only one portion of the status. The stoplight report is important to use because it draws attention to project activities that are over or under a predetermined value. Also, because the stoplight report is graphical, it is easier to understand the project areas you should focus on immediately to gain control of and return to the original plan.

Using a stoplight report

Before you can use the stoplight report, you must identify who on your project team will use it so that you can determine the level of detail needed, distribution frequency, style, and format of the stoplight report. Some users of the report will want to see just the schedule variance, some the cost variance, and some both.

Review the stoplight report in Chapter 12 - Defining Communication Tools That Manage Project Communications, and then complete the following steps:

1. Incorporate the stoplight report into the weekly project status meetings with your team. Review the report with your team and confirm the project and task colors, and then adjust where applicable. This lets you confirm with team members the various project colors and project status once a week. The stoplight report also provides the project team with information about the color for their portion of the project. If they are working on a section that is red or yellow, they will know that they need to do something different to get the project back to green status.
2. Present the stoplight report to your customers and leadership. The stoplight report is easy to explain because of the colors in the report and how easy it is to read. You can schedule a separate meeting or present the report at a scheduled status meeting, but being able to speak to the colors on the stoplight report is you and your team's responsibility. You will need to specifically speak to why a task is red, yellow, or green and discuss the reasons or action plans to get red or yellow tasks back on track.

Tip

A best practice you can use during the early reporting of the stoplight report is to explain the criteria used to create each report. This lets the customer know what the various colors mean, and if they have concerns about the criteria, they have the opportunity to change it early in the reporting cycle. If you choose to hide the criteria, or share it too late in the reporting cycle, you may find yourself in a situation where you are reporting the wrong thing. The stoplight report could be showing a green status when the customer believes it is red. It all depends on the limits.

3. Focus on project work activities that are red or yellow and decide where and how to get the activities to a green status. This process will occur throughout the project life cycle.

4. Store the final stoplight report in the document control system for long-term storage, archiving, and retrieval purposes.

Summary

The tools that we described in this chapter are the best choices for reporting project performance and status information, while executing and controlling the project. These tools will help you understand what is happening on the project and what you need to do to get the project under control when project areas are going off track.

The communication tools in this chapter span a wide variety of project reporting, including daily progress reports, checkpoint reports, and project status reports, delivered weekly on small to midsize projects.

Using the reporting communications tools outlined in this chapter will benefit you, your customers, and the project team. The reports are simple, easy to create, and informative for presenting project information to customers, leadership, and anyone involved in the project.

Chapter 23

Using Communication Tools During the Closeout Process

IN THIS CHAPTER

♦ Mastering the Formal Acceptance document
♦ Mastering the Lessons-Learned document
♦ Mastering the User Acceptance document

In this chapter, we explore project communication tools you'll use during the project's closeout process. Specifically, the communication tools in this chapter focus on closing the project and ensuring that everything is complete, approved, and achieved to the customer's satisfaction.

The project closeout process is twofold. First, there is the technical closeout that focuses on delivery of the final product, and second is the administrative closeout. During the technical closeout, you close out and archive all technical documents, files, and paperwork, for long-term storage. You put away or shut down anything the team used to build the project. The project's administrative closeout phase includes many different areas, such as closing contracts, purchase orders, and budgets; reallocating staff; defining warranty period terms; closing payroll and any legal issues or conditions. You must understand how critical this project phase is and that communicating effectively during the closeout process is important—any mistakes during this phase could be costly. If you handle the closeout incorrectly, you could face legal ramifications, impacting you and your company.

The communication tools included in this chapter consist of the formal acceptance document, lessons-learned document, and the user acceptance document.

Mastering the Formal Acceptance Document

Before mastering the *formal acceptance document*, you must understand how it can help and support you on your project. The following project scenario highlights its importance and why the formal acceptance document is critical to every project.

A large shoe manufacturing company, based out of London, England, has just launched a project to create a new shoe inventory system in their stores worldwide. Because the shoe manufacturing company produces shoes, not software, they decided to contract the work and hired a local consulting firm to manage and develop the inventory system. You are a project manager for the software consulting company and decide to manage this project. After a yearlong effort, you successfully set up the project around the world. You are now in the project's closeout process, and you are ready to take on your next challenge. However, you just realized that you neglected to get the customer's final project approval. You captured the go/no-go decision to release the application into the production environment, but never followed up by getting the formal acceptance document. Your management is excited about the launch and happy everything is going well; however, after three weeks into production, the application starts to fail. The application opens in one store, but immediately shuts down. In another store, no one is able to log on to the application, so the staff cannot use it. You have a mess on your hands, and your leadership wants some answers. They ask you for the customer's formal acceptance document that shows they accepted the software as complete and ready for worldwide implementation.

Customer questions include:

- How are the problems going to be resolved?
- Who is going to pay for the problems to get resolved?
- How long will it take to fix the issue?

Management questions include:

- How could you have captured formal customer approval?
- What could you have done to prevent this situation from occurring?

The answer these questions, you should use a formal acceptance document. A formal acceptance document transfers ownership at the end of the project from you and your team to the product customer. The formal acceptance document is usually a single-page document, sometimes handled through email that is compulsory on all projects as evidence that the customer accepted the final product.

Cross-Reference
We recommend that you review the formal acceptance document in Chapter 14 - Defining Communication Tools to Manage Project Procurement for more information.

Creating the formal acceptance document

The formal acceptance document is simple to create and requires little to no effort from you. Usually, the formal acceptance document is one page. It may be an email that includes **Approve** and **Reject** buttons; anything that provides evidence that the customer accepted and approved the project. Even a single-page document provides enough basic information for the person signing it to understand exactly what they are accepting. Developing the document with limited information, or in a manner that allows customers to avoid responsibility, can cause serious issues for you or the company. You should always have the legal department overlook the acceptance document.

Successful project managers must ensure they are diligent about having their customers sign the formal acceptance document. Lawyers use the formal acceptance document in lawsuits and court cases as evidence that the customer accepted and approved the work; thus, helping to get companies and project managers, specifically, out of trouble if a project ever goes to court. The formal acceptance document provides an agreement between two parties that the work is complete and everyone is satisfied with the results. You need to ensure that the customer approves and sign offs on the project's formal acceptance document. This may mean stopping the project completely until everyone signs off—dramatic, but sometimes necessary. At the beginning of the project, make sure that everyone agrees on who will give final project approval, and then, at a minimum, those individuals sign off on the formal acceptance document. If you do not get signoff from everyone on the list of approvers, from an auditing perspective, the project is not signed off or approved. If the project goes forward, you are taking a risk.

Project customers play an important role in the formal acceptance process. Customers should play a big role in this process and work diligently with you to provide project approval and acceptance when it completes. The project is not a success unless the customer signs the formal acceptance document. Customers should understand exactly what they are accepting when signing off on the formal acceptance document. By signing, they accepted and approved the project and all associated responsibilities. Customers rarely have anything to do with creating the formal acceptance document. Their roles are to review the formal acceptance document and agree to what fields and information it contains, and then sign it when the project completes.

The steps for creating a formal acceptance document vary among project managers. Instead of providing step-by-step instructions for creating a formal acceptance document, we're provided a formal acceptance document template that you can use.

Figure 23.1 — Formal acceptance document shows an example of a formal acceptance document. As you can see, this document is simple to create by using the template and filling in the blank fields. The example seeks customer approval for project delivery, but you can change the document depending on your project needs.

Figure 23.1 — Formal acceptance document

Formal Acceptance Document

Project ID/#: _____   Project Name: _____   Acceptance Date:
_____

Project Client/Owner Name: _____   Customer/ Owner Department Name:
_____

Project Manager Name: _____   Project Management Office Rep:
_____

Project Acceptance or Information:

    Acceptance or Reject Delivery of project: Accept: _____   Reject: _____ (*)

    * If rejected please explain the reason:

_____
_____

Further Comments:

_____
_____

Project Detail information:

Planned Start Date: _____   Actual Start Date: _____

Planned Finish Date: _____   Actual Finish Date: _____

Actual Budget ($): _____   Final Costs ($): _____   Over or Under Budget: _____

Signatures/Approvals Section:

Project Manager Approvals: _____

        Print Name

        _____

        Signature

Project Client/Owner Approvals: _____

        Print Name

        _____

        Signature

Using the formal acceptance document

Before implementing the formal acceptance document, you must identify who on your project team will use it so you can determine the level of detail needed, distribution frequency, style, and format of the formal acceptance document.

Before using the formal acceptance document, review the material in Chapter 14 - Defining Communication Tools to Manage Project Procurement, and then complete the following steps:

1. Make sure the customer agrees to sign off on the document when you request their signatures at the end of the project. Early in the project, make sure the customer agrees with what is stated in the formal acceptance document so there aren't any problems when it comes time to get their signatures.

2. When the project is complete, deliver the formal acceptance document to everyone on the formal acceptance approval list.

3. Store the signed and approved formal acceptance document in the document control system. Make sure that team members have security rights and the formal acceptance document is ready to immediately access by anyone on the team.

Mastering the Lessons-Learned Document

Before mastering the *lessons-learned document*, you must understand how it can help and support you on your project. The following project scenario highlights its importance and why the lessons-learned document is critical to every project.

A large software company decides to launch a new software operating system that will change the way businesses use tablet computers. The software company is promising new features and capabilities that hardware companies have never seen before. The company predicts that when the tablets hit the shelves, "they are going to sell like crazy." You are one of the most senior project managers in the company, and leadership has asked you to lead the project, so you quickly begin planning the project's activities. As the project progresses, everything is going along nicely; there are no major issues until you approach the software development phase. Your two top developers have run into some problems that prevent them from moving forward. You research the situation, and it turns out there is a minor misunderstanding between the two developers; your work resolves the situation and the project continues. Then, another situation arises between the two developers, and you step in again, resolve it, and put the incident behind you.

As the project moves into the test phase, a couple of minor problems occur, which are quickly resolved and the project continues. Again, you do not capture anything formally about the minor test phase problems because you thought they were minor and nothing to worry about. As the project moves into the user acceptance phase, a major problem occurs and the project stops dead in its tracks. Users cannot use the software, and the issues that the two developers were discussing during the development phase, which you ignored, have just derailed your project. You try to remember what the disagreement was about, but your memory is not what it used to be. You wonder if that was a major warning sign that you should have taken more seriously. You call the two developers into a meeting, but so much time has passed that they cannot remember what the issues were about either. Leadership is applying pressure to get the user acceptance testing phase going again. While the issues remain unresolved, the project is losing thousands of dollars a day. Leadership is trying to get into the details of the issues that occurred during development, and are looking for documentation to understand how they can help resolve the issue. Leadership asks the following questions:

- What happened during the development phase?
- Who was responsible?
- How was it resolved?
- Who took ownership of the resolution?
- Who approved the resolution?

To answer these questions, you should have used a lessons-learned document. The lessons-learned document captures the lessons everyone learned while executing and working on the project. The lessons-learned document provides a wealth of project information that only a project team member working on a project can provide because they experience the events as they occur. It is impossible for an outsider to provide the same project information that someone working on the project can provide, especially if they are not part of the team. Every project should have a lessons-learned document so they can provide best practices and lessons-learned information so that the same information is not repeated.

Tip
Collect lessons-learned information during the entire project life cycle; do not wait until the end. A best practice is to capture the data during weekly status meetings.

Cross-Reference

We recommend that you review the lessons-learned document in Chapter 14 - Defining Communication Tools to Manage Project Procurement for more information.

Creating the lessons-learned document

Creating the lessons-learned document occurs throughout the project life cycle. A common mistake is waiting until the end of the project to collect lessons-learned data when the team has long forgotten it or has since moved on. Chances are slim that team members will remember from the beginning of the project what went right and what went wrong about key questions to capture lessons-learned information. Asking someone to remember the details of something that happened six months ago is not practical; people are busy and will not remember that far back in time. The recommended approach for collecting and compiling lessons-learned information is to capture it throughout the project life cycle.

Tip

Using a lessons-learned document is better than using a daily log. The lessons-learned document has more information and often includes resolutions to prevent the mistakes from happening in the future.

Project customers should be involved in providing lessons learned-information throughout the project life cycle. A project customer who is active on a project will be part of the events and situations that occurred, so capture their thoughts about events to include in the project's lessons-learned document.

The steps for creating a lessons-learned document vary among project managers. Instead of providing step-by-step instructions for creating a lessons-learned document, we've provided an example table of contents.

Table 23.1 – Example of a lessons-learned table of contents

#	Section	Description
1	Areas of Success	The project areas that were successful, such as budget, schedule, quality, human resources, and general project management.
2	Areas of Improvement	The project areas that needed improvement, such as budget, schedule, quality, human resources, and general project management. Add anything the project team, customers, or you felt needed improving in this section.
3	General Lessons Learned Information	Document the project's lessons-learned information that does not fall in other categories, such as resource assignments, working conditions, and overtime issues.
4	Final Thoughts	Document any other thoughts or recommendations you have in this section.

Using the lessons-learned document

Before using the lessons-learned document, identify who on your project team will use it so you can determine the level of detail needed, distribution frequency, style, and format of the lessons-learned document. By understanding this information about the lessons-learned document, you can communicate the appropriate details to the project team and customers.

Before using the lessons-learned document, review Chapter 14 - Defining Communication Tools to Manage Project Procurement, and then complete the following steps:

1. Make sure you have established a process for collecting lessons-learned data during the project life cycle. This includes adding time to weekly status meetings, setting up generic templates or websites to collect project information.

2. Collect the lessons-learned information from project team members. Collect lessons-learned information during project status meeting. This is the one time when team members are together and can provide project information. Some project managers may want to hold separate meetings to collect lessons-learned information.

3. After you collect and compile the lessons-learned information throughout the project, create a lessons-learned presentation for an end-of-project meeting. This presentation provides everyone involved a summarized view of areas that were successful and areas that needed improvement.

4. Schedule a lessons-learned meeting and present your project's lessons-learned data. During this meeting, you not only present what you collected during the project life cycle, but you also collect new material presented at the meeting. Occasionally, project team members or customers will wait until this meeting to voice their concerns or present lessons-learned information. In these situations, all you can do is collect the new information, compile it with the other information, and discuss it during the meeting.

5. Store the lessons-learned materials in the document control system for long-term storage, archiving, and retrieval purposes. This allows you to store all your project information in one location. Lessons-learned information is important and relevant to store.

Mastering the User Acceptance Document

Before mastering the *user acceptance document*, you must understand how it can help and support you on your project. The following project scenario highlights its importance and why the user acceptance document is critical to every project.

A large manufacturing company decides to update and improve their current performance appraisal system. The company has grown in four years from 20 employees to 158 employees and is still growing. The current system cannot handle the staff increase the finance department puts on it. The employees feel the method by which management is appraising their performance is stale and no longer valid. This method is long overdue for a change. An updated performance system will have new rules and policies for appraising employees. The company's leadership team performed a feasibility study on the new performance system and agrees to update it. As lead project manager for the finance group, you think this project would be fun to manage and have asked if you can lead it. Management approves, and you immediately start working on the project.

As you begin the start-up activities, you pick the project methodology, who and what customers will be involved, and the overall project layout. Everyone will benefit from this project and you are excited to lead it. As you start the project's first phase, the customers provide their requirements and you jointly develop the business requirements document. The customer signs off on the business requirements document, and you store the document and approvals in the document control system. The project moves into the technical phase, and the same process occurs where the customer reviews the documents, approves them, and the project moves onto the design phase. As the project completes and moves into the production environment, something goes wrong. The screens and the user interface for the new application are not usable. One of the biggest problems is that it is hard to enter data into the application. The reports do not print correctly and on many reports the data does not fit onto the page. The application is a disaster and the company has wasted hundreds of thousands of dollars. You, as project manager, made the biggest mistake of your professional career, and management is looking for someone to blame. Management wants to understand who approved such a terrible, unworkable product for final delivery. As you scramble and look back over the course of the project, you review the information in the document control system and find the customer only provided their approval for the first two project phases. However, you realize that you sent documents to the customers for approval, but they never returned or approved them. You search and search, but you quickly realize you forgot to secure the customer's approval on the project phases after the technical phase. You know the mistake you made, but management is asking some tough questions, such as:

- What formal documentation should you have used to capture the customer's signatures?
- What process and procedures would you have followed to prevent the project from moving into the next phase?

To answer these questions, you should have used a user acceptance document and followed through to ensure all customers signed it before moving on to the next phase of the project. User acceptance documents capture the customers' formal acceptance and approval at each phase of the project. The user acceptance documents are critical for project audits when you seek approvals between project phases. Auditors request evidence of approval at a specific stage in the project and need approval on the project itself. These two approvals are different. If you use the user acceptance document and ensure at every phase there is a sign-off process, you are doing what is expected to manage your project.

Cross-Reference
We recommend that you review the user acceptance document in Chapter 14 - Defining Communication Tools to Manage Project Procurement for more information.

Creating the user acceptance document

Creating and using the user acceptance document is critical for all projects, and you must ensure that customers are happy with the product or deliverable at each phase of the project. Whether a construction, software, manufacturing, or research project, the customers play a role in the overall success and adoption of the product; therefore, their approval is important. If the customer doesn't like the end product or deliverable, they may never approve it or use it. For example, on a construction project, it is in the best interest of the contracting company and the design company to ensure the owners are happy with the building before turning it over to them. If the owners decide to build another building and give your company future project work, it is best to ensure you have a good relationship with the owner to secure future projects. A happy owner will most likely want to work with the same construction company again in the future.

Project customers should be active in the user acceptance process. Project customers are rarely involved in creating the user acceptance document, but they need to be involved in it. Ensure your customers accept and approve the processes for using the document. The most important task for each customer is signing the user acceptance document at the end of every project phase and each major project deliverable. Without their approval, stop the project until all approvals are received. Because it is important to keep the project moving, leadership may choose to allow the project team to continue without everyone's approval. In that case, you cannot stop the process for obtaining approvals, but the team can continue with their activities. Sometimes, the issues are small and not worth stopping the project to get remaining signatures. There could be valid reasons, such as holidays or vacations that prevent a customer or project team member from providing approval. When this happens and you continue the project without all the approvals, accountability falls on leadership and not you. Make sure your leaders accept accountability, and then continue executing the project.

Note
It is important to know from an auditor's perspective that this breaks all auditing rules. Most projects state that without sign-off from all parties, the project does not move forward.

The steps for creating a user acceptance document can vary among project managers. Instead of providing step-by-step instructions for creating a user acceptance document, we provided a template that you can complete.

Figure 23.2 — User acceptance document is an example of a user acceptance document. This document is simple to create by completing the template. This partial example shows a document seeking customer approval for a project deliverable, not a project phase. The document is easy to update for seeking customer approval on a phase and not a deliverable. You are responsible for updating the document depending on project needs.

Figure 23.2 — User acceptance document

Date: _____

This acceptance form acts as formal document of the _____ deliverable on the _____ project.

By signing off on this document, you agree to the following terms outlined below.

Please approve each statement below:

_____ The deliverable is of the highest quality the project can afford.

_____ I have fully tested the deliverable (if applicable) and it passes my tests and is ready from my perspective to be moved into a production environment. If the deliverable is a document, I have read it and agree to the contents of the document.

Signature: _____

Printed name: _____

Using a user acceptance document

Before using a user acceptance document, identify who on your project team will use it so you can determine the level of detail needed, distribution frequency, style, and format of the user acceptance report.

Before using the user acceptance document, review the material in Chapter 14 - Defining Communication Tools to Manage Project Procurement, and then complete the following steps:

1. Ensure the customer agrees to sign off on the user acceptance document when the project completes a particular phase. To ensure this, you will literally stop all project activities until everyone signs the document. Work with the customers so they are comfortable with the contents of the document during the project's planning process. When you receive their buy-in and approval, they will use this document to approve project deliverables.

2. Enforce the use of the user acceptance documents with your team as you transition from project phase to project phase. Each team leader needs to work with you to produce a user acceptance document for their phase. For example, from the design phase to the build phase in a software project, the lead designer might create a user acceptance document for the customers to sign and approve for the project's design phase. Enforce the use of these documents with your team members by adding them as a formal step in the phase closeout process.

3. Store your project's approved user acceptance documents in the document control system after getting official sign-off from customers. This includes ensuring that team members have security rights and the system is ready for immediate use by anyone on the team. You may need to request that the security team confirm your team members' access to the document control system to allow them complete access to the project files.

Summary

In summary, the tools described in this chapter are the best choices for closing out and getting final approval on the project. Closing a project should be something a project manager handles carefully. Usually, there is little time between finishing one project and starting on the next. As such, project managers sometimes miss important sign-offs on their projects. There is no excuse for this, but it does happen. Using the tools outlined in this chapter can prevent you from missing sign-offs on your projects.

The tools in this chapter include some of the popular tools, such as the formal acceptance document, lessons-learned document, project closure notification, and user acceptance document. These tools are common to many project managers today and are used across most industries.

One of the most important tools in the project closeout process is the lessons-learned document. You normally collect lessons learned during the project's closeout process, but as we discussed in this chapter, you should collect this data throughout the project. Collecting lessons-learned information throughout the project and presenting that information along the way is valuable toward avoiding making the same mistakes multiple times.

Using the reporting communications tools outlined in this chapter will benefit you, your customers, and project team. The reports are simple to create and informative for presenting information to various parties.

Part IV – Project Management BI & PMP® Exam Questions

Chapter 24

Project Management Business Intelligence

IN THIS CHAPTER

- ♦ Introducing Business Intelligence as a Tool for Project Communications
- ♦ Planning to use Business Intelligence as a Project Management Communications tool
- ♦ The Project Management Business Intelligence process
- ♦ Using Business Intelligence reports

In this chapter, we explore business intelligence (BI) by using project management data. Projects and project management generate a lot of data for every project. Receiving, understanding, and acting on project information are a challenge for all project stakeholders. Project managers are faced with the challenge of getting their message across to the vital stakeholders in a world of communication "noise" where there is a distinct danger that their messages may go unheard. Business intelligence has evolved to address just this need. BI converts large amounts of data—from disparate sources and formats—and combines it into reports and interactive visualizations that people can quickly interpret, understand, and act on. Couple this with the trend towards all-electronic communications and the use of apps and web portals for information sharing and collaboration, and it becomes clear that BI should be considered a new tool in your project management communications tool box.

Introducing Business Intelligence as a Tool for Project Communications

Business intelligence (BI) is an often-used term in organizations today. Wikipedia defines BI as "a set of theories, methodologies, architectures and technologies that transform raw data into meaningful and useful information for business purposes." BI has two main purposes: to enable data analysis, and to serve as a communications tool. BI is often said to convert "data to information," and combine and simplify large amounts of data in ways that people can quickly interpret, understand, and act on.

The key benefits of BI are flexibility and insights.

- Flexibility: BI tools are made to be flexible in terms of the data that they can ingest and combine from different data sources, formats, and locations. This is a distinct advantage to business users who grapple with data of all shapes, sizes, and formats, but who need to use the different data to make decisions or provide updates. Having tools that can span and normalize the data for different purposes is invaluable.

- Insights: Perhaps the best known and most valuable aspect of BI is the ability for the business user to derive new insights into the data through statistical operations and data visualizations (for example, charts, graphs, and dashboards).

In a world where a large proportion of work is being done using all-electronic media, and where apps and web portals are integral to how people interact and collaborate, BI is emerging as both a normal and vital extension to the communications spectrum.

Tool Value
In the project management context, BI provides a tool for reporting project data.

This book talks in great detail about the many communication tools and instruments that might be applied in a given project. For certain communication types and stakeholders, the various documents, reports, and files may be overwhelming and confusing. This is where BI might be useful. Using BI techniques and tools, you can quickly and economically bring together data from various sources, combine related data sets, create simplified data visualizations, and share the reports for viewing and consumption by various stakeholders. Because projects are rarely exactly alike, the flexibility of BI to connect to vastly different data sources and yet still create views that people can understand and act on is invaluable.

Project Scenario:

You are the project manager for several concurrent projects that are all for the same owner. You are managing the project schedule using project management software and tracking risks, issues, change requests, and lessons learned in separate spreadsheets. The owner of the projects is a senior executive, and while she is very experienced with project management tools and concepts, she does not have the time or inclination to carefully read all of your documents and logs each week. She feels that the weekly project status reports are too infrequent and static to keep her as informed as she would like to be about her projects. Instead, she wants to independently check where the projects are in terms of task completion, when the projects are expected to complete, how the projects are tracking with respect to effort and cost, and the current status of the risks, issues, and change requests. You decide that BI might meet this expressed need. Using the BI tools you have access to, you collect the relevant data from the various applications, create some simple visualizations to report the key attributes, and then post the new view to a central location that the project owner can access. The project owner loves the fact that she can view the simple charts that you created to get a quick feel for how the projects are progressing, and with just a few clicks of the mouse, she can find out more details. You feel good because you have used the reports you are already maintaining to provide an extra layer of project communication that addresses a key stakeholder's needs. You decide that you will keep BI in mind as a communications tool for use in future projects.

Planning to use Business Intelligence as a Tool for Project Management Communications

Before using BI, you need to create a plan. When creating your BI plan, there is a best practice that you can follow to give yourself the best chance of success. You may know them already, they are the same questions that reporters ask when they are investigating a story: who, what, where, when, and so on.

Let's look at these questions now in the context of using BI as a tool for project management communications.

When would you use BI as a project management communications tool?

- When you want to combine and summarize large amounts of data from different sources and tools to create a simplified view of various project attributes. Typically, you only use BI for projects that are long and/or complex.

Who is going to use this tool?

- When the BI reports and views have been created, any project stakeholder may use them to gain insights and make decisions. However, the key audiences for this kind of report are typically project owners, sponsors, and executives who are time constrained yet want to "drill in" to areas of interest within the project information.

Why are you going to use this tool?

- To meet the project communication needs of certain stakeholder groups to provide a modern and interactive interface and access to a combined view of project information.

How are you going to use this tool?

- By using BI tools supported by your organization, you will collect relevant data from the various project communication tools and create simple visualizations to report key attributes, and then share the new view in a central location that is accessible by the target project stakeholders.

How will you distribute the information?

- BI reports can be shared through email, stored in a central location, and posted to a project portal for central access.

What decisions can or should you make from BI?

- BI reports can be used to inform the viewer about project progress, current risks, issues, and change status, and to direct attention to items that are out of the ordinary.

What information does BI provide for your project?

- BI reports can be created for almost any project attribute. The only limits are the availability of the data that you want to report, the features of the BI tools being used, and the imagination and skill of the person creating the reports. BI is a flexible tool, so new reports or adjustments can be quickly and easily made.

What historical or legal information do you need to store?

- BI can be used to access and report all sorts of current and historical project information, but in the scenarios envisaged here, the information being reported would mostly include project tasks and status. This data may be sensitive or confidential, so careful thought must be given to how the reports are distributed, and by what means and to whom they are sent or shared.

What are the staffing requirements (roles) to run and maintain BI?

- Using many of the BI tools available today, you should be able to build simple BI reports. The "do-it-yourself" BI approach has the advantage of informing you as you build the reports and allows you to quickly improve the quality and impact of the reports being created as they are built. However, if you have a large workload or need support, you could employ a specialized BI analyst to create the reports.

- BI is an important way to visually express performance and progress statistics. There are many tools that can be used for this kind of visualization. One of the more common and accessible BI tools is Microsoft Excel. In the following pages, we use Excel to provide examples of how project management information can be expressed using BI.

You should take advantage of using BI and processes whenever possible on your projects. This provides your customers, leadership, and project teams a completely different way to look at project data and be exposed to data insights and views that they may never have seen before.

The Project Management BI Process

The project management BI process is a simple eight-step process for you to follow in order to set up and prepare your project to use BI.

The following table **(Table 24.1 — Project Management BI Process)** outlines the eight common steps for using project management BI on a project.

Table 24.1 — Project Management BI Process

#	Step Name	Description
1	Locate/Collect	You and your team document where all the relevant project files are located. Some files may need to be moved from their current locations to ensure that they are accessible when the data is pulled into the BI tools. Storing all project files together in a centrally accessible location is good practice, and doing so makes reporting from the data much easier.
2	Prepare	Prepare the data for use with BI tools.
3	Ingest/Consume	Use the BI tools to consume the data. This step takes data from the various files, locations, and formats, and feeds the data into the BI tools.
4	Shape	Because the project data comes from a variety of source files, locations, and formats, changes are often required to match data formats and descriptive items. Shaping may also be needed to filter out unneeded information, leaving behind just the data required for reporting.
5	Visualize	Once the data has been consumed and shaped, it is ready for visualization. There are many visualization techniques that can be applied to express project information, including charts, graphs, and tables. In the next section, we share some examples.
6	Share	Share the reports with the target stakeholders. There are a variety of means to share the reports, ranging from emailing a copy, pasting snapshots into other reports, and posting them to a shared drive or team site. BI reports are created to increase the readers' understanding of the complex data that is fed into them, so report sharing is arguably the most important step in the BI process.

#	Step Name	Description
7	Consume	Project stakeholders access the reports, and use the controls and options to gain a quick and deep understanding of the state of the project. The BI report consumption method depends on the means by which the BI reports are shared.
8	Refresh	BI reports can be refreshed during the project life cycle.

These eight steps are applicable to any project manager wanting to implement BI on their projects.

Using Business Intelligent Reports

In this section we briefly discuss how project summary dashboard reports assess project health and progress and guide project decisions.

The project summary dashboard provides a wealth of project information.

Figure 24.1 — Project summary dashboard shows an example of a project dashboard using the reports we created in the previous section.

Figure 24.1 — Project summary dashboard

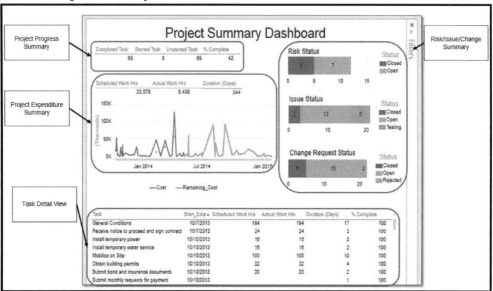

Let's look at some of the key characteristics of this dashboard in **Table 24.2 — Project summary dashboard**.

Table 24.2 — Project summary dashboard

Report Information	Decisions & Assessment
The top-left of the report provides a "by-the-numbers" progress summary of task completion status, percentage complete for the overall project, and the work planned and expended.	Looking at this section, project stakeholders can quickly get a feel for the number of completed tasks and the work hours expended versus the percent complete. If the proportions are consistent, the project is likely making progress as expected. If the proportions are unbalanced—for example, if the % complete was 25%, but the actual work hours were reported as more than 50% of the scheduled work hours—something is likely going wrong on the project.

Report Information	Decisions & Assessment
The top-right of the report provides a summary view of project risks, issues, and change requests.	Project stakeholders can get a feel for how many risks, issues, and change requests exist for the overall project and how well the project team is addressing these items as they arise. If the number of risks, issues, or changes is too small or too large, or they are all "open" or don't change status from week to week, it's a sign that these items are not being managed effectively. To drill into the details for these items, stakeholders can view the project dashboards.
The middle-left section of the report shows actual and planned project expenditure over time.	The cost timeline is based on the actual and planned work effort for project tasks. Looking at this example, we see some busy (and, therefore, more expensive) weeks, but other than a narrow spike in April or May, there are no large anomalies. The remaining cost seems to be in proportion with past expenditure, and is well distributed over the remaining duration. If the cost was concentrated towards the end of the project, it would be a sign that there may be something wrong with project scheduling.
The lower section of the report provides a full listing of project tasks, showing the start dates, work effort, durations, and percent complete.	This section of the report shows project stakeholders more project task details. Using the tabular data, they can see scheduled and actual work hours and look for inconsistencies. If a task is 50% complete, but has consumed 75% of the scheduled work hours, it might be a sign that something is going wrong on this task. The scroll bar to the right of this section lets the viewer browse all project tasks in this view.

Report information decisions and assessment—project risk dashboard

Additional popular dashboards that you are encouraged to create are the risk and issues dashboards. You and leadership can make many project decisions using project risk and issue information.

Figure 24.2 — Project risk summary dashboard shows a sample of a project risk dashboard. This dashboard is a very powerful and important communication tool to use for your projects.

Figure 24.2 — Project Risk Summary Dashboard

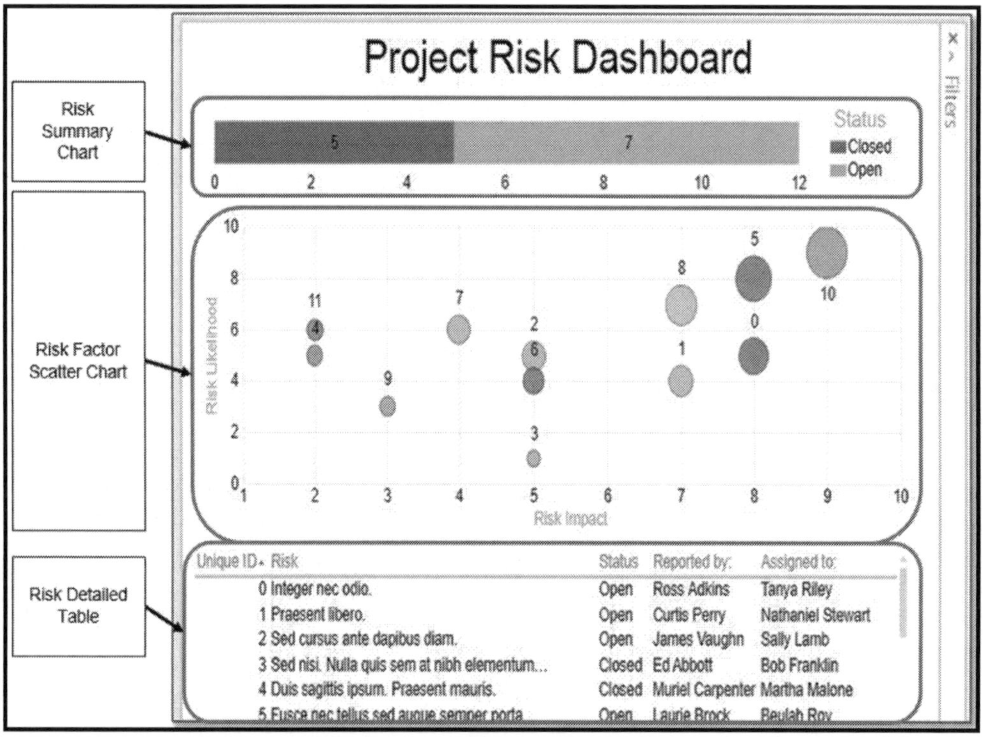

Let's look at some of the key characteristics in the following table.

Table 24.3 — Project Risk Summary Dashboard table

Report Information	Decisions & Assessment
The top-left of the report provides a "by-the-numbers" progress summary of task completion status, percent complete for the overall project, and the work planned and expended.	Project stakeholders can quickly get a feel for number of completed tasks and the work hours expended versus the percent complete. If the proportions are consistent, the project is likely making progress as expected. If the proportions are unbalanced—for example, if the percent complete was 25%, but the actual work hours were reported as more than 50% of the scheduled work hours—something is probably going wrong with the project.
The top-right of the report provides a summary view of project risks, issues, and change requests.	Project stakeholders can get a feel for how many risks, issues, and change requests exist for the overall project, and how well the project team is addressing these items as they arise. If the number of risks, issues, or changes is too small or too large, or they are all "open" or don't change status from week to week, this is a sign that the items are not being managed effectively. To drill into the details

Report Information	Decisions & Assessment
	for these items, stakeholders can view the detail dashboards.
The middle-left section of the report shows actual and planned project expenditure, over time.	This cost timeline is based on the actual and planned work effort for project tasks. Looking at the example, we can see some busy (and, therefore, more expensive) weeks, but other than a narrow spike in April or May, there are no large anomalies. The remaining cost seems to be in proportion with past expenditure, and is well distributed over the remaining duration. If the cost was concentrated towards the end of the project, it would indicate that there may be something wrong with project scheduling.
The lower section of the report provides a full listing of project tasks, showing start dates, work effort, durations and percent complete.	This section of the report shows project stakeholders more project task details. Using the tabular data, they can see scheduled and actual work hours and look for inconsistencies. If a task is 50% complete, but has consumed 75% of the scheduled work hours, it might be a sign that something is going wrong on this task. The scroll bar to the right of this section lets the viewer browse all project tasks in this view.

These reports are just two of the many different project dashboard reports that can be created for your project. As you spend more time and embrace the project management BI on your projects, you will find that these two dashboards are just two of the many dashboards available for use.

Summary

In summary, project managers generate a lot of data on every project—data that is often wasted or not reported. Understanding what to do with this information is challenging for project managers and stakeholders.

Project Managers should start to embrace this idea of Project Management BI and spend the time reviewing all the project information available to them. In time, and as more and more data is created and better tools become available, project managers will have a world of information at their fingertips and be in a much better position to drive successful projects.

Chapter 25

Sample PMP® Exam Questions for Project Communications

IN THIS CHAPTER

♦ Sample PMP® Exam Questions for Project Communications

In this chapter, we explore ten common exam questions about project communications that you might encounter when preparing for your PMP® certification. A PMP® certification is important and we wanted to provide some possible exam questions. Project communications, as we have said throughout the book, is a critical component in project management. There will likely be a large number of communication questions in the exam, so we thought providing a small sample of possible questions would help you get started when preparing for the exam.

Sample PMP® Exam Questions: Communications

Table 25.1 – Exam Questions provides some sample communications questions you might encounter on when preparing for your PMP® certification. These questions focus solely on project communications and will help you practice and prepare to get your certification.

Table 25.1 Exam Questions

#	Question	Responses
1	A communications method that sends out information, with no certification requirements, is referred to as?	a. Interactive communications b. Pull communications c. Push communications d. Paralingual communications
2	Which of the following is true about the "plan communications" process?	a. Uses communications requirements analysis as a key tool and technique b. Leverages meetings as a key input c. Uses the stakeholder register as a key tool and technique d. Develops communications models as a key output
3	A team had seven total stakeholders. Yesterday, a new stakeholder came on board. How many additional communications channels were added?	a. 21 b. 28 c. 1 d. 7
4	A project manager is concerned that communications technology factors may impact the communications choice for a key infrastructure development project. Which of the	a. Ease of use b. Project environment c. Integrated change control

	following would not be considered a communications technology factor?	d. Sensitivity and confidentiality of information
5	A project manager is involved in a key status meeting. She fears that levels of commitment among stakeholders are dropping. Which communications strategy will help her least?	a. Listening for paralingual clues
		b. Carefully watching body movements of the participants
		c. Carefully recording verbal feedback
		d. Looking for lack of eye contact as a clue to true feelings
6	A project manager has a number of key communications activities to perform this week. Which activity would not generally require a formal written approach?	a. Sending a memo to team members clarifying schedules
		b. Transmitting communications that define a complex problem to a virtual team
		c. Sending out documentation across long distances to reach all worldwide team members
		d. Documenting a recent performance appraisal about a core team member
7	Which of the following activities would be considered a candidate for lessons learned?	a. Documentation on how the team will use earned value
		b. A checklist that will be added to the quality management plan
		c. Configuration management procedures to be included in the scope management plan

		d. A review of the scope statement template used by the team
8	The "managing communications" process is dependent upon which key input to perform effective performance reporting?	a. Work performance information
		b. Work performance reports
		c. Work performance data
		d. Work Authorization Systems
9	An issues log would serve as a critical input to perform which process?	a. Planning communications
		b. Managing communications
		c. Controlling communications
		d. Manage Issues
10	Which key communications vehicle documents the status of events that may pose a positive or negative impact to the project's time, cost, or scope?	a. Work performance information
		b. Risk reports
		c. Issue reports
		d. Variance reports

Summary

In summary, it is important to practice and know all areas that could be covered to get your PMP® certification; not just communications. This chapter provides a glimpse into ten possible exam questions about project communications. While you don't know whether these sample questions will be on the exam, they will get you thinking about these types of questions.

Cross-reference

See Chapter 27 – Appendix for answers to the PMP® exam questions.

Chapter 26

Bibliography

IN THIS CHAPTER

- ♦ Bibliography
- ♦ Trademark & Attributions

Bibliography

- Chapter 6, page 8/Chapter 16 page 5: ...shows a product vision statement template in a format that was created by Geoffrey Moore in his book, Crossing the Chasm.

- Chapter 10, page 13, Table 10.2 – Example of a Design Specification Document Table of Contents: Permission to reprint this design specification document is granted by Bradford D. Appleton. The full document template can be found at: www.bradapp.com/docs/sdd.html

Trademarks and Attributions

- **Apple:** Proper Trademark Notice and Attribution

1. Distribution Within the United States Only

a. On product, product documentation, or other product communications that will be distributed only in the United States, use the appropriate trademark symbol (TM, SM, ®) the first time the Apple trademark appears in the text of the advertisement, brochure, or other material.

b. Refer to the Apple Trademark List for the correct trademark symbol, spelling of the trademark, and generic term to use with the trademark. Generally, the symbol appears at the right shoulder of the trademark (except the Apple Logo, where the logo appears at the right foot).

Chapter 27

Appendix

IN THIS CHAPTER

- ◆ Sample PMP® Exam Answers and Explanations
- ◆ Project Management Communications Tools List

Sample PMP® Exam Answers and Explanations

Table 27.1 – PMP® Exam Answers provides the answers to the PMP® exam questions in chapter 25. Not only have we provided the answers we have also provided the justification around those answers below.

Table 27.1 – PMP® Exam Answers

#	Answer
1	C
2	A
3	D
4	C
5	C
6	A
7	D
8	B
9	C
10	B

Answers Explained:

1. **Option C:** *Push communications* is a method that sends information with no certification requirements. *Pull communications* are placed in a public area for access by team members, as required. *Interactive communications* is defined as communications between two or more individuals. *Paralingual communications* references tone of voice.

2. **Option A:** *Communications requirements analysis* is a key tool and technique for the *plan communications* process. Meetings and communications models are tools and techniques used to plan communications. The stakeholder register is a key input.

3. **Option D:** *Communications channels* are calculated using the formula $((n * (n-1))/2$. In this scenario, we began with seven stakeholders. Doing the math, $((7*(7-1))/2 = 21$ channels. A new stakeholder was added increasing the total stakeholder number to eight. Doing the math, we now have $((8*(8-1))/2 = 28$ channels. This is an increase of $28–21 = 7$ channels.

4. **Option C:** *Communications technology factors* are defined as technology factors that impact the choice of communications for a project. There are five documented communication technology factors. These factors include the urgency for information, technology availability, ease of use,

sensitivity and confidentiality of information, and the project environment. *Integrated change control* is not a communications technology factor.

5. **Option C:** According to sources acknowledged by the Project Management Institute, 55% of all communications is considered non-verbal, while 45% is considered verbal. *Paralingual communications* as defined in answer #1 is also considered a non-verbal source. In this question, options A, B, and D are all non-verbal, or paralingual. Option C is a verbal source. Option C, while important, only gives the project manager 45% of the story; the other options give 55%. In essence, this is a bit of a math question! And, 55% is greater than 45%!

6. **Option A:** You need to differentiate among various types of communications and classify them as formal written, formal verbal, informal written, or informal verbal. This question provides a list of communication activities and asks you to identify the activity that does *not* require a formal written approach. Options B, C, and D fall under the definitions for a formal written approach. Option A, however, uses two key terms associated with an informal approach. The key words are *memo* and *team*.

7. **Option D:** *Lessons learned* include actions that occurred in the past or that are currently happening. They do *not* include ideas or future plans. In this scenario, Options A, B, and C are futuristic; they are planned, but have not occurred. Option D is the only item that occurred in the past and is a candidate for lessons learned.

8. **Option B:** The *managing communications* process occurs during the *executing process* and implements the communications management plan. This process depends on complete work performance reports generated during the monitoring and controlling project work process. *Work performance data* is raw information that is difficult to share comprehensively. *Work performance information* is more advanced than work performance data, but is still not comprehensive enough to share total project status. A *work authorization system* is a means to control the project's flow of work during the executing process and has no real connection to this scenario.

9. **Option C:** An *issues log* is a means of effectively performing the process of controlling communications. The need for an issues log can be discussed during the planning communications process. The issues log itself may be generated as an output of managing communications. It serves as an input to effectively control communications. Managing issues sounds correct, but it is not a formal process.

10. **Option B:** Risk reports document events that may pose a positive or negative impact to the project's time, cost, or scope. An issue report is no longer potential risk; it is a risk that occurred. Options A and D do not match the description.

Project Management Communication Tools Master List

Table 27.2 – Project Management Communication Tools Master List provides a cross reference for every tool in the book. The value of this table is that it provides the opportunity for project managers to be able to select the right tools for their projects, at a single glance. The breakdown of the tools—by knowledge area or processes—provides a single reference to draw upon when deciding which tools to use for what project area. Other benefits of the table include the various social media tools that can be used with each tool. With the rise of social media, project managers need to know which tools to use for which platform. Finally, the table shows the communication purpose—why someone would use the tool for social media, and what would be the communication purpose. For example, the change control plan is used to inform and instruct across the various social media tools.

Let's spend some time now and review this table.

Table 27.2 – Project Management Communication Tools Master List

Tool Name	Part II Chap	Part III Chap	Knowledge Area	Life Cycle Process	Social Media Tools / Communication Purposes				
					Inform	Inspire	Instruct	Persuade	Motivate
Agile Estimating Tools	7	16	Scope	Integration	Yammer, Socialcast, Facebook		Yammer, Socialcast, Facebook		
Agile Information Radiators	12	22	Communications	Execute & Control Reporting	Yammer, Socialcast, Facebook				
Agile Project Meetings	6	20	Integration	Execute & Control Admin	Yammer, Socialcast, Facebook	Yammer, Socialcast, Facebook	Yammer, Socialcast, Facebook		Yammer, Socialcast, Facebook
Agile Product Vision Statement	6	16	Integration	Integration	Yammer, Socialcast, Facebook	Yammer, Socialcast, Facebook	Yammer, Socialcast, Facebook		Yammer, Socialcast, Facebook
Agile User Story	7	16	Scope	Integration	Yammer, Socialcast, Facebook	Yammer, Socialcast, Facebook	Yammer, Socialcast, Facebook		
Agile User Story Backlogs	7	16	Scope	Integration	Yammer, Socialcast, Facebook	Yammer, Socialcast, Facebook	Yammer, Socialcast, Facebook		
Baseline Schedule	8	18	Time	Planning Developing	Yammer, Socialcast, Facebook				
Budget Spreadsheet	9	19	Cost	Planning Reports	Yammer, Socialcast, Facebook			Yammer, Socialcast, Facebook	
Business Case	7	16	Scope	Integration	Yammer Socialcast, Facebook			Yammer Socialcast, Facebook	

Tool Name	Part II Chap	Part III Chap	Knowledge Area	Life Cycle Process	Inform	Inspire	Instruct	Persuade	Motivate
Change Control Plan	10	18	Quality	Planning Developing	Yammer Socialcast, Facebook		Yammer Socialcast, Facebook		
Change Readiness Assessment	12	17	Communications	Planning Admin	Yammer Socialcast, Facebook		Yammer Socialcast, Facebook		Yammer Socialcast, Facebook
Change Request Form	15	20	Stakeholder Management	Execute & Control Admin	Yammer Socialcast, Facebook		Yammer Socialcast, Facebook		
Circle of Communications Chart	11	16	Human Resources	Integration	Yammer Socialcast, Facebook				
Communication Plan	12	16	Communications	Integration	Yammer, Socialcast, Facebook		Yammer, Socialcast, Facebook		
Comprehensive Test Plan	10	18	Quality	Planning Developing	Yammer, Socialcast, Facebook		Yammer, Socialcast, Facebook		
Control Chart	10	20	Quality	Execute & Control Admin	Yammer, Socialcast, Facebook				
Customer Requirements	7	16	Scope	Integration	Yammer, Socialcast, Facebook		Yammer, Socialcast, Facebook		
Daily Progress Report	12	22	Communications	Execute & Control Reporting	Yammer, Socialcast, Facebook		Yammer Socialcast, Facebook		
Dashboard Report	15	17	Stakeholder Management	Planning Admin	Yammer, Socialcast, Facebook		Yammer, Socialcast, Facebook		Yammer, Socialcast, Facebook
Design Specifications	7	18	Scope	Planning Developing	Yammer, Socialcast, Facebook		Yammer, Socialcast, Facebook		
Document Control System	14	16	Procurement	Integration	Yammer, Socialcast, Facebook		Yammer, Socialcast, Facebook		
Earned Value Analysis	9	19	Cost	Planning Reports			Yammer, Socialcast, Facebook	Yammer, Socialcast, Facebook	Yammer Socialcast, Facebook
Earned Value Estimating Tool	9	19	Cost	Planning Reports	Yammer, Socialcast, Facebook		Yammer, Socialcast, Facebook	Yammer,, Socialcast, Facebook	Yammer Socialcast, Facebook
Executive Summary	7	16	Scope	Integration	Yammer Socialcast, Facebook		Yammer, Socialcast, Facebook		
Expected Monetary Value	13	18	Risk	Planning Developing	Yammer, Socialcast, Facebook		Yammer, Socialcast, Facebook	Yammer, Socialcast, Facebook	

Social Media Tools / Communication Purposes

Tool Name	Part II Chap	Part III Chap	Knowledge Area	Life Cycle Process	Inform	Inspire	Instruct	Persuade	Motivate
Feasibility Study	7	16	Scope	Integration	Yammer Socialcast, Facebook		Yammer, Socialcast, Facebook		Yammer, Socialcast, Facebook
Formal Acceptance Document	14	23	Procurement	Project Close	Yammer Socialcast, Facebook		Yammer, Socialcast, Facebook	Yammer Socialcast, Facebook	
Gantt Chart	8	22	Time	Execute & Control Reporting	Yammer, Socialcast, Facebook		Yammer, Socialcast, Facebook		
Histogram Report	11	22	Human Resources	Execute & Control Reporting	Yammer, Socialcast, Facebook		Yammer, Socialcast, Facebook		
Issue List	13	21	Risk	Execute & Control Monitoring	Yammer, Socialcast, Facebook		Yammer, Socialcast, Facebook		
Lessons Learned Document	14	23	Procurement	Project Close	Yammer, Socialcast, Facebook		Yammer, Socialcast, Facebook		
Logic Network Diagram	8	19	Time	Planning Reports	Yammer, Socialcast, Facebook		Yammer, Socialcast, Facebook		
Pareto Chart	12	22	Communications	Execute & Control Reporting	Yammer, Socialcast, Facebook		Yammer, Socialcast, Facebook		
Project Calendar	12	18	Communications	Planning Developing	Yammer, Socialcast, Facebook		Yammer, Socialcast, Facebook		
Project Charter	6	16	Integration	Integration	Yammer, Socialcast, Facebook		Yammer, Socialcast, Facebook		Yammer, Socialcast, Facebook
Project Kickoff Meeting	6	16	Integration	Integration	Yammer, Socialcast, Facebook	Yammer, Socialcast, Facebook	Yammer, Socialcast, Facebook		Yammer, Socialcast, Facebook
Project Management Plan	6	16	Integration	Integration	Yammer, Socialcast, Facebook		Yammer, Socialcast, Facebook		
Project Meeting Minutes	6	21	Integration	Execute & Control Monitoring	Yammer, Socialcast, Facebook		Yammer, Socialcast, Facebook		
Project Newsletter	15	20	Stakeholder Management	Execute & Control Admin	Yammer, Socialcast, Facebook	Yammer, Socialcast, Facebook			Yammer, Socialcast, Facebook
Project Organization Chart	11	16	Human Resources	Integration	Yammer, Socialcast, Facebook		Yammer, Socialcast, Facebook		
Project Presentations	12	20	Communications	Execute & Control Admin	Yammer, Socialcast, Facebook	Yammer, Socialcast, Facebook			Yammer, Socialcast, Facebook

Social Media Tools / Communication Purposes

Tool Name	Part II Chap	Part III Chap	Knowledge Area	Life Cycle Process	Inform	Inspire	Instruct	Persuade	Motivate
Project Proposal	14	16	Procurement	Integration	Yammer, Socialcast, Facebook			Yammer, Socialcast, Facebook	
Project Schedule	8	18	Time	Planning Developing	Yammer, Socialcast, Facebook				
Project Status Meetings	6	20	Integration	Execute & Control Admin	Yammer, Socialcast, Facebook			Yammer, Socialcast, Facebook	
Project Status Report	6	22	Integration	Execute & Control Reporting	Yammer, Socialcast, Facebook			Yammer, Socialcast, Facebook	
Quality Management Plan	10	16	Quality	Integration	Yammer, Socialcast, Facebook		Yammer, Socialcast, Facebook		
Quality Metrics	10	19	Quality	Planning Reports	Yammer, Socialcast, Facebook				
Responsibility Matrix	11	17	Human Resources	Planning Admin	Yammer, Socialcast, Facebook		Yammer, Socialcast, Facebook		
Risk Assessment Form	13	21	Risk	Execute & Control Monitoring	Yammer, Socialcast, Facebook				
Risk Matrix Tool	13	19	Risk	Planning Reports	Yammer, Socialcast, Facebook				
Risk Model	13	17	Risk	Planning Admin	Yammer, Socialcast, Facebook				Yammer, Socialcast, Facebook
Risk Register	13	19	Risk	Planning Reports	Yammer, Socialcast, Facebook		Yammer, Socialcast, Facebook		
Scatter Chart	10	19	Quality	Planning Reports	Yammer, Socialcast, Facebook			Yammer, Socialcast, Facebook	
Spider Chart	12	22	Communications	Execute & Control Reporting	Yammer, Socialcast, Facebook			Yammer, Socialcast, Facebook	
Stakeholder Management Plan	15	16	Stakeholder Management	Integration	Yammer, Socialcast, Facebook		Yammer, Socialcast, Facebook		
Stakeholder Register	15	16	Stakeholder Management	Integration	Yammer, Socialcast, Facebook				
Stop Light Report	12	22	Communications	Execute & Control Reporting	Yammer, Socialcast, Facebook	Yammer, Socialcast, Facebook			Yammer, Socialcast, Facebook

Tool Name	Part II Chap	Part III Chap	Knowledge Area	Life Cycle Process	Social Media Tools / Communication Purposes				
					Inform	Inspire	Instruct	Persuade	Motivate
System Requirements	7	18	Scope	Planning Developing	Yammer, Socialcast, Facebook		Yammer, Socialcast, Facebook		
User Acceptance Document	14	23	Procurement	Project Close	Yammer, Socialcast, Facebook				
Work Breakdown Structure (WBS)	7	18	Scope	Planning Developing	Yammer, Socialcast, Facebook		Yammer, Socialcast, Facebook		
Work Package	12	21	Communications	Execute & Control Monitoring	Yammer, Socialcast, Facebook		Yammer, Socialcast, Facebook		

Chapter 28

Index

A

Agile Epic User Story Example, 405

Agile Estimating Tool, 20, 134

Agile Estimating Tools, 132–33, 387, 395, 402

Agile Information Radiators, 20, 103, 264, 266–67, 414, 417

Agile Product Vision Statement, 20, 100, 104, 106, 389, 393, 550

Agile Project Management Communication Tools, xxviii

Agile Project meetings, 100, 102–3, 414, 417, 550–51

Agile User stories, 131–32, 135, 137–38, 387, 419

Agile User Story, 20, 100, 135, 404, 550

Agile User Story Backlog, 20, 131, 138–42, 410, 419

B

Baseline Schedule, 175–78, 197, 208, 365, 487–89, 517, 519, 523, 527, 587

Baseline Schedule Tool, 176, 178, 488

BI reports, 21, 647

Budget Spreadsheet, xxvii, 8, 92, 199–204, 214, 268, 338, 519–22, 548

Business Case, 143–44, 173, 420–21

Business Case documents, 143–45, 155

Business Intelligence (BI), xxviii–xxix, 1, 21

Business Travel, 69, 71

C

Calculating earned value analysis performance, 207

Case Study - A real-world project communication lesson, 75

Case Study - A virtual project team member conflict scenario, 79

Case Study - Kingdome roof replacement, 35

Change Control Board, 363–65, 367, 491–93, 560–61

Change Control Boards, 491–92

Change Control Plan, 115, 361–67, 384, 487, 490–93, 517

Change Control plan table of contents, 363, 491

Change Control process, 9, 148, 362–63, 365, 490–93, 560, 562

Change Management, organizational, 272–73, 275

Change Readiness Assessment, 263, 272, 274–76, 305, 471–72, 474, 486

Change Readiness Assessment Document, 272, 274–76, 472–74

Change Readiness Assessment Template, 275, 473

Change Request Form, 368

Circle-of-Communications Chart, 6–7, 23, 36–37, 40, 243–46, 252, 261, 269, 387, 422–23, 469

Closing Process group, 18

Communicating in writing, 65

Communicating Project Information, xxx–xxxi, 1, 7–8, 22, 31, 45, 49, 65, 85, 268, 283, 475, 568

Communicating verbally, 64

Communicating visually, 66

Communicating with the virtual project team, 76

Communication Links, 53–54, 68, 252–53

Communication Links and Figure, 53

Communication Links Chart, 53–55, 57

Communication Management, 11

Communication Management plan, 7, 32, 116

Communication Plan, xxxi, 1, 6–8, 17, 25, 31–33, 48, 93, 263, 268–71, 317, 387, 424–26, 468–69

Communication Plan Matrix, 270–71

Communication Plan Table of Contents, 32–33, 268–69

Communication Requirements, customer's, 32–33, 270

Communication Requirements Matrix, 7, 38–41, 43, 246, 268–69

Communication Requirements Matrix tool, 40–41, 270

Communication Rhythm, 377, 469, 522

Communications, Formal, 64, 66, 244–45, 422

Communications management, 8

Communication Tools for Human Resource Management, 454–55, 479, 481

Communication Tools that Manage Project Scope, 131

Comprehensive Test Plan, 215–16, 218, 487, 494–96, 517

Cone of Uncertainty, 396

Control Chart, 215, 219–22, 461–62, 549, 563–66

Cost Calculations for earned value reports, 524

Cost Estimates, 102, 135, 139, 144, 212, 407, 531, 548

Cost management, 8

Cost Management, 8, 10, 25–26, 113–14, 116, 199–200, 205, 211, 214, 248, 449

Cost Performance Index, 207

Cost variance, 207

Creating a Baseline schedule, 488

Creating a Budget spreadsheet, 520

Creating a Change control plan, 490

Creating a Comprehensive test plan, 494

Creating a Control chart, 563

Creating a Customer requirements document, 427

Creating a Dashboard report, 374, 475–76

Creating a Feasibility study, 438

Creating Agile epic user stories, 403

Creating Agile Planning Poker, 399

Creating Agile relative sizing, 395

Creating Agile team velocity, 401

Creating a Logic network diagram, 532

Creating an Agile product vision statement, 389

Creating an Earned value estimating tool, 529

Creating an Expected monetary value, 500

Creating a Project calendar, 502

Creating a Project communication plan, 23, 31

Creating a Project Estimate Tool, 530

Creating a Project Forecast, 530

Creating a Project management plan, 450

Creating a Project newsletter, 568

Creating a Project organization chart, 454

Creating a Project proposal, 456

Creating a Project schedule, 505

Creating a Quality management plan, 460

Creating a Responsibility matrix, 479

Creating a Risk assessment form, 583

Creating a Risk matrix, 541

Creating a Risk model, 483

Creating a Risk register, 538

Creating a Role report matrix, 43

Creating a Scatter chart, 545

Creating a System Requirements document, 508

Creating a Work Breakdown Structure, 513

Creating a Work package, 586

Creating Design Specifications, 497

Creating Detailed Agile user stories, 407

Creating Project Presentations, 570

Creating Schedules, 505

Creating the Agile User story product backlog, 410

Creating the Agile User story release backlog, 413

Creating the Agile User story sprint backlog, 415

Creating the Change readiness assessment, 472

Creating the Circle-of-communications chart, 422

Creating the Communication plan, 424

Creating the Document Control System, 431

Creating the Earned Value analysis performance tool, 523

Creating the Executive Summary, 436

Creating the Issues List, 578

Creating the Project Charter, 441

Creating the Project kick-off meeting, 445

Creating the Stakeholder management plan, 466

Creating the Stakeholder register, 463

CRUD Matrix, 256, 259–60, 479

Customer Requirements Document Table of Contents, 146–47

Customer Requirements Table of Contents, 428

Customers, Stakeholders, and Leadership on Social Media, 83, 94

Customer's Requirements, 25, 127, 131, 135, 146–49, 152, 224, 282, 298, 343, 412, 427–29, 447

D

Daily Progress report, 263, 277–79, 305, 574

Dashboard Report, 361, 372–74, 384, 471, 475–77

Dashboards, 21, 196, 264, 267, 372–74, 466, 475–77

Design Specification Document, 131, 150–53, 223–26, 498

Detailed Agile User Story Example, 408

Developing Lessons Learned Information, 45

Differences in Business Styles, 72

Discovering Etiquette, 72

Document Control System, 116, 156, 159, 164, 315–16, 337–42, 355–56, 358, 430–35, 507, 515–16, 530–31, 534, 539–40, 581–82

E

Earned Value Analysis (EVA), 195, 199, 205–10, 213–14, 519, 523–24, 526–27, 548

Estimating Tool, 10, 199, 211, 213–14, 395, 519, 529–30

Example of a Basic Network Diagram, 186

Example of a Budget Spreadsheet (Cost by Group), 201

Example of a budget spreadsheet (hours/project costs), 521

Example of a Business Case Document Table of Contents, 144

Example of a change assessment readiness template, 274, 473

Example of a change control plan table of contents, 363, 491

Example of a change request form, 368

Example of a Circle-of-Communications Chart, 245

Example of a Communication Plan Matrix, 270

Example of a Communication Plan Table of Contents, 269

Example of a Comprehensive Issues List, 313

Example of a Comprehensive Test Plan Table of Contents, 217, 495

Example of a Control Chart, 219

Example of a CRUD Responsibilities Matrix, 259

Example of a Customer Requirements Document Table of Contents, 147

Example of a Customer Requirements Table of Contents, 428

Example of a Dashboard Report (using Microsoft Project), 477

Example of a Design Specification Document Table of Contents, 225

Example of a Design Specifications Document Table of Contents, 151

Example of a Detailed Status Report, 129

Example of a Feasibility Study Table of Contents , 439

Example of a Gantt Chart, 179, 181

Example of a Histogram Report (Hours Worked per Resource), 249

Example of a Histogram report and bar chart, 248

Example of a Logic Network Diagram, 186, 188, 533

Example of an Earned Value Performance Report, 525

Example of an Executive Summary Document's Table of Contents, 155

Example of an S-Curve chart (performance reporting), 526

Example of a One-Page Project Presentation slide, 288

Example of a Pareto chart (delivery problems), 280

Example of a Project Calendar, 286, 503

Example of a Project Calendar (software project), 284

Example of a Project Communication Plan, 425

Example of a Project Dashboard, 372

Example of a Project Newsletter, 376

Example of a Project Organization Chart, 253–54

Example of a Project Proposal Table of Contents, 354

Example of a Project Status Meeting Agenda, 574

Example of a Quality Management Plan Table of Contents, 228

Example of a Responsibility Matrix, 481

Example of a Responsibility Matrix Chart shows a RACI, 257

Example of a Risk Assessment Form, 318

Example of a Risk Matrix, 323

Example of a Risk Model, 328, 484

Example of a Risk Register, 333

Example of a Scatter Chart (No Correlation), 236

Example of a Scatter Chart (Old Faithful Eruptions), 237

Example of a Scatter Chart (Positive Correlation), 236

Example of a Spider Chart (more complex example), 294

Example of a Stoplight Report, 297

Example of a System Requirements Table of Contents, 509

Example of a Table of Contents for a Lessons-Learned document, 348

Example of a table of contents for a Stakeholder Management Plan, 382

Example of a User Acceptance Document, 357

Example of a WBS Integrated with the Planning Process, 168–69

Example of a Weather Spider Chart, 294

Example of a Work Package Form, 303

Example of Budget Spreadsheet, 203–4

Example of Budget Spreadsheet (Hours/Project Costs), 203

Example of Circle of Communication Chart, 36

Example of Data for Creating a Scatter Chart Diagram, 545

Example of Earned Value Analysis Report, 209

Example of Expected Monetary Value, 308–11

Example of Expected Monetary Value (rain on new patio), 308

Example of Feasibility Study Tables of Contents shows a table of contents example, 157

Example of Formal Acceptance Document, 343

Example of Logic Network Diagram Task Dependencies, 187

Example of Project Issues List, 313

Example of Quality Metrics, 536

Example of Scatter Chart, 236–37, 239–40

Example of Scatter Chart (negative correlation), 237

Example of Scatter Chart (Schedule and Budget Tracking), 239

Example of Stakeholder Register Ttable of Contents, 379

Example of System Requirements Table of Contents, 161

Example of the Expected Monetary Value Formula, 309

Example of the Shewhart Cycle represents a typical Shewhart cycle, 230

Example of Typical Trending Curves for Earned Value Calculations, 209

Example of WBS, 171, 300–301

Example of WBS (highlighting work packages), 300

Example of Work Packages, 169–70

Example of Work Packages in the Logic Network Diagram, 169–70

Exam Prep Answers and Project Management Master, xxix

Executing Process group, 18

Executive Summary, 131, 154–55, 158, 387, 425, 436–37, 439

Executive Summary document, 154–56, 436–37

Expected Monetary Value, 307–11, 318, 324, 335, 487, 500–501, 517, 583

Expected Monetary Value Calculation, 308, 324

Exploring Foreign and Virtual Communications, 50, 69

Exploring Virtual Communications, 75

Exploring Virtual Team Member Qualifications, 80

F

Face-to-Face Communications, 50–51, 78, 468

Feasibility Study, 131, 157–59, 173, 387, 438–40, 469

Feasibility Study Table of Contents, 439

Fibonacci Sequence, 133, 139, 398–400

Fibonacci Sequence Example, 400

Fibonacci Sequence number, 133–34, 399

Fibonacci Sequence tool, 133

Foreign Countries, 50, 70–71, 82

Formal Acceptance Document, 337, 342–46, 356, 359, 480, 492–93

Formal Acceptance Document template, 345

G

Gantt Chart, 175, 179–84, 186, 193, 197, 247, 285, 296, 587

H

High-Tech, Low-Touch Information Radiator Examples, 266

Histogram Report, 247–51

Human Resource Management, 11, 422, 454–55, 479, 481

I

Information radiators, 102, 264–67, 392

Interacting Face-to-Face, 49

Introducing Agile Methodology, 20

Introducing Agile Planning Poker, 134

Introducing Agile product backlog, 139

Introducing Agile relative sizing, 133

Introducing Agile story points, 133

Introducing Agile team velocity, 134

Introducing high-tech, low-touch Agile information radiators, 265

Introducing low-tech, high-touch Agile information radiators, 264

Introducing Project Management Business Intelligence, 1, 21

Introducing the Change Control Plan, 362

Introducing the Project Newsletter, 375

Introducing the Stakeholder Management Plan, 381

Introduction to Agile Estimating Tools, 132

Introduction to Agile Information Radiators, 264

Introduction to Agile Product Vision Statement, 99

Introduction to Agile Project Meetings, 99–100

Introduction to Earned Value Analysis, 205

An Introduction to Project Communications, xxxi

Introduction to the Agile Product Vision Statement, 104

Introduction to the Agile release backlog, 139

Introduction to the Agile User Story, 131, 135

Introduction to the Agile User Story Backlog, 131, 138

Introduction to the Baseline Schedule, 176

Introduction to the Budget Spreadsheet, 200

Introduction to the Business Case, 131, 143

Introduction to the Change Readiness Assessment Document, 272

Introduction to the Circle-of-Communications Chart, 244

Introduction to the Communication Plan, 268

Introduction to the Comprehensive Test Plan, 216

Introduction to the Control Chart, 219

Introduction to the Customer Requirements, 131, 146

Introduction to the Daily Progress Report, 277

Introduction to the Design specification document, 131

Introduction to the Design Specification Document, 150, 223

Introduction to the Document Control System, 338

Introduction to the Earned Value Estimating Tool, 211

Introduction to the Executive summary, 131

Introduction to the Executive Summary, 154

Introduction to the Expected Monetary Value, 308

Introduction to the Feasibility study, 131

Introduction to the Feasibility Study, 157

Introduction to the Formal Acceptance Document, 342

Introduction to the Histogram Report, 247

Introduction to the Issues List, 312

Introduction to the Lessons-Learned Document, 347

Introduction to the Logic Network Diagram, 185

Introduction to the Pareto Chart, 280

Introduction to the Project Calendar, 283

Introduction to the Project Charter, 99, 107

Introduction to the Project kick-Off Meeting, 99

Introduction to the Project Kick-Off Meeting, 110

Introduction to the Project Management Plan, 99, 113

Introduction to the Project Meeting Minutes, 99, 118

Introduction to the Project Organization Chart, 252

Introduction to the Project Presentation, 288

Introduction to the Project Proposal, 353

Introduction to the Project Schedule, 192

Introduction to the Project Status Meeting, 99, 122

Introduction to the Project Status Report, 99, 126

Introduction to the Quality Management Plan, 227

Introduction to the Quality Metrics Tool, 232

Introduction to the Responsibility Matrix, 256

Introduction to the Risk Assessment Form, 317

Introduction to the Risk Matrix, 322

Introduction to the Risk Model, 327

Introduction to the Risk Register, 331

Introduction to the Scatter Chart, 235

Introduction to the Spider Chart, 292

Introduction to the Stoplight Report, 296

Introduction to the System Requirements Document, 131, 160

Introduction to the User Acceptance Document, 356

Introduction to the Work Breakdown Structure, 165

Introduction to the Work Package, 300

Issues List, 307, 312–16, 335, 577–79, 589

K

Kanban Board, 265

Knowledge areas, xxiv, xxvi–xxvii, xxix, xxxi–xxxii, 2, 6, 8–9, 14, 20, 22, 26–27, 99, 116, 118, 277

L

Learning Virtual Communication, 69

Lessons Learned, 33, 45

Lessons-Learned process, 350–52, 501

Logic Network Diagram, 169–70, 175, 185–90, 197, 519, 532–34, 548

M

Managing virtual project teams, xxxi, 76

Mapping Social Media Tools to Project Management Life Cycle Processes, 86

Mastering Agile Estimating Tools, 395

Mastering Agile User Stories, 403

Mastering Agile User Story Backlogs, 410

Mastering Project Meeting Minutes, 580

Mastering Project Presentations, 570

Mastering the Agile Product Vision Statement, 389

Mastering the Baseline Schedule, 488

Mastering the Budget Spreadsheet, 520

Mastering the Business Case, 420

Mastering the Change Control Plan, 490

Mastering the Change Readiness Assessment, 472

Mastering the Change Request Form, 559

Mastering the Circle-of-Communications Chart, 422

Mastering the Communication Plan, 424

Mastering the Comprehensive Test Plan, 494

Mastering the Control Chart, 563

Mastering the Customer Requirements Document, 427

Mastering the Dashboard Report, 475

Mastering the Design Specifications, 497

Mastering the Document Control System, 431

Mastering the Earned Value Analysis Tool, 523

Mastering the Earned Value Estimating Tool, 529

Mastering the Executive Summary, 436

Mastering the Expected Monetary Value, 500

Mastering the Feasibility Study, 438

Mastering the Logic Network Diagram, 532

Mastering the Project Calendar, 502

Mastering the Project Charter, 441

Mastering the Project Kick-Off Meeting, 444

Mastering the Project Management Plan, 449

Mastering the Project Newsletter, 568

Mastering the Project Organization Chart, 454

Mastering the Project Proposal, 456

Mastering the Project Schedule, 505

Mastering the Project Status Meeting, 573

Mastering the Quality Management Plan, 460

Mastering the Responsibility Matrix, 479

Mastering the Risk Assessment Form, 583

Mastering the Risk Modeling Process, 483

Mastering the Scatter Chart, 544

Mastering the Stakeholder Management Plan, 466

Mastering the Stakeholder Register, 463

Mastering the System Requirements Document, 508

Mastering the Work Breakdown Structure, 513

Mastering the Work Package, 586

Measuring a project's earned value, 207

Meeting agenda, project kick-off, 111

Monitoring & Controlling Process group, 18

Motivating virtual project teams, 78

N

Newsletters, 21, 32–33, 79, 246, 375–77, 381, 455, 568–69

Organization chart, 36–37, 252–54, 454–55

P

Pareto Chart, 263, 280–82, 305, 461–62, 501

Planned Budget Sample for a Software Development Project, 206

Planning a project kick-off meeting, 112

Planning a project management plan, 116

Planning a project status meeting, 124

Planning a project status report, 128

Planning a user story, 137

Planning for Project Communications in Foreign Countries, 70

Planning Poker, 134, 399–400, 553

Planning Poker Deck Using a Fibonacci Sequence Example, 400

Planning Process group, 17

Planning Project Communication, 5, 7, 246

Planning Risks and Contingencies, 217

Planning the Product Vision Statement, 136

Planning the Project Meeting Minutes, 120

Planning the Project Status Meeting, 573

Planning to Agile Information Radiators, 266

Planning to give a better project presentation, 290

Planning to use a Baseline Schedule, 178

Planning to use a Business Case, 144

Planning to use a Change Control Plan, 365

Planning to use a Change Readiness Assessment, 274

Planning to use a Change Request Form, 370

Planning to use a Circle-of-Communications Chart, 246

Planning to use a Communication Plan, 270

Planning to use a Comprehensive Test Plan, 218

Planning to use a Control Chart, 221

Planning to use a Daily Progress Report, 278

Planning to use a Dashboard Report, 374

Planning to use a Design Specification Document, 152

Planning to use a Feasibility Study, 159

Planning to use a Formal Acceptance Document, 345

Planning to use a Gantt Chart, 181

Planning to use a Histogram Report, 249

Planning to use a Lessons-Learned Document, 351

Planning to use a Logic Network Diagram, 188

Planning to use an Agile Estimating Tool, 213

Planning to use an Executive Summary, 155

Planning to use an Issues List, 315

Planning to use a Pareto Chart, 282

Planning to use a Product Vision Statement, 106

Planning to use a Project Calendar Tool, 285

Planning to use a Project Newsletter, 377

Planning to use a Project Proposal, 355

Planning to use a Project Schedule, 195

Planning to use a Quality Management Plan, 229

Planning to use a Quality Metrics Tool, 233

Planning to use a Risk Matrix Tool, 325

Planning to use a Risk Model, 329

Planning to use a Scatter Chart, 239

Planning to use a Spider Chart, 293

Planning to use a Stakeholder Management Plan, 382

Planning to use a Stakeholder Register, 379

Planning to use a Stoplight Report, 298

Planning to use a System Requirements Document, 163

Planning to use a user Acceptance Document, 358

Planning to use a WBS, 170

Planning to use a Work Package, 301

Planning to use Customer Requirements, 148

Planning to use Earned Value Analysis, 208

Planning to use the Expected Monetary Value, 310

Planning to use the Project Organization Chart, 254

Planning to use the Responsibility Matrix, 260

Planning to use the Risk Assessment Form, 320

Planning to use the Risk Register, 334

Plan to Communicate, Communicate the Plan, 1, 5

PMBOK Exam Questions, xxviii

PMBOK Exam Questions (Project Communications), xxviii

PMP® Exam Questions, xxxii

Preparing and Delivering Presentations, 61

Preparing and Planning for Project Communications in Foreign Countries, 70

Preparing and Presenting Presentations, 49

Preventing Common Communication Problems, 30

Procurement management, 13, 337

Product Backlog, 102–3, 137, 139–40, 398, 401, 409–15, 550

  initial, 140, 413, 419

Product Vision Statement, 104–6, 136, 138, 389–93, 395, 403–4, 410, 550

Product Vision Statement Template, 104, 390

Project Calendar, 7, 186, 263, 283–87, 305, 487, 502–4, 517

Project Charter, 17, 99–100, 107–9, 112, 441–43, 469

Project Charter Table of Contents, 442

Project Communication Plan, 7, 9, 23, 31–32, 270–71, 422, 425

Project Communication Requirements Matrix, 7, 23, 33, 38

Project Communication Tool RACI, 29

Project Communication Tools by Knowledge Areas, xxxi

Project Communication Tools by Process Groups, xxxii

Project Dashboards, 196, 372–74, 475–77, 486

Project information, distributing, 49, 64

Project integration management, 9, 99

Project Kick-off Meeting, 77, 99, 106, 110–12, 130, 387, 444–46, 448, 469

Project Kick-off Meeting Agenda Template, 446

Project Knowledge Area, xxx, 8, 22, 113, 115

Project Level and Top Level, 165–66

Project Level and Top Level of a WBS, 166

Project Management Business Intelligence, xxviii–xxix, 21

Project Management Communication Tools Master List, 664

Project Management Institute, 99–100, 104, 107, 110, 113, 132, 135, 138, 143, 146, 154, 157, 160, 176, 179

Project Management Life cycle processes, 83, 86

Project Management Methodologies, 341, 475

Project Management Plan, 18, 99, 113, 115–17, 130, 331, 354, 387, 449–50, 452–53, 458, 469

Project Management Plan Table of Contents, 113–14, 451

Project Meeting Minutes, 99, 118, 120–21, 577, 580–82

Project Meeting Minute's template, 120

Project Meeting Minute's template, 581

Project Newsletter, 17, 361, 375–77, 384, 549, 568–69, 576

Project Organization Chart, 243–44, 252–55, 261, 387, 454–55, 458, 469, 479

Project Procurement, 13, 19, 337, 359, 431, 435, 456, 459

Project Proposal, 108, 337, 353–55, 456–59, 469

Project Proposal Table of Contents, 457

Project RACI, 8, 28, 256, 259

Project Risk, 12, 307, 310, 317, 324, 330, 333, 483, 485, 500–501, 538–39, 541–42, 578–79, 583, 585

Project Risk Dashboard, 21

Project Risk Models, 328, 483

Project Risk Summary Dashboard, 650

Project scenario, 1, 152, 245, 318, 362, 389, 395, 403, 410, 436, 513, 550, 563, 586

Project Schedule, 9, 16–17, 115, 175–80, 183–85, 188, 192–97, 296–98, 447, 502–3, 505–7, 523, 525–27, 533, 581

Project Scheduling Tool, 115, 177, 180, 188, 192, 195, 285, 489, 506, 533–34

Project Scope, 131, 363, 365, 378–79, 403–4, 427, 429, 436–39, 497–98, 508, 511, 513, 515–16, 524, 527

Project scope management, 9

Project Status Meetings, 99, 122–25, 203, 315, 573–76, 578, 581

Project Status Report, xxxiv, 23, 33, 45, 65, 78, 99, 126–30, 268, 317, 375, 568, 575

   single, 128

   ten-page, 425

Project Summary Dashboard, 21, 648

Q

Quality Control, 215–16, 228–29, 461–62

Quality Management, 10

Quality Management Plan, 115–16, 215, 227–31, 387, 449, 460–62, 469

Quality Management Plan Table of Contents, 461

Quality Metrics, 232–34, 460, 535–37, 548

R

Release planning meetings, 106, 135–39, 264, 398, 404, 406, 408, 412, 550, 553

Reporting from a baseline schedule, 178

Reporting from a budget spreadsheet, 203

Reporting from a business case, 144

Reporting from a change readiness assessment, 275

Reporting from a change request form, 370

Reporting from a comprehensive test plan, 218

Reporting from a daily progress report, 279

Reporting from a dashboard report, 374

Reporting from a Gantt chart, 181

Reporting from a histogram report, 249

Reporting from a logic network diagram, 188

Reporting from an issues list, 315

Reporting from a project newsletter, 377

Reporting from a project organization chart, 254

Reporting from a project proposal, 355

Reporting from a project schedule, 196

Reporting from a quality management plan, 230

Reporting from a risk assessment form, 320

Reporting from a risk model, 330

Reporting from a scatter chart, 239

Reporting from a spider chart, 294

Reporting from a stakeholder management plan, 382

Reporting from a stakeholder register, 380

Reporting from a stoplight report, 298

Reporting from a system requirements document, 164

Reporting from a WBS, 170

Reporting from earned value analysis, 208

Reporting from expected monetary value, 310

Reporting from project presentations, 290

Reporting from quality metrics, 233

Reporting from the change control form, 365

Reporting from the circle-of-communications chart, 246

Reporting from the communication plan, 270

Reporting from the design specification document, 152, 225

Reporting from the estimating tool, 213

Reporting from the executive summary, 155

Reporting from the feasibility study, 159

Reporting from the formal acceptance document, 345

Reporting from the lessons-learned document, 351

Reporting from the Pareto chart, 282

Reporting from the project calendar tool, 285

Reporting from the responsibility matrix, 260

Reporting from the risk matrix tool, 326

Reporting from the risk register, 334

Reporting from the user acceptance document, 358

Reporting information from a project management plan, 116

Reporting information from a project status meeting, 125

Reporting information from the project charter, 109

Reporting information from the project's meeting minutes, 120

Reporting using a project status report, 128

Reporting using the product vision statement, 106

Responsibility Matrix, 243, 256, 260–61, 455, 462, 471, 479–82, 486

Responsibility Matrix Chart, 257–58

Responsibility Matrix Template, 480–81

Reviewing Project Scenario, 3

Risk Assessment Form, 12, 307, 317–18, 320–21, 324, 327, 330–35, 577, 583–85, 589

Risk Assessment Matrix Template, new, 542

Risk Management, 2, 12, 59, 113, 307, 335, 483

Risk Matrix, 268, 307, 310, 322–26, 335, 483, 541–43, 548

Risk Matrix Chart, 324, 542

Risk Model, 307, 327–30, 335, 471, 483–86

Risk Models, 327–28, 485

Risk Model Spreadsheet, 485

Risk Model Template, 330, 484

Risk Register, xxvii, xxxiv, 116, 307, 331–35, 517, 538–39

Risk Register Template, 334

Risk Scores, 327–30, 333, 483–85, 583–85

Risk Tolerance Levels, 58–60, 296

  Understanding Stakeholder, 49

Role Report Matrix, 6–7, 23, 41–44, 246, 268–69

S

Sample Gantt Chart, 181

Sample Logic Network Diagram, 189–90

Sample Logic Network Diagram for a Book-Publishing Project, 190

Sample PMP® Exam Questions: 654

Sample PMP® Exam Questions for Project Communications, 653

Sample Project Schedule, 193–94

Scatter Chart, 215, 235–41, 519, 544–48

Scatter Chart Diagram, 544–45

Schedule and Cost Forecasting Report, 209

Sending & Receiving Model, 55

Sending Model, 56

Shewhart Cycle, 230–31, 536

Shewhart Cycle chart, 230

Shewhart Cycle process, 230

Significance of gestures, 72

Social Embarrassment, 72

Social media, xxix–xxxi, 83–87, 89–91, 94–96, 389, 395, 403, 550

Social Media and Networking Tools Mapped to Project Management Life Cycle Processes, 86

Social Media and Project Management Communication Tools, xxviii, xxxi, 83

Social Media Experts, 83, 95–96

Social Medial Tools, 264

Social Media to Life Cycle Process Mapping, 87

Social Media Tools, 83–84, 86–87, 89–95, 104, 107, 110, 113, 133, 135, 138, 143, 146, 154, 157, 160

    five, 89

    major, 389, 395, 403

    using, 83–84, 90, 94–95

    various, xxxi

Social Media Tools change, 90

Social Media Tools/Communication Purposes, 92

Social Media Tools Map, 86

Software Design Specification Template, 498

Specifications, functional, 173, 517

Spider Chart, 80, 263, 292–95, 305

Sprint Backlog, 102–3, 140–41, 410, 415–19, 550, 552–53

Sprint Burndown chart, 141, 417–19

Sprint Planning, 100–101, 141, 551–53

Sprint planning meeting, 101–2, 140–41, 408, 415–16, 419, 551–52

Sprint Review, 101, 551, 555–56

Sprint Review meeting, 101, 554–56

Stakeholder communication strategy information, 467

Stakeholder Management, 9, 14, 99, 146, 272, 361, 381–82, 384, 467

Stakeholder Management plan, 361, 381–84, 387, 466–69

Stakeholder Management Plan Table of Contents, 467

Stakeholder Register, 361, 378–82, 384, 387, 463–67, 469

Stakeholder Register Template, 464

Stop Light Report, 44, 263, 296–99

  all-red, 299

  creation, 298

  using, 296

Story Points, Agile, 132–34, 139–41, 266, 397–99, 401–2, 408, 412, 414, 418, 553

Struggling with Proper Project Communication Planning, 23, 25

System Requirements, 160, 163–64, 257, 487, 490, 508

System Requirements Document, 131, 160–61, 163–64, 173, 508–9, 511–12, 517

System Requirements Document Template, 509

T

Table of Contents for a Project Kick-Off Meeting Agenda, 447

Table of Contents for a Stakeholder Management Plan, 381

Technical Requirements, 160–61, 354, 430, 458, 508

Time Management, 9

Time Scale Diagrams, 186

Typical PMI Life Cycle Process Chart, 15

U

Understanding Communication Links, 49, 53

Understanding PMI's Project Life Cycle Process, 1, 15

Understanding PMI's Project Management Knowledge Areas, 1, 8

Understanding PMI's Project Process Groups, 15

Understanding the Shewhart cycle, 230

Understanding the Stakeholder Risk Tolerance Level, 58

Understanding the value of face-to-face communications, 51

United Arab Emirates, 488

United Kingdom, 72

United States, 75, 233, 424

United States and Canada, 494

United States of America, 73

User Acceptance Document, 218, 337, 342, 356–59, 425–26, 430, 443, 453, 459, 462, 527, 533, 537, 539

User Acceptance Document process, 358

User Acceptance Testing (UAT), 245, 289

User Stories, Agile, 100–102, 132–37, 139–41, 265–66, 395–401, 403–10, 412–19, 551–53, 556

User Story Template, 135

Using a Baseline schedule, 489

Using a Budget spreadsheet, 522

Using a Change control plan, 492

Using a Dashboard report, 477

Using Agile, 399

Using Agile epic user stories, 406

Using Agile product vision statement, 393

Using Agile story points, 399

Using a Logic Network Diagram, 533

Using an Expected Monetary Value, 501

Using an Issues List, 579

Using a Project Calendar, 503

Using a Project Organization Chart, 455

Using a Project Schedule, 507

Using a Quality Management Plan, 462

Using a Risk Assessment Form, 584

Using a Risk Matrix, 542

Using a Risk Model, 485

Using a Risk Register, 539

Using a Scatter Chart, 546

Using a System Requirements document, 511

Using a Work Breakdown Structure, 516

Using a Work Package, 587

Using Business Intelligent Reports, 648

Using Communication Tools, 106, 109, 112, 134, 137, 142, 145, 149, 156, 159, 276, 279, 282, 310, 312

Using Communication Tools for Project Reporting, 187–88, 191, 204, 206, 210, 213, 234, 239–40, 324, 326, 334, 519

Using Communication Tools to Plan and Develop Project Deliverables, 153, 164, 178, 196, 218, 226, 287, 311

Using Design Specifications, 498

Using Detailed Agile User Stories, 409

Using Project Presentations, 571

Using Social Media, 83–84, 89–91, 94, 96

Using the Agile User Story Product Backlog, 412

Using the Agile User Story Release Backlog, 415

Using the Agile User Story Sprint Backlog, 419

Using the Business case, 421

Using the Change Readiness Assessment, 474

Using the Circle-of-Communications Chart, 423

Using the Communication Plan, 425

Using the Control Chart, 566

Using the Document Control System, 435

Using the Earned Value Analysis Performance tool, 527

Using the Earned Value Estimating Tool, 530

Using the Executive Summary, 437

Using the PMBOK, xxv

Using the Project Newsletter, 569

Using the Responsibility Matrix, 481

Using the Stakeholder Management Plan, 467

Using the Stakeholder Register, 464

V

Verbal Communication, 57, 64

Virtual Communicating Methods, 76

Virtual Communications, 31, 75, 82

Virtual Project Teams, xxxi, 75–76, 78

Virtual Team Member Qualifications, xxxi, 80

Virtual Team Members, 75, 77–80, 110

Virtual Teams, xxxi, 31, 49, 65, 75–77, 82

W

WBS (work breakdown structure), 9, 17, 131, 165–73, 208, 213, 300–302, 407, 432, 458, 498, 513–17, 526–27, 529, 586–87

WBS Dictionary, 167

What is social media? 83

The work package, 167

Work Package Benefits, 300

Work Package Form, 300, 302–3

Work package level, 167–68, 458, 515, 529

Work Packages, 165–70, 172, 208, 213, 263, 300–304, 312, 354, 458, 506, 514–16, 577, 586–87, 589

Made in the
USA
Columbia, SC